Praise for *Roosevelt's Centurions*

"Well-paced, thoughtful, and often shrewd, this leading historian's engaging look at FDR's role as America's chief war strategist spotlights how he chose and worked with military leaders through the war's twists and turns." —*World War II* magazine

"A magisterial work that merges an expansive military history with an intimate political biography." —Albany *Times Union*

"Persico describes the president and his military team so vividly that they seem to come alive and rise from the pages." —Schenectady *Daily Gazette*

"Fascinating ... a gripping tale of war as seen from FDR's White House." —*The Charlotte Observer*

"Joseph E. Persico has done it again! *Roosevelt's Centurions* is a riveting, analytic recounting of FDR as top World War II strategist. Nobody before has written on Roosevelt as talent scout with the brilliant insight of Persico." —DOUGLAS BRINKLEY, author of *Cronkite*

"To a remarkable degree we inhabit a world originated by Franklin D. Roosevelt—on World War II battlefields, in the gilded halls of diplomacy, and above all inside FDR's fertile, inscrutable imagination. Joe Persico brings all this to life with stunning originality, insight, and narrative drive." —RICHARD NORTON SMITH, author of *The Colonel*

By Joseph E. Persico

Roosevelt's Centurions

Franklin and Lucy

Piercing the Reich

My American Journey (co-author)

Eleventh Month, Eleventh Day, Eleventh Hour

Roosevelt's Secret War

Nuremberg

Casey

The Imperial Rockefeller

Edward R. Murrow

My Enemy, My Brother

The Spiderweb

ROOSEVELT'S
CENTURIONS

ROOSEVELT'S CENTURIONS

FDR and the Commanders
He Led to Victory
in World War II

Joseph E. Persico

RANDOM HOUSE TRADE PAPERBACKS
NEW YORK

2014 Random House Trade Paperback Edition

Copyright © 2013 by Joseph E. Persico
Maps copyright © 2013 by David Lindroth, Inc.

Published in the United States by Random House Trade Paperbacks,
an imprint of Random House, a division of Random House LLC,
a Penguin Random House Company, New York.

RANDOM HOUSE and the HOUSE colophon are
registered trademarks of Random House LLC.

Originally published in hardcover in the United States by Random House,
an imprint and division of Random House LLC, in 2013.

Library of Congress Cataloging-in-Publication Data
Persico, Joseph E.
Roosevelt's centurions : FDR and the commanders he led to victory in
World War II / Joseph E. Persico.
p. cm.
Includes bibliographical references and index.
ISBN 978-0-8129-7497-3
eBook ISBN 978-0-679-64543-6
1. Roosevelt, Franklin D. (Franklin Delano), 1882–1945—Military leadership.
2. Generals—United States—History—20th century. 3. Admirals—United States—
History—20th century. 4. World War, 1939–1945—United States. 5. World War,
1939–1945—Campaigns. 6. World War, 1939–1945—Diplomatic history. I. Title.
E806.P467 2012
973.917092—dc23
2011048698

Printed in the United States of America on acid-free paper

www.atrandom.com

2 4 6 8 9 7 5 3 1

Book design by Donna Sinisgalli

Preface

WARS ARE DIFFERENT NOW, BUT THE HUMAN FACTORS AND FORCES at the highest levels change little. The story of Franklin Roosevelt and his top military command sheds light on the perennial issues that confront America when we are challenged. How should we fight our foes? Where and when? At what price? Who decides the wisest course when the best minds disagree? Who should be our allies? And what do we fight for?

FDR answered the final question in his last testament. On Wednesday, April 11, 1945, the day before he died, Franklin Roosevelt was at work on a Jefferson Day speech: "Today we are part of the vast Allied force—a force composed of flesh and blood and steel and spirit—which is today destroying the makers of war, the breeders of hate in Europe, and in Asia." But FDR always looked ahead; he was a man of the future, and the world to come was on his mind. "Today, science has brought all the different quarters of the globe so close together that it is impossible to isolate them one from another," he wrote, accurately predicting the emergence of the global civilization that has become the reality of the twenty-first century.

The leaders he chose to fight for his ideals seem distant now, either Olympian—Eisenhower, MacArthur, Patton—or dimmed by time—Marshall, Arnold, King. Yet each of these men held the lives and destinies of young Americans and the course of democracy itself in their hands. Who they were and how they did what they did—how they fought and how they thought—repays our attention, for they were at work in the greatest war in the history of man.

And at the center—always at the center, in command, smiling yet steely—was Franklin Roosevelt. Now seen as a marble man, a demigod, he was in fact all too human, and to understand him as he was—a man, not a myth—arms us well to judge his successors as they struggle with issues of war and peace and power.

Had he lived another day, he would have told America: "Today we are faced with the preeminent fact that, if civilization is to survive, we must cultivate the science of human relationships—the ability of all peoples, of all kinds, to live together and work together, in the same world, at peace."

That is the world that the commander in chief and his centurions fought for. Their story is told here.

Contents

x   Contents

Introduction

On March 4, 1933, Franklin Delano Roosevelt stood on the East Portico of the Capitol behind a massive Great Seal of the United States. Four rows of dignitaries, many arriving in black silk top hats, took their places behind him. His son James had been positioned strategically should the paraplegic president, supported only by leg braces, begin to fall. FDR's hand rested on the Roosevelt family's 1686 Bible as Supreme Court chief justice Charles Evans Hughes swore in the thirty-second president of the United States. Along with the civilian powers and duties of the office that Roosevelt assumed that day, he became, under Article II, Section II of the Constitution, "the commander in chief of the Army and Navy of the United States." Ironically, and admirably in a democracy, this oath usually places a military amateur over the most star-studded generals and admirals in uniform. Roosevelt reveled in the authority. Throughout his life, he had displayed an interest in military matters. As a boy he had indulged dreams of attending the Naval Academy at Annapolis, but his doting mother could not bear the thought of long separations from her only child. As a birthday present, FDR once presented his grandson Curtis Roosevelt with the Navy bible, *Jane's Fighting Ships*. His love of the sea reached its fullest expression when, at age thirty-one, President Woodrow Wilson appointed him assistant secretary of the navy. When the United States entered the First World War in 1917, he pleaded with Wilson to be allowed to resign and get into uniform, but the president turned him down. Nevertheless, against the resistance of his superior, navy secretary Josephus Daniels, FDR managed to wangle a mission to the Western Front in the summer of 1918. While there he wore a vaguely military dress of his own design, khaki pants tucked into leather puttees, a gray knee-length coat, a French army helmet, and a gas mask looped around his neck. Though never under fire, he described in a letter home the aftermath of battle. After slogging through oozing mud and around water-logged shell holes, he wrote of "discarded overcoats, rain-stained love letters . . . and many little mounds, some wholly un-marked, some with a rifle stuck bayonet down in the earth with a tag of wood or wrapping paper hung over it and a pencil scrawl of an Amer-ican name."

Fifteen years later, as president, even as he wrestled with the eco-nomic tailspin of the Great Depression, FDR, alarmed by the rise of Nazism, fascism, and Japan's imperial ambitions, fought to increase military spending, eventually winning congressional approval for a $4 billion creation of a true two-ocean Navy. In 1938, while the coun-try slipped back into the economic doldrums, the president angled for congressional approval to build 20,000 war planes annually. When in 1940 his Army chief of staff, General George Marshall, lobbied for funds to double the size of an Army that ranked somewhere between those of Portugal and Bulgaria, FDR doubled the request.

On September 1, 1939, a transatlantic phone call from William Bullitt, the U.S. ambassador to France, woke the president from a deep sleep to alert him that Germany had invaded Poland. The second world war in a generation had begun. Soon Roosevelt began to unravel the Neutrality Laws that had tied his hands from aiding the Allies fighting against Hitler. When in late December 1940 an anxious Winston Churchill informed him that Britain, facing imminent invasion, was nearly flat broke and "we will no longer be able to pay cash for shipping and supplies," FDR hatched, in the unknowable recesses of his imagi-nation, a scheme for giving Britain fifty overage destroyers which he justified by obtaining in exchange several bases of minimal usefulness. This decidedly unneutral act was followed a year later by Lend-Lease, which allowed America to pour billions in arms and equipment into Britain and the Soviet Union, employing the flimsy rationale that the "loaned" material would be returned after the war. In July 1941 he im-posed an oil embargo on fuel-short Japan, which, it can be argued, contributed to the Japanese decision to attack Pearl Harbor.

To keep the sea lanes open to Britain, FDR stretched the definition of the Western Hemisphere to limits that would have astonished President James Monroe and his doctrine. In a fireside chat in September 1941, Roosevelt revealed how far he was prepared to go, telling his radio listeners, "When you see a rattlesnake poised to strike, you do not wait until he has struck before you crush him." The press quickly branded his words the "Shoot on Sight" policy. In effect, the president had launched an undeclared war against Germany on the high seas.

Thus by the time that Japan struck Pearl Harbor on December 7, 1941, and Germany declared war on the United States four days later, Franklin Roosevelt was already a commander in chief firmly in control of the nation's war-making apparatus like no president since Abraham Lincoln during the Civil War. FDR wore the mantle as comfortably as the battered, upturned fedora that had become his trademark. In his address to a joint session of Congress the day after Pearl Harbor, seeking a declaration of war, he underscored his military powers, saying, "as commander in chief of the Army and Navy I have directed that all measures be taken for our defense." At a cabinet dinner, he turned to his secretary of state, Cordell Hull, who was about to introduce him, and told Hull to present him not as president, but as commander in chief.

Roosevelt's direction of America during the war must be judged by how well he performed the three roles he assumed. The first was as recruiter in chief, choosing the generals and admirals he deemed capable of winning a war. How apt were his selections of Marshall to run the Army, Admiral Ernest J. King to command the Navy, General Henry H. "Hap" Arnold to build an Air Force, Dwight D. Eisenhower to command the invasion of Western Europe, and other figures in key roles, Generals Douglas MacArthur, Omar Bradley, and Joseph Stilwell among the most prominent? He valued the sober, sensible workhorses, like Marshall and Eisenhower, but he was also drawn to the show horses with the dash and panache of a George S. Patton, or a Mark Clark, perhaps as a vicarious escape from his own immobility. He directed the war from an environment of controlled chaos, largely self-created. His secretary of war, Henry L. Stimson, only slightly exaggerating, noted,

"He has no system. He goes haphazard and scatters responsibility among a lot of uncoordinated men and consequently things are never done."

Secondly, FDR must be judged as strategist in chief. He was not a military meddler in a league with Churchill, who poked his nose into the smallest details and fired generals left and right. Roosevelt was largely content to have the professionals wage the tactical war. But, on the strategic level, he retained for himself the consequential decisions. If, however, he felt a military chief was foot-dragging or wrong, he did not hesitate to step in, as when he pressured a resistant Admiral King to adopt the convoy system to thwart the massive kills German U-boats were scoring against merchant shipping in the Atlantic. He indulged a practical bent, once describing as part of his war on U-boats in the Atlantic a scheme for installing helicopter pads on the decks of merchant ships. "The helicopters," he explained, "could hover over the convoys, spot German submarines, drop a depth charge or two and then, if they had difficulty landing on a wobbly deck, could be plucked from the sea in great nets trailing behind the base ship."

Even after the American people seethed with vengeance over the sneak attack on Pearl Harbor, FDR never wavered from his position that the war against Germany retained priority. He took this stance because he believed that the defeat of Germany would bring about the defeat of Japan, but the defeat of Japan would not bring about the defeat of Germany. During the conflict, Europe received 85 percent of the nation's war output. What was left went to the Pacific.

In likely his most controversial decision, and against the will of his military chiefs, who unanimously supported an invasion across the English Channel to defeat Germany, he chose to engage America in the European war, initially not against the Germans on the continent but against the French in North Africa. Eisenhower would describe this decision as "the blackest day in history." Churchill was obsessed with controlling the Mediterranean to preserve the lifeline of the British Empire, though he cleverly sold his support for a North African invasion as wise military policy and not simply as a nakedly imperialist objective. He and his military chiefs also buttressed their case by maintaining that at this point the Allies lacked sufficient sea transportation to build a powerful enough invasion force in England and that untested American troops were not yet ready to storm Fortress Europa. To FDR, eager to have American troops engaged *somewhere* in 1942, North Africa presented an attractive compromise. Then, after Erwin Rommel's Afrika Korps had been driven out of North Africa, FDR made his next strategic decision, again influenced by Churchill. The prime minister persuaded him of the advantages of invading Sicily and then Italy proper. Marshall warned that if Sicily were attacked, the drain of resources would make it "difficult if not impossible" to make the cross-Channel campaign as originally planned, in 1943. Indeed, the Sicilian invasion force, 166,000 men landed within three days, roughly equaled the armies that would land at Normandy on D-Day, nearly a year later. Nevertheless, FDR remained lukewarm about Italy. He told his secretary of war, Henry Stimson, that he did not want to go further than Rome. But he did. The bloody slog up the Italian boot was still going on when the war ended. FDR's decisions on North Africa, Sicily, and Italy, right or wrong, clearly established who was in charge of the U.S. war effort. As former chief historian of the Army Kent Roberts Greenfield has calculated, during World War II, FDR made over twenty major decisions that went "against the advice, or over the protests of his military advisers."

In another major override of his professionals, Roosevelt supported Douglas MacArthur's insistence that the general be allowed to reconquer the Philippines after he had lost the islands early in the war. Admiral King, strongly supported by Admiral Chester Nimitz, the man FDR had sent to command the Central Pacific, believed that by island hopping across the ocean, bypassing certain islands, most notably the Philippines, Japan could eventually be strangled, which would obviate the need for a bloodbath on Japanese beaches. FDR had to resolve the controversy in 1944, a presidential election year, and MacArthur claimed to tell Roosevelt privately, "If your decision be to bypass the Philippines and leave its millions of wards of the United States and thousands of American internees and prisoners of war to continue to languish in their agony and despair—I dare to say that the American people would be so aroused that they would register most complete resentment against you at the polls this fall." FDR let MacArthur have his invasion.

The president's most stunning strategic surprise was sprung at Casablanca in January 1943 when, as he glanced at handwritten notes on his lap, he announced, "The elimination of German, Japanese, and Italian war power means the unconditional surrender by Germany, Italy, and Japan." Churchill would subsequently waffle on how he felt about unconditional surrender. Joseph Stalin at the Big Three conference at Tehran in 1943 argued that negotiated terms would hasten the day of German capitulation. Eisenhower said of unconditional surrender, "If you were given two choices—one to mount the scaffold and the other to charge twenty bayonets—you might as well charge twenty bayonets." Roosevelt's pronouncement, however, left Hitler's propaganda minister, Joseph Goebbels, ecstatic. "How can any German," he said, "whether he likes it or not, do anything but fight on with all his strength?" Nevertheless, FDR insisted on total unconditional capitulation to his dying day.

Another far-reaching decision occurred when FDR told his military aide, General Edwin "Pa" Watson, "This requires action." Roosevelt had just been informed by Albert Einstein of the unimaginable power of the atom. With these words, Roosevelt set in motion the quest for an atomic bomb, producing a chain reaction that changed the course of history.

Finally, FDR must be judged as the home front leader charged with motivating, marshaling and inspiring a people at war, by sustaining the belief that their sacrifices were worth enduring, even dying for. The smoke had not yet cleared from the wreckage of Pearl Harbor when he set the tone, vowing, "No matter how long it may take us to overcome this premeditated invasion, the American people . . . will win through to absolute victory."

This work deals with paths taken over sixty years ago. Revisiting the decisions calls to mind what one writer has said of "revisionism," that it is the "itch of historians to say something new about something already known." The contemporary reader knows how things turned out and it often seems they had to turn out that way. The challenge before the historian is to bring the reader back to the point when we did not know how things would turn out and when the forks in the road were still hidden. There is little point in writing history, or reading it for that matter, if no idea, no reinterpretation, no fresh conclusion is worth exploring. Most of the conclusions reached in this work are underpinned by primary sources. The president's private and public papers at the Franklin D. Roosevelt Presidential Library at Hyde Park are a treasure trove revealing the president's wartime leadership. The files of FDR's Map Room, which became the White House nerve center during the war, provide firsthand, eyewitness, day-by-day accounts as we watch the war unfold. We see the president sparring with Marshall, dispatching Harry Hopkins, measuring Eisenhower, clashing with Stalin and agreeing with, disputing, and being cajoled by Churchill. These original sources have been buttressed by the review of the papers of George Marshall, Dwight Eisenhower, Joseph Stilwell, and George Patton along with several others. My reading of the contemporary newspaper coverage of the war provided a you-are-there perspective.

No human endeavor matches the destructive scale of warfare. Over sixty nations were involved in World War II. The fronts on which the United States fought reached halfway around the globe, from the rim of Asia to the middle of Europe, spanning 12,590 miles. The "good war" cost an estimated 62 million to 78 million military and civilian deaths worldwide, ranging from 301,000 in a country as small as the Netherlands to over 23 million in the Soviet Union. The shattering of normal life, the dying, the homelessness, the hunger, the maiming, the sum total of misery inflicted on individuals and families, the destruction of property including cultural treasures, is incalculable. The historian Max Hastings has described World War II as the "most disastrous human experience in history."

Franklin Roosevelt stood at the vortex of this calamity. The ultimate question pursued in this work is whether the fulfillment of his roles, recruiter, strategist, and home front leader, hastened victory, with the concomitant saving of millions of lives, or whether they delayed the end with unnecessary death and destruction. Further, did the final victory achieve the lofty aims to which he pledged himself, to create a community of nations at peace, governed by democracy, freed from colonialism, oppression, despotism, and the baleful enterprise of war? We seek the answers in the story that follows.

ALBANY, NY
JULY 19, 2011

ROOSEVELT'S
CENTURIONS

CHAPTER 1

The Day We Almost Lost the Army

WHEN HE ENTERED A ROOM ONE SENSED, NO MATTER WHAT HE WORE, that here was a soldier. On July 9, 1941, General George Catlett Marshall, Army chief of staff, appeared before the Senate Committee on Military Affairs wearing a gray civilian suit, tall, shoulders squared but not conspicuously, chin receding slightly, thin lips compressed in a line of firm resolution, a figure exuding dignity and authority. Marshall was embarked on a mission that he regarded as vital as any in his forty years in uniform, to save the still anemic United States Army from emasculation. Unless the committee could be persuaded to report favorably on a bill to extend the draft, the nation's first peacetime draftees would soon complete their required one year of service and head home. Because President Franklin Roosevelt desperately wanted the draft extended, he had sent the less politically divisive Marshall to Capitol Hill to serve as point man before the committee. Marshall began his testimony, "If the term of service of the National Guard and of the selectees is not extended," he warned, ". . . under existing limitations of the law, almost two-thirds of our enlisted men and three-fourths of our officer personnel will have to be released after completing 12 months of service." He mounted a strong finish, citing the disaster of an expired draft on a vital garrison, "the great naval base of Pearl Harbor."

DEBATE OVER THE INITIAL DRAFT LAW the year before had been stormy. Upstate New York Republican congressman James Wadsworth introduced the legislation on June 20, 1940, two days before France gave up the fight against Nazi Germany. His championing of military service had a long pedigree. His great-grandfather, William Wadsworth, had been a brigadier general in the War of 1812. His grandfather, also James and a Civil War general, was killed in the Battle of the Wilderness. Wadsworth himself had served in the Spanish-American War. Wadsworth's measure, HR 10132, bore the ringing title "A Bill to Protect the Integrity and Institutions of the United States Through a System of Selective Compulsory Military Training and Service." The bill eventually called for a single year of Army service for men aged twenty-one through thirty-six. It sought to strengthen readiness, while keeping America out of the war raging in Europe by barring draftees from serving outside the United States, except in America's overseas possessions.

In the America of 1940, public interest in a far-off conflict remained low. Moviegoers were flocking to the season's hits, Walt Disney's *Fantasia*, W. C. Fields and Mae West in *My Little Chickadee*, and Katharine Hepburn and Cary Grant in *The Philadelphia Story*. Young Americans danced to the beat of Glenn Miller, Artie Shaw, and Benny Goodman and girls swooned to a new rage, Frank Sinatra, crooning "I'll Never Smile Again." Sports fans flocked to watch their heroes of the diamond, the gridiron, the tennis court, and the ring, Joe DiMaggio, Sammy Baugh, Don Budge, and Joe Louis. Initially, public opinion over the draft split down the middle according to a Gallup poll taken less than a month before the bill's introduction. But as Europe's dominoes began to fall before the Nazi onslaught—Denmark, Norway, Holland, Belgium, and, most shockingly, the swift collapse of France—American public opinion began to shift. By August, some six weeks after HR 10132's introduction, the latest Gallup poll showed 71 percent of Americans favoring a peacetime draft.

Still, opponents were vigorous and organized. Senator Claude Pepper of Florida spoke in favor of the bill and found himself hanged in effigy outside the Capitol by the Congress of American Mothers. "Pauline Revere," in colonial garb, rode a white horse up the Capitol steps and carried a sign that read, "Mobilize for Peace and Defeat Conscription." The isolationist America First Committee boasted among its members former President Theodore Roosevelt's outspoken daughter Alice Longworth, aviation hero Charles Lindbergh, and Hollywood star Lillian Gish. America Firsters argued that should beleaguered Britain fall, the wisest course for America was to find an accommodation with Germany rather than embroil the country in another European war.

Tempers frayed as the debate in Congress dragged on. Martin Sweeney, an isolationist Ohio Democrat, denounced the bill as a Roosevelt ruse to drag America into the conflict. Mr. Beverly Vincent, a representative from Kentucky, called Sweeney a traitor and "a son-of-a-bitch." Sweeney took a swing at Vincent, who counterpunched with a hard right to Sweeney's head. The House doorkeeper described the fracas as the best fistfight he had witnessed in his fifty years in his post.

On September 14, after being amended thirty-three times, the draft bill carried handily by 47 to 25 votes in the Senate and by 232 to 124 in the House. Two days later, the president signed the first peacetime draft.

Registrants for the draft far exceeded the Army's needs and a national lottery was to be held to determine who would go first. The date for the lottery posed a dilemma for FDR. He was facing his precedent-shattering run for a third term and his Republican opponent, the rumpled, affable, astute Wall Street lawyer Wendell Willkie, had found his campaign issue: FDR, Willkie charged, was a warmonger. Roosevelt's political advisors pleaded with him to wait until the election was over before staging the lottery. FDR, so often accused of political sleight-of-hand, said no. He scheduled the lottery for October 29, one week before the election.

At noon, the paraplegic president, held upright by his leg braces, stood before a ten-gallon fishbowl filled with 8,500 numbers stuffed into cellulose capsules. What followed suggested the rites of a mystical fraternal society. The fishbowl containing the capsules was the one used for the World War I draft lottery. An aide blindfolded Secretary of War Henry Stimson with a strip of yellow linen from a chair used at the signing of the Declaration of Independence. Another aide stirred the capsules with a ladle carved from one of the rafters in Independence

Hall. The old-fashioned Stimson, his silver hair parted in the middle, mustache bristling, exuding respectability, reached into the bowl, drew out a capsule, and handed it to the president, who read the number aloud, "One-fifty-eight!" A woman's cry broke from the audience. Mrs. Mildred Bell's twenty-one-year-old son held that number.

On the day after the lottery, Roosevelt, fearing that Willkie's "warmonger" label might stick, used a campaign speech at the Boston Garden to promise, "While I am talking to you fathers and mothers, I give you one more assurance. I have said this before, but I shall say it again and again and again; your boys are not going to be sent into any foreign wars." To Sam Rosenman, FDR's close confidant, and the playwright-speechwriter Robert Sherwood, he had commented earlier, "If someone attacks us, it isn't a foreign war, is it?" FDR's son James confronted his father about the "dishonesty of his war stand." FDR explained, "If I don't say I hate war, then people are going to think I don't hate war. If I say we're going to get into this war, people will think I want us in it. If I don't say I won't send our sons to fight on foreign battlefields, then people will think I want to send them. . . . So you play the game the way it has been played over the years, and you play to win." In the end, backing the draft proved no obstacle to the president's reelection. On November 5, FDR defeated Willkie by five million votes in the popular count and by 449 electoral votes to his opponent's 82.

The draft became a popular phenomenon. Comedian Bob Hope and movie siren Dorothy Lamour starred in a film called *Caught in the Draft*, a wacky comedy about the futility of trying to beat the system. A comic strip called *Draftie* appeared. Jokes about reveille, marching, mess halls, and leather-lunged sergeants became staples for radio comedians. Young men and their families quickly mastered the thirteen draft categories ranging from 1A, the fittest, to 4F, unfit for the military. Those classified 1A began receiving letters from the government that began, "Greeting: . . . you are hereby notified that you have now been selected for immediate military service."

Baseball team owners split over the issue of deferments for their players. Warren Giles of the Cincinnati Reds professed that as far as the draft was concerned, his stars would "go just as fast as the batboy."

Harry Grabiner of the Chicago White Sox argued that baseball and its stars were vital to maintaining America's morale. In the end, standouts like the Cleveland Indians' Bob Feller, the New York Yankees' Phil Rizzuto, and the Detroit Tigers' Most Valuable Player, Hank Greenberg, were all classified 1A. So was the world heavyweight champion, Joe Louis.

Ten days after the lottery, 100,000 young Americans were out of civvies and into khaki and olive drab.

ALMOST A YEAR PASSED. The twelve-month draftees were beginning to approach their discharge date when Congressman Wadsworth introduced another HR 10132 to extend their service. Once again, opponents mobilized, and the issue was debated throughout the summer of 1941 in Senate and House hearings. A full-page ad appeared in *The New York Times* signed by 240 educators who proclaimed, "In our view, peacetime conscription and American democracy are incompatible . . . never before in American history has it been necessary."

Jim Wadsworth gathered a group of skeptical fellow House Republicans to a private dining room in Washington's Army-Navy Club to hear Marshall make his case. One balky congressman told Marshall, "You put the case very well, but I will be damned if I am going to go along with Mr. Roosevelt." The usually unflappable Marshall exploded: "You are going to let plain hatred of the personality dictate to you to do something that you realize is very harmful to the interest of the country!" Marshall countered their doubts until two o'clock in the morning. *Time* magazine reported, "The President has sent in General George C. Marshall, Army Chief of Staff, to carry the ball. Good soldier Marshall pounded down the field through center, off tackle, around the ends. . . . By now, General Marshall had smashed all the way to the one-yard line."

Not quite yet. The Senate Military Affairs Committee held hearings on July 17. The lead-off witness that day was Norman Thomas, the preeminent Socialist in the land, bland and bow-tied, looking every bit the Presbyterian minister he had once been. The Socialist Party's four-time candidate for president branded Marshall an FDR dupe. "To an extent that he may not realize, the prestige of General Marshall's name, his plans for the organization of his opinions, are being used in a great game of politics," Thomas charged, "the logical end of which is a war which 70 or possibly 80 percent of the American people do not want." He heaped scorn on FDR's recent claim that even Iceland was in the Western Hemisphere and thus needed to be defended by the United States. What was next, Thomas asked, "perhaps some lonely posts in Siberia . . . occupation of the Sahara Desert?"

Warned that passage of the bill was imperiled, FDR gave up a weekend at his beloved Hyde Park home and stayed in Washington to plot the next move. On July 21, he summoned reporters and before rolling cameras and radio microphones warned that if Congress failed to act, "beginning this autumn . . . the Army of the United States will begin . . . to melt away." He recalled the nation's perilous birth. "The risks and weaknesses caused by dissolving a trained Army in times of national peril were pointed out by George Washington over and over again in his messages to the Continental Congress."

Hearings continued throughout a steaming summer. On July 28, Mrs. Rosa Farber, an opponent speaking for the Mothers of America before the House Committee on Military Affairs, asked, had the members forgotten the song popular when the draft had first been enacted, "Good-bye Dear, I'll Be Back in a Year"? "You talk about breaking faith with draftees," Georgia Democratic congressman Eugene Cox struck back. The congressman, described as "resembling a paunchy, aging matinee idol," asked, "But what about breaking faith with the Nation? When our country calls, who will refuse to answer? . . . Let us say to the world that we are Americans and that we mean business."

As the possibility grew that men awaiting their discharge might be kept in uniform, scrawled letters began to appear on barrack walls, latrines, and mess halls in Army posts across the country: OHIO. Passersby assumed that men from the Buckeye State were serving there. Actually, the letters stood for "Over the Hill in October." Impatient draftees reasoned that Uncle Sam had entered into a contract with them and by October they would have met their end of the bargain. They now threatened to go home, regardless of what Congress did.

As the final August 12 vote on the extension bill neared, according to the latest Gallup poll, 51 percent of Americans believed the draftees' tour should be extended while 45 percent thought they should be released. On the eve of the House vote, Turner Catledge, the *New York Times* political analyst, warned, "the Administration has not yet sufficiently impressed Congress and the country with the gravity of the emergency so far as it affects the self interest of the United States."

Shortly before final debate in the House, Democrat John McCormack, the majority leader, called the president's press secretary, Stephen Early, with disturbing news. McCormack warned that he could not guarantee delivery of his Democratic members for passage of the extension bill. Forty-five Democrats planned to oppose it. Thirty-five more were undecided. He had "lost control of his people," McCormack admitted.

FDR, convinced that he had personally pressed his case as far as he dared and with a secret mission occupying his thoughts, quietly slipped out of the capital aboard the presidential yacht, *Potomac,* for what he claimed would be ten days of fishing. *The New York Times* reported, "For probably the first time in American history, the whereabouts of the President of the United States has been unknown for three days to the American people and to most, if not all, ranking government officials." The *Times* noted, "With Winston Churchill also vanished from the public eye, speculation reached a new high mark."

On August 12, House members prepared to vote on HR 10132. The speaker, Sam Rayburn, clad in his customary funereal dark suit, mounted the rostrum. To Rayburn, a fifty-nine-year-old bachelor, the House was his home, the first and last love of his life. He had come to this chamber twenty-eight years before, the end point of an extraordinary climb from Texas cotton fields tilled by him and ten siblings, through his election to the Texas legislature, to now, essentially becoming the second most powerful man in the country. At 10 A.M., Rayburn, anticipating a grueling day, called the House to order two hours earlier than usual. Fortunately, the ordinarily sweltering capital was cool with rain threatening. Reporters filled every seat in the press gallery. Depending on how one viewed the issue, the lawmakers were voting to save the Army, or to rebuff that warmonger in the White House.

The House resolved itself into the committee of the whole with Andrew Jackson May, a Kentucky Democrat and the chairman of Military Affairs, known as "Millions for Defense May," presiding. The parliamentary maneuver freed Speaker Rayburn to work the House floor and cloakroom for passage, wielding his massive power and collecting on favors due.

Pennsylvania congressman Charles Isiah Faddis, who had risen to lieutenant colonel in the First World War, took the floor and spoke of a letter that a fellow representative, Clare Hoffman, had sent to members the day before, "warning me," Faddis said, "to be careful of my political scalp." He went on, "To think that any man who is a member of this body would take into consideration and weigh against the security of his nation whether or not he was going to be returned to the House of Representatives. My God! What have we come to? To what depths have we sunk?" Usher L. Burdick, a North Dakota Republican, bejowled, white-haired, and avuncular, scoffed at the suggestion that America faced imminent danger. "Germany has not yet been able to swim the English Channel," Burdick noted of the long awaited Nazi invasion of Britain after France fell. "It is nothing but a pipe dream to think that Germany could land troops in the United States." Another extension opponent, Congressman James W. Mott, an Oregon Republican, called conscription "the method which has long been employed by Hitler, by Mussolini, by Stalin and by the totalitarians who control the Japanese government." Congressman Robert E. Thomason, a Texas Democrat, shot back, rattling off a litany of Nazi conquests: Czechoslovakia and Poland in 1939; Norway, Denmark, Holland, Belgium, France, and the occupations of Romania, Hungary, and Bulgaria in 1940; Greece and Yugoslavia in 1941. Germany "now dominates and has in enslavement over 200 million people." We are not getting nearer to war, Thomason declared, "war is getting nearer to us."

Outside, the sky darkened as the debate wore on and the rain tapered off. The session was now approaching its tenth hour with no break for lunch or dinner. Bleary-eyed members ducked out to the speaker's lobby, the one place where, amid the clatter of the Associated Press and United Press news tickers, they could have a smoke. Rayburn's adroit parliamentary footwork managed to beat back amendment after amendment intended to weaken or sink the bill, including motions to cut the extension to six months, give soldiers free travel home, and to release men whose families depended on them for support. Though all were defeated, Rayburn's head count revealed that he still lacked the votes to pass the bill.

Sol Bloom, a diminutive, feisty representative from Manhattan and the chairman of the House Foreign Affairs Committee, briefly left the chamber. The theatrical Bloom had in his twenties already amassed a fortune bringing midway attractions to the 1893 Chicago World's Fair before he turned to politics. He entered the cloakroom and lit a cigar to calm his nerves. There he found a colleague who said that he was going to change his vote from "yea" to "nay." According to Bloom, he blocked the man, threatening, "you'll have to knock me through the doorway if you want to return to the floor. I'm going to stand right here."

Rayburn replaced Chairman May and resumed the speaker's role. "The question is on the passage of the bill," he called out. Initially it appeared that the bill had passed with 204 yeas to 201 nays, with 27 not voting. But New York congressman Andrew L. Somers announced, "I change my vote and vote nay," which left the proponents with only a one-vote edge. Dewey Short, a Republican opponent of the measure from Missouri, impressive, dignified, a former minister and a member of the isolationist Committee to Keep America Out of War, seized a tactical stratagem to reverse the outcome. Short called for a "recapitulation," which would require the clerk, Hans Jorgenson, to go through the entire House membership to repeat their original vote. Rayburn allowed the recapitulation, recognizing that Short had blundered. Had he called for a "reconsideration," instead of a "recapitulation," members would have been able to change their vote. An electric hush gripped the chamber during the forty-five minutes it took Jorgenson to call the roll. In the end, the 203 to 202 vote held. Rayburn gave a

whack of his gavel that resounded throughout the chamber and announced, "The vote stands and the bill is passed." The clock above the
speaker's rostrum showed 8:39 P.M. A cacophony of applause, boos,
cheers, jeers, clapping, and hissing erupted from the gallery. The Senate
had already passed a similar bill by the more comfortable margin of 45
to 30 among those who voted. Immediately after the House vote, the
members approved a resolution conforming the two bills. The next day
The New York Times editorialized that the extension meant draftees
will "give their time in order that an unprepared American Army may
not be butchered in a war brought on by its own weakness."

Six days later, on August 18, FDR, back in Washington and flush
with success after a secret meeting at Argentia, Newfoundland, with
Prime Minister Churchill, signed the draft extension into law.

Less than four months later, America was at war.

★

GEORGE MARSHALL, SO ESTEEMED BY CONGRESS, had come into
Franklin Roosevelt's official circle on the very day that, for the second
time in two decades, Europe had erupted into war. On September 1,
1939, FDR was asleep in his bedroom when his valet, Irvin McDuffie,
woke him saying the White House switchboard had the president's ambassador to France, William Bullitt, on the line. Bill Bullitt was the
president's kind of guy, ebullient, bursting with ideas, charming and
rich, popular in Paris as the party-loving "champagne ambassador." In
1933, Bullitt had been Roosevelt's choice as the first American ambassador to Moscow since the 1917 revolution. This morning Bullitt's tone
was grim. He had just talked to America's envoy in Poland, he said, who
informed him that Germany had sent its army across the Polish border
and that over 1,000 aircraft were raining destruction on Warsaw. "Then
it's happened," Roosevelt replied resignedly. The president had his valet
prop him up in bed and instructed the switchboard to call the secretaries of state, war, and navy and his military chiefs. Soon, office lights
began to blaze throughout the sleepy capital. To Roosevelt, the moment
had an eerily familiar ring. During the four years of the First World
War, while serving as President Wilson's assistant secretary of the navy,

he had become accustomed to the phone jangling at his bedside in the small hours with reports of ship sinkings and sabotage attempts.

Marshall was at his official residence, number one General's Row at Fort Myer, in northern Virginia, when the call came from the War Department that Europe was once again at war. The Marshalls had just moved in and the bare-walled government housing was still a turmoil of unpacked boxes. They had been living temporarily in a handsome home on Wyoming Avenue loaned to them by a wealthy World War I comrade of Marshall's, Colonel George Patton. With the call to Fort Myer, the even tenor of peacetime Army life had been shattered in a blink for Marshall, Patton, and every American in uniform.

At eleven the following morning, Marshall was summoned to the Oval Study on the second floor of the White House where FDR preferred to work more often than in the formal Oval Office in the West Wing. Along with the president were Secretary of War Henry H. Woodring; his assistant, Louis A. Johnson; the acting secretary of the navy, Charles Edison; and the chief of naval operations, Admiral Harold R. Stark. Somber of mien this day, the usually genial president studied his visitors from behind a massive desk holding bottles of medicine, a clock in the shape of a ship's wheel, a bronze bust of the president's wife, Eleanor, four cloth donkeys, and a can holding the two packs of Camel cigarettes that the president smoked daily, among other bric-a-brac. Nautical prints decorated the walls and model sailing ships lay becalmed along the tops of cabinets. By now, Marshall had been running the Army informally at Roosevelt's direction for nearly six months. Earlier this day, wearing an unlikely white Palm Beach suit, he had been officially sworn in by Woodring as chief of staff, the head of the U.S. Army. He thereupon was promoted to temporary four-star general with a salary of $9,770 a year plus an annual expense allowance of $2,200, still lagging woefully behind the personal fortune of his friend George Patton.

The man whom Roosevelt had raised to the pinnacle of the American military was then fifty-nine, two years older than FDR. George Catlett Marshall was the third child of George and Laura Marshall, born on New Year's Eve in 1880, six years after brother Stuart and five years after sister Marie. Nothing in his boyhood augured the life he would one day lead. By the time George was born, his father had moved the family from Kentucky to Uniontown, Pennsylvania, a community prospering through its blue-collar industries—iron, steel, radiators, coke, and bricks. The elder Marshall initially succeeded in the coal and wood business, and George's boyhood passed comfortably in a big house on West Main Street while he attended a private school. The elder Marshall was sensitive to social position and rarely missed an opportunity to remind people that the family was related, however remotely, to John Marshall, the distinguished nineteenth-century chief justice of the U.S. Supreme Court. Young George grew to slightly above average height, rather spindly, with sandy hair parted in the middle in the style of the day. He was, to his father's distress, a poor student with one exception. "If it was history, that was all right," he later recalled, "I could star in history." The boy occasionally showed an entrepreneurial spark, at one point breeding a prize tomato for sale to local grocers and raising fighting cocks.

All his life Marshall would be marked by a stony reserve. The root may lie in the boy's acute sensitivity to what he regarded as humiliating experiences. "People made fun of me a great deal," he remembered of his youth. In the most painful incident, his father had assigned George the regular chore of hosing down the street in front of the house, usually littered with horse manure. As he performed the dreaded task, boys passing by taunted him with upturned posteriors and rude noises. The girls giggled. On another occasion, he and a pal fashioned a raft from scrap lumber and floated their "ferry" on a local stream, charging pennies for the ride. One day, a group of girls came aboard and refused to pay. "I was humiliated," Marshall remembered, "and what made it worse, my chum, Andy, began laughing at me," while the girls stuck out their tongues. Reserve, to a degree, armors one from revealing inner vulnerability and that may have been how Marshall's guardedness began.

The Marshalls' comfortable life came to a halt when the father lost heavily in a land speculation. His checks bounced, he was sued by creditors, and Mrs. Marshall let the servants go. To save money the family began taking its meals in a cheap hotel. After dinner, Mrs. Marshall would ask the cook for scraps, to feed the dogs, she said, but actually to put meat in a stew. Young George was yanked from the private academy and put into a public school. Eventually, the family fortune was sufficiently recouped to enable him to enroll again in a private school. He forever recalled this brush with poverty as "painful and humiliating . . . a black spot on my boyhood." He said later, with unintended condescension, "every boy in a democracy should attend, at least for a period of time, a public school."

Marshall's older brother, Stuart, had been sent off to Virginia Military Institute in Lexington, and after completing high school George applied to VMI as well. He was admitted on the strength of Stuart's record and the family's old Virginia name. Though run along military lines with uniforms, barracks, drill, and hazing, VMI was not principally a preparatory school for aspiring Army officers. At the time young Marshall matriculated, no more than ten VMI graduates were on duty in the Regular Army. What the school did offer was a solid education in the sciences and engineering.

VMI was steeped in the Confederate past and most of Marshall's fellow students were southerners. He was sixteen at the time, still tall, gangly, and shy. His classmates "pretty much kept the pressure on me because of my northern accent," he recalled with lingering resentment. First-year students, "rats," were subjected to semi-sadistic hazing. In Marshall's second week, an upperclassman ordered him to squat over an upright bayonet. Weak from a recent bout of typhoid, he sunk onto the blade, suffering a wound that required hospitalization. When released, he said nothing to anyone about the incident. Out of respect for his silence, the upperclassmen called off hazing in the school for the rest of that year. His aura of quiet authority quickly catapulted him to leadership of his class, where he ranked first in military aptitude. In the only sport he played, intercollegiate football, he made All-Southern tackle, a canny performer better able to outthink his opponents than overpower them. By his senior year, he had attained the highest cadet rank, senior first captain. The form of his character had by now become fixed and never really changed: the formality, the habit of command, and above all the impenetrable reserve.

Marshall had entered VMI with no particular military vocation. On August 12, 1898, with America's victory in the Spanish-American War, a resurgence of patriotism gripped the nation as at no time since the Civil War. Back briefly for a visit to Uniontown, the young cadet watched returning veterans parade through the streets, hailed as conquering heroes and eyed admiringly by the women. Local boosters painted Main Street red, white, and blue. Flags and banners fluttered from verandas and storefronts. Marshall later admitted that these heady days provoked his "first great emotional reaction" and had a "determining effect on my choice of profession." The decision made, he began angling for a commission in the Regular Army. In the spring of 1901, as graduation neared, Marshall's father began an aggressive campaign to help his son, buttonholing anyone with whom he had the slightest political connection. The elder Marshall's lobbying was matched by an unexpected burst of brazenness on the part of his often silent son. George journeyed to Washington and without an appointment went to the White House to see President William McKinley. After watching serial groups of people ushered into the president's quarters, an idea struck him. "As a man and his daughter went in . . . I attached myself to the tail end of the procession and gained the President's office. . . . After the people had met the President, they also went out, leaving me standing. Mr. McKinley, in a very nice manner, asked what I wanted and I stated my case." Marshall did not recall any specific result from his gambit with McKinley, but on January 4, 1902, he was commissioned a second lieutenant in the U.S. Army.

Earlier, in his final year at VMI, George Marshall had fallen in love. She was four years older and lived just outside the gate of the school. Marshall had become enchanted by the piano playing he heard emanating from the home of Elizabeth "Lily" Carter Coles. Months after an arduous courtship and after receiving his commission he married the titian-haired, fair-skinned, brown-eyed Lily, by all accounts a beauty.

Marshall began to follow the slow slog of an officer in the peacetime Army: a tour in the Philippines, then service in the Oklahoma Territory. The snail-like pace depressed him. It took him eighteen years to make major, only three grades above his original rank. He wrote to the VMI superintendent, his former math instructor, that the path upward was clogged by "large numbers of men of nearly the same age all in the single grade." But he stayed on. His career finally took flight when the country went to war against Germany on April 6, 1917. Marshall was posted to France as chief of operations (G-3) for the First Division. On his arrival at the port of Saint-Nazaire he had been met by a French officer. As the two drove off Marshall decided to dust off his college French. Commenting on the sunny weather, he said to his escort, "Je suis très beau aujourd'hui." As the Frenchman eyed him oddly, Marshall realized what he had said: I am very beautiful today. "I never spoke French again except when forced to," Marshall recalled.

On October 3, 1917, Marshall's division braced for an inspection by the commander of the American Expeditionary Forces, General John J. "Black Jack" Pershing. The general, a stickler for discipline and military decorum, began pacing before the troops, cataloguing the First Division's failings. To everyone's disbelief, Marshall interrupted. "There is something to be said here," he began, "and I think I should say it because I've been here the longest." He then began respectfully but firmly to rebut what he thought were Pershing's unfair criticisms. Nothing records Pershing's reaction, but on subsequent visits to the division he always sought out Marshall and asked his opinion of the division's preparedness. Subsequently, he brought Marshall to Chaumont, AEF headquarters, and appointed him to his operation's staff.

On the last day of the war, November 11, 1918, certain American generals, in a last-minute bid for glory, ordered their troops out of the trenches to face German Maxim machine guns hours, even minutes before the cease-fire set for 11 A.M. At least 320 American doughboys lost their lives that morning fighting an enemy that had already conceded defeat. Marshall was nearly killed by a bomb blast in the last half hour.

Marshall remained at Pershing's side for the next five years serving as aide-de-camp. And then the slow round of peacetime postings resumed: Tientsin, China; an instructorship at the Army War College; command of an infantry division. On September 15, 1927, Lily, his beloved wife of twenty-five years, was hospitalized with a weak heart and thyroid condition. She underwent an operation while Marshall was delivering a lecture at the base. A guard summoned him to the telephone and later remembered how Marshall, "spoke for a moment over the phone then put his head on his arms on the desk in deep grief." He lifted his head only to say, "I just had word my wife . . . has just died." Two months later, appointed assistant commandant of the Infantry School at Fort Benning, Georgia, Marshall fought off heartache and loneliness through compulsive work and a joyless schedule of social activities for his staff. He organized riding competitions, hunts, pageants, amateur theatricals, anything to keep his mind and body engaged. Still, his distress was evident. He lost weight and for a time developed a nervous tic that trembled in the corner of his mouth.

Then his life changed. In 1929, Marshall had gone to a dinner in Columbus, Georgia. There he eyed a tall, regal woman, a former actress named Katherine Boyce Tupper Brown, a widow with three children, Molly, seventeen, Clifton, fifteen, and Allen, thirteen. He offered to drive Mrs. Brown home and took her along a circuitous one-hour route whose purpose was all too evident to the widow. In time, they drew closer, but before allowing the relationship to ripen into marriage, Katherine wanted her children's approval and invited Marshall to visit the family at a summer resort. Soon after the invitation's arrival, Marshall received a note in a schoolboy's hand that said, "Don't be nervous, it is O.K. with me. A friend in need is a friend indeed." The note was signed by Allen Brown. George and Katherine were married on October 15, 1930. General Pershing served as best man. Marshall's relations with his stepchildren were warm, and he developed a particular affection for Allen.

During the Great War, Marshall had witnessed mistakes by raw, unseasoned officers that were paid for in men's lives. Believing that similar failings would occur in the next war, he wanted, he said, "a technique and methods so simple and so brief that the citizen officer of good common sense can readily grasp the idea." Thus, while posted at

Benning, Marshall authored an infantry tactic in which half a platoon would carry out a steady fire to keep the enemies' heads down while the other half swept around to outflank the hunkering foe. Fire and Flank was to become part of the American infantryman's catechism.

After a slow but steadily rising career, something inexplicable happened threatening to derail Marshall. In 1933 he was assigned as senior instructor with the Illinois National Guard. For a Regular Army officer so drab a posting represented a military graveyard. Here was a man who seventeen years before had been described by his then commanding officer, Lieutenant Colonel John Hagood, as "a military genius." Answering the annual efficiency report question as to whether he would want Marshall to serve under him in battle, Hagood responded, "I would prefer to serve *under* his command." Former vice president Charles G. Dawes, who had also served with General Pershing in the Great War, went to him pleading that the then Army chief of staff, Douglas MacArthur, change Marshall's assignment. "He can't do that," Dawes argued. "Hell no! Not George Marshall. He's too big a man for the job. In fact he's the best goddam officer in the U.S. Army." Pershing went to MacArthur pleading Marshall's case. Marshall himself requested a more suitable assignment. MacArthur's curt reply was, "Request refused." During service in this military Siberia, Katherine Marshall recalled, "George had a gray, drawn look, which I had never seen before, and have seldom seen since."

Marshall's prospects began to revive when Franklin Roosevelt became president. He did not vote for FDR. He never voted for anybody. But he seized on a Roosevelt initiative. In one of FDR's earliest New Deal efforts to combat unemployment, the president created the Civilian Conservation Corps. The CCC would take restless young men off city streets, feed them decent food, engage them in wholesome exercise, and put structure into their lives. They would control flooding, combat forest fires, and spruce up parks, beaches, and historic sites. Only the Army possessed the expertise to organize the eventual 2.5 million young men who entered the CCC. Involvement in a civilian effort to clear brush was not a coveted assignment for a career officer, but Marshall sensed the chance to do something useful in a country mired in depression. He plunged into the work, setting records in creating new camps. He later described this chapter of his life as "the most instructive service I have ever had . . . the best antidote for mental stagnation an Army officer in my position can have."

In 1935, Secretary of War George Dern received a message in Roosevelt's unmistakable handwriting. "General Pershing asks very strongly that Colonel George C. Marshall (Infantry) be promoted to general," Roosevelt had written. "Can we put him on the list of next promotions?" Again, Douglas MacArthur, still Army chief of staff, blocked Marshall's way. Marshall, he said, should wait until he could first be appointed to command infantry. Finally, in August 1936, with MacArthur out as chief of staff, Marshall received his first star. Thirty-four years after entering the Army, he had become a brigadier general.

More than two years later, on November 14, 1938, Marshall had his first opportunity to deal personally with the president. He was invited to the White House with the secretary of the treasury, the solicitor general, the assistant secretary of war, and an Air Corps representative (before the service was renamed the Air Forces). Germany's growing airpower had begun to trouble FDR. He told his visitors that he wanted Congress to appropriate an unimaginable sum to build the nation's peacetime Air Force to 24,000 planes a year, though he said with a sly smile that he would settle for 12,000. He believed the buildup necessary to protect the hemisphere "from the North Pole to the South Pole." The nation, he said, faced the greatest threat of foreign intervention since pronouncement of the Monroe Doctrine in 1823. Pleased with what he regarded as an unassailable case, FDR turned to Marshall and said, "Don't you think so, George?" Marshall shrank from the president's casual use of first names for people he scarcely knew, finding the practice condescending. He himself usually referred to even his close associates by their last names. Marshall answered, "I am sorry, Mr. President, but I don't agree with that at all." The president had glossed over what expansion of airpower on that scale would require in training pilots, building airfields, and producing ammunition, he said. He also believed that FDR had overstated the danger to the Western Hemisphere. After the meeting, as he walked down the White House steps, a fellow officer quipped that Marshall could expect his next posting to be Alaska, maybe even Guam.

Later, the president confessed that his bid for a huge aircraft expansion had little to do with hemispheric defense. What he really wanted was to produce enough planes to supply France and Britain, enabling them to deter the threat of Hitler's ever more powerful Luftwaffe. It would take time for a straight shooter like Marshall to follow the labyrinthine twists of Franklin Roosevelt's mind. Yet FDR, who was constantly told "yes," was drawn to a man who dared tell him "no." Marshall's bluntness did not torpedo his career that day.

On Sunday, April 23, 1939, the general was at his home in Leesburg, Virginia, engaged in his favorite weekend relaxation, cutting brush, pruning trees, planting vegetables, and maintaining a compost heap in which he took inordinate pride. He was called away to take a call summoning him to the White House. He was ushered into FDR's upstairs study and, to his surprise, found that they were alone. Not even Marshall's civilian superior, the secretary of war, was present. After a forty-minute monologue, FDR finally got to the point, his intention to make Marshall the Army chief, jumping over four other generals senior to him. Marshall did not immediately leap at what should have represented the apex of a professional soldier's career. Instead, he told Roosevelt that, if he took the job, he intended to speak his mind in a way that might not always be welcome. "Is that all right?" he asked. The president waved aside any concern and said, yes, of course it was all right. Marshall pressed on, "You said *yes* pleasantly, but it may be unpleasant." Again, Roosevelt dismissed Marshall's reservations. FDR had made the signal appointment of his wartime leadership. And he rarely addressed Marshall by his first name. Told of her husband's selection, Mrs. Marshall immediately wrote to the president. "For years I feared that his brilliant mind and unusual opinions were hopelessly caught in more or less of a treadmill," she said. "That you should recognize his ability and place in him your confidence gives me all I have dreamed of and hoped for."

With the passage of the years Marshall's once sandy hair had now turned gray; his posture was still erect, his blue-eyed gaze penetrating.

He could not be described as handsome. The long line of the upper lip was too thin, too grimly set. The nose was snubbed, and the chin receded slightly. His features combined plainness with something nevertheless arresting, rather like an American Gothic as depicted by Grant Wood. He spoke with quiet confidence, using few but emphatic hand gestures. The overall impression was of massive authority, carried unaffectedly as though he had been born to lead.

He was to a remarkable degree a man who had molded his own character. As a boy he had dodged activities in which he could not excel. In his maturity, he forced himself to master the very tasks for which he had little natural ability. He recognized that his obsession with work risked a danger to his physical and mental well-being and he forced himself to take time off, treasuring the moments when he could escape to Leesburg. His natural temperament was highly flammable, but years of self-discipline had enabled him, most of the time, to mask the passions that swirled beneath the controlled exterior. Inclined like most people to want to be agreeable, he steeled himself to saying "no," even to his closest Army associates, warning them to measure up or move out. Officers who failed him experienced his scalding anger, or worse, cold contempt. He was impervious to the guile of sycophants. Pressure on him to advance a particular officer's fortune was likely to backfire. Dwight Eisenhower, while still a middle grade officer, recalled, "I was in his office one day when someone called him on the telephone, apparently to urge the promotion of some friend in the Army. His answer was, 'If the man is a friend of yours, the best service you can do him is to avoid mentioning his name to me.'" Eisenhower further noted that Marshall resented any efforts to "pass the buck" to the chief. Officers who could handle details were a dime a dozen, Marshall remarked, "but they left to him the necessity of making every decision." Eisenhower noted, "Another type General Marshall disliked was the truculent personality—the man who confused firmness and strength with bad manners and deliberate discourtesy." The ultimate sin in Marshall's eyes, Eisenhower remembered, was for "those with too great a love of the limelight."

The general lived plainly, his routines invariable. He rose every morning at 6:30 and rode horseback for an hour. He was, however, not part of the horsey set. Riding was strictly for exercise. He remained in superb physical condition except for a pulse rate that occasionally became erratic, the arrhythmia induced by a malfunctioning thyroid gland and relieved by exercise. By eight he had breakfasted and was at his office at the War Department in the Munitions Building on the corner of 20th Street and Constitution Avenue in Northwest Washington. The building had originally been thrown up as temporary office space in 1918 to handle the wartime explosion of government. His desk was bare except for a blotter and a wooden in-basket and another out-basket. On one wall hung an oil portrait of General Pershing, on the opposite wall a painting of a World War I battle scene. His daily needs were met by his orderly, Master Sergeant James Powder, nearly six feet five and broad as a bull. The name had been anglicized from its Polish origins and his roots ran back to an ancestor who had fought with Napoleon in Russia. Powder kept the general supplied with handfuls of dime-store reading glasses that Marshall constantly lost. When the general's muscles knotted under stress, Powder massaged them. Marshall worked late, then brought home more work in a bulging briefcase before going to bed long after dark. Powder saw to it that when Marshall did retire he would find a candy bar and a selection of paperbacks at his bedside.

While Roosevelt had recognized Marshall's qualities, the two men still did not mesh easily. The chief of staff was determined to end the problem that had almost driven him to the brink of resignation years before: too many mediocre officers in their sixties standing in the way of abler colonels in their fifties. "The situation had resulted in the accumulation of large numbers of these senior officers who I felt were not suitable for combat command," Marshall concluded. He was determined to clean out the deadwood if he were to modernize the army. But approaching sixty, he believed himself in a poor position to fault other officers for being too old. He decided that he must resign and allow the president to appoint a younger chief of staff. "I would forfeit my career in the effort to make it possible," he decided. Marshall went to the White House to deliver his decision. FDR's confidant, Harry Hopkins, was also present. The president appeared to be listening to Marshall, but said nothing. He then launched into an hour-long monologue utterly unrelated to the subject at hand. Afterward, Marshall asked Hopkins if FDR had understood his intention. Hopkins responded, "The President just laughs at you." Marshall kept his job and went on to force out nearly three quarters of division and corps commanders whom he judged over the hill.

The Army chief found the president's habit of deflecting unwanted issues by monopolizing the conversation with irrelevancies maddening. Roosevelt had once explained this behavior at a reception for senators and congressmen. His secretaries, he said, would set up a ten-minute slot for a visitor, but "I get enthusiastic, and the result is that at the end of ten or fifteen minutes my visitor hasn't had a chance to get in a word edgewise. . . . If you do come in, say to me, quite frankly, 'Now listen, before you talk, Mr. President, let me have my say.'" Marshall observed that this advice was rarely hazarded and never heeded by FDR. While a nonstop talker, the president blocked attempts to record what he said. "I brought in [General John] Deane once to keep some notes," Marshall remembered. "He brought a big notebook and the President blew up. Next time Deane brought in a book so little he couldn't use it." Marshall concluded that the only way to break through the president's verbal barrage was by interrupting. On one occasion, Roosevelt began railing against a magazine critical of him, saying that he wanted it banned from Army bases. "I felt that he was going too far, and I told him so," Marshall recalled. But FDR insisted. "It finally got to the point where I told him that if he did this thing, I would resign and tell the nation why I resigned." The president let his demand wither.

Marshall was long in overcoming his conclusion that FDR, with his breezy manner, slapdash administration, and verbosity, was little more than a glib politician. On the other hand, Roosevelt had to endure Marshall's somber visage upon delivering a presidential wisecrack that had the rest of the room roaring with laughter. In time, if affection never grew between them, mutual respect did. Underneath the geniality and flippancy, Marshall discovered that FDR, faced with hard decisions, was tough-minded and courageous. For FDR's part, not only did he value Marshall's sober judgments but he knew that the universal respect the man commanded could win acceptance for his own policies from resistant political opponents. Roosevelt antagonists in Congress once spent four hours trying to trap Marshall into saying that FDR was a warmonger. He bore the pressure with forbearance and courtesy, but never yielded. Driving back to his office, he closed his eyes and said to an aide, "If I can only keep all personal feelings out of my system, I may be able to get through with this job." FDR told House speaker Sam Rayburn at a private lunch, "I am not always able to approve [Marshall's] recommendations. . . . But when I disapprove his recommendations, I don't have to look over my shoulder to see . . . whether he is going to the Capitol, to lobby against me." Rayburn explained why Marshall was so effective with Congress: "because when he takes the witness stand we forget we are Republicans or Democrats. We just remember that we are in the presence of a man who is telling the truth."

FDR could be maddening with his fluctuations, course reversals, and bewildering thought processes. But in Marshall he had found a sturdy oak able to bear the weight of his shifting predilections, a compass that always gave him a true bearing, whether he chose to heed it or not. In George Marshall, the president had made his single wisest choice for the military eventualities, as yet unknown, that loomed over the horizon.

✳

THE ARMY THAT GEORGE MARSHALL took over in 1939 was, for a country the size of the United States, pitifully weak. A nation with a population of 131 million had 174,000 men in uniform, ranking somewhere between Portugal and Bulgaria. Troops trained with broomsticks for rifles, stovepipes for mortars, trucks for tanks, firecrackers for gunfire, and eggs for hand grenades. So strapped was the Army that a field grade officer had to fill out a requisition for streetcar fare from the War Department to the Capitol. Marshall's task was to transform this small, stagnant, ill-equipped force into a first-rate fighting army. He was to do so in a country in which, even seven weeks after Germany had struck Poland, a poll showed that 95 percent of Americans wanted nothing to do with Europe's conflict.

CHAPTER 2

———— ★ ————

An End of Neutrality

$\mathbf{F}$RANKLIN ROOSEVELT CONTINUED TO MAINTAIN AT LEAST THE POSE of neutrality in a world plunged into war. He knew all too well that after America's involvement in the First World War public sentiment had swung around to the belief that the country had been bamboozled into entering that conflict. On April 2, 1917, President Woodrow Wilson had taken the country into war on a tide of impassioned eloquence. Face flushed, chin trembling, Wilson, reading from a speech he had typed himself, told a hushed joint session of Congress, "We have no selfish ends to serve. We desire no conquest, no dominion. We seek no indemnities for ourselves, no material compensation for the sacrifices we shall freely make." The president proclaimed in his cadenced, high church delivery that the United States was entering a far-off conflict with one noble purpose: "The world must be made safe for democracy." The applause when he closed was thunderous.

Over 8.5 million combatants and over 21 million civilians died in the War to End All Wars. But almost as soon as it was over, Wilson's fine ideals were trampled underfoot by victorious and vengeful allies. So harsh were the terms against Germany at the 1919 Versailles conference that they created fertile soil for the charismatic demagogue Adolf Hitler to rise to power.

In March 1934, sixteen years after the war, an article, "Arms and the Men," appeared in *Fortune* magazine and struck an immediate chord. The account stoked long simmering suspicion that America had been finagled into the Great War. The following month, a book, *Merchants of Death,* appeared and claimed to provide evidence of conspiracies among industrial tycoons to enrich themselves through arms sales. The book became an instant bestseller and a Book-of-the-Month Club selection. The Senate decided to act. Senator Gerald Nye, a forty-two-year-old Republican from North Dakota, a champion of farmers, headed what became known as the Senate Munitions Committee. Nye's panel held ninety-three hearings. It summoned powerful men to testify, J. P. Morgan Jr. and Pierre du Pont among them. In the end, the committee proposed nationalizing the arms industry to remove the profit. Franklin Roosevelt, in office since 1933, could hardly appear to be supporting capitalist malefactors who supported war to line their pockets. Nevertheless, he resisted completely abdicating his sworn responsibility to protect the country. He compromised, agreeing that, yes, arms making should be government-regulated, but he balked at unilateral U.S. action. "It is not possible," he said, "effectively to control such an evil by the isolated action of any one country." So out of fashion was military preparedness at the nadir of the Great Depression that FDR slashed the Army below its already skeletal strength.

Fearing another involvement in Europe's squabbles, Congress passed the first of the Neutrality Acts. The bill sailed through with heavy majorities in both the Senate and the House. Under the law, FDR was required to embargo the export of arms to any warring nation. Roosevelt signed it without a murmur. A year later the law was tightened further to ban even loans or credit to belligerents. That August, running for his second term and seeking to burnish his credentials as a man of peace, Roosevelt spoke at the sixty-two-year-old Chautauqua lecture series in western New York where he branded as "fool's gold" profits to be made from war. "If we face the choice of profit or peace," he declared, "the nation will answer, must answer, 'we choose peace.'" His patrician voice rising, he began describing his experience of war during the mission he had made to the European front in 1918. "I have seen war. . . . I have seen blood running from the wounded, I have seen men coughing out their gassed lungs. I have seen the dead in the mud. . . . I have seen children starving. I have seen the agony of mothers and wives." Then with a ringing tremolo he exclaimed, "I hate war ... I shall pass unnumbered hours, thinking and planning how war may be kept from this nation." His claim to have been a firsthand eyewitness to the horrors of war may have been exaggerated, but his portrayal of it was accurate enough. In 1937, Congress extended the law to exclude trade not only in armaments, but in any materials undergirding the prosecution of war, such as copper, steel, and oil.

While the United States sought to isolate itself behind a moat of neutrality, the world continued to become a more dangerous place. Japan, which had been nibbling at pieces of China since 1931, launched full-scale war there in 1937. In 1938 England's prime minister, Neville Chamberlain, France's premier, Edouard Daladier, and Italy's strongman, Benito Mussolini, sat down with Adolf Hitler in Munich and proceeded to carve up Czechoslovakia like a chicken on a plate. The Czechs had not been allowed at the table. Half past midnight on September 30, the negotiators agreed to cede the Czechs Sudetenland, home to ethnic Germans, to Germany, exactly the goal that had brought Hitler to Munich. On Chamberlain's return, as he stepped from his car at 10 Downing Street, he was greeted by cheering throngs. London's *Daily Mail* hailed him as the "Prince of Peace." He became a strong candidate for the Nobel Peace Prize. While Chamberlain was being celebrated in Parliament, one member, Winston Churchill, sat on his hands, noting grimly, "The government had to choose between shame and war. They chose shame and they will get war." FDR sent Prime Minister Chamberlain a cryptically noncommittal message: "Good man."

GEORGE MARSHALL AT THIS TIME again displayed the vision that combined military with social objectives. Roosevelt wanted to put men to work and Marshall wanted to strengthen the Army. In September 1938, Marshall proposed an idea to FDR's reliable weather vane, Harry Hopkins. Why not divert some of the money going to relieve unemployment to producing arms? Hopkins liked the plan and the two men went to see FDR. Roosevelt bought the idea and Marshall's creativity further impressed the president. The deed was done. FDR gave Admiral William Leahy, then chief of naval operations, $275 million to allot to the job-making Works Progress Administration. "It was relief money," the president said slyly, "relief of the Navy." Shipbuilding would put people to work just as surely as raking leaves.

At the same time, the president continued to guard his flanks against any appearance of warmongering. His secretary, Missy LeHand, placed in his reading file a letter that she said he must read. The missive was written in a neat longhand, dated April 15, 1939, and signed by Anthony A. Clay of Lyndhurst, New Jersey. "You certainly are using your energies trying to get us into the European mess," Clay began. "Why not mind your own business. I was for you 100% but I'm against you now. . . . Why not try keeping quiet. Every mother's son will certainly appreciate it. . . . Remember we were supposed to have 'made the world safe for Democracy' last time. Instead all we did was to kill off our men, lend our money (and we didn't get it back) . . . If you believe in God, you'll keep this country prepared, but don't look for war in other shores." Clay concluded, "I think you are vain enough to throw us into a war so that you could get the power you crave."

✯

FDR TRIED TO SMOKE OUT HITLER's intentions. "You have repeatedly asserted that you and the German people have no desire for war," he said in a letter to the führer. ". . . I am convinced that the cause of world peace would be greatly advanced if the nations of the world were to obtain a frank statement relating to the present and future policy of governments. . . . Are you willing to give assurance that your armed forces will not attack or invade . . ." (There followed a list of virtually every nation in Europe from Belgium to Yugoslavia and several Middle East countries as well.) FDR had directed his plea for peace to Hitler, a man who a week before attacking Poland had said, "Our enemies are little worms. . . . Close your hearts to pity! Act brutally! . . . The stronger man is right."

Roosevelt found it difficult to reconcile a Germany run by bullies with his boyhood experiences. He had spent more time in Germany than in any other foreign country. At age nine, his parents enrolled him for six weeks in a German school to learn the language. At age nineteen, Franklin and his mother, while sailing the Norwegian fjords, were invited for tea aboard Kaiser Wilhelm II's gleaming white yacht the *Hohenzollern.* Before leaving Franklin lifted an imperial pencil as a souvenir because it "bore the teeth marks of the Kaiser."

On the day Germany invaded Poland in 1939, a grim-faced Roosevelt, in his shirtsleeves to relieve the 86-degree temperature, met with reporters in the Oval Office. One asked, "Can we stay out of this?" "I not only sincerely hope so," FDR replied, ". . . every effort will be made by this administration to do so." Two days later, Neville Chamberlain, noting that Hitler had refused Britain's ultimatum to withdraw its troops from Poland, told his countrymen, "consequently this country is at war with Germany. You can imagine what a bitter blow it is to me that all my long struggle to win peace has failed."

FDR's secretary of state, Cordell Hull, during a conversation with the British ambassador to Washington, commented, "The most incomprehensible circumstance in the whole modern world is the ability of dictators, overnight almost, to stand 35,000,000 Italians and 65,000,000 Germans on their heads and so dominate their mental processes that they arise the next morning and insist on being sent to the first line trenches without delay." Still, FDR wondered how far he dared go to curb aggression abroad. A poll published in *The Washington Post* seven weeks after Hitler struck Poland reported that 62 percent of Americans believed that "the United States should do everything possible to help England and France win the war except go to war ourselves."

Within a month of Hitler's attack, FDR felt confident enough to seek to open a crack in the Neutrality Laws. He called a special session of Congress to spring an idea first suggested by his financial éminence grise, the canny, wealthy Bernard Baruch, an investor who had sold out before the crash of 1929. Following Baruch's suggestion, FDR urged Congress to allow belligerents to buy American arms and materials as long as they paid in cash and transported them aboard their own ships. The intended beneficiaries were Hitler's foes, Britain and France. This "Cash and Carry" scheme, as it came to be called, was a have-your-cake-and-eat-it situation: aid your friends, but stay out of the line of fire. By November 1939, Congress amended the Neutrality

Acts, lifting the embargo. The Allies could now buy all the guns, tanks, and airplanes they could pay for and carry home. Shortly afterward, FDR described his juggling act to William Allen White, crusading editor of the *Emporia Gazette* in Kansas: "my sage old friend, my problem is to get the American people to think of conceivable consequences without scaring the American people into thinking that they are going to be dragged into this War."

On January 3, 1940, FDR, leg braces locked, leaning on the rostrum of the dais before the House of Representatives, delivered his State of the Union address. He attempted to straddle the divide separating isolationists and interventionists. "I can understand the feelings of those who warn the nation that they will never again consent to the sending of American boys to fight on the soil of Europe. . . . Nobody expects such an undertaking . . . but there is a vast difference between keeping out of war and pretending that this war is none of our business."

After Poland's defeat the European war fell into an uneasy calm, the "Phony War" to the British, the "Sitzkrieg" to Germany. That facade of peace collapsed on April 9, 1940, at 4:20 A.M. when Hitler's troops swept over Denmark's undefended border with Germany. The struggle was over before the Danes could finish breakfast. Simultaneously, Nazi amphibious forces landed in Norway, establishing bridgeheads from Oslo to Narvik. The Norwegians lasted two weeks. A *Fortune* magazine poll the following month revealed that 40 percent of the respondents still favored neutrality, or at last nonbelligerence. Only 19 percent believed that America should intervene if the Allies appeared headed for defeat. Roosevelt's private thoughts about defeatists and isolationists were unequivocal. Chatting with his Hyde Park neighbor and treasury secretary, Henry Morgenthau Jr., about his ambassador to Britain, Joseph P. Kennedy, FDR said the man was "an appeaser and will always be an appeaser. . . . If Germany or Italy made a good peace offer tomorrow, Joe would start working on the King and his friend, the Queen. . . . He's just a pain in the neck to me." Morgenthau, a Jew, was particularly appalled that Joe Kennedy blamed the war on "the Jewish conspiracy."

FDR was pleased to see the back of the future president's father when Joe Kennedy quit his post on October 23, 1940, and came home.

✶

In May, Hitler struck neutral Belgium, the Netherlands, and Luxembourg. On the morning that the Low Countries were invaded, George Marshall listened aghast at what the unpredictable FDR intended. He wanted to cut the military budget by $18 million. Keenly aware that one sure route to the president's thinking was through Morgenthau, the general found the treasury secretary at his Pennsylvania Avenue office on a Saturday morning, May 11, 1940. Marshall explained the huge increases he felt the military needed, over $50 billion, with $640 million to double the size of the Army to 280,000 men, not Roosevelt's cuts. "It makes me dizzy," Marshall confessed. Morgenthau answered, "It makes me dizzy if we didn't get it." Marshall then asked the seasoned treasury secretary's advice on how to play Roosevelt to win support for this buildup. "When you go to see the President," Morgenthau counseled, "stand right up and tell him what you think and stand right there. There are too few people who do it and he likes it."

The following Monday morning, Marshall and Morgenthau, with other key advisors, trooped into the president's office. "It was quite evident he was not desirous of seeing us," Marshall recalled. As usual FDR kept up a steady chatter unrelated to the subject at hand until Morgenthau finally broke through FDR's verbal smoke screen. "Mr. President," he said, "will you hear General Marshall?" FDR responded impatiently, "Well, I know exactly what he would say. There is no necessity for me hearing him at all." The president made a gesture as if to terminate the meeting. A desperate Marshall, unable so far to get in a word, saw the crucial moment slipping through his fingers He remembered Morgenthau's advice. "A man has a great advantage psychologically when he stands looking down on a fellow," Marshall recalled of that conversation. "I took advantage, in a sense, of the President's condition. . . . 'Mr. President, may I have three minutes?'" he asked. Roosevelt's quicksilver mood shifted and he said affably, "Of course, General

Marshall." The Army chief expressed his shock and dismay upon learning of the cuts Roosevelt intended. "I don't know quite how to express myself about this to the President of the United States, but I will say this," Marshall went on. Then, leaning his six-foot frame over the president's desk, he exclaimed, "You have got to do something and you've got to do it today." Marshall then criticized the bureaucratic hodge-podge created by Roosevelt's loose management habits. A flagrant example was FDR's placement of airplane production in the hands of the secretary of the treasury, not the military. "With all frankness," Marshall began, "none of you are supermen and Mr. Morgenthau has no more chance of managing this thing than of flying. We had lunch and he gave orders he was not to be interrupted. He was interrupted three times by the matter of closing down the stock exchange!" Morgenthau later noted that he was "tremendously impressed with General Marshall. He stood right up to the President." Three weeks later, Roosevelt approved a defense appropriation of $100 million, twice what Marshall had initially requested. The president's undecipherable swings recalled the Walt Whitman lines from *Leaves of Grass*:

> *Do I contradict myself?*
> *Very well then, I contradict myself,*
> *I am large. I contain multitudes.*

While FDR struggled to maintain his balance on a tightrope strung between neutrality and intervention, a conspicuous head rolled in Britain. As one Nazi attack after another tore the Munich hopes for peace to shreds, Neville Chamberlain fell from hero to dupe. Cries for his removal echoed throughout Parliament. During a debate over war policy on March 7, 1940, a Tory backbencher, Leo Amery, delivered the death blow. Quoting Oliver Cromwell's contempt for the Long Parliament, Amery shouted, "You have sat here too long for any good you have been doing. Depart, I say, and let us have done with you. In the name of God, go." On May 10, Chamberlain resigned and the king summoned Churchill, then first lord of the admiralty, to Buckingham Palace to form a new government. As he finally fell into bed at three the next morning, the new prime minister described his reaction after spending ten years in the political wilderness: "I felt as if I were walking with destiny, and that all my past life had been but a preparation for this hour and this trial." Three days later, addressing Parliament, Churchill unsheathed his best weapon in those dark days, his command of the English language. "You ask what is our policy?" he told the members. "I will say it is to make war, by sea, land and air. . . . To wage war against a monstrous tyranny, never surpassed in the dark, lamentable catalogue of human crime." What did he offer his people for taking on this burden? Only "blood, toil, tears and sweat."

Just five days into office, Churchill, about to board a plane to embattled France, fired off a thinly veiled warning to FDR. "I trust you must realize, Mr. President, that the voice and force of the United States may count for nothing if they are withheld too long. You may have a completely subjugated Nazified Europe." Three days later in another radiogram to FDR he raised a chilling possibility. "Excuse me, Mr. President, for putting this nightmare bluntly," he said, but should he himself fall from power, ". . . I could not answer for my successors who in utter despair or helplessness might well have to accommodate themselves to the German will." FDR answered in the only way he believed possible at this stage. He could not aid Britain further without congressional approval. Still, through "Cash and Carry," the British were able to order 69,600 old machine guns, 20,000 antiaircraft weapons, half a million Enfield rifles, and millions of shells and rounds of cartridges, much dating from U.S. World War I stocks. It was small stuff compared to Britain's needs. But FDR directed Morgenthau, who handled these transactions, to give the delivery "an extra push every morning and every night until it is on board ship." The transfers would absorb 20 percent of America's ordnance and ammunition.

Churchill began spouting inspiration in one breath and cold fact in the next. On June 4, 1940, he roused Britons in a speech before the House of Commons. "We shall fight on the beaches, we shall fight on the landing grounds, we shall fight in the fields and in the streets; we shall fight in the hills," he promised, "we shall never surrender." But the next day, after the last British troops had been evacuated from Dunkirk in France, on the English Channel, he inventoried the disaster: "We had lost the whole equipment of the Army. . . . Never has a great Nation been so naked before her foes."

France, its vaunted Maginot Line along the German border simply bypassed by a Nazi sweep through Luxembourg, Belgium, and Holland, took another blow on June 10 with Mussolini's opportunistic declaration of war against its neighbor. On June 10, FDR's son Franklin Jr. was to graduate with a law degree from the University of Virginia at Charlottesville. The president decided to attend and before his departure spent time cruising the Potomac writing a speech in longhand suitable for the occasion. Upon his arrival at the campus, pelting rain drove the commencement ceremony inside to the campus gym. That afternoon, wearing a crimson hood, the president faced nearly a thousand graduates, undergraduates, faculty, and families. Earlier he had been much taken by an image used by Bill Bullitt, his ambassador to France, to describe Italian perfidy. Borrowing Bullitt's phrase, FDR intoned with cold fury, "The hand that held the dagger has struck it into the back of its neighbor." Mussolini later retorted with a pun linking FDR's middle name, Delano, to the Italian word *ano,* meaning anus.

"With Roosevelt's speech," *Time* magazine reported, "the U.S. had taken sides. Ended was the myth of U.S. neutrality." France's current premier, Paul Reynaud, wanted to know what the president's outrage meant in material terms. Thanking America for its planes and armament thus far, Reynaud struck a Churchillian note: "Today, the enemy is almost at the gate of Paris. We shall fight in front of Paris. We shall fight behind Paris; we shall close ourselves in one of our provinces to fight and if we should be driven out of it we shall establish ourselves in North Africa to continue the fight. . . ." His plea closed with a call for all-out aid from America, "short of an expeditionary force." Again, Roosevelt responded that his hands were tied: "only the Congress can make such commitments." However, as with Britain, FDR managed to turn over to the French 2,000 75-mm guns that the United States had originally purchased from the French in the First World War. Roosevelt's secretary of war, Henry Stimson, who at age fifty had fought in the World War I trenches and had a healthy distaste for Teutonic swaggering, was largely free from FDR's need to consider the public pulse. He voiced what the president would have said if he thought the country ready for it. Delivering the commencement speech at Yale, Stimson urged, "repeal the provisions of our ill-starred so-called Neutrality . . . throw open all of our ports to the British and French naval and Merchant Marine . . . [provide] aid to Britain on a scale that would be effective. . . . combat the defeatist arguments . . . as to the unconquerable power of Germany."

It was too late for France. The French army that had fought so valiantly in the trenches for four years in the Great War collapsed in less than six weeks. William Shirer, then in France reporting for CBS News, described the mortifying spectacle that took place on June 21 at the same spot in the Forest of Compiègne where at 5 A.M. on November 11, 1918, Germany capitulated. "Adolf Hitler today handed his armistice terms to France," Shirer wrote. "The humiliation of France was complete. . . . Hitler told the French that he had not chosen this spot at Compiègne to taste revenge; merely to right an old wrong. From the demeanor of the French delegates I gathered that they did not appreciate the difference."

His French ally's ignominious fall did not deter Winston Churchill's pugnacity, though by now Hitler's armies stood on the shore of the English Channel. On July 16, Hitler told his inner circle that since Britain was being stubborn, "I have prepared a landing operation against England." "Hitler knows that he will have to break us in this island or lose the war," Churchill told the House of Commons on June 18, 1940. "Let us therefore brace ourselves to our duties, and so bear ourselves that, if the British Empire and its Commonwealth last for a thousand years, men will still say: This was their finest hour."

ON JUNE 11 CHURCHILL SENT TWO MESSAGES to FDR asking for fifty or more old destroyers. Roosevelt again replied that he could not do so without the authorization of Congress. Furthermore, the United States needed the ships for its own defense. Yet, as so often, an idea once planted kept churning in the president's brain. He called in Admiral

Harold Stark, the Navy chief. Why not take twenty motor torpedo boats that were being built for delivery to the U.S. Navy and sell them to Britain? FDR asked. Stark, who always found Roosevelt's will overwhelming, acquiesced. The secretary of the navy sent a message alerting the president to a brewing insurgency among isolationists. Democratic senator David I. Walsh of Massachusetts, chairman of the powerful Naval Affairs Committee, exhibiting the common Irish American antipathy toward the English, was "in a towering rage about sale of Navy stuff to Allies. He is threatening to force legislation prohibiting sale of anything . . . the whole Committee is in a lather," the navy secretary warned. Walsh went directly to the press, charging that FDR wanted to sap America's strength to benefit foreigners. The torpedo boat deal was "a grievous wrong especially to American youth who may be called upon to fight for the defense of our country." Roosevelt, undaunted, asked his attorney general, Robert Jackson, to look into the legality of the deal. Jackson knew what answer the president wanted, but proved to be a lawyer before a partisan. The torpedo boat deal, he advised FDR, was "absolutely illegal." Walsh then pushed through the Senate on June 28 an amendment to a bill forbidding disposal of *any* military matériel unless the chief of staff or the chief of naval operations certified such equipment as "not essential to the defense of the United States." FDR canceled the deal and learned a hard lesson. The British might be in dire straits and with all his heart he wanted to come to their aid. But he still had to fight undiminished isolationist opposition in the Congress.

Still, the idea of handing over ships simmered. The president called to the White House one man he could count on to be straight with him, his cantankerous secretary of the interior, Harold Ickes. "If I should guess wrong, the results might be serious," he said. "If we should send some destroyers across they would be of no particular use to the Allies, but they might serve further to enrage Hitler." Ickes countered, "If you do send some help with bad consequences to ourselves, the people will blame you just as they will blame you if you don't send the help and the Allies are crushed." Roosevelt raised another snare. "We could not send these destroyers unless the Navy could certify that they were useless to us for defense purposes." Herein lay the contradiction: how could he get the Navy to declare the destroyers obsolete, "in view of the fact that we were reconditioning more than one hundred of them to use for our own defense purposes?"

The president let almost three weeks go by when his restless imagination hatched another angle. He invited Morgenthau, Stimson, Sumner Welles from the State Department, and the Republican Frank Knox, whom he had appointed secretary of the navy, to lunch on August 13, and served the usual dull fare offered by Eleanor's choice for housekeeper and chef, Mrs. Henrietta Nesbitt. Harold Ickes, the secretary of the interior, described the Nesbitt fare as "fried mush with what was called maple syrup but which was not the real thing." After the lunch, Morgenthau recorded in his diary what FDR had spawned. "The plan on the destroyers is that England is to give us land in Newfoundland, Bermuda, Trinidad, and some other places in exchange for the fifty destroyers." During the meeting, the president had raised a tactical quandary. As Morgenthau recorded it, "should he conclude the deal with the English first, and tell the Congress afterward, or tell Congress first?" Most voices urged him to act and then tell Congress.

Attorney General Jackson was directed to find a legal rationale for the president's brainstorm. In an opinion submitted to FDR on August 27, Jackson faced the legal barrier head-on: "May such an action be concluded by the President or must it be negotiated as a treaty subject to ratification by the Senate?" Given continuing isolationist sentiments, getting the required two-thirds approval of the Senate would hardly be a sure thing. But, Jackson advised, "The power of the Commander in Chief of the Army and Navy of the United States which is conferred upon the President by the Constitution but is not defined or limited. . . . It will hardly be open to controversy that the vesting of such a function in the President also places upon him a responsibility to use all constitutional authority which he may possess to provide adequate bases and stations. . . . It seems equally beyond doubt that present world conditions forbid him to risk any delay." As for the president's power to give a belligerent nation fifty American ships of the line, Jackson reached back to an 1883 law which held that no naval vessels could be sold "for less than such appraised value, unless the President of the United States shall otherwise direct in writing." In Jackson's legal opinion not only did the president have the power to act, he would be negligent if he did not act. The path was now clear to work FDR's will with or without congressional assent. Merely for information, Roosevelt sent to Congress on September 3 a message leading off with the more appealing aspect of acquiring bases in British possessions rather than the nakedly belligerent act of sending one side fifty American warships in the midst of a war. FDR characterized the bases deal as "the most important action in the reinforcement of our national defense that has been taken since the Louisiana Purchase." Secretary Stimson described FDR's coup as "the President at his best."

The day after the deal was signed with the British, FDR held his 677th press conference, a weekly occurrence that Merriman Smith of the United Press described as a combination of "a high school track meet, bear baiting, and third degree administered by heavy-handed plain clothes men." The reporters flashed their press passes to the Secret Service and gathered in a semicircle around the president's desk in the Oval Office, notebooks in hand. He was immediately hit with the question "Any value placed upon the destroyers?" The president answered, "Some people will say, undoubtedly—this is still off the record—that, from the point of view of dollars and cents it is not a good deal. And others will say, 'My God, the old Dutchman and Scotchman in the White House has made a good trade. . . . Personally, I think it is a good trade." When Smith, as the senior correspondent, sensed that FDR was finished, he uttered the customary "Thank you Mr. President," and the reporters made a mad scramble through the door to their phones in the press room. Admiral Stark ordered the first destroyers to set sail on September 6 for Halifax, Nova Scotia, where British crews would take over.

Churchill, upon learning that the destroyer deal had gone through radioed FDR, "I need not tell you how cheered I am by your message or how grateful I feel for your untiring efforts . . . for you know that the worth of every destroyer that you can spare to us is measured in rubies." Most satisfying to the prime minister was that his fondest wish, to draw America into the war, had to be advanced by an act as provocative as Roosevelt's scheme. Harold Ickes, in his diary, described how the coup was received in Germany. "Hitler screamed with rage when the destroyer deal went through and announced he was going to turn everything he had on England with a view to overwhelming it without further delay. It was actually claimed in some quarters that England would be suing for peace before last week came to an end, but the British seem to be fighting on as bravely as ever."

Barely had the destroyers passed from American to British ensigns when FDR's mind began churning again. He had sought escape from the chill of Washington in December aboard the heavy cruiser *Tuscaloosa*, headed for the Caribbean. With him were Admiral Ross McIntire, his personal physician; Captain Daniel Callaghan, his current naval aide; and his truest sounding board, Harry Hopkins. Officially, the president was inspecting West Indies bases. But he spent most of his time basking in the tropical sun, fishing, playing poker, watching movies, and swapping stories with his staff. He would later explain what these trips meant to him: "In Washington the working day of the President averages about 15 hours. But at sea, the radio messages and the occasional pouch of mail reduce official work to not more than two or three hours a day. So there is a chance for a bit of sunshine or a wetted line or a biography or a detective story or a nap after lunch." Mostly he prized time for reflection, "between the really big things of life and those other things of moment which . . . are forgotten in a month."

On December 9, a Navy seaplane came alongside the *Tuscaloosa*, then anchored off the island of Antigua. The White House pouch that the plane delivered included a letter from Churchill listing a bleak inventory of British military losses, ships sunk by U-boats now approaching 1,500, arms abandoned, and war plants destroyed during the Blitz. "The moment approaches when we shall no longer be able to pay cash for shipping and supplies," he wrote. In short, Britain was broke. What his country needed from America was "a decisive act of constructive non-belligerency." To FDR, Britain's plight was not an abstraction. Earlier, he had received from Churchill another reminder of the ordeal of ordinary Britons. The prime minister wrote of the raid of May 13, 1940, "The most destructive attack of the whole Blitz. . . . Over three thousand people were killed or injured." The wife of an English friend, Arthur Murray, a former member of Parliament who was considered a distant relative, wrote, "Mr. President (Cousin Franklin), I am going this after noon to sort out . . . bundles of warm clothes for the children and women who have been evacuated. . . . This is the first few names on my list: John Hudson (aged 10) one parent killed in air raid, other missing. George Tilton (aged 12) mother killed, father in army abroad, Elsie Burrey (age 7) both parents killed; Harry Young, mother missing, father killed at Dunkirk. And the list goes on."

Impatient to help Britain strike back, Roosevelt sought a loophole in the remaining Neutrality Laws. Why not send B-17s to Britain for "combat testing"? he asked George Marshall. More fastidious about the law, Marshall spent hours as he rode his horse along the Fort Myer paths, wrestling with the appropriateness of the president's scheme. He finally gave in. "We turned over fifteen Flying Fortresses to the British," he later wrote. "I was a little bit ashamed of this because I felt that I was straining at the subject to get around the resolution of Congress." Eventually he managed to assuage his doubts and justify the move. "We let them have planes for experimental purposes. And we should have done it earlier because we found difficulties with the planes that the Air Corps had not perceived at all." Further, the plane transfer was psychologically satisfying. The British "wanted them to bomb Berlin to meet the demands of their people," Marshall concluded, ". . . to pay the Germans back."

The president viewed donating the B-17s as merely a gesture. He wanted far more done. Aboard the *Tuscaloosa*, Hopkins watched FDR sitting in a deck chair, a navy blue blanket covering his thin knees, reading and rereading Churchill's letter over the course of two days. Then, "one evening he suddenly came out with it—the whole program. He didn't seem to have any clear idea how it could be done legally. But there wasn't a doubt in his mind that he'd find a way to do it." On his return to Washington, FDR laid out his plan to Henry Morgenthau. "I have been thinking very hard on this trip about what we should do for England, and it seems to me that the thing to do is to get away from the dollar sign . . . we will give you the guns and ships that you need, provided that when the war is over you will return to us in kind the guns and ships that we have loaned you." The scheme was pure Roosevelt, its origins obscured. The novelist John Steinbeck noted of the president, "He simply liked mystery, subterfuge, and indirect tactics . . . for their own sake." As FDR's speechwriting aide Robert Sherwood concluded, "I tried . . . to look beyond his charming and amusing and warmly affectionate surface into his heavily forested interior. But I could never really understand what was going on in there. His character was not only multiplex, it was contradictory to a bewildering degree."

The president's military team, Stimson, Knox, Marshall, Stark, and others, had also been mulling over options. The admiral's position was emphatic. At the current rate of ship losses, Britain would go under in six months. Stimson asked Stark how the United States could come to Britain's rescue. The Neutrality Acts would have to be repealed, Stark answered. U.S. merchant ships should be allowed to carry supplies to British ports. These merchantmen would require naval escorts, which would likely draw America into the war. But that was a necessary risk. FDR was not yet resigned to that inevitability. On December 17, he invited the press in to talk about Britain's plight. One approach certainly would not work, he told them, "for us to pay for all these munitions, ships, plants, guns, etcetera and make a gift of them to Great Britain." That might be a bit much for the American taxpayer to swallow. "I have been at it now for three or four weeks, exploring other methods." He repeated essentially what he had told Hopkins. Several months before, Harold Ickes, the interior secretary, had come up with an analogy that had stayed with Roosevelt. He now retrieved it. "Well, let me give you an illustration," he told the reporters. "Suppose my neighbor's home catches fire, and I have a length of garden hose four or five hundred feet away. If he can take my garden hose and connect it up with his hydrant, I may help him to put out his fire. . . . I don't say to him before that operation, 'Neighbor, my garden hose cost me $15, you have got to pay me $15 for it. . . .' I don't want $15. I want my garden hose back after the fire is over." And if the garden hose were damaged beyond repair? "It seems to me you come out pretty well if you have them replaced by the fellow that you have lent them to." There it was in a nutshell: lend munitions to Britain "and get the munitions back at the end of the War."

Lend-Lease, as the proposal came to be called, proved one of the most creative ideas of Roosevelt's wartime leadership. His brainchild circumvented all disputes over arms sales, gifts, cash loans, or repayment of war debts. He put his crack legal team, including the clever Ben Cohen, even Supreme Court justice Felix Frankfurter, to work to transform a concept into law. HR 1776 was introduced in both houses of Congress on January 10. The president enlisted an early and impressive ally, his recent presidential adversary, Wendell Willkie, who came out in support of the bill. Other Republicans were less accommodating. The Montana isolationist senator Burton K. Wheeler in a radio debate described Lend-Lease as another "New Deal triple A foreign policy: plow under every fourth American boy." FDR called a press conference and fired back. He characterized Wheeler's attack as "the most untruthful, as the most dastardly, unpatriotic thing that has ever been said. Quote me on that! That really is the rottenest thing that has been said in public life in my generation."

THE PRESIDENT SAW HIS NEXT TASK as winning popular support for his initiative. On Sunday, December 29, 1940, as 9 P.M. approached, people began leaving restaurants, shops, and movies, headed home for what was becoming a national habit. The president delivered his fireside chats over the radio in a style that combined folksiness with patrician elegance. An extraordinary 60 percent of Americans tuned in on this night. FDR was wheeled into the White House diplomatic cloakroom where he stubbed out a cigarette, squared the pages of his speech, and faced a forest of microphones. There was no hope for peace with Germany. "A tiger," he warned, "could not be tamed by stroking it. There can be no appeasement with ruthlessness." Lest his countrymen believe the oceans could insulate them, he said, "If Britain goes down . . . all of us in the Americas would be living at the point of a gun." He then uttered an electric phrase, urged on him by Felix Frankfurter, that would immortalize the speech: "We must be the great *arsenal of democracy.*" Americans "must display the same sense of urgency, the same spirit of patriotism and sacrifice as we would show were we at war." In the days that followed he anxiously awaited public reaction. Letters and telegrams supporting his call for wartime fervor ran 100 to one in his favor.

Three weeks later, on January 20, for the first time in the nation's history, a president took the oath of office for a third time. As the Supreme Court's chief justice prepared to swear him in, Roosevelt leaned forward and said in a mock whisper, "I don't know how you feel about this, but I'm getting sick of it."

THAT MONTH, FDR INFORMED CHURCHILL that he was sending a personal emissary to London. The British embassy in Washington alerted the prime minister that the man coming was the president's closest confidant and had performed some sort of role in shaping the social programs of FDR's New Deal. Harry Hopkins had, in fact, emerged from the world of settlement houses, welfare agencies, and public health organizations. The name meant nothing to Churchill. He nevertheless sent Brendan Bracken, voluble, savvy, and something of a surrogate son, to meet Hopkins's plane and bring him to Ditchley, the stately home of wealthy Churchill supporter Ronald Tree. Chequers, the prime minister's official country residence, dating from 1480, which was once occupied by Cromwell and where every painting, chair, and bedstead spoke of history, was too likely a target of Luftwaffe bombers. On Saturday, January 11, Churchill hosted a dinner for his guest. After the ladies had withdrawn, and the men had their coffee, brandy, and cigars, Churchill sought to display his social conscience to Hopkins. "After the war we must make a good life for the cottagers," he said. The man he spoke to was frail, wraithlike, with the pallor of a cadaver. He had been diagnosed with stomach cancer the year before and given six months to live. Sir Charles Wilson, Churchill's personal physician, elevated to Lord Moran, upon observing Hopkins noted, "His lips are blanched as if he had been bleeding internally, his skin yellow like a stretched parchment and his eyelids contracted to a slit so that you can just see his eyes moving about restlessly, as if he was in pain. He looks like a Methodist minister." The passion that erupted from this unlikely frame stunned the prime minister. Sunken eyes blazing, Hopkins began, "The President didn't send me here to listen to any of that stuff. All he wants to know is how you propose to beat that son of a bitch in Berlin." "Mr. Hopkins," Churchill said, "we had better get into the library." The two men withdrew alone, talking until four in the morning. In subsequent encounters, Hopkins's instinct for getting to the point led Churchill to call him "Lord Root of the Matter." At a later dinner, Hopkins raised his glass and said, "I suppose you want to know what I am going to say to President Roosevelt on my return. Well, I am going to quote you one verse from that Book of Books. 'Whither thou goest, I will go, and where thou lodgest, I will lodge: thy people shall be my people . . . even to the end.'" Churchill wept. He later wrote of Hopkins, "His was a soul that flamed out from a frail and failing body." Hopkins's judgment of Churchill was, "Jesus Christ! What a man!"

A wily FDR, recognizing Wendell Willkie's usefulness, was only too pleased when his recent opponent informed him that he had obtained permission to visit Churchill. The president gave him a note to deliver to the prime minister that began, "I think this applies to your people as it does to us," and he ended with these lines from the poet Longfellow, written in the president's bold longhand:

> Sail on, O ship of state,
> Sail on, O Union strong and great!
> Humanity with all its fears,
> With all the hopes of future years,
> Is hanging breathless on thy fate!

After fifty-eight days of heated debate, Roosevelt prevailed. Lend-Lease passed the House by 260 votes to 165. On March 8, the Senate voted in favor by 60 to 31. Three days later, FDR signed the bill into law, smiling broadly as he handed out ceremonial pens. Soon after he told reporters what the British were asking for in their first Lend-Lease shopping list. "It included 900,000 feet of garden hose," apparently for fighting fires ignited by German bombing or to maintain the English love of gardening. The reporters erupted in laughter.

Hitler now said of Lend-Lease, "it will come to war with the United States one way or another." His High Command issued a statement that the program "may be regarded as a declaration of war on Germany." A Nazi mouthpiece, the *Boersen Zeitung*, branded the program a Jewish plot. "The Jew Frankfurter did them no service by getting around and undermining American neutrality," the newspaper exclaimed. Hitler added that he regretted not yet having aircraft to bomb American cities. That would teach a lesson to American Jews.

Long before, as a candidate for the presidency in 1932, FDR had defined his concept of leadership in a speech to the San Francisco Commonwealth Club. "Government includes the art of formulating a policy, and using the political technique to attain so much of that policy as will receive general support; . . . the greatest duty of a statesman is to educate," he said. Lend-Lease was the concrete expression of the president's philosophy at its apogee, a bold burst of imagination that would change history.

THE COMMANDER IN CHIEF ACCEPTED that he lacked enough Navy to fully cover both the Atlantic and the Pacific Oceans. The comforting illusion that these vast seas insulated America from entanglement in foreign wars began to vanish as German victories in Europe opened numerous ports on the Atlantic for Germany. While Congress resisted spending money to aid foreign governments, FDR's call for a strong Navy sailed through both houses with scarcely a murmur, even as the country still felt the drag of the Great Depression. Congress approved a $4 billion bill for creating a two-ocean Navy—17 battleships, 18 aircraft carriers, 27 cruisers, 115 destroyers, and 43 submarines. Nearing completion was the USS *North Carolina*, a 35,000 ton, 704 foot leviathan, boasting three massive turrets from which nine 15-inch guns jutted. When the vessel slid down the ways at the Brooklyn Navy Yard, the *North Carolina* became the first new American battleship launched in eighteen years. The entire upgraded fleet, however, would not be complete until 1946. Until then, the central question persisted: how were the ships currently available to be allotted between the two oceans? As early as 1938, even before war broke out in Europe, a board of Army and Navy strategists, believing that war was imminent, presented its recommendation. Of course, the Hawaiian Islands had to be defended. However, if Japan did attack in the Pacific, the distant Philippines might have to be excluded from the defense perimeter. The board ominously warned that Japan's overwhelming advantage in aircraft carriers made Pearl Harbor particularly vulnerable to air attacks that "could damage major fleet units without warning." The board's recommendation was unanimous and emphatic. The president must concentrate America's naval might in the Atlantic. An aggressive Nazi Germany might advance along the Western Atlantic and threaten South America, which FDR saw as the hemisphere's Achilles' heel.

Though his advisors had recommended the "Atlantic First" policy, the president had not yet made a final decision. On May 22, 1940, he called in General Marshall and the Navy chief, Admiral Stark. Stark, in a profession where hard men abounded, has been described by the naval historian Samuel Eliot Morison as a military thinker, a diplomat, a man "gentle in manner and unobtrusive in personality . . . [who] with his pink complexion, benevolent countenance, rimless spectacles and thick shock of white hair, looked more like a bishop than a sailor." And then there was the nickname, "Betty." That day the military advisors agreed; the United States should not become engaged in the Pacific beyond the 180 degree meridian, a point about 1,000 miles west of Hawaii and indeed omitting the Philippines. A month later, France surrendered to Germany and Nazi access to the Atlantic increased.

While the Atlantic took precedence, the president, on October 8, speaking in an unguarded moment while a primitive hidden recording device in the Oval Office captured his words, gave his frank assessment of Japanese intentions. He referred to a telegram reportedly received by the "Chief of the Japanese press association," stating that there would be no war between America and Japan on one condition: the United States must recognize Japan's dominance in Asia. America should demonstrate its acceptance of this state by demilitarizing all its naval, air, and Army bases in Wake Island, Midway, and Pearl Harbor. "God," Roosevelt thundered, "that's the first time that any damn Jap has told us to get out of Hawaii.... The only thing that worries me is that the Germans and Japs have gone along, and the Italians too, for—oh gosh—five, six years without their foot slipping, without their misjudging foreign opinion.... And the time may be coming when the Germans and the Japs will do some fool thing that would put us in. That's the only real danger of our getting in—is that their foot will slip."

SOON AFTER FDR HAD BEEN ELECTED to his third term in November 1940, the Army and the Navy submitted a new naval strategy to him. The pivotal list of four options was known as Plan Dog, for the military's phonetic alphabet for the letter. Plan Dog's government-gray prose dealt with what would become one of the fateful strategic decisions of the war. Under Dog, the Navy was to take the offensive in the Atlantic but remain on the defensive in the Pacific. This strategy appeared validated after the disastrous night of April 3–4, 1941, during which a German submarine wolf pack struck a British convoy just south of Iceland. Ten plodding merchant vessels went under that night. Roosevelt thereafter ordered a substantial part of the Pacific Fleet transferred to the Atlantic—three battleships, one carrier, four light cruisers, and two destroyer squadrons. His decision was not welcomed in every quarter. Secretary of State Cordell Hull and Pacific Fleet admirals warned "that the disappearance of the American fleet from the Pacific would be taken by the Japanese as a go ahead signal for their southward expansion." But the die was cast. Britain's Atlantic lifeline was to be kept open at all costs. The Western Hemisphere must be protected, while the Japanese could be handled with America's left hand.

ON APRIL 11, 1941, the fastidious and able Henry Stimson entered the president's cluttered study. He rated Roosevelt "the poorest administrator I have ever worked under." Further, as no one else dared to, FDR called him "Harry." Stimson knew well Roosevelt's penchant for dominating a conversation, which FDR admitted to a friend that he did. He controlled the situation by "telling stories and doing most of the talking!" Stimson's cabinet colleague Cordell Hull had advised him, "I used to get a little bite to eat first myself so that I could talk while he was eating." On Stimson's visit this day the president, gesturing toward a heap of books, asked the secretary to hand him his favorite atlas. Turning the pages to the Atlantic Ocean, he drew a pencil line down the middle from Iceland through the waters between Brazil and West Africa. In one bold stroke, FDR had swept Greenland and Iceland, 2,100 miles from the United States, into the Western Hemisphere. "He is trying to see how far over in the direction of Great Britain we could get!" Stimson wrote in his diary later that evening. "His plan then, is that we shall patrol the high seas west of the Meridian line . . . by the use of patrol planes and patrol vessels, we can patrol and follow the [Allied] convoys and notify them of any German raiders or German submarines that we may see and give them a chance to escape." The word "patrol" created a semantic morass. A reporter asked the president the difference between a patrol and a convoy. "I think you know what a horse looks like. I think you also know what a cow looks like," Roosevelt said as if addressing a particularly dense student. "You can't turn a cow into a horse by calling it something else. . . ." A patrol meant having warships reconnoiter a sector of the sea "to find out whether there are any possibly aggressive ships within that area." On the other hand, a convoy meant warships escorting merchant vessels to protect them.

In a private conversation, Henry Morgenthau heard FDR say "he is going to have a patrol from Newfoundland down to South America and if some submarines are laying there and try to interrupt an American flag and our Navy sinks them, it's just too bad. . . . We simply say, 'so sorry' and the next day we go ahead and do it again." Morgenthau, leading the interventionists, found FDR still too cautious. "The President is loath to get into this War," he wrote in his diary, "and he would rather follow public opinion than lead it." Given his acute political antennae, Roosevelt's caution was probably well advised. A Gallup poll in

April showed a clear majority opposed to having American convoys shepherd merchant vessels through the war zones. Convoys invited contact and contacts provoked shooting, which led to war.

Roosevelt summoned Admiral Stark to the White House and produced the map he had shown Stimson and retraced his demarcation. "I don't think anyone could beat him," Stark later recalled of the performance. "He could sit and plot all the towns that could be passed on a flight down Brazil and over to India." He could also cite "the height of the mountains, depths of the oceans, the plains they watered and tides." Roosevelt now considered turning merchant ships into combat vessels. He described to Averell Harriman his scheme for installing helicopters on the decks of merchant ships that could drop depth charges on German submarines. Harriman, who had known the president since their days at Groton, dismissed such occasional ideas as FDR's "romancing." Ironically, while FDR may have been ready to carry out a barely subliminal shooting war, Hitler, eager not to give Roosevelt a provocation for entering full-scale war, ordered all German surface warships and submarines in the Atlantic not to fire at American vessels, even in self-defense.

The newly mapped borders of the hemisphere took on tangible form when FDR announced in April 1941 that the United States was taking over protection of Denmark's Greenland, its landmass running from the North Atlantic beyond the Arctic Circle. He had obtained agreement to do so from the foreign minister of Denmark's government-in-exile. At his next press conference, FDR, sounding like a college lecturer, informed reporters, "I have talked to a number of geographers and geologists, etc., and from the point of view of very, very ancient history, the Island of Greenland, in its fauna and flora and its geology, belongs much more closely to the American continent than it does to the European continent." Securing this vast trackless island was necessary, Roosevelt maintained, because German planes were reconnoitering over Greenland possibly in preparation for an assault against the Western Hemisphere. Thus, American protection was vital "to bring Greenland within the system of hemispheric defense."

A German battleship, bearing the proud name *Bismarck,* was

about to test the president's willingness to engage German warships. On May 24, 1941, the *Bismarck* attacked the battle cruiser HMS *Hood* and sank her. Of her crew of 1,416, three British sailors survived. Subsequently, the German vessel managed to give avenging British ships the slip. FDR guessed that the *Bismarck* was headed for the Caribbean, a direct challenge to the Western Hemisphere. He gathered his military team to his study where they found him sitting next to an open window to temper the oppressive heat. He wanted a strategy for dealing with the supposedly approaching *Bismarck*. "We have some submarines down there," he told them. "Suppose we order them to attack her. Do you think the people would demand to have me impeached?" As Sam Rosenman saw Roosevelt's dilemma, "Should he order submarines to attack it? What would the people say if he did? There would obviously not be enough time to ask Congress." Ultimately, the Royal Navy solved the president's quandary. On May 27, British battleships and cruisers sank the *Bismarck* far from the Caribbean, 700 miles off the coast of France. Over 2,000 German sailors died while 110 survived.

After absorbing Greenland into the Western Hemisphere, FDR took a more militant step in neighboring Iceland. Some 25,000 British troops posted there were essentially hors de combat. On June 7, the president ordered 4,400 U.S. Marines to Reykjavik, soon followed by 4,200 Army troops. The British soldiers were now free to fight elsewhere. Roosevelt was essentially baiting a trap. He instructed Admiral Stark that if any German force came within fifty miles of Iceland, this act would represent hostile intent toward the Americas and was to be met with force.

FDR soon embarked on his next step in shredding neutrality just short of war. On the evening of May 27, soon after learning of the *Bismarck*'s sinking, the president, wearing black tie, was wheeled into the East Room of the White House to a point just inside the door to shorten exposure of his crippled condition. The ostensible occasion was to celebrate Pan American Day. Latin American ambassadors with their well-groomed wives, and other officials from Canada to the Argentine, awaited his remarks. After uttering a few pro forma paeans to hemispheric solidarity, he started speaking not simply to the few hundred guests perched on small gilt chairs in the East Room, but to an estimated 65 million Americans listening on the radio. With Nazi power stretching from Norway to the Mediterranean, he warned, "what started as a European war has developed, as the Nazis always intended it should develop, into a world war for world domination." The United States, he charged, was under de facto attack. "Some people might wish to think we had not been attacked until bombs fell on New York or San Francisco. . . . But if you hold your fire until you see the whites of their eyes, you will never know what hit you." He conjured up a Nazi octopus, its tentacles strangling Europe, enveloping North Africa, and creeping west toward the Azores, only seven hours' bombing distance from South America. In the days before the speech, he had pored over a Justice Department memorandum describing his powers if he found the country menaced. Until now, the United States had faced a limited threat, he explained. But now, the country faced "an *unlimited* national emergency." After finishing the speech, one that ratcheted the country closer to outright war, FDR retired with friends to the Monroe Room. He asked Eleanor to bring Harry Hopkins and Hopkins's guest, the songwriter Irving Berlin, to join him. FDR's gift for shifting gears had always astonished Sam Rosenman. "He was an expert at dividing his day into periods of work and play, of excitement and relaxation." After telling millions of his fellow Americans that they faced the danger of war, all that FDR wanted was for Berlin to sing and play his hits, starting with "Alexander's Ragtime Band." Finally the president returned to his bedroom and Robert Sherwood, who with Sam Rosenman had helped craft the address, stopped by to say good night. He found the president awash in a sea of telegrams. "They're ninety-five percent favorable," he said with a grin. "And I figured I'd be lucky to get an even break on this speech."

In mid-June 1941, a Brazilian vessel, the *Ozorio,* spotted crowded life rafts bobbing in waters of the South Atlantic. An American freighter, the *Robin Moor,* en route to East Africa, had been torpedoed three weeks earlier by a German submarine. On June 20, in response to the sinking the president sent a message to Congress charging that the submarine commander had to have known what nation's vessel he was attacking. Given this provocation, occurring so soon after his tough-fisted declaration of an "unlimited national emergency," Roosevelt might have been expected to respond with force. He condemned the sinking of the ship as "ruthless," and described in harrowing detail the hunger and exposure the survivors had suffered. He echoed the charge made before the Pan American Union condemning Hitler's "plans for world domination," but he ended with only a limp phrase he had written in by hand at the end of the formal text: "We are not yielding and we do not propose to yield." He demanded compensation and kicked the German consular staff out of the country. But he did not make the incident another *Lusitania*. It was as if after the saber-rattling speech, he was closely calibrating how much further he dared go. His administration hawks, among them Harry Hopkins, Henry Stimson, Henry Morgenthau, and Harold Ickes, had only to please a constituency of one, the president. FDR had to govern a country embracing isolationists, interventionists, and everybody in between. His tacking from belligerence to prudence revealed something that isolationists did not believe and that interventionists did not want to accept. He would keep the United States out of the war if, at the same time, he could sufficiently strengthen Britain to hold out against Germany.

CHAPTER 3

———✦———

From Barbarossa to the Atlantic Charter

FRANKLIN ROOSEVELT WAS THE FIRST WORLD LEADER TO KNOW DE-
finitively that Hitler planned to attack the Soviet Union. Sam E. Woods,
an affable, party-loving commercial attaché posted to the American
embassy in Berlin, had cultivated a German friend with high-level connections in the Nazi Party and government ministries. One afternoon,
meeting in a darkened movie theater, his contact slipped Woods a copy
of a directive dated December 18, 1940, revealing Operation Barbarossa, Hitler's code word for the invasion planned for the summer of
1941.

Only fifteen months before, the Soviet Union and Nazi Germany,
the cobra and the mongoose of world powers, had signed the
Ribbentrop-Molotov peace pact, to the shock of communists around
the world who could not conceive that two such antagonistic regimes
could ally themselves. Initially, the pact had paid off for Russia when
sixteen days after Hitler invaded Poland from the west, the Russians
swept in from the east to grab their slice.

By early January 1941, the State Department, after having the
FBI vet Sam Woods's intelligence for credibility, passed the information to the president. FDR instructed his then ambassador in Moscow, Laurence Steinhardt, to warn Stalin of Barbarossa. In March he
sent undersecretary of state Sumner Welles to see the Soviet ambassador in Washington, Konstantin Oumansky, a boorish former capitalist-
baiting journalist, to sound the alarm. Rather than warn Stalin,
Oumansky called the German ambassador in Washington, Hans

Thomsen, and told him that the Americans were sowing rumors to sabotage the friendship between their two countries. Oumansky was merely echoing Stalin's deep-dyed mistrust of the West planted immediately after World War I when British and American troops had been dispatched to Russia to help strangle the Bolshevik revolution in its cradle. Stalin could not overcome his conviction that Hitler's predicted invasion could be anything more than a capitalist plot, even after dozens of warnings from reliable sources had reached the Kremlin.

On the night of June 21, a German deserter in occupied Poland passed through the Soviet army lines and gave himself up. His unit, he told his captors, was part of a vast force poised to invade Russia at three the next morning. As the hour neared, a German army of over 3.8 million men roared out of Poland, Romania, and East Prussia into the Soviet Union while 2,700 planes effectively shot the Red Air Force out of the sky, all achieved with total surprise. Stalin was shaken by the deception and went into a funk approximating a nervous breakdown. For several critical days, Russia was leaderless.

ROOSEVELT HAD WATCHED the trajectory of the Russian Revolution with growing dismay. When in February 1940, at Eleanor's prodding, he had agreed to receive a delegation from the far-left-leaning American Youth Congress at the White House, he told a hostile audience that he had initially hoped the Soviet regime might bring about a better life for its millions. But by now, he told the young idealists, much to their chagrin, "The Soviet Union . . . is run by a dictatorship as absolute as any other dictatorship. It has allied itself with another dictatorship, and it has invaded so infinitesimally small a country that could do no possible harm to the Soviet Union." He was referring to the Red Army assault on Finland in December 1939.

Still, FDR moved gingerly when the Germans struck Russia. The day afterward, he issued a cautious statement describing Nazi Germany as the number one world threat, but did not mention the attack on the Soviet Union. A common attitude in America at the time was a-pox-on-both-your-houses. Senator Harry Truman told a *New York Times* reporter, "If we see that Germany is winning we ought to help Russia and if Russia is winning we ought to help Germany and that way let them kill off as many as possible."

The president finally decided that the United States must come to the aid of the lesser evil. On July 31, five weeks after the Nazi aggression, he spent forty minutes with the dour Ambassador Oumansky and a Russian general, Filip Golikov, who presented him with a long list of what Russia wanted from the United States. Three days later, an impatient FDR sent a memo to Wayne Coy, an assistant he had charged with expediting the aid, saying, "If I were a Russian, I would feel that I had been given the run-around by the United States. . . . With my full authority use a heavy hand—act as a burr under the saddle to get things moving." The president summoned General Marshall and the Air Corps chief, Hap Arnold, and told them that he wanted forty of the P-40 fighters initially meant for Britain's Royal Air Force flown instead to Fairbanks, Alaska, where Soviet crews would take them over. Further, he wanted 160 fighters and bombers taken from the U.S. Army Air Corps and given to the Soviets. Alarmed, Marshall and Arnold warned that this diversion would cripple American airpower, since only some ninety P-40s were flyable. But FDR had made up his mind. He wanted Russia fortified.

IT WOULD BE DIFFICULT TO CONJURE anyone with a more visceral hatred of communism than Winston Churchill. He had once declared, "The Nazi regime is indistinguishable from the worst features of communism." His antipathy had sharpened since the war. While German bombers were leveling British cities during the Blitz, while Britons waited to be invaded any day, Russia was shipping oil to Germany. However, all of Churchill's detestation of Bolshevism vanished overnight when Germany invaded Russia. Even before, as rumors of the impending attack mounted, Churchill told dinner guests at Chequers, "We should go all out to help Russia." He then uttered his memorable phrase, "If Hitler invaded hell, I would make at least a favorable reference to the Devil in the House of Commons."

After the invasion, Churchill believed, in light of his previous loathing of the Soviet Union, that he owed the British public an explanation for his reversal. He spoke over the BBC. "No one has been a more consistent opponent of Communism than I have for the last twenty-five years," he said. He was not changing his spots, he explained. His concern was not for the godless communist regime, but for "the . . . Russian soldiers standing on the threshold of their native land . . . where mothers and wives pray for the safety of their loved ones . . . where maidens and children play . . . I see the 10,000 villages of Russia where the means of existence is wrung so hardly from the soil. . . . It follows therefore that we shall give whatever help we can to Russia and the Russian people."

In desperate need of support from the West, Stalin felt he had to explain why he had earlier entered a vipers' embrace with the Nazis. Nearly four months after Hitler struck, he spoke frankly to FDR's envoy, Averell Harriman, at a vodka-soaked dinner in the Kremlin during which forty-two toasts were raised. His treaty with Hitler, Stalin insisted, was all Britain's fault. The British had always been hostile to his regime. When, in 1938, Neville Chamberlain failed to consult him over the dismemberment of Czechoslovakia at Munich, he saw through the ploy immediately. Hitler was being appeased solely to turn the Nazis' hostility away from the West and instead direct it to the East, toward his nation. Feeling himself betrayed and fearful of standing alone against a powerful Germany, Stalin claimed to have no choice but to ally himself with Hitler. Before the dinner was over, however, he did admit to Harriman that his erstwhile partner's betrayal had caught him completely unaware.

IN THE SUMMER OF 1941, Hap Arnold received a call from Marshall alerting him to prepare for a trip. Where to? Arnold asked. Marshall, even more terse than usual, said only that the Air Forces chief should pack warm clothing and expect to be gone about ten days. Admiral Ernest King, also invited, had a clearer picture of what was going on. Nearly three months before, on April 19, 1941, Grace Tully, FDR's principal secretary, had called King, telling him that the president expected him at Hyde Park the next day, no later than 3 P.M. On King's arrival, FDR waved him into his manually controlled Ford where just the two of them, trailed by the Secret Service, rode up a steep, rutted path passing through a grove of Christmas trees that the president proudly pointed out were for sale. They arrived at the top of a hill unfolding a broad vista of the Hudson River and entered Stone Cottage, a rustic Dutch-style hideaway that the president had built for himself. FDR rolled his wheelchair to a table where he spread out a map of the coast of Newfoundland. He had been in frequent correspondence with Churchill, he told King, but was now eager to meet him face-to-face. He furtively told King that when he was ready to discuss his plans further, he would send him a message containing an innocuous reference to "ice." Nothing further was said about the matter for three months, until July 25, when King was again summoned to Hyde Park. FDR explained that he wanted the admiral's flagship, the heavy cruiser USS *Augusta,* adapted to his special needs. They were going to Placentia Harbor off the tiny town of Argentia in Newfoundland where the U.S. Navy maintained an outpost under the destroyer-for-bases deal.

On August 3, a misty Sunday morning, Marshall and Admiral Stark arrived in New York and were ferried to the *Augusta,* where Admiral King greeted them. Soon after, Hap Arnold, still in the dark, came aboard the cruiser. Secretive behavior, concealing his hand, fooling the press, gave FDR a boyish delight. While his chiefs were gathering on the *Augusta,* he told the White House staff, including his Secret Service detail, that he needed to unwind and was going off aboard the yacht *Potomac,* for ten days of fishing off Cape Cod. He explained to his mother, "The heat in Washington has been fairly steady and I long to sleep under a blanket for the first time since May." The story rang true. The men going along with FDR, the amiable General Edwin "Pa" Watson, a military aide, the president's physician, Admiral McIntire, and Captain John Beardall, his current naval aide, were all avid anglers. He repeated the story to Eleanor. "Then he smiled and I knew that he was not telling me all that he was going to do," she concluded. The president was much amused when, on August 4, *The New York Times* reported, "Dropping the cares of official duties for a long-sought rest at sea, President Roosevelt sailed tonight from the New London Submarine Base for a week's salt-water vacation."

To WINSTON CHURCHILL THE PROSPECT of meeting personally with Franklin Roosevelt presented an opportunity that he dared not misplay. How closely did FDR see Britain's fate intertwined with that of his own country? How strongly did Roosevelt feel about the menace of Hitler and the Nazi regime? Once, Churchill's son Randolph, on leave from the army, had visited his father and found the prime minister stark naked, shaving himself before a mirror. Churchill turned and said, "I think I see my way through." Puzzled, Randolph asked, "Do you mean we can avoid defeat?" Churchill tossed his razor into a basin and answered, "Of course I mean we can beat them." "I don't see how we can do it," Randolph replied. Churchill, mopping his pink cheeks, responded, "I shall drag the United States in." During the previous year, Roosevelt had been moving, crablike, closer to Britain and war. Now on a remote, windswept bay in Newfoundland, Churchill intended to clinch the deal.

On August 4, the prime minister and his military chiefs boarded the Royal Navy's most formidable battleship, *Prince of Wales,* and began a zigzag course across the Atlantic to elude U-boats. Sailing with the party was Harry Hopkins, on his way back from a meeting with Stalin. From the ship's radio room, Churchill sent FDR a message using the by now familiar address between them, "Former Naval Person." "Harry returned dead-beat from Russia," the prime minister reported. "We shall get him in fine trim on the voyage." He then reminded FDR of the auspicious date of his embarkation. "It is twenty-seven years ago today that the Huns began their last war. We must make a good job of it this time. Twice ought to be enough." Just before Churchill set to sea, Averell Harriman had met in London with the prime minister and was surprised by the man's anxiety over meeting FDR. Twice Churchill took Harriman aside and asked plaintively, "I wonder if he will like me?"

That same August 4, FDR's *Potomac* put into the Yacht Club at New

Bedford Harbor in Massachusetts. There FDR welcomed aboard Princess Martha of Norway and her three children. The princess had fled her country after its defeat by Germany and FDR had brought her initially to Hyde Park, then to the White House, until he found her a suitable estate in Maryland. Martha was perfect company for the president. He dearly loved a royal, and she, at age forty, was regal-looking. "Exactly as a princess should," one observer noted. Martha, on this occasion as on others, fulfilled the president's pleasure in the company of adoring, admiring, undemanding women, unlike his earnest, ever crusading wife.

At 6:30 P.M., after a picnic ashore, the president and the princess parted and FDR returned to the *Potomac,* where he actually did fish for a while. Afterward, he shed a flashy sport shirt for a crisp white shirt and tie as the *Potomac* put out to sea. An aide draped his Navy cape with a velvet collar and braided frogs over the president's shoulders. For a man wheelchair-bound, putting on an overcoat was a clumsy affair. The cape had proved a perfect solution. Later that evening, a signalman aboard the *Augusta* picked up a flashing light message from the *Potomac*: "will come alongside at first light." Early the next morning, the president was bundled by his faithful security chief, Mike Reilly, aboard a whaleboat and spirited aboard the cruiser. Meanwhile, Ed Starling, chief of the White House Secret Service, positioned himself in a deck chair on the *Potomac*'s fantail, wearing a battered fedora, brim upturned, a cigarette holder clenched between his teeth, and a cloak draped over his shoulders. As the *Potomac* sailed through the Cape Cod Canal, onlookers waved and shouted at the man they assumed was their president.

The *Augusta,* escorted by five destroyers in wartime darkened-ship condition, steamed the Atlantic through a thick fog in heavily traveled shipping lanes at a brisk 22 knots, reaching Placentia Bay on August 7. As minesweepers finished clearing the bay, the *Augusta* dropped anchor. Soon after, a destroyer, the USS *Mayrant,* approached the cruiser. The *Augusta*'s captain had been alerted that one of the *Mayrant*'s officers, Ensign Franklin Roosevelt Jr., was coming aboard. The sight of the son who bore so close a resemblance to himself gladdened the president's heart. He took Franklin Jr. to his cabin. "Here," he said, handing him a gold-braided aiguillette. "I got Pa Watson to bring this up for you." He then appointed his son "junior naval aide," and reminded him that the aiguillette, which he described as "golden spinach," was to be worn over his right shoulder because he was now a presidential aide, and not on the left side as on lesser staff.

Hap Arnold had arranged for Air Corps Major Elliott Roosevelt to fly down from Gander Lake to Argentia to join the *Augusta*. FDR also appointed Elliott a presidential aide and gave him the gold aiguillette. Though the United States was still at peace, three Roosevelt brothers, Franklin Jr., Elliott, and Marine officer James, were in uniform. John, the youngest brother, would join the Navy as soon as the country entered the war. Elliott asked his father what he expected when he and Churchill met. "Watch and see if the PM doesn't start off by demanding that we immediately declare war against the Nazis," FDR answered.

That evening, the president summoned Marshall, Stark, and Arnold to his cabin, telling them that he wanted his policy clearly understood. Any hostile ship entering the Atlantic west of Iceland and the Azores must be assumed to have hostile intent. "If they closed to within shooting distance, we must start shooting first." Further, "We must do everything possible to provide for delivery of aircraft to England, establish weather and radio stations, help train ferry pilots."

ON FRIDAY, AUGUST 8, CHURCHILL, still aboard the *Prince of Wales,* settled into an armchair to watch Laurence Olivier and Vivien Leigh in *Lady Hamilton* (retitled *That Hamilton Woman* for the U.S. release). The story of Lord Horatio Nelson's brave and ultimately fatal battle at Trafalgar told against the backdrop of his passionate love affair with the beauteous but married Emma Hamilton brought tears to Churchill's eyes. Just as then, his England was again threatened. At dawn the next morning, the gray mass of the *Prince of Wales* loomed out of the fog into a sunlit sea. "She was magnificent," Admiral King recalled as the warship came into view, "crew manning the rail, the Prime Minister on the bridge." The strains of "Stars and Stripes Forever," played by the

Prince of Wales band, floated within earshot of the *Augusta*. The British ship anchored astern of the cruiser and Churchill was ferried to the gangway. King later wrote of his surprise upon first glimpsing the great man up close. He was "short and stout with a florid complexion." He wore a faintly military-looking cap with a double-breasted, gold-buttoned jacket and a black bow tie, the uniform of an Elder Brother of Trinity House, and looked like a figure out of an old nautical print. Churchill was piped aboard the *Augusta* with the traditional sideboys and wailing of the boatswain's pipe.

The man whom Roosevelt was finally to meet was then sixty-six, seven years older than the president. In dress, manner, and speech he appeared a figure out of the nineteenth rather than the twentieth century. As a young man, he had stood with the crowds celebrating Queen Victoria's Golden Jubilee in 1887. He had graduated from Britain's Royal Military Academy, Sandhurst, and gone to South Africa during the Boer War. His capture there and his lively account of his escape instantly propelled him to national hero. By age twenty-seven he had won a seat in Parliament. Subsequently, he filled impressive posts: home secretary, minister of munitions, chancellor of the exchequer. While first lord of the admiralty during the Great War his career suffered a near fatal blow for his promotion of the campaign in the Dardanelles that ended in bloody disaster at Gallipoli in Turkey. He was thereafter relieved of his post and went into the trenches in France as an officer in the Grenadier Guards. Accustomed to the good life, he arrived at the front with a staff car loaded with personal possessions, including a bathtub riding atop the vehicle. He was a man of dizzying mood shifts, swinging easily from euphoria to depression. While at the front, he wrote his wife, Clementine, "I am so devoured by egoism." Yet, he once confided to Lord Moran, his personal physician, "I don't like standing near the edge of a platform when an express train is passing through. I don't like to stand by the side of a ship and look down into the water. A second's action would ruin everything, a few drops of desperation."

There were parallels in the lives of the two leaders. Both loved the sea, Churchill again having held the post of first lord of the admiralty before becoming prime minister. Roosevelt had served as assistant secretary of the navy in the First World War. Both were moved by pomp and pageantry, heroic verse, and voices raised in old church hymns. Churchill was addicted to cigars, FDR to cigarettes, and both enjoyed a drink, the prime minister more avidly than Roosevelt. Both were the sons of wealthy American mothers, Churchill through his father's marriage to the beauteous Brooklyn-born heiress Jenny Jerome, and FDR the son of Sara Delano Roosevelt, whose family had made a fortune in the Chinese opium trade. Both men were unabashedly theatrical. Mike Reilly detected that Churchill liked to stage dramatic entrances, just as did FDR. Roosevelt's charm was inbred and near instinctual. Churchill's manner was more understated until he began to speak, when he became captivating. The prime minister was moody, volatile, more intellectual, less opaque, while FDR presented a buoyant facade that even his closest associates could never fully penetrate.

FDR had prepared for his first encounter with Churchill down to the last detail. He insisted on wearing his metal leg braces, which Mike Reilly called his "painful prison," rather than using his wheelchair. He wore the clumsy device so that he could stand when he met the prime minister. Reilly worried that "Even the slight pitch of the *Augusta* meant pain and the possibility of a humiliating fall." To further mask his impairment Roosevelt had his braces painted black to blend in with his shoes and socks. As he awaited Churchill's arrival, the memory of an unpleasant encounter long ago lingered. He and Churchill had briefly crossed paths at Gray's Inn during FDR's visit to Europe during World War I, in which, Roosevelt remembered, he "acted like a stinker and was one of the few men in public life who was rude to me." The prime minister came aboard the *Augusta* finding FDR standing upright, clutching the right arm of son Elliott. As Churchill stepped forward to greet him, the ship's band struck up "God Save the King." Studying each other, they smiled and each extended a hand. "At last we've gotten together," Roosevelt said, beaming. Churchill responded, "We have." The president mentioned the earlier meeting at Gray's Inn without elaboration. Churchill at first responded that he didn't remember the occasion. But detecting the disappointment in the president's expression, he quickly recovered. Yes, he said, he remembered Roosevelt in "all his youth and strength."

Admiral King hosted a buffet lunch after which the president and prime minister retired to the captain's cabin. Elliott Roosevelt was a witness to the conversation that ensued. Churchill went directly to the point. "My information . . . is that the temper of the American people is strongly in our favor. That in fact they are ready to join the issue." The president answered carefully, "You can find counter-indications." The debate on Lend-Lease, Churchill insisted, demonstrated proof of America's sympathy. FDR, still confronting isolationist sentiment at every turn, answered, "If you are interested in American opinion, I recommend that you read the *Congressional Record,* every day."

That evening the president took over the officers' wardroom where, amidst a field of gold braid, his guests dined on broiled chicken, spinach omelet, and chocolate ice cream, plain fare much like the meals FDR ate at the White House. As black stewards cleared the table the president asked Churchill his assessment of the war. Elliott Roosevelt has left a vivid portrayal of Churchill in full feather. "He reared back in his chair, he slewed his cigar around from cheek to cheek and always at a jaunty angle, he hunched his shoulders forward like a bull, his hands slashed the air expressively . . . he held us enthralled." Elliott was accustomed to seeing his father dominate every conversation. "But not tonight," he recalled. "Somebody else was holding the audience, holding it with grand, periodic speeches, never quite too florid, always ripe and fruity to the point where it seemed you'd be able to take his sentences in your hands and squeeze until the juice ran out." As Churchill rolled on, FDR fiddled with his pince-nez and doodled on the tablecloth, "But never an aye, nay, or maybe," Elliott remembered, "came from the Americans sitting around that smoke-filled saloon." When Roosevelt and Churchill later huddled alone, the prime minister went straight to the issue. "I would rather have an American declaration of war now and no supplies for six months," he said, "than double the supplies and no declaration."

While the principals met privately, Marshall and his colleagues sat down with Churchill's military staff, during which time the Americans were dismayed by a repeated British refrain. The right strategy, the British argued, was the Middle East—keep the Suez Canal open, protect the sea lanes to India. Marshall sat, stolid, poker-faced. He and Arnold had earlier agreed that any approach other than large armies and vast airpower unleashed against occupied Europe was futile. Yet they hesitated to hand out advice from the sidelines to men who had been fighting for almost two years and who had arrived at Argentia on a ship still bearing the scars of its duel with the *Bismarck.* The reluctance of the British to strike at Hitler's vitals on the continent foreshadowed confrontations that would echo for months to come.

Sunday morning, August 10, dawned sunlit with the great ships riding steadily at anchor in a smooth sea. The president and his retinue had transferred to the *Prince of Wales.* Marshall, King, and Arnold headed for their assigned places, behind seats set up for Roosevelt and Churchill. The ship's fantail was jammed shoulder to shoulder with American bluejackets and British tars standing at attention, deliberately mixed together. Suddenly, all eyes were drawn to the figure of Roosevelt, one arm clutching Elliott, the other holding a cane, as he lurched unsteadily past an honor guard of Royal Marines, his face registering pain. One British witness described him as "A St. George who has trampled the dragon under him." Cautiously, the president lowered himself, unaided, into his seat. He regained his smile as he and Churchill chatted beneath a turret sprouting four massive guns, their muzzles fourteen inches wide. An American and a British chaplain began conducting a joint service at a small altar set between flags of the two countries. A chorus of voices rose singing two hymns that Churchill had selected, "O God Our Help in Ages Past" and "Onward Christian Soldiers." Roosevelt had selected "Eternal Father, Strong to Save." Of the service FDR would later remember, "I think everybody, officers and enlisted men, felt that it was one of the great historic services. . . . I know I did." To Churchill, the close-packed ranks of British and American sailors "sharing the same book and joining fervently in the prayers familiar to both . . . seemed to stir the heart. It was a great hour to live."

After the service the British sailors were treated to gifts rare in wartime Britain, a box of tropical fruit and American cigarettes, "compliments of Franklin D. Roosevelt, Commander in Chief of the United States Navy." That afternoon, the two leaders, with staff, conferred again, and as Admiral King noted, Churchill "seemed to be talking, talking, talking and Roosevelt listening."

The following Monday afternoon, the prime minister decided to relax and explore Placentia Bay. Sailors watched a dumpy figure slip into a whaleboat headed for a nearby bluff. Churchill immediately took over the tiller and began barking orders. Elliott Roosevelt has captured the scene, describing the prime minister, "clad in a one piece jumper with short sleeves and trousers cut off above the knees. From where we stood, he looked like some outsize fatboy, lacking only a toy bucket and spade for his afternoon's romp on the beach." Having scaled the bluff, Churchill mischievously began tossing pebbles among officers sunning themselves on the beach below. "Highjinks in high places," Elliott observed. On his return a British aircraft flew low over the *Prince of Wales* and dropped a box on the deck. In it were the latest decrypts of German enciphered messages cracked through the code-breaking triumph, Ultra, messages that Churchill impatiently snatched. The box had been weighted so that if the plane went down, the box would sink too.

What took place between Roosevelt and Churchill in their private sessions has remained largely unknown and unrecorded, although one agreement did seep out to their staffs. The month before, 40,000 Japanese troops had seized Indochina's rubber plantations. FDR had retaliated by freezing Japanese assets in the United States and cutting off the export of aviation gasoline to Japan. Yet whatever threat Japan represented, Roosevelt and Churchill agreed that Hitler, not the Japanese, remained the paramount menace.

During Argentia, Roosevelt took time to write his confidant and distant Hudson River cousin, the fifty-year-old spinster Margaret "Daisy" Suckley. "He is a tremendously vital person," he wrote in describing Churchill, "and in many ways like an English Mayor LaGuardia. Don't say I said so. . . . I like him and lunching alone broke ice both ways." Churchill would later describe Roosevelt, "with all his sparkle and iridescence" as like "opening a bottle of champagne."

The prime minister was still angling for the objective that had brought him to Newfoundland, to draw the United States into the war. To FDR, however, Argentia had an immediate priority. He saw the ideal setting for proclaiming a noble, ringing purpose for the conflict. At Roosevelt's prompting, their two staffs wrestled over the language of what the president called the "Atlantic Charter." With Churchill's concurrence, the charter vowed that their nations sought the territory of no other nation; supported the right of all peoples to choose their own form of government; pledged to support free trade, disarmament, and to create an international body to achieve world peace and security. These goals were to follow upon "the final destruction of Nazi tyranny." Self-determination was particularly dear to Roosevelt. At a lunch with Elliott before Churchill's arrival, he had said, "America won't help England in this war simply so that she will be able to ride roughshod over colonial peoples." Elliott answered, "I can see there will be a little fur flying here and there, in the next few days." FDR said, "We'll see. We'll see." At this point, Churchill would have agreed to almost anything to win FDR's favor and he swallowed the charter, anticolonialism and all, much like King Henry IV of France, who said, "Paris is well worth a mass." But an inevitable collision awaited the two men regarding empire. As Churchill would later put it in a speech at Mansion House, "Let me, however, make this clear, in case there should be any mistake about it in any quarter: we mean to hold our own. I have not become the King's First Minister in order to preside over the liquidation of the British Empire."

As for how far the president was willing to go to support Britain militarily, he promised Churchill that American warships would not only protect British convoys, but would seek out and actually attack German submarines. However, at this point, a formal declaration of war was out of the question. Congress would turn it down flat, FDR advised. The most recent poll, taken just as he was departing for Argentia, revealed that 74 percent of the American people wanted to stay out of the war against Germany. On August 12, under drizzly leaden skies, the *Prince of Wales* weighed anchor, its band playing "Auld Lang Syne."

Within four months the formidable dreadnought would be no more, sunk by Japanese bombers in the South China Sea.

The Argentia conference had been in its second day and Americans still had not known where their president was. The ruse of a fishing trip and the double on the *Potomac* had succeeded. Not until August 14, when the White House issued the full text of the Atlantic Charter, did the public learn that the president had met secretly in remote Atlantic waters with Britain's prime minister. The lofty sentiments of the charter had little discernible impact on the country. The percentage of people who opposed going to war with Germany before the conference remained essentially unchanged afterward.

When Churchill returned to London, he admitted to the cabinet that the president "was skating on pretty thin ice in his relations with Congress." He assured his government, however, that "Roosevelt was determined to come in . . . the President had said that he would wage war but not declare it, and that he would become more and more provocative. If the Germans did not like it, they could attack the American forces." He told the South African leader, Field Marshal Jan Christiaan Smuts, that Roosevelt had told him, "I may never declare war; I may make war."

As soon as the president arrived back in Washington, he made good on his pledge to Churchill. He summoned the then chief of naval operations, Admiral Stark, and ordered him to organize escort convoys covering two thirds of the distance across the Atlantic. Penetration this deep into the war zone meant that clashes with German submarines were all but inevitable. Stark believed he deserved clearer guidance. What action should the Navy take if American warships encountered German U-boats? How far was the Navy to go in fending them off? In short, what rules of engagement applied? He put these queries to the president, but no answers were immediately forthcoming. When in a subsequent meeting Stark continued to press the point, FDR answered only, "Betty, please don't ask me that."

CHAPTER 4

───────── ✦ ─────────

An Undeclared War

On September 4, 1941, the USS *Greer*, a World War I vintage destroyer, camouflaged in shades of gray, steamed a northeast course from Boston to Iceland to deliver mail to lonely soldiers and Marines stationed on that remote post, when 175 miles from its destination lookouts on the *Greer* heard a hum overhead and saw a British two-engine patrol plane paralleling their course. The plane signaled to the *Greer* that a submarine had been spotted ten miles ahead. The destroyer located the submerged U-boat through sonar and began updating its position to the plane. Thus guided, the aircraft swooped down and dropped four depth charges, which missed the target, and then flew off to refuel. Meanwhile the U-boat had discovered the *Greer*'s presence and the commander, assuming that the destroyer had attacked him, maneuvered into firing position. From the *Greer*'s bridge a crewman spotted a narrow wake indicating an approaching torpedo. The destroyer now began firing its own depth charges, none of which scored. Breaking off the encounter, the destroyer proceeded to Reykjavik.

The day after the attack the president held a press conference at which a reporter immediately asked if the United States was now in a "shooting war." "Once upon a time there were some school children who lived in the country," a smiling FDR began. "They were on their way to school, and somebody fired a number of shots at them from the bushes. The father of the children took the position that there was nothing to do about it—not even search the bushes—since the children had not been hit . . . some radio and news commentators took the same view with regard to this attack on the *Greer*." Describing the actions of the *Greer* captain, he added, "You might say that the school teacher ordered a search of the bushes."

On September 11, the president was wheeled into the East Room past a poster that exhorted, "Keep 'Em Flying." He was about to deliver a fireside chat to an audience estimated at some sixty million Americans. He wore a gray seersucker suit with a black mourning band circling his left arm, marking the death of his beloved mother four days before. He had once observed, "What vitality I have is not inherited from the Roosevelts. . . . Mine, such as it is, comes from the Delanos." "The United States destroyer, *Greer*," he began, "proceeding in broad daylight toward Iceland . . . was flying the American flag. Her identity as an American ship was unmistakable. She was then and there attacked by a submarine. . . . I tell you the blunt fact that the German submarine fired first upon this American destroyer without warning, and with deliberate design to sink her." What FDR said was true as far as it went. Yes, the German U-boat commander, spotting an American destroyer in his periscope and rocked by depth charges, reached the not unreasonable assumption that it was the American ship that had attacked him and not an unseen British aircraft.

Roosevelt again turned to metaphor, that you don't wait for a rattlesnake to strike before you crush it. "These Nazi submarines and raiders are the rattlesnakes of the Atlantic." He went on, "That means, very simply, very clearly, that our patrolling vessels and planes will protect all merchant ships—not only American ships, but ships of any flag. If German or Italian vessels of war enter the waters, the protection of which is necessary for the American defense, they do so at their own peril. . . . The orders which I have given as Commander-in-Chief are to carry out that policy at once."

The New York Times headlined its front-page story on the speech the next day, "Roosevelt Orders Navy to Shoot First." Upon hearing FDR's talk, Churchill described the Nazis' dilemma: "Hitler will have to choose between losing the Battle of the Atlantic, or coming into frequent collision with the United States warships." To the German navy's chief, Admiral Erich Raeder, FDR's hard line meant "There is no longer any difference between British and American ships." After the fireside chat, Admiral Stark wrote a friend, Hitler "has every excuse in the world to declare war on us now, if he were of a mind to." The president had made a persuasive case. A Gallup poll conducted after the rattlesnake speech found 57 percent of Americans agreeing that our warships should "shoot on sight," while 35 percent said "wait until attacked."

ON THE NIGHT OF OCTOBER 16–17, fifty merchant ships laden with weapons and supplies for Britain plowed the North Atlantic escorted by five American destroyers. Suddenly, powerful explosions rent the night and great tongues of fire lit the sky. A submarine wolf pack had penetrated the destroyers' protective perimeter and scored six hits on the slow-moving freighters. The fire from one stricken ship was so bright that it illuminated the USS *Kearny,* a new $5 million destroyer. Within minutes a torpedo smashed into the *Kearny*'s engine room, killing eleven sailors outright. The *Kearny* limped back to port in Iceland. Admiral King wrote of the attack, "the *Kearny* incident is but the first of many that, in the nature of things, are bound to occur." No undue fuss should be made over the loss, Admiral King cautioned Stark. "I suggest we go slow in this matter of making heroes out of these people who have, after all, done the jobs they are trained to do." Within two weeks another convoy escort vessel, the USS *Reuben James,* took a torpedo midships and broke in half. As the ship sank, its depth charges exploded, heaving survivors bodily out of the sea. Of a 160-man crew, only 45 survived. The U-boat captain, an ace with thirty-four sinkings to his credit, claimed he thought he was attacking a British destroyer.

On a rainy Washington evening ten days after the *Kearny* attack, Secret Service agents lifted FDR from his limousine and carried him into a rear entrance of the Mayflower Hotel. Grace Tully recalled the first time she had seen the president of the United States handled like a sack of flour. She had turned away and cried. Since FDR never complained and usually smiled and cracked jokes while being lugged about,

Tully, like the rest of the staff, eventually became inured to his condition. On this night, the president was to speak at the annual Navy Day Dinner. So often favoring gray suits, he looked resplendent this evening in black tie as he looked down from the dais upon Washington's elite, congressional leaders, cabinet members, and military chiefs. As the Marine Corps Band finished "Hail to the Chief," the president's genial demeanor vanished. Alluding to the recent American ship losses, he began, "We have wished to avoid shooting, but the shooting has started. And history has recorded who fired the first shot. In the long run, however, all that will matter is who fired the last shot." He then added with a note of conspiracy, "I have in my possession, a secret map made in Germany by Hitler's government, by planners of the New World Order. . . . It is a map of South America and a part of Latin America as Hitler proposes to reorganize it. . . . The geographical experts of Berlin have ruthlessly obliterated all the existing boundaries; they have divided South America into five vassal states. . . . And they have so arranged it that the territory of these new puppet states includes the Republic of Panama, and our great lifeline, the Panama Canal."

The next day, the president held a press conference at which a reporter asked if he might see the map. No, the president responded in mock horror. It had notations on it that "would dry up the source of further information." A second reporter pressed on, "What would you say to the charge of the suspicion that the map . . . had been foisted on you in some way? That it was also a forgery or a fake of some sort?" FDR answered placidly that the map had come to him from "a source that is undoubtedly reliable. . . . There is no question about that." The map had come into his hands through William J. Donovan, a World War I Medal of Honor winner and a wildly successful Wall Street lawyer now heading the president's fledgling espionage service, the Office of the Coordination of Information, subsequently to become the Office of Strategic Services, the OSS. The map had been slipped to Donovan by William Stephenson, who headed a British intelligence operation in the United States, blandly named the British Security Coordination, whose prime objective was to lure the United States into the war. What

Roosevelt had touted as a plan to break up South America into Nazi vassal states was in reality nothing more than an old map of routes used by German commercial airlines between major Latin American cities. How much FDR knew of the true nature of the map is unknown. But once handed to him, any evidence that bolstered his claim that the Germans intended to subjugate America's southern neighbors preparatory to an attack on the United States was not to be scrutinized to death.

✶

WHILE THE PRESIDENT'S ATTENTION WAS FOCUSED on the Battle of the Atlantic, General Marshall had been carrying out the commander in chief's order to estimate what it might take to "defeat our potential enemies," Germany and Japan. On September 25, Marshall took into the president's office a seventeen-page document classified top secret and bearing the thudding title "Army and Navy Estimate of United States Overall Production Requirements." The document, shorthanded as "Rainbow 5," seized the president's attention. To defeat Germany, the United States must create 216 infantry divisions, 51 motorized divisions, raise an Army of 8.8 million men, and vastly expand the Navy, at a cost of $150 billion. The earliest that this force could be ready to fight was July 1, 1943. Roosevelt's occasional speechwriter Robert Sherwood was permitted to see Rainbow 5, and noted, "It is, in my opinion, one of the most remarkable documents of American history, for it set down the basic strategy of global war before this country was involved in it."

To keep Rainbow 5 under wraps, only thirty-five copies had been circulated. Somehow one copy was leaked to Senator Burton Wheeler, who was convinced that the contingency plan proved FDR's intention to drag the country into war. Wheeler passed the purloined copy to FDR's archenemy, Colonel Robert McCormick, publisher of the *Chicago Tribune*. On December 4, the *Tribune*'s front page shouted, "FDR's War Plans! Goal Is 10 Million Armed Men, Proposes Land Drive by July 1, 1943." If Roosevelt's "Shoot on Sight" policy meant undeclared war on Germany on the high seas, the *Tribune*'s story on Rainbow 5, as available in Berlin as in America, seemed the equivalent of a declaration of war by land.

GEORGE MARSHALL FOUND THE PRESIDENT'S unabashed preference for the Navy exasperating. "I was the one," Marshall once commented, "who pulled the statement on the President that I wished he would not speak of the Navy as 'us' and the Army as 'they.'" On September 20, 1941, when the military draft had been extended barely a month before, Marshall was stunned to hear the president say that he intended to *reduce* the Army. It had become fashionable among military thinkers to proclaim a new age of warfare. As propounded by the cerebral and influential columnist Walter Lippmann, modern wars would be decided by navies and air forces, backed by industrial mobilization, while ground forces would assume a subordinate role. An agitated Marshall told his staff that he was going to the White House to educate the president on the fallacy of the Lippmann view that "an army was passé, no longer needed."

He was greeted by the usual display of amiability as the president waved him to a chair, though the salutation "George" was still not employed. Preparing ships, aircraft, and their crews might seem more complex than putting a uniform on a man and giving him a gun. But this was not so, Marshall argued. Once sailors and pilots were trained, they were essentially required only to push the right buttons. Infantrymen faced a far more daunting task. In combat they were, in Marshall's view, "at their worst as to a state of fatigue from long marches, from mud, rain, dust, heat and then they have to operate . . . in a place they have never seen before. . . . Whereas in the Navy, a man can take a bath and put on clean underwear, and go to his fixed battle station. In the infantry regiment, for example, he has no fixed place that he can go to. It is all in a state of transition and change. . . . And also he is under heavy fire in most cases. He is also probably surrounded by very frightening casualties which are right there for him to see. All this requires a very high state of discipline and a higher state of technique in training." Marshall granted that "the airplane is very photogenic. The Navy is very photogenic." But success ultimately depended on foot soldiers. "If you wanted to hold an air base, you need these ground forces and without them, you were, in a sense, impotent." Contrary to popular impression, "the lengthiest preparation was required for what was ordinarily supposed to be the simplest military set-up, that is, a regiment of infantry," Marshall concluded.

Two weeks after Marshall spoke to him, the president was still talking about reducing ground forces, while seeking a stronger hand at sea. He pressed Congress to drop Section 6 of the Neutrality Act, which prohibited arming merchant vessels. On November 8, after a close vote in the House and a thirteen-vote edge in the Senate, Congress gave FDR what he wanted. At the same time, he wanted to bolster airpower. His conversion to airpower had been slow in coming. Roosevelt had first flown when, as assistant secretary of the navy, he had gone aloft in a dirigible during his mission to the European war zone in 1918. His belief in aerial warfare thereafter waxed and waned. In the summer of 1919, he was asked what he thought of the future of airplanes, and told the Senate Military Affairs Committee, "I don't know whether the Chief of Naval Operations will agree with me, but . . . in the future, aviation might make surface ships practically impossible to be used as an arm." A few years later, however, he seemed lukewarm. At a speech to the Kiwanis Club of New York, he advised, "it is highly unlikely that an airplane or a fleet of them could ever successfully attack a fleet of Navy vessels under battle conditions." He did make aviation history on July 2, 1932, when he boarded a Ford Tri-Motor at the rudimentary Albany Airport en route to Chicago and became the first presidential candidate to fly to accept his party's nomination.

By the mid-1930s he had become a thoroughgoing airpower convert. On the very day that he had appointed Hap Arnold chief of the then Army Air Corps, he told cabinet members and the new chief that creating "a new field artillery regiment, building a new barracks somewhere in Wyoming, and constructing another arsenal would not deter Hitler in the slightest. What would were airplanes, now, lots of them." If necessary, he said, the government might have to take over ownership of a sizable share of American plane manufacturers. Listening to the president, Arnold believed that he was witnessing the moment when the U.S. Air Corps "achieved its Magna Carta."

HENRY HARLEY ARNOLD HAD BEEN BORN on June 25, 1886, in Gladwyne, Pennsylvania, just northwest of Philadelphia. His father was an austere physician who ruled his family with an iron hand, not permitting his children to speak at the dinner table except after a three-hour Sunday service at the Baptist church, and then only when called upon by their father. Arnold remembered his mother as "a staunch member of the Montgomery County D.A.R. [who] steadily reminded us that a number of our ancestors—four on her side, and three on my father's—had taken part in [the Revolutionary] War." However authority-ridden the household, "I grew up in one of the happiest environments in America," Arnold remembered. He was the doctor's son, a mark of status in a small town. The family called him "Harley."

His older brother, Tom, was slated to go to West Point and Harley to become a Baptist minister. Tom balked at attending the academy so it fell to his younger brother to apply instead. Harley, no scholar, passed the examination, much to the family's surprise. He was sworn in as a plebe on July 23, 1903. However stern his upbringing, young Arnold turned out to be a mischievous cadet, frequently gigged for breaking rules and staging pranks, once launching fireworks from the roof of his barracks. He never rose above 66th in a class of 110, and was passed over for his choice of the cavalry and commissioned instead a second lieutenant in the infantry in 1907. He served in routine assignments on Governors Island in New York Harbor and in the Philippines. Bored at his latest post, he fired off an application to the Ordnance Department to do "aeronautical work." The first time Arnold had ever seen an airplane was in 1909, only six years after the Wrights had introduced a new age with the first powered flight at Kitty Hawk. Arnold had been taking a meandering trip through Europe between assignments and coincidentally pursuing a young woman with whom he had fallen in love, Eleanor Pole, whom he would eventually marry. While strolling down a Paris street, he recalled, "All of a sudden, there it was, a queer contraption hanging overhead. I managed to find out with my best West Point French that this was the flying machine in which Monsieur Louis Blériot had, on the 25th of July, 1909, just a few weeks previously, flown from Calais across the English Channel to Dover."

Arnold was stunned when in April 1911 "an official letter arrived from the War Department. Would I be willing to volunteer for training with the Wright brothers as an airplane pilot?" Arnold took the order to his commanding officer, who responded, "Young man, I know of no better way for a person to commit suicide." Arnold was unfazed. Soon, with War Department Special Order 95 tucked into his breast pocket, he took a train for Dayton, Ohio, to learn how to fly from the men who had invented flight. He was much taken with Orville and Wilbur Wright, finding them unpretentious and eager to initiate their acolyte into the new frontier of the air. After ten days of instruction in a moth-like 12 horsepower Wright model B, he soloed. As the flimsy craft rolled to a stop, Arnold recalled thinking, "I could fly. I was an aviator." Eager to test the limits of aviation, he tried to race a trolley doing 45 miles an hour. The trolley won.

From the first moment, Arnold was as at home in the sky as an eagle. Soon after completing flight training, he set a world's record for altitude, 3,260 feet. Within a year he had broken that mark, reaching 6,540 feet. He became the first Army pilot to fly the U.S. mail. After a bug lodged in his eye he became the first pilot to wear goggles. He flew the first plane from which a rifle was fired. He won the first Mackay Trophy for outstanding aeronautical achievement after a successful flight from College Park, Maryland, to the Washington, D.C., barracks at Fort Myer, and back to College Park. He became the first flier to use radio to guide artillery fire on the ground, all these feats accomplished within four months of earning his wings. Later he would credit the Wright brothers, saying, "they gave me a sense that nothing is impossible."

A year and a half later, on November 5, 1912, a cocksure Arnold was piloting another Wright Flyer when it unaccountably stalled and began spinning toward earth as he "gave up everything as lost." Grabbing furiously at the controls, he managed to pull out of the tailspin just eighty feet from the ground and landed safely. Later, at his barracks, his comrades popped champagne corks to celebrate Arnold's escape from almost certain death. But despite his jaunty manner, something had snapped during those terrifying moments. The next day he went to see his commanding officer and confessed, "At the present time my nervous system is in such a condition that I will not get in any machine." On another occasion he complained, "I cannot even look at a machine in the air without feeling that some accident is going to happen." To a fellow flier he announced, "That's it. A man doesn't face death twice." Arnold's fear of flying was hardly irrational. Of the first twenty-eight pilots trained by the Army, ten were killed in crashes and twelve quit within months. After his close shave, Arnold requested twenty days leave to calm his frayed nerves and managed to get himself assigned to ground duty in the Signal Corps in Washington. His flying career, it seemed, was over.

Four years later, in 1916, Arnold found himself in a lackluster job as supply officer at the Signal Corps Aviation School in San Diego, California. During the intervening years he had not set foot in a plane, even as a passenger. In his new post, he was surrounded by fliers chattering excitedly about the latest advances in aircraft design, the hottest plane being the Curtiss Jenny, a far better and safer model than Arnold had flown when he quit. The enthusiasm around the school began to ignite old passions and on October 18, 1916, after five months of doling out supplies, Arnold yielded to the itch to fly again. He began cautiously, nothing fancy. But as he began to feel his mastery over the aircraft, he flew upside down, put the plane into a roll, did a spin and a loop. He cut the engine and deliberately stalled. Forty minutes later he landed and climbed from the cockpit beaming. His fear of flying had ended.

The ascent of the airplane as a weapon of war had been swift. During a fairground stunt in January 1911, a pilot reportedly threw a section of gas pipe filled with black powder that exploded on striking the ground, presumably the first aerial bombardment. Just four years later, rickety German bombers launched a raid on Compiègne in France.

Within a year, both sides had air squadrons. During the U.S. Army's campaign in September 1918, against the Saint-Mihiel salient, a pugnacious, independent-minded officer, Brigadier General Billy Mitchell, sent relays of 500 planes, 1,500 in all, against the enemy lines. The U.S. Air Service grew to a force of 750 planes. From the moment America entered the war, Arnold applied repeatedly for a combat assignment. Instead, he wound up flying a desk in Washington, a blow to his pride arousing a fear that his career had ended. The air wing itself emerged from the war with mixed notices. One official report concluded, "The airplane is one of the most short-lived of all implements of war."

Arnold, in the following years, fell under the spell of Billy Mitchell, now deputy chief of the Air Service. Mitchell was preaching the David and Goliath potential of small planes to destroy great battleships. Not surprisingly, career seadogs found his claims laughable. Josephus Daniels, former secretary of the navy and young FDR's superior in World War I, declared that he "would stand bareheaded on the bridge of any battleship during any bombardment by any airplane, by God, and expect to remain safe!"

Mitchell kept pressing for a practical demonstration to test what would happen if aircraft attacked even the stoutest battleship. On July 21, 1921, he finally won his stubborn appeals for a trial. The target was a decommissioned German battleship, the *Ostfriesland*. After being hit by 1,000-pound bombs, the battle wagon sank. Planes sent a German submarine and destroyer to the bottom as well. Though the tests convincingly confirmed Mitchell's boasts about the future of airpower, he could not discipline a sharp tongue. After the Navy dirigible *Shenandoah* crashed in a storm, killing its crew members, Mitchell issued a public statement accusing Army and Navy leaders of "almost treasonable administration of the national defense." His rashness provided his long-smoldering enemies with their chance. In 1925, Mitchell was court-martialed for insubordination. Career officers were warned that if they testified on Mitchell's behalf they would jeopardize their careers. Arnold not only testified for the defendant, but spent hours helping Mitchell prepare his defense, to no avail. Mitchell was found guilty.

A year later, a statement praising men of Mitchell's vision and condemning a backward Army bureaucracy appeared surreptitiously. The Army inspector general traced the statement's authorship to Arnold. In writing it, he had used a government typewriter and government stationery and was charged with misappropriating public property. The Army inspector recommended that he too be court-martialed, a death blow to his career. His commanding officer, Major General Mason Patrick, gave Arnold a choice: resign or face trial. Arnold chose to be tried. In the end, Patrick backed down, unwilling to put the Air Service in the dock on the heels of Mitchell's conviction. Nevertheless, he relieved Arnold of his duties and transferred him to a moribund air unit at Fort Riley, Kansas, as air advisor to the cavalry.

By his drive and indomitability Arnold managed to put his career back on track. He had crossed George Marshall's path nearly a quarter century earlier while both were serving in the Philippines. During maneuvers, Marshall, then a young lieutenant, was commanding 5,000 men and planning a simulated amphibious landing. Arnold saw Marshall just as the latter was drafting an attack order for the White Force, which won the mock battle. Afterward, Arnold told his wife, "I had just met a man who was going to be Chief of Staff of the Army one day." Marshall's first impression of the young flier was equally admiring. Fairly early in his career Marshall had begun keeping his Little Notebook of promising officers. Arnold made the list.

For a time Arnold ran the Aviation Section's information services, writing speeches for senior officers and dealing with the press. This experience taught him the uses of public relations and the art of cultivating powerful people. At age thirty-one he became the youngest colonel in the Army. When given command of March Field in Riverside, California, he seized an opportunity to befriend Hollywood royalty. Movie mogul Jack Warner became his pal, as did Will Rogers. A fair exchange grew. Arnold wanted favorable publicity for his service and movie stars enjoyed hobnobbing with glamorous, handsome young fliers. He pinned wings on Mary Pickford and recruited Jean Harlow and Wallace Beery to attend the opening of the March Field theater. Ira Eaker, who would rise during World War II to become one of Arnold's top deputies and had known him since the First World War, recalled, "Colonel Arnold was the most handsome Army officer, with the possible exception of General Pershing, I had ever seen. He was six feet tall, erect, wore his uniform with pride and grace. He had a quick, engaging smile, but a reserve and dignity that did not encourage familiarity."

Another March Field friend brought Arnold to Franklin Roosevelt's notice. The president's son Elliott, an early aviation enthusiast, was a licensed pilot, worked in the aviation industry, and served as aviation editor for the Hearst newspapers. Arnold so impressed young Roosevelt that he sent his father a letter urging that he be promoted to brigadier general, which he was, at least to temporary rank, on February 11, 1935.

In 1938, FDR named Major General Oscar Westover to command the Army Air Corps, under whom Arnold served as second in command. The position opened again when Westover, piloting a small plane, crashed and was killed on September 21. Roosevelt hesitated in moving Arnold up to the top spot. Washington gossip had it that while serving in Hawaii Arnold had often made a drunken fool of himself. In truth, he was a sparing drinker and had never served in Hawaii. In the meantime, Harry Hopkins returned to Washington from an inspection of the American air industry, where he heard more glowing reports of Arnold's leadership. Given Hopkins's endorsement and Marshall's good opinion, the president named Arnold chief of the Air Corps eight days after Westover's death.

By now the Arnold persona was set. The face he presented to the world was one of affability and high spirits. To his peers he was "Hap," always smiling. The smile, however, was explained by a slight anomaly in which a facial muscle pulled the left corner of his mouth into a permanent expression of amusement. Despite the ever present smile, he pushed his people relentlessly and found subpar performance intolerable. He was an antibureaucrat who saw regulations as walls to be breached, not limits to be observed. Arnold kept on his desk a carved plaque saying, "The difficult we do today. The impossible takes a little longer."

That September, FDR took Harry Hopkins with him to visit his son James, who was about to undergo surgery in Rochester, Minnesota. The car radio was on, tuned to coverage of a mass Nazi Party rally in Nuremberg. Hearing the translation of Adolf Hitler's harangue, interspersed with the audience's shouts of "Sieg Heil! Sieg Heil! Sieg Heil!," Roosevelt switched off the radio and turned to Hopkins. An idea suddenly popped into the president's head, genesis unknown. He told Hopkins that he wanted him to start scouting immediately for sites on the West Coast where aircraft could be manufactured. Hopkins later regarded this decision as the moment when, if it came to war, FDR believed, "air power would win it."

Hap Arnold had become adept enough at Washington power moves to commission his early champion, Elliott Roosevelt, as a captain in the Air Corps. "I was severely taken to task and all kinds of stories were circled," Arnold noted, "about preferential treatment for the well placed." He felt his action was justified when young Roosevelt became the first to fly over the Greenland ice cap and brought back remarkable photographs. "That picture tore away the veil of mystery in which the Greenland icecap had been shrouded for centuries," Arnold remembered, and proved that planes could fly over polar routes.

Like FDR, Arnold was no respecter of organization charts. One member of the president's staff complained that Roosevelt would give the same job to six people and give one staffer six jobs. One of Arnold's subordinates claimed that it was his chief's penchant to "give the wrong person the wrong assignment at the wrong time." Laurence Kuter, an aide, remembered, "Hap Arnold never sat still. . . . My hope of getting as much as one hour of concentrated attention . . . was greatly optimistic. After ten or fifteen minutes, the General would begin to fidget . . . and bolt out of his office." Arnold's machinations showed a talent worthy of the president himself. As pressure for an expanded Air Force grew, he warned manufacturers that they had to step up production because more pilots were being produced than planes. Simultaneously, he told aviation training schools that they had to turn out more pilots because there were more planes coming on line than pilots.

No sooner had Arnold cracked the presidential circle than he stepped on a land mine. Much to Hap's astonishment, Henry Morgenthau, the secretary of the treasury, had seized control of airplane procurement, brushing aside the secretary of war and the Air Corps. While testifying before the Senate Military Affairs Committee with its still vocal contingent of isolationists, Arnold was asked, "Does the Secretary of the Treasury run the Air Corps? Does he give orders about Air Corps procurement?" What lay behind the isolationists' concern was a fear that FDR wanted "to supply our foreign friends with airplanes," as Arnold put it. Which was true of the president and the interventionist Morgenthau. Arnold, in principle, also supported strengthening the British and the French air forces. But he told the committee, "between helping to arm our future allies and giving everything away, a realistic line must be drawn, or there would never be a United States Air Force, except on paper." Morgenthau alerted FDR to Arnold's less than unconditional support for strengthening friendly air corps. At a White House meeting in March 1940, Arnold felt a distinct chill as he took his seat alongside the other military chiefs and cabinet secretaries. As he described the fateful meeting, "The President in unmistakable language, covered the necessity for cooperation and coordination concerning foreign sales for aircraft. . . . And then, looking directly at me, he said, there were places to which officers who did not 'play ball' might be sent, such as Guam." The fixed smile on Arnold's face could not conceal his anguish. "I felt that I was about to lose my job," he later wrote. "I had a genuine worry because I had lost the President's confidence at probably the most critical period of my professional career."

He became persona non grata. Nine months of exile passed when, out of the blue, a White House secretary informed Arnold that the president wanted him over for a small dinner. As Arnold recalled his arrival, "I was received genially by the President who was sitting beside a table upon which the fixings for cocktails were set up." Without a flicker of reference to their earlier falling-out, an ebullient FDR asked, "How about my mixing you an Old Fashioned?" Arnold never knew precisely what or who ended his banishment, a not uncommon experience for those who aroused the president's displeasure. Most likely Hopkins's and Marshall's admiration for Arnold had achieved his rehabilitation. As Laurence Kuter described the bond between Marshall and Arnold, "There was no back slapping, no banter or chit-chat that you would expect between old pals. . . . They were simply two senior officers who had known each other for thirty years with mutual friendship. I never heard them call each other by nickname or first name." For Arnold, however, his youthful prankishness had never disappeared entirely. He sent a friend, a comedian named Vince Barnett, using a phony name, to the office of the sober-sided Marshall. Barnett, speaking in a thick, unplaceable accent, identified himself as a wealthy immigrant eager to get into the aviation business. The stunned general demanded, "Who are you? How did you get in here?" Barnett answered with a sly wink, "You know what I want. You can fix it for me!" He then plunked down a wad of bills on Marshall's desk. "Get out! Get out!" Marshall shouted. At that point, Arnold, who had been eavesdropping behind the office door, came in laughing uproariously. Marshall's response to the caper is unknown, but Arnold kept his job.

Hap Arnold had barely arrived in London in April 1941 on a mission to determine what aircraft the RAF needed when he experienced firsthand the destructive force of German air raids. He wrote, "Hundreds of people were killed and injured in the raid that night, but the papers gave each casualty only a small official notice, 'Killed in Action.'" The Londoners' resilience impressed him. "There were bright flowers in window boxes right in the midst of ruins. . . . People were groping in the wreckage of their homes for salvage. . . . Six thousand bombs were dropped that night, 600 people killed; 4,000 injured. . . . [Yet] the people maintained their calm and worked hard at cleaning up the city."

The president's commitment to airpower became evident in an incident occurring during the summer of 1940. Arthur Travers Harris, commander of the RAF's 5 Group Bomber Command, believed that bombing could win wars, which earned him the moniker "Bomber Harris." While Harris was in Washington, FDR invited him to the White House. Harris, blunt in appearance, manner, and speech, was unawed at being ushered into America's inner sanctum, where he heard FDR ask what America could do at this point to best help the RAF. Harris answered without hesitation that he wanted more pilots to ferry planes across the Atlantic to Britain. Roosevelt handed the assignment to Arnold. Hap had just the pilot in mind to organize such a program, Jacqueline Cochran, a pioneer female flier. Cochran set to work creating the Women Airforce Service Pilots, WASPs, and began an uphill battle to prove that a woman could fly a plane as well as a man.

Regular Army officers had long treated the Air Corps as a stepchild, dismissed as a leech trying to siphon off more of the military budget than it merited. FDR was about to change that disequilibrium. On May 5, 1941, he announced that an unprecedented 20,000 planes would roll off the assembly line that year. Automobile factories were to allot space for plane production and make 500 bombers a month. The next day, *The New York Times* reported that the president was demanding that heavy bombers "must be turned out even at the expense of other defense efforts." Absolute command of the air by the democracies, he said, "must and can be achieved."

FDR had a gift, trained or unconscious, to detect a kindred soul. He was not close to Arnold personally nor did he display the genuine affection that he felt toward a Harry Hopkins or a Pa Watson. Yet Arnold was steel beneath an affable facade, serious while capable of whimsy, comfortable using wiles to pursue his ends, at once a visionary and a pragmatist. Despite the yawning gulf in their backgrounds, the two men were not all that different. On June 20, 1941, Roosevelt revised Army Regulation 95-5, elevating the Army Air Corps to the Army Air Forces. The change meant that the new branch's earlier Magna Carta had now been strengthened by a partial declaration of independence. In a single lifetime, Hap Arnold had witnessed airpower's rise from the kitelike contraptions of the Wright brothers to a major, possibly *the* major, weapon of modern warfare.

FOR ALL HIS GROWING SUPPORT FOR AIRPOWER, the Navy remained FDR's true love. His attraction to all things nautical had been planted by his father, James Roosevelt, who taught his son to sail their fifty-one-foot yacht, the *Halfmoon,* in the waters off the family's summer home on Campobello Island in eastern Canada. The elder Roosevelt eventually gave Franklin his own boat, the *New Moon,* aboard which he cruised northeastern waters, often by himself, while a student at Harvard. The president once revealed to his current naval aide, Captain John McCrea, "One of my earliest ambitions was to go to Annapolis, but my mother vetoed that hard."

After Woodrow Wilson's election as president in 1912, the incoming administration's prospective secretary of the navy, Josephus Daniels, wanted Roosevelt to leave his seat in the New York State Senate and become the Navy's assistant secretary. FDR leaped at the offer. Navy careerists found the sea-loving assistant secretary far more congenial than his superior. While Daniels struggled with naval nomenclature, referring to "decks" as "floors," "overheads" as "ceilings," and "ladders" as "steps," Roosevelt used the Navy's idiom comfortably and naturally. He pursued his duties with an independence that occasionally left Daniels in the dark as to what his ambitious assistant was up to. At one point, FDR let a major contract for constructing naval barracks and only sought Daniels's permission after the job was done.

The skipper of the World War I destroyer *Flusser,* Lieutenant William F. Halsey Jr., recalled taking the assistant secretary on a tour of naval installations in Frenchman's Bay, Maine, during which Roosevelt asked if he could take the ship through a narrow strait between Campobello and the mainland. He knew this stretch well, Roosevelt assured Halsey. "All I had been told was that he had some experience in small boats," Halsey remembered of that day. "The fact that a white-flanneled yachtsman can sail a catboat out to buoy and back is no guarantee that he can handle a high-speed destroyer in narrow waters." Halsey was uneasy. Damage to his vessel could ruin a ship captain's future. He stood close by as he yielded command to FDR. "As Mr. Roosevelt made his first turn," Halsey remembered, "I saw him look aft and check the swing of our stern. My worries were over. He knew his business." Halsey would become a beneficiary of a Roosevelt penchant. As president, he exercised final approval of all assignments for officers of flag rank. He kept at hand a well-thumbed copy of the *Naval Register* and could describe the strengths and weaknesses of an astonishing number of men. As Frank Freidel, a Roosevelt biographer, noted, "Numerous officers commented . . . upon the fact that they had not seen FDR since the World War, and that he still remembered their names and faces." If FDR recalled an officer favorably, he might appoint him even if his name had not appeared on the nomination list suggested to him.

ONE EVENING, FDR's son Elliott had gone up to say good night to his father, and took the opportunity to ask, "How come we were shipping scrap iron to Japan? Surely we knew that scrap iron to Japan meant dead Chinese." In fact, between 1935 and 1940, the United States had sold 200 million tons of scrap iron to Japan. After a long pause, the president answered his son. "We're a nation of peace. It means we're not looking for war, it means we don't want war, it means we're not prepared for war." Besides, he pointed out, scrap iron was not classified as war matériel, and consequently anybody was free to sell it to Japan. Elliott began to protest, but his father went on. "If we were suddenly to stop our sales of scrap iron to Japan, she would be within her rights in considering that we had performed an unfriendly act. . . . She'd be entitled to consider such an action on our part sufficient cause to break off relations with us. . . . We are in essence and in fact appeasing Japan," the president openly admitted. Nevertheless, soon after the conversation with Elliott, and alarmed by Japanese covetous eyes on British and French possessions in Asia, FDR, in September 1940, did embargo iron and steel scrap shipments to the Japanese.

CHAPTER 5

Pearl Harbor

THE PRESIDENT SPENT THE EVENING OF DECEMBER 6, 1941, IN HIS private quarters in the company of Harry Hopkins, as close to Roosevelt as any man and now living in a bedroom next to the Lincoln Study. The ailing Hopkins, so fleshless, so pallid, was yet so lively that his appearance suggested an animated cadaver. FDR was editing a peace overture to Emperor Hirohito drafted by Cordell Hull, his secretary of state. The message cautiously raised recent disquieting acts by Japan, but concluded with "the fervent hope that your Majesty may, as I am doing, give thought in definite emergency to ways of dispelling the dark clouds." A young naval aide to the president, Lester R. Schulz, on only his second day on the job, tapped tentatively on the president's door to deliver the first thirteen parts of a fourteen-part coded message from Tokyo to Japan's embassy in Washington, entitled "Final Memorandum," that had been broken by U.S. cryptographers. Roosevelt took the message from Schulz without a word and started to read. After several minutes, he turned to Hopkins and said, "This means war." Schulz, recognizing that he was an eyewitness to history, listened intently to what the two men said.

That evening typesetters at *The New York Times* hurried to finish locking their chases for the Sunday, December 7, edition. The paper's front page would carry the daily digest entitled "The International Situation," reporting that the president had dispatched a personal appeal to Emperor Hirohito urging peace; that the Red Army had driven back the German invaders from Rostov; and that the Finnish president,

Risto Heikki Ryti, now allied with Germany, warned America and Britain that their support of the Russians "was clasping hands with a leper." Another front-page story would report that football's Rose Bowl was being challenged for dominance by the new Sugar Bowl. Most heartening, after over a decade of Depression, the digest indicated that the index of business activity had just scored a record high.

On Sunday morning, on the other side of the world, another sun-splashed day dawned over the demi-paradise of the Hawaiian Islands. The sky was a soft blue dotted by billows of cottony clouds. Church bells announcing Sunday services sounded across Pearl Harbor where over ninety Navy ships rested at anchor or were tied alongside piers and in dry dock. Sailors coming off the morning watch went below for breakfast, then prepared to attend church or just sleep in. Admiral Husband E. Kimmel, the Pearl Harbor naval commandant, had ordered a slow Sunday routine, allowing the men to spend time ashore with friends, wives, and children before putting out to sea the next morning for training exercises.

THAT SAME MORNING, after finishing breakfast and glancing at the Sunday papers, George Marshall began his fixed weekend habit, having the Fort Myer stables send up his favorite sorrel, Prepared, for a horse-back ride. Marshall turned the horse down a bridle path, passing through Arlington National Cemetery and along the government's experimental agricultural station where, one day, the Pentagon would rise. For Marshall a morning free of the ceaseless pressures of his job was treasured.

THE PRESIDENT HAD BEEN AWAKE since 8:30 that Sunday morning and finished his customary breakfast, orange juice, soft-boiled eggs with bacon, toast, and coffee. His current valet, Navy petty officer Arthur Prettyman, delivered the Sunday papers, the thick *New York Times*, two Washington papers, and the rabidly anti-Roosevelt *Chicago Tribune*. Prettyman wheeled the president into the bathroom, where FDR shaved with an old-fashioned straight razor. He dressed casually, putting on a baggy sweater that belonged to his son Jimmy. The day was glorious with the sun streaming through the White House east windows. The temperature was a brisk 43 degrees, but warm enough for golfers to tee off at Washington's Burning Tree course.

FDR checked his schedule with satisfaction. Tension in the White House had been unremitting ever since Secretary Stimson had urged him six days before to cut short his vacation at Georgia's Warm Springs and get back to Washington. This day, however, his calendar showed only an appointment with the Chinese ambassador, Hu Shih, and that not until 12:30. Otherwise, he was free to pursue his passion since boyhood, his stamp collecting. But first, his chronic sinusitis was acting up and he had called Admiral McIntire to treat him. McIntire left his first-floor dispensary and hurried along the eerily quiet White House corridors, the clacking of his heels audible as he mounted the stairway to FDR's study. Outside, only the bells of St. John's Church across Pennsylvania Avenue on Lafayette Square broke the stillness. As McIntire entered the president's room, FDR rolled back his large, handsome head to let the doctor administer eyedrops. The admiral was another naval officer who had prospered because, while serving aboard a cruiser during World War I, he caught the eye of the assistant secretary of the navy. FDR was in a garrulous mood this morning, spinning a stream of stories about the old days, going on long after the doctor had finished treating him. Two pleasant hours passed before McIntire finally left.

Hu Shih arrived promptly at 12:30 and was ushered into FDR's study, a room in casual disarray, with teetering stacks of books and piles of papers tied with string carpeting the floor. The Chinese envoy was dispatched in the trademark Roosevelt fashion. FDR began by reading to Hu the cable he had sent to Hirohito the night before, punctuating his recital with asides of "I got him there; that was a telling phrase; that will be fine for the record." Hu Shih left after a half hour during which time the president had talked nonstop while the Chinese scarcely had an opportunity to state his business.

FDR could finally turn to his philately. The State Department mailroom, receiving correspondence from all over the world, had instructions to send the most interesting stamps to the White House. The president called Prettyman to bring him the tools of his avocation, his album, scissors, magnifying glass, stickers, and the collector's bible, *Scott Stamp Catalogue*. He was supposed to be attending a formal lunch downstairs, but had begged off. "I was disappointed but not surprised," Eleanor Roosevelt recalled. "The fact that he carried so many secrets in his head made it necessary for him to watch everything he said, which in itself is exhausting."

Hopkins came in, greeted effusively by the president. As Roosevelt's grandson Curtis Roosevelt described their relationship, "FDR enjoyed Harry's company. He was funny, always had a flip remark. He shared with the president this capacity to make anything amusing, rather than serious, unlike my grandmother." For lunch, the president chose to have something simple served on a removable tray attached to the wheelchair that he himself had adapted from an ordinary kitchen chair. He poked desultorily at his food. The White House chef, Henrietta Nesbitt, notorious for uninspired fare, had been described by the president's son Jimmy as "the worst cook I ever encountered." Hopkins, still in his bathrobe, stretched out on a couch, bantering with the president while FDR munched on an apple. At 1:57 the quiet was shattered by the jangling of the telephone. The White House operator apologized for interrupting the president on a Sunday but said that the navy secretary, Mr. Knox, insisted that he speak to the president.

"Put him on," FDR said.

Knox's voice was strained. "Mr. President," he said, "it looks as if the Japanese have attacked Pearl Harbor."

"No!" FDR gasped.

Knox said that he had few details so far but would get back when he knew more.

FDR told Hopkins what he had just heard. Hopkins replied that it had to be a mistake, Japan would never dare attack Hawaii. "No, this was exactly the sort of thing the Japanese would do," the president answered—talk peace while plotting war. Within the hour Admiral Stark, the chief of naval operations, called the president confirming the worst. The attack had been devastating, with the fleet seriously damaged and many hundreds of lives lost. Word of the attack plunged the White House into a frenzy with aides rushing in and out and phones endlessly jangling while the president remained an oasis of calm amidst the clamor. "His reaction to any great event was always to remain calm," Eleanor once observed. "If it was something that was bad, he just became almost like an iceberg, and there was never the slightest emotion that was allowed to show."

The president's secretary, Grace Tully, used his bedroom phone to take further calls from Stark and other officials updating the inventory of disaster. She typed up her shorthand notes while the president's military aide, Pa Watson, hunched over her shoulder, impatient to bring the latest word to the president. FDR managed to get a call through to Joseph B. Poindexter, the governor of Hawaii, who was in the midst of giving him a firsthand account of the assault when the governor's voice was drowned out by a roar. After Poindexter again became audible, the president turned to his aides and relayed what he had just heard: "My God, there's another wave of Jap planes over Hawaii."

THAT MORNING, well before the president had learned of the attack, Colonel Rufus S. Bratton, head of the Far East section of Army intelligence, had in hand all fourteen parts of the Japanese Final Memorandum, though FDR had not yet seen the final part. Tacked onto the end of the message was a separate note to Japanese ambassador Kichisaburo Nomura, instructing him to deliver the Final Memorandum to the White House at precisely 1 P.M. Washington time, which would be 7 A.M. in Hawaii. Why such precision? Bratton wondered. His unease led him to call General Marshall at Fort Myer, who was coming out of his shower after his ride. Bratton urged him to come to the War Department at once. After speeding through the capital's deserted streets, Marshall reached his office by 10:30 and found Bratton brandishing the Japanese message. The general sat at his desk, adjusted his dime-store glasses, and began to read. He too found the preciseness of the instruction to Nomura alarming. It was now 11 A.M., and 5 A.M. in Hawaii.

The Final Memorandum stated that all negotiations between Japan and the United States had come to an end. Marshall, divining the possible meaning of such finality, calculated that he had about two hours to warn all Army commands in the Pacific. He wrote out a message in longhand reading, "The Japanese are presenting at 1 pm Eastern Standard Time today what amounts to an ultimatum. Also they are under orders to destroy their code machines immediately. Just what significance the hour set may have we do not know but be on the alert accordingly."

Admiral Stark had also gone to his office that Sunday, as was his habit. He too received copies of decoded Japanese traffic, but judged the Final Memorandum as merely a rehash of previously expressed Japanese positions. Marshall called Stark before sending his message to Army posts and asked if the admiral wanted the Navy to receive the same alert. Stark hesitated. He had already sent one "war warning" to the fleet on November 27 and was reluctant to be heard crying wolf. In the end he agreed to tack onto Marshall's warning the words, "Show this to your naval officers." Colonel Bratton took Marshall's message with Stark's addendum to the War Department's signal room assuring the general that it would reach its addressees in eight minutes. Once informed that his message had gone out Marshall returned home.

What would turn out to be a warning of historic proportions suffered a fate difficult to conceive in the world of modern communications. The Army's circuit between Washington and Honolulu had broken down. Marshall's message was then sent via the commercial cable company Western Union, and given no particular priority. The cable, received in Honolulu at 7:33 A.M., was delivered by a messenger on a bicycle who had to take shelter from the attack. By the time Marshall's alert reached Army posts, hours, not eight minutes, had elapsed. Pearl Harbor had already gone up in smoke.

Marshall arrived at the White House, grim-faced, bearing the burden of knowing that a chance to put Pearl Harbor's defenses on battle alert had been bungled. He found the president issuing orders with cool dispatch. FDR asked him the best way to deploy troops in the event of a land assault on Pearl Harbor and added as an afterthought that he wanted the Army to protect the Japanese embassy and consulates throughout the country from being sacked by outraged Americans. He told Knox and Stimson to draft orders putting the country on a wartime footing.

At 5 P.M., FDR summoned Grace Tully to his study. "Sit down, Grace," he said. "I am going before Congress tomorrow. I'd like to dictate my message. It will be short." As she propped her steno pad on her knee, the president lit a cigarette, inhaled deeply, and began to speak, as Tully remembered, "in the calm tone in which he dictated his mail . . . only his diction was different as he spoke each word incisively and slowly, carefully specifying each punctuation mark and paragraph." "Yesterday comma December 7 comma 1941 dash a date which will live in world history dash . . ." FDR subsequently crossed out "world history" and wrote in longhand "infamy." The call for a declaration of war against Japan was brief, 521 words.

As night fell, FDR ate a snack with Harry Hopkins and Tully in his study. He was then taken into the Oval Office where he nimbly shifted himself from the wheelchair to the seat behind his desk. By 8:30 P.M. members of the cabinet, at the president's direction, began trooping in. Labor Secretary Frances Perkins recalled the mood. "The President nodded as we came in but there was none of the usual cordial, personal greeting," she noted. "This was one of the few occasions he couldn't muster a smile. . . . He was calm, not agitated. He was concentrated, all of his mind and all of his faculties were on one task of trying to find out what had really happened." Roosevelt also summoned congressional leaders from both parties to come to the White House at 10 P.M., among them Sam Rayburn, the House speaker; Joseph W. Martin, the House minority leader; Alben W. Barkley, the Senate majority leader; Charles McNary, the Senate minority leader; and Tom Connally, chairman of the Senate Foreign Relations Committee. Conspicuously absent among the invited was Roosevelt's Hudson River neighbor, the ranking minority member of the House Foreign Affairs Committee,

Representative Hamilton Fish III, who had fought the draft extension just months before. Stewards lugged in additional chairs, forming a semicircle around the president. Through the windows facing south over the Ellipse, the moon could be glimpsed riding behind the clouds over a capital that had begun the day at peace and ended it in war. In front of the White House, illuminated by floodlights, people had gathered, singing, "America the Beautiful," "God Bless America," and "My Country, 'Tis of Thee."

FDR, surprisingly in the wake of an attack in the Pacific, began by reasserting his conviction that the war in Europe remained primary, telling his visitors that he detected a plot by the Axis powers in launching the attack, "to divert the American mind from and the British mind from the European field and divert American supplies from the European theater to defense of the East Asian theater." Turning to Pearl Harbor he observed that the sneak attack had a strong Japanese odor, presaged by Japan's long-ago war with Russia. The attack on the Hawaiian Islands, he said, was "equaled only by the Japanese episode of 1904, when two [Russian] squadrons, cruisers . . . without any warning, I think on a Sunday morning by the way, Japanese cruisers sank all of them." Similarly, on November 26, 1941, a Japanese task force of six aircraft carriers, two battleships, two cruisers, and nine destroyers had steamed out of Tankan Bay in the Japanese Kuril Islands headed to deliver "a mortal blow" to Pearl Harbor. Before the attack, the president had inadvertently confirmed to the Japanese that their deception was working. He had summoned to the Oval Office the Japanese ambassador, Nomura, and a special envoy, Saburo Kurusu, and warned them that he possessed information that a large Japanese force was moving from Shanghai toward Indochina, indicating that the Americans knew nothing of the task force steaming toward Hawaii.

Aides continued to set fresh bulletins on the attack before the president. He looked up from one to announce, "It looks as if out of eight of our battleships, three have been sunk, and possibly a fourth. Two destroyers were blown up while they were in drydock. Two of the battleships are badly damaged. Several other smaller vessels have been sunk or destroyed. . . . I have no word on the Navy casualties, which will undoubtedly be very heavy, and the best information is that there have been more than 100 Army casualties and 300 men killed and injured." Senator Connally, a lean, crusty Texan, sitting closest to the president, slammed his fist on FDR's desk and demanded, "How did it happen that our ships were caught like lame ducks at Pearl Harbor? How did they catch us with our pants down? They were all asleep!" The president answered, "I don't know Tom, I just don't know."

The long day was not yet over. Edward R. Murrow, the thirty-three-year-old preeminent radio broadcaster of the time, had been invited earlier with his wife, Janet, to a White House supper. Mrs. Roosevelt insisted on going ahead with the plan, though, she explained to them, Franklin would not be able to join them. After she served a meal of scrambled eggs and pudding, the Murrows prepared to leave, but were told that the president wanted to see Ed later. Murrow then waited with Harry Hopkins in the latter's bedroom to be summoned. A distraught Hopkins flung himself across his four-poster bed and cried, "Oh God, if I only had more strength!" To Murrow the emaciated Hopkins looked like "a death's-head."

Not until nearly 1 A.M. was Murrow ushered in to see FDR, whom he found wearing a shapeless gray jacket, his face drawn, as he nibbled a sandwich and sipped a beer. Also present was William Donovan, then building the nation's first intelligence arm for the president. FDR asked Murrow, recently returned from London, how Britain was bearing up under its ordeal. The broadcaster assured him that the British could take it. Roosevelt then began listing, with cold fury, the losses at Pearl Harbor. When he described the planes destroyed he pounded his fists on his desk, bellowing, "On the ground, by God, on the ground!" The final count would be 18 ships sunk or seriously damaged, 347 planes destroyed or badly shot up, and 2,403 lives lost, almost half of them aboard the sunken battleship *Arizona*. Japanese losses amounted to 29 of the 343 attacking torpedo planes and bombers, one full-size and two midget submarines. The official Japanese agency, Domei News, reported that the crippled U.S. fleet "would be regarded as utterly inadequate to accomplish any successful outcome in an encounter with the thus far intact Japanese fleet."

Born that day was a conspiracy theory alleging that Roosevelt, so eager to get the United States into the war, contrived to leave the U.S. fleet in Pearl Harbor supine, unresisting, unwarned, thus inviting the Japanese attack. In a later broadcast addressing the theory, Ed Murrow described the demeanor of the president and other leaders that fateful night: "If they were not surprised by the news from Pearl Harbor, then that group of elderly men were putting on a performance which would have excited the admiration of any experienced actor. I cannot believe that their expressions, bearing and conversation were designed merely to impress one correspondent who was sitting outside in a hallway." Quizzed later on what he had heard on delivering the Final Memorandum to the president the night before the attack, Lieutenant Schulz answered, Pearl Harbor had never been mentioned. "The only geographical name I recall was Indochina. . . . There was no indication that tomorrow was necessarily the day."

IN ENGLAND ON THE EVENING OF DECEMBER 7, Kathleen Harriman, the twenty-four-year-old daughter of Averell Harriman, found herself with her father, American ambassador to Great Britain John Winant, and Winston Churchill, all gathered to celebrate her birthday. To the elder Harriman, "The Prime Minister seemed tired and depressed. He didn't have much to say and was immersed in his thoughts, with his head in his hands part of the time." Near nine o'clock, Churchill's valet, Sawyers, came in carrying a small portable radio, a present from Harry Hopkins. The prime minister turned on the radio and caught the tail end of a report of fighting on the Russian Front and a tank battle raging in Libya. The announcer then said, "The news has just been given that Japanese aircraft have raided Pearl Harbor, the American naval base in Hawaii."

After a stunned silence, Churchill rose, headed for the door, and said over his shoulder, "We shall declare war on Japan!" Ambassador Winant trailed after him. "Good God," he said, "you can't declare war on a radio announcement." Churchill stopped, and asked, "What shall I do?" Winant suggested a transatlantic phone call to the president to find out exactly what had happened. Winant had barely been put through to FDR when Churchill grabbed the phone. "Mr. President," he asked, "what's this about Pearl Harbor?" "It's true," Roosevelt responded. "They have attacked us at Pearl Harbor. We're all in the same boat now." Churchill ended the conversation saying, "This certainly simplifies things. God be with you." He would later describe his feelings about this moment. "So we had won after all! Yes, after Dunkirk, after the fall of France . . . after the threat of invasion . . . we had won the war . . . Hitler's fate was sealed, Mussolini's fate was sealed. As for the Japanese they would be ground to powder." The next morning, a staff member asked Churchill if, with the Americans now in the war, he would still be so ingratiating toward them. Churchill answered, "Oh, that is the way we talked to her while we were wooing her; now that she is in the harem, we talk to her quite differently."

GEORGE MARSHALL AND HAROLD STARK sat among the first rows in the jammed House of Representatives, awaiting the commander in chief's arrival. Stark's eyes were red-rimmed, his face haggard. He had been at his office without sleep ever since word of the attack, fielding questions about how the debacle at an American naval bastion could have happened. Shortly after noon, a hush followed by an explosion of applause filled the chamber as the president, on crutches, made his way painfully to the rostrum. As the clapping finally died down, he began delivering the speech that he had dictated to Grace Tully the day before. He spoke for only six minutes and thirty seconds, during which time he was interrupted twelve times by applause. He closed, "No matter how long it may take us to overcome this premeditated invasion, the American people in their righteous might will win through to absolute victory!" The cheers and clapping were deafening. The inimitable voice uttering the words in patrician outrage and steely determination would forever echo in the memory of those old enough to have heard them that day and in a thousand repetitions in the decades since. The Senate passed the declaration of war within thirty-three minutes by a vote of 82 to 0 and the House by 388 to 1. Republican Jeannette Rankin of Montana cast the lone dissenting vote as she had also done in World War I. Rankin's vote was greeted with boos and hisses.

★

LEARNING OF THE JAPANESE attack on the United States, Adolf Hitler crowed, "Now, it is impossible for us to lose the war. We have an ally who has never been vanquished in three thousand years." Roosevelt, as he would have wished, could not expect to get a declaration of war against both Germany *and* Japan that day. One enemy was quite enough for the American people. Hitler, however, solved the problem for FDR. On December 11, he delivered, in the Reichstag, a ninety-minute harangue. "Roosevelt comes from a rich family and belongs to the class whose path is smoothed in the democracies," Hitler said. "I was the only child of a small, poor family and had to fight my way by work and industry. When the Great War came, Roosevelt occupied a position where he got to know only the pleasant consequences." By contrast, Hitler pointed to his four years in the trenches. Further, Roosevelt had failed to end the Depression in America, while the führer had put Germany back to work almost overnight. Finally, Hitler charged, Roosevelt was a tool of diabolic Jews who had maneuvered to turn him against the Third Reich. He then proclaimed a state of war existing between Germany and the United States.

A question would long intrigue historians: why did Hitler do it? Why, with Germany already embroiled in a brutal conflict in the Soviet Union and at war with the British in North Africa, did Hitler take on another world power? Through the Tripartite Pact of September 27, 1940, Hitler had pledged to Japan that should America and Japan clash, Germany would "at once open war against the United States." Hitler, however, was hardly known for honoring international agreements. He declared war on the United States because he believed it was inevitable. The War Department's Rainbow 5 contingency plan for mobilization in the event of war with Germany had been exposed by the *Chicago Tribune* and its sister publication, the *Washington Times-Herald*. In his declaration of war, Hitler practically quoted from the *Tribune,* saying, "there has been revealed in America President Roosevelt's plan by which, at the latest in 1943, Germany and Italy are to be attacked." By declaring war on the United States, Hitler did not believe that he had acted rashly, but that he was getting the jump on an inevitable enemy.

CONTROVERSY OVER WHO WAS TO BLAME for Pearl Harbor would never die. In the five years following the attack, nine investigations would be carried out by the Roosevelt administration, the Army, Navy, and Congress. Within days of the assault, FDR dispatched Navy Secretary Frank Knox to Pearl Harbor, who, after his investigation, prepared two reports, one for public consumption and the other to be kept secret. In the secret version Knox said that he asked Admiral Kimmel and General Walter C. Short how they could have been caught by surprise. The Navy, he noted, had not even taken such rudimentary precautions as placing torpedo nets around the harbor. Both men explained that they could not believe the enemy would strike from "the great distances which the Japs would have to travel to make the attack." As Kimmel later put it, "I never thought those little yellow sons of bitches could pull off such an attack so far from Japan." In his confidential report, Knox admitted that "no attempt by either Admiral Kimmel or General Short to alibi the lack of a state of readiness for the air attack" had been made.

By 10 P.M. on December 14, Knox was back in Washington and despite the late hour went directly to FDR's study to brief an impatient president. His nineteen-page report began, "Army preparations were primarily based on fear of sabotage while the Navy's were based on fear of submarine attack." Well before the attack, General Short had considered three alternative conditions of readiness: one, a defense against sabotage, espionage, and subversive activities; two, defense against air surface and submarine attack; three, "a defense against all out attack." The general had chosen option one, and perhaps understandably. Ever since countries in Europe had fallen so swiftly to Hitler, FDR had been convinced that their collapse could only be explained by internal subversion. Thus, military outposts, including Pearl Harbor, were continually pressed to guard against spies and sabotage. At Pearl Harbor, this emphasis had resulted in General Short's decision to mass his planes practically wingtip to wingtip and place a security cordon around them, which prompted the president's outrage upon learning how many aircraft had been so easily destroyed on the ground. As Knox read from his report, FDR took notes. "Essential fact is that Jap purpose was to knock U.S. out of the war before it began. Made apparent by deceptions practiced," he wrote. As for the performance of the Army and Navy, "The U.S. services were not on the alert against surprise air attack on Hawaii. This calls for a formal investigation, which will be initiated immediately by the President. . . . We are entitled to know . . . if there was any dereliction of duty prior to the attack." FDR wrote at the end of his notes, "Given me by F.K. 10 pm December 14 when he landed from Hawaii. FDR." By December 18, the president had appointed Associate Supreme Court Justice Owen J. Roberts to head a formal investigation, a shrewd choice for removing politics from the debate since Roberts was the sole remaining justice who had been appointed by a Republican president. Its work finished, the Roberts Commission laid the blame for the catastrophe squarely on Kimmel and Short, finding both guilty of dereliction of duty. Angered, both officers demanded to be court-martialed so that they could defend their actions. The requests were denied principally because their defense must inevitably depend on what they had been told through the Magic code-breaking operation, which the government was not about to admit existed.

The most exhaustive investigation, held by a joint congressional committee, completed after the war and with a report numbering some 15,000 pages, was scathing in its verdict. The report concluded, "The Commanders in Hawaii were clearly and unmistakably warned of war with Japan. . . . They failed to defend the fortress they commanded—Their citadel was taken by surprise." While granting that some of the responsibility "might appear to rest in Washington, the ultimate and direct responsibility for failure to engage the Japanese on the morning of December 7, with every weapon at their disposal rests essentially and properly with the Army and Navy commands in Hawaii." As for the culpability of the civilian leadership, beginning with the president, an exhaustive forty-volume 1946 inquiry by a Senate committee reported, "all evidence conclusively points to the fact that they discharged their responsibilities with distinction, ability, and foresight. . . . The President, the Secretary of State and high government officials made every possible effort, without sacrificing our national honor and endangering our security, to avert war with the Japanese." The committee also dealt with various conspiracy theories claiming that Roosevelt had engineered America's entry into the war. "The Committee found no evidence to support the charges made before and during the hearings that the President, the Secretary of State, the Secretary of War, or the Secretary of the Navy tricked, provoked, incited, cajoled or coerced Japan into attacking this Nation in order that a declaration of war might more easily be obtained from the Congress."

Nearly sixty years on, the guilt for Pearl Harbor would still stoke heated debate. On May 25, 1999, the U.S. Senate passed a nonbinding resolution by a vote of 52 to 47 posthumously exonerating Kimmel and Short of responsibility for the debacle and recommending restoration of their ranks. Senator Strom Thurmond, a sponsor of the bill, called the men the "two final victims of Pearl Harbor." But neither then President Bill Clinton, nor his successor, George W. Bush, followed the resolution's recommendation.

Given the wealth of intelligence, including almost immediate access to communications to and from the Japanese Foreign Office obtained through Magic, how, it might reasonably be asked, could the president not have known of the impending attack? In hindsight, the clues seem to point to that conclusion like lights on a runway. Yet not one of the 239 messages passing between Tokyo and the Japanese Washington embassy decoded by Magic ever mentioned Pearl Harbor. Based on the intelligence FDR did have in hand, if asked if Japan was going to attack somewhere in the Pacific, he would almost certainly have responded "Yes." He had said as much when on November 25 he told his military leaders, "We are likely to be attacked perhaps next Monday." Asked if he knew where such an attack would take place, he could honestly answer "No." Admiral Stark and General Marshall's

"Memorandum for the President," submitted just ten days before Pearl Harbor, warned only of possible attacks on the Burma Road, Thailand, Malaya, the Netherlands East Indies, the Philippines, and the Russian Pacific Maritime Provinces. The only Japanese fleet movements reported to Washington before December 7 were heading south along the China coast toward Indochina and Thailand, not east toward Hawaii. Further, General Marshall had advised the president that Pearl Harbor was virtually invincible, "the strongest fortress in the world. . . . Enemy carriers, naval escorts and transports will begin to come under attack at a distance of approximately 750 miles."

So tightly was the Japanese secret held that even the envoys in Washington, Kurusu and Nomura, claimed that they were kept in the dark. They had been instructed only, they claimed, to keep negotiations going to the last minute. After the war, Nomura complained that he had been the "worst informed ambassador in history."

To believe that FDR had foreknowledge of the attack but deliberately failed to act would require that the recipients of Magic besides himself, the secretaries of state, war, navy, the chiefs of the Army, Navy, and Air Forces, along with intelligence officers reviewing the decrypts, even code clerks who decoded the Japanese traffic, had all conspired to remain silent about an attack that would cost the lives of over 2,400 of their fellow Americans and cause the near annihilation of the Pacific Fleet. The scenario defies credibility. However, some respectable authors and scholars, and some not so respectable, have answered "Yes" to the perennial question "Did FDR know that the Japanese were going to attack Pearl Harbor?" Why this insistence in the face of the evidence? Likely because conspiracy theories present tightly wound, suspenseful drama, while the truth is often messy, contradictory, confusing, and dull. No shred of proof exists that Franklin Roosevelt wanted war with Japan. Undeniably, Roosevelt wanted the United States in the war, but in the European conflict that he was already waging, undeclared, on the high seas of the Atlantic. To FDR, who had diverted much of the fleet from the Pacific to the Atlantic, Japan's belligerency amounted to an unwanted diversion while Hitler's regime threatened Western democratic civilization. Nevertheless, the "Roosevelt knew of Pearl Harbor" hypothesis has entered the eerie world of undying conspiracy theories along with the assassinations of Presidents Abraham Lincoln and John F. Kennedy. A major failing afflicting Roosevelt and his chief advisors was that they received only raw Magic decrypts. As the cryptology pioneer William Friedman put it, "There was nobody in either the Army or Navy intelligence staffs in Washington whose most important if not sole duty was to study the whole story which Magic messages were unfolding . . . nobody whose responsibility was to try and put the pieces of the jig-saw puzzle together." Granted, the surprise attack on Pearl Harbor was the most stunning intelligence failure in American history, perhaps in all history. But what cold, hard fact makes certain is that Pearl Harbor was not a conspiracy, but a catastrophe.

THE SURPRISE ATTACK PRODUCED AMONG Americans reactions ranging from legitimate outrage to baseless hysteria. On the day war was declared, Henry Stimson noted in his diary that he had been called by an assistant, "Saying that an enemy fleet was thought to be approaching San Francisco." That same night sirens wailed from San Francisco to Los Angeles after a policeman reported an unidentified aircraft reconnoitering the Pacific coast. General Joseph Stilwell recorded in his diary an alert put out by the Army, "Reliable information that an attack on Los Angeles is imminent." Along the coast of Washington, Oregon, and California, citizens armed themselves with shotguns, even pitchforks, and formed improvised patrols to drive off expected invaders. Mayor Fiorello La Guardia in New York City ordered civil defense plans drawn up to protect Manhattan "from such an attack as surprised Pearl Harbor."

Given the president's obsession with internal subversion, Japanese in the United States, both those born in America, the Nisei, who were American citizens, and immigrants from Japan, the Issei, came under instant suspicion. William Donovan, serving as intelligence chief, was eager to show his mettle and informed FDR that Japanese soldiers disguised as civilians were mobilizing to move against San Diego. Another source reported that ground glass had been found in shrimp canned by

Japanese workers and that Japanese saboteurs had sprayed arsenic on vegetables, even that a Japanese farmer near Ventura, California, had planted a flower bed so that it formed an arrow pointing to a nearby airfield. California's governor, Culbert Olson, and the state's attorney general, Earl Warren, one day to be a liberal chief justice of the U.S. Supreme Court, called for interning all Japanese in America. Cooler heads argued against heedless action. FBI director J. Edgar Hoover, no civil libertarian or lover of foreigners, advised, "The necessity for mass evacuation is based primarily upon public and political pressure rather than factual data." General Ralph Van Deman, respected chief of military intelligence in World War I, described calls for evacuation as "about the craziest proposition I have heard of yet."

However, the subsequent drumbeat of defeat in the Pacific did little to allay the belief that Japanese running loose in America presented a real danger. Franklin Roosevelt, more than ever, feared internal subversion. He told his daughter, Anna, that he wanted her and her children, Buzzie and Sis, to leave Seattle, where they were then living, and come to the East Coast. FDR drew his attorney general, Francis Biddle, into the evacuation debate. Biddle was uncomfortable, believing that the internment raised serious constitutional questions. But the attorney general, who had known FDR since their Groton School days, read his chief well. "I do not think he was much concerned with the gravity or implications of this step," Biddle later reflected. "He was never theoretical about things. What must be done to defend the country must be done." The president reached back to the Alien Enemies Act of 1798 for authority to issue Executive Order 9066 on February 19, seventy-four days after Pearl Harbor. The order would eventually uproot over 114,000 men, women, and children of Japanese ancestry, even citizens, and banish them to remote, barren "relocation centers" that FDR himself described as concentration camps. The Supreme Court upheld the constitutionality of his order. Relocation of Japanese in the United States raised a curious anomaly. Some 140,000 persons of Japanese descent lived in the Hawaiian Islands. Sixteen days after issuing 9066, the president told Frank Knox that he wanted them removed as well. On March 13, FDR approved a plan prepared by the Joint Chiefs of Staff ordering "the commanding General, Hawaiian Department, to evacuate to the mainland of the United States for internment in concentration camps, Japanese residents of the Hawaiian islands, either United States citizens or aliens." In the end, the removal was abandoned as impractical. Thus, Japanese residents of Pasadena and Fresno were uprooted while most of those living in and around Pearl Harbor, where Japan had actually made war, stayed put. For a leader to be ranked alongside Washington and Lincoln as one of America's greatest presidents, FDR's signature on Executive Order 9066 would remain an ineradicable stain on his presidency.

WITHIN SEVENTY-TWO HOURS AFTER Frank Knox reported his first-hand investigation of Pearl Harbor to FDR, heads began to roll. Admiral Kimmel, General Short, and the Air Forces chief for the Hawaiian Department, Major General Frederick Martin, were all relieved of duty. Someone had to be picked quickly to take over the Pacific Fleet. The admiral then running the Navy's Bureau of Navigation, Chester W. Nimitz, had earlier caught FDR's eye. Despite its dull-sounding mission, the bureau controlled a subject dear to FDR's heart, key assignments and promotions in the Navy. Nimitz was a fifty-six-year-old whose blue eyes, silver hair, and firm chin suggested an admiral sent over by central casting. Months before Pearl Harbor, FDR had offered Nimitz a plum, command of the U.S. Fleet, making him second only to the chief of naval operations in the Navy hierarchy and jumping him over numerous senior officers. Sensitive to the pitfalls of commanding men who had once been his superiors, Nimitz begged off. After the attack of December 7, FDR called Knox and said, "Tell Nimitz to get the hell out to Pearl Harbor and stay there until the war is won." When Nimitz informed his wife that he was now commander in chief of the Navy for the Pacific, she happily remarked, "You always thought that would be the height of glory." Nimitz replied, "The fleet is at the bottom of the sea." On New Year's Eve, Nimitz stood on the deck of the submarine *Grayling* to take command of a Navy with its morale at rock bottom.

✳

ADMIRAL ERNEST J. KING WAS CREDITED with once saying, "When they get in trouble they send for me, the sons of bitches." King denied ever using these words but once said, "If I had thought of it I would have said it." The man lacked that helpful qualification for success in the Navy at the time, personal acquaintance with Assistant Secretary of the Navy Roosevelt during World War I. As King's Atlantic Fleet chased and was occasionally chased by U-boats in prosecuting FDR's undeclared war at sea, the president came to see a great deal of Ernest King, and liked what he saw, a tough, smart, aggressive sailor. When the president's son Elliott asked his father what he thought of King, FDR offered the highest praise in his book: "He's a grand Navy man." The president decided to make King the most powerful leader in the Navy's history. On December 16, 1941, King, Stark, and Knox were called in to see the president. FDR announced that he intended to name King commander in chief, U.S. Fleet. The crusty admiral was not instantly pliant. He objected to the Navy shorthand for the job, CINCUS, pronounced "Sink Us," an infelicitous title for the head of a navy. He preferred commander in chief, pronounced "Cominch" in Navy speak. FDR resisted. It treaded on his turf as commander in chief of all the country's military forces. But Roosevelt wanted King and ultimately agreed to the change. At this point, Stark's presence posed an awkward situation, his having been chief of naval operations, and King's superior. But he had the unhappy fate of commanding the Navy at the time of Pearl Harbor and his star had lost its luster. For a time the two admirals found themselves within shouting distance of each other's offices in the Navy Department's sprawling headquarters on Constitution Avenue. Inevitably they were stepping on each other's toes. On the organization chart, King was responsible for current war plans and Stark for future plans. When King went to the president and raised the issue of inevitable conflict and confusion over the duplicated roles, FDR waved him aside airily. "Don't worry. We'll take care of that." Subsequently, a job was created for Stark as commander in chief, U.S. Naval Forces Europe, and he was packed off to London.

In the coming months FDR codified King's unprecedented powers through Executive Order 9096, which directed that the duties of the commander in chief, U.S. Fleet, and the duties of the chief of naval operations "may be combined and devolve upon one officer." King was also designated "principal naval adviser to the President." Further, he was elevated to four-star rank, full admiral. The president's military triumvirate was now complete, Marshall running the Army, King the Navy, and Arnold the Air Forces, a team that would remain in place throughout the war.

Whenever Ernie King's name came up, phrases sprang to mind: "hardboiled," "tough as nails," "hothead." One of his daughters described her father as the most even-tempered man she knew: "He's always in a rage." Roosevelt joked that Ernie King shaved himself with a blowtorch. King had been born in Lorain, Ohio, in 1878, four years before the president, the son of a worker in a railroad repair shop. Headstrong and impetuous, the boy announced one day in the eighth grade that he was quitting school. His father told him that was fine, but once he left, he could not go back. Young King worked for a time in his father's shop and showed a natural mechanical bent. However, he also soon regretted his impetuosity, and went back to high school, where he graduated as valedictorian in a class of thirteen.

At age ten, young Ernie had read an article about the U.S. Naval Academy in a magazine called *The Youth's Companion*. Thereafter, Annapolis was never far from his thoughts. After graduating from high school, he went up against thirty competitors in his congressional district and won an appointment to the academy to start on August 15, 1897. The institution was located near Annapolis, a slumbering fishing village where the Severn River emptied into the Chesapeake Bay. The town was graced with antebellum mansions and the bracing smell of salt air, which confirmed for young King that he was far from his inland Ohio home. From his arrival at Annapolis, the ambitious and utterly assured King set the goal of attaining the highest student rank, battalion commander, earning the four distinctive stripes on his sleeve. And he made it. He also played football with no particular distinction, though he was a talented ice skater. With his rosy cheeks and glowing health, his mates nicknamed him "Dolly" or "Beauty," both of which he detested. Handsome and cocksure, he preferred "El Rey," Spanish for "the King."

The great American adventure for young men of King's generation arrived in 1898, with the Spanish-American War. King dropped out of Annapolis to serve on the cruiser USS *San Francisco*, where he came under fire during the siege of Havana. He returned with an anchor tattooed on his left arm and a dagger on his right and visited Lorain as a conquering hero. He reentered the academy and in 1901 flung his cap in the air, the midshipmen's graduation tradition. He graduated fourth in his class. He claimed that he had deliberately chosen not to become first in the class academically because that distinction would make him a target for rivals for the rest of his naval career. He was now a slim six footer, weighing 165 pounds, a weight that would never change.

While still a midshipman, King had been dazzled by a vivacious beauty, Martha "Mattie" Egerton, the girl most sought after by midshipmen. King decided he must win her, and did. They were married four years after his graduation. However, in time King recognized that for all her charm, good looks, and high spirits, Mattie's horizons were limited to home and children and she showed scant interest in the fortunes of a career naval officer. The physical attraction that had first drawn them like magnets must have endured at least for a time, however, since the couple had seven children, six of them girls. In a marriage lacking shared concerns his eye began to roam. The vain King was chagrined when he began losing his hair, attributing the problem to wearing undersized hats that cut off circulation to his scalp.

Over the course of his career, King captained five warships, with command at sea the sine qua non for success in the Navy. He became legendary as a profane, hard-drinking, party-loving skipper with a split personality. On liberty ashore, he would carouse freely with his junior officers, imbibing and gambling to a point that they nicknamed him "Uncle Ernie." So easygoing was the mood that subordinates, emboldened by liquor, dared to rag their captain and slap him on the back in boozy camaraderie. The next morning it was as if the night before had never happened. King became aloof, exacting, and contemptuous toward any man who showed a hangover.

His approach to leadership style was the opposite of textbook theory. As his biographer Thomas Buell wrote, "Praise was given grudgingly and then only in private. Censure was swift, before a cloud of witnesses." One King officer, Kleber Masterson, recalled, "He didn't need a megaphone. He'd just stand on the edge of that bridge and they could hear him from one end to the other of the flight deck, even in a high wind, because he could really bellow when he was mad." One aide labored over an organization plan for weeks only to have King tell him, "Take this to the head [the toilet] with you." Another crew member recalled, "King was the only Naval officer I ever knew who would actually curse his subordinates." Buell explained that King, early in his career, had decided he was too soft and that if he was to succeed he would have to suppress a compassionate nature, not an interpretation that many Navy men who served with him would endorse. What no one ever questioned, however, was that for all the ruffled feathers and bruised egos he inflicted, nobody ran a ship more competently or achieved better performance than Captain King.

"His weaknesses," according to a friend who had known King since Annapolis, "were other men's wives, alcohol, and intolerance." According to Buell, "King had a way of talking that made a woman feel that she was very special, that he understood her, and that he admired her wit and beauty." But the gallant could violate the bounds of propriety. Well-bred women learned to avoid sitting next to King at dinner parties, where his hands had a habit of disappearing beneath the table. On balance, however, he was notoriously successful, and as King once told a friend, "You ought to be very suspicious of anyone who won't take a drink or doesn't like women."

By the summer of 1939, King's career appeared to have reached its last anchorage. Admiral Stark, at the time his superior, could not get the sixty-year-old King a final seagoing command, which for a Navy careerist was akin to shutting off oxygen. Instead, he was assigned to the General Board in Washington, respectable enough but a Navy pasture nonetheless. To one friend he referred to himself as "a has been." To another he broke into tears at a cocktail party while recounting his fate. King nevertheless impressed the then secretary of the navy, Charles Edison, with the energy and imagination that he brought to the board's unglamorous work. "I believe that Rear Admiral E. J. King is outstanding of this type and," Edison reported to the president, "would do wonders for the fleet and service." Roosevelt hesitated to bring King back to an active post, concerned about accounts that he was a heavy drinker, the sin of which Hap Arnold had been unjustly accused. Ultimately placated on this score, FDR rescued the admiral from oblivion, appointing him commander in chief, U.S. Atlantic Fleet, and adding another star, bringing him to full admiral, the Navy's highest rank. At this point King could be described as a controlled alcoholic. Upon his appointment the rigorously self-disciplined admiral became the most sparing of drinkers overnight. He would occasionally sip a glass of sherry, or have a beer, but no more. Like many converts, King became more Catholic than the pope. He told another officer with a drinking problem who had served under him on the *Lexington,* "your trouble is that intoxicating liquor and business do not mix. . . . While I have seen fit to be blunt—even brutal, it may be of interest to you to know that I, myself, went on the wagon in regard to hard liquor . . . for the duration, and very likely after." The man FDR appointed was hardly in tune with the president's social philosophy. Ernie King's politics were worthy of a nineteenth-century Tory. Democracies, he once observed, "put a premium on mediocrity and tend to emphasize the defects of the electorate."

King loved the trappings of power. After Roosevelt had made him chief of the entire Navy, he demanded a personal plane, a two-engined Lockheed Lodestar. He established his headquarters aboard a luxurious 257-foot yacht that had once belonged to the Dodge family and that King rechristened *Dauntless.* He kept the vessel moored at the Washington Navy Yard, since, as he claimed, he had to be able to put to sea at a moment's notice. Yet, except for the briefest interruptions, *Dauntless* would remain tied up at the Navy Yard for the rest of the war.

Aboard the vessel King followed an unvarying routine: up at 7 A.M.,

exercise for ten minutes, breakfast alone at 7:30, a glance at the newspapers, where he turned first to the comic strips and laughed uproariously at the antics of Dagwood and Blondie. Next he went to the ship's
fantail where the bugler sounded "attention," and King took the salute
of his spit-and-polish crew. Finally, he was driven to his office in the
Navy Department building on Constitution Avenue in a Cadillac given
to him by the vice president of the A&P grocery chain. "Main Navy," as
the department headquarters was known, teemed with civilian employees and Navy personnel from admirals to yeomen third class jostling elbows. Messengers delivering mail by tricycle jammed the
corridors and young working mothers dropped off babies at the department nursery. The origins of this bureaucratic chaos could be laid
at the feet of the president. FDR enjoyed telling reporters how, as assistant secretary of the navy during the First World War, he had to find
temporary space for the fast-swelling Navy Department. "Well, that
was finished in the spring of 1918. That is twenty-three years ago. . . .
There was nothing temporary about it; and then it was so good that we
went ahead and put the Munitions Building right alongside."

All commotion in the Navy Department ceased abruptly on the
third floor where King maintained stately offices, which he ran with
the discipline of the ship's captain he had been. He usually left the office at four and did not return to *Dauntless* for dinner until about six,
telling no one where he was in between. Besides the yacht, King was
provided with an official residence, the Naval Observatory on Massachusetts Avenue, today home to the vice president, where he planted
his wife and daughters, whom he visited only on Sundays. A congressman wanted to know why the government, while providing King with
a handsome home, also needed to give him a ship at an annual cost to
the taxpayers of $250,000. King saw that nothing came of the inquiry.

The historian Frederick Lewis Allen has left a vivid portrait of King
at the apex of his career. At a briefing for editors and writers seated
around a table that Allen described as "majestic," he described King as
"a tall man, bald, gray with a very fine face, small blue eyes, a beautiful
longish thin nose, a fine mouth, and tiny crow's feet at the corners"
who spoke "in stiff generalities. . . . One felt that he had been per-

suaded, as a matter of obscure duty, to speak to a group of people whom he saw no compelling reason for informing." Allen claimed to understand King's grudging performance. "He was neither a professor of naval interpretation nor a salesman with a glad eye; he was the man who had to run the United States Navy."

Much in King lacked admirability, a dictatorial personality fed by colossal vanity. Except for rather fawning behavior toward FDR, the admiral's equals found the man testy, subordinates bullying. Might the president have chosen a Navy chief of equal ability minus the wear and tear on King's associates? Yes, but FDR, with his love of all things nautical, had seen in King the crusty sea captain of legend and was well pleased with his choice.

WINSTON CHURCHILL HAD REJOICED at U.S. entry into the war. But which war? After Pearl Harbor, the American public was focused on the Pacific. The blow to prestige, the lives lost, the ships destroyed, had been inflicted not by Germany, but by Japan. To Churchill this emphasis posed a danger. While Asia contained swaths of the British Empire, it was the war in Europe, the prime minister believed, that threatened Britain's very existence. He was determined that FDR, as agreed upon at Argentia, must hold to a Europe-first strategy. He decided to go to Washington to protect his interest.

Five days after Pearl Harbor, the prime minister and his war council were aboard the newly commissioned battleship HMS *Duke of York,* which was making its way through gale winds and fifty-foot seas while steering a zigzag course across the Atlantic. The ship arrived at Norfolk where Churchill was whisked away by a U.S. Navy Lockheed Lodestar for a forty-five-minute flight to Washington. As the plane taxied to a halt, he could glimpse FDR in a White House limousine. As at Argentia, Churchill was wearing the uniform of an Elder Brother of Trinity House. He waved to an honor guard, entered the automobile, and shook hands with a beaming FDR as they were driven over the 14th Street Bridge to the White House.

FDR's visitor was to a marked degree still a nineteenth-century aristocrat. Churchill's wife, Clementine, describing her husband, once noted, "He's never been in a bus, and only once on the Underground. That was during the General Strike, when I deposited him at South Kensington. He went round and round, not knowing where to get out, and had to be rescued eventually." The prime minister struck the White House like a tornado, immediately making himself at home and issuing demands. Eleanor Roosevelt had assigned him the Lincoln Bedroom, which he turned down. "Bed's not right," he told her. Instead he chose the Rose Bedroom where Britain's Queen Elizabeth had slept two years before. He pulled aside FDR's butler, Alonzo Fields, and instructed him, "Now Fields, we want to leave here as friends, right? So I need you to listen to me. One, I don't like talking outside my quarters. Two, I hate whistling in the corridors. And three, I must have a tumbler of sherry in my room before breakfast, a couple of glasses of Scotch and soda before lunch, and French Champagne and well aged brandy before I go to sleep at night." His breakfasts were equally prodigious, a menu of melon, bacon and eggs, toast, followed by a cutlet.

The prime minister's mission bore the code name Arcadia. The first session started late because Churchill was not an early riser. George Marshall was present at this initial encounter and took notes. According to him, the two countries' leaders agreed on one point, much to Churchill's relief: the United States needed to be involved soon at some level in the European conflict. American bombers, even a few, would do the trick for starters and offer the psychological benefit of disconcerting Germany. The leaders further agreed that the United States would put three American divisions into Ireland, ostensibly for training, thus freeing up British soldiers tied down there for combat. As they spoke, Churchill drove home his points with a rhythmic drumming of his pencil on the table.

The prime minister, his eye ever on the Mediterranean, suggested just the place where American troops should first be engaged, North Africa. The rump French government in Vichy, he believed, might be persuaded to allow American troops to land in its colony of Morocco if promised food and fuel and a place at the peace table after the war, a fanciful scenario, since the Germans held Vichy by the throat. Marshall recorded in his notes that FDR, without buying into Churchill's idea, nevertheless believed it "very important to morale . . . to have American troops somewhere in active fighting across the Atlantic."

The Americans meeting Churchill for the first time were starstruck by the short, dumpy, yet heroic figure in their midst. When he spoke it was with shoulders hunched and eyes downcast, gesturing with small hands that, as one witness put it, "gave one the impression they had not been used." Eleanor Roosevelt's liberal protégé, Joseph Lash, found himself seated next to the prime minister at a White House lunch and recalled, "I was too awestruck to open my mouth." There was no necessity, Lash said. "The language cascaded out of him. . . . He is exuberant, enormously strong personality, exciting, full of temperament, witty, his phrases resonant with the vigors of the best English stylists, his talk full of imagery." His eating habits were atrocious. Another observer remembered, "He would slurp his soup, spill things, pick up food with his fingers . . . and would quite uninhibitedly unzip his siren suit to scratch his crotch." One morning the president wheeled himself into the prime minister's bedroom to find his guest stepping from his bath, stark naked. A flustered FDR began to leave. Churchill stopped him, saying, "The Prime Minister of Great Britain has nothing to conceal from the President of the United States."

On Christmas Day FDR took Churchill to Foundry Methodist Church where the prime minister was charmed by a carol he had never heard before, "O Little Town of Bethlehem." After an unexceptional Christmas dinner prepared by Mrs. Nesbitt, Churchill withdrew early to prepare for a signal event. He would be the first foreigner invited to address a joint session of Congress since the Marquis de Lafayette in 1824. He feared that he might face an unsympathetic audience since several isolationists resented FDR's presumed maneuvering to get the United States into the war.

When he rose to speak in the House chamber, Churchill lamented that his mother, the American Jenny Jerome, "whose memory I cherish across the vale of years," was not alive to witness this day. Then, with an impish grin, he uttered words that put the audience in the palm of his hand. "I can not help reflecting that if my father had been American and my mother British, instead of the other way around, I might have got here on my own." While his motive in coming to Washington was to keep FDR fixed on Europe, he read the country well enough to know what the people wanted to hear at this point. He spoke of the dastardly attack on Pearl Harbor, and with a theatrical flourish exclaimed, "What kind of people do they think we are? Is it possible they do not realize that we shall never fail to persevere against them until they have been taught a lesson that they and the world will never forget?" The chamber echoed with foot stomping and cheers. Churchill spoke for thirty-five minutes. As he sought to depart through the crush of lawmakers crowding in on him, he flashed the "V for Victory" sign, which was returned by hundreds of upraised hands, and more cheers.

On the second day in the White House, Lord Moran, Churchill's personal physician, was summoned to the prime minister's bedroom, where he found a much distressed patient. "It was hot last night," Churchill explained, "and I got up to open the window. It was very stiff. I had to use considerable force and I noticed all at once that I was short of breath. I had a dull pain over my heart. It went down my left arm. It didn't last very long, but it never happened before. What is it? Is my heart all right?" Moran recognized the classic symptoms of a heart attack. "That would mean publishing to the world," Moran realized, "that the PM was an invalid with a crippled heart and this at the moment when America has just come into the war, and there is no one but Winston to take her by the hand." He judged the coronary minor and told his sixty-seven-year-old patient, "You've been overdoing things." And there the matter ended.

Though necessary to each other, Churchill and Marshall were not immediately in step. Marshall argued for a unified command structure, believing that allies committed to the same struggle could not each fight the war in their own way. Someone ultimately had to be in charge. In the Pacific, four nations, the United States, Britain, Australia, and the Netherlands, were separately pitted against Japan. Marshall maintained that the situation called for one theater commander. Churchill's back was instantly up and he went over Marshall's head to the president. On December 28, Marshall was summoned to the Rose Room and found Churchill "in bed and propped up. I didn't want to sit down and look up, so I stood up and looked down," Marshall recalled. "The issue was if, under . . . unity of command, an Army officer could give orders to a Navy officer . . . he got off quite a spiel. . . . The implication was that it was inconceivable for an Army officer to have anything to do with the Navy. He said a ship was a very special thing and that it was difficult to put the Navy under an Army commander." As Churchill cited naval giants from the past, "I told him I was not interested in Drake and Frobisher, but I was interested in having a unified front against Japan," Marshall countered. The prime minister disappeared into the bathroom, came out wearing only a towel and saying "I would have to take the worst with the best." Marshall left uncertain whether he had won or lost his point. "We had a meeting right after that," he recalled, "in which Churchill agreed to the unity of command." Marshall had learned a useful lesson. Winston Churchill would fight for his position with bulldog tenacity. But he was not immune to reason.

The White House managed to catch its breath when its exacting guest departed temporarily for a trip to Canada and a brief respite in Pompano Beach, Florida, accompanied by General Marshall. Churchill by now judged Marshall as the American he must court most assiduously, second only to the president. Members of the PM's circle began to measure the general, among them Lord Moran, who possessed not only medical expertise, but a keen eye for character. Moran concluded, "Marshall remains the key. . . . In truth it was impossible not to trust Marshall. . . . It is what Marshall was, and not what he did, that lingers in the mind."

Soon Churchill and Marshall were exchanging thoughts not only on the grand strategies of war, but on its moral ambiguities. "One evening the general came to see me and put a hard question," Churchill recounted in his memoirs. Marshall was preparing to send nearly 30,000 American troops to Northern Ireland. The British had two converted transports available for the job, the liners *Queen Mary* and *Queen Elizabeth*. Since the ships could carry up to 16,000 men, but had lifeboats, life rafts, and other flotation devices for only 8,000 men, how many troops should they put on board? Marshall asked. "If it were part of an actual operation, we should put all on board they could carry," Churchill answered. "If it were only a question of moving troops in a reasonable time, we should not go beyond the limits of lifeboats, rafts, etc. It is for you to decide." As it turned out, early transports sailed with enough rescue capacity to accommodate all the troops. But as the war wore on the ships were packed to the gunwales, with or without enough rescue equipment.

FDR found that his and Churchill's diurnal habits clashed like mismatched gears. The president's custom was to turn lights out by 10 P.M. By then, Churchill was just hitting his stride and expected an American audience to stay up, along with his own people, to hear his acute assessments of the military situation and enjoy his brilliance as a raconteur until two, even three in the morning. He would then sleep till noon. FDR was generally awake by 8:30.

So eager had Churchill been at Argentia to draw the United States into the war that the old colonialist had swallowed hard and accepted FDR's insistence on the Atlantic Charter language, pledging "the right of all peoples to choose the form of government under which they will live." But the prime minister's heart was not in it. On a day when they met in the president's study to discuss Asian strategy, FDR unexpectedly raised the issue of independence for the crown jewel of the British Empire, India. According to Lord Moran, "There was a violent explosion. . . . The P.M. looked with pride on the story of our Indian Empire. Henry Lawrence and Clive and Dalhousie were men after his own heart, whereas the President, whose feelings went back to the American War of Independence, saw only a subject people in the grip of a conqueror." As tempers cooled, Churchill conceded that he was ready to grant full independence, "but after the war." At present, with Japan at the gates of India, with the ever festering feuds between Hindus and Muslims, lifting imperial rule would constitute "an act of madness," to be paid for in a bloodbath. British colonial policy was not to be decided by public opinion in America, Churchill announced. There the matter rested, to remain unresolved for the remainder of the war.

★

ROOSEVELT WANTED A PHRASE EQUAL in rallying power to the "New Deal" to trumpet the newly forged alliance arrayed against the Axis. The customary communiqué to be released at the end of a diplomatic conference offered the ideal moment. One phrase had struck FDR. He immediately had himself wheeled into the Rose Room where the prime minister was again taking a bath. Why not, the president suggested, entitle their statement the "Declaration of the United Nations." Though Roosevelt had never had much published beyond a paper he delivered, he fancied himself a writer and the coinage pleased him. Churchill rolled the phrase over his tongue and savored it. On January 1, the two leaders and their associates gathered for a New Year's Day celebration. FDR was effusive, urging drinks on his guests and raising his glass in impromptu toasts. Mrs. Roosevelt knew that the president prided himself on the draft communiqué that he had left in the upstairs living quarters. She suggested that Franklin have it brought down and read it to his guests. The president demurred modestly, but upon being coaxed sent Harry Hopkins to retrieve the declaration. With a dramatic flourish, he read the opening lines drawn from Byron's *Childe Harold's Pilgrimage*, "Here, where the sword united nations drew . . ."

On January 14, 1942, the White House staff sighed with relief as their guest prepared to leave. Churchill and his party boarded a Boeing flying boat to Bermuda where the *Duke of York* lay moored waiting to bring them home. Arcadia had achieved Churchill's goal, Germany remained the primary threat. Further, two nations with two armies, two navies, and two air forces had agreed to merge their leadership and thus avoid dissipating their strength in confusion, rivalry, and overlapping effort. Marshall sat down with his British counterpart, Field Marshal Sir John Dill, recent chief of the Imperial General Staff; Admiral King, a borderline Anglophobe; Admiral Sir Dudley Pound, first sea lord; Air Marshal Sir Charles Portal, chief of the Air Staff; and Hap Arnold. Out of these talks arose the Allied architecture for fighting the War. "Joint," in military parlance, meant integrating the roles of different branches within the same nation. Marshall, King, and Arnold formed the American Joint Chiefs of Staff. The other organizational form adopted at Arcadia was "Combined," meaning unity among the

armed forces of more than one country. Thus was born the Anglo-
American Combined Chiefs of Staff. FDR was clear as to where he
wanted the combined chiefs to sit: between their German and Japanese
enemies, in Washington, of course. Field Marshal Dill established
headquarters in the capital where he and Marshall, mutually admiring,
sought to create a truly Allied military force. While filled with regard
for his counterpart, Dill's judgment of Marshall's countrymen was
harsh. He wrote back to the new chief of the Imperial General Staff,
Alan Brooke, "This country is the most highly organized for peace you
can imagine. . . . I have never seen so many motor cars, but I have not
seen a military vehicle. . . . Never have I seen a country so utterly unprepared for War and so soft."

On January 26, just days after Churchill's departure from Washington, a former restaurant dishwasher, twenty-three-year-old Private
First Class Milburn Henke from Hutchinson, Minnesota, stepped off a
troop transport, the first American GI to arrive in Ireland. Winston
Churchill's dogged campaign to have the United States in the European conflict had found a flesh-and-blood symbol.

THE PRIME MINISTER'S VISIT had left another imprint on the White
House. In London, his frequent destination was the Map Room, located underground at Storey's Gate. Here at a glance he could trace the
lines of battle, movements of the fleet, and air armadas across the
world. On coming to the White House, he had instructed his naval
aide, Commander Charles "Tommy" Thompson, to bring along a portable version of the Map Room, which was hung opposite Churchill's
bedroom. FDR, seeing British officers scurrying about, became curious and started visiting the Map Room with Churchill. Eleanor Roosevelt observed them, "like two little boys having fun with their boats in
the bathtub." FDR decided that he must have a map room.

Captain John McCrea had joined the White House staff two days
after Churchill's departure to become FDR's latest naval aide. Before
assuming his duties, McCrea had been tutored by Admiral King on the
nature of reflected power. He should not be surprised, he told the cap-

tain, "the number of people, your senior, who heretofore have never given you a tumble, who will now address you as 'John, old boy.'" McCrea was also alerted that the job demanded a strong back since he could often find himself pushing FDR's wheelchair. Upon selecting McCrea, FDR instructed him as to what he expected from a naval aide. "Briefly, I would like you to be my eyes and ears in the Navy Department," he said. "I'm sure you won't burden me with nonessentials, but I must confess that little things about the Navy will be of more interest to me than the same sort of things about the other services." McCrea soon learned the eclectic stretch of his duties. The president once had his aide escort him to St. John's Church across Lafayette Park from the White House. When time neared for the collection, McCrea drew a dollar bill from his wallet. He felt a jab in his side, "Say John," FDR whispered, "by any chance do you have a couple of extra dollars I may borrow for the collection? I don't have a cent with me." McCrea found two singles and slipped them to the president just as the collection plate arrived. McCrea was amazed a week later when the president said, "John, what do you think of people who don't pay their just debt?" and handed him $2.

McCrea's first significant assignment was FDR's airily delivered order to create a map room, just like Churchill's in London. The captain first went to the chief White House usher, Howell Crim, to find out where they might find space. On the ground floor, between Admiral McIntire's infirmary and the Diplomatic Reception Room, they found a onetime women's cloakroom—as McCrea described it, "about the size of a couple of modest living rooms." The room possessed one attraction: it was opposite the elevator that the president used coming down from the upstairs living quarters.

Other than finding a location, McCrea had not the foggiest idea of how to proceed. He learned of a Navy lieutenant junior grade who had spent weeks as an observer in Churchill's Map Room. McCrea immediately used White House prerogatives to have the young officer transferred to Washington where he learned that he had hired a movie star. Lieutenant JG Henry "Robert" Montgomery had become a popular leading man, appearing in *Private Lives, Night Must Fall,* and *Here*

Comes Mr. Jordan. Montgomery took to his new duties with imagination. The walls of the former cloakroom were soon papered with blow-ups of maps covering the Atlantic, Pacific, and European battlegrounds. He devised color-coded pins and flags to plot the locations of armies and fleets. He adopted symbols to track the movements of the three principal Allied leaders: a cigarette holder for FDR, a cigar for Churchill, and a pipe for Stalin. A special flag marked the location of the destroyer on which FDR's son Franklin Jr. served. A sign on the Map Room door warned, "No Admittance," and the list of officials cleared to enter was short. Besides the president, it included Harry Hopkins, Secretary Stimson, Marshall, King, Arnold, and Admiral McIntire. The navy secretary, Frank Knox, complained bitterly to the president after he was blocked from entering. Though the gregarious Hopkins was popular with young officers staffing the Map Room, he posed one hazard to this sanctum, tossing his still lit cigarettes into the wastebaskets. The Map Room became the White House nerve center, manned twenty-four hours a day. The president, coming out of Admiral McIntire's infirmary after getting his sinuses packed or his legs massaged, headed straight for the room, often twice a day. McCrea had the maps hung low, making it easier for the wheelchair-bound president to study them. FDR reveled in the secrecy surrounding the Map Room. As Grace Tully observed, "the President took to that sort of thing like a duck to water."

CHAPTER 6

★

The President and General MacArthur

AT 4 A.M. A RINGING PHONE WOKE UP GENERAL DOUGLAS MACARTHUR in the palatial apartment he occupied in the Manila Hotel. His chief of staff, Major General Richard K. Sutherland, was calling to tell him that Pearl Harbor had been attacked, and urged MacArthur to come at once to One Calle Victoria, the Philippine Islands military command center. According to one account, MacArthur's first move was to snap on a reading lamp, reach for his mother's Bible, read a few passages, and pray. Arriving at the command center, he received a call from George Marshall's war plans director in Washington, Lieutenant General Leonard T. Gerow, warning, "I wouldn't be surprised if you get an attack there in the near future." Previously, intelligence reports that the Philippines were a likely target had led Admiral Stark, then chief of naval operations, to issue his November 27 war warning. MacArthur was among the recipients.

After Sutherland's call, there ensued one of the most baffling sequences of events in MacArthur's long career. At the moment, MacArthur had only thirty-five B-17 bombers, described quixotically by a War Department official as "the greatest concentration of heavy bomber strength anywhere in the world." Hap Arnold alerted the Philippines command to disperse its aircraft. FDR had raged about the planes destroyed "on the ground" at Pearl Harbor. Now, nine hours later, Arnold did not want a repeat performance in the Philippines.

Six days before Pearl Harbor, MacArthur had already informed General Marshall that he was moving his B-17s beyond the reach of

Japanese airfields located on Formosa. The bombers were to be shifted from Clark Field, seventy miles north of Manila, to a base hastily carved out of a Del Monte pineapple plantation on the island of Mindanao, 500 miles to the south, where presumably they would be safe and from which they could, as MacArthur put it, "deliver their own blows." Three days later, on December 4, MacArthur's deputy Sutherland, a haughty Yale graduate, made a blistering call to the headquarters of Major General Lewis Brereton, MacArthur's air chief. "You know General MacArthur ordered those B17s down to Mindanao," he shouted. "Why the hell aren't they down there? We want them moved!"

By December 5, only sixteen bombers had been moved to the Del Monte strip. Nine hours after Pearl Harbor had been attacked, fifty-four Japanese Mitsubishi bombers from Formosa swooped down from 18,000 feet and began wreaking havoc on the nineteen B-17s still parked on Clark Field, just as had happened to the planes at Pearl Harbor. As the Japanese flew off, not a single American bomber was left flyable. While judgments against Short and Kimmel were swift and career-wrecking in the wake of Pearl Harbor, MacArthur managed to survive this "second Pearl Harbor" without a scratch. No investigation was ever ordered.

He appeared to live a charmed life and could not have had a more fitting birth for a martial romantic. The way MacArthur told the story, "My first recollection is that of a bugle call." The memory is possibly true, though, more likely, another of MacArthur's theatrical flights. He was, in fact, born on January 26, 1880, on a military post then called Fort Dodge in Arkansas, where his father, Captain Arthur MacArthur, served with Company K, 13th Infantry. No matter what Douglas MacArthur would achieve in a meteoric life, his father would remain for him a star whose brilliance he would never outshine. Arthur MacArthur had been just fifteen when the Civil War broke out in 1861, a small, pale, fine-boned boy with a squeaking adolescent voice who looked like anything but a soldier. Yet he joined the Union army and won a commission with the Wisconsin 24th Infantry. In the Battle of Missionary Ridge in Tennessee, with Union soldiers cut down like mown grass, the 24th was ordered to take the crest of the ridge. As one after another of the regiment's color-bearers fell, young MacArthur seized the flag, shouting, "On Wisconsin," and gained the summit where, silhouetted against the sky, he waved the banner, crying out for Union troops huddled below to join him. The teenaged officer won the Medal of Honor for conspicuous valor. In all, Arthur MacArthur fought in thirteen battles, was wounded twice, and at nineteen became a full colonel, the youngest officer holding that rank in the Union army; he was known thereafter as "the boy colonel." When peace came he stayed in the Army but reverted to the regular rank of captain, which he held at the time of Douglas's birth. Douglas and his older brother, Arthur, lived a storybook Old West life in the Arkansas wilds. Shirtless and shoeless, wearing fringed rawhide leggings and colorful headbands, they spurred their Navajo ponies across the plains, shooting whatever small game they could flush out.

That Douglas would enter West Point seemed ordained. But it was not certain. He twice failed to win presidential appointments, first under Grover Cleveland and then William McKinley. Rejection only spurred on his greatest champion, his mother, Mary Pinkney MacArthur, known as "Pinky." She was a petite, stunning beauty, whose honey-eyed Virginia graces concealed a steel core and naked ambitions for her sons. After Douglas's failure to win a presidential appointment to the academy, Pinky took up residence in Milwaukee, leaving her husband 328 miles behind at his post in St. Paul, Minnesota. Her goal was to persuade the district congressman, Theobald Otjen, a friend of her father-in-law's, to appoint Douglas to the academy. Otjen, besieged by other aspirants, arranged for a competitive examination. On the eve of the exam, after young MacArthur had crammed for weeks, his mother took her jittery son by the shoulders and lectured him: "Doug . . . be self-confident, self reliant, and even if you don't make it, you will know you have done your best. Now, go to it." Douglas beat his competitors handily, scoring 99.3 compared to the 77.9 scored by the second-place applicant. In later years MacArthur would say of his mother's counsel, "It was a lesson I never forgot. Preparedness is the key to success and victory." When, on June 13, 1889, MacArthur stepped off the train at West Point, Pinky was with him. As he reported for plebe processing, his mother was taking rooms at the nearby Craney's Hotel, where she would live for the next four years practically within earshot of her boy.

The first three weeks at the academy, called "Beast Barracks," meant hell for plebes, an unremitting ordeal of brutal hazing. MacArthur was ordered by upperclassmen to perform "spread eagles," similar to what George Marshall had undergone at VMI. In MacArthur's case, he had to squat over broken glass for an hour, flapping his arms like a bird. He remembered repeating the motion two hundred times before he passed out temporarily, then staggered back to his tent and went into convulsions. Congress investigated hazing after another West Point cadet died. MacArthur was called to testify and, protecting the academy, would only admit that hazing could be cruel after being hard pressed by the committee. During the hearing his mother sent him a note saying, "Never lie. Never tattle," advice he believed he had followed.

Enthusiastic about sports, Douglas's performance was nevertheless middling. In 1901, he scored the winning run in a 4 to 3 Army baseball victory over Navy. But he had got on base by a walk and a teammate's hit drove him home. He also managed the football team for a season. His consuming ambition, however, was to place first academically. He graduated on June 11, 1903, at age twenty-three, a recruitment poster cadet, six feet tall, slim, erect as a rail, and with his slicked-back, center-parted hair, a turn-of-the-century beau ideal. He took the two top academy honors, militarily as first captain, and was indeed academically first in his class. His classmates voted him most likely to succeed. After receiving his degree, he turned and handed it to his beaming father, General Arthur MacArthur.

MacArthur's first posting was to the Philippines, beginning a life-long love affair with the islands and where salient traits of the MacArthur persona began to emerge. Appearance meant everything to him—not easily maintained in the sweltering heat of Manila. He showered as often as four times a day and changed his uniform just as often. He installed a full-length mirror in his quarters, turning before it to measure his image from various angles. When he went into town he wore a chalk white uniform, and when he could afford it rented a carriage and driver.

Just months into the Philippine assignment, MacArthur claimed to have made his first kill when he was ambushed by rebels, *insurrectos,* and took a bullet through his campaign hat. According to his account, he then drew a revolver and shot two of his attackers dead. In MacArthur's frequent retelling of the story, an Irish sergeant, eyeing the bullet-pierced bodies, said, "Begging the lieutenant's pardon, but all the rest of the lieutenant's life is pure velvet." No evidence confirms the story, but MacArthur made it a staple of his reminiscences.

World War I would be the making of Douglas MacArthur. He helped organize a new division, the 42nd Infantry, composed of men from twenty-six states. "The 42nd Division stretches like a rainbow from one end of America to the other," he declared. Thus was born the banner under which the unit would win fame, the "Rainbow Division." We see MacArthur in France on March 9, 1918, planning one of the first raids by tyro doughboys against an enemy trench, a conspicuous figure, striding along the ramparts, disdaining the regulation steel helmet, choosing instead a visored cap with the wiring removed to achieve a jaunty crushed look. He wore a bulky sweater with the letter "A" for Army woven into the front. Around his neck he coiled a four-foot-long scarf, knitted by his mother. A fellow officer asked MacArthur why he dared flout dress regulations. "It's the orders you disobey," he answered, "that make you famous." One objective of a raid was to nab prisoners for interrogation. As darkness fell, MacArthur, face daubed with mud, clambered over the parapet. He was leading a raid at least three pay grades below his rank and doing so without seeking permission from his commanding officer. Armed only with a riding crop, a cigarette holder jutting from clenched teeth, he moved forward. The raid was a marginal success with several doughboy casualties suffered and one German officer captured. A comrade wrote of MacArthur that he found it hard to imagine "this sensitive, high-strung personage slogging in the mud, enduring filth, living in stinking clothing and crawling over jagged soil under criss-crosses of barbed wire." But to a military romantic, bloodshed, hardship, and squalor were transmuted into finer elements, courage, heroism, and glory.

By the war's end he was Brigadier General MacArthur, the youngest man holding that rank in the American Expeditionary Forces. He had been promoted in spite of the fact that his name was not on the list of nearly fifty officers General Pershing had recommended for their first star. MacArthur's ceaseless lobbyist, Pinky, the military equivalent of a stage mother, had bombarded Secretary of War Newton Baker, Pershing, and anyone else who might be useful with letters reminding them of the virtues of Douglas, the cadet who had finished at the top of his class. During the Great War, he had deliberately shared the doughboys' perils and hardships. He encouraged the men to call him "Buddy," and they in turn idolized him. It was only in subsequent years that he created the aloof, godlike persona of current memory.

MacArthur's rise continued unabated after the war. He attained the prestigious appointment of West Point superintendent. There he introduced progressive, innovative reforms, sending instructors to learn modern educational methods, ordering every cadet to partici-pate in at least one intramural sport, requiring cadets to read a daily newspaper, write poetry, even to learn to dance the waltz and the two-step. At age forty-two he was back serving in the Philippines, having married and subsequently divorced a vivacious, spoiled, and wayward thirty-one-year-old divorcée, Louise Cromwell Brooks, one of the world's richest heiresses. In Manila, he became involved in an affair with an exquisite, doll-like sixteen-year-old Eurasian, Isabel Rosario Cooper, whom he in effect shipped to the United States along with his personal effects in 1930 when President Herbert Hoover elevated MacArthur, then fifty, to the Army's summit as chief of staff. The affair turned messy and threatened MacArthur's career when the sensation-alist Washington columnist Drew Pearson learned what was going on and ran with the story. Again, MacArthur survived, after Isabel exacted $15,000 to keep quiet.

MacArthur came to Franklin Roosevelt's attention during the darkest chapter in the general's life while FDR was serving as governor of New York. Six years after World War I, Congress had approved an average $1,000 bonus to be paid to veterans in 1945. But with the Great Depression spreading joblessness, homelessness, and hunger across the land, Wright Patman, a Texas congressman, introduced legislation to make the bonus payable immediately. By the spring of 1932, over 10,000 veterans, a ragged army called the Bonus Expeditionary Force, descended on Washington to lobby for passage of Patman's bill. They occupied abandoned buildings on Pennsylvania Avenue and camped in makeshift shacks on the Anacostia Flats, a fetid sprawl of marshland on the far side of the Potomac River. When Congress rejected the bill, demonstrations by the veterans turned violent, and the situation overwhelmed the capacity of the Washington police to maintain order. President Hoover called in his Army chief of staff, MacArthur, and told him that he wanted the Bonus Marchers driven out of the capital and back onto the Anacostia Flats. Rather than delegating the assignment to the general in command of the troops in Washington, MacArthur decided to take on the mission himself, much against the advice of fellow officers including his assistant, a promising major named Dwight Eisenhower. Many years later, Eisenhower told the historian Stephen Ambrose, "I told that dumb son of a bitch he had no business going down there. I told him it was no place for the chief of staff."

A legend would emerge that MacArthur, wearing his most bemedaled uniform and astride a white steed, led the charge against men with whom he had fought in the trenches. The horse was fiction, but MacArthur did send his valet to fetch him his dress uniform as he prepared to take charge. On July 28, as reported on the front page of *The New York Times*, "at 4:30 this afternoon the regulars came, cavalry leading the way, and after them, the tanks, the machine guns and the infantry." What happened next would be subject to disputed views that would color judgments of Douglas MacArthur for years to come. After the veterans had been driven from the city by clouds of tear gas, the points of bayonets, and the flat side of sabers, an alarmed President Hoover sought to safeguard the women and children squatting at the Bonus Marchers' camp. He ordered that troops were not to cross the Anacostia Bridge and were not to force evacuation from the camp. The key question in judging MacArthur's subsequent conduct is whether he did or did not receive Hoover's order. Brigadier George Van Horn Moseley, MacArthur's assistant Army chief of staff, who was to deliver Hoover's instructions to MacArthur, later claimed that his chief "was very much annoyed at having his plans interfered with in any way until they were executed completely." Yet, on other occasions, Moseley boasted that he had made sure MacArthur never got the order. Other officers on the scene, including Major Eisenhower, confirmed that "The President's message just didn't get to [MacArthur]." A worried Hoover sent another message. But as MacArthur later wrote in his *Reminiscences,* "I was in the midst of crossing the river." It was too late to turn back. That night, Washingtonians peered east across the river at a sky turned red as the routed marchers burned their shacks and retreated. To MacArthur, as he wrote in his memoirs, the Bonus Marchers were pawns of "the American Communist Party," who "planned a riot of such proportions that it was hoped the United States Army . . . would have to fire on the marchers. In this way the Communists hoped to incite revolutionary action." Whatever the facts, the sight of MacArthur, in full regalia, routing ragged veterans whom he had once asked to call him "Buddy" presented an unattractive spectacle.

Even before Roosevelt had become president, during a lunch with the head of his "brain trust," Rexford G. Tugwell, the then governor received a blistering phone call from Louisiana's demagogue senator, Huey Long, accusing FDR of being in bed with Wall Street. Hanging up, FDR turned to Tugwell and remarked that Huey Long was "one of the two most dangerous men in the country." Tugwell asked who the other was. "The other is Douglas MacArthur," Roosevelt answered. In the summer of 1932, after Franklin Roosevelt had been nominated by the Democrats to run, and observing the hapless Hoover's fate in the handling of the Bonus Marchers, he remarked to Felix Frankfurter, the future Supreme Court appointee, "Well, Felix, this elects me." Upon taking office, one of Roosevelt's earliest acts was to invite the veterans to the White House where he led them in singing doughboy favorites, "Mademoiselle from Armentières" and the plaintive "There's a Long, Long Trail A-Winding."

Surprisingly, upon taking office, FDR kept MacArthur on for a year after his term as chief of staff would have expired. They had a rough start. The budget that FDR inherited from the Hoover administration had already slashed military appropriations to the bone. Roosevelt, with the Depression worsening, cut Regular Army funds further,

51 percent below customary peacetime support. An alarmed George Dern, secretary of war, brought MacArthur with him to the White House to try to reverse FDR's decision. Dern argued that Germany and Italy were rearming and that Japan had threatened China, which only inflamed a president struggling against an economic debacle. As MacArthur remembered the moment, Dern's opinions "were answered by a tongue-lashing that left the secretary white-faced and wordless." When MacArthur took up the case, "the President turned the full vials of his sarcasm upon me. He was a scorcher when aroused." MacArthur would later write in his memoir, "In my emotional exhaustion, I said something to the general effect that when we lost the next war, and an American lying in the mud with an enemy foot on his dying throat, spat out his last curse, I wanted the name not to be MacArthur, but Roosevelt." "You must not talk to the President that way," a livid FDR shot back. MacArthur sputtered an apology and offered Roosevelt his resignation. After a dead silence, FDR said coolly, "Don't be foolish, Douglas. You and the Budget must get together on this." As Dern and MacArthur left, the secretary complimented the general on "saving the Army." But as the emotionally drained MacArthur later described the moment, "I just vomited on the steps of the White House."

The relations between the general and his commander in chief continued to remain wary. According to MacArthur's mistress, Isabel, he privately referred to Roosevelt as "that cripple in the White House." Yet, when MacArthur's term as chief of staff ended, Roosevelt's praise was effusive. "Douglas," he said, "if war should suddenly come, don't wait for orders to come home. Grab the first transportation you can find. I want you to command my armies." FDR recognized MacArthur as a vainglorious peacock, but never lost sight of the paramount issue: the man was gifted in the profession of arms.

AFTER LEAVING THE POST OF CHIEF OF STAFF, MacArthur commenced the cushiest chapter in his life. Manuel Quezon, the excitable, flamboyant, onetime *insurrecto,* soon to be president of the Philippines, felt the breath of Japanese expansionism threatening his country. At this point, the islands were a U.S. protectorate recently given commonwealth status and promised independence in 1946. In 1934, Quezon traveled to Washington to ask Roosevelt for the one man he believed could save his country, Douglas MacArthur. Thereafter Quezon offered and the general accepted the post of military advisor to the Philippine commonwealth, which included a penthouse atop the Malacañang Palace and a lavish annual salary of $33,000 a year, in addition to his Army pay, over five times General Marshall's annual compensation of $8,000. In the fall of 1935, the general, with his ailing eighty-three-year-old mother and Eisenhower, set sail on the SS *President Hoover* to the islands that had earlier captivated him and his father before him. Quezon elevated MacArthur to the rank of field marshal in the Philippine army. The practical Eisenhower tried to persuade MacArthur to refuse the title since he found it pompous, even ridiculous, "to be the Field Marshal of a virtually nonexisting army." Despite Eisenhower's entreaty, MacArthur ordered a glittering uniform with a white high-collared tunic spangled with medals, stars, and ribbons, a gold cord looped over his right shoulder, a cap with the gold-braided visor that was to become his signature head gear, and black pants, attire suggesting a figure out of Gilbert and Sullivan. During his early months in the Philippines MacArthur lost his adoring mother and married his second wife, Jean Marie Faircloth, a wealthy, vivacious, petite woman, surprisingly still single at age thirty-eight. Clare Boothe Luce, the charming and deceptively tough-minded wife of *Time* magazine's publisher, Henry Luce, interviewed MacArthur in Manila and leaves a vivid portrait describing the man: "the whiteness of MacArthur's skin. . . . His narrow sloping shoulders, his trembling hands, surprisingly small for a man his size, and the way he combed his thinning black hair . . . across his head in a losing struggle to conceal advancing baldness."

No one was a closer or keener observer of MacArthur in the Philippine years than Dwight Eisenhower. Two oft repeated stories persist regarding this odd pairing. In the first, MacArthur disparages Eisenhower as "the best clerk I ever had." And in the second, Eisenhower tells a friend, "I studied dramatics for seven years under General MacArthur." Neither story is proven, yet neither seems improbable given the character of the lordly superior and his down-to-earth subordinate. "Probably no one had tougher fights with a senior man than I did with MacArthur," Eisenhower recalled of their association. "I told him time and again: 'Why in the hell don't you fire me. Goddammit, you do things I don't agree with and you know damn well I don't.'" Yet, years later, when he had eclipsed his old chief, Eisenhower told a reporter, "if that door opened at this moment, and General MacArthur was standing there, and he said, 'Ike, follow me,' I'd get up and follow him."

✴

As summer came to Washington in 1941, before Pearl Harbor, FDR, ever the student of geopolitics, had gone over his maps of the Pacific with Stimson and Marshall amidst growing alarm over Japan's belligerence. On July 27, while MacArthur was enjoying breakfast in his penthouse overlooking Manila Harbor, an aide from One Calle Victoria brought him a message stamped "Urgent." "Effective this date," it read, "there is hereby constituted a command designated as the United States Army Forces in the Far East. . . . You are hereby designated commanding general of the new force." MacArthur's life of chocolate soldiering had ended and real soldiering resumed. FDR's message added further that Filipino soldiers were to be swept into the United States Army along with regular American troops. MacArthur telegraphed Roosevelt, assuring him that absorption of the Filipinos into the force "had changed a local feeling of defeatism into the highest state of morale" he had ever seen. In the event of war with Japan, War Plan Orange called for withdrawal of U.S. forces from a vast swath of the Pacific, including the Philippines. Magic intercepts now revealed that the Japanese military had its eye fixed on the oilfields of the Dutch East Indies. Roosevelt wanted to make a stand against Japanese expansionism, whereupon War Plan Orange was reversed. On July 31, 1941, Marshall gathered his staff at the Munitions Building and announced the shift: "It is the policy of the United States to defend the Philippines."

There matters stood for the next five months, until Japanese fighters and bombers appeared and turned Clark Field into a twisted, smoking graveyard.

CHAPTER 7

———— ✦ ————

Philippines Lost, China on the Brink

Early in 1942, correspondence drafted in General Marshall's office in clear, incisive, tightly reasoned language began appearing on FDR's desk. The author was a little known officer whom Marshall had recently taken into the War Plans Division. In a group photo he was identified as "D. D. Ersenbeing." The White House usher's visitor's log listed him as "P. D. Eisenhauer."

Dwight Eisenhower hungered for a field command, especially after spending seven exhilarating and exasperating years under the thumb of Douglas MacArthur. In the fall of 1939, while still in the Philippines, he had begged for reassignment. "General," he told MacArthur, "in my opinion, the United States cannot remain out of this war for long. I want to go home as soon as possible to participate in the preparatory work." MacArthur, who looked upon requests to leave his service not only as a mistake but as a betrayal of trust, sought to dissuade Eisenhower, arguing that his duties in the Philippines far exceeded anything that a mid-level officer could be doing in the States. Eisenhower remained unmoved and finally won his release. On December 13, 1939, he boarded the SS *President Cleveland* to sail home.

In the fall of 1941, fate delivered Eisenhower to the right place at the right time just as General Marshall ordered the biggest maneuvers in American history, nearly half a million soldiers practicing war in Louisiana. Reporters covering the maneuvers lavished praise on an obscure colonel as the author of a brilliant strategy that led the Third Army, in mock battle, to triumph over the Second Army. Dwight

Eisenhower, deviser of the plan, and George Marshall had met briefly eleven years before when the former was interviewing World War I veterans for a history of the war to be published by the American Battle Monuments Commission. Subsequently, the two men encountered each other briefly but only at formal military ceremonies. In those days Army officers feared the little black book that George Marshall kept in his desk drawer. Forrest Pogue, Marshall's biographer, noted, "Members of his staff watched with fascination as he took it out from time to time, crossed off one name and moved up or added that of another." As Eisenhower's name kept cropping up, Marshall asked John McCloy, assistant secretary of war, to visit the Third Army in Houston, Texas, to take a look at this paragon. McCloy reported back, "That man Eisenhower makes more sense than any of the others down there." But, McCloy warned, if Marshall was thinking of putting him behind a desk, Eisenhower was "very sensitive to the fact that he had not gotten involved in combat in World War I."

Marshall summoned trusted senior officers, including General Mark Clark, two years behind Eisenhower at West Point, and said, "I've got to relieve the fellow in War Plans who is somehow identified with Pearl Harbor." He turned to Clark and asked him to come up with ten candidates to fill the job. "I'll give you one name and nine dittos," Clark answered. "Dwight D. Eisenhower." On December 12, Eisenhower, now a brigadier general, was at home with his wife, Mamie, looking forward to visiting their son John, a cadet at West Point. The phone rang. "Is that you, Ike?" a familiar voice asked. Walter Bedell "Beetle" Smith, an up-from-the-ranks colonel and secretary to the Army general staff, was calling from Washington. "The Chief says for you to hop a plane and get up here right away," Smith said. "Tell your boss that formal orders will come through later." Eisenhower informed a disappointed Mamie that the trip to the academy was off. Two days later, he entered Marshall's office in the Munitions Building with no idea what lay ahead. Marshall greeted his visitor simply as "Eisenhower," though he was universally known throughout the Army as "Ike." Marshall rarely employed the American male icebreaker, the instant use of first names.

One exception was George Patton, whom Marshall called "Georgie." Eisenhower would remain "Eisenhower."

Ike remembered of this early encounter that Marshall possessed "an eye that seemed to me awfully cold." With Pearl Harbor just a week past, Marshall asked, "What should be our general line of action" in the Pacific. Eisenhower answered that he needed a few hours to think it over and left, looking for an empty desk somewhere.

He sat down at the nearest free typewriter, rolled in a sheet of paper, and began typing with one finger, "Steps to Be Taken." When he returned shortly, he told Marshall, "General, it will be a long time before major reinforcements can go to the Philippines, longer than the garrison can hold out if the Japanese invaded." In effect, the Philippines were a lost cause. "Our base must be in Australia," Eisenhower advised, "and we must start at once to expand it." As for his old chief, Eisenhower recommended that MacArthur should hold out on the island of Corregidor at the south end of Manila Bay and go down fighting with his men. Marshall thought for a moment, then responded, "I agree with you," but added, "Do your best to save them." Eisenhower made one last recommendation: "Influence Russia to enter the [Pacific] war" in order to tie down Japanese divisions in Manchuria.

TWO DAYS AFTER JAPANESE BOMBERS had ravaged Clark Field, Lieutenant General Masaharu Homma started putting troops ashore on the island of Luzon and began moving south toward Manila. Two days later Homma landed more troops on the southern part of Luzon and headed north, creating a pincer around the Philippine capital. Two more landings followed in quick succession while a Japanese naval blockade completed the island's isolation. Attacked from three sides, MacArthur declared Manila an open city, ceding it to the advancing Japanese. The MacArthur family left its penthouse apartment on Christmas Eve with the tree still decorated. The general told his staff that they had four hours to pack before leaving the capital. His wife, Jean, took a few dresses, an extra pair of shoes, and one brown coat. She dumped her favorite jewelry into a cardboard box and packed a few toys for their four-year-old son, Arthur MacArthur IV. The boy's birth had made MacArthur a parent at age fifty-eight, and he became the apple of his father's eye. Piling into a battered Packard, the MacArthurs were driven to Manila Harbor to board a small steamer, the *Don Esteban,* along with MacArthur's top staff, President Quezon, and 100 other passengers. Loaded aboard the crammed vessel were MacArthur's two automobiles and one of General Sutherland's. They were bound for Corregidor, the rocky island off the tip of the Bataan Peninsula. By New Year's Day, Japanese officers were tramping through MacArthur's penthouse and Army headquarters at One Calle Victoria.

However dire the circumstances, MacArthur believed that Washington shared his conviction that defense of the islands was imperative. "The yielding of the Philippines by default," he warned, "would mark the end of white prestige and influence in the East." The United States might as well "withdraw in shame from the Orient." The reality, however, was that the most MacArthur could hope for was a trickle of aid slipped through the Japanese noose by submarines and blockade runners.

BACK IN WASHINGTON, Eisenhower found his life consumed by the desk job he had dreaded. He wrote a friend, LeRoy Lutes, "it is now eight o'clock New Year's Eve. I have a couple hours work ahead of me, and tomorrow will be no different from today. I have been here about three weeks and this noon I had my first luncheon outside the office. Usually it is a hot dog sandwich and a glass of milk." He proved a workhorse with a short fuse. He vented his temper in his diary. "MacArthur is as big a baby as ever," he wrote on one occasion. ". . . he still likes his bootlickers . . . a refusal on his part to look facts in the face." Marshall had made clear early what he expected of his new deputy. "Eisenhower," he told him, "the Department is filled with able men who analyze their problems well but feel compelled to bring them to me for final solutions. I must have assistants who will solve their own problems and tell me later what they have done." Ike's workday was stretched further when Marshall moved him up from deputy to chief of the War Plans Division, succeeding General Gerow. The relative newcomer was now essentially charged with planning when, where, and how the U.S. Army should fight the war.

Ike found Marshall a boss of brutal honesty. On one occasion, the chief of staff called him in to discuss promotions for other officers. He would be spending the war in Washington behind a desk, Marshall warned, so he should forget about his own advancement. Eisenhower snapped back that he did "not give a damn about promotion plans." If he was to be chained to a desk, "So be it." He strode out of Marshall's office and as he left he glanced back and thought he caught the faintest trace of a smile on that sober face. Much to his astonishment, within days a clerk brought him a directive revealing that he was to get another star, promotion to lieutenant general. Even years later, Ike would remember, "The nearest that [Marshall] ever came to saying [anything] complimentary to my face was 'you're not doing badly so far'!"

While Eisenhower was chained to his desk, his father died. "I have felt terribly," he wrote a friend. "I should like so much to be with my mother these few days. But we're at war! I loved my Dad. I think my mother the finest person I have ever known." The next day he noted, "My father was buried today. I've shut off all business and visitors for thirty minutes—to have that much time, by myself, to think of him."

The American people became fixed on MacArthur's struggle in the Philippines. Yet, at the highest echelons, beginning with the president, the war in Europe still retained priority. Eisenhower, though tied up with Pacific planning, fully subscribed to the Europe First doctrine. He jotted down in a notebook, "We've got to go to Europe and fight, and we've got to quit wasting resources all over the world . . . we've got to begin slugging with air [power] at Western Europe; to be followed by a land attack as soon as possible."

Though the United States military was tautly stretched, FDR nevertheless wanted Lend-Lease aid increased to the Russians, and it fell to Eisenhower to find out what they needed. He invited a procurement officer from the Soviet embassy to his office to find out. The encounter was not pleasant. When the Russian officer handed Eisenhower his wish list, Ike asked what each item was to be used for. "I don't think that is any of your business," he replied. "We want them and that is that." Eisenhower told the officer that he needed more time to study the request. He then stomped down the hall to Marshall's office and let fly his temper. "I recommend we throw the guy out," he fumed. "The hell with him." Marshall nodded sympathetically, but gave Ike the White House line: "we have to handle them with kid gloves—or they'll do a France on us. . . . Do your best to get along with them." Fear that the Soviet Union, which had already made one peace pact with Nazi Germany, might do so again and leave the fighting to the Western allies was to become the president's rationale for endless concessions to Russia that would continue until the war's last day and with repercussions lasting well beyond 1945.

IN A BOMBPROOF REFUGE IN THE MALINTA TUNNEL on Corregidor island, MacArthur's deputy, Richard Sutherland drew up, at President Quezon's direction, Executive Order No. 1, which awarded MacArthur half a million dollars. The largesse was based on a bonus agreement worked out in 1935. The money was to be paid from the Philippines treasury based on the amount of potential income MacArthur had foregone by serving six years as the island's military advisor, a dubious sacrifice given a career officer's middling salary in the Regular Army. The transaction might have appeared unseemly coming from a poor country now on its knees. However, the Army's adjutant general had ruled in 1935 that such payments were legitimate, and the president, aware of the arrangement, did nothing to block it. Whether the American public would have been sympathetic is a moot point since knowledge of MacArthur's bonanza would not surface publicly for thirty-seven years.

His military fortunes, however, were faring far worse than his personal fortune. The general, as it turned out, made a disastrous tactical error. Initially, he had intended to throw the Japanese invaders back into the sea on the Luzon beaches. When that approach proved too late, MacArthur decided to pull his forces back onto the Bataan Peninsula. However, his logistical support could not keep pace with troop movements. Consequently, weapons, medicine, and above all, food, were left behind. Tons of supplies remained piled up on the Manila docks or went up in flames after Japanese air attacks. Further undermining MacArthur, President Quezon ordered that all food stockpiled in warehouses should remain there to feed his people. MacArthur thus found himself compelled to sustain 80,000 troops and 26,000 refugees with food for fifty days at most. He cut rations by half, a starvation diet for men beginning to be ravaged by malaria and enervating tropical diseases who were expected to fight crack, well-fed Japanese divisions.

While in raw numbers MacArthur's forces outnumbered the invaders, his Filipino soldiers were abysmally trained and lacked basics such as helmets, entrenching tools, even blankets. MacArthur's second in command, Major General Jonathan M. Wainwright, described the Philippine army as a mob, "incapable of stopping battle tested Japanese troops." Nine days into the New Year, MacArthur left his Corregidor headquarters and hopped aboard a PT boat bound for Bataan to fire up the troops. "My heart ached as I saw my men slowly wasting away," he wrote of this moment. "Their long bedraggled hair framed gaunt bloodless faces. Their hoarse, wild laughter greeted the constant stream of obscene and ribald jokes issuing from their parched, dry throats. They cursed the enemy and in the same breath cursed and reviled the United States." This was to be his only trip to the men defending Bataan.

Despite his desperate situation, hope died hard for MacArthur. On January 15, 1942, in the dim light of Malinta Tunnel he drafted a message that he ordered to be read to every soldier under his command. "Help is on the way," he promised. "Thousands of troops and hundreds of planes are being dispatched. . . . It is imperative that our troops hold until these reinforcements arrive." Marshall had assured him that "Our heavy bombers have been arriving in the theater at the rate of three a day." Over 42,000 troops were being shipped out from the West Coast. However, Marshall was referring to sending these reinforcements not to the Philippines but to Australia. MacArthur either misunderstood or chose to misread Marshall in his determination to sustain hope in his beleaguered army. Ingratiating himself with the president, he cabled on January 30, "Today . . . your birth anniversary, smoke begrimed men covered with the murk of battle, rise from the foxholes of Bataan and the batteries of Corregidor, to pray reverently that God may bless immeasurably the President of the United States."

IN WASHINGTON, THE DESPERATION OF THE PHILIPPINES' predicament came like a thunderclap in a cable President Quezon sent on February 8. The president had had lunch that day with his Marine son, Jimmy, and was looking forward to seeing the hit movie *Woman of the Year* that evening when he was informed that Stimson and Marshall insisted on seeing him. The secretary of war, sprightly despite his seventy-four years, handed the president two messages, one from Quezon and the other from MacArthur. "Militarily it is evident that no help will reach us from the United States in time . . . to prevent the complete overrunning of the entire Philippine Archipelago," Quezon wrote. This abandonment was occurring despite the fact that "my people entered the war with confidence that the United States would bring us such assistance so as to make it possible to sustain the conflict with some chance of success." Quezon was essentially charging the Roosevelt government with desertion. He asked, "Shall we further sacrifice our country and our people in a hopeless fight?" And gave his own answer. The United States had promised the Philippines independence by 1946. The Japanese invaders were offering the islands the same terms. Quezon's solution stunned the usually imperturbable FDR. The United States, the Filipino leader pleaded, should grant his nation full independence immediately and "The Philippines be at once neutralized." By neutralization he meant "all occupying troops, both American and Japanese, be withdrawn by mutual agreement with the Philippine government." After reading Quezon's missive, the president read what MacArthur had to say. "You must determine whether the mission of delay would be better furthered by the temporizing plan of Quezon or by my continued battle effort," he wrote. MacArthur's recommendation shocked FDR. "So far as the military angle is concerned,"

the general wrote, "the plan of President Quezon might offer the best possible solution of what is about to be a disastrous debacle." He was, in effect, ready to accept defeat.

In his memoirs, written twenty-two years after the event, MacArthur described what Quezon had told him at the time. "For thirty years I have worked and hoped for my people. Now they burn and die for a flag that could not protect them. I cannot stand this constant reference to Europe. . . . America writhes in anguish at the fate of a distant cousin, Europe, while a daughter, the Philippines, is being raped in the back room." MacArthur also used his memoirs to revise his reaction to Quezon's neutralization plan. "I remonstrated with Quezon as best I could against the proposals involved, and said bluntly, I would not endorse them," a statement completely at odds with what he cabled Roosevelt at the time.

Roosevelt's reaction to the Quezon solution was swift and unambiguous. "We can't do this at all," he told Stimson and Marshall. He cabled MacArthur and Quezon, in a draft prepared by Eisenhower, "American forces will continue to keep our flag flying in the Philippines so long as there remains any possibility of resistance." He closed with a promise that MacArthur would one day echo as his own. "Whatever happens to the present garrison," he pledged, ". . . we are now marshalling outside the Philippine Islands to return to the Philippines and drive the last remnant of the invader from your soil." Until now, Marshall had never been entirely sure of the character of his commander in chief. As he later reflected, "I immediately discarded everything in my mind I had held to his discredit. . . . I decided he was a great man." A chastened Quezon replied that he would abide by FDR's decision. MacArthur, in his answer, was rather more vivid. He, his wife, and son, "will share the fate of the garrison." He would defend Bataan to the death, and if driven back, take the same last-ditch stand on Corregidor. "I have not the slightest intention in the world of surrendering or capitulating the Filipino elements of my command." He wanted Quezon evacuated but not himself and during the night of February 20 the Philippines president, his family, and coterie were smuggled to Australia by the U.S. Navy.

Roosevelt was embarked on a war in which military aptitude had to be husbanded. He could not indulge MacArthur's sentimentality. Further, if MacArthur were captured, the prospect of America's most famous soldier paraded as a prisoner in Tokyo was intolerable. FDR urged MacArthur to prepare to evacuate to Australia to carry on the fight. MacArthur replied that he would not think of it.

By 1941, CHINA, A NATION OF 489 MILLION, the world's largest population, with an army of 5.7 million, had been engaged in fighting Japan for four years. China had a powerful hold on the imagination of Franklin Roosevelt, convinced as he was that this behemoth could become a strong American ally. Roosevelt's affection for the country had deep family roots. His mother, born Sara Delano, was the middle child of nine siblings whose father, Warren Delano II, had made a fortune in the Chinese tea and opium trade. Delano did not justify his opium dealings from "a moral and philanthropic point of view." But he could not see how it differed much from "the importation of wine and spirits into the United States." Young Sara spent much of her girlhood in a sumptuous villa swarming with servants and overlooking Hong Kong Harbor. The home where young Franklin grew up, in Hyde Park, was filled with Chinese vases, wall hangings, even a gong to announce dinner. His lifelong passion for stamp collecting had begun as an eight-year-old with Hong Kong and Chinese issues given to him by his mother. He once told his treasury secretary, Henry Morgenthau, in discussing Asian policy, "Remember that I have a little over a century in Chinese affairs," then added, "China during the past hundred years has not changed much."

When, in 1937, the Sino-Japanese War began in earnest, Japan's successes had been swift. By the fall of 1938, Japan had taken Shanghai and the capital, Nanking. Canton and Hankow quickly fell as the Chinese government retreated inland to Chungking. The military performance of the Japanese was brilliant but barbaric. Japan's indiscriminate bombing of Chinese cities and machine-gunning of helpless citizens outraged the president. The abstract figure of 200,000 Chinese civilians murdered in Nanking took on telling reality when Americans saw newsreel images of people summarily shot in the back of the head, an old woman wailing over the dead, and most indelibly, a lone Chinese infant screaming amid the smoke and ruin of the city. In the years following, FDR had pursued the tightrope act of trying to support China without provoking war with Japan.

The embattled Chinese leader, Generalissimo Chiang Kai-shek, knowing Morgenthau's closeness to FDR, used the treasury secretary as a conduit to put through a request for 500 American planes, claiming that if so armed he could retake Canton and Hankow, strike at Japanese bases on Formosa, and even attack Japan itself. Chiang's American aviation advisor, a pugnacious former U.S. Army Air Corps captain, Claire Chennault, was sent to Washington to plead the generalissimo's case, and boasted that with these planes China could "burn out the industrial heart of the [Japanese] empire with fire bomb attacks on the teeming bamboo heaps of Honshu and Kyushu." Morgenthau, in a meeting with the Chinese ambassador, T. V. Soong, Chiang's brother-in-law, told him that "asking for 500 planes is like asking for 500 stars." Still, Morgenthau remembered FDR earlier remarking, "It would be a nice thing if the Chinese would bomb Japan." On December 18, 1940, the treasury secretary had brought Chiang's request to the president. "Is he still willing to fight?" FDR asked. "That is what the message is all about," Morgenthau assured him. "Wonderful," Roosevelt answered. "That's what I've been talking about for four years."

The next day, after meeting with his cabinet, FDR asked Morgenthau, Stimson, Knox, and Secretary of State Hull to join him in the Oval Office. He ran a finger across a map provided by the Chinese government showing airbases only a tantalizing 650 miles from Tokyo. Raids on the Japanese capital were feasible, he said, and ordered, "The four of you work it out." Roosevelt biographer James MacGregor Burns, in describing Roosevelt's attraction to the bold stroke, once wrote that "he liked to try new things, to take a dare, to bring something off with a flourish." Enabling the Chinese to strike back, while the United States maintained its neutrality, fit the Burns portrayal perfectly.

A snag developed when Chennault visited Morgenthau's home in the shadow of Washington's Embassy Row. He was still 100 percent behind bombing Japan, Chennault said, but the president could not expect poorly trained Chinese fliers to hop into B-17s and hit Tokyo. American pilots would have to fly the missions from China. To Stimson the scheme was beginning to look "half-baked." On Sunday, December 22, he invited Marshall, Morgenthau, and Knox to his home to "try to get some mature brains into this, before we are committed to do it." American planes, flown by American pilots, bombing Japanese cities, they finally agreed, constituted an egregious act of hostility by a neutral nation supposedly hoping to avoid war with Japan. Morgenthau, undeterred, then placed a scaled-back alternative before FDR. Why not give China 100 P-40 fighter planes, allow Army Air Corps pilots to resign from the service and volunteer to fly for China and pay them $600 per month, plus $500 for every Japanese plane destroyed. FDR bought the idea. Thus was born the World War II legend, the American Volunteer Group commanded by Chennault, more colorfully known as the Flying Tigers.

When Lend-Lease passed in March 1941, FDR added China to the list of recipients. On July 26, 1941, he clamped the oil embargo on a fuel-thirsty Japan. Doubtless, these provocations—the embargo, American planes and pilots flying for China, American arms supplied to China, and FDR's demand for Japan's complete withdrawal from China—contributed to the Japanese decision, taken less than five months later, to drive the United States from the Pacific.

★

ON A SUNDAY MORNING IN DECEMBER 1941, Major General Joseph Warren Stilwell, commanding the III Corps of the Fourth Army, had invited his staff for coffee, sandwiches, and a relaxing day at his residence in Carmel, California. The easy conversation and banter stopped as the general took a call from the War Department. Pearl Harbor had been attacked, he was told. Stilwell began firing off orders to his staff, who rushed off to their posts, still clad in slacks, shorts, and sport shirts. The War Department call made Stilwell responsible for defending three hundred miles of the Pacific coast where five million Americans lived, and where much of the country's aircraft manufacturing plants and oil refineries were located. He quickly found himself caught up in a vortex of panic and rumor. His intelligence staff informed him, "The main Japanese fleet is 164 miles off San Francisco." Another alert warned, "Reliable information that attack on Los Angeles is imminent." Two weeks later, Stilwell received another call from the War Department. He was told to get himself to Washington at once.

A bleak winter sky shrouded the capital as Stilwell's plane touched down on an ice-slick runway. No stickler for the prerogatives of rank, he flagged down a cab and told the driver to take him to the Munitions Building. There he went to the office of a former classmate from the Army's Leavenworth Command and General Staff School, Dwight Eisenhower. After warm greetings between "Ike" and "Joe," Eisenhower sent him to be briefed on the situation in North Africa. Apparently, Stilwell assumed, the Army had a role for him in an invasion of that coast, an operation the British had already code-named Gymnast.

Stilwell wrote his wife describing the maelstrom he encountered in wartime Washington. The town, he said, "is a rush of clerks in and out of doors, swinging doors, always swinging, people with papers rushing after other people with papers, groups in corridors whispering in huddles, everybody jumping up just as soon as you start to talk, telephones ringing, rooms crowded, with clerks all banging away at typewriters." It was just as well that he was leaving. "Six months of this," he said, "and I'd be screaming in my sleep."

But North Africa was not to be Stilwell's destination.

The fifty-eight-year-old general was an ornery cuss with a biting tongue that had won him the nickname "Vinegar Joe." The journalist and historian Theodore White has painted a sharply etched portrait of Stilwell at the time. He was "wiry, ugly in the most attractive fashion," White wrote, "his face wrinkled and gnarled, yet full of vitality." Another observer described his lean, hard frame as resembling "a knotted rope." He was undiplomatic, tactless, impatient, incapable of suffering fools gladly, and a first-rate general. While in Washington, Stilwell had his first face-to-face exposure to President Roosevelt. He was appalled, finding FDR "a rank amateur in all military matters . . . apt to act on sudden impulses." Even more disturbing to him was the way he observed Roosevelt acting toward Churchill during the British leader's White House visit. He wrote in his diary, "The Limeys have his ear, while we have the hind tit."

FDR pondered for some time over who could realize his vision of China as a world power before Japan completely trampled the country underfoot. Marshall recommended Hugh A. Drum, a pompous lieutenant general with a visibly high regard for himself. Drum made clear that China was too minor a canvas for his talents. On the other hand, Joe Stilwell's expertise and affection lay in China. He had spent four tours of duty there, culminating in his appointment as military attaché to the U.S. embassy in 1938. He had been assigned a sprawling viceroy's mansion but spent little time there, shunning the social circuit and setting out to get the feel of the country by bus, boat, even on foot through China's vastness. During this period Stilwell had come to know Chiang Kai-shek, who had risen to his present eminence from humble birth, the son of a peasant. Stilwell's judgment of the generalissimo was unhesitating: "He is utterly ignorant of what it means to get ready for a fight with a first class power."

Marshall asked Stilwell, who was still being briefed on the European war, if he would consider going to China. Vinegar Joe registered his enthusiasm in his diary, writing, "Me? No thank you. In China they remember me as a small fry colonel that they kicked around. They saw me on foot in the mud, consorting with coolies, riding soldier trains." Nevertheless, Henry Stimson invited Stilwell to his home, where they talked for nearly two hours before a fire in the secretary's wood-paneled library. Finally, the secretary got around to asking Stilwell if he would reconsider China. The good soldier paused before speaking and then answered that he would go wherever he was sent. Stimson asked him how he rated chances for success in China. Victory was possible, Stilwell answered, "if I have command." Stimson asked him how they should go about getting him that power. "Ask Chiang if he'll do it," Stilwell responded. But one thing had to be made clear: "I exercise command."

Vinegar Joe was taken to see FDR again. He arrived at the White

House on February 9 at 12:20 P.M. and was taken to the president's study just as Roosevelt was finishing lunch. FDR began a monologue, fueled principally by his sympathy for China and embellished by stories of his mother's life there. Stilwell failed to fall under the Roosevelt spell. He and his family were all Republicans and his brother was a vocal Roosevelt hater. Roosevelt, accustomed to easy verbal seduction, could not have failed to detect the resistance in the unyielding visage before him. Despite the palpable lack of rapport, the president decided that if Stimson and Marshall had confidence in this crotchety soldier, he would do for China. Before Stilwell left, he asked Roosevelt if he had a message for Chiang Kai-shek. "Tell him we are in this thing for keeps," the president said. "We intend to keep at it until China gets back all her lost territory." Later that day, Stilwell recorded in his diary his latest reaction to the commander in chief. "Very pleasant and very unimpressive. As if I were a constituent in to see him." His final verdict on FDR: "just a lot of wind."

Later in February Stilwell found himself in China again face-to-face with Chiang Kai-shek. The general's arrival coincided with a dark hour in the Allies' fortunes. The British had lost Hong Kong. Then, on February 15, Singapore, the "impregnable" naval fortress, surrendered, with 138,000 British losses, a dispiriting number. Churchill called Singapore the "greatest disaster to British arms which our history affords." The fear at the time was that Germany and Japan could join forces and divide the world between themselves. As reported in *The New York Times*, the Allies "have voiced the opinion to President Roosevelt that Japan is preparing to move a heavy part of her fleet into the Indian Ocean in the hope that the Germans will drive eastward from Bulgaria in order to make a junction." The British colony of Burma, positioned between China and India, now assumed strategic significance. The Japanese might drive through Burma to link up with the Germans. The colony had further importance. With the Chinese Pacific coast blockaded by Japan, Burma, if it could be kept free, could provide a back door for supplying Chiang Kai-shek from India. Key to this effort was the Burma Road, running from Lashio, a town in the middle of Burma, for 730 miles to Chungking in China. Another link was planned to extend the road from Lashio to the Indian city of Ledo, thus opening a road between the two countries. Roosevelt wanted this supply route finished. Its completion was another of Stilwell's tasks.

Chiang Kai-shek initially appeared welcoming to Roosevelt's representative. He pledged to FDR that Chinese armies in Burma "are all under the command of General Stilwell." In response, the president reassured Chiang that "this government is proceeding vigorously to find practicable ways and means of continuing to support you." The generalissimo gave Stilwell a handsome home clinging to the hillsides of Chungking and provided a staff of twenty-nine servants, including gatekeepers, gardeners, cooks, houseboys, and water bearers. The plain-living Stilwell quickly cut the staff, finding the number ridiculous, and because he suspected rightly that this retinue was intended to spy on him for Chiang.

Vinegar Joe and the generalissimo's honeymoon was short-lived. While Stilwell held nominal command, Chiang continued to fire off orders to his generals without informing him, even countermanding him. Rather than performing as commander in chief, Stilwell was treated merely as an advisor whom Chinese officers could disregard with impunity while they pursued their primary mission, using their position to enrich themselves. A unit commander would receive the payroll for his men and decide how much to dispense to them and how much to keep for himself. The Burma Road, rather than a lifeline, was proving more of a gold mine for corrupt Chinese officials. Sixteen separate agencies "supervised" the road, their staffs overloaded with relatives and hangers-on. So vast was the thievery that, on average, in order for 5,000 tons of material to reach Chungking, 14,000 had to be loaded aboard trucks in Burma. The commander of the Chinese Fifth Army, allegedly under Stilwell, put it this way to the British governor of Burma, Sir Reginald Dorman-Smith: "the American general only thinks that he is commanding. In fact, he is doing no such thing. You see, we Chinese think that the only way to keep the Americans in the war is to give them a few commands on paper. They will not do much harm as long as we do the work." He might have added, and as long as American aid kept pouring in.

Within a month of Stilwell's arrival in China, the harassed general unloaded his frustration upon Stimson and Marshall. "Under existing conditions," he wrote, "cannot continue to command of 5th and 6th armies without being stooge for Chinese who can bypass me for anything they want to do and then blame me for the result." His pessimism was understandable after Stilwell's first Burmese campaign. The Japanese were driving on Lashio, from which goods were to be transported along the Burma Road into China. Chinese forces, some fighting bravely, others a fleeing mob, failed to stem the enemy advance. Stilwell found himself retreating on foot along primitive trails clogged with refugees and littered with the dead and dying. He judged the campaign "a hell of a beating."

DURING THE EARLY WEEKS OF 1942, as MacArthur's forces on Corregidor yielded to malnourishment, tropical disease, and 300 Japanese bombing raids, the general began to contemplate how it must end for him. He told Sid Huff, his former naval aide, whom he had recycled into an Army lieutenant colonel, "They will never take me alive." He pulled from his pocket a small, wooden-handled, double-barreled Derringer and told Huff, "This belonged to my father when he was in the Philippines." He then sent the colonel to find bullets for the pistol. Returning with two rounds, Huff watched MacArthur open the weapon, load it, and put the pistol back into his pocket.

Franklin Roosevelt did not particularly like Douglas MacArthur and MacArthur reciprocated the sentiment. Yet both men, circling each other like wary lions, were shrewd enough to recognize their mutual usefulness. FDR had to make a decision: where would MacArthur be of most use? To Marshall, acutely aware of the paucity of superior generals, there was little doubt. MacArthur had to be pulled out of the Philippines. But so delicate was the matter, with its whiff of the captain leaving his sinking ship, that Marshall took special pains to placate MacArthur's ego. He used Eisenhower as his messenger to deliver a cable to the code room in a sealed envelope. "The most important question concerns your possible movements should your forces be unable longer to sustain themselves in Bataan and there should remain nothing but the defense of Corregidor," he wrote MacArthur. Then came the carefully calibrated wording: "Under these conditions, the need for your services there might be less pressing than at other parts in the Far East." To make absolutely clear that MacArthur had not chosen to abandon his men, Marshall promised that he would receive a "direct order of the President to you," which was soon forthcoming. "The president directs that you make arrangements to leave Fort Mills and proceed to Mindanao," it read. "From Mindanao you will proceed to Australia where you will assume command of the United States troops."

MacArthur received this message while sitting with his wife and little boy in a bomb-scarred cottage on Corregidor. According to one witness, after reading the cable MacArthur "walked around like a man numbed or crazed. He seemed to age in years in the space of a few minutes. The order to leave hit him like the death of a loved one." He turned to his wife and said that this was one order he intended to disobey. That evening, he called his staff together and read a reply that he intended to send to the president refusing to leave the Philippines. There ensued a heated discussion that dragged on for hours, with MacArthur maintaining that he would not leave, while his aides insisted that disobeying an order from the commander in chief would end his career, not in glory, but in a court-martial. MacArthur finally yielded and sent a reply acknowledging the president's order. The one sop to his pride that he requested was to decide when and how he should leave. "Please be guided by me in this matter," he wrote Roosevelt. "I know the situation here in the Philippines and unless the right moment is chosen for so delicate an operation, a sudden collapse might result."

Eisenhower, from his perch in the War Plans Division, pondered the wisdom of extricating MacArthur. He wrote in his diary, "I'm dubious about the thing." FDR, he believed, was being pushed by public opinion, not military considerations. MacArthur, he thought, should stay put. He did not believe, as did Roosevelt's military aide General Pa Watson, that getting MacArthur off "The Rock" was worth "five Army corps." Eisenhower closed his entry, "Bataan is made to order for him. It's in the public eye, it has made him a public hero, it has all the essentials of drama." The diarist's view may have reflected lingering resentment over his treatment at the hands of MacArthur or a shrewd reading of the man's penchant for the theatrical, or both.

Most wrenching for MacArthur as his departure neared was the arrival at the Corregidor cottage of a skeletal soldier wearing a badly wrinkled uniform with two faded stars on his collar tabs, Lieutenant General Jonathan Wainwright, whom he had summoned from Bataan. "Skinny" Wainwright had been a plebe at West Point four years behind MacArthur, and was now his second in command in the Philippines. MacArthur motioned Wainwright to a wicker lounge chair and said, "Jonathan, I want you to understand my position very plainly. . . . I'm leaving for Australia pursuant to repeated orders of the President. . . . I want you to make it known throughout all elements of your command that I'm leaving over my repeated protests." Wainwright, he explained, was now in charge. "If I get through to Australia you know I'll come back as soon as I can." MacArthur rose, took Wainwright's hand. "Good-bye, Jonathan," he said, and promised the weary soldier a promotion as soon as he returned, which he expected would happen by July 1. With that, Wainwright headed back to beleaguered Bataan.

MacArthur's departure has been best described by himself in a lengthy statement released by his staff on March 11. Though written in the third person, the account bore the unmistakable mark of MacArthur's pen. Manila Bay, he wrote, "had just been bathed in the warm sunlight of one of the sunsets for which it is famous. . . . Suddenly the silence of the newborn night was destroyed by the roar of powerful motors burst upon the drowsy bay." The roar was produced by Squadron 3, four PT boats under the command of Lieutenant John D. Bulkeley, a dashing bearded figure MacArthur referred to as "Buck." Seventeen members of MacArthur's staff began to board the gray, sleek-hulled, seventy-seven-foot-long PTs. Bulkeley carried Jean MacArthur's single suitcase aboard, little Arthur clutched a stuffed animal, and his Cantonese nanny, Ah Cheu, brought aboard all her possessions wrapped in a handkerchief. Justifying the servant's presence on the crowded vessel, MacArthur explained that it "would have been certain death had she been left behind." Once out of Manila Bay, with Bulkeley at the helm of PT-41, the waters turned ugly, adding to MacArthur's mortification at leaving his men as he became deathly seasick, retching over the side and finally retreating to a bunk belowdeck. In describing the hazards the PT boats faced in slipping past Japanese patrols, MacArthur wrote, "Memories of frontier days when beleaguered garrisons sent the youngest and most hardy through enemy lines to bring reinforcements came to mind. . . . But this was a 62-year-old man, a commanding general, a veteran of many wars." The PTs arrived at Mindanao, from where MacArthur's party was flown to Australia in two B-17s, landing at Batchelor Field some forty miles from Darwin early in the morning of March 17.

MacArthur was immediately besieged by reporters. "The President of the United States," he told them, "ordered me to break through the Japanese lines and proceed from Corregidor to Australia for the purpose, as I understand it, of organizing the American offensive against Japan." He then uttered the words that would forever be associated with his name. "I came through and *I shall return.*" He later wrote in his reminiscences of the impact of the phrase in the Philippines, "it was daubed on the walk of the *barrios,* it was stamped on the mail, it was whispered in the cloisters of the church. It became the battle cry . . . that no Japanese bayonet could still."

In the United States, MacArthur's leaving the Philippines did nothing to tarnish his heroic image. Streets were named for him, babies were christened "Douglas" and "MacArthur." His photo appeared on bubble gum cards that boys collected. If the move aroused any disapproval, it was against the president. Mr. and Mrs. A. M. James of Texas telegraphed FDR, "We the parents of boys who fought so valiantly under General MacArthur protest his removal with all the sorrow and bitterness at our command. . . . We believe this to be a political move to bolster the morale of some of our allied nations. . . . It is more regrettable that you should take it upon yourself to deprive [the soldiers] of their idolized commander."

All who served under him did not see a selfless commander. Before he left the Philippines this doggerel surfaced from the pen of a disenchanted soldier, sung to the tune of "The Battle Hymn of the Republic":

Dugout Doug MacArthur lies ashakin' on the Rock
Safe from all the bombers and from any sudden shock
Dugout Doug is eating of the best food on Bataan
And his troops go starving on . . .

While MacArthur, in his vanity, could be exasperating, no one close to him ever doubted his physical courage, beginning with doughboys who watched him stride fearlessly above the trenches in World War I. The slur "Dugout Doug" offered a handy alliteration rather than a description. However, Marshall urged the president "To offset any propaganda by the enemy directed against his leaving his command and proceeding to Australia in compliance with your orders" by approving the Medal of Honor for MacArthur. Soon after the general's arrival in Australia, on March 26, Australia's prime minister, John Curtin, hosted a banquet where the U.S. ambassador, Nelson T. Johnson, read aloud President Roosevelt's citation awarding MacArthur the medal. The Australians, grateful to have this paragon sent to their defense, applauded wildly. For MacArthur, receiving this decoration meant deep satisfaction. Throughout his life, he had sought to emulate his revered father. Now they became the first father and son to receive the Medal of Honor. Back on Corregidor the mood was less festive. FDR's naval aide, John McCrea, handed Roosevelt a signal from the Philippines: "Wainwright states that doubtful if he can hold out beyond fifteenth of April because of lack of food."

By early May, the Japanese were pounding at the entrance to Corregidor's Malinta Tunnel, now jammed with the wounded and refugees. Wainwright managed a final message to Roosevelt. "With broken heart and head bowed in sadness but not in shame," he informed FDR that all was lost. He must surrender. The American flag came down over Corregidor and on May 6, 11,000 men laid down their arms. MacArthur, getting the news, was furious that Wainwright had given up. He cabled Marshall that his successor must be "temporarily unbalanced and his condition renders him susceptible to enemy use." For public consumption, however, he issued a statement to the press declaring, "The Bataan forces went out as it would have wished, fighting to the end in its flickering forlorn hope. No army has ever done so much with so little, and nothing became it more than its last hour of trial and agony. To the weeping mothers of its dead, I can only say that the sacrifice and halo of Jesus of Nazareth has descended upon their sons and that God will take them unto Himself." Afterward, he wept openly.

At this point, neither the president, MacArthur, nor the American people knew the fate of those left behind as the Japanese herded 75,000 Americans and Filipino prisoners from Bataan eighty-five miles to a prison camp deep in Luzon. The brutality they underwent reflected Japanese contempt for soldiers who surrendered. Stragglers were shot, beheaded, bayoneted, or run over by Japanese vehicles. As one captive later described the ordeal, "Through the dust clouds and blistering heat we marched . . . without food, we were allowed to drink dirty water from a roadside stream. . . . Prisoners fell out frequently and threw themselves moaning beside the roadside. The stronger were not permitted to help the weaker." Of 78,000 American and Filipino prisoners eventually taken, nearly 12,000 perished on what history would call the Bataan Death March. The first American newspaper accounts of the atrocity would not surface until almost two years later.

AMID THE DESPAIR of the first six months of war—the disaster at Pearl Harbor, the debacle in the Philippines, the loss of Wake Island and Guam—one ray of light pierced the gloom. Soon after the attack of December 7, FDR revived a long simmering obsession. "The President was insistent that we find ways and means of carrying home to Japan proper, in the form of a bombing raid, the real meaning of war," Hap Arnold remembered. In the weeks that followed, FDR never dropped the matter. On January 28, he sat in his second-floor office scanning the faces of Marshall, King, and Arnold. What were they doing, he demanded, about bombing Japan? Could not the United States strike from bases in China or eastern Russia? Arnold explained that "it would take a few months to get the gasoline and fields available." Roosevelt thumped his desk impatiently. They were showing no imagination, he said, being overcautious. What about striking from the Aleutians or Mongolia? FDR asked. "By the time we had the planes," Arnold recalled, "the Japs had moved so far inland in China that a raid from bases in China was out of the question." The sailor in FDR now began to press Admiral King for seaborne alternatives. King went to his operations officer, Captain Francis C. "Dog" Low, who along with another Navy man, Donald Duncan, proposed a daring stroke. The Navy's carrier aircraft lacked the range to reach Japan. But a long shot, never tried before, just might work. Long-range bombers might be able to fly from the deck of a carrier and hit Japan. The proud King took the rare step of calling on Hap Arnold, whom he usually treated as a stepchild on the Joint Chiefs. Would the deck of a carrier be long enough to launch a heavy, land-based plane, say a B-25 bomber? King asked. "I assured him it was [possible] provided the carrier deck was large enough to accommodate the number of B-25s that should be sent out on such a mission," Arnold replied. Soon King and Arnold, smiling broadly, were ushered into the president's office. Their staffs working together had hammered out a bold gamble. Upon hearing it, FDR pronounced the idea "grand." The remaining issues were practical. Which carrier? How many planes? Launched what distance from Japan? And who should lead the raid? Arnold, back in his office pondering the choice, recalled a pilot involved in a disciplinary incident years before. At the time, his adjutant had warned him, "Colonel, there is a man down at Ream Field whose conduct has been so bad it requires your personal attention." Subsequent investigation revealed that a second lieutenant, James H. Doolittle, had made a bet with a fellow flier. As they watched another pilot taxi out to the runway for takeoff, Doolittle, already a veteran flier in World War I, told his companion, "I'll bet you five bucks I can sit on his landing gear while he lands." The bet agreed upon, Doolittle trotted out to the plane and asked if he could go along for a ride. No sooner had the plane leveled off when the pilot watched in disbelief as his passenger popped out of the cockpit, scrambled under the wing struts, and lowered himself to a sitting position on the axle between the landing wheels. The unnerved flier brought the plane back to earth, as gently as possible. As it came to a stop, Doolittle hopped off, went to his companion, and said, "Pay me!"

Jimmy Doolittle was an unusual combination of daredevil and thinker who held a Ph.D. from the Massachusetts Institute of Technology in aeronautical engineering. He became a test pilot and rose to the rank of colonel in the Air Corps. Here was the man Hap Arnold settled on to head "Special Aviation Project #1," the mission to bomb Japan. The risks were appalling. Once, reflecting on the responsibility of putting men in harm's way, Doolittle had observed, "an air force commander . . . sent every mission out with a better than fair idea of what his losses would be—about half your boys were killed, about half of them made prisoner. . . . You were obliged to usurp, if I may say so, almost deific prerogatives." Doolittle himself was about to face these odds or worse. Still he had little trouble recruiting volunteers for Project #1. Soon the skies above Eglin Field, Florida, roared with the sound of B-25s, repeatedly taking off from a 750-foot-wide white rectangle painted on the runway while sagging under the weight of dummy bomb loads and extra fuel tanks. Finally, sixteen bombers and crews were selected to make the raid on Japan, which Doolittle intended to lead. They were to fly from the carrier USS *Hornet*, commanded by Admiral Marc Mitscher. The *Hornet* would be protected by Vice Admiral Bill Halsey's Task Force 16, which included another carrier, the *Enterprise*, four cruisers, eight destroyers, and two tankers. Halsey was a rule-bending sailor who had won FDR's heart. Faced with restrictions on drinking aboard a Navy vessel, he had ordered his flight surgeon to requisition 100 gallons of "medicinal" bourbon, claiming that after a hazardous mission, "there is no substitute for a tot of spirits, as the Royal Navy well knows." His concessions to the seadog image were that he was tattooed and once owned a parrot. War correspondents tagged the feisty admiral "Bull" Halsey, a monicker the straight-shooting admiral detested as posturing and melodramatic.

Once their bomb loads were dropped, the planes from the *Hornet* were to head for designated fields in China. As a security precaution,

Marshall radioed General Stilwell, "Desire that there be no *repeat no* publicity of any kind connected with the special bombing mission. It is our purpose to maintain an atmosphere of complete mystery including origin, nationality, destinations and results of this type efforts." Further, "you are directed also to make earnest request upon the generalissimo [Chiang Kai-shek] to observe this policy."

On April 17, a yeoman handed Admiral King in his Main Navy office a message reporting that the *Hornet* was about to reach its launch point. King grabbed his hat and rushed to the White House where he informed an anxious FDR that Project #1 was under way.

The operation had not gone off flawlessly. Doolittle calculated, optimally, that the *Hornet* should be no more than 650 miles from Japan before the B-25s left the carrier's deck. But 800 miles out, a radioman aboard the *Enterprise* intercepted radio signals from a nearby Japanese patrol vessel. Should this ship alert Tokyo of an approaching task force, the element of surprise would be lost and the mission likely doomed. Doolittle decided that he must launch immediately. Pilots poured from the ready room, clambered into the cockpits, and started their engines as sailors began undoing the restraining cables that moored the B-25s to the deck. Doolittle climbed into the lead plane as a 40-mile gale wind lashed the bombers, streaking their windshields with rivulets of sea spray. At the signal from the flight controller Doolittle's bomber lumbered down the deck at full throttle, cleared the *Hornet*'s bow, and sank perilously close to the choppy waves before rising in a steady upward path. The other fifteen planes successfully followed and assembled on headings for Tokyo, Osaka, Kobe, and Nagoya. In the event of excessive cloud cover or other obstruction, Yokohama and Yokosuka were to be backup targets.

"JAPAN REPORTS TOKYO, Yokohama, Bombed by 'Enemy Planes' in Daylight" ran the headline on Saturday morning's front page of the April 18 *New York Times*. A listening post maintained by the Columbia Broadcasting System had intercepted a Japanese newscast in English reporting, "Just after noon on the 18th the first enemy planes appeared over the city of Tokyo." The report went on to say, "The enemy planes did not attempt to hit military establishments and only inflicted damage on grammar schools, hospitals and cultural establishments.... Casualties in the schools and hospitals were as yet unknown."

FDR HAD BEEN IN THE SNUGGERY at Hyde Park working with Sam Rosenman on a fireside chat on inflation when a call from the White House informed him that the Doolittle mission had succeeded. The president maintained an official silence in the days that followed even though the raid had already been reported in the media. Finally, on Tuesday, April 21, a chipper Roosevelt called in the press. Immediately, a reporter asked, "How about the story about the bombing of Tokyo?" Where had the planes come from? During their earlier conversation at Hyde Park, Rosenman had said, "Mr. President, you remember the novel of James Hilton, *Lost Horizon,* telling of that wonderful timeless place known as Shangri-la?" FDR now answered the reporter, "I think the time has come to tell you. They came from Shangri-la. They came from our new base at Shangri-la." The reporters greeted the president's evasion with laughter.

Damage caused by the four 500-pound bombs that each of Doolittle's B-25s dropped had been militarily inconsequential. Fifty people were killed, mostly civilians, and a hundred houses damaged with not a dent made in the Japanese war machine. Before the raid, an aide to navy chief Admiral Isoroku Yamamoto had said, "the idea that Tokyo, the seat of the Emperor, must be kept absolutely safe from air attack amounted almost to an obsession." That sense of inviolability had been shattered in minutes. The raid, if merely symbolic, produced exactly what Roosevelt wanted. He could now exclaim, "We're striking back."

The fate of Doolittle's raiders would not be known for months. Because of his decision to launch 150 miles before the ideal point, the B-25s burned too much fuel to land at their designated Chinese airfields. Two of them were forced down in Japanese-occupied China. The others ran out of gas and their crews parachuted into friendly territory held by the Chinese, and one crew jumped into Russia. Almost a year to the day after the raid, a solemn FDR told Americans in a radio address, "It is with a feeling of deepest horror . . . that I have to announce the barbarous execution by the Japanese government of some of the members of this country's armed forces who fell into Japanese hands as an incident of warfare." All the men captured were in uniform and presumably, as prisoners of war, under the protection of the Geneva Convention, to which Japan was a signatory. Of the eight fliers taken prisoner, three were tried by the Japanese as war criminals and shot by a firing squad. Another flier died in captivity of malnutrition and dysentery. After Japan's defeat a United States military tribunal tried and convicted four Japanese officers implicated in the executions and sentenced them to prison. Astonishingly, of the eighty men who flew off the deck of the *Hornet,* seventy-three survived.

CHAPTER 8

———————— ✦ ————————

Europe a Debate, Pacific a Victory

Men in uniform might fight the war but whom they fought
against, where they fought, how armed, and where they might die was
determined by faceless figures laboring behind desks, attending meetings, drafting strategies, and pushing paper. Churchill and Marshall,
during the prime minister's visit to Washington after Pearl Harbor, had
wrangled over how two allies each with their own land, sea, and air
forces and separated by the Atlantic Ocean should wage war. The solution had been the creation of the Combined Chiefs of Staff composed
of the military chiefs of the United States and Britain. FDR had argued
successfully for locating the Combined Chiefs in Washington, especially since the United States would increasingly bear the greater burden in manpower and treasure. As Lord Moran put it in his diary,
Roosevelt "got what he wanted in an uneven contest. . . . Our people
are very unhappy about the decision." Given their first allegiance to
their own nations, the Combined Chiefs meshed remarkably well,
largely because of the civility between Marshall and Britain's representative, Field Marshal Sir John Dill, an essentially egoless man, liked and
respected by his American colleagues, whose only concession to form
was to carry a swagger stick and speak the most upper-class English
that most Americans had ever heard.

Dill and Marshall were so in tune that they devised a stratagem to
defeat Roosevelt's tendency to communicate directly with Churchill,
leaving Marshall in the dark. When British communications officers
saw messages from the president to the prime minister, they sent Dill a

copy, which he then passed along to Marshall. "I had to be very careful," Marshall later commented. "If the arrangement were known Dill would be destroyed in a minute."

Marshall found awkward his position as both head of the American Army and the senior officer presiding over meetings of the Joint Chiefs of Staff. "In a sense, I would have two votes," he noted. The arrangement rankled the prickly, status-conscious Navy chief, Ernie King. On one occasion, King deigned to leave his office and went unannounced to see Marshall. Marshall happened to be tied up with the obstreperous Australian foreign minister, H. V. Evatt. While King fidgeted in the reception room, Evatt was laying into Marshall for allegedly underestimating the Japanese threat to his country. After essentially throwing Evatt out, Marshall came out to greet King and "I found that he had left in a huff and gone back to his office at the other end of the Munitions Building." Marshall, keenly aware of King's ego, accepted that he had to go to the other end of the building to see the admiral. He explained to a sullen King what had held him up, adding, "if you and I begin fighting at the very start of the War, what in the world will the public have to say about us?" King sat silent, hands folded for what seemed to Marshall an eternity. "Well, you have been very magnanimous in coming over here," King finally said. "And we'll see if we can get along." "And we did get along," Marshall later commented. King found Marshall variously, depending on the day, "an able man" or "stupid."

King continued to be sensitive to rank. At JCS meetings, whenever the junior member, Air Forces chief Arnold, asked King a question, the admiral would direct his answer to Marshall. King saw Arnold as Marshall's "yes man" who "didn't know what he was talking about." Eisenhower, while still in the War Plans Division, wrote in his diary, "Admiral King is an arbitrary, stubborn type with not too much brains and a tendency toward bullying his juniors." Yet Ike, along with the president and Marshall, recognized King's saving virtue. "I think he wants to fight," he also wrote in the diary, "which is vastly encouraging."

The person toward whom King was deferential was FDR, recognizing that though the president was a civilian, he could be astonishingly expert on naval matters. At one point Roosevelt demanded that King and Navy Secretary Frank Knox provide him with "the relative advantages of 13,600-ton heavy cruisers vs. the 11,000-ton heavy cruisers." On another occasion he asked, "What is the relative anti-aircraft fire of five of the new destroyers compared to one cruiser?"

For FDR, war was the paramount priority, but simultaneously he had a country to run. In early 1942, trade unions began pressuring him to derail Republican attempts in Congress to weaken the New Deal's Wages and Hours law. The farm bloc was pushing him to support a bill to keep agriculture prices high, and he had to fend off criticism that Eleanor was sticking her nose into government business. One day, with much on his mind, Roosevelt snapped at Grace Tully when she told him that General Marshall insisted on coming over right away. Upon Marshall's entering the president's study, FDR greeted him with forced geniality. Marshall responded with his customary stiffness. The three service chiefs, the general explained, were engaged in a competition for access to the president, which was making a shambles of coordination between the services. He explained further his discomfort at essentially exercising two votes in JCS deliberations. What the president must do, Marshall urged, was name an impartial chief of staff to preside over the JCS. A puzzled FDR answered, "Why? You are my chief-of-staff." Marshall reminded him that he was chief of staff of the Army only. "We must have a neutral man to preside," Marshall continued. Roosevelt protested. Why did they need another bureaucratic layer? "I'm the Chief-of-Staff," he insisted, "I'm the Commander-in-Chief." Marshall, with a faint smile, answered, "You are not Superman."

The general kept pressing his case for a JCS arbiter throughout the following months. Mostly he wanted a chief of staff to help discipline FDR's haphazard organizational improvisations. The head of the Army Air Forces, Hap Arnold, had won his seat at the JCS table precisely through a spur-of-the-moment impulse by the president. As Marshall later described what happened, "Of course, General Arnold was under me because the air corps was part of the Army. . . . But when the President came out with this message in which he referred to his military leadership of myself, Admiral King and of General Arnold as head of the air corps . . . the matter was settled right then." Arnold, de facto, had become a member of the Joint Chiefs. Similarly, the Marine Corps, as part of the Navy, enjoyed FDR's favoritism. During a visit by General Thomas Holcomb, the Marine Corps commandant, FDR complained, "First thing you know, *we're* going to be left out of things. *We* are not represented on the joint chiefs of staff." On another occasion he asked General Holcomb, "How would you like to be a member of the Joint Chiefs of Staff?" Holcomb replied tactfully that he did not know how the other chiefs might react to this idea.

Marshall may have had another less conscious motive for urging a JCS chief of staff, which, given his innate reserve, he was not eager to express. His workload was killing, averaging fifteen-hour days. In his few free hours, he sought refuge at his country retreat in Leesburg, where he exhausted himself in physical labor. Even there he enjoyed little respite. One Sunday afternoon while he was trimming a tree under his wife's supervision, the phone rang, as it did as often as fifty times a day. He climbed down to take a call from the War Department alerting him that a German raider was threatening oil refineries off Venezuela. He climbed back up the tree only to be called three more times, the last time by the president. At that point, "I just gave up the whole business and changed my clothes and got into the car and drove back to Washington."

In his quest for a JCS chairman, Marshall went to Harry Hopkins, the surest back door to the president's thinking. They agreed that the candidate should be a Navy admiral to counter Marshall's dual role. This solution, however, might raise a question: who would be the country's top naval officer, an admiral serving as the president's military chief of staff, or King, the overall Navy chief? The candidate Marshall and Hopkins favored was well known to FDR, another officer fortunate enough to have come into Roosevelt's orbit in the old days when he was assistant secretary of the navy. William Leahy, then a lieutenant, had commanded the yacht *Dolphin,* which Roosevelt once commandeered to evacuate his wife and children from Campobello to Washington during a 1916 polio epidemic. Leahy subsequently reached the Navy's summit when Roosevelt appointed him chief of naval operations in 1937. While pinning a Distinguished Service Medal on

Leahy, Roosevelt said, "Bill, if we have a war you're going to be right back here helping me to run it." In 1939, FDR gave him the posh post of governor of Puerto Rico. The idyll was short-lived. In January 1941 Roosevelt sent Leahy to perform a diplomatic tightrope act as ambassador to the Vichy French government. FDR's instructions to him were to forestall "the possibility that France may actually engage in war against Great Britain and in particular, that the French fleet may be utilized under the control of Germany." Not an easy task, since the Vichy leadership was servile to its German conquerors and Leahy considered the Vichy leader, Marshal Philippe Pétain, the eighty-four-year-old World War I hero, a "feeble, frightened, old man" and his cabinet "jellyfish." When finally the president consented that the JCS did need a chief of staff, he sent for sixty-seven-year-old Bill Leahy. The admiral prepared to leave France in May 1942 at a trying time in his life. As he embarked aboard the Swedish liner *Drottningholm*, the body of his wife, who had just died, lay belowdecks. The loss devastated Leahy, who told a *New York Times* reporter that he "had lost his incentive." He viewed the call home from the president as a blessed distraction from his grief. Soon after, FDR announced Leahy's appointment to a mouthful of a title: chief of staff to the commander in chief of the Army and Navy of the United States.

On July 21, 1942, FDR called a press conference, a day so sweltering that he appeared wearing a damp short-sleeved sport shirt with no jacket. A reporter asked, "Mr. President, can you tell us what the scope of Admiral Leahy's position will be?" FDR answered, dismissively, "I haven't got the foggiest idea, and it has nothing to do with the price of eggs." As the reporters pressed him further, he spoke of the avalanche of paper that flowed across his desk: "I should be helped . . . by somebody else doing . . . indexing work, and summarizing work, and at the same time somebody in whose judgment I have got a good deal of confidence. And it is going to save me a great many hours of work . . . if I can get somebody else to do the legwork." As the *New York Times* reporter wrote, "The President made clear that as commander-in-chief of the armed forces, he himself would continue to direct world strategy."

FDR's seemingly breezy style toward the deputies who ran the war for him masked a toughness. Harry Hopkins drew a comparison with another wartime president, Abraham Lincoln. The records of some current generals and admirals, Hopkins observed, "look awfully good, but [they] well may turn out to be the McCellans of this war," referring to the foot-dragging Civil War general George McClellan. "The only difference between Lincoln and Roosevelt is that I think Roosevelt will act much faster in replacing those fellows."

George Marshall was out of town when he picked up a newspaper, stunned to read that FDR had essentially portrayed Leahy's position as a clerk, a legman, a paper pusher. FDR's behavior was likely intended to salve the ego of his present military aide, Pa Watson. Watson was a big, handsome Virginian and professional "good ol' boy," with a soothing drawl, a raconteur's gift, and a talent for letting people down gently. He had become "Pa" at West Point by impressing his fellow cadets with his precocious paternal manner. Watson had been awarded a Silver Star for bravery during World War I and subsequently displayed a political bent, helping to promote Woodrow Wilson's Fourteen Points at Versailles. Beyond his duties as military aide, Watson exercised a powerful White House post, appointments secretary, which meant that anyone hoping to see FDR had first to get past Pa Watson. In shielding the president, the man was superb, his gambits as gatekeeper matching the president's talent for conversational obfuscation. Roosevelt's naval aide, Captain McCrea, has provided a striking account of Watson at work. Upon getting a phone call Watson would say, for example, "Ernie, I can't tell you how good it is to hear your voice. What have you been doing with yourself? You want to see the President? I'm soooo sorry. But he is so busy that I stand outside his door and say to myself, isn't there some way I can spare him this interruption? Now, I know the boss well enough to know that there isn't anyone he would rather see than you. But he just can't make it any day soon. I'll tell the President of your call at the risk of catching hell for not letting you in. Ernie, it's been so good to talk to you." He would then hang up, telling McCrea, "Jesus, John, if I let that guy in, I'd find myself on duty with the troops in about forty-eight hours."

In his determination to have a strong JCS chief of staff, George Marshall could not concern himself overly with Pa Watson's ego. For Leahy's first meeting with the chiefs, he directed his staff to prepare a place for the admiral at the head of the table. "King was furious when Leahy came in and sat down as presiding officer," Marshall recalled. Still, Bill Leahy, modest, spare, bald-headed, with a face resembling a faintly bemused owl, possessed of an innate dignity and impartiality, quickly won over the chiefs. Most significantly, they soon recognized that he had Roosevelt's ear. FDR had Leahy installed in an office in the newly constructed East Wing of the White House where he would arrive early to sift through a mass of color-coded papers—pink, white, and orange—all addressed to the president and never, it seemed, stamped less than "Urgent" or "Top Secret." Every morning as FDR shaved, Leahy brought him papers he deemed worthy of presidential attention. As time went on, he became a familiar figure in the White House, courted by reporters who watched as FDR emerged from the elevator with a cheery, "Good morning, Bill." He now possessed the next best source of power: proximity to power. When the United States hosted Combined Chiefs of Staff meetings with the British, Leahy presided.

Manpower was a subject that FDR harped on continuously with Leahy. As the president told reporters at a press conference, "There are a million men rejected, which is about fifty percent . . . of all those who were called." He went on to inventory the failures. "About a hundred thousand of them were turned down because they couldn't meet the fourth grade educational requirements." Others were rejected for dental defects, poor eyesight, poor hearing, heart disease, mental illness, defective feet, even 57,000 for venereal disease. He wanted more men in uniform.

✭

IN THE SPRING OF 1942, FDR faced the burning question: with Britain driven off the continent since 1940, with the United States technically at war with Germany yet nowhere fighting the enemy, with the president impatient to engage Hitler, where and when should the Americans strike first? The answer was hotly debated in Washington and London, and guessed at in Berlin. Roosevelt depended heavily upon Marshall for guidance, who turned to his smart, energetic, overworked chief of the War Plans Division, Dwight Eisenhower. To Eisenhower, they were about to make "the great decision of the war." As FDR jocularly spoke of the choice in a letter to a friend, Russell C. Leffingwell, "Some people want the United States to win so long as England loses. Some people want the United States to win so long as Russia loses. And some people want the United States to win so long as Roosevelt loses."

In notes he kept for himself, Eisenhower had written on January 27, 1942, six weeks after joining the War Plans Division, "we must win in Europe." The Pacific, he judged, was "important, but not a vital area." But where to attack in Europe? Eisenhower considered Italy and concluded, "the difficulty of attacking Germany through the mountainous flanks was obvious." As for the British proponents of Gymnast, a campaign in North Africa, "The first disadvantage was the distance of the North African bases from the heart of Germany." Norway? Eisenhower was well aware of how easily the Germans had driven a British-French force from that nation in June 1940. To Eisenhower the only strategy that made sense was to cross the English Channel, invade France, then drive through the relatively flat 550 miles from the French coast to Berlin. "It's going to be a hell of a job," Eisenhower wrote, "but so what?... We can't win by sitting on our fannies giving our stuff in driblets all over the world, with no theater getting enough."

In March of 1942 Eisenhower took a plan to Marshall. By arranging the necessary transportation, armaments production, recruitment, and training, an invasion could be mounted across the English Channel at Calais or Cherbourg by April 1, 1943, at which time one million American troops could be in England. The British Isles also offered the only practical bases for the air cover indispensable to a successful land assault. Then, striking a note that would particularly appeal to the president, Ike maintained that a "successful attack in this area will provide the maximum of support to the Russian front." He also anticipated what to do "if the imminence of Russian collapse requires desperate action." A small-scale toehold should be swiftly secured on the continent, perhaps at the port cities of Cherbourg and Le Havre. This contingency operation, code-named Sledgehammer, could be launched as early as September 1, 1942. Marshall asked Eisenhower the chances for Sledgehammer's success. "I personally estimate," Eisenhower said, "that, favored by surprise, the chances of a fairly successful landing are about 1 in 2." Fifty-fifty odds were not heartening and Marshall saw the operation at best as a "sacrifice play," a "desperate operation to save Russia." Nevertheless, it was worth the gamble, he believed, "even if we were to lose divisions in the process, but thereby keep the Russians in the war." Eisenhower agreed, adding, "we should not forget that the prize we seek is to keep 8,000,000 Russians" fighting. Ike had another rationale for pressing a cross-Channel attack. The British were continuing to argue for Gymnast, which, Eisenhower warned, "would eliminate the possibility of a major cross Channel venture in 1943." In the meantime, a buildup for a full-scale invasion from Britain code-named Bolero, and the actual cross-Channel invasion, called Roundup, would take place in 1943. Marshall, upon reviewing Eisenhower's proposal, said, "This is it. I approve." Next, Admiral King and General Arnold had to be brought aboard. Finally, the president and Prime Minister Churchill must be convinced. The JCS signed on readily. On April 1, an anxious Marshall, flanked by expected allies Harry Hopkins and Secretary of War Henry Stimson, sat across from the president in his study watching him turn the pages of Eisenhower's proposal, pausing to inject an occasional question. Finally, he nodded, saying "the United States would no longer be treated like a sort of stepchild" by the British. He wanted Marshall and Hopkins to go to London to sell the cross-Channel option to Churchill and his military chiefs. Marshall did not anticipate an easy road. He had come to believe that the British propensity was to fight wars around the edges. The prime minister himself, during the First World War, had championed the disastrous 1915 expedition to the Dardanelles, thousands of miles from the trenches of the Western Front where the war had to be won. Marshall did not want to see a Mediterranean diversion in this war.

✫

ON APRIL 4, 1942, two men identified only as Mr. A. H. Hones and C. G. Mell boarded a Pan American airliner in Baltimore for a flight to Bermuda, then to Scotland and on to London. Hones and Mell were cover names respectively for Hopkins and Marshall. They carried a message from FDR to Churchill saying, "what Harry and George Marshall will tell you all about has my heart and mind in it." The following day Roosevelt cabled Churchill, indicating his hopes for the short-term Sledgehammer, which would achieve his immediate goal to have Americans fighting Germans soon. "Your people and mine," FDR wrote, "demand the establishment of a front to draw off pressure on the Russians. And these people are wise enough to know that the Russians are today killing more Germans and destroying more equipment than you and I put together."

Harry Hopkins was one of the rare men whom Marshall addressed by his first name. Hopkins's courage astonished him. His chain-smoking companion had had part of a cancerous stomach removed, which left him unable to absorb enough protein. Thus he lived in a state of chronic semistarvation. "I know that the previous two weeks he had ten blood transfusions," Marshall remembered of their departure, "and he had been found crawling up the back stairs at Hyde Park because he wasn't strong enough to walk up." Upon their arrival in London, Hopkins had to collapse in his hotel room to recover his strength. Marshall went by himself, driven in a dun-colored auto, to meet the prime minister. Accustomed to Washington, a city at war but untouched by war, Marshall was overcome by what he saw. His driver wound through heaps of rubble, around craters, past buildings piled high with sandbags and bristling with barbed wire. Low in the sky he glimpsed the bloated shapes of barrage balloons set in place to slice the wings off enemy planes attempting low-level bombing. He arrived at 10 Downing Street, a house built on the cheap by a profiteering contractor named Downing 260 years before.

Marshall's conversation with the prime minister was cordial but inconclusive. Churchill was not going to commit himself to anything until his military chiefs had heard the American proposals. The next morning, April 9, Marshall met for two hours with his British counterpart, General Sir Alan Brooke, chief of the Imperial General Staff, a physically unimpressive figure with thin sloping shoulders, spindly legs, a profile like a hatchet, and the disconcerting habit of rapidly darting his tongue about his lips. Appearances aside, Brooke commanded universal respect in Britain. He descended from the "Fighting Brookes" who had served England since the reign of Queen Elizabeth I. Brooke barely concealed an air of soldierly superiority. He had commanded a full corps in the 1940 campaign in France, while Marshall had never taken an army into battle. Brooke later recorded in his diary, Marshall "gave us a long talk on his views concerning desirability of starting a Western Front next September." Brooke was leery, however, of what at this early stage the Americans could commit: "the total force which they could transport by then only consisted of two and a half divisions, no very great contribution!" At the end of the encounter, each man had taken the measure of the other. Brooke concluded, "I liked what I saw of Marshall, a pleasant and easy man to get along with, rather over filled with his own importance. But I should not put him down as a great man." Marshall, for his part, found Brooke "icy and condescending."

Finally, on April 14, with Hopkins's condition improved, he and Marshall met with the prime minister on a gloomy London afternoon. Churchill had by now studied the American proposal, entitled "Operations in Western Europe," which the British kept referring to, as if to maintain some distance, as the "Marshall Memorandum." Churchill and his military leaders were stunned by the gargantuan logistics effort envisioned for Bolero, over a million American troops, thousands of ships and planes to be mustered in England for an invasion across the English Channel. In the end the British appeared to have been won over. As Churchill later wrote, "We all agreed there should be a cross channel operation in 1943." He further told FDR's emissaries, "our two nations are resolved to march forward into Europe together in a noble brotherhood of arms, in a great crusade for the liberation of tormented peoples." Marshall and Hopkins prepared to return to Washington, convinced that they had Churchill's proxy in their pocket. The Third Reich was to be defeated by an invasion launched from England into France.

WHILE THE PRESIDENT AND HIS military chiefs continued to plan for a campaign in Western Europe, another war remained to be fought. The Pacific Ocean in early 1942 presented a featureless battlefield of sixty million square miles interrupted by countless islands. The issue before the president was how to allot responsibility for conducting operations over so boundless an arena. Douglas MacArthur, now in Australia, set up his headquarters in Melbourne and settled his family into Lennons Hotel in Brisbane, where they occupied four suites. Here was a living legend, a Caesar whom the American public would gladly embrace as their champion in the Pacific war, and initially George Marshall was willing to give MacArthur responsibility for the whole ocean and all the islands in it. The Navy, however, despite being caught asleep at Pearl Harbor, had been preparing to fight a war against Japan for over twenty years. Admiral King let his fellows in the JCS know that he had no intention of yielding the whole ocean to Douglas MacArthur, a man whom he regarded as a vainglorious know-nothing in naval matters. MacArthur for his part could not imagine himself subordinate to an admiral. As commander in chief, FDR faced a Solomon-like decision. The arrangement worked out in the end split the Pacific in two. MacArthur became Supreme Commander of the Southwest Pacific Area with authority over operations in Australia, New Guinea, and the Philippines, which facilitated his pledge to return to the islands. Admiral Chester Nimitz, designated Commander in Chief, Pacific Ocean Area, would run the rest of the theater, including New Zealand and on up to the Arctic, roughly following a boundary along longitude 160 degrees east. King had won at least a co-captaincy for the Navy in the Pacific. This division created an anomaly unprecedented in U.S. military history, with MacArthur commanding Army and naval forces in his sector and Nimitz controlling Navy, Army, and Marines in his sector. Generals would be giving orders to admirals and admirals giving orders to generals. FDR approved the scheme on March 31, 1942. Though satisfied with the president's decision, King found himself driven at times to distraction by FDR's assumption of expertise in naval affairs. On one occasion, the president bypassed his Navy chief entirely, directly instructing a King subordinate on how to deploy patrols to block further Japanese advances in the Pacific.

For all Roosevelt's sentimental attachment to the Navy his priority remained the invasion of Europe. After Pearl Harbor, the War Department had taken the position that "the United States should adopt the *defensive* in the Pacific and devote its major offensive effort across the Atlantic." The Pacific was to take a backseat in this war. For most Americans, however, the real battle remained in the Pacific where the hulks of battered ships, the fresh graves of men lost, and the subsequent fall of the Philippines, Guam, and Wake Island kept the bitterness over Pearl Harbor alive.

The first great clash in that theater, the Battle of the Coral Sea, was to mark a seismic shift between fleets in naval warfare, the first engagement in which opposing vessels never fired on each other, indeed never saw each other. The blows were landed entirely by planes launched from American and Japanese carriers. Admiral Nimitz had dispatched two carriers, the *Lexington* and the *Yorktown*, to head off a Japanese invasion force headed for New Guinea. On May 8, 1942, the *Lexington*, "Lady Lex," to her crew, suffered aerial torpedo and bomb blasts that set her vast stores of aviation gasoline aflame. At 5:07 P.M. the crew began to abandon ship, after which the destroyer *Phelps* sent the mortally stricken carrier to the bottom with five torpedoes.

The sinking of the *Lexington* provided a rare glimpse into the pathways of Franklin Roosevelt's mind. A few weeks after the loss, with the public still uninformed, Elmer Davis, FDR's scrupulously honest head of the Office of War Information, alerted Admiral King that he intended to reveal the story of the *Lexington*'s fate to the press. The public, Davis maintained, had the "right to know." King managed to wring one concession from Davis. He asked him not to release the account until first clearing it with the president. King immediately called FDR's naval aide, Captain McCrea, at the White House and instructed him "to do the necessary" to kill the story. McCrea put through a call to Hyde Park where the president had gone for the weekend, and spoke to the chief White House operator, Louise "Hackie" Hackmeister, who was reputed to recognize a voice after hearing it once. "Has Mr. Elmer Davis talked to the President today," McCrea asked, "and if not, has he got a call in for him?" He begged Hackie not to put Davis's call through until he himself had an opportunity to speak to the president. FDR at the time was dealing with a guest and as soon as he was free, Hackie informed him that McCrea wanted to speak to him. The naval aide told FDR of King's strong desire, for the time being, to muzzle Davis's account of the *Lexington*. Roosevelt's response took McCrea aback. "You should be up here today, John," FDR said cheerily, "the weather is perfect. The Hudson River Valley can turn on wonderful weather from time to time." He then ended the conversation. McCrea quickly reported this seemingly pointless exchange to King.

On Sunday morning, McCrea warily picked up *The Washington Post* from his front porch to see if Davis had released his story of the *Lexington* disaster. Surprised at finding nothing, he again called Hackie. "Tell me," he asked, "did the President talk to Mr. Elmer Davis yesterday?" She told him that she had advised the president to expect a call from Davis, to which he replied only, "I'm going to take a nap and don't wish to be disturbed." She further informed McCrea that after his nap FDR had gone for a drive "to take advantage of the fine weather." He then received guests, mixed cocktails, had dinner, and went to bed, never mentioning Elmer Davis or his expected call. FDR, using one of his stock stratagems, creative inactivity, made sure that the fate of the *Lexington* would not be disclosed until he believed the public was ready to hear it.

THE PRESIDENT HAD A LIFELONG penchant for the secretive, the covert, the clandestine, that had surfaced early in an ingenious code he devised as a Harvard student to mask his love life. As president he created a small spy ring operating out of the Oval Office, run by a well-connected journalist, John Franklin Carter, the operation secretly funded and barely known even within the president's circle. Spying in the mold of an E. Phillips Oppenheim thriller excited his imagination, but the technical world of radio wave interception, mathematical analysis, permutations, combinations, and gadgetry to break codes bored him. Almost a year before Pearl Harbor an exasperated Henry Stimson had insisted to Pa Watson that he had to see the president on an urgent matter. The staid secretary of state found FDR still in bed at 10:30 that morning leafing through *The New York Times,* the remains of his customary breakfast set aside. The president must recognize, Stimson began, the priceless value of code breaking. While not the stuff of espionage melodramas, it offered an extraordinary window into what was going on, not only in Japan, but in Germany as well. The Japanese ambassador to Berlin, Hiroshi Oshima, was an army general from a prominent family of whom the journalist-historian William Shirer noted, "Oshima often impressed this observer as more Nazi than the Nazis." The ambassador had easily won Hitler's trust and was told virtually everything happening in the Third Reich. Oshima, a conscientious diplomat, would then cable back to his Foreign Ministry in Tokyo whatever he had learned. Thanks to Magic, the triumph of American cryptologists, this intelligence could be on the president's desk almost as soon as it arrived in Japan. "I told him that he should read certain of the important reports," Stimson urged, knowing "He hadn't read them."

Belatedly, the president recognized the value of signals intelligence, "sigint" in the trade. Magic decrypts were like seeing one's opponent's hand in a card game rather than guessing at it. FDR had recently been shown decoded cables reporting an ominous move in the Pacific. He cabled MacArthur on June 2, 1942: "It looks at the moment as if the Japanese fleet is heading toward the Aleutian Islands or Midway and Hawaii with a remote possibility it may attack Southern California or Seattle by air." The information had originated in a cramped windowless basement, the Combat Intelligence Unit, in the 14th Naval District Administration Building at Pearl Harbor. An unlikely Navy commander, Joseph J. Rochefort, his workaday uniform including a red smoking jacket and carpet slippers, padded about an office with overspilling file drawers, teetering piles of books, and folders strewn across his desk. Rochefort's unmilitary presence was tolerated by his smartly uniformed superiors because he had lived in Japan, spoke the language fluently, and was a workaholic who slept on a cot and drove his team of cryptanalysts through twelve-hour shifts seven days a week producing intelligence that was now about to change history. Through Magic, the cryptanalysts had long been breaking the Japanese diplomatic cipher. But the enemy's naval code, JN-25, had proved harder to crack. Within a month of Pearl Harbor, however, code breakers had begun to strip away the layers of ciphering to reveal the Japanese navy's secrets underneath.

On May 24, Rochefort trotted up to the office of the Pacific Fleet commander, Admiral Chester Nimitz, telling a wary Nimitz that his team had uncovered what the Japanese navy was referring to as "the decisive battle" of the war. Earlier signals intelligence had produced information that Japan might be considering using poison gas in the Central and Eastern Pacific, including the Hawaiian Islands. Marshall warned Pacific commanders, "Imperative this information be kept secret because of danger of revealing source." Further Magic decrypts of JN-25 revealed a far more likely scenario. Admiral Isoroku Yamamoto, his country's premier strategist, the mastermind behind Pearl Harbor, planned a decisive blow to drive the United States from the Pacific. His strategy was to lure Nimitz's remaining Pacific Fleet into battle against the strongest force Japan could muster. With the U.S. fleet dispatched, the road would be open for the conquest of the Hawaiian Islands and conversion of the Pacific into a Japanese sea. Yamamoto's first intention was to occupy a sparsely populated, strategically placed island at the far end of the Hawaiian chain. Though Magic had revealed Japanese plans, the name of the island was as yet unknown to the Americans since the Japanese referred to it only by a code name,

"AF." A Rochefort colleague, Commander W. J. "Jasper" Holmes, devised an ingenious ruse to surface the identity of AF. Holmes had a
hunch that the Japanese target could be Midway. He suggested that the
island's radio station contact Pearl Harbor via an uncoded message,
saying that Midway's water distilling plant had broken down. Japanese
monitors on Wake Island picked up the message. Fresh water would be
a necessity on an island they shortly expected to occupy. Thus a Japanese station on Wake Island informed the Imperial Navy in Tokyo that
AF would be short of water. Holmes had been right, AF was Midway.

Nimitz, cautious and fearing a feint against a small island while the
Japanese struck hard at Hawaii, still needed convincing. He called in
his intelligence chief, Commander Edwin T. Layton, asking what he
thought of Rochefort's too-good-to-be-true revelations. Layton was a
conservative officer not easily stampeded by the wonders purportedly
achieved by Rochefort's unlikely crew in the basement of the administration building. However, upon studying the decoded messages, Layton became a believer. "They'll come in from the northwest on bearing
325 degrees and they will be sighted at about 175 miles from Midway,"
Layton told his chief, "and the time will be about 0600 Midway time."
Nimitz, whose battle philosophy was to take "calculated risk," decided
to gamble on Rochefort. He assigned Admiral Raymond A. Spruance,
now commanding Task Force 16, to exploit the Magic breakthrough.
Ray Spruance was a hard man, opposed to Roosevelt's New Deal, and
contemptuous of soft-headed welfare schemes that he believed only
allowed the lower orders to keep propagating. None of that mattered
now. The admiral was a scrapper, a hard charger. He knew how to mo-
tivate men, strolling the flight deck of his flagship, the carrier *Enterprise,* often hatless and tieless with sleeves rolled up. Instead of
observing the decorum that can prevail in the wardroom of a great
capital ship, particularly a flagship, Spruance was a regular guy who
chatted easily with junior officers, oblivious of rank. As for the mission
now assigned him, the naval historian Samuel Eliot Morison described
Spruance as a commander who did not make mistakes.

★

YAMAMOTO'S CARRIER TASK FORCE weighed anchor from the Inland Sea south of Hiroshima on an auspicious date, May 27, 1942, Navy Day in Japan, the thirty-seventh anniversary of Admiral Togo's epic 1905 defeat of the Russian fleet at the Battle of Tsushima. Yamamoto's fleet was formidable: eleven battleships, sixteen cruisers, fifty-three destroyers, and the centerpiece, four aircraft carriers—the *Akagi,* meaning the Red Castle; the *Kaga,* Increased Joy; the *Hiryu,* Flying Dragon; and the *Soryu,* Green Dragon. Yamamoto himself rode the *Yamato,* a gargantuan dreadnought, the largest battleship afloat, the length of three football fields, home to 2,800 sailors and mounting 18-inch guns that could hurl a 3,200-pound projectile twenty-seven miles. The *Yamato* dwarfed American *Iowa*-class battle wagons.

Yamamoto was short, stocky, his head closely shaven, missing two fingers of his left hand that had been blown off during the Russo-Japanese War. Though a thoroughgoing professional he indulged an earthy, fun-loving streak ashore, gambling and patronizing two favorite geishas. He was, further, the rare Japanese who understood the United States. He had spent three years studying at Harvard, subscribed regularly to *Life* magazine, and was an ardent admirer of Abraham Lincoln. When Japan chose war, he had supported and masterminded the Pearl Harbor attack because he recognized the United States as a sleeping giant that must be driven from the Pacific before its strength became aroused. However successful the attack on Pearl Harbor had been, the Japanese had missed a crucial objective, destruction of the American carrier fleet, which had been out to sea on December 7. Since the United States had not been driven from the Pacific, Yamamoto now counted on the Midway operation as a final knockout punch. So confident was he that his fleet would succeed that Japanese soldiers assigned to the campaign began giving Midway as their mailing address.

THE SUN CAME UP OVER CALM WATERS early in the morning of June 4. Three carriers under Admiral Spruance, the *Enterprise,* the *Yorktown,* and the *Hornet,* were steaming toward their rendezvous with the unwitting Yamamoto. An American reconnaissance pilot spotted the enemy task force and at 6:03 A.M., the loudspeaker on the *Enterprise* blared, "Two carriers and battleships bearing 320 degrees, distant 180 miles [from Midway] course 135 speed 25." At 7:02 A.M., from his command post on the superstructure of the *Enterprise,* Spruance gave the order, "Launch the attack." At 10:24 A.M., Japanese lookouts reported to an astonished Yamamoto and his commander of the Japanese carriers, Admiral Chuichi Nagumo, aboard the *Akagi,* that a swarm of American planes was fast approaching. Within five minutes, the unimaginable happened. American dive-bombers, crewed by men who not long before had been insurance salesmen, teachers, accountants, and college students, began streaking toward the decks of the Japanese carriers. As their bombs struck home, the enemy carriers, laden with gas, began geysering brilliant orange flames into the sky. American pilots scanned the sea and radioed back the score. Four of the carriers were mortally wounded. Nagumo had to scramble ignominiously down the side of his doomed ship onto a motor launch that carried him to safety aboard the cruiser *Nagara.* A stunned Yamamoto turned the hulking *Yamato* back toward Japan.

The American interception had not been without cost. The carrier *Yorktown,* badly crippled, was sunk two days later by a Japanese submarine and lost sixty planes. But for the Japanese the Battle of Midway was a calamity. Four of her best carriers had vanished. Japanese pilots circled the flaming flight decks of doomed ships before plunging into the sea. All told, Japan lost 322 planes and their invaluable crews. So feared was the demoralizing effect of the catastrophe on the Japanese public that survivors of Midway were isolated and kept under guard. The loss went well beyond men and arms. An unbroken chain of Japanese victories had been snapped. American code breakers toiling in a cramped basement amid the clatter of teletypes, key punchers, collators, and tabulators, puzzling over seemingly meaningless jumbles of random letters, had enabled a surprise attack that amounted to a Japanese Pearl Harbor. Admiral Nimitz generously described Midway as "essentially a victory of intelligence." America had progressed from retreating before the enemy to stopping the enemy, and now to the prospect of defeating the enemy. The war in the Pacific had turned around.

After Midway, FDR invited three of the Navy's participating pilots, Lieutenants O'Hare, Thach, and Flatley, to the White House and asked what they needed. After having faced the impressive maneuverability and speed of the Japanese Zero, their leader responded that they wanted "something that will go upstairs faster." Within six months, the Grumman aircraft company was producing an improved F6F Hellcat, faster, higher climbing, and better armed than the Zero.

Part of Yamamoto's Midway strategy had been to mislead the Americans by sending a portion of his fleet as a decoy to the Aleutian Islands. Clueless to what had befallen the main task force, Japanese transports pushed north toward possibly the most forlorn soil under the American flag, the cloud-shrouded, wind-swept, biting-cold islands of Attu and Kiska, U.S. territories since the purchase of Alaska from Russia. On Attu the Japanese captured ten men manning a weather station and a clutch of Aleut Eskimos. They found Kiska uninhabited. In Japan, the press trumpeted the seizure of Attu and Kiska as a signal victory, the Rising Sun now flying over U.S. territory, small consolation after the disaster at Midway. To American planners, enemy occupation of these dreary outposts was viewed as a pinprick to be left uncontested for another year.

FDR had long since become inured to the knee-jerk enmity of his Groton School classmate Colonel Robert McCormick and the anti–New Deal newspapers he published. Roosevelt once charged that the *Tribune* "prints lies and deliberate representations in lieu of news. . . . I do not trust the *Chicago Tribune* farther than you can throw a bull." The story in the *Tribune* three days after the Battle of Midway was, to the president, unconscionable, possibly treasonous. Once Admiral Nimitz had decided to gamble on the reliability of the Magic decrypts, he had sent a secret message to naval units in the Pacific unveiling the Japanese plan and setting the order of battle. Commander Morton T. Seligman, a former executive officer of the *Lexington,* showed the Nimitz communication to a *Tribune* war correspondent, Stanley Johnson. The reporter, recognizing that he had a scoop, filed a story to his paper. Essentially the same article appeared in the *Tribune*'s sister dailies, the *Washington Times-Herald* and the New York *Daily News*, published by McCormick's cousin, Joseph Patterson. Johnson's report produced the headline in the *Tribune* that enraged FDR: "Navy Had Word of Jap Plan to Strike at Sea." The story went on to recount that "The advance information enabled the American Navy to make full use of the air attacks on the approaching Japanese ships." The article went on to enumerate precisely the ships in the Japanese task force, even mentioning the four carriers by name. The explicitness of the report screamed aloud that the American Navy had access to Japanese codes. While the Roosevelt White House wanted to crow to the American people about the tide turning at Midway, exposure of Magic would represent a disaster. Roosevelt huddled with Marshall and King to devise a damage control strategy. As Marshall saw it, they must not draw too much attention and "Treat the operation as normal rather than extraordinary." Thus, on the day the *Tribune* story broke, Admiral King went before the press and downplayed the victory. "After General Doolittle's raid on Japan, General Marshall and I both felt, knowing the Japanese psychology, that some reprisal in kind was inevitable in order that they might save face," King explained stonily. How was the United States able to foresee this reprisal? a reporter asked. That was simple, King explained. American submarines plying the Western Pacific had spotted the Japanese task force.

Still, so obvious was it that McCormick's papers had risked exposing Magic that the cry of "traitor" rose up against the colonel. One congressman speaking on the floor of the House denounced the *Tribune* for giving away a secret that would doubtless lead the Japanese to change their codes. In the paper's hometown, Chicago, a grand jury convened to consider possible violations of the Espionage Act. Colonel McCormick and his reporter, Johnson, faced indictment for treason. The temptation was great for FDR to give his nemesis his comeuppance. But Roosevelt was far too shrewd a player to sacrifice a precious covert weapon for the fleeting satisfaction of seeing a foe brought down. The Navy was ordered to refuse to cooperate with the grand jury and the matter withered.

Incredibly, the Japanese remained oblivious to what any cabdriver in Chicago could guess, that the Americans were breaking their naval code. Yamamoto's fleet continued using JN-25 to the end of the war, and the United States went on breaking it.

CHAPTER 9

———⋆———

North Africa: FDR Versus the Generals

In the spring of 1942, as the debate raged as to where United States forces should first fight the Germans, Winston Churchill had taken his stand. Simply stated: the Mediterranean remained vital to preserving the lifeline of the British Empire, and all his positions flowed from this belief. As he put it, he found "control by Britain of the whole North African shore from Tunis to Egypt" indispensable, "thus giving . . . free passage through the Mediterranean to the Levant and the Suez Canal." While he seemed to have gone along with Hopkins and Marshall during their London mission in endorsing the Americans' determination to strike Germany through an invasion across the English Channel, the prime minister, as far back as his first stay at the White House, had attempted to infect Roosevelt with an alternative. Two days before Christmas in 1941, in a private meeting amid the swirling smoke of his cigar and the president's cigarette, the prime minister hazarded an earlier North African plan. He already had enough men and the necessary transport, he said, to land 55,000 troops on the coast within twenty-three days. Their objective would be to trap Germany's Afrika Korps, under the brilliant Erwin Rommel, between Egypt, where the British were located, and the northwest African coast. This was a variation on the operation code-named Gymnast. Churchill claimed that he "had the feeling that the President was thinking very much along the same lines as I was about acting in French Northwest Africa."

Worried about FDR's susceptibility to Churchill's powers of persuasion, George Marshall went to the president and pointed out what he regarded as the hole in Churchill's thesis. Success in North Africa would require a "French invitation for a direct occupation of French Morocco," an unlikely outcome, since Vichy France, which controlled the colony, was under the thumb of Nazi Germany. Yet realizing that Churchill might win the argument, he had briefly considered General Stilwell for Gymnast before the hapless Vinegar Joe had been dispatched to China.

Though Roosevelt and his chiefs believed they had won Churchill's consent for the short-term Sledgehammer operation and the long-term Bolero buildup for a major invasion of France, the prime minister was really shifting the sands under their feet. Five days after promoting Gymnast he warned FDR of the necessity to prevent a junction of the Japanese and the Germans linking up in the India-Burma sector. The way to cut that link was by controlling the Mediterranean, not by crossing the Channel. He proceeded to belittle Sledgehammer, warning that seizing a toehold in France would only create a "bomb and shell trap." Besides, so puny a venture would barely draw a single German soldier from the Russian Front. If Roosevelt wanted American troops fighting in 1942, "Where then could this be achieved?" he asked. Answering himself, he said, "Where else but in French North Africa."

Marshall struggled to keep the president's eye fixed on the cross-Channel invasion. Dismayed when FDR started to talk about sending 100,000 troops to Australia, Marshall laid it out flatly. "If the Bolero project is not to be our primary consideration," he warned, "I would recommend its complete abandonment." The tactic worked. On May 6, 1942, FDR answered Marshall, "I do not want Bolero slowed down." As if to lock Roosevelt in place, the Army chief traveled to West Point on May 29 and delivered a commencement speech assuring 1,830 cadets, "American soldiers will land in France."

WHILE MARSHALL WAS AT WEST POINT, a new figure arrived at the White House, square-headed, the face an impassive slab behind a ferocious mustache. Vyacheslav Molotov, the Soviet foreign minister, nicknamed at home "the Hammer," studied Franklin Roosevelt through cold eyes from behind a decidedly unproletarian pince-nez. He had come directly from England where he had pressed Winston Churchill to open a second front. Churchill has left a vivid picture of the Russian, whom he hosted at Chequers. Molotov demanded keys to all the bedrooms assigned to his retinue, who were told to keep the doors locked. Stolid, unsmiling Russian women were posted outside each room day and night. English chambermaids upon making up the rooms found pistols under the pillows.

By now, Churchill had so firmly concluded that the Russo-German war was Britain's insurance policy for survival that the once rabid anticommunist was ready to grant Stalin almost anything, even recognizing Russia's seizure of the independent states of Estonia, Latvia, and Lithuania. The dizziness of Churchill's turnaround from past views was evident in a memorandum that Eleanor Roosevelt had found written by him in 1919 maintaining that the Red revolution must be strangled at birth. "Large sums of money and considerable forces have been employed by the Allies against the Bolsheviks during the year," he wrote at the time, noting that over 8,000 American troops were in Siberia fighting the Reds. The president's wife had written across the top of this faded document, "It is not surprising if Mr. Stalin is slow to forget." The president too was ready to make apparently boundless concessions to keep the Red Army engaged. He told Henry Morgenthau, "I would rather lose New Zealand, Australia or anything else than have the Russians collapse."

On Molotov's arrival at the White House, a valet unpacking his luggage in the Rose Room discovered sausage, black bread, and, again, a pistol. That evening, FDR huddled with the foreign minister, Harry Hopkins, and Molotov's American counterpart, Secretary of State Cordell Hull. The Russian's words were as blunt as his appearance. When, he wanted to know, could the Western Allies launch a campaign of some thirty-five divisions that might draw as many as forty German divisions away from the Russian Front? Stalin expected an answer. "If you postpone your decision," Molotov warned, "you will have eventually to bear the brunt of the war." Hitler might well seize the breadbasket

of Ukraine and the oilfields of the Caucasus. Finally, somewhat mollified by FDR's charm and lubricated by plenty of drink, the foreign
minister went to bed seemingly content. His dogged pressing of Russia's positions won him among the White House staff the nickname
"Stone Ass." The next morning talks resumed, this time with Marshall
present. The president still feared that Hitler and Stalin might reach
some sort of rapprochement. He was after all looking at a man who
only a little more than two and a half years before had sat down in
Moscow next to the German foreign minister, Joachim von Ribbentrop, with Stalin as a witness, and signed the Russo-German peace
pact. FDR put the question to Marshall: could the United States "say to
Mr. Stalin that we were preparing a second front?" Marshall, recognizing that the answer struck at the heart of America's future intentions in
Europe, was slow to respond but finally answered, "Yes." Roosevelt
turned to Molotov and said that he could now assure Stalin, "we expect
the formation of a second front this year." Were they talking about the
same thing? FDR did not specify where such a "second front" might
occur—somewhere in Europe as Molotov presumed, or somewhere
else, maybe North Africa as Churchill wanted? And was the president
thinking in terms of thirty-five divisions, or something on the modest
scale of Sledgehammer, maybe five Allied divisions at most? Under
this cloudy understanding, Molotov departed. On a later occasion,
Churchill asked Stalin if he knew what Molotov had done in his free
time in the United States. Stalin answered, "The only surprise to me is
that he did not go to Chicago where he could have gotten in with the
other gangsters."

ON JUNE 19, 1942, FDR sat in his manually controlled Ford Phaeton
alongside a primitive landing strip near Hyde Park watching a small
aircraft drop from the sky and come to a bumpy halt practically next to
the car. Out stepped a stubby figure waving a cigar. Winston Churchill
was making his second wartime visit to the United States. As he entered
the Ford, FDR took off with a start, proudly demonstrating the hand
controls as he took the prime minister on a breakneck tour of the Roo-

sevelt estate, trying to give his Secret Service escort the slip. Noting Churchill's tenseness, FDR told him to relax as he whipped around hairpin curves. He asked Churchill to feel the muscle in his right arm while he steered with the other hand. He had biceps, he said, that a boxing champ had envied. Arriving at the Roosevelt family seat, the president led the prime minister through rooms of homey furnishings, brass sculptures of Scotty dogs, paintings of sailing ships, and an easel with an enormous portrait of FDR's mother. They entered a nook off the portico, the Snuggery. Roosevelt pointed out a new gadget, a twelve-inch RCA television set with a magnifying glass in front to enlarge the picture. On first receiving the set, Roosevelt had for a few minutes watched flickering images beamed from an experimental station in New York and then lost interest.

On Sunday, after breakfast, Churchill handed Roosevelt a memo-randum prepared by the prime minister's staff, again raising doubts about Sledgehammer. Britain, the report read, "would not favor an op-eration that was certain to lead to disaster for it would not help the Russians . . . and expose to Nazi vengeance the French population in-volved." FDR was not yet ready to fold. Later, while Churchill splashed happily in a warm bath, the president called in his naval aide, Captain McCrea, and began to dictate a message that the captain was to phone to Marshall and King. Did they think Sledgehammer could work? "If you answer in the affirmative, I will press it vigorously with the Brit-ish." He went on, "I do not believe we can wait until 1943 to strike at Germany." That month *Time* magazine noted that six months after Pearl Harbor the United States had "not taken a single inch of enemy territory, not yet beaten the enemy in a major battle on land, nor yet opened an offensive campaign." The president then proposed an alter-native to his chiefs that would have warmed Churchill's heart. If Sledgehammer could not be carried off, "then we must attack at an-other point. Gymnast might not be decisive, but it would hurt Ger-many."

During Churchill's Hyde Park stay, FDR had spent a sleepless night wrestling with unresolved decisions. In the morning, he had himself wheeled, unannounced, into the bathroom where Churchill was again soaking in a tub. Later, describing the encounter to his secretary, Grace Tully, he noted impishly, "you know, Grace . . . he's pink and white all over." Tully, upon seeing a photo of Churchill's infant grandson, remarked that the child "is certainly a dead ringer for you." Churchill answered, "Quite, Miss Tully, but you know I look like all babies and all babies look like me." At another point, he wrote of the impression FDR had made on him, describing "His powerful torso and leonine head, in such vivid contrast to his handicap, of which he seemed to take no notice at all, to the point that others were not overly conscious of it, his animated features and strong but melodious voice."

Upon the two leaders' return to Washington on June 21, Churchill called Sir Alan Brooke, telling him to come to the White House at once. Upon entering FDR's study, Brooke, still wearing rumpled weekend tweeds, apologized "for being so badly dressed." FDR answered, "Why not take your coat off like I have, you will feel far more comfortable." From then on, Brooke, while still unimpressed by America's military leaders, became smitten with Roosevelt. He also revealed a subtle insight into the American character. "Accustomed to their vast pioneer [past] and expanding economy, to setting themselves impossible targets and then going all out to achieve them," he wrote in his diary, "they could not understand the hesitations of their allies. To them, ifs and delays were merely signs of half-heartedness." The American objective was simply to win the war, Brooke understood, and the sooner the better. The British objective was to win the war in a way that would preserve his country's greatness and empire. Brooke also discerned a difference between FDR and Churchill in their behavior toward their generals. "The President had no great military knowledge and was aware of this fact and consequently relied on Marshall," Brooke noted. Further, Marshall did not shrink from knocking down FDR's cockeyed ideas. "My position was very different," Brooke admitted. "Winston never had the slightest doubt that he had inherited all the military genius of his great ancestor, Marlborough," the eighteenth-century victor at Blenheim. He continuously hatched schemes from the brilliant to the far-fetched, the latter not easily derailed by Brooke.

That Sunday morning, Captain McCrea had gone to the Map

Room to check the overnight cables. He was preparing to leave when an aide handed him a freshly decoded message. McCrea read it with a frown and headed for FDR's second-floor study where the president, Churchill, and Brooke were having breakfast. On arriving, McCrea wordlessly handed FDR the message. Roosevelt, nimbly shifting from his wheelchair to the seat behind his desk, began reading. With a somber expression he handed it back to McCrea, who gave the cable to the prime minister. As McCrea recalled the moment, "Churchill's pink cheeks faded visibly." Rommel, the Desert Fox, had taken the British fortress of Tobruk in Libya. "I can't understand it," an anguished Churchill said. "I simply can't understand it." Here was a disaster matching the humiliation of Singapore where British troops had surrendered to a far smaller Japanese force. Now Rommel's outnumbered soldiers were herding 30,000 British Tommies into POW cages. For this victory, Hitler subsequently elevated Rommel to field marshal.

Roosevelt reacted without hesitating: "What can we do to help?" Brooke later wrote, "I remember vividly being impressed by the fact and real heartfelt sympathy that lay behind those words." Churchill's reply was swift: "Give us as many Sherman tanks as you can spare and ship them to the Middle East as soon as possible." Roosevelt summoned Marshall and repeated Churchill's request. The general was visibly disconcerted. "Mr. President," he said, "the Shermans are only just coming into production, the first few hundred have been issued to our own armored divisions. . . . It is a terrible thing to take weapons out of a soldier's hands." Roosevelt's Dutch jaw jutted and Marshall shifted his tone. "Nevertheless," he said, "if the British need is so great, they must have them." The decision nearly denuded American armored forces as 300 tanks were loaded aboard the fastest freighters available. When a ship carrying the tanks' engines was torpedoed off Bermuda, Roosevelt ordered Marshall to send out another shipload.

That same Sunday, Harry Hopkins stopped by to see Churchill. "There are a couple of American officers the President would like you to meet," he said. At 5 P.M. Generals Dwight David Eisenhower and Mark Clark were ushered into the prime minister's room. He later recorded his reaction. "I was immediately impressed by these remarkable but hitherto unknown men." The conversation turned to the merits of a cross-Channel invasion. The debacle at Tobruk worked in Churchill's favor. The defeat shifted attention, for the moment, from crossing the Channel to salvaging the Mediterranean. Four meetings were held that Sunday, each ending with Churchill hammering home his point: Morocco and Algeria must be invaded. Of course, he reassured the Americans, doing so would complement and not displace the invasion of France. Marshall was not deceived. A shift to North Africa, he knew, would drastically drain logistical support for Bolero, the mobilization for a cross-Channel campaign in 1943. His hopes sank further when, after the final gathering that day, FDR asked him to stay behind. What did Marshall think, the president asked, of dispatching a large American force to gain control of the Middle East from Egypt to Iran? That, he told the president, "was an overthrow of everything they had been planning for." In a rare exhibition of emotion, he refused to discuss the matter further and stalked out. Weeks before, he and Admiral King had sent the president a tightly reasoned, five-page, single-spaced analysis of Gymnast's pitfalls, concluding, "The occupation of Northwest Africa this summer should not be attempted." Now the president was talking about moving even further afield. As Churchill prepared to leave Washington, Marshall made another impassioned plea to FDR. "The operation, Gymnast," he said, "has been studied and restudied. It is a poor substitute for Bolero." A month later, FDR again sent Marshall and Hopkins to London, this time with Admiral King, to reargue with the British chiefs of staff the case at least for the small-scale operation in France that year. After fruitless debate, his envoys cabled Roosevelt that the British were adamant. Sledgehammer in 1942 was dead. They now fell back to the next battle line, to salvage Bolero for 1943.

IN MID-1942, FDR APPROVED Marshall's creation of a new command, the European Theater of Operations, United States Army. To command ETOUSA he jumped over a long list of senior officers to pick a man who had never commanded troops in battle, who had never heard a shot fired in anger, who had never gone to war. He had earlier brought

Dwight Eisenhower into the War Department within days of Pearl Harbor, and though grudging in praise, Marshall quickly recognized the wisdom of his choice. Upon public announcement of a chief of the ETOUSA command on June 25, the press instantly seized upon the news as signaling "definite plans for a second front" to be launched from Britain. Within a month of Eisenhower's appointment, readers of *Life* opened the magazine to find a half page photo of an affable-looking soldier in khakis leaning back in his chair, and gesturing with a cigarette. The story identified Eisenhower as a "big, bland Kansan," and "the closest thing the United States has to a Pershing in this war." When he set up headquarters in London's Grosvenor Square, the area was instantly dubbed "Eisenhower Platz."

Ike, now fifty-one, was in his twenty-seventh year in the Army. Nothing in his origins foretold a career in the military. The first Eisenhauer (the original spelling) to come to America was Hans Nicholas, who emigrated to Pennsylvania from Elterbach, Germany, in 1741, part of a migration of persecuted Mennonites who sought refuge in the United States. Mennonites were uncompromising pacifists. Jacob Eisenhauer, the general's grandfather, prospered in Pennsylvania as a hardworking, thrifty, God-fearing farmer, whose holdings were appraised at a handsome $13,000 before the Civil War. Jacob, bearded as an Old Testament prophet, abhorred slavery and supported Lincoln, yet as a pacifist would not fight in the war. After peace returned, he moved the family to Kansas where great tracts of land could be had cheaply. The family, now called "Eisenhower," settled near Abilene, a town only recently emerging from its Wild West past when cheap hotels, barrooms, gambling halls, and bordellos lined its unpaved streets. As in Pennsylvania, Jacob prospered, branching out from farming to real estate, banking, and starting a creamery. His wife bore him six sons who lived to maturity; the eldest, David, would become Ike's father. David Eisenhower could have enjoyed a prosperous if hardworking life had he bent to his father's will. As with all his sons, Jacob promised David $2,000 and 160 acres of good farmland when he married. But David detested farming. He went off instead to a small religious college, Lane University in Kansas. There he met a bright, strong-willed woman with the independence of mind to enter college from a culture that eyed educated women with suspicion. Soon after, David and Ida Stover married. She was eventually drawn to the Jehovah's Witnesses, another sect, like the Mennonites, that opposed war. Thus, on both sides of his family, Dwight Eisenhower descended from pacifists.

David's unwillingness to till the soil meant that his family lived for a time in circumstances bordering on destitution. He failed as a merchant, then left Abilene for Denison, Texas, leaving his wife and first child, Arthur, behind. There, he found menial work in the railroad yards greasing the rolling stock and other machinery. Ida eventually joined him in a run-down, soot-streaked house, more like a shack, located near the yards. There, a second son, Edgar, was born, and, on October 14, 1890, a third, Dwight. After four years, Jacob, the Eisenhower patriarch, came to Denison to see for himself how his firstborn was faring, and was so appalled that he took the family back to Abilene. Jacob installed David as plant manager in the Belle Springs Creamery, which he had helped found, a job his son would hold for the rest of his life. Subsequently, four more sons were born, Roy, Earl, Milton, and Paul, who died in infancy. Dwight Eisenhower would have almost no memories of his Texas childhood.

The eight-member family lived from paycheck to paycheck in a crowded house lacking indoor plumbing in which smoking, dancing, and card playing were banned. As Ike would later remember those days, "we were poor. But the glory of America is that we didn't know it then. I didn't know it because so was everybody around us." His parents, though strict, were loving, caring, and he never heard "a cross word pass between them." Dwight began his education in a one-room schoolhouse where he displayed a gift for mathematics and writing and became enamored of history, especially the battles of the ancient Greeks and Romans. Sports, however, were his consuming passion. All the Eisenhower boys were athletes, Edgar having been voted the best football player in school. Dwight too was a natural, a fierce competitor at baseball and football, the latter a game that he would never cease to love. He did make one appearance on stage as Launcelot Gobbo, Shylock's clownish servant, in *The Merchant of Venice*, earning a review as "the best amateur humorous character on the Abilene stage in this generation." Fistfights were common in Abilene schoolyards and Dwight proved a bare-knuckled scrapper, though he claimed he never looked for trouble. All in all, Eisenhower led a Huck Finn boyhood. Yet beneath the easygoing facade lurked a steely determination and an explosive temper not always disciplined. He became "Ike" in high school and it stuck for life.

We look to the boy for the seeds of the man. All his life, Eisenhower was to display a near fanatic sense of responsibility. One day he had been whittling and put the knife on a windowsill in his father's toolshed. His three-year-old brother, Earl, whom he was supposed to be watching, climbed on a chair, fell, and the blade pierced the child's eye. Nearly sixty years later, Eisenhower expressed "my feeling of regret . . . heightened by a sense of guilt" for failing in his responsibility. He proved an indefatigable worker, toiling as a farmhand, laboring amid the din of a factory that made steel grain bins, and in the creamery with his father, wrestling blocks of ice for hours, then switching to the baking heat of the company's furnace room. He won the unlikely friendship of Bob Davis, an illiterate woodsman and guide, who taught Ike how to duck hunt, fly-fish, survive in the wild, and play winning poker. The science of the game, as Davis taught it, not drawing to a four-card flush in a two-man game with an opponent who had openers, came naturally to young Eisenhower. Calculating the percentages, figuring the odds, measuring the risks, became ingrained in his decision making for life.

He never intended to stay in Abilene. But as one of six boys, and with brother Edgar already off to college, he lacked the money to escape. A friend, Everett "Swede" Hazlett, had applied to Annapolis, which sparked Ike's interest principally because the Naval Academy offered a free education. In an early display of resourcefulness, he began to pry letters of recommendation from everybody who was anybody in Abilene. To expand his odds, he took the examination for both Annapolis and West Point. He came in second for the Naval Academy. When the boy who came in first failed his physical, Ike stood in line for the appointment. Kansas senator Joseph Bristow, for unexplained reasons, decided that young Eisenhower was better suited for West Point. For his parents, Ike's acceptance at a prestigious institution stirred mixed feelings. They abominated war and their boy was going off to become a warrior. His mother broke down in tears as he boarded the train east.

He arrived at the citadel looming over the Hudson River in the summer of 1911 with $5 in his pocket, one of 285 plebes. Beast Barracks, with upperclassmen barking inane, mean-spirited orders, was his introduction to academy life. "We were all harassed and at times resentful," Ike remembered, tempted to take "the next train out." His resentment faded when the entire class assembled on West Point's Plain to be sworn in as cadets. As a "raw-boned, gawky Kansas boy from the farm country," he later remembered, "when we raised our right hands and repeated the official oath . . . a feeling came over me that the expression 'the United States of America' would now henceforth mean something different. . . . From here on it would be the nation I was serving not myself."

The high-spirited plebe racked up a perilous number of demerits for keeping a messy room, arriving late for chapel, violating the dress code, smoking, and gambling. He indulged a mischievous streak. Ordered to report to an upperclassman in dress coat, he showed up in nothing else. At one point the academy commandant broke him from cadet sergeant to private for dancing "improperly." He went "over the wall" to a nearby town to a soda fountain, which, if discovered, could have meant expulsion. The onetime high school sports star had built himself up to a muscle-hard 174 pounds over a five-foot-eleven frame, an aggressive, smart, fierce competitor bent on football glory. It was not to be. In a game against Tufts, he suffered an excruciating twisted knee followed shortly afterward by a horseback injury doing further damage to the cartilage, tendons, and ligaments. His football—and baseball—playing days were over.

One incident at the academy illuminates the Eisenhower character in the making. As an upperclassman, he began hazing a plebe who accidentally bumped into him. Assuming the traditional bullying, bellowing stance, Ike laid into the cadet. "Mr. Dumgard," he shouted, "what is your P.C.S.?"—West Point jargon for Previous Condition of Servitude. "You look like a barber," he said. The youth responded sheepishly, "I *was* a barber, Sir." Ike returned to his quarters and announced to his roommate, "I've just done something that was stupid and unforgivable. I managed to make a man ashamed of the work he did." He never hazed another plebe. He graduated in 1915, ranked a respectable 61st in a class of 164. Unlike MacArthur, he never fully applied his considerable intelligence in pursuit of academic laurels. He had no desire, he said, to be judged a grind and preferred to be seen as one of the guys, respected, well liked, and not above his fellows.

He was commissioned a second lieutenant in the infantry a year after the world had been plunged into the Great War, which had not yet included America. He was posted to the 19th Infantry Regiment at Fort Sam Houston, Texas. There he met a pert, saucy eighteen-year-old debutante, Mamie Geneva Doud, daughter of a wealthy Denver meatpacker who rented a mansion for his family in warm San Antonio for the winter months. Mamie Doud was spoiled, accustomed to grand homes, servants, chic parties, and traveling in the family's huge electric automobile. Eisenhower, at this time, was an essentially penniless Army officer of the lowest commissioned rank. Still, the magnetism between them proved strong. Despite the economic gulf, Ike won over Mamie's parents, who detected the mettle beneath the affable facade. The couple was married on July 1, 1916, in the Douds' Denver home, Ike resplendent in his dress white uniform, Mamie in white lace.

Eisenhower suffered professional frustration during the early years of his career. While fellow West Pointers had gone south in 1916 on the punitive expedition to capture the Mexican revolutionary Pancho Villa, Eisenhower received a lackluster assignment as instructor for an Illinois National Guard unit and coached football at a boys' school. When, on April 6, 1917, President Woodrow Wilson led the United States into the First World War, to "make the world safe for democracy," Eisenhower awaited what every career infantry officer wants, combat command, rapid promotion, and the opportunity to become a hero. Instead, while Douglas MacArthur and George Patton were reaping these very rewards in France, Ike was made supply officer for the newly formed 52nd Infantry. After repeatedly failing to win a transfer, an overjoyed Ike was finally ordered to train for battle with the Army's newest innovation, tank warfare. His unit was scheduled to be sent to France in November 1918. On November 11, Eisenhower awoke to the cheers of doughboys shouting that the war was over. Postwar, he continued with the tank corps, which brought him into contact with the wounded and decorated Patton. The two hit it off immediately, consumed by a shared conviction that in pioneering the tank they stood in the vanguard of modern warfare. On one occasion the enthusiasts disassembled a tank, including the engine, and put it back together in perfect running order.

Ike was by now a doting father. His son, christened Doud Dwight, and called Little Ike, turned three in 1920. Eisenhower spent every free moment with the boy, hoisting him on his shoulders to watch football games, parades, and mock battles between roaring, smoke-belching tanks. Ike's fellow officers presented the child with a miniature tanker's uniform and made him their mascot. Just before Christmas in 1920, Little Ike came down with scarlet fever, caught apparently from the family's maid. The boy never recovered and died in his father's arms two days into the new year. The loss to both parents was devastating and permanent. Forty-five years later, Ike wrote in his memoirs, "Today when I think of it . . . the keenness of our loss comes back to me as fresh and as terrible as it was in that long dark day soon after Christmas 1920."

Eisenhower continued to trudge the milestones of the peacetime army, attending the prestigious Command and General Staff School at Fort Leavenworth, Kansas, where he graduated first in his class, then the Army War College at Fort McNair, the capstone of every ambitious career officer's education. In 1930 his path took a fateful turn. He was spotted by the then Army chief of staff, Douglas MacArthur, and in 1932 became MacArthur's personal assistant. When FDR sent MacArthur to the Philippines as chief military advisor to the commonwealth in 1935, Eisenhower went with him. There he toiled under this military narcissist's near overpowering ego, until he finally managed to extricate himself in the fall of 1939. Filipino president Manuel Quezon had tried to lure Ike to stay on with an offer of a $100,000 annuity, not perhaps in MacArthur's league, but munificent enough. Ike was more tempted by a totally unexpected opportunity that had considerable humane appeal. As Nazi persecution drove more and more Jews out of Germany, Jewish leaders offered Eisenhower a $60,000-a-year salary, ten times his Army pay, to resign his commission and travel Asia in search of countries willing to take in the refugees. He turned down the offer. The vow he had taken on the Plain at West Point was to remain his calling.

The Eisenhower marriage was not unruffled. When, before the Philippines assignment, Ike had been posted to sweltering, bug-infested, disease-ridden Panama with its bats, cockroaches, snakes, and mildew, Mamie stuck it out as long as she could bear it, then left for her family's home in Denver to have her second baby, John, born on August 3, 1922. Describing the Panama posting she once said, "I could hear the monkeys scream in the jungle and I felt like screaming too." Again, and for similar reasons, she stalled for a year before joining Ike in the Philippines. Long separations would continue to stress the marriage, particularly in the years to come.

AFTER FDR LEARNED THAT Sledgehammer was dead, he remained determined that American troops must be fighting somewhere in 1942. At this point, Marshall and King attempted what can be described as strategic blackmail. King heaped scorn on the British, saying that they would never invade Europe, "except behind a Scotch bagpipe band." On July 10, while FDR relaxed at Hyde Park, Marshall sent him a message saying that if the British opposed an Allied landing on the continent in 1942, "it is our opinion that we should turn to the Pacific and strike decisively at Japan." Roosevelt's reply was swift and emphatic. He scribbled his reply to Marshall on a pad of White House stationery: "that is exactly what Germany hoped the United States would do after Pearl Harbor. . . . It does not in fact provide use of American troops in fighting except in a lot of islands whose occupation will not affect the world situation." And finally, "It does not help Russia." Marshall's alternative was "disapproved as of the present." He signed with a flourish, "Roosevelt C in C," making clear who was in command.

On July 30, FDR summoned Admiral Leahy in his role as chairman of the JCS and instructed him to deliver jarring news to the chiefs. Gymnast, the invasion of North Africa, was on. It is "now our principal objective," FDR emphasized. The president's decision appalled his military leaders. Eisenhower complained bitterly, "I'm right back to December 15," 1941, the time when, while in the War Plans Division, he had first pressed for the cross-Channel invasion. Roosevelt's choice of North Africa over Europe struck Ike as the "blackest day in history." FDR, though surrounded by gold braid and gold stars, had made manifest in this first far-reaching decision who ultimately decided U.S. strategy. Prussian general Carl Philipp Gottfried von Clausewitz, the venerated military thinker, would likely have questioned FDR's judgment. Clausewitz preached "always to be very strong: first in general and then at the decisive point." To American military leaders, North Africa hardly seemed a decisive point. Gymnast was renamed Torch, and planning began in earnest.

ADMIRAL KING BELIEVED THAT THERE EXISTED a special bond between himself and FDR. "Many times in his study at the White House, especially when Churchill was there," King recollected, "I would not say anything but when the President would look at me, I would shake my head slightly so that other people would not see it." Stimson, the secretary of war, saw a different King. As he wrote in his diary, after a strategy session with the president, "King wobbled around in a way that made me rather sick with him. He is firm and brave outside the White House, but as soon as he gets in the presence of the President, he crumbles up."

War in the Pacific had been relegated to a defensive role, principally to protect Australia and New Zealand from the Japanese southward sweep. Roosevelt was never comfortable with a static posture. He wanted in the Pacific what he had just ordered for North Africa: U.S. troops on the offensive, striking back. He had a natural ally in King. The admiral had grudgingly bowed to the Europe First decision. But, as he wrote his fellow chiefs in May 1942, "the Pacific problem is no less so, and is certainly more urgent—it must be faced *now*." King was convinced of the need to safeguard the two former British colonies, which he described as "white man's country." They must not be overrun "because of the repercussions among the non-white races of the world."

During the summer of 1942, King and FDR studied the charts on the Map Room wall and began hatching an offensive campaign for the Pacific. The island of Guadalcanal in the Solomon Islands, ninety miles long, twenty-five miles wide, and 1,000 miles northeast of Australia, held a certain appeal. Though thinly populated and economically insignificant, its occupation by the Japanese could prove disastrous. Commander Rochefort and his code breakers discovered that the Japanese were building an airfield on Guadalcanal and its expected completion by August would enable enemy bombers to seize control over the shipping lanes through which tens of thousands of American troops were pouring in for the defense of Australia. FDR and King decided that Guadalcanal presented the place to strike even before Marshall and the rest of the JCS were brought into the picture. King directed Chester Nimitz, in whose sector Guadalcanal lay, to prepare for the invasion.

Douglas MacArthur had been pressing for the logistics to support his own offensive all along, charging that his Southwest Pacific command was being starved of matériel. His complaint was not groundless. The Pacific was never to receive more than 15 percent of the nation's war output. After the victory at Midway, MacArthur had sent Marshall a blast accusing Washington of failing to back him adequately. "Not just the fate of Australia was at stake," he argued, "but the United States itself will face a threat of proportions as she has never faced in the long years of its existence." The invasion of Guadalcanal, outside his control, would provide little solace to MacArthur. The Marines, under FDR's beloved Navy, would do the job. To lead the attack, Roosevelt chose Major General Alexander Archer "Archie" Vandegrift, another officer who had caught FDR's eye some twenty-five years before when the Marine was a scrappy thirty-year-old captain.

On the morning of August 7, 1942, Rear Admiral Richmond Kelly

Turner, commander of the Guadalcanal landing force, standing on the bridge of the troop transport *McCawley*, raised his binoculars and pronounced the island "a truly beautiful sight that morning." A Marine officer described Guadalcanal rapturously: "Blue green mountains towering into a brilliant tropical sky all crowned with cloud masses. . . . The dark green of jungle growth blends into the softer greens and browns of coconut groves and grassy plains and ridges." Given the signal, 16,000 green-clad Marines began clambering down sagging rope nets into Higgins boats, which could deposit the troops ashore in three feet of water. In the first hours, the landing went unopposed.

On the night of August 8–9, the day after the Marines landed, a Japanese fleet commanded by an intrepid admiral, Gunichi Mikawa, entered the channel between Guadalcanal and Savo Island determined to oust the invaders. Though the night was black, Mikawa pushed his ships at perilous speed and caught the American fleet patrolling the beachhead off guard. After a half hour of Mikawa's well-aimed torpedoes and pinpoint shelling, four heavy cruisers had been destroyed, three American and one Australian. The Japanese attack left 1,023 men dead and another thousand struggling to survive in oil-slicked, shark-infested waters. No Japanese ships were lost. Two days later, the duty officer woke Admiral King aboard his flagship/residence, the *Dauntless*. Told of the magnitude of the defeat, King refused to believe it. He handed the message back and told the officer, "They must have decoded the dispatch wrong. Tell them to decode it again." The report proved accurate. After the battle, Captain McCrea, with King's confirmation in hand, broke the news to FDR, at Shangri-La in Maryland's Catoctin Mountains, a former summer camp for children and at that time a training retreat for budding spies in the OSS (today's Camp David). Savo Island represented the worst disaster that the Navy had suffered in history, a sorry beginning for the campaign that the president and King had spawned.

The Marines may have waded ashore in safety on August 7, but there the cakewalk ended. The Japanese had deeply entrenched themselves and expended their lives in suicidal charges against the Marines before yielding an inch. Besides the enemy, the Marines, joined by

Army infantry, fought sapping heat, torrential rains, mud, and swarms of malarial mosquitoes. Six months later, the battle still raged.

Out of Guadalcanal came a story that tickled FDR. A Marine allegedly complained that he had never had the chance "to kill a Jap." His commanding officer told him to climb a nearby hill and shout, "To Hell with Emperor Hirohito." That should bring the enemy out of hiding. The Marine did so and a Japanese soldier came out of the jungle shouting, "To Hell with Roosevelt!" The Marine didn't shoot him, as he later explained to his buddies, because, "I couldn't kill a Republican!" The president regaled his visitors with the story at every opportunity.

CHAPTER 10

Sea War, Air War

On August 14, 1942, a Map Room aide brought FDR a cable marked "Personal for the President's eyes only." Roosevelt's envoy to the Kremlin, Averell Harriman, was reporting on Churchill's bitter experience after traveling to Moscow to court Joseph Stalin, a mission the prime minister later described as "like carrying a large lump of ice to the North Pole." The Western Allies had led the Soviet premier to believe that their armies would invade Europe in 1942, thus sparing the Red Army from facing the Wehrmacht alone. Thanks to FDR's yielding to Churchill to invade North Africa first, Europe was not going to happen. Harriman went on to say, "Stalin took issue at every point with bluntness almost to the point of insult." The Soviet leader told Churchill "that we had broken our promise about Sledgehammer." Stalin then taunted the prime minister "about being too much afraid of fighting the Germans, and if we tried it like the Russians, we would not find it so bad." In succeeding sessions Churchill tried to convince Stalin that France was not the only place to strike at Germany. He tore a sheet of paper from a pad and drew Stalin a crude sketch of a crocodile. "Why stick your mouth in the crocodile's mouth," he asked, "when you can go to the Mediterranean and rip his soft underbelly?" He began to tick off the benefits. First a North African campaign would "hit Rommel in the back; second, Spain would be . . . disinclined to back Germany; third, it could instigate fighting against the German occupiers in France; and fourth, it would "expose Italy to the whole brunt of the war." Churchill in his own report to FDR spoke of informing Stalin of the death of Sledgehammer. "I am sure that the disappointing news I brought could not have been imported except by me personally," he wrote. Now they know the worst." On August 16, as the prime minister's party boarded a Liberator bomber to fly home, Field Marshal Sir Archibald Wavell, who had earlier commanded British forces in the Middle East, recited, to Churchill's wry amusement, a ballad he had composed:

> *Prince of the Kremlin, here's a fond farewell.*
> *I've had to deal with many worse than you.*
> *You took it though you hated it like hell;*
> *No second front in 1942.*

Soon after Churchill's return, and seemingly proving his point about the folly of a cross-Channel operation in 1942, came word of Dieppe. The operation, code-named Jubilee, was designed to make an amphibious landing across the English Channel at the French port city, putting over 6,000 men ashore to test landing tactics and equipment, particularly a new vessel, the Landing Craft Tank or LCT, to see if off-loaded tanks could make it across open beaches. Though the raid had never been intended as a permanent incursion, its outcome might serve as a dress rehearsal for a full-scale invasion of the continent. The mission was assigned essentially to the Canadian 2nd Division with some British and American Rangers participating.

The landing took place in the half-lit dawn of August 19 and ended eight hours later in unmitigated disaster. The Germans had reacted swiftly, scattering and driving the invaders back into the sea. An eyewitness report by a Canadian correspondent described "Wild scenes that crowded helter-skelter one upon another in crazy sequence" as the attackers "stormed through the flashing inferno of Nazi defenses." The final Canadian tally was over 1,000 dead, 633 wounded, and 2,547 missing or captured, 67 percent of the attacking force. Soon after, a relieved FDR learned that only four of the fifty American Rangers who had taken part in the debacle failed to get back to England. However short-term its intent, the failure of Dieppe was a slap at Marshall's vigorously argued case that Allied forces could stay on the continent. To Churchill, the failure of Jubilee in France vindicated the decision to launch Torch in North Africa.

DWIGHT EISENHOWER HAD INITIALLY GONE to London as chief only of the American forces in Europe. On August 6, 1942, FDR, with British consent, vastly expanded his authority, appointing him Commander-in-Chief, Allied Expeditionary Forces. Like people in positions of power who must endure the blandishments of sycophants, the machinations of rivals, the clash of outsize egos, the power grabs, the ideas promoted, the ingenious along with the scatterbrained, he needed one person with whom he could let his hair down and confide thoughts never to be repeated elsewhere. For Ike this person was Navy commander Harry Butcher. The Eisenhowers and Butchers had been friends in the States for sixteen years, since Ike was a major. Butcher had risen at CBS to become a vice president. Their wives now lived across from each other in the same Washington apartment building. Ike had managed to persuade a puzzled Ernie King to assign "Butch" to London as his naval aide. Besides serving as confidant, sounding board, public relations fixer, and bridge partner, Ike directed Butcher to keep a diary, so that "I can tell you everything that happened." "Butcher's job is simple," Ike remarked. "It is to keep me from going crazy." The diary, published after the war, would provide a remarkably candid insider view of the Eisenhower camp.

One of Butcher's earliest duties was to find a retreat from the commotion at Ike's London headquarters on Grosvenor Square. He located a tiny house, Telegraph Cottage, twenty-five minutes from London on a private road adjoining a golf course where Ike could escape occasionally to play a few holes. Butcher rented the house for $32 a week. Kay Summersby, Eisenhower's British driver, said it was "as picturesque as an English Christmas card." One of Ike's early visitors to Telegraph Cottage was his old tanker comrade George Patton, who wrote to his wife, Beatrice, that "Ike was fine," but he was disturbed that he "spoke of lunch as 'tiffin,' gasoline as 'petrol' and of antiaircraft as 'flack.' I truly fear that London has conquered Abilene." He also wrote Beatrice, "if there are any pretty women in England they must have died. They are hideous." One exception was the striking Summersby, born Kathleen McCarthy-Morrogh, daughter of a retired British army officer, raised in County Cork, Ireland, as she put it, in an "obsolete world." Kay had gone to London and, after a fling as a fashion model and movie extra, and a failed marriage, joined the Motor Transport Corps the day after Britain went to war. While chauffeuring several high-ranking Americans, she was handed a trip ticket to pick up an American general she had never heard of named Dwight Eisenhower. Soon, Eisenhower took her on as his permanent driver and Kay Summersby found herself, along with Butcher and Ike's personal aide, Sergeant Mickey McKeogh, a member of the general's inner circle. In her later memoir, Summersby described a small party held at Telegraph Cottage to celebrate Eisenhower's fifty-second birthday where he was given a black Scottie pup as a present. Everyone tried suggesting names for the dog. According to Summersby's account, Ike suddenly shouted, "I've got it." The pup was to be called "Telek." When asked why, he answered, "It's a combination of Telegraph Cottage and Kay. Two parts of my life that make me very happy." Contact between officers and women had to be carefully calibrated during the war. While Eisenhower was in London, General Marshall gigged Major General Lewis Brereton, commanding general of the U.S. Army Air Forces in the Middle East, warning that he had information "indicating that your relations with your secretary have given rise to facetious and derogatory gossip. . . . I wish you to release your secretary and if practicable see that she returns to her permanent residence." Thus far, nothing had given rise to any such speculation about Eisenhower and Summersby, who was widely regarded as intelligent, competent, and good company.

EISENHOWER'S APPROACH AS COMMANDER of forces representing several nations and military branches began to emerge early. As one observer put it, "Few who watched him carefully indulged the fantasy that he was a genial, open, barefoot boy from Abilene who just happened to be in the right place when lightning struck." One constant was Eisenhower's determination to make his diverse subordinates pull together, as he put it, "like a football team." He wrote his son that warfare at the highest echelon was "no longer just a question of going out and teaching soldiers how to shoot or how to crawl up a ravine or dig a foxhole—it is partly politics, partly public speaking, partly essay writing, partly social contact." According to one durable tale, after a fracas between one of his men and a British officer, Ike broke the American and sent him home. The Briton protested, "He only called me a son of a bitch, Sir." "I am informed," Eisenhower is said to have answered, "that he called you a British son of a bitch. That is quite different."

WHILE FDR WAS IMPATIENT to see Americans fighting Germans abroad, he still feared subversion, sabotage, and espionage at home. Was it not by subverting France, Belgium, the Netherlands from within, he believed, that Hitler's victories had come so cheaply? Operation Pastorius, named for the first German immigrant to come to America in 1683, confirmed his suspicions. Eight Germans, two of them American citizens, who had all lived in America had returned to Germany lured by the prospect of prospering in a resurgent fatherland under Nazism. The eight were recruited by the Abwehr, the German intelligence service, and underwent training in tactics to sabotage the American war machine. Once trained, they boarded U-boat 202, the *Innsbruck,* armed with drawings of key American bridges, railroad yards, the New York City water supply system, the Niagara Falls hydroelectric plant, and other vital installations. They carried the then formidable sum of $174,000 in American currency to cover expenses and bribes. The eight were split into two teams, one to land in Florida; the other, under George Dasch, a former itinerant waiter in America, was rowed ashore on June 13, 1942, during a fog-shrouded, pitch-black night on Long Island near Amagansett. Their ineptitude was stunning. John C. Cullen, a twenty-one-year-old rookie Coast Guardsman, armed with only a flashlight, spotted four men emerging from the mist. Dasch pulled a gun, shoved $250 into Cullen's hand, and ordered him to "Forget about this." Cullen hightailed it back to the Coast Guard station and reported this bizarre encounter to his superiors, who brought in the FBI.

The would-be saboteurs made it to New York City where they began Pastorius with a night on the town, squandering the Abwehr's money on first-class hotels, expensive restaurants, fancy clothes, and women. Dasch, with the debacle at Amagansett still fresh in his mind, decided that if they turned themselves in they would be greeted as heroes and might even be presented to the president. From their hotel he phoned the FBI insisting that he had to talk directly to J. Edgar Hoover. Less than two days after the landing, Dasch found himself in the bureau's headquarters spilling everything. The rest of his team was easily rounded up, and thanks to Dasch's informing the FBI arrested the other four men, who had put ashore at Ponte Vedra Beach, south of Jacksonville. Hoover reported the arrests to the president as another coup by his agency, omitting the fact that Dasch had surrendered and squealed on his comrades.

FDR might have looked on Pastorius as a clutch of bumblers who never got nearer to an American installation than their hotel bar. He could have had them tried for conspiracy, imprisoned, and deported after the war. Instead he displayed the hardness beneath the congenial exterior. He told his attorney general, Francis Biddle, regarding the two American citizens, "It seems to me that the death penalty is almost obligatory." As for the six German citizens, "this is an absolute parallel of the case of Major [John] André in the Revolutionary War and of Nathan Hale. Both of these men were hanged." Roosevelt further informed Biddle that he wanted all eight tried, not in a civilian court, but by a military tribunal free of the endless appeals and loopholes civilian prosecution afforded. On July 8, the eight defendants were shaved by prison barbers, lest they put the razor to their own wrists, herded into two armored vans, and taken to Assembly Hall #1 on the fifth floor of the Department of Justice where they faced a tribunal of seven generals chosen by FDR and were charged with violating the Articles of War by conspiring to commit espionage and sabotage. Enterprising vendors set up stands selling hot dogs to the crowds that gathered at the department's iron gate to catch a glimpse of the enemy. In twenty-six days the court rendered its verdict. All eight were condemned to death. The president approved the verdicts but reduced Dasch's sentence to thirty years and that of Ernest Burger, a U.S. citizen who had also fingered his erstwhile comrades, to life in prison. On August 8 the other six men were electrocuted on the third floor of the District of Columbia jail. Just eight weeks had elapsed from the time they had slipped from U-boat 202.

The country was with the president. Approving telegrams and letters poured into the White House mail room typified by a mother with three sons in the Army, who wrote, "It's high time we wake up in this country and show the world we are not a bunch of mush hounds."

★

WHILE THE AMERICAN PLANNERS in the European theater were still waging land battles largely on paper, clashes paid for in blood were being fought on the Atlantic, and the Allies were losing. Admiral Karl Dönitz, with his few hundred U-boats, sowed havoc in the shipping lanes that constituted the Allies' lifeline. Contrary to popular impression, most kills were not scored while a submarine lurked unseen beneath the sea. Submerged U-boats could achieve only 7.5 knots. But on the surface at 17.7 knots they could easily position themselves to torpedo merchantmen lumbering along at 6 to 9 knots. In March 1942, German submarines sent 88 tankers and cargo vessels to the bottom. In May a record 120 more were sunk, an average of 4 a day. The U.S. Navy calculated that U-boat sinkings of just two freighters and one tanker equaled the amount of matériel that 3,000 cargo planes could carry. Marshall warned King, "another month or two of this will cripple our means of transport."

An exasperated FDR sent Admiral King a chart comparing losses from ships sailing independently versus those sailing in convoys, 118 sinkings among the former against 20 for the latter. At the bottom of the page he penned, "This furnishes excellent proof of what I have been talking about for many weeks." He ended, "I think it has taken an un-conscionable time to get things going. . . . We must speed things up." Eisenhower, while in the War Plans Division, had written in his diary that King's predecessor, Harold "Betty" Stark, may have been "just a nice old lady," but King was "a deliberately rude person, which means he's a mental bully," and predicted, "this fellow is going to cause a blow-up sooner or later." King had undeniably been sluggish in adopting tactics to protect shipping. As U-boats stalked the American coast, brightly lit cities from Boston to Miami unwittingly provided sharply defined silhouettes of merchantmen for German raiders to torpedo. Night after night, people living along the Atlantic coast watched the flames of stricken ships in their death throes. King, prodded by the president and Marshall, finally managed to have the city lights dark-ened, over the howls of resort owners who feared the effect on the tourist business. Roosevelt continued to pressure King to hasten the convoy system. By April the admiral finally instituted partially escorted convoys, though he complained that he lacked sufficient escort vessels to protect more merchantmen. What he needed, he claimed, was "a very large number—roughly 1,000" destroyer escorts. "I am doing my best to get them quickly," he assured FDR. King's overbearing conduct and foot-dragging did not permanently trouble FDR, who could read-ily have replaced him. While the admiral grated on the nerves of his associates, the president regarded the rasp-tongued Navy chief as a fighter, and in this war that was FDR's imperative.

The layman president proved ahead of King in another naval ini-tiative. Roosevelt told him that he wanted smaller, cheaper aircraft car-riers, CVEs or pocket carriers, sped into production to fight U-boats in the Atlantic and to provide air support in the Pacific. King responded in a reply dated May 15, 1942, that he saw no pressing need for such a vessel. Roosevelt, in his freewheeling style, turned to a go-getter, sixty-year-old Henry J. Kaiser, whose unorthodox methods were cranking out Liberty ships like links of sausages, sometimes in days. Kaiser, on his own, had designed a small carrier and took his sketches to King's Bureau of Ships where this interfering landlubber was thrown out on his ear. The president, nevertheless, gave Kaiser the green light and ordered King to get on board. Throughout the war the CVEs, fast, cheap, and deadly against the enemy, were to vindicate FDR's vision.

BRITISH CODE BREAKERS, operating out of an ugly Victorian stone heap called Bletchley Park, had read every message passing between U-boats and the German naval high command since May 1941. These decrypts were relayed to an underground bunker near the Horse Guards Parade in London where trackers, mostly young women, moved ship models on an ocean map, helping the navy to devise course changes to confound the wolf packs. Disaster, however, struck in February 1942 when German cryptologists added a fourth rotor to their Enigma coding machine, stymieing Bletchley Park. Suddenly, Allied sub hunters were struck deaf, dumb, and blind. There followed the worst ship losses in the Battle of the Atlantic. By the end of 1942, Bletchley Park solved the latest riddle and was again able to warn ships away from U-boats. This breakthrough, together with the dimming of lights along the Atlantic coast, the introduction of convoys, and coordinated air-sea assaults led Admiral Dönitz to confess to the Japanese ambassador, Oshima, that his U-boat losses had begun to spiral perilously.

GENERAL HAP ARNOLD's attitude toward FDR had remained one of near reverence ever since Roosevelt had given Arnold a seat on the JCS, thus making his branch practically coequal with the Army and Navy. In June 1942, Arnold entered the president's study beaming. The United States had been at war for six months and had yet to drop a single bomb on a German target. Arnold told FDR that he was arranging an attack on German airfields in Holland, and added with relish that the raid would take place on the Fourth of July. The target chosen represented exactly the kind of air war FDR wanted to conduct, precision bombing against military installations. Horrified by what the Japanese had done to Chinese cities, the president had appealed to the combatant nations as soon as war broke out in September 1939 to refrain from "the inhumane barbarism of bombing civilians." He believed his approach could work, given America's possession of the Norden bombsight, in effect an early analog computer invented by a Dutch American optical genius. The sight, according to lore, could guide a bomb into a pickle barrel from 30,000 feet. Another tale told was that bombardiers were ordered to wreck the bombsight with a pistol shot if they were going down over enemy territory.

British strategists, with almost three years of air war under their belts by the summer of 1942, took an opposite approach from the president's. They believed in area bombing, essentially a euphemism for indiscriminate raids on population centers. They dismissed the vaunted Norden bombsight. As one RAF officer lectured Arnold, it was far different dropping a dud into a practice circle in the desert on a clear day with no one shooting at you, than trying to hit a target in daylight under hostile fire. Further, the bombsight was blinded by cloud cover. Even in clear weather the device required the bombardier to hold a steady course, without taking evasive action, for a full twenty seconds before releasing the bomb load, making the plane a sitting duck for enemy fighters and for antiaircraft batteries that could hurl flak four miles into the sky. British damage assessment photography revealed abysmal bombing results against factories, bridges, and other pinpoint targets. One out of every five bombs dropped missed its objective by more than a mile. Precision bombing even in broad daylight, the RAF concluded, was a waste of time.

Underscoring this conviction, in February 1942 the British brought back from his Washington post Arthur Harris, portly, mustachioed, a man who could easily pass for a public school headmaster, to take charge as air chief marshal of RAF's Bomber Command. Harris had begun the war as a flier dropping propaganda leaflets, which he came to deride as "toilet paper." He thereafter became an early convert to carpet bombing. Heavy civilian losses, he believed, would break German morale and the raids would likely hit some military targets in the process. Beginning in March 1942, Harris scraped together every flyable bomber, even crews still in training, to send armadas of 1,000 planes against Lübeck in March, Rostock in April, Cologne in May, and Bremen in June. "Give me 20,000 bombers," Harris boasted, "and I will finish Germany in a week." The British populace, their cities still scarred from the Blitz, cheered "Bomber Harris."

The Independence Day raid that Hap Arnold promised FDR proved a modest toe dipping for the American Air Forces in Europe. Twelve Douglas A-20s hit a Dutch airfield and two were lost, a percentage that would not change significantly in the future no matter how many fighter escorts protected the bombers. By July, Arnold began in earnest to marshal his air fleet against occupied Europe. General Carl "Tooey" Spaatz, a disciple of precision bombing, was to command the new U.S. Eighth Air Force flying out of England. Arnold and Spaatz grew up in neighboring towns in Pennsylvania and had met during the First World War. Spaatz, with hawklike features and a pencil-thin mustache, was a dapper, poker-playing, guitar-strumming singer of bawdy songs and more popular with subordinates than the short-fused Arnold. Eisenhower criticized Spaatz on this score, finding him "not tough and hard personally to meet the full requirements of his high position," and too generous in handing out promotions. Heading the Eighth Air Force's bomber command was Ira Eaker, a short Texan, soft-speaking but iron-willed. Spaatz and Eaker traded places running the Eighth in England with Spaatz first in charge until Eaker took over in December 1942.

Arnold and his team believed that the British simply had not understood how to carry out targeted attacks. Hap's boosterism occasionally tried even General Marshall's patience, once prompting him to explode, "I'm tired of hearing from that goddamned high school staff you have down there." FDR, nevertheless, remained in Arnold's corner. Early on he urged him to send his heavy bombers against a sharply defined objective, the German U-boat pens along Brittany and the Bay of Biscay. The bombs, however, failed to penetrate the thick slabs of concrete protecting the subs tied up below.

The weapon that Arnold, Spaatz, and Eaker counted on most was the four-engine B-17, in development since the 1930s. The official debut of the bomber had been ignominious. In 1935 a B-17 flown by the Air Corps's leading test pilot, Major Ployer Peter Hill, crashed before an assemblage of Air Corps and industry leaders, killing Hill and setting back hopes for the plane for months. Successful modifications went forward and one observer gazing up at a now airworthy B-17, bristling with thirteen mounts, remarked, "With all those guns, it looks like a fort that can fly." Thus it became the "Flying Fortress." By 1941, B-17s turned over to the British under Lend-Lease had proved themselves in combat. Not until August 1942, however, did the Eighth Air Force employ B-17s flown by American pilots under American command. Their maiden raid struck a rail yard in occupied France, returning without a plane lost, at best beginner's luck. Before the war ended, 12,731 of these doughty aircraft would be built.

Flying was the more glamorous way of fighting the unglamorous business of war. Among the movie stars that Hap Arnold had met during his earlier posting to California was Clark Gable while the actor was filming *Mutiny on the Bounty*. Gable wanted to get into the fight and asked to see Arnold. The actor, showing up with a studio press agent, explained that he preferred the Air Forces. The agent broke in, "We'd like him to go in as a captain." Arnold said nothing. The agent kept arguing his case. Finally, the air chief blew up. Turning his gaze directly on Gable, he said, "You don't just come into a service as a captain when you've had no military service." The actor signaled the press agent that it was time to leave. That evening, Gable called Arnold at his quarters. "I've been thinking about what you told me," he said, "and I agree. I should start as a private." The Hollywood star did, in fact, begin as an enlisted man and by war's end had risen to the rank of major with a creditable record.

LONG YEARS BEFORE AMERICA had gone to war, in 1927, twenty-five-year-old Charles A. Lindbergh had achieved fame worldwide for his solo crossing of the Atlantic in the mothlike *Spirit of St. Louis* in thirty-three and a half hours. Ten years later, on April 20, 1937, President

Roosevelt invited Lindbergh to the White House just as "Lucky Lindy" was emerging as an influential voice in isolationist circles. FDR wanted to take the measure of so popular a figure who might become a potential rival. The still boyish-looking paragon of Yankee virtue had already raised FDR's eyebrow. While in Germany, Lindbergh had sent Hermann Göring, second only to Hitler in the Nazi hierarchy, the gift of a silver dish upon the birth of Göring's daughter, Edda. Subsequently, on October 19, 1938, Göring pinned on Lindbergh the Service Cross of the Order of the German Eagle with the Star, "by order of the Führer," the highest honor accorded a foreigner. The decoration was presented just two weeks after Germany, under the Munich Pact, had seized a slice of Czechoslovakia and at a time when persecution of the Jews was becoming blatant. Lindbergh fought off criticism for accepting the medal, claiming that the presentation had been sprung on him without warning at a dinner given by the American ambassador in the U.S. embassy. To have rejected the medal, he maintained, would have been an insult straining already tense U.S.-German relations. Lindbergh left the fifteen-minute April meeting with FDR pleased, he claimed, that he had not fallen victim to the fabled Roosevelt charm. Instead, he found FDR "a little too suave, too pleasant, too easy." He confided to friends that talking to Roosevelt was like talking to a man wearing a mask.

Hap Arnold was a practical man. Politics was not his game; building the Air Corps was. He had received letters from Lindbergh since 1938 "full of striking information," particularly about the swift growth of the German air force. "I shall count it a great personal favor and believe you will be performing a patriotic service if you can supply me with any data on the subject," he wrote. In effect, the Lone Eagle became Arnold's aerial spy. After the horrifying and fatal kidnapping of his twenty-month-old son, Lindbergh had exiled his family to Europe. After his return to the United States in 1939 he contacted Arnold. The two men agreed to meet at West Point where Arnold's son was a cadet. They managed to slip unrecognized into the bleachers on the Plain where the Army baseball team was playing Syracuse University. Over the rest of the afternoon, "Lindbergh gave me the most accurate picture of the Luftwaffe, its equipment, leaders, apparent plans, training methods, and present defects," Arnold recalled.

On September 15, 1939, Lindbergh was scheduled to make a nationwide radio speech warning America to stay out of Europe's war. He first showed the speech to Arnold, whose brow furrowed as he read it. Lindbergh was now a colonel in the Air Corps Reserve and Arnold suggested that he drop the politics. Lindbergh went ahead and made his speech anyway. Less than a year later, on May 19, 1940, he unfurled his isolationist banner in a widely broadcast radio address. The Roosevelt administration, he charged, was stoking "a defense hysteria." The only way the country could be ensnarled in Europe's war was if the "American people bring it on through their own quarreling and meddling with affairs abroad." The warmongers, he claimed, were "a small minority of the American people, but they control much of the machinery of influence and propaganda." The barb was unsubtly aimed at American Jews. Roosevelt listened to as much of the speech as he could stomach, turned off the radio, and said to Henry Morgenthau, "If I should die tomorrow, I want you to know this. I am absolutely convinced that Lindbergh is a Nazi." He told Henry Stimson that Lindbergh's speech "could not have been better put if it had been written by Goebbels himself."

On April 25, 1941, the war of words came to a head. Roosevelt had asked John Franklin Carter, who ran FDR's small spy ring out of the Oval Office, to do some research on the Civil War. Armed with Carter's facts, FDR met with the press that afternoon and gleefully leapt to answer a reporter's question, likely planted by himself. The journalist asked why in this period of national emergency had the famed Colonel Lindbergh not been called to serve his country? According to the *New York Times* account, "The President put the colonel into the category of defeatists and appeasers, and he likened such people to the Copperheads of the Civil War [who] agitated for peace in 1863 on the ground that the North could not win." Within the week, Lindbergh resigned his reserve commission. Still, three days after Pearl Harbor, he sought to go on active duty. FDR was not a forgiving man and the request was denied. Arnold, however, hated to lose the expertise and judgment of a peerless aviator. Lindbergh became a consultant to aviation manufacturers and Arnold, with Marshall's complicity, looked the other way when Lindy tested the P-38 fighter, in the course of which he shot down two Japanese Zeros.

CHAPTER 11

---✦---

Torch: The Political Education
of Dwight Eisenhower

NORTH AFRICA WAS NOT AN EMPTY MILITARY LANDSCAPE BY THE time Torch had been decided upon. In late 1940, the Italian dictator, Benito Mussolini, advancing his dream of a reincarnated Roman Empire, invaded Egypt. His armies pouring from the Italian colony of Libya drove 60 miles to within 250 miles of Cairo, poised to conquer the onetime colony where British political influence still predominated. On December 9, 1940, the British commander in Africa, General Sir Archibald Wavell, strengthened by fresh troops from Australia and India, struck back, driving the Italians out of Egypt almost 250 miles into Libya and taking 115,000 prisoners. With his grandiose dreams in tatters, Mussolini went to Hitler for help before Libya might be completely lost to Italy. On February 12, 1941, the führer dispatched a large force to the Libyan capital, Tripoli, to stiffen the Italians' spine. Commanding the expeditionary force, the Afrika Korps, was a general who had won Germany's highest military honor, the *Pour le Mérite*, in the Great War and who at the age of forty-nine had distinguished himself in the conquest of France. General Erwin Rommel swiftly turned back Wavell's advance into eastern Libya.

A vast reach of North Africa was held by the French. The armistice signed in June 1940 had given Germany 60 percent of France, a wide swath running down the center from the Belgian border to Spain and Switzerland. Paris was occupied and the French government, emasculated and humiliated, withdrew to Vichy as the capital of a rump

France. Under the armistice terms, Vichy was allowed to keep its fleet, the world's third largest, far greater than Germany's, to maintain a 120,000-man army in its unoccupied remnant, and retain control of Morocco, Algeria, and Tunisia. The Germans exacted a price for these concessions. Vichy was to fight off any Allied invasion of its colonies.

That was the situation until November 1942: French colonies of uncertain loyalties still autonomous in North Africa, and Rommel's forces hammering at the gates of Alexandria, Egypt. On November 4, 1942, the tide turned. An ecstatic Winston Churchill cabled FDR that General Bernard Law Montgomery had won a stunning victory at El Alamein close to Alexandria, news that set church bells ringing in London for the first time since the war had begun. El Alamein produced for the British not only a victory, but a paladin, "Monty," their new shining knight. A short, scrawny man of furrowed features and a bristling mustache who favored a nonregulation beret, sheepskin jacket, and sweater had become the agent of restored national pride. In an instant the stains of Dunkirk, Singapore, and Tobruk seemed to fade. Defeat in the war had been thwarted and victory appeared a possibility. Britain had come close to losing this hero in the Great War. After graduating from Sandhurst, Britain's military academy, Montgomery fought in the trenches of the Western Front where a German sniper felled him. So serious was his wound that the field surgeon had a grave dug for the blood-soaked lieutenant. He survived. Years later his wife died, leaving him with a young son. He never remarried. The army became his life. Unprepossessing in appearance perhaps, Montgomery matured into a general of soaring self-confidence, along with a testiness in dealing with superiors and equals. The official British history of the Mediterranean war described his "arrogance, bumptiousness, ungenerosity . . . [and] schoolboy humour." A fellow officer, General Brian Horrocks, found him "rather like an intelligent terrier who might bite at any moment." Another contemporary concluded "he is not quite a gentleman." Yet to men in the ranks he displayed a different face. His habit in the desert was to roar up in a jeep, jump out, and tell the dusty sun-baked Tommies, "Break ranks and come close. . . . Sit down. Take off your helmets so I can get a look at you." He told them what a fine-looking lot they were and that he was honored to command them. The men loved him.

Eisenhower had first felt Monty's prickliness months before El Alamein. Ike had attended a lecture that Montgomery was giving on field exercises. Ike, a heavy smoker, lit up and Montgomery sniffing the air demanded, "Who's smoking?" Eisenhower answered, "I am." "I don't permit smoking in my office," Monty snapped. Ike stubbed out the cigarette wordlessly, but exhibited signs of his patented slow burn, lips compressed, veins in his temple bulging, his neck turning bright red. The moment was the first in a long history of skirmishes in which Ike would seek to balance Montgomery's hubris against his genius, petulance against brilliance.

FDR WAS EMPHATIC ON ONE POINT. Torch must principally be an American show. Initially he wanted only U.S. troops involved. The French resentments toward the British ran deep. They believed that Britain had abandoned them at Dunkirk. The RAF, in a raid on a Renault plant near Paris, had killed 500 French civilians. Most enraging, on July 3, 1940, barely two weeks after the fall of France, Winston Churchill, fearing that the formidable French fleet might fall into German hands, had ordered an attack on the port of Oran. The Royal Navy sank the French battleship *Bretagne,* seriously damaged two others, and in five minutes killed 1,250 French sailors. FDR feared that British involvement in Torch would stiffen the French will to fight back to maintain what little was left of their pride. Churchill's suggestion was to put British troops in American uniforms, saying that he would be "proud to have 'em wear 'em." Eisenhower turned down the offer, one he believed would backfire once revealed.

In an effort to neutralize or at least minimize French resistance, Ike's deputy, Major General Mark Clark, volunteered for a covert mission. Tall, confident in speech, manner, and bearing, with a profile suggesting an American eagle, the perfect Anglo-Saxon appearance belied one surprise in Clark's background: his mother was the daughter of a Jewish pawnbroker. At West Point he had himself baptized as an

Episcopalian. The current plan was for him to slip into North Africa via submarine and try to persuade anti-Vichy French leaders not to resist Torch. Before departing London, Clark wrote a letter to his wife, Renie, telling her that he was embarking on a potentially mortal mission and scrawled across the envelope, "Deliver only in the event that I do not return." Clark was put ashore on the Algerian coast by the British submarine *Seraph* and then rendezvoused in a remote villa with a French general, Charles Mast, chief of staff of the French XIX Corps. He warned Mast that the Allies would be putting a half million men into North Africa, a gross exaggeration, but a persuasive argument for the French not to fight. Clark managed essentially to defuse Mast's forces. But how the rest of the still sizable French army in the colonies would react to the invasion remained disquieting.

The timing of Torch posed a dilemma for FDR. He faced midterm elections on November 3 and hoped that a victory in North Africa would boost the Democrats' fortunes. When Roosevelt pressed Marshall for a date, "he held up his hands in an attitude of prayer, and said, 'Please make it before election day,'" Marshall remembered. Marshall in turn asked Eisenhower when he could move. Ike came up with the date of November 8, five days too late for Roosevelt's election day hopes. What impressed Marshall, who stiffened at any hint of political pressure intruding upon military decisions, was Roosevelt's reaction. "When I found out we had to have more time, he never said a word, he was very courageous." As the invasion date approached, Marshall informed the president that Eisenhower judged "the chances of overall success in the operation . . . are considerably less that fifty percent."

ON THE EVENING OF NOVEMBER 7, people in Casablanca, Oran, and Algiers heard the approaching drone of aircraft. They eagerly snatched at leaflets that came fluttering from the sky bearing the flag of the United States, a photo of President Roosevelt, and a message. Simultaneously, the same words were being broadcast via radio into their homes, delivered in FDR's surprisingly fluent French from a recording he had cut a few days before in the Cabinet Room of the White House.

"My friends, who suffer day and night under the crushing yoke of the Nazis," Roosevelt began, "I wish to speak to you as one who was with your Army and Navy in France in 1918." FDR closed assuring North Africans that "We come among you solely to defeat and rout your enemies. . . . We assure you that once the menace of Germany and Italy is removed, we shall quit your territory at once. . . . Do not obstruct I beg of you, this great purpose." He ended with a Gallic flourish, "Vive La France Eternelle!" As morning approached, people living along the beaches could hear the splash of approaching landing craft.

Roosevelt's remarks heralded the arrival of a two-pronged flotilla of unprecedented magnitude. One half, Task Force 34, comprising 600 ships, was traveling 4,500 miles from U.S. ports, and the other half, equally powerful, was sailing 2,800 miles from Britain. To mislead German intelligence, deception teams had staged lectures on frostbite for the troops, had ships conspicuously loaded with cold weather gear, delivered a party of reporters to Scotland to observe ski training, and openly went looking for Norwegian currency. Part of the task force would strike from the Atlantic near Casablanca in Morocco. The rest, carriers, battleships, and transports bound for Algeria, would have to pass through the Strait of Gibraltar, only eight miles wide and under constant surveillance by German lookouts positioned on rooftops in La Línea, Spain. Further, numerous German and Italian submarines patrolled the strait. Astonishingly, the armada slipped past Gibraltar without incident. Torch would disembark Americans at Casablanca and Oran, and joint American and British forces at Algiers, 107,000 troops in all. The French possessions were defended by 200,000 troops ostensibly loyal to the Vichy government. Thus America's entrance into the European war began in bitter irony. France, the country whose support had helped America win its independence, whose people had given Americans the Statue of Liberty, alongside whom doughboys had fought with French *poilus* to defeat Germany in World War I, was to become the first enemy against whom American soldiers would fire.

At H-hour Allied troops began clambering down rope nets slung alongside the hulls of the transports into LCVPs, Landing Craft Vehicle, Personnel, known as Higgins boats after their New Orleans creator,

a fiery Irishman named Andrew Jackson Higgins. Higgins had originally designed his boat for logging operations. As he explained it, "We
needed shallow draft boats that could go . . . over logs, sand and mud
bars, through swamps and jungles and in rough open sea." Logging
may have been Higgins's original impetus, but no craft could have been
better conceived for the campaigns to be fought in a two-ocean war.
Cheaply mass produced of plywood, except for a metal ramp that
dropped from the bow, the thirty-six-feet-long-by-ten-feet-wide Higgins boat could deliver thirty-six men in full packs directly onto or
close to the beach. FDR, with his own mechanical bent, had given
thought to something similar. Admiral Leahy recalled a meeting at
Shangri-La where the discussion had turned to amphibious operations. "The President took a pencil and sketched out his own ideas of
these crafts," Leahy recalled, which bore a remarkable resemblance to
the Higgins boat. Even with the president's backing, Higgins's path to
production had not been smooth. The Navy's hidebound Bureau of
Ships, a bureaucracy within a bureaucracy, resisted his design, arguing
that the davits on ships used to lower small craft into the water were
designed maximally for thirty-foot boats. In the end Higgins won out
and began producing his boats en masse.

On the day of the invasion, FDR, along with Harry Hopkins,
Harry's chic new wife, Louise, the president's birdlike distant cousin,
Margaret "Daisy" Suckley, two of Daisy's young nieces, and Grace Tully,
had gathered at Shangri-La in Maryland. Tully sensed a tenseness in
the president unlike his usual effervescence in the company of young
women. Earlier he had marked a passage from the 39th Psalm that
read, "O spare me, that I may recover strength, before I go hence and be
no more." The brittle mood at Shangri-La was broken by the ringing of
a phone. Tully answered and told the president that the War Department was calling. "The boss's hand shook," she recalled, "as he took the
telephone from me." He listened wordlessly, then burst out, "Thank
God, thank God. That sounds grand. Congratulations." He set the
phone down, the relief on his face palpable. "We have landed in North
Africa," he said. "We are striking back!" That afternoon, Mrs. George
Marshall had gone to a football game with Hap Arnold's wife, disap-

pointed that her husband, without explanation, had bowed out at the last minute. In the midst of a downfield march a voice boomed out over a loudspeaker, "Stop the game! Important announcement! The President of the United States announces the successful landing on the African coast of an American Expeditionary Force. This is the Second Front." "Like the waves of the ocean," Mrs. Marshall remembered, "the cheers of people rose and fell, then rose again in a long sustained emotional cry. The football players turned somersaults and handsprings down the center of the field, the crowd simply went wild."

EISENHOWER'S ODDS FOR THE SUCCESS of Torch proved pessimistic. Two Allied destroyers were lost at Oran, but the French fought for only two days before surrendering the port. Algiers was quickly subdued. At Casablanca, the fighting, though fierce, was brief. Finally, on November 11, the French quit and signed an armistice. Victory had been swift, but hardly a dustup. The Allies saw 1,100 men die, mostly Americans. The French dead totaled over triple that number. Hitler instantly tore up his armistice with France and seized the rest of unoccupied France. German and Italian troops began pouring across the Mediterranean into Tunisia, 68,000 within a month of the Torch landings, followed by another 110,000 in the months to follow. If Roosevelt and Churchill chose to drive the Axis from North Africa first, rather than in Europe, they were going to have to fight for it. The demands of Torch had further set back Bolero, cutting the cross-Channel buildup from a planned 1,470,000 to 427,000 men. For Roosevelt the timing of Torch exacted a political price. Had the invasion occurred before rather than after election day, its success might have given FDR a political boost. Instead, the Democrats lost forty-five seats in the House and nine in the Senate.

THE MORNING AFTER THE CASABLANCA LANDINGS, soldiers resting from unloading landing craft on the debris-strewn beach spied an older officer striding toward them, scowling and spewing obscenities.

Wading into the surf, George Patton yelled in a reedy, high-pitched voice, "Come back here! I mean all of you . . . goddamit on the double!" He then put his shoulder to a beached boat and ordered them to help set it free. Wait for the next wave, he instructed, then "Lift and push, now push, goddamit, push!" Patton later described his performance that morning. "One soldier who was pushing a boat got scared and ran onto the beach. I kicked him in the ass with all my might and he jumped right up and went to work." Disgusted at the slow pace, "I hit another man who was too lazy to push a boat."

Two days later, Patton received French officers at his headquarters in Casablanca's Hotel Anfa to accept their surrender. He began to read armistice terms prepared by the War Department. As he read one demeaning clause after another, the humiliation and anger on the faces of the defeated Frenchmen became visible. Suddenly, with a flourish and a grin, Patton tore up the document. "You and I fought side by side in the First World War," he said. "I am sure we can work together now on the basis of mutual trust." Here was a man capable of the coarsest vulgarity and yet acts of nobility and magnanimity. He was also an anomaly in the Regular Army. Few career officers were to be found in the *Social Register*. Many had been drawn to the military academies precisely because they were smart but poor boys eager for a free education. George Smith Patton Jr. *was* in the *Social Register*. He chose to follow a tradition that had been burned into his being. Among his soldier ancestors were General Hugh Mercer, mortally wounded in the Revolutionary War Battle of Princeton; Colonel George Patton, a great-uncle; and Colonel Waller Patton. His grandfather, also George Smith Patton, was one of four brothers who attended Virginia Military Institute and who studied under Stonewall Jackson. Grandfather Patton's boldness in the Civil War's third Battle of Winchester cost him his life at age thirty-one. Patton's father, also George, was a VMI graduate but chose the law, becoming district attorney of Los Angeles and ultimately a wealthy man. George Jr., born November 11, 1885, grew up on the family's sizable estate, Lake Vineyard in California. The property had originally been amassed by one of the more colorful figures in Patton's family tree, his maternal grandfather, Benjamin Davis Wilson, a tough, self-made rancher known as "Don Benito" because his first wife was Mexican and because he treated Indians fairly.

To his parents, young George appeared alarmingly slow. He had to be tutored at home until age eleven, when he was still barely able to read and write. His passion instead was horses and, while still a child, he had become an accomplished rider. A learning disability still undiagnosed in his day, dyslexia, explained his backwardness in school. His spelling was atrocious: "remidy" for remedy, "obriged" for obliged, "staid" for stayed. In spite of the handicap he did catch fire in one realm of scholarship. From age fifteen, he began to devour volumes of history, Shakespeare's tragedies, Sir Walter Scott, Kipling, the lives of kings and conquerors, knights and villains, and biographies of Confederate generals.

In 1903, at age eighteen, Patton also entered VMI, but only long enough to give his father time to pull every string within his considerable political reach to get his son into West Point. Young George entered the academy in the summer of 1904. Like Douglas MacArthur's mother, Patton's mother and a favorite aunt, Nannie, took up residence nearby. Again, he proved no great shakes as a scholar but plunged himself into his current passion, fencing. He began referring to himself as "Master of the Sword." He scorned defensive postures. The thrust was his move. He gave his own estimate of his skills: "I am the best of the best in class." He also pushed a lanky frame to the limit and set a school record in the 220-yard hurdles. But his academic deficiency caught up with him. He failed math and had to repeat his plebe year. In letters and diaries he revealed mood swings from bluster to insecurity on a manic-depressive scale. "I am a characterless, lazy, stupid, yet ambitious dreamer," he once wrote, "who will degenerate into a third rate second lieutenant and never command anything more than a platoon." On another occasion, he wrote, "You have done your damndest and failed. Now you must do your damndest and win. Remember that is what you live for. Oh you must! You have got to do something. Never stop until you have reached the top or the grave." He shocked his fellow cadets by foolhardy displays of bravery. When he was assigned to raise and lower targets on the rifle range, he suddenly rose from the pit and faced the firing line, as bullets whizzed past him. He later explained to disbelieving fellow cadets that he had done so to test his courage under fire.

While at West Point, George met a young woman, Beatrice Ayer, comely, musically gifted, a composer who played the piano, mandolin, and guitar. Patton's soldierly appearance, Beatrice soon learned, was an obsession. Her suitor admitted that he might change uniforms fifteen times a day "in order to be clean and neat always." During the West Point–Yale football game of 1908, Beatrice watched with mixed pride and amusement as George, now regimental adjutant, "pranced up and down the field at inspection, chest bulging and chevrons shining. . . . Our only anxiety was that he might break in two at the waistline."

Patton was tagged a "quiloid" by his fellow cadets, one who took pleasure in putting others on report for the most trifling infractions. While Eisenhower reproached himself for humiliating a cadet during hazing, Patton reveled in it. "I reported more men than any other officer of the day this summer," he boasted. Not surprisingly, according to his keenest biographer, Carlo D'Este, "To the end of his West Point days he remained virtually friendless, a shameless man on the make." Upon graduating he ranked 46th in a class of 103. The wealthy Frederick Ayer was not immediately persuaded that Beatrice's brash young man was suitable for his lovely and gifted daughter. However, after seeing a statement of Second Lieutenant Patton's finances, Ayer came around. After the couple married on May 26, 1910, Patton's father-in-law began providing a monthly income, which insured further that George Patton would continue to live the high life.

In 1912, the Army granted Patton time to train for the Olympic games in Stockholm where he competed in the modern pentathlon. He scored well in fencing, pistol shooting, and swimming and finished a respectable fifth place. Posted to Fort Myer, he began scouring the Virginia-Kentucky horse country and accumulated a stable of seven horses, including registered thoroughbreds. He competed in flat races, steeplechases, and played polo. In April 1913, he was thrown from a horse and struck his head, not the first or last in a series of head injuries.

When a Bosnian radical, Gavrilo Princip, assassinated Austria's Archduke Franz Ferdinand on June 28, 1914, touching off the Great War, Patton, dismissing America's neutrality, saw the main chance and went directly to General Leonard Wood, Army chief of staff. Give him a year's leave of absence, Patton pleaded, and he would fight in Europe and "I will never apply to the United States for help if I get in trouble or am captured." Wood turned him down. "We don't want to waste youngsters of your sort in the service of foreign nations," he said.

On a pitch-dark night on March 9, 1916, a charismatic Mexican revolutionary, Pancho Villa, led an attack on the town of Columbus, New Mexico. When the Mexicans rode off, eighteen Americans lay dead. President Woodrow Wilson responded to a public outcry for the Mexican's head and ordered General John "Black Jack" Pershing to mount a punitive expedition. George Patton saw another chance for martial stardom. He took no detours, went directly to Pershing, and talked himself into an assignment as the general's aide. In his first test under fire, Patton encountered three armed Mexicans fleeing on horseback from the courtyard of a hacienda, all of whom, Patton claimed, shot at him. One of the Mexicans fell in a hail of bullets. It did not matter that at least five other troopers had fired on the ill-fated Villista, including three shots by Patton. It was the bumptious lieutenant who caught the journalists' eye. *The New York Times* carried a graphic account of Patton's derring-do. A Boston paper's headline read, "Mexican Bandit Killer Well Known in Boston." Whether or not Patton killed anyone that day is uncertain, but reporters had detected what would always be true: George Patton was good copy.

His dream of covering himself with glory loomed even brighter when Woodrow Wilson won a declaration of war against Germany on April 6, 1917. Patton was promoted to captain and attached to Pershing's staff, a choice assignment, possibly influenced by the fact that Black Jack had become romantically involved with Patton's attractive sister, Nita, twenty-seven years the general's junior. His fellow officers assumed that George Patton would become the brother-in-law of the commander of the American Expeditionary Forces. It was not to be. Pershing found someone younger in Paris, a twenty-three-year-old Romanian artist, Micheline Resco, and the affair with Nita ended.

On September 16, 1916, before the United States had entered the war, German soldiers peering from trenches near the villages of Flers and Courcelette watched in disbelief at what appeared to be giant iron tortoises rumbling toward them, belching cannon fire and sooty exhaust, easily traversing the deepest shell holes and knocking protective barbed wire flat. The British had introduced tank warfare. When America entered the war, Pershing handed Patton a plum assignment, making him the first U.S. officer to serve in the newly formed Tank Corps. Patton eventually commanded 400 tanks, driving his crews mercilessly. "Why you God damned sons of bitches," he roared, "do you think the Marines are tough? Well you just wait until I get through with you. Being tough will save lives."

During the doughboys' first major offensive, closing the Saint-Mihiel Salient, Patton came upon the village of Essey and encountered the commanding general of the Rainbow Division's 84th Brigade, a soldier whose panache matched his own. Douglas MacArthur was urging his men on and as Patton described the moment, "They were all in shell holes except the General." A creeping barrage, like a rainfall of metal, began nearing the two officers. "Each one wanted to leave, but each hated to say so," Patton said of the experience, "so we let it come over us." Had a well-placed shell found its mark amid these outsize egos, the effect on a world war to be fought twenty-three years later could have been incalculable.

On September 26, 1918, at the beginning of America's greatest World War I battle, the Meuse-Argonne Offensive, George Patton found himself under intense German fire. "I felt a great desire to run," he recalled. "I was trembling with fear." He nevertheless called for volunteers to storm an enemy position. Six men answered and five were killed instantly. A ditched tank, raked by machine-gun fire, failed to provide sufficient cover for Patton. He felt a dull thud and as he later described the wound, the bullet had struck his left hip and emerged "just at the crack of my bottom about two inches to the left of my rectum." After his brush with death, Patton wrote home, "I have been cited for decoration either the Medal of Honor or the Military Cross. I hope I get one of them." "I would rather be a second lieutenant with the DSC [Distinguished Service Cross] than a general without it."

On his thirty-third birthday, November 11, when an armistice was due to end the war within hours, a frustrated Patton found himself still in the hospital. Unable to endure the ignominy of being flat on his stomach with a wound to his buttocks, Patton bribed an orderly to let him out of the hospital and commandeered a car to take him to the front, arriving just as the war ended. After the war, posted to Boston, he would unbuckle his pants at fashionable tea parties and invite the ladies to inspect his battle scar.

During the Great War Patton had begun to reveal a mystical streak. In the moment before he was wounded, he had overcome his fear, he said, by thinking, "It is time for another Patton to die. . . . I thought of my progenitors and seemed to see them looking at me." He would one day describe to his daughter, Ruth Ellen, visions of himself as a Viking warrior, prone on a shield, being carried from an ancient battlefield, or as he told his grandson, as a soldier in besieged Carthage so overcome with thirst that "he drank urine out of his helmet." His firsthand experience of war moved him to compose poetry revealing an ambivalence swinging between horror and fascination. After one battle, walking among the unburied dead of both sides, their faces gray in the moonlight, he pondered that all these men had been made in God's image and wrote:

> Yet that damned Boche looked just like Him,
> leastwise he looked to me
> so why God should be partial
> I don't rightly see.

Yet when the war ended he wrote a more bloodthirsty verse, "Peace—November 11, 1918."

We can but hope that e're we drown
'Neath treacle floods of grace,
The tuneless horns of mighty Mars
Once more shall rouse the Race
When such times come, Oh! God of War
Grant that we pass midst strife,
Knowing once more the whitehot joy
Of taking human life.

He had become a man of puzzling contradictions, admitting fear, yet reluctant to withdraw from the field of battle, vain and at the same time insecure, a swaggering warrior who believed he had to rehearse a "war face" in his mirror before facing his troops, unhesitating in sending men to their death, yet capable of shedding tears for the dead, a romantic living in the twentieth century, yet more likely at home around King Arthur's Round Table. In many ways, George Patton was a dreadful human being, a Jekyll-Hyde, tolerated for his courage and genius. Martin Blumenson, who edited Patton's papers, perhaps best caught the Patton essence: "Like most great men, General Patton was at heart a child. . . . His impetuousness and occasional impatience were manifestations of a childlike character."

The return to peace dropped Patton from full colonel to captain before he clambered back up to major. In 1919, now posted to Camp Meade, he met Dwight Eisenhower, five years younger than himself and clearly in awe of Patton's war record. Eisenhower and Patton, one a poor kid from Kansas, the other a society swell, were joined initially only by their common uniform and belief in tank warfare. Patton, flagrantly egotistical, and Eisenhower, reflexively modest, somehow clicked.

During the mid-1930s George Patton lost his way, a warrior without a war, rather like a ship without a rudder. He was fifty years old, seemingly dead-ended professionally. He began drinking heavily, engaged in binge eating, once putting away an entire box of chocolates at a sitting and having to enter a hospital to have his stomach pumped. He began exhibiting the sexual restlessness of a vain middle-aged man, finding fault with his wife and complaining about her hair turning gray. While serving in Hawaii, and at the very moment when a proud Beatrice was about to have a novel published, George fell in love. Jean Gordon, his wife's twenty-one-year-old half-niece, had besotted him. When his Beatrice fell ill, he left her behind and took Jean on a trip to one of the other islands. Only his wife's love and maturity saved the marriage. "Your father needs me," Beatrice told her children. "He doesn't know it right now, but he needs me more than I need him." Womanizing was to become a Patton way of life. Amused fellow officers repeated one of his dictums, "A man who does not screw will not fight."

IN 1940, EISENHOWER, fearing that with war in the air he would again be deskbound, resumed a correspondence with Patton. The older officer, after thirty-one years in the Army, had finally made brigadier general. About to be given command of an armored division, Patton offered Ike a job, writing, "no matter how we get together we will go places." Eisenhower wrote back, "It would be great to be in the tanks once more, and even better to be associated with you again." The two families came to know each other well. Patton's profanity, amusing to some, abhorred by others, tolerated by those who accepted his compensating brilliance, shocked Ike's young son John. "He not only swore profusely around ladies, but also encouraged all three of his children to do the same," John recalled. When Patton's boy, again named George, "would come out with an appropriate piece of blasphemy, Patton would roar with pleasure."

In 1942, Patton received a career-reviving assignment. He was to command II Corps during Torch. "Patton is by far the best tank man in the Army," George Marshall observed. "I realize he is a difficult man but I know how to handle him." In July 1941 Patton's scowling "war face" appeared on the cover of *Life* magazine.

FDR HAD COME TO KNOW GEORGE Patton early in his presidency when the flamboyant soldier was stationed with the cavalry at Fort Myer. He immediately liked what he saw, dash, daring, fresh ideas, qualities not unlike his own. Eighteen days before Torch, FDR called in Patton and Admiral Kent Hewitt, who was to command naval forces in the Casablanca phase of Torch, two of the fifteen to fifty people the president saw on a typical day. As Patton described the meeting, "Admiral Hewitt and I arrived at 2:00. He greeted us with 'come in skipper and old cavalryman, and give me the good news.'" FDR proceeded to give Hewitt "a lot of advice about how to moor a ship to keep it head to wind by a stern anchor. He had done this once with a yacht." The admiral raised his immediate concern: Prime Minister Churchill wanted to swap certain British for American vessels as part of Torch, which "would be fatal at this late date." The admiral was treated to vintage Roosevelt. FDR told him to come up with a counterproposal, but to take his time, "we can stall until it's too late." As the two men rose to leave, Roosevelt asked Patton "whether he had his old cavalry saddle to mount on the turret of a tank and if he went into action on the side with his saber drawn." Patton's final words, uttered in a voice choked with emotion, were "Sir, all I want to tell you is this, I will leave the beaches either a conqueror or a corpse." FDR sent a copy of Patton's account of the meeting to be kept in the Roosevelt Library at Hyde Park, writing on it, "Patton is a joy."

THE STORY DID NOT RATE the front page. An article under the headline "Himmler Program Kills Polish Jews" was buried on page 10 of the November 25, 1942, issue of *The New York Times*. The Polish government-in-exile in London had issued a statement containing eyewitness accounts of what was happening to the Jews in Poland, the most vivid provided by Jan Karski, a courier between the Polish underground and the exiled government. The *Times* article described Jews packed 150 to a freight car, the floor thick with lime to kill the smell, since "wherever the trains arrive half the people are dead. Those surviving are sent to special camps at Treblinka, Belzec, and Sobibor." The *Times* reporter, James MacDonald, quoted from a Polish government report that the Nazi goal was that "half of the remaining Polish Jews must be exterminated by the end of this year," in addition to the 250,000 already killed. The slaughter thus far was a "first step toward complete liquidation."

The *Times* was hardly the first to produce evidence of Nazi savagery within occupied Europe. As early as March 12, 1939, five months before the war began, William C. Bullitt, U.S. ambassador to France, had managed to obtain a verbatim transcript of remarks made by Hitler at a gathering of his inner circle. In the document, marked "Secret and Personal," the führer is quoted saying, "enemies of the German people must be exterminated radically. . . . We will settle accounts with the 'dollar Jews' in the United States. We will exterminate this Jewish democracy and Jewish blood will mix with the dollars."

That anti-Semitism characterized a segment of American life in the 1930s cannot be denied. A 1938 Roper poll asked Americans, "What kinds of people do you object to?" Thirty-five percent of respondents named the Jews. Waspish State Department officials who handled visa requests applied the immigration laws not just strictly but meanspiritedly against Jews seeking to flee Germany. A bill introduced in Congress to enable Jewish refugee children under age sixteen to be granted at least tourist visas never made it out of committee. The saga of the SS *St. Louis* reveals the atmosphere at the time. The Hamburg-Amerika liner, carrying 930 Jewish refugees, left Germany for Cuba on May 13, 1939. Arriving at Havana, only a handful were allowed to disembark. The captain then circled the Florida coast for days, within sight of Miami, waiting for permission to dock. State Department and immigration authorities threw up legal obstacles with chilling exactitude. With nowhere else to go the ship returned to Europe where many of its passengers were abandoned in countries soon to be overrun by the Nazis, thus sealing their fate.

Soon after France fell in 1940, FDR heard reports of French hostages executed en masse. On October 25, 1941, he issued a statement saying, "The practice of executing scores of innocent hostages in reprisal for isolated attacks on Germans in countries temporarily under the Nazi heel, revolts a world already inured to suffering and brutality. . . . Frightfulness can never bring peace to Europe. It only sows the seeds of hatred which one day will bring fearful retribution." In 1942, the world learned that the Czech village of Lidice had been obliterated and 1,331 of its inhabitants murdered to avenge the assassination in Prague of Reinhard Heydrich, deputy chief of the Gestapo.

A failure to act more vigorously, especially in the matter of the *St. Louis*, or in pressuring the State Department to admit more Jews, might suggest that Franklin Roosevelt exhibited the genteel anti-Semitism of his class. His son Jimmy once observed that FDR's social circle was drawn almost wholly from his own set. "I now think he travelled with that group as an escape, back to the world of Groton, Harvard and Hyde Park," Jimmy concluded. "These people had everything so they didn't want anything from father. He was more comfortable with them than he was with his political associates, who constantly pestered him with their problems."

Some of Roosevelt's ideas about the dilemma the Jews faced might raise an eyebrow. "One of the things that he couldn't understand which was very interesting to me," Sam Rosenman remembered, "was why some Jew didn't assassinate Hitler . . . why the Jews submitted to these things in Germany. Even though they couldn't do anything about it as a mass, why wasn't one fellow able to get at Hitler and kill him?" When Henry Morgenthau approached FDR over the deepening tragedy of the Jews, FDR, the avid amateur geographer, suggested they be settled in the Cameroons on Africa's western coast, where they would find "some very wonderful highland, tableland, wonderful grass. . . . All of that country has been explored and it's ready." He presented another idea with a certain prescience. "I would actually put a barbed wire around Palestine, and I would move the Arabs out of Palestine," he suggested. "Each time we move out an Arab, we would bring in another Jewish family. . . . There are lots of places to which you could move the Arabs. All you have to do is drill a well because there is this large underground water supply."

In his administration, FDR's regard for the Jews was self-evident.

They represented only 3 percent of the U.S. population at the time, yet he filled 15 percent of his top administration posts with Jewish appointees, including members of the cabinet and Supreme Court. Henry Morgenthau Jr., Sam Rosenman, and Bernard Baruch were all close to him personally. Under FDR's tenure, the United States took in more Jewish refugees from Germany and Austria than all other countries of Europe and the Western Hemisphere combined.

As irrefutable evidence piled before him on the fate of Jews in Europe, Roosevelt's stance hardened. Speaking to the American people in a fireside chat in October 1942, he warned, "I now declare it to be the intention of this government that at the successful close of this war we shall include provisions for the surrender to the United Nations of war criminals. . . . It is not the intention of the government or of the governments associated with us to resort to mass reprisals. It is our intention that just and sure punishment shall be meted out to the ringleaders responsible for the organized murder of thousands of innocent persons and the commission of atrocities which have violated every tenet of the Christian faith."

The surrender of the French colonial government to the Allies in North Africa, where 350,000 Jews lived among 25 million Arabs, was about to test Roosevelt's commitment.

ADMIRAL FRANÇOIS DARLAN REPRESENTED every detestation against which the Allies were fighting. He had prospered in the Vichy regime. His chief, the aged Marshal Pétain, hero of the First World War, raised him to vice premier and commander of all Vichy armed forces as well as high commissioner for French North Africa. Pétain had ordered the French to collaborate in building Hitler's "new order," and Darlan eagerly advanced the old man's wishes. On May 13, 1941, *The New York Times* reported, "Reichsfuehrer Hitler has received the French Vice Premier Admiral François Darlan, in the presence of German Foreign Minister Joachim von Ribbentrop," in Berchtesgaden. When the Germans demanded that 150,000 skilled French workers be conscripted to Germany, Darlan offered no objection. When French resistance fighters killed a German officer in Nantes, Darlan turned over thirty of his own people to be shot in reprisal. He arranged for French ships to deliver 200 tons of food to Rommel's forces in Tunisia weekly. As high commissioner of North Africa, Darlan mimicked Germany's racial dogmas. He shipped back to Germany Jews who had sought refuge in France's colonies. He threw Jews and political dissidents into jails similar to Germany's concentration camps. Purely by coincidence, Darlan happened to be in Algiers visiting his son, Alain, who had been stricken with polio, when the Allies invaded North Africa. Those who despised Nazism were about to be stunned by Darlan's treatment there.

WITH MOROCCO AND ALGERIA LARGELY subdued, Eisenhower, from his Gibraltar headquarters, now fixed his sights on the rest of North Africa, particularly Tunisia, which the Germans were speedily fortifying. He dispatched General Mark Clark to Algiers to work out a deal with Darlan to defuse any residual French resistance. The man Clark met in the vice premier's baroque summer palace was an unprepossessing figure, described by a Clark aide as a "short, bald-headed, pink-faced, needle-nosed sharp-chinned little weasel." As Clark laid down the Allies' demands, Darlan daubed at a sweaty brow with a handkerchief. Darlan must issue a cease-fire order covering Morocco and the unconquered parts of Algeria, Clark said, or he would have him shot. Darlan nodded and issued the order. A pleased Eisenhower embraced Clark's deal, which took French forces out of the North African war while he allowed Darlan to remain as high commissioner. In granting this concession, Eisenhower had made a political decision without consulting Washington. His action ignited a firestorm. An outraged Henry Morgenthau wanted Eisenhower relieved from command. One of Churchill's associates asked, "Is this then what we have been fighting for?" The CBS broadcaster Edward R. Murrow, the most widely regarded American voice reporting from Europe, asked his listeners, "Are we at some future time to occupy Norway and turn it over to a Quisling?" referring to the Nazis' Norwegian puppet leader.

Eisenhower found himself twisting in the wind. As he wrote a fellow officer, "war carries with it a lot of things that were never included in our textbooks, in the Leavenworth course or even in the War College." He wrote another friend, "I walk a soapy tightrope in a rainstorm with a blazing furnace on one side and a pack of ravenous tigers on the other." He was now smoking over two packs a day. He cabled FDR and the Combined Chiefs of Staff a defense of his actions. Upon receiving Ike's explanation, the president called in Harry Hopkins and Robert Sherwood and read Ike's message aloud, making dramatic pauses, as if delivering a speech. "The actual state of existing sentiment here does not, repeat, not agree even remotely with some of [our] prior calculations," Eisenhower had written. Too many Americans believed that the French in North Africa would be so overjoyed with their "liberation," he added, that they would immediately make common cause with the invaders. Instead, Eisenhower found most North Africans sticking by their constituted leader, François Darlan. Anyone who stood in his shoes for "ten minutes," Ike went on, "can be convinced of the soundness of the moves we have made." North Africa had given Dwight Eisenhower a crash course in realpolitik.

FDR came to Eisenhower's rescue. On November 16, 1942, his press secretary, Stephen Early, distributed a handout to White House correspondents that read, "I have accepted General Eisenhower's political arrangements made for the time being in Northern and Western Africa." He was, however, endorsing "only a temporary expedient . . . to save American and British lives, and French lives. Pressed later by a reporter, FDR quoted "a Serbian proverb about how it was permissible crossing a stream to ride on the back of the devil until you got to safety." Roosevelt wrote Eisenhower personally, "I am therefore not disposed to in any way question the actions you have taken." Nevertheless, Eisenhower must bear in mind FDR's verdict on the unpalatable new French ally: "we do not trust Darlan." To give the beleaguered general greater public support, Roosevelt directed Eisenhower to release previously censored casualty figures, even before the next of kin had been notified, which showed that losses for Torch, initially estimated at 18,000, had totaled only 1,800. Thus, Ike's Darlan deal could be said to have saved 16,200 men from death, injury, or captivity.

On December 23, Ike invited Darlan to join him for lunch along with Mark Clark and other Americans. The admiral had earlier written to Ike, "I am but a lemon which the Americans will drop after it has been squeezed." His fear was about to be confirmed. FDR had offered to send Darlan's son to Warm Springs to treat the boy's polio. His father could resign his present post, Eisenhower explained, and go with Alain to America. The usefulness of "the little man," as the Americans called him, was over. His brief interval ended with unexpected suddenness. On the day before Christmas, as bells tolled from the English chapel in Algiers, a dark-haired youth appeared at Darlan's headquarters and asked to see the high commissioner. Darlan was out to lunch and on his way back to his quarters; the youth stepped in front of him and pulled a Rubis revolver, fatally shooting him in the head and stomach. The assassin was twenty-year-old Fernand Bonnier de la Chapelle, a monarchist with a hatred of the Vichy regime. Bonnier was summarily tried by a French military tribunal and executed by firing squad at dawn the day after Christmas.

In an effort to expunge the stench of the Darlan deal, Roosevelt urged Eisenhower to free Vichy political prisoners and end the persecution of the Jews, though he soft-pedaled the latter point. Ike, he advised, must be sensitive to the racial dynamics of North Africa. For one thing, the bulk of French forces recruited to fight alongside the Allies in North Africa would be Islamists. Eisenhower had to calculate, FDR advised, "the effect of a statement such as I have indicated on the Moslems and Arabs."

One Frenchman, as towering in height as in ego, gagged on the Darlan deal. When France fell, Charles André Joseph Marie de Gaulle, a forty-nine-year-old brigadier general, had refused to surrender and escaped to England in a plane provided by Churchill. To the prime minister, de Gaulle "carried the honor of France." But the man could be a prickly guardian of that honor. As Churchill's physician, Lord Moran, described his initial encounter with de Gaulle, "I first met him in the hall at Chequers . . . an improbable creature, like a human giraffe, sniffing down his nostrils at mortals beneath his gaze." De Gaulle was currently head of the French Committee of National Liberation

operating out of London and commander of Free French Forces composed of Frenchmen who had escaped from occupied Europe and men
from the country's colonies. De Gaulle was detested by fellow officers
in France. While they had swallowed their defeat and pledged allegiance to Marshal Pétain, he had continued the fight. If his was an act
of courage, then their staying behind and surrendering made them
cowards. They chose instead to think of de Gaulle as an officer who had
disobeyed a lawful order and fled his country, making him a deserter.

He had expected to be an active partner in Torch. However, de
Gaulle's stratospheric ego and his presumption that, by his own declaration, he was France's leader, irritated Roosevelt. As FDR put it, who
had elected Charles de Gaulle to anything? In preparing for Torch, the
president had asked General Marshall's guidance on "how to deal with
General de Gaulle and his followers." Marshall's advice was to deceive
the haughty Frenchman. "I am proposing," he suggested, "that General
Eisenhower commence formal discussions with General de Gaulle regarding plans for landing on the continent this fall, the purpose being
to 'cover up' our real purpose in Torch." A week into the North African
invasion, Churchill sought to mollify de Gaulle, hosting a lunch in the
family quarters at 10 Downing Street during which the prime minister's wife, Clementine, tried unsuccessfully to charm their guest. Instead, de Gaulle unleashed his pent-up resentments. "You have been
fighting this war since the first day. . . . Up to this very moment," he
charged, while "not a single one of Roosevelt's soldiers has met a single
one of Hitler's soldiers. . . . Yet you let America take charge of the conflict." Here was Charles de Gaulle in a nutshell, a plausible case delivered in offensive terms. The tactlessness turned Churchill and FDR,
otherwise natural allies, into de Gaulle's antagonists.

CHAPTER 12

The Home Front

THE AMERICANS WHO STORMED THE BEACHES OF CASABLANCA AND Oran were white. Conspicuously absent were black GIs in segregated units who were relegated to loading ships, driving trucks, and repairing roads. Their absence was not explained by an unwillingness to fight. Blacks, free and slave, had served in colonial militias as far back as 1652. Five thousand blacks fighting under General George Washington helped win America's independence, if not their own. Over 37,000 black soldiers died in the Civil War wearing Union blue; eighteen blacks won the Medal of Honor. Over 367,000 blacks served in World War I. In every cause, these men had fought in the belief that what could not be achieved in a cotton patch or cornfield might be won on the battlefield, entitlement to full rights as American citizens. Thus far, the hope had proved forlorn. In one egregious example, General Andrew Jackson had promised free land to blacks who fought with him at New Orleans in the War of 1812; the promise was broken.

On New Year's Eve 1939 black leaders made a plea to FDR to "appoint fifty Negroes to the Naval Academy . . . and that the army train 100 Negroes to be Air Corps officers." At that time, though blacks comprised approximately 10 percent of the U.S. population, only 1.5 percent had been allowed to join the Regular Army. FDR accepted that if he moved vigorously to desegregate the armed forces, he would run into widespread white prejudices, challenge segregation laws enacted in the southern states, and most daunting, arouse the enmity of southern chairmen of congressional committees upon whom he depended for New Deal support. Illuminating the tone of the times, Army chief George Marshall answered an inquiry from Massachusetts senator Henry Cabot Lodge Jr. saying, "It is the policy of the War Department not to intermingle colored and white enlisted personnel." He added that the buildup of the armed forces was "not the time for critical experiments which would inevitably have a highly destructive effect on morale." Further, the armed forces already provided "separate but equal facilities." Implied but not spoken was the conviction of Marshall and other officers who fought during the First World War that black units had performed poorly in it. The second-highest-ranking American officer in that war, just below General Pershing, Lieutenant General Robert Lee Bullard, had written, "Our government seemed to expect the same of them as of white men. Poor Negroes! They are hopelessly inferior. . . . If you need combat soldiers, especially if you need them in a hurry, don't put your time upon Negroes."

Thus, twenty-four years later, black soldiers were confined to menial tasks that bore out George Bernard Shaw's observation, "America makes the Negro clean its boots and then proves the moral and physical inferiority of the Negro by the fact that he is a shoeblack."

On the same day that Marshall defined U.S. military policy on race to Senator Lodge, FDR, at Eleanor's badgering, agreed to see another three civil rights leaders in the Oval Office, A. Philip Randolph of the Brotherhood of Sleeping Car Porters, Walter White, head of the NAACP, and T. Arnold Hill, acting secretary of the National Urban League. What his visitors did not know was that the president had turned on a rudimentary recording device in place since 1940, the microphone hidden in his desk lamp. He had ordered the system after having been damagingly misquoted following a private meeting in the Oval Office. The surviving transcript of what was spoken with the black leaders is spotty, sometimes inaudible, but it offers a rare view not only of FDR's attitudes on race, but of the unguarded Roosevelt, away from crowds, cameras, or reporters. A. Philip Randolph, his voice rolling and deep, began. "Mr. President . . . the Negro people, they feel they are not wanted in the armed forces of the country, and they feel that they have earned their right to participate in every phase of the

government by virtue of their record in past wars since the Revolution." FDR's response amounted to what later black generations would
call gradualism. "Now suppose you have a negro regiment and right
over here on my right in line would be a white regiment," he said. "Now
what happens after a while in case of war? Those people get shifted
from one to the other . . . gradually working in the field together you
may back into [integration]." Roosevelt then turned to Navy Secretary
Frank Knox, who did not pussyfoot. "We have a factor in the Navy that
is not so in the Army," Knox said, "and that is that these men live aboard
ship. And in our history we don't take negroes into a ship's company."
The president tried to make light of the issue. "If you could have a
northern ship and a southern ship it would be different. [He laughs]
But you can't do that."

The black leaders left the encounter thinking that they had at least
pried open a crack in the wall of segregation. But their hopes were
dashed a few days later when Stephen Early, Roosevelt's press secretary,
a southerner and a racist, told reporters after the meeting with FDR
that the black leaders had expressed contentment with the status quo.
Outraged blacks then issued a counterblast accusing the White House
of a "stab in the back of democracy." The Negro press accused the administration of hypocrisy. FDR sent Harry Hopkins to find out discreetly what might mollify blacks. As a result, the highest-ranking black
officer in the military, Colonel Benjamin O. Davis Sr., the grandson of
a slave, was promoted to brigadier general and William H. Hastie, the
black dean of Howard University Law School, was invited to join Secretary Stimson's staff to promote Negro interests. Nine months after
the meeting, acting only as fast as he believed politically tenable, FDR
issued Executive Order 8802 "to prevent discrimination in employment by holders of defense contracts on account of race, creed, color
or national origin."

After the war, George Marshall manfully admitted that "one of the
greatest mistakes I made" had exacerbated the race issue. Because of
severe winters, training camps in the North were more expensive to
construct than in the South. Further, heavy snow and bitter cold
reduced the months available for training. Consequently, Marshall

opted to have black troops train in the South. As he later confessed, "we ran into things that were utterly beyond our control—that is the local customs of the town, the laws regarding the street, bus services . . . which violently excited the negroes from the North who were unaccustomed to such matters of segregation . . . [yet] we couldn't do away with feeling and reactions and customs in the Deep South."

Racist prejudice was hardly confined to the United States. When Marshall polled military posts abroad about deploying black troops, the reactions were dismally uniform. Australia: "recommends withdrawal of all colored troops." Panama: "The President of the Republic demanded [black soldiers'] immediate withdrawal." Alaska: "The mixture of the colored with the native Indian and Eskimo stock is highly undesirable." Hawaiian Islands: "Colored troops . . . assignment to Hawaii was most undesirable." At the time that the great democracy was celebrating its liberation of North Africa, the armed forces were still as segregated as a public bathroom in Mississippi.

FDR OFTEN AWOKE IN THE MORNING to find in his in basket memoranda left by Eleanor promoting another of her liberal causes, which usually ran ahead of her husband's thinking. Well before Pearl Harbor, in the spring of 1941, his wife had allied herself with Edith Nourse Rogers, only the sixth woman ever elected to Congress. Rogers wanted the military opened to women. She herself had served in France with the American Red Cross during World War I and was all too aware of how women who had served as volunteers and contract employees had been sidelined after the war, denied pensions, disability benefits, and other privileges granted to male veterans. The idea of women in the military was not unprecedented. Lucy Mercer, with whom FDR had a love affair during World War I, had enlisted in the Navy as a yeoman, 3rd class, a "yeomanette." However, in 1941 resistance against women serving ran only slightly behind objections to a racially integrated Army. Congresswoman Rogers was unfazed. On May 28, 1941, with Eleanor Roosevelt's enthusiastic support, she introduced HR 4906, a bill to establish a women's army auxiliary corps. The "auxiliary" qualifier had been insisted upon by the Army to remove any impression that in matters of pay, rank, and duties the WAAC was to be considered part of the military. Under the bill's language, women were to serve *with* but not *in* the service. The bill languished for months in the House Military Affairs Committee where it met with predictable objections. Military service was not ladylike; women lacked the strength, skills, and emotional temperament to perform duties required of the armed services; women should stay at home and mind their husbands and children; the presence of women would pose a threat to morality on military bases. The pragmatic George Marshall, however, had become a convert and asked what sense it made to put men through grueling combat training only to have them end up typing, filing, or answering the phone. Each job filled by a woman, he argued, would free a soldier for soldiering. A year would pass, Pearl Harbor would be attacked, and manpower shortages would become acute before Rogers's bill passed. On May 15, 1942, FDR signed HR 6293, updated legislation creating the new force. Volunteers had to be between the ages of twenty-one and forty-five with no dependents, stand at least five feet tall, and weigh 100 pounds or more. They were not to command men. To distance them further from the Army, WAAC officers would bear ranks such as first, second, and third officer, rather than the usual lieutenant, captain, and major. And rank for rank they were to be paid less.

Oveta Culp Hobby, former parliamentarian of the Texas legislature, co-publisher of the *Houston Post*, and wife of former Texas governor William Pettus Hobby, worked for the War Department's Women's Interests Section. Marshall had depended on the politically astute Hobby to help navigate the WAAC bill through the shoals of a reluctant Congress. With FDR's blessing, Mrs. Hobby, at age thirty-seven, became director of the women's auxiliary on the day the bill became law. The original WAAC strength was set at 25,000 but enlistments came in a flood and within six months the quota was raised to 150,000. Within less than a year of the corps' establishment, WAACs were serving at 240 military installations around the globe. On their first anniversary, FDR told the American people, "There were many in the beginning who smiled and some who violently opposed the thought of women serving with our armed forces. Today, those who have and know the work they are doing . . . have only admiration and respect for the spirit, dignity and the courage they have shown." He signed a bill dropping the "auxiliary" and redesignated the organization the Women's Army Corps, making it a regular component of the Army. Its officers now carried full army rank, Oveta Culp Hobby was promoted to colonel, and WACs received equal pay and benefits. Prejudices, however, died hard. Within the same year, the WACs were subjected to accusations of sexual promiscuity, drunkenness, and a claim that the Army was issuing them condoms, the latter belief particularly outraging the Catholic Church. Eleanor Roosevelt protested, "Will we ever get over believing Nazi propaganda?" The House Military Affairs Committee, the FBI, and Army intelligence conducted investigations that found the allegations baseless. Mrs. Roosevelt ultimately leaned on the Navy, which formed the WAVES (Women Accepted for Volunteer Emergency Service). The Marines and Coast Guard soon followed suit, creating female auxiliaries.

Likely the most accomplished and certainly the most glamorous women in uniform were the Women Airforce Service Pilots, the WASPs, a service that Hap Arnold, overcoming male prejudice, had created under the leadership of a pioneer aviatrix, Jacqueline Cochran, to fly noncombat missions. Over 1,500 WASPs ferried planes, delivered cargo, flew aerial weather reconnaissance, and towed targets for antiaircraft practice. "It was common for commanding officers to say they would rather have the WASPs ferry airplanes across the United States than male pilots," Arnold noted, "because the WASP normally reached her destination a day or two ahead of the time required by a male pilot to do the same job." In explanation Arnold offered, "The WASP didn't carry an address book with her." These women, however, were never acknowledged as members of the Air Forces and were carried instead as civilian employees. As time went on and more male pilots were trained than needed, the WASPs suffered a particularly unkind cut. Hap Arnold, yielding to political and budgetary pressure, declared, "the WASPs have completed their mission," and he disbanded the service. WASPs in their time had flown sixty million miles ferrying 12,650 planes representing seventy-eight different models both within the United States and abroad. Thirty-eight of the women pilots lost their lives. Arnold frankly admitted why the WASPs were grounded. "In my own mind it was because the airline pilots were a bit jealous of the women flier and were apprehensive about what might happen after the war."

✷

THE PRESSURES ON THE PRESIDENT after Pearl Harbor began to intrude on his lifelong habits. He loved to swim, which allowed his muscular chest and biceps to compensate for the withered legs. During the war he stopped using the White House pool and settled for a rubdown. The White House itself had begun to take on the trappings of war. In the evening, Arthur Prettyman, the president's valet, closed heavy blackout curtains in FDR's bedroom. Every room had a bucket of sand and a shovel in it to fight fire. Gas masks hung in several locations. As a deception to conceal construction of a bombproof bunker capable of sheltering 100 people, an East Wing was extended from the White House in 1942. Wartime precautions reshaped the president's travels.

On Saturday evening, October 31, 1942, eight days before the North Africa landings, the president, looking forward to a weekend respite at Hyde Park, was bundled into his limousine and driven along an unfamiliar route. Where, he asked, were they going? Secret Service agents told him that he would soon find out. The limo rolled down a ramp at 14th Street leading to a railroad siding beneath the Bureau of Engraving and Printing. The security staff had devised the arrangement to replace previous routes to exposed sidings scattered around Washington. William Hassett, presidential assistant and omnipresent traveling companion, described the precaution as "a very necessary consideration in these dangerous and troubled times." Amidst bales of paper and barrels of ink that would eventually become U.S. currency, the president was taken aboard the *Ferdinand Magellan,* his private railway car furnished with a sitting room, five staterooms, an observation deck, a small kitchen stocked with FDR's favorites, wild duck, terrapin, and fine wines, and a dining room seating twelve. While in transit, the president remained in contact with the outside world through wire service teletypes, radio transmitters, receivers, and coding machines towed in a car behind the train's engine. The *Ferdinand Magellan* had been heavily armored, including bulletproof windows three inches thick, and weighed three times as much as a conventional Pullman. The Bureau of Engraving and Printing annex was to remain FDR's railway point of departure from Washington for the rest of his life.

In February 1942 the president began dictating to Grace Tully a thirteen-page radio address to be delivered on Washington's birthday. He called in Harry Hopkins and Robert Sherwood to help polish the language and told them, "I'm going to ask the American people to take out their maps. I'm going to speak about strange places that many of them never heard of—places that are now the battleground for civilization. I'm going to ask the newspapers to print maps of the whole world. I want to explain to the people something about geography. . . . I want to tell them in simple terms of ABC so that they will understand what is going on and how each battle fits into the picture. I want to explain this war in laymen's language." The speech went through seven drafts before achieving the spontaneous tone that the president wanted. On February 23, he descended into a basement studio in the White House and before a clutch of microphones began his role as geographer in chief. "From Berlin, Rome and Tokyo," he said, "we have been described as a nation of weaklings—'playboys.'" In a rising crescendo, he intoned, "Let them tell that to General MacArthur and his men. Let them tell that to the sailors who today are hitting hard in the far waters of the Pacific. Let them tell that to the boys in the Flying Fortresses." Then, with an ear-to-ear grin, he said, "Let them tell that to the Marines!"

FDR also saw himself as the nation's morale and recreation officer. A month into the war, he wrote Judge Kenesaw Mountain Landis, the major league baseball commissioner, "I honestly feel that it would be best for the country to keep baseball going. . . . I know you will agree with me that individual players who are of active military or naval age should go, without question, into the services." Yet, on balance, he concluded, "if 300 teams use 5,000 or 6,000 players, these players are a definite recreational asset to at least twenty million of their fellow citizens—and that in my judgment is thoroughly worthwhile."

However grave the moment, he maintained the Roosevelt insouciance. Two days before Torch, bantering at the regular Friday morning press conference with some 200 reporters, he said, "What I am a little afraid of is that somebody will raise the issue that was paramount a few years ago, as to whether one should 'crumble' or 'dunk' the donut. (roaring laughter) Now those are very important things in our national life. And it's part of the grand sense of humor of the American people, and it's all to the good." At another press conference, a reporter asked, "Mr. President, does the ban on the highways include the parking shoulders?" A puzzled FDR asked, "parking shoulders?" The reporter went on, "Yes, widening out on the edge, supposedly to let the civilians park as the military goes by." "You don't mean necking places?" the president responded again to prolonged laughter. He good-naturedly scolded the press, condemning "typewriter strategists" who found fault with the war's conduct. "One of the greatest of American soldiers, Robert E. Lee," he noted, "once remarked on the tragic fact that in the war of his day all of the best generals were apparently working in newspapers instead of in the Army. And that seems to be true of all wars."

Putting enough men in uniform presented a constant challenge. Of every ten men examined for military service, five were rejected, many the result of abysmal health conditions during the Depression. Tens of thousands were unacceptable for psychiatric reasons. To fill mounting levies, physical requirements were gradually lowered. Males could be as short as five feet and weigh as little as 105 pounds. Recruits needed only to have twelve of their original thirty-two teeth. The joke among draftees was that the Army had not tested their eyes, only counted them. A hotly contentious issue arose over how far to lower the draft age. Parents resisted having teenaged sons conscripted for combat. Nevertheless, George Marshall needed soldiers. He went to Congress, investing his considerable prestige to achieve what FDR felt he could not hazard politically, urging that the draft age be lowered to eighteen. Marshall succeeded. An impressed FDR slipped into rare familiarity with the reserved general and wrote him, "Dear George, you won again."

America's industry went on a wartime footing with impressive speed, a cornucopia pouring forth artillery, tanks, ships, planes, rifles, machine guns, mortars, ammunition. The Air Forces chief, Hap Arnold, cited examples of the quick turnaround: the conversion of "a piano company into an outfit that could turn out airplane wings within a few months," a toy factory making "accessories for our airplanes," a pickle plant producing airplane skis, and "a manufacturer of girdles and corsets [who] made parachutes." The war created so much employment that the decade-long Depression vanished overnight. No longer need Americans fear, as FDR once put it, that "Grass will grow in the streets of a hundred cities, weeds will overrun the fields of millions of farms."

In raising an armed force dominated by conscripts, the president believed that the troops should know why they had been torn from civilian life. General Marshall, sharing that conviction, dismissed the value to servicemen of current morale talks by poorly prepared officers "presented after lunch and the man was tired and he went to sleep." A forty-five-year-old Sicilian immigrant, born Francesco Rosario Capra, and who, as Frank Capra, had created such film classics as *Mr. Deeds Goes to Town, Lost Horizon, It Happened One Night,* and other runaway hits, had enlisted in the Army, eager to serve the adopted homeland in which he had succeeded so extraordinarily. One day, to his puzzlement, Capra, now a major in the Signal Corps, was told to report to General Marshall in Washington. He was ushered into the surprisingly tranquil office in the Munitions Building of the nation's senior military figure. Remembering how he had been told to behave before the chief of staff, Capra sat wordlessly as Marshall thumbed through a document. Finally, putting the paper down, the general looked up and came directly to the point. Could Capra make films convincing soldiers that what they were doing was worth fighting for, even dying for? Capra respectfully demurred. He was, he explained, a maker of entertaining movies. He had never made a documentary in his life. "Capra," Marshall answered, "I have never been chief of staff before." Within weeks

Major Capra returned with the first in a series of films, *Why We Fight*. Marshall was astounded by the work's believability, and Capra's subsequent episodes tracing the rise of the dictators, their threat to freedom, and America's stake in defeating them. He found the director's films "amusing, they were serious, they were tremendous in their scope." He wanted every serviceman to see *Why We Fight* before being shipped overseas. The president had in mind an even more substantial morale booster, one reflecting the social philosophy of the New Deal. Five days after Torch, he told the American people that he intended "to enable the young men whose education has been interrupted to resume their schooling and afford equal opportunity for the training and education . . . after their service. . . ." He had planted the seed of the GI Bill.

IN THE FALL OF 1941, drivers along Virginia Highway 27 paralleling the Potomac River noted that the fields of a onetime government experimental farm were being churned by huge earth-moving equipment. Within sixteen months there rose on this plot a colossus. It had been built to consolidate in one place officers and employees of the military scattered in offices throughout Washington, including twenty-three locations for the Army alone and its 24,000 clerks. The shape of the building, chosen by the American architect George Bergstrom, was five-sided, a pentagon. So huge was the structure that if built as a rectangle, one office could be a mile distant from another. The five concentric rings, with five floors aboveground and two below, were built to accommodate over 40,000 personnel, from four-star general George C. Marshall to the lowliest civilian clerk typist. Its labyrinthine corridors totaled seventeen miles, spawning apocryphal tales of the Western Union messenger boy who entered the maze and emerged three days later as a lieutenant colonel; of the secretary who reported to work as a virgin and became so hopelessly lost that she eventually emerged as a mother. So huge was the Pentagon that it could only be seen in its entirety from the air or from nearby mountaintops.

The feat of building this Goliath in less than a year at a cost of an economical $75.2 million was largely the work of Colonel Leslie Groves, an Army engineer, paunchy, soft-looking at 250 pounds, thick-maned with a sparse mustache, who fueled himself with chocolate bars, and had ranked fourth in the West Point class of 1918. A fellow engineer, Lieutenant Colonel Kenneth D. Nichols, described Groves as "the biggest sonovabitch I've ever met in my life; but also one of the most capable individuals. He had an ego second to none. . . . He had absolute confidence in his decisions and he was absolutely ruthless in how he approached a project to get it done."

On September 17, 1942, Colonel Groves had gone before the House Military Affairs Committee to testify on what he hoped would be the last time that he had to defend his construction spending. Afterward, he was intercepted in a Capitol corridor by his superior, Lieutenant General Brehon B. Somervell, an energetic and forceful military engineer who handled the logistical needs of the Army. Groves had been eagerly awaiting a promised assignment that would get him out of Washington and overseas. "About that duty," Somervell said, "you can tell them 'no.'" A flustered Groves asked, "Why?" The secretary of war, Somervell answered, had selected him for another task. "If you do the job right," Somervell added, "it will win the war." Groves, still in the dark, was about to undertake a mission that would demand every shred of ego, professionalism, and ruthlessness that he possessed.

The seed of Groves's new assignment had been planted over two years before. At that time, Leo Szilard, a Hungarian physicist and Jewish refugee, had traveled in a 1935 Plymouth driven by Edward Teller, a fellow countryman and also a physicist, to the summer retreat of Albert Einstein at Peconic, Long Island. Szilard, a pioneer in nuclear fission, a short, round-faced man with unruly dark hair and a limp, intended to convince Einstein to write President Roosevelt, advising him of the extraordinary destructive potential of a new weapon and warning him that Germany could well harness this terrible power first. Persuaded, Einstein signed a letter drafted by Szilard, initially written in German, which Einstein read best, and translated into English. The physicists now needed someone possessing a personal connection to the president to deliver the letter. They found their man in Dr. Alexander Sachs, an economist with the financial firm Lehman Brothers, who had contributed ideas to FDR's speeches in the 1932 presidential campaign and was still occasionally called upon for advice. Sachs, now forty-six, was a self-important figure with a thick halo of curly hair and a receding chin who resembled a cerebral Harpo Marx. He managed to obtain an appointment with FDR through Pa Watson for October 11, 1939. Well aware of the president's penchant for dominating a conversation, the cheeky Sachs reminded Roosevelt that he had come from New York at his own expense and expected to get his money's worth. He bore a letter of earth-shaking consequence, he explained, and launched into a parable for the anecdote-loving president. A young inventor, Sachs said, had once written to Napoleon that he could move ships without wind, which would enable the emperor to invade England in any season. "Bah! Away with your visions," was supposedly Napoleon's response to Robert Fulton and his steamboat. Given what he was about to say, Sachs urged the president not play Napoleon to his Fulton. The letter he carried from Einstein read, "it may be possible to set up a nuclear chain reaction in a large mass of uranium by which vast amounts of power . . . would be generated." This process could produce an explosive, Einstein went on, and "A single bomb of this type, carried by boat and exploded in a port, might well destroy the whole port together with some of the surrounding territory." He ended warning FDR that Germany had already seized Czechoslovakia with its uranium mines and had "stopped the sale of uranium," keeping the element for itself.

Sachs elaborated on Einstein's brief message, reading aloud an 800-word summary of the latest scientific thinking on atomic fission. He closed quoting Francis Aston, a scientist who had expressed the hope, regarding the power of the atom, that mankind would not "use it exclusively in blowing up his next door neighbors." The president thought for a moment, and said, "Alex, what you are after is to see that the Nazis don't blow us up."

"Precisely," Sachs replied. FDR summoned Pa Watson, and, handing him Sachs's papers said, "This requires action." He added that he also wanted Pa to "prepare a nice note of thanks to Professor Einstein," a copy of which Grace Tully was to place "in our very confidential files."

On December 6, 1941, the president agreed to see Dr. Vannevar Bush, his science advisor; Dr. James B. Conant, president of Harvard; Dr. Arthur Compton, a Nobel laureate in physics; and two other physicists, Dr. Lyman J. Briggs and Dr. Ernest Lawrence. The men sitting around the president had one message and it was best argued by Compton, who was meeting the president for the first time. "If atomic bombs could be made, only one plan was possible," Compton warned. "We must get them first." Roosevelt asked a few questions that impressed the group with his grasp of the strategic implications of what they were telling him. The meeting was so secret that it was not recorded in the White House usher's log. As his visitors prepared to leave, Roosevelt asked them to give him an answer within six months as to whether an atomic bomb was feasible. The next day, Japan attacked Pearl Harbor.

Within less than six months, Bush and his colleagues came back with their answer. Theoretically, an atomic bomb was possible. Roosevelt wrote Bush on March 11, 1942, "I think the whole thing should be pushed not only in regard to development but also with due regard for time. This is very much of the essence." FDR handed responsibility to Henry Stimson and the War Department for what became known as the Manhattan Project, the name derived from a fictional engineering district in New York City.

Leslie Groves now learned what General Somervell had obliquely alluded to the previous September. This get-things-done, pile-driving administrator was to head the Manhattan Project. Groves, while a superb manager, was not a scientist and recognized the need for a physicist to lead the science at the heart of the project. At a luncheon in October 1942, hosted by the president of the University of California at Berkeley, he met a thirty-eight-year-old theoretical physicist, J. Robert Oppenheimer, tall, bony, with a domed forehead, blue eyes of startling intensity, a figure described by a colleague as looking like "a young Einstein." Oppenheimer impressed Groves as the physicist he needed. He concluded, "He's a genius. . . . Why, Oppenheimer knows about everything. He can talk to you about anything you bring up. Well, not exactly. . . . He doesn't know anything about sports." But the physicist's background gave the conservative engineer pause. Oppenheimer's wife, brother, and sister-in-law had all been members of the Communist Party. Groves was nevertheless single-minded: he would do whatever he had to do and take whomever he needed to build an atomic bomb. The place chosen for pursuing this objective was a barren chalk dry mesa in New Mexico 7,200 feet above sea level, affording spectacular views for miles. At the time, the property was the site of a boys school called Los Alamos, which the government bought for a little over $400,000.

As America entered the second year of the war, over eighty reporters, elbow to elbow, crowded around the president's desk cluttered with family knickknacks and faced a contented-looking FDR. He waved them closer. He had news, he said. The phrase "New Deal" had been burned into public consciousness as the rallying cry of his presidency. But that banner, he said, was now outdated and time had come for a change. He then began a well-rehearsed ramble. "It was because there was an awfully sick patient, called the United States of America," he went on, "and they sent for the doctor. . . . There were specific remedies that the old doctor gave the patient." He then proceeded to read from a scribbled note on his desk a formidable list of New Deal accomplishments: Social Security, unemployment insurance, the Securities and Exchange Commission, the WPA, FDIC, AAA, the whole alphabet soup of social experiments, over thirty in all. He then updated the patient's prognosis. "Two years ago on December seventh, he was in a pretty bad smashup—broke his hip, broke his leg in two or three places. . . . And they didn't think he would live. And then he began to 'come to.'" What the patient needed now was a new physician, "Dr. Win-the-War. . . . And I think that is almost as simple, that little allegory, as learning again how to spell 'cat.'" No sooner had the president signaled the shift when his foes jumped on him. The chairman of the Republican National Committee, Harrison E. Spangler, asked, "Can a leopard change his spots?" and expressed "great sympathy for [FDR] in his desire to forget the record of his administration for the past eleven years." Indiana congressman Charles A. Halleck said he hoped the president meant "getting rid of the Hopkins-Frankfurter-Wallace scheming in Washington," the latter referring to Vice President Henry Wallace.

Dr. Win-the-War did not abandon his social impulses entirely. In the summer of 1943 FDR went on the air and told the American people, "While concentrating on military victory, we are not neglecting the planning of the things to come." He went on, echoing Lincoln's Second Inaugural Address, "to care for him who shall have borne the battle," "we are today laying plans for the return to civilian life of our gallant men and women in the Armed Services. They must not be demobilized into an environment of inflation and unemployment to a place on a bread line or on a corner selling apples." He formally proposed the GI Bill of Rights. A year later, the bill passed in Congress without a single nay vote. In a well-staged Oval Office drama, Roosevelt used ten pens to sign the GI Bill, then handed them to supporters of the new law, the first presented to Congresswoman Edith Nourse Rogers, the champion of veterans ever since her World War I service with the Red Cross in France. The bill's provisions eased the way for veterans to get a loan to buy a home or go into business. It provided unemployment payments until an ex-serviceman could get on his feet. Its crowning promise was in education. What he wanted, FDR had said, was "an opportunity for members of the armed services to get further education or trade training at the cost of their government." Before the war, less than 5 percent of young Americans went to college. The cost for a single year on a campus could absorb the entire annual pay of an average worker. Attending college remained a prerogative of the upper class.

Postwar, the GI Bill prompted an educational revolution. Half of America's sixteen million veterans took advantage of the bill in some form, from attending Harvard to learning to repair refrigerators. Two years after the war, 50 percent of male students in college were there on the GI Bill. It freed an entire generation from a future of low expectations. Hundreds of thousands of veterans who would have gone back to clerking in grocery stores, cutting hair, or pumping gas went on to become physicians, physicists, engineers, teachers, lawyers, journalists, and thus entered the American middle class. One veteran, Larry Montrell, commented after the war, "Almost everything important that happened to me later came from attending college" on the GI Bill. Roosevelt's vision managed to combine the medicine of Dr. New Deal *and* Dr. Win-the-War.

CHAPTER 13

Unconditional Surrender

NEW YEAR'S EVE 1942: AS THE CLOCK ON THE MANTEL STRUCK TWELVE, FDR gazed with a paternal smile at members of the Roosevelt family and a few close friends. He raised his champagne glass in a toast: "To the United States of America and to United Nations victory this year." Afterward, he invited the guests to join him in watching a movie. As they followed behind his wheelchair to a makeshift theater rigged in the new East Wing, he said over his shoulder that they were about to see the new Humphrey Bogart, Ingrid Bergman hit, *Casablanca*.

FDR had been plotting a meeting of the Big Three—himself, Churchill, and Stalin—for months. However, the battle for Stalingrad was reaching its climax and the Soviet leader begged off, claiming that he could not leave his country at so critical a moment. If it was to be only himself and Churchill, the president still wanted to go forward. The site agreed upon was Casablanca in French Morocco. The astute Harry Hopkins divined FDR's motive: "the reason the President wanted to meet Churchill," he said, "was because he wanted to make a trip." While war raged around the globe, FDR remained confined to a wheelchair at the White House, Hyde Park, or Shangri-La. "He wanted no more of Churchill in Washington," Hopkins observed. "He wanted to see our troops . . . he liked the drama of it!" The journey would provide an adventure for the president, but, more crucially, it would resolve the war's overarching question; as Hopkins put it, "We are off to find where we shall fight next."

Just after dark on a Saturday night, January 9, 1943, the president's limousine rolled down the ramp below the Bureau of Engraving and Printing and stopped alongside the *Ferdinand Magellan*. The faithful Mike Reilly carried the president the few yards into his private car. The bodyguard was aptly suited for the task, a burly Irishman from the Montana mining country, an amalgam of toughness and sentimentality. At 10:30 P.M., the engine began to creak forward amidst hissing clouds of steam. The trip by rail to Hyde Park was an old story for the engineer. Yet, just outside Baltimore, the brakeman was sent to throw switches setting the train back toward the capital. The initial northward direction had merely been a feint, tickling FDR's pleasure in the clandestine. Two days later, the train arrived at Miami's Dinner Key where the president boarded a Navy launch that took him to a massive flying boat, the Dixie Clipper, a Boeing 314, the largest commercial aircraft at that time. Roosevelt, now aged sixty, dreaded flying. His wife, Eleanor, recalled of this journey, "It was his first long trip by air across the water, and I hoped he would be won over." When she had suggested to her sea-loving husband "that the clouds could be as interesting as waves," he snapped back, "You can have your clouds." He had flown ten years before to Chicago to accept a presidential nomination, an aviation first at the time. He was now about to become the first president to leave the country in wartime while in office, the first to fly the Atlantic, the first to enter a war zone. He was accompanied by a small coterie, among them Admiral Leahy, Admiral McIntire, and Harry Hopkins. The Joint Chiefs were flying to Casablanca separately.

Not until Roosevelt was aboard the plane did the pilot, Howard Cone, Pan American Airways' ablest and a naval reserve lieutenant, learn that the "Mr. Jones" on his manifest was the president. After a smooth ascent and the lulling drone of the engines, FDR began to relax. He "acted like a 16-year-old," Hopkins remembered. However, as the skies became turbulent at 15,000 feet, Admiral McIntire watched FDR turn ghastly pale and "worried about the President's bad heart," an early and rare admission that Roosevelt had a coronary condition. McIntire felt compelled to administer what the president later dismissed as "a few whiffs of oxygen."

The trip to Casablanca was circuitous and leisurely, during which

time FDR played solitaire and took naps. The seaplane stopped at Trinidad, crossed the Equator to Belem, Brazil, and proceeded to Bathurst
in the British West African colony of Gambia. FDR in a letter to Daisy
Suckley described what he had just seen of British colonialism, and it
appalled him: "Crowds of semi-dressed natives—thatched huts—great
poverty and emaciation . . . an awful pestiferous hole." At Gambia the
party shifted to an Army Air Forces C-54 transport, arriving at Casablanca as dusk fell on January 14, five days after the handicapped president had left Washington for the journey of 7,541 miles. As he was
lowered to the ground, he could glimpse bomb craters, confirming that
he had indeed entered the war zone. He was taken to a khaki-colored
Daimler automobile and whisked five miles to a slight rise of land
opening onto a glorious aspect of the Atlantic coast. The motorcade
passed through a high wire mesh fence and entered a burst of color,
bougainvillea, begonias, and palm trees. In the center rose a gleaming alabaster hotel, the Anfa, where Patton had received the French
surrender. Surrounding the hotel were eighteen villas owned by rich
Moroccans. Earlier, when his staff had been arranging the conference,
the president told them that he was prepared to sleep in a Bedouin tent.
Instead, he was taken to the most opulent villa in the compound, Dar es
Saada. Upon being shown his bedroom, FDR looked at the frilly décor,
the pastel colors, the wide bed and sunken black marble bathtub, and
declared, "Now all we need is the madam of the house." Churchill's
villa, the Mirador, stood a convenient fifty yards away. Harold Macmillan, part of the prime minister's circle and one day to be Britain's prime
minister, upon viewing the scene wrote, "I christened the two personalities the Emperor of the East and the Emperor of the West and indeed
it was like a meeting of the later period of the Roman Empire."

FDR's military chiefs had arrived two days before, with Marshall so
unsure of local conditions that he arrived wearing a broad-brimmed
hat with a veil of mosquito netting, gloves, and long pants, only to find
his British counterparts in sun helmets and shorts. To Marshall, the
North African campaign had been a lamentable detour and he continued to favor a strike at Germany's vitals through France. He told his
British counterparts that he was "most anxious not to become com-

mitted to interminable operations in the Mediterranean." But the British, having won the Torch debate and ever determined to regain control of the Mediterranean, had already begun to press for Sicily next.

On the evening of his arrival, FDR invited Churchill and his staff to dinner along with his own advisors. As described by one witness, "Since the PM is short and stockily built, his chin isn't very much above the soup plate. He crouched over the plate, almost had his nose in the soup plate, wielded the spoon rapidly. The soup disappeared to the accompaniment of loud gurglings." After dinner, Churchill resumed his fixed habits, staying up all hours and consuming copious amounts of alcohol with no apparent diminution of his mental and verbal facility. Another guest described Churchill's consumption as a "noble procession of wines . . . champagne, port, brandy, cointreau," capped by "two glasses of whiskey and soda." Unfortunately, Admiral King, who had tempered his drinking since becoming the American Navy's chief, lacked Churchill's capacity for holding his liquor and his wits. At the dinner General Brooke, Britain's chief of the Imperial General Staff, described the high point as occurring when King, obviously feeling no pain, became "more and more pompous, and with a thick voice and many gesticulations" instructed the assemblage on how to solve North Africa's political problems. "Most amusing to watch," Brooke observed.

One indulgence the principals had granted themselves was to have their sons present. Air Forces Colonel Elliott Roosevelt, Navy Lieutenant Franklin Roosevelt Jr., Churchill's son, Randolph, a captain in the Special Services Brigade, and Hopkins's son, Robert, a combat photographer, were all seconded to Casablanca. When the first evening's session finally broke up at 3 A.M., Elliott accompanied his father to his bedroom where the weary but exhilarated FDR noted, "The English mean to maintain their hold on their colonies. They mean to help the French maintain *their* hold on *their* colonies." He then added with a laugh, "Winnie is a great man for the status quo. He even *looks* like the status quo, doesn't he?" Yet, for all his determination to end colonialism, FDR's offhand remarks revealed the mores of a vanishing era. When the subject of the Caribbean came up he said, "Oh yes, those West Indies Islands. We're going to show you how to look after them, and not only you but the Portuguese and Dutch. Every nigger will have his two acres and a sugar patch."

The man responsible for security at Casablanca, the barbed wire, searchlights, a swimming pool converted into an improvised air raid shelter, the guard dogs, whom one Britisher described as "biting everyone impartially," was General Patton. Patton by now was well on his way toward cementing his reputation as a terror and a bully. During the North African campaign, he visited the command post of one of his divisional commanders, Terry Allen. Spotting slit trenches around Allen's perimeter, Patton demanded to know why he was being so cautious. For protection against German bombing attacks, Allen explained. Patton then demanded to know which trench was Allen's. As the perplexed officer pointed it out, Patton walked to the edge, opened his fly, urinated in the trench, and said, "There, now try to use it."

Dwight Eisenhower arrived at Casablanca one day after the president. Recently, Marshall had been urging FDR to promote Ike to four-star general. The president answered not yet, not until he saw a "damned good reason." During a meeting between Ike and FDR the president kept demanding to know why the campaign to take North Africa had bogged down. When would it end? Clearing North Africa had in fact fallen beyond schedule, which did not augur well for Eisenhower's promotion. Feeling the pressure, Ike hazarded a long shot and said May 15, still almost four months off. Eventually, the president did relent and Eisenhower was elected to a select company of only twelve American officers who had been awarded four stars, among them Ulysses S. Grant, William T. Sherman, John J. Pershing, MacArthur, and Marshall.

Ike also had a long talk with Churchill at the latter's villa and soon detected which way the winds would blow at Casablanca. Churchill argued vigorously for making Sicily the next stepping-stone. Besides protecting Britain's Mediterranean lifeline, he maintained that Sicily could mark the beginning of Italy's withdrawal from the war, and provide an Allied toehold in Europe proper. Of course, he added, knowing Eisenhower's position in the cross-Channel camp, Sicily would not interfere with planning for the invasion of France. "He could become intensely oratorical, even in discussion with a single person," Ike re-called. "He used humor and pathos with equal facility, and drew on everything from the Greek classics to Donald Duck, cliché and forceful slang to support his position." Churchill's obsession with Sicily, Eisen-hower sensed, would prompt another battle for FDR's soul.

Eisenhower had arrived at Casablanca with his comely driver, Kay Summersby, who wore a tailor-made uniform resembling that of a WAC officer though at this point she was technically a civilian. Her as-sociation with the general had come close to ending the previous fall when she sailed aboard the *Strathallan*, a converted British ship that was torpedoed on December 21, 1942, off Oran en route to delivering reinforcements. She had been rescued and subsequently reentered Eisenhower's entourage. The woman possessed an observing eye. Upon meeting Churchill for the first time, she noted, "I was astounded by the cherubic face superimposed on the bulldog head. . . . His eyes were a vivid blue, at times those of a gurgling infant, at other times of a cold wartime leader. I was impressed by his clear baby like skin. As a woman I was more attracted to that characteristic than to any other." She also noted his preferred form of dress, "his famous siren suit. . . . The best way I can describe it is that it was very similar to a baby's one piece sleeping suit. He liked it because he could thrust his stubby legs in it, pull it up and push his arms into the sleeves—and zip and he was dressed." Summersby did not go unnoticed by FDR, with his keen eye for a handsome woman. He was given a picnic at Casablanca, which Summersby attended along with Franklin Jr., whom his father claimed had fallen for Kay. Further, Roosevelt took for granted an intimacy be-tween Ike and Summersby. The woman was not universally welcomed at Casablanca. General Marshall, she noted, "would have been just as happy if I did not exist."

Two days into the conference, Marshall and his JCS colleagues met with their British counterparts to thrash out where to strike next. Mar-shall saw any diversion from Bolero as a "suction pump," draining re-sources necessary to build an invasion force in Britain strong enough to cross the Channel. A concerned FDR, in seeming agreement, told his chiefs on January 20, "I have a general feeling that we are placing the operation across the channel in 1943 as the last one to be accomplished." Reassuringly, Churchill at one point told the chiefs of staff, "I never meant the Anglo-American Army to be stuck in North Africa. It is a springboard and not a sofa." Marshall and the Americans learned to their dismay that Churchill still intended to point the springboard not at the heart of Europe, but at Sicily. The year before, the British had thwarted the Americans' desire for crossing the Channel in 1942. Here at Casablanca, they were balking at 1943. As before, Churchill managed to swing the president around to his view and FDR accepted the case for Operation Husky, as the Sicilian venture was code-named. Marshall, the good soldier, accepted the president's decision, but with a caveat. He told FDR, Churchill, and the military staffs of both countries that a cross-Channel invasion of France "would be a difficult if not impossible operation to undertake once we have committed ourselves to operation Husky." Major General Albert Wedemeyer, a member of Marshall's planning group, was more succinct, saying, "we came, we listened and we were conquered."

Almost as soon as he had met with the president, Eisenhower and his retinue left for his current headquarters in Algiers. FDR had been much impressed by the man. As he would later say in a speech before the White House Correspondents' Association, "I spent many hours in Casablanca with this young general—descendant of Kansas pioneers. I know what a fine tough job he has done.... Mr. Churchill took the lead at Casablanca in proposing him for the supreme command of the great Allied operations which are imminent."

Against the pleas of his chiefs, FDR insisted on visiting the front, or getting as near as practical. The morning of January 21 had dawned cool but started to warm up under a brilliant sun. Along a route stretching from Casablanca to Rabat crewmen could be seen hosing down dust-streaked tanks, half-tracks, and artillery. Sergeants bellowed orders at 40,000 cleaned-up and shaven soldiers to align themselves shoulder to shoulder along the entire route. The GIs, unsure of why the sudden spit and polish, grumbled about "another bunch of brass hats" on a junket. A collective gasp went up as a smiling, waving figure in a battered fedora, a cigarette holder clamped between his teeth, passed within six feet of them in a jeep, driven by Oran Lass, a staff sergeant from Kansas City, Missouri. Cries of "Jee-zuzz!" rose as the men recognized their president. With FDR were Patton, Mark Clark, and Harry Hopkins. The boxy vehicle carrying them had come into being two years before after a snap decision by George Marshall. At the time, the general had been tied up in a meeting at the Munitions Building when Major Walter Bedell Smith, now secretary of the general staff, broke in to tell Marshall that a salesman from the Willys Motor Company insisted on showing him something. What did he want? Marshall demanded. Smith unrolled a design for a low-slung general purpose vehicle that could seat four to five persons. "Well, what do you think of it?" Marshall asked. "I think it's good," Smith replied. "Do it," Marshall ordered and went back to the business at hand. Thus the jeep was born. Soon after, the vehicle's ruggedness was demonstrated by Willys's chief test driver, who drove one up the steps of the Capitol and back down. Ultimately, 653,568 of the infinitely useful vehicles would be built. The origin of the name is widely believed to derive from the designation GP, for General Purpose vehicle. But the truth remains clouded, since "jeep" was used for certain military vehicles well before the one that became enshrined as a World War II icon.

The president's party passed by men of the 9th Infantry Division, then entered an open field where Sergeant Joseph Baer from Sharon, Wisconsin, had set up an Army field kitchen and twenty small tables with metal folding chairs. Around the tables sat fifty men, some with crutches, who wore the Silver Star and Purple Heart. As a soldier's mess kit heaped with ham, green beans, sweet potatoes, bread, butter, and jam was set before FDR, he was clearly having the time of his life. He later described the moment to Elliott: "You could hear 'em say, 'Gosh, it's the old man himself!'" He described an Army band playing "'Chattanooga Choo-Choo,' 'Alexander's Rag-Time Band,' and that one about Texas, where they clap their hands." "'Deep in the Heart of Texas'?" Elliott answered. He was at least spared "Home on the Range." Somehow it had become embedded that he loved the song. The fact was, as Bill Hassett put it, "the President abominated the song." As FDR said, "The copyright has run out."

After the field lunch the president was shifted to the Daimler and the motorcade proceeded to Port Lyautey, the site two months before of three days of fierce hand-to-hand fighting. Behind a white picket fence stood precise rows of crosses above freshly dug graves, one half of the cemetery for fallen GIs and the other half for the Frenchmen they had fought. FDR directed General Clark to place huge wreaths on each side. He removed his hat and bowed his head as the mournful strains of "Taps" floated over the hallowed ground. On the return to Casablanca, George Patton rode beside the president. As Roosevelt later described their conversation, Patton told him "at least five times that he hoped to die with his boots on." Patton, usually a critic rather than an admirer of politicians, later wrote that Franklin Roosevelt "really appeared as a great statesman."

The purpose of Casablanca had been settled. And again the British had prevailed. At noon on January 24, the press corps was summoned to a garden behind the Hotel Anfa bursting with beds of crimson flowers. Some fifty reporters, photographers, and newsreel cameramen jockeyed for position in front of two white leather chairs, a microphone propped between, and less grand seats placed on each side. Corporal Hopkins, the Army photographer, scurried about framing his shots. The hotel door opened and Lieutenant Colonel Elliott Roosevelt stepped out supporting his father, who wore a lightweight gray suit. He chatted endlessly as he was lifted onto his seat, his customary tactic for diverting attention from his handicap. Reporters covering him for the first time gaped in wonder at the fleshless legs, surprised to discover how severely impaired the president was.

A minute later Churchill appeared wearing a blue pin-striped suit, a bow tie, a homburg, and a watch chain draped across a modest paunch, looking as if he were about to enter Parliament. In his lapel he wore a "V for Victory" pin. Churchill was followed by two Frenchmen competing for command of the Free French Forces, Generals Henri Giraud and Charles de Gaulle, who flanked FDR and the prime minister. The president asked Churchill if he would like to take off his hat. No, he answered, he needed it to keep the sun out of his eyes. He suggested that the president might wear one, to which FDR replied, "I was born without a hat and didn't see any need for one now."

Roosevelt began to read the official end-of-conference communiqué in the starchy, bloodless prose of diplomacy. He then glanced at a sheaf of handwritten notes in his lap, looked up, and assumed the bemused expression he reserved for moments when he intended to surprise. "I think we have all had it in our hearts and our heads before," the president began in a folksy manner, "but I can't think that it has ever been put down on paper by the Prime Minister and myself." He went on, "we had a general called U.S. Grant. . . . In my and the Prime Minister's early days, he was called 'Unconditional Surrender' Grant." He paused, his voice became somber. "The elimination of German, Japanese, and Italian war power means the unconditional surrender by Germany, Italy, and Japan." There it was, out in the open. This war was not to be ended by negotiations, not by terms of an armistice, not by give-and-take among belligerents, but only when the enemy lay prostrate at the feet of the victors. Reporters dropped to their knees, balancing their notebooks and scribbling furiously.

As FDR finished, Churchill is reported to have chimed in, "I agree with everything the President has said." However, in later statements he would claim he had been caught off guard. According to Robert Sherwood, Churchill subsequently told him, "I heard the words 'unconditional surrender' for the first time from the President's lips at the conference. . . . I would not myself have used these words, but I immediately stood by the President." The prime minister's claim of being surprised appears disingenuous. The term "unconditional surrender" had a recent history. Almost eight months before Casablanca, an American advisory committee had been formed to deal with "Post War Foreign Policy." On May 6, 1942, Norman Davis, a member of the panel much admired by FDR and once an advisor to Woodrow Wilson, briefed Roosevelt on how the war should end, "with the assumption that unconditional surrender will be expected of the principal defeated states." Before his departure for Casablanca, on January 7, FDR held one last meeting with his military chiefs. He was concerned, he told them, that "Mr. Stalin probably felt out of the picture as far as Great Britain and the United States were concerned." Roosevelt's haunting fear was that an isolated Stalin might enter into another peace pact with Hitler. He added that he had an idea for overcoming Stalin's "loneliness." He was "going to speak to Mr. Churchill about the advisability of informing Mr. Stalin that the United Nations were to continue until they reach Berlin and that their only terms would be 'unconditional surrender.'" Further, FDR had discussed the issue with Churchill at Casablanca on January 20, four days before the press conference. Afterward the prime minister cabled London asking what his war cabinet thought about his issuing a statement "of the firm intention of the United States and the British Empire to continue the war relentlessly until we have brought about the unconditional surrender of Germany and Japan." The cabinet agreed unanimously.

Elliott Roosevelt provides a lively account of the subject over a lunch the day before the final press conference involving himself, FDR, Churchill, and Harry Hopkins. According to Elliott, unconditional surrender came up again and Churchill exulted, "Perfect! I can just see how Goebbels and the rest of 'em'll squeal." Two days later, FDR had put the thoughts on paper that he intended to use at the press conference marked, "Notes for my use—dictated by me on January 22," expressing "the simple formula of placing the objective of this war in terms of unconditional surrender by Germany, Italy and Japan." That FDR's utterance was a spontaneous outburst or that Churchill heard the expression for the first time from the president's lips in that sunlit Casablanca garden contradicts the facts.

The deeper question persists as to whether the policy was wise, a controversy debated to the present day. Roosevelt's early experience had shaped his thinking. As assistant secretary of the navy in World War I, he had seen a negotiated armistice leave the virus of German militarism intact, enabling Hitler to exploit the claim that the Fatherland had not been beaten on the field of battle in World War I, but "stabbed in the back" by defeatist politicians and communist agitators. This time, Germany's defeat must be utter and undeniable, Roosevelt believed. He had taken the American people into war, they were told, to defeat evil. The posters rousing them to enlist, to build more planes, to ration food, to collect scrap, to believe that "loose lips sink ships" featured a Germany with octopus tentacles reaching out to swallow up Europe and bucktoothed, demonic Japanese. Their president was not asking Americans to sacrifice their sons to negotiate with the devil, but to destroy the devil. Unconditional surrender raised a stirring battle cry, a call to defeat villainy and right wrongs. Finally, unconditional surrender, in FDR's view, offered Stalin proof that the Western Allies would not make a separate deal with the Nazis and leave the Soviet Union dangling alone.

The president's rationale was not embraced in all quarters. Churchill fluctuated from echoing Roosevelt to a later secret message to Anthony Eden, his foreign secretary and a future prime minister, saying, "We certainly do not want, if we can help it, to get [the enemy] fused together in a solid block." Churchill's seeming contradictions make sense if one accepts evidence that he supported unconditional surrender, but regretted FDR's public utterance of the phrase, which left no room for maneuver in the future. Churchill's chief of military intelligence, Major General Sir Stewart Graham Menzies, predicted that, faced with unconditional surrender, the Germans would fight "with the despairing ferocity of cornered rats." As Eisenhower framed the dilemma, "If you were given two choices—one to mount the scaffold and the other to charge twenty bayonets—you might as well charge twenty bayonets." If Roosevelt had pushed for unconditional surrender in no small measure to placate the Soviet Union, he was in for a rude disappointment. First, Stalin was angered that he had not been consulted beforehand. Second, a ringing phrase was no substitute for what he wanted: a second front. Third, he too feared that unconditional surrender would stiffen German backs just as the war was turning around at Stalingrad. Roosevelt himself never retreated from unconditional surrender, sticking to his "pig-headed Dutchman stance" to the last. His close advisor, Sam Rosenman, noted, "I do not remember any time when the President wavered on it." Unconditional surrender, however, was eagerly embraced in one camp. Dr. Joseph Goebbels, the Nazi propaganda chief, crowed, "If our Western enemies tell us 'we don't deal with you. Our only aim is to destroy you,' how can any German, whether he likes it or not, do anything but fight on with all his strength."

★

THE EMPEROR OF THE East and the Emperor of the West, along with their generals, admirals, and aides, had met twenty times and shared thirteen meals at Casablanca. Churchill, following his work-hard-play-hard habits, "ate and drank enormously all the time, settled huge problems, played bagatelle and bezique by the hour and generally enjoyed himself," observed Harold Macmillan. For Roosevelt, Casablanca had meant escape from the literal and figurative prison of his wheelchair, allowing him to go where the war was being fought and mix with the men who were fighting it. Harry Hopkins's take on Casablanca was right. The president essentially had wanted an adventure.

As the conferees began to scatter, Churchill persuaded FDR to join him for a five-hour, 150-mile drive in the Daimler along Route 9, insisting, "you cannot come all this way to North Africa without seeing Marrakech," the so-called Paris of the Sahara, with its "fortune tellers, snake charmers, masses of food and drink, and on the whole the largest and most elaborately organized brothels in the African continent." They stayed at another sumptuous villa, the stucco russet-colored La Saadia, where FDR allowed his security detail to lug him in a wicker chair up sixty circular steps to a tower affording a spectacular view that Churchill had painted before the war. The prime minister's physician, Lord Moran, watched the effort to elevate the president, noting his "paralyzed legs dangling like the limbs of a ventriloquist's dummy."

The next day, wearing his zippered flying suit, Churchill accompanied FDR to a waiting plane that would retrace the six-day journey back to the United States. As the plane lumbered into the sky, Churchill seized the arm of Kenneth Pendar, the American vice consul in Marrakech, and said, "If anything happens to that man, I couldn't stand it. He is the truest friend, he has the farthest vision, he is the greatest man I have ever known."

★

ON JANUARY 25, the day after Casablanca, the Red Army scored a signal victory in the struggle for Stalingrad. Two Russian armies joined forces in the middle of the city, dividing the enemy and dooming Germany's Sixth Army, a force that in 1940 had roared triumphantly across Holland and Belgium. Eight days later, Field Marshal Friedrich Paulus, commanding the Sixth, whose men had been ordered by Hitler to "hold their positions to the last man to the last round," suffered the ignominy of surrendering his 90,000 troops, including twenty-seven generals, to a twenty-one-year-old Russian lieutenant. Subsequently, the bedraggled "Ubermenschen" were paraded past grim-faced Muscovites in a parade that lasted for hours. Hitler, in a last-ditch attempt to buck up Paulus, had promoted him to field marshal; thus the Russians had the satisfaction of seeing an officer of the highest rank in the German army herded among the defeated.

CHAPTER 14

★

From Pacific Islands to Desert Sands

THE PRESIDENT WAS IMPATIENT WITH THE PACE OF FIGHTING IN the Pacific. After four months of grueling jungle combat, Guadalcanal, key to defending Australia, remained unconquered. Instead, after the Navy's thumping off Savo Island, the usually upbeat Chester Nimitz, commander in chief of the Pacific Fleet and of ground forces in his zone of the ocean, warned Roosevelt, "It now appears that we are unable to control the sea in the Guadalcanal area . . . the situation is not hopeless but it is certainly critical." On Saturday, October 23, 1942, FDR gathered the Joint Chiefs and told them that before the weekend was over he expected them to find whatever could be stripped from other sectors "to make certain that every possible weapon gets into that area to hold Guadalcanal." Bill Hassett, FDR's correspondence secretary, wrote in his diary on November 1, "The President was really apprehensive about Guadalcanal Island and our losses there, particularly the loss of our fourth carrier," the *Hornet*.

FDR's interest was both strategic and personal. Guadalcanal was essentially a Marine Corps show and the Marines formed part of his favored Navy. His eldest son, now Lieutenant Colonel James Roosevelt, 1st Marine Battalion, was fighting on the island. Jimmy would eventually stand on a Guadalcanal parade ground as Nimitz pinned the Navy Cross on him, a decoration ranking second only to the Medal of Honor in the Navy, for his part in a raid on Makin Island where "at great risk to himself . . . he continually exposed himself to heavy machine gun and sniper fire" and "personally saved three men from drowning in heavy surf."

George Marshall made a practice of sending casualty figures to the president to make the abstract movements of pins on the Map Room walls take on a flesh-and-blood reality, otherwise, he feared, "you get hardened to these things." The reality was brought home forcefully to FDR when, in November 1942, his naval aide, John McCrea, came into the study with a report that instantly shifted the president's customary breezy aplomb to a somber mien. The light cruiser *Juneau*, limping away from an engagement off Guadalcanal, had been torpedoed and some 700 crewmen went down with her. A hundred men who initially survived were left adrift, dying from exposure, thirst, and attacks by sharks. In the end, only ten of the crew lived. Sometime afterward, McCrea brought to FDR a list of names for new destroyers. One was designated the USS *Sullivan*. A puzzled Roosevelt asked, who was Sullivan and "what did he do for the Navy?" McCrea explained that among the *Juneau*'s losses were five brothers from Iowa, Albert, Francis, George, Madison, and Joseph Sullivan. "It occurs to me that the people collaborating on this list didn't use much imagination," the president commented. He took out his pen, crossed out "Sullivan" and wrote in "The Sullivans." "A good change I say," McCrea added. Thereafter the Navy tightened its policy against family members serving on the same ship.

ON NOVEMBER 20, CHURCH BELLS pealed across New Jersey, the home state of pugnacious sixty-year-old Admiral William "Bull" Halsey, to celebrate a day in his honor. Repeated Japanese attempts to replenish the garrison on Guadalcanal had been rebuffed, with so many ships and planes destroyed on both sides that the strait between that island and Savo Island became known as "Iron Bottom Sound." Still, in the end, an exultant Halsey told his staff, "We've got the bastards licked." Guadalcanal had essentially been won. As glowing reports reached the Map Room, Robert Sherwood went in to see the president, urging him to make a public announcement of victory. Roosevelt, usually the eternal optimist, resisted, fearing Americans would become complacent. On November 17, at a forum with editors of the *New York Herald Tribune,* he cautiously allowed that "It would now seem that the turning point in this war has at last been reached." Though serious resistance had been quelled, the last Japanese would not evacuate Guadalcanal until February 1943. The battle was costly. For the United States, in over six months of naval clashes, two carriers, eight cruisers, and fourteen destroyers went to the bottom. Japanese ship losses were comparable. In a hell hole of jungle rot, mud, and vermin, the Japanese had been willing to expend 24,000 lives, while 5,775 of the 60,000 U.S. Marines and soldiers engaged were killed or wounded.

Before the conquest of Guadalcanal, at a meeting of the Joint Chiefs late in 1942, FDR complained that at the current rate they would need 2,000 years to reach Japan. Later, at Casablanca, he told his staff that moving island by island "would take too long to reduce Japanese power. Some other method of striking at Japan must be found." Nimitz, Halsey, and other Pacific admirals, upon contemplating the vastness of the ocean and the myriad islands within it, favored "leapfrogging," invading certain Japanese-held islands while cutting off others and leaving them to wither. Marshall endorsed the strategy. But MacArthur showed less enthusiasm. One of the island chains that might be leapfrogged, he feared, was the Philippines to which he had sworn to return.

With Guadalcanal won, North Africa invaded, and the British victory at El Alamein, Winston Churchill felt secure enough to say at the Lord Mayor's Luncheon at Mansion House on November 10, 1942, that while it was premature to proclaim the beginning of the end, the Allies had reached "the end of the beginning."

★

ADMIRAL KING WAS SOON TO MARK his sixty-fourth birthday, the Navy's mandatory retirement age. For King, at the summit of his career, commanding a mighty navy in history's greatest conflict, retirement was anathema. Still he could not penetrate the thicket of FDR's mind to know if he might be kept on or be permanently dry-docked. He had Navy doctors give him a rigorous physical examination and passed easily, which emboldened him to tackle the retirement issue head-on. He called in his chief yeoman and dictated a letter to the president: "I should bring to your notice the fact that I shall attain the age of sixty-four years on November 23 next," he wrote, then added, "I am, as always, at your service." He had the letter typed on his four-star letterhead stationery, hand-delivered to the White House, and held his breath. FDR returned the letter with a handwritten note at the bottom, "So what, old top? I may send you a birthday present." Ernie King had received the present he hoped for.

King's dictatorial reign of the Navy was to continue. At one point, he lost patience with so many of his officers preferring khaki dress, making them look as though they were in the Army, rather than wearing the classic Navy blue double-breasted uniform with gold trim and gold buttons. He concocted a uniform of his own design, single-breasted, the color of dishwater, with black trim and black buttons. He issued an order mandating use of the uniform and banning khaki. Navy officers hated the garb from the start, and King could enforce its use only among staff officers within his sight. Even he eventually recognized the futility of his sartorial initiative when, during a group photo session, a photographer mistook him for an enlisted man and complained that he was blocking the shot. End of the experiment in Navy gray.

THE MOUNTAINOUS ISLAND of New Guinea lay like a jagged crescent across from the northern coast of Australia. On its southeastern edge, just 300 miles from Australia, lay the city of Port Moresby. The port, if taken, would provide Japan with a staging area for a Japanese invasion of Australia. The Australians and MacArthur wanted Port Moresby as a forward line of defense to cut off such an invasion. For Douglas MacArthur, the port held another attraction; it could become a launch pad for fulfilling his obsession, to drive north and free the Philippines. His determination to do so was steeled when a handful of haggard escapees from the Bataan Death March came to him and recounted the horrors they had endured. "The Japanese will pay for that humiliation and suffering," he promised the survivors. At this time, perhaps accepting the brutal nature of the war against the Japanese, the usually preening MacArthur stopped covering his chest with medals, ribbons, and badges and began displaying only his general's stars. However, he still moved about like a potentate. When leaving his headquarters in Melbourne he was always accompanied by tommy-gun-toting bodyguards in a nation where the police went unarmed. His limousine carried a four-star flag and the license plate "USA 1." The plate on his wife's limousine read "USA 2." Whenever he flew it was in his comfortably appointed bomber escorted by a flying wedge of P-38 fighters.

On July 21, 1942, a Japanese force had landed at Buna on the northeastern shore of New Guinea intending to press south to Port Moresby. MacArthur fought back and by November was able to launch a three-pronged attack on Buna by American and Australian troops to block the Japanese advance. He did not think much of the Australians. They were, he complained, "unable to match the enemy in jungle fighting. Aggressive leadership is lacking."

Hap Arnold left a less than admiring report of MacArthur after visiting his headquarters. MacArthur delivered a nonstop, two-hour monologue claiming that the pick of the Japanese army was fighting him, that they were superior to the Germans, and that "the Australians were not even a good militia." MacArthur poured out his resentment that the president and the War Department were starving his sector in favor of the European theater, a conviction not entirely unfounded. During Operation Torch in North Africa, Eisenhower's forces had been allotted fifteen tons of supplies per man while MacArthur in his campaigns received only five tons. Upon leaving MacArthur, Arnold wrote of him in his diary, "a brilliant mind—obsessed by a plan he can't carry out—dramatic to the extreme.... Hands twitch and tremble—shellshocked."

The war in New Guinea was fought through sucking, ankle-deep mud and fetid vegetation, in temperatures frequently exceeding 100 degrees, where men clambered on their hands and knees over stony, sharp-edged ridges in drenching rains that rotted their clothing to rags. According to U.S. Army medical records, men fell victim to "Malaria, dengue fever, scrub typhus, bacillary and amoebic dysentery . . . jungle rot, dhobie itch, athlete's foot, and ringworm." Christmas 1942 passed in this pesthole virtually unnoticed. Not until April 1944, after nearly two years of combat, would the island be effectively conquered, though fitful Japanese resistance would not sputter out until the end of the war. Battles fought over places barely remembered today—Buna, Sanananda, the Kokoda Trail—cost 3,095 American and Australian dead, nearly twice the bloodshed at Guadalcanal. The ultimate Allied victory in New Guinea had two consequences: first, Australia was saved, and secondly, in the debate over Pacific strategy MacArthur strengthened his argument that Japan could be reached by a thrust northward toward the Philippines versus the King-Nimitz approach of leapfrogging across the Central Pacific.

ON APRIL 15, 1943, FDR contacted his Navy secretary, Frank Knox, with a knotty proposition. He had just been informed by Nimitz of the most spectacular coup by American code breakers since Midway. With this fresh intelligence, American forces could have Japan's greatest military strategist in its cross-hairs. Navy radiomen in the Pacific had intercepted a coded signal from the Japanese Southeastern Air Fleet and forwarded it to cryptanalysts at Pearl Harbor. Admiral Isoroku Yamamoto, the principal Japanese strategist, would be flying in a bomber escorted by six fighters from Rabaul on New Britain Island, the main Japanese naval base in the Pacific, to three posts near Bougainville in the northern Solomon Islands. Given the recent reverses in the Pacific, the admiral was coming to boost the morale of his forces, comfort the sick and wounded, and decorate the brave.

Admiral Nimitz immediately grasped the possibilities of the coding breakthrough. American forces on Guadalcanal had taken an airbase, Henderson Field, named after a Marine pilot, Major Lofton Henderson, killed in the Battle of Midway. Yamamoto's itinerary would place his plane within range of Henderson's fighter aircraft. The opportunity to eliminate so renowned a figure, however, amounted almost to the assassination of a chief of state. Further, the intelligence on Yamamoto's movements was so pinpointed that attacking him might signal that the Americans were breaking JN-25, the Japanese naval code. Thus Nimitz had bucked the decision as to what to do up to the president. Navy Secretary Knox suggested that Roosevelt seek guidance from clergymen he respected. The clerics consulted raised no objections and Roosevelt gave the green light to Nimitz, who passed along to Bull Halsey the signal, "Good luck and good hunting."

At 6 A.M., on the morning of April 18, Yamamoto, in a crisp green uniform, boarded the Mitsubishi twin-engine bomber at Rabaul. Simultaneously, eighteen Army P-38 Lightning fighters fitted with extra belly tanks to increase their range took off from Henderson Field flying at low level under the radar. An hour and a half and 500 miles later, the fateful rendezvous took place. Cannon fire from the fighters quickly set the Mitsubishi ablaze, which fell from the sky, tearing a gash in the Bougainville jungle. Yamamoto was killed outright. The death of Japan's paragon was judged the equivalent of America losing Eisenhower in Europe or Nimitz in the Pacific. So heavy was the blow that when Yamamoto's fate became known in Germany, Hitler had a posthumous medal struck in his honor.

BY THE END OF AUGUST 1943, the Japanese had been driven from the windswept wastes of Attu and Kiska in the Aleutians. They fought to the death on Attu, with only twenty-eight of the 2,500 defenders surrendering. On August 15, a massive Allied force of over 34,000 troops landed on Kiska only to find that the enemy had abandoned the island. Militarily, the Aleutians amounted to little, except to the 1,200 Americans who lost their lives there and their families. At least Japan no longer occupied an inch of U.S. soil. The retaking of the Aleutians, added to the far greater defeats at Midway, Guadalcanal, and New Guinea, confirmed Yamamoto's earlier foreboding. America had to be driven from the Pacific in the first six months. It had not. Instead, the giant had been awakened and Japan now faced the full might of America's military and industrial power while struggling to keep pace.

✶

George Marshall had bent to the British and—most disappointedly—to his president's will that the place to start the European war was North Africa. The month before the Casablanca conference, he had made an attempt again to steer the president toward the continent, saying that he "opposed dabbling in the Mediterranean as wasteful," and that North Africa should be wrapped up as quickly as possible so that the Allies could get back to Operation Bolero, the serious business of building a force powerful enough to cross the Channel. Now, three months after Torch, the American army still faced the cold winter rains and churning mud of the Atlas Mountains to reach its next objective, Tunisia. At Casablanca, Marshall had undergone another bitter setback, one that exemplified FDR's oft quoted remark that he was "a juggler, and I never let my right hand know what my left hand does." Marshall had counted on FDR's alleged impatience with peripheral adventures that could only delay the cross-Channel invasion. But now, the undecipherable president had gone along with Churchill's arguments that even after North Africa was won, Western Europe would still have to wait. The invasion of Sicily, Operation Husky, was to be undertaken next.

At this point, the map of North Africa revealed an Allied pincer movement in the making. The British Eighth Army, under Montgomery, was pushing west from Libya against Rommel's Afrika Korps. The Americans and British, after taking Morocco and Algiers, were regrouping to move eastward into Tunisia, converging with Montgomery's forces, and thus trapping the Axis armies between them. Soon after Torch, Rommel had gone to Hitler's East Prussian headquarters, the *Wolfsschanze* (Wolf's Lair), in a mosquito-infested woods near Rastenburg. His intention was to warn the führer, "If the Army remained in North Africa, it would be destroyed." Upon delivering the message, Rommel was taken aback by Hitler's reaction. His words, Rommel recalled, acted "like a spark in a powder barrel. The Führer flew into a fury. . . . I began to see that Adolf Hitler simply did not want to see . . . what his intelligence must have told him was right." Instead of abandoning Africa, Hitler intended to pour more German troops into Tunisia by ship, plane, and glider and defend it to the last.

For a while it seemed that Hitler's determination to fight on in Africa made sense. On February 14, 1943, Rommel launched a westward offensive in Tunisia against American and British troops, driving a wedge through a gap in the rugged Western Dorsal mountain range at a point called the Kasserine Pass. The Americans particularly took a fearful mauling and GIs surrendered in droves. The performance at Kasserine prompted George Marshall to compare the character of the American soldier with his enemy. As he saw it, "The Germans are natural fighters; we must accept that. . . . If you left a sergeant with a few men, he fought like he had a lieutenant general in command. . . . Too often our fellows, when they were new at the game, would think that somebody else ought to come right away and reinforce them or take over. . . . They were far from home and the ordinary military quality is not dominant in the American anymore. It's no longer the question of taking the gun down off the mantelpiece and fighting against the savages."

Kasserine made clear to Eisenhower, the commander in North Africa, that heads must roll. Leading the II Corps in the sector where the Kasserine debacle occurred was Major General Lloyd R. Fredendall, a fifty-nine-year-old dropout from West Point who later won a commission through an Army competitive examination. Described by a colleague as "small in stature, loud and rough in speech, he was outspoken in his opinions and critical of superiors and subordinates alike." Though thirty-six years in the Army, Fredendall had never led men in battle before Torch. Ike initially had regarded the man as a fighting gamecock and cabled Marshall three days after Torch, "I bless the day you urged Fredendall upon me." Now he would have to eat those words. He sent Major General Ernest N. Harmon to help Fredendall straighten out the Kasserine mess. Harmon sent back a merciless evaluation to Eisenhower. He described Fredendall as "a son of a bitch" unfit for command, and a coward to boot. Field Marshal Harold Alexander finished off Fredendall, telling Ike, "I'm sure you must have better men than that." Ike faced the most disagreeable act a commander must perform in wartime. He flew to Fredendall's headquarters, a comfortable bunker hewn from solid rock by Army engineers seventy miles from the front, a refuge Fredendall rarely left. Ike relieved him of command on March 5, but let Fredendall down easy. He was promoted to lieutenant general, given a job training troops in the States, and received a hero's welcome upon coming home.

Eisenhower dealt with his old tank partner George Patton as if handling a stick of dynamite. The man's military gifts were indisputable. At a point when Ike wrote down his assessment of his officers, he granted Patton a "deep sense of duty, courage and service" and rated him a superb combat commander. At the same time he recognized Patton as dangerously combustible. "He talks too much and too quickly and sometimes creates a very bad impression. Moreover, I fear that he is not always a good example to subordinates." Nevertheless, Eisenhower needed a fighter not a saint to replace Fredendall. The tempestuous, profane, flammable Patton was given command of II Corps, sending a shock wave through the unit's lackadaisical GIs. Patton ordered troops, even in the combat zone, to wear neckties and leggings. Rear echelon men, cooks and clerks, were to wear steel helmets at all times in the fearsome African sun. An officer's pay would be docked $50 and an enlisted man's $25 for infractions. What grumbling GIs dismissed as "chickenshit" was Patton's way of notifying the corps that a new commander was in the saddle and that pre-Kasserine slovenliness was over.

As throughout his career, Patton continued to exhibit bewildering contradictions. On one occasion when Marshall came to North Africa he and Eisenhower watched him conduct an amphibious training exercise during which Patton rushed at the first wave shrieking, "And just where in the hell are your goddamned bayonets!" He then unleashed a torrent of abuse and obscenities that caused Marshall and Eisenhower to turn away in embarrassment. Yet, when the same Patton sent his aide, Captain Dick Jenson, to the front, "to get him blooded" and the young man was killed, Patton fell on his knees and wept openly before his men. As he recorded in his diary, "I kissed him on the brow and covered him up."

✶

IN THE MIDST OF THE NORTH AFRICAN campaign, Eisenhower temporarily dispatched his aide, chum, poker partner, and diarist, Commander Harry Butcher, to Washington to tend to some stateside business. Butcher carried out his tasks and was planning to return when, on March 26, he was told to come to the White House. The president wanted a briefing on North Africa for which Butcher was to be allotted ten minutes. He was ushered into the private study, where FDR sat behind a desk stacked with the New York and Washington afternoon newspapers. "The President greeted me," Butcher recalled, exclaiming "that nothing pleased him more than to realize that the Navy was taking care of a general." After ten minutes, Butcher glanced at his watch, expecting to be dismissed. Instead, the president embarked on a soliloquy lasting over a half hour in which he displayed a fine awareness of Ike's problems with Lloyd Fredendall and his satisfaction with the latter's replacement by his favorite, the dashing George Patton. He amusedly told Butcher how Patton had told him at least five times at Casablanca that he hoped to die with his boots on. FDR surprised Butcher with his detailed grasp of the North African campaign, wanting to know why Army intelligence got it wrong in predicting that a major German offensive would be launched in the north rather than in the south at Sidi bou Zid. He laughingly recounted the story of a truckload of Italian officers in dress uniforms, including plumed helmets, riding into a Tunisian POW camp to surrender. "On the other hand," he noted, "the Germans we capture are truculent and mean." With that, the president bade a thoroughly charmed Butcher goodbye and thereafter informed the Senate that he wanted Patton's promotion to lieutenant general speedily approved.

✶

IT WOULD TAKE A CONSCIOUS EFFORT to pair two more unalike generals than George Patton and Omar Bradley: Patton, well born, Bradley, descended from hardscrabble Missouri farmers, losing his father at age fourteen; Patton, a hard drinker, and Bradley who never touched a drop until age thirty-three; Patton vulgar before the troops and cultivated on loftier occasions; Bradley never uttering a coarse word at any time; in short, braggadocio and theatrics versus modesty and understatement. Eisenhower ordered Bradley, a 1915 West Point classmate, to Tunisia to serve as Patton's deputy. The two men had lived across the street from each other twenty years before during Hawaiian service, but had never worked together. As Bradley later reflected on his new superior, "When Patton talked to officers and men in the field, his language was studded with profanity and obscenity. I was shocked." Bradley interpreted these antics as Patton saying, "I'd rather be looked at than overlooked." Bradley found Patton a Jekyll-Hyde personality, yet on balance, "an amazing figure."

By late April 1943, Eisenhower had decided to pull Patton from the Tunisian front to map preparations for the Sicilian campaign. Bradley, at age fifty, took command of II Corps. He too was rated by Eisenhower as "a godsend. . . . About the best rounded, well-balanced senior officer we have in the service. . . . I feel there is no position in the Army that he could not fill with success." A. J. Liebling, war correspondent for *The New Yorker,* dubbed this unprepossessing, spindly, knobby-chinned officer who dressed no differently than his men, "the GI General." Liebling recalled Bradley standing on a hillside before a map pinned to an easel and in a Missouri twang briefing reporters on his plan for victory in Tunisia with all the drama of "a teacher outlining the curriculum for the next semester." The homespun modesty, however, concealed a ruthless drive, which Bradley began to display as his forces pushed the Axis forces up the Cap Bon Peninsula toward Tunis, the capital.

On April 7, Joseph Randall, a slightly built sergeant from State Center, Iowa, and a boyish British soldier, William Brown from Devonshire, one coming from the west and the other from the east, shook hands on the road linking the Tunisian towns of Gafsa and Gabès.

Bradley's II Corps had linked up with Montgomery's Eighth Army. The Germans and Italians, with their backs to the sea, retreated further toward Tunis, their last foothold in North Africa. On May 12, Colonel General Hans-Jürgen von Arnim, a hereditary Prussian soldier, surrendered his army. Over a quarter of a million Axis troops, including eleven German generals, marched into POW cages. Rommel, who had been transferred since March 9, was spared the ignominy of seeing his once fearsome Afrika Korps lay down its arms.

After six months, the battle for North Africa was over. Was it worth it? The campaign had cost the Allies 10,290 dead and 21,363 missing or captured. Another 38,688 were wounded, many maimed for life. The British had maintained that the Allies, particularly the untested Americans, were not yet prepared to strike against the continent in 1942 and instead had pressed successfully for Torch. With victory, the Mediterranean lifeline of the British Empire had been secured. But for the Americans? The chiefs of staff, Marshall, King, and Arnold, along with the theater commander, Eisenhower, had never wanted Torch. They had merely acquiesced when FDR allowed himself to be persuaded by the British that in 1942 U.S. troops were not ready to take on Fortress Europa, that the sea lanes to Britain were too long for an invasion buildup, and amphibious transport too short for successfully crossing the English Channel. Yet the distance was just as far from American ports to North Africa as to Britain. Further, the case that American GIs were too green is countered by the fact that when Europe was finally invaded, nearly twenty months later, 60 percent of the American troops were facing combat for the first time. Further, these initially untested Americans, along with the British, had ultimately bested the vaunted Afrika Korps, as tough troops as they would meet in France on D-Day.

Another alternative to North Africa might plausibly have been considered, one that would have met British objections to Sledgehammer yet would still have put Allied troops into Europe in 1942. Imagine if the convoys approaching North Africa, instead of turning south toward Morocco and Algeria, had turned north and struck the Vichy-controlled south of France between Toulon and Cannes, exactly as they would twenty months later in Operation Anvil. The first enemy that American troops faced in North Africa were French, the same flag they would have faced in the south of France. Actually, the Allies would have initially faced less opposition there, since Vichy had fewer troops in France than in North Africa. Admittedly, such a landing would have prompted the Germans to tear up the Vichy armistice and rush troops into unoccupied France. But this is essentially what they did anyway, pouring troops if not into southern France, then into North Africa. Likely, the Vichy French would have surrendered in France proper as quickly as they did in North Africa. Instead, the Allies had to fight across Casablanca to Tunis, a distance of 1,000 miles, the equivalent of fighting from Normandy to well beyond Berlin.

The wisdom of Roosevelt's decision to go along with Churchill and make North Africa the American entryway into the European war still eludes the final judgment of history. Nor can the alternative suggested above be proven to have worked. But what is never tried cannot be disproven. Marshall later made an often quoted statement that seemed to endorse FDR's conviction that American troops had to be engaged *somewhere* in 1942, even North Africa. "We failed to see that the leader in a democracy has to keep the people entertained," he said. "That may sound like the wrong word, but it conveys the thought." Did Marshall mean that he ultimately embraced FDR's decision, or might he have meant that, regrettably, political showmanship trumped military logic? He may also have made this statement because it would be unthinkable for a chief architect of a military campaign, as was Marshall, to admit to families who lost loved ones in North Africa that the enterprise was ill conceived and likely unnecessary. The historian Stephen Ambrose insists that Marshall went to his grave "convinced that a mistake had been made in North Africa." What is generally agreed upon is that the unanticipated fierceness of the German resistance in North Africa, as Churchill himself admitted, threw "out all previous calculations," about when the continent could be invaded. Even Hitler noted that the North African campaign delayed the invasion of Western Europe by at least six months. His prediction was to prove too conservative. As planning for the invasion of Sicily began sucking up manpower, ships, and planes, the possibility of invading Western Europe, already lost for 1942, now appeared lost for 1943 as well.

AT 6:45 P.M. ON MAY 11, 1943, an eager Franklin Roosevelt, his limousine parked on the siding beneath the Bureau of Engraving and Printing, sat in his wheelchair facing the *Ferdinand Magellan.* The president had been listless of late, his skin gray, eyes baggy. But as a rotund, rosy-cheeked figure in an improbable yacht squadron uniform emerged from the train, all FDR's cares vanished. Franklin Roosevelt and Winston Churchill beamed like long-lost chums as they entered FDR's private car. Churchill had just sailed the Atlantic aboard the *Queen Mary,* now a troopship, accompanied by over 100 generals, admirals, advisors, diplomats, and a Royal Marine detachment. As the prime minister would later confess in his memoirs, "the main purpose for which I crossed the Atlantic," his third wartime trip to Washington, code-named Trident, was to win FDR's support for an invasion of the Italian mainland even before the Sicilian campaign had begun.

The day after Churchill's arrival, the president invited him and the top military chiefs and civilian advisors of both countries into his study, a gathering Churchill described as "the most powerful group of war authorities that could be assembled in any part of the world." FDR greeted his guests arms outstretched and smiling broadly. As they sat down, General Sir Alan Brooke found his attention drawn to the haphazard array of items on the president's desk, a "bronze bust of Mrs. R, bronze ship's steering wheel clock, four cloth toy donkeys, one tin toy motorcar, one small donkey made of two hazel nuts, jug of iced water, pile of books, circular match stand and inkpot." Churchill wasted no time in getting to the point. They must invade mainland Italy as soon as Operation Husky had subdued Sicily. He described the twin rewards: drawing Italian troops out of the Middle East, thus influencing Turkey to come in on the Allied side; more importantly, forcing Italy to leave the war, thus breaking up the Axis partnership, which would "cause a chill of loneliness over the German people." Roosevelt's poker-faced military advisor, Admiral William Leahy, saw through the prime minister's circumlocution. "Churchill made no mention of any British desire to control the Mediterranean . . . which many persons believed to be a cardinal principle of British national policy."

A brief for invading Italy was not what Roosevelt wanted to hear from the prime minister. He "had always shrunk," he said at this gathering, "from the thought of putting large armies in Italy." His words heartened Marshall, echoing his own conviction that "landing ground forces in Italy would establish a vacuum in the Mediterranean" that would swallow up the resources necessary "to execute a successful cross Channel operation." As Brooke later noted in his diary, "the Americans are taking up the attitude that we led them down the garden path by taking them to North Africa. That at Casablanca we again misled them by inducing them to attack Sicily. And now they do not intend to be led astray again."

There followed a separate meeting of the Combined Chiefs at their unlikely headquarters, the Public Health Building on Constitution Avenue. Afterward, Brooke and Marshall chatted in the corridor where the American remarked, "I find it hard even now not to look on your North African strategy with a jaundiced eye." Brooke responded, "What strategy would you have preferred?" The Army chief was unhesitating, "Cross channel operations for the liberation of France and advance on Germany; we should have finished the war quicker." Brooke's reply illuminated the chasm between the American and British objectives. "Yes, probably, but not the way we hope to finish it." Besides his intent to control the Mediterranean, events in Russia had shifted Churchill in a new direction. As the Russians turned the tide after Stalingrad and, with only intermittent reversals, began driving west, the prime minister became obsessed with ending the war as far east as possible, before the Red Army could sweep across Europe. Possession of Italy, enabling drives into Austria and the Balkans, was far more desirable, in his judgment, than trooping across France. Churchill's barely concealed maneuvers to derail Bolero, the cross-Channel strategy, prompted a joke in London circles. The prime minister gets a call at 10 Downing Street and asks who is calling. A voice answers, "This is Joe at this end," to which Churchill asks, "Joe who?" "Joe Stalin." Churchill asks, "Where are you?" Stalin answers, "Oh, I'm at Calais."

As the Trident conference continued, the British kept pressing their case, mounting arguments from handsome leather-bound policy guides but counting principally on their most potent weapon, Churchill's eloquence and bulldog tenacity. As a Map Room aide, Navy Lieutenant Junior Grade George Elsey, observed, "The President sat back and listened carefully; Churchill never sat back . . . the Americans could not match the voluble Brits, especially Churchill!" One week into Trident, the prime minister received his second invitation to address a joint session of Congress. The first time, soon after Pearl Harbor, he had been defiant in the face of all too possible defeat. But with Germany beaten in Tunisia just the week before, with 5,000 Nazi prisoners jammed belowdecks on the *Queen Mary* during his journey to America, he faced U.S. lawmakers and leaders, thumbs hooked in his vest, and crowed, "For [this] we have to thank the military intuition of Corporal Hitler." The Allies had "arrived at this milestone in the War, we can say, 'One continent is released.'"

Thirteen days into the conference, Churchill's physician, Lord Moran, watched his patient pacing his room and muttering, "The President is not willing to put pressure on Marshall. He is not in favor of landing in Italy. It is most discouraging. I only crossed the Atlantic for this purpose. I can not let the matter rest where it is." Nor did he. In the end, the two powers reached a compromise. As recalled by Leahy, Roosevelt, while agreeing on Italy, told Churchill that he wanted the Channel operation at the earliest possible date, and not later than 1944. Eisenhower was to be instructed to "eliminate Italy from the War immediately." But how, where, and how far up the Italian boot must the campaign advance? All this was left hanging. As for the cross-Channel operation, Churchill still dragged his feet, conceding only that, of course, "an invasion of Europe must be made at some time in the future." But "adequate preparations could not be made for such an effort in the spring of 1944." General Brooke even suggested 1946. Emerging from one heated session, the ever-irascible Admiral King complained,

"We ought to divert our forces to the Pacific." At FDR's insistence, however, a date for invading Western Europe was agreed to, May 1, 1944. British General Frederick Morgan, Eisenhower's chief of staff, was handed the task of drawing up the master plan, determining the transports, landing craft, planes, divisions, and desirable points of attack. The operation was to be called Overlord, a term of Churchill's invention.

Aware of the Americans' barely concealed lack of enthusiasm over Italy, the prime minister worried that the agreement might slip away. He played one last card. On May 25, the day before he was to depart from Washington, he "appealed personally to the President to let General Marshall come to Algiers with me." As his rationale, he explained that he was going to discuss the Mediterranean with Eisenhower at the latter's headquarters in Algiers and that he wanted Marshall present as "a United States representative on the highest level." He did not want it to appear "that I had exerted an undue influence" on Eisenhower. Roosevelt warily agreed. Churchill decided not to sail the *Queen Mary*, but to fly. The intimacy of a long plane ride should give him time to work his wiles on Marshall. He knew that if he could convert Marshall to Italy, Marshall would keep Roosevelt committed. The general, already exhausted by Trident, was scheduled to make another long trip to the Pacific theater and hoped to squeeze in a few days' relaxation at home before having to pack again. Secretary Stimson was appalled by Churchill's gall. He wrote in his diary that dragging the dog-tired Marshal "on a difficult and rather dangerous trip across the Atlantic Ocean where he is not needed, except for Churchill's purposes, is I think going pretty far."

WINSTON CHURCHILL'S MACHINATIONS were not the only tension FDR faced during Trident. He still clung to the sentimental notion of China becoming a world power that could lead Asia from colonialism to independence once the war was won. However, Joe Stilwell, the man he had sent to serve as his chief emissary to Generalissimo Chiang Kai-shek, kept delivering bad tidings, and not without cause. The Air Forces chief, Hap Arnold, had flown to the Pacific in February 1943 to get a firsthand view of the air war in China. On Chiang, he agreed with Stilwell. "The Generalissimo does not impress me as being a big man," he wrote in his diary. "He casts aside logic and factual matters as so much trash." The will of the Chinese, Chiang had assured him, would overcome any military deficiencies. The generalissimo's only strategy, Arnold found, was "Aid to China! Aid to China!" And planes, planes, planes. He delivered to FDR a memorandum prepared by Stilwell, which the president read with mounting dismay. "If a Chinese soldier fires," Stilwell reported, "and kills anyone on the enemy side, he himself gets shot. That is common talk. . . . It indicates how anxious the Chinese are not to interrupt business." Besides Chiang's reluctance to engage the Japanese army, Stilwell described in minute detail endemic corruption in Chiang's military forces. In one example, the commander of the Chinese Fifth Army was given funds to pay 45,000 troops, though he had only 25,000, allowing him to put "about $6,000 United States gold in his pocket every day." Under the "coffin racket," "The division commander gets $15.00 per coffin. He keeps $7.00." Other middlemen "kept nibbling at the remaining $8.00 until finally a local carpenter got $2.00 for making the coffin." To Stilwell the Chinese army was "A gang of thugs with the one idea of perpetuating themselves and their machine. . . . Hands out for anything they can get." Chiang's efforts to tame graft and injustice were spasmodic and arbitrary, Stilwell reported. Seeing a file of peasants, ropes around their necks, being dragged off to serve in the army, Chiang stopped them and after hearing their tales of brutality, personally began beating the recruiting officer half to death with his walking stick.

In a letter to his wife, Stilwell vented his frustration in a ditty:

Pappy's done his bit,
He's shoveled all the shit,
He's just a sap,
He took the rap,
The wringer got his tit.

Despite the dreary assessments, the president remained fixed on making something of China. He advised Arnold on which Chinese targets to bomb. If the Shanghai power plant were destroyed, "it would slow up Japanese production for six months," he said. FDR further believed that he better understood the Oriental mind than did the brusque Stilwell. After reading Vinegar Joe's catalogue of calamities, he told Marshall, "Stilwell has exactly the wrong approach in dealing with Generalissimo Chiang who, after all, can not be expected, as a Chinese, to use the same methods we do. When Stilwell speaks about the fact that the Generalissimo is very irritable and hard to handle, upping his demands, etc. he is of course correct. But when he speaks of talking to him in sterner tones," Roosevelt concluded, "he goes about it just the wrong way."

During Trident, the president had ordered Stilwell to Washington with another old China hand, the cocky aviation champion, now Major General, Claire Chennault. Chennault, who with the president's enthusiastic support had created the Flying Tigers before the United States entered the war, had since risen to command the American 14th Air Force operating in China. There was bad blood between Chennault and Stilwell, which had begun over what the flier called "that whorehouse of mine." He had been alarmed by the number of his men put out of action by venereal disease, and as he saw the solution, "The boys have got to get it, and they might as well get it clean as get it dirty." He had dispatched an Air Forces plane to fly twelve Indian prostitutes, cleared by doctors, to China and set them up in a brothel. When Stilwell learned of the enterprise, he exploded. U.S. planes, crews, and gasoline were not intended for carting whores over the Himalayas. As Chennault's nominal commander, he ordered that the bordello be shut down. As *Time* magazine's Asia correspondent, Theodore White, described Stilwell, he "had the morality of Oliver Cromwell—he was pure, absolutely pure of graft, adultery, lying, thieving or any transgression of the Ten Commandments."

From this earthy spat, the quarrels between Stilwell and Chennault had escalated into the strategic sphere, principally over proper distribution of scarce equipment flown from India over "the Hump" into

China. Stilwell was still trying to stick to what he regarded as military fundamentals: keep the supplies coming his way in order to open a land route across Burma, thus enabling a strengthened China to take on the Japanese army. Chennault had boasted to FDR that, given enough planes and supplies, he could "accomplish the downfall of Japan" without a ground campaign. Stilwell referred to Chiang Kai-shek behind his back as "Peanut," whereas Chennault played him like a harp. He won over a priceless ally, the generalissimo's closest partner, his wife, the feline, slit-skirted, brainy seductress, Madame Chiang, born Mayling to the prominent Soong family, a Wellesley graduate who had lived fifteen years in the United States and understood Americans. At the time of Trident, FDR was in a fight with the labor leader John L. Lewis, and asked Madame Chiang, who had shown up uninvited at the White House, how she would handle the situation. As Eleanor Roosevelt recalled the moment, "the beautiful small hand came up very quietly and slid across her throat." The generalissimo, tired of the squabble between Stilwell and Chennault, had earlier sent a cable to FDR essentially dumping the problem onto his lap, which led to the president bringing the two Americans to Washington. After meeting with British generals, Stilwell wrote in his diary, "Nobody was interested in the humdrum work of building a ground force but me. Chennault promised to drive the Japs right out of China in six months, so why not give him the stuff to do it." Finally, Stilwell had a meeting with FDR and Churchill, but when he "tried to speak my piece," Roosevelt waved him aside and "Churchill kept pulling away from the subject and it was impossible." Afterward he noted in his diary, "Churchill has Roosevelt in his pocket. . . . The Limeys are not interested in the war in the Pacific, and with the President hypnotized, they are sitting pretty." In the end Claire Chennault ran circles around Vinegar Joe at the Trident conference. Roosevelt told the flier to skip channels and in the future to communicate with him directly.

The one person who seemed to grasp Stilwell's true worth was George Marshall, who saw a splendid potential corps commander going to waste. "I wanted Stilwell to resign his command and let me give him another command," Marshall later admitted. But at the time he dared not use up any more of his credit with FDR, which was primarily invested in keeping the president focused on the cross-Channel operation. And so Vinegar Joe, an essentially friendless but "splendid fighting man," was shipped back to China to resume Roosevelt's dream of making China a great power in a poisonous partnership with Chiang Kai-shek.

THE LENGTHS TO WHICH CHURCHILL and Roosevelt would go to appease Joseph Stalin became glaring in a grisly story that began to unfold on April 13, 1943. During the period in 1939 in which Stalin and Hitler had been partners in carving up Poland, the Russians had taken 180,000 Poles prisoners, mostly soldiers, but officers, policemen, government officials, and intellectuals as well. During a 9 P.M. newscast on the April date, Radio Berlin reported that German forces occupying the area of Smolensk in Russia had found in the Katyn Forest a massive pit eighty-four feet long and forty-eight feet wide filled with "twelve layers of bodies of Polish officers numbering about 3,000 . . . their hands tied, all of them had wounds in the back of their necks caused by pistol shots." If true, the discovery offered a windfall for the German propaganda chief, Joseph Goebbels, allowing him to tell the world that the behavior of the Russians was no better than what the Nazis were accused of doing. According to the German account, the massacre had occurred in 1940 when the Russians still occupied Katyn.

FDR was in Monterrey, Mexico, on a goodwill tour, when eight days after the Radio Berlin accusation Cordell Hull forwarded to him a blistering message from Stalin. The dictator lashed out at "the campaign of calumny against the Soviet Union initiated by the German Fascists regarding Polish officers they themselves slaughtered in the Smolensk area on German occupied territory." Subsequently, the head of the London-based Polish government-in-exile, General Wladyslaw Sikorski, called for a Red Cross investigation. Stalin shot back that Sikorski was fomenting mistrust to defame the Soviet Union. Before leaving Mexico, Roosevelt moved to placate his angered ally. He cabled a message to "Mr. Stalin, Moscow," saying that General Sikorski "has made a stupid mistake in bringing this issue to the international Red Cross." Hull managed to persuade FDR to remove the word "stupid" before sending the message.

The Russians put up a showy defense in 1944, naming a prominent Soviet surgeon, Dr. Nikolai Burdenko, to head an investigation of the Katyn slaughter. Three American journalists and Averell Harriman's daughter Kathleen attended Burdenko's inquiry and accepted evidence exonerating the Soviet Union. But FDR and Churchill had known the truth well before. On May 24, 1943, after the German revelation of Katyn, Churchill received a report prepared by Owen O'Malley, the British representative to the Polish government-in-exile. O'Malley deduced the time of the killings from the clothing worn by the Poles. He also noted that Katyn had been a favored Soviet site for executing czarist enemies. Most damning was the fact that the prisoners' letters to their families ceased abruptly in April 1940 when the Katyn Forest was still in Soviet hands. "In light of all the evidence," O'Malley concluded, the guilt of the Russians was unassailable. A practical man, however, he accepted that the need to maintain solidarity with the Soviet Union outweighed all else. "We have been obliged to behave as if the deed was not theirs," he said. But his conscience bothered him. In turning a blind eye to evil, O'Malley asked if they were not "falling under St. Paul's curse on those who can see cruelty and not burn." Churchill was prepared to risk St. Paul's curse. He forwarded O'Malley's report to Roosevelt, penning a note that it was "a grim, well written story, but perhaps a little too well written." He asked the president to send the report back and closed saying, "We are not circulating it officially in any way." FDR was all too willing to keep the Faustian bargain: don't anger the Russian Bear with Western moralizing, just keep him fighting on our side. Thus the dead Poles were buried not only physically but politically, their true fate subservient to a presumed larger cause.

What actually had happened? Lavrenty Beria, chief of the Soviet secret police, the NKVD, wrote Stalin on March 5, 1940, warning that the Polish prisoners "are attempting to continue their counter-revolutionary activities and are carrying out anti-Soviet agitation." Stalin all too eagerly embraced Beria's suggested solution, "The supreme penalty, shooting." Soon after, their Russian captors began luring Polish prisoners from three camps with promises that they were being transferred to more hospitable conditions and could look forward to returning home soon. One group of Poles was reportedly taken to Smolensk, some to an abattoir in the city, and others to the Katyn Forest twelve miles to the west. All were dispatched by the preferred Soviet method of execution, a shot in the back of the head. The final number of Poles killed is estimated between 9,000 and 11,000.

A half century would pass before the Soviet Union publicly acknowledged responsibility for the atrocity when President Mikhail Gorbachev presented the Polish government with boxes of documents that he admitted "indirectly but convincingly established the guilt" of Stalin's regime.

CHAPTER 15

★

Italy Invaded, Germany Blasted

FDR WAS AWARE THAT HE HAD DISAPPOINTED HIS MILITARY CHIEFS by surrendering to Churchill's arguments to invade North Africa first, which inevitably delayed Bolero. At the Casablanca conference, Marshall and the other cross-Channel proponents lost a second round when FDR, again siding with Churchill, agreed to the invasion of Sicily next. Churchill's latest argument for the operation, called Husky, was one he knew FDR would embrace. Sicily, he maintained, could tie down German divisions, thus relieving pressure on the Soviet Union. Marshall, ever the good soldier, swallowed the decision. But he wanted to know what was to follow Husky. "Is Sicily to be a means to an end," he asked, "or is Sicily to be an end in itself?" Eisenhower's deputy, Mark Clark, was more trenchant. "In reality, we will get no place by doing [Sicily]," he wrote in his diary, "and the result will not be commensurate with the effort and the losses involved." Whatever appreciation was expected from Stalin failed to materialize. "Sicily cannot replace the second front in France," he wrote the prime minister.

Nevertheless, Husky went forward. At a White House dinner honoring French General Giraud, FDR, speaking off the cuff, picked up on Churchill's pet phrase and said conspiratorially, "I have just had word of the first attack against the soft underbelly of Europe," and added, "I am going to ask you to say nothing about it after you leave here, until midnight ends." He closed, "Last autumn the Prime Minister of England called it 'the end of the beginning.' I think you can almost say that this action is the beginning of the end."

★

EISENHOWER, AS COMMANDER IN CHIEF of Allied forces, was in overall charge of Husky and under him, leading the Seventh Army, he picked George Patton, who was finally to achieve what he believed he had been born to do, lead a great legion in battle. Eisenhower had handed Patton the command with his customary mix of confidence and uneasiness. "You frequently give the impression that you act merely on impulse and not upon sturdy reflection," he wrote Patton. "People that know you as I do are quite well aware of the fact that much of your talk is a smokescreen, but some of those in authority, who have a chance to meet you only occasionally, do not have this knowledge. My advice is therefore . . . count to ten before you speak." Eisenhower's second in command, British General Sir Harold Alexander, retained overall charge of his nation's and Canada's forces, while operations on the ground rested with the theatrical Bernard Montgomery heading the Eighth Army. Monty was not a pliant subordinate, especially toward American superiors. His shifts of mood could be mercurial. After the RAF turned down his request for a personal plane, he went to Eisenhower, who came through with a B-17. Upon first seeing the plane on the tarmac, Monty described Eisenhower as a "great and generous man." Just before Husky, he offered this description of himself: "I know well that I am regarded by many people as being a tiresome person. I think this is probably true. I try hard not to be tiresome."

Husky had multiple objectives: to deprive the Axis of strategically placed airfields and sea lanes, to trap enemy forces on the island before they could withdraw to the Italian peninsula, creating something of a German Dunkirk, and as a possible bonus, to bring about the fall of Mussolini's fascist regime. The paramount objective, if unspoken, was Churchill's continuing determination to gain total control of the Mediterranean.

If Sicily is seen as a triangle, Montgomery's mission was to drive up its right-hand leg to the Strait of Messina, thus sealing off the enemy's escape to the mainland. The Americans were to land on the triangle's southern leg and move inland, acting as a shield to protect Montgomery's left flank, a subordinate role Patton found galling. The armada moving toward Sicily on July 10, 1943, was like nothing the world had ever witnessed. Pounding through a wind-whipped sea, lulling the Germans into believing that this was no night for an invasion, were over 3,000 vessels—warships, transports, tankers, minesweepers, and landing craft delivering eventually 150,000 men, 600 tanks, and 1,800 heavy guns. Aboard the Western Task Force flagship, USS *Biscayne*, George Patton, conspicuous in a green-lacquered helmet bearing two stars, a short well-cut leather jacket, riding breeches, and gleaming boots, with an ivory-handled revolver slung at his side, gazed through binoculars seeking to spot the Sicilian shoreline. His mouth was a thin arc curving downward, set in the practiced Patton scowl. Near midnight on July 9, over 3,000 paratroopers from the American 82nd Airborne Division, faces blackened with cork, began to flutter earthward from C-47 Dakota transports. By 3 A.M., American troops were untangling themselves from rope ladders and dropping into the landing craft. With extraordinary luck, the winds died down just as morning dawned, providing calm seas for a smooth debarkation for the infantry. Uncertain of the waters, some coxswains dropped their ramps too soon, leaving men weighted down under eighty-pound packs to drown in waters over their head. The Americans began landing along the island's southern shore at six points around the ancient city of Gela.

On the right, on the Catania Plain, stiff German resistance bogged down Monty's push for Messina. To advance this objective, a concerned General Alexander ordered Patton to continue to maintain the shield alongside Montgomery. Playing a supporting role failed to fulfill George Patton's vision of martial glory. On the northern coast of Sicily lay the island's capital, Palermo, to him, a far more tempting prize. Though in the opposite direction from which Alexander had ordered him to move, Patton began to shift his forces toward Palermo. Outraged by Patton's disobedience, Alexander directed him to halt and drive east to bolster Montgomery. Afterward, Patton would claim that he had received Alexander's order but that it was "garbled in transmission." He drove ahead and took Palermo on July 22. Patton's ambition was now revealed in all its nakedness. Huddled with Bradley over a map just outside Palermo, he pointed east and said, "I want you to get into Messina as fast as you can. . . . Even if you've got to spend men to do it. I want to beat Monty into Messina." Bradley later recalled of this encounter, "I was very much shocked."

As Sicily was being conquered, the pain awaiting Italians on the mainland became clear when on July 19, in broad daylight, 570 B-17, B-24, and B-26 bombers dropped over 1,000 tons of bombs on the rail yards at San Lorenzo and Scalo del Littorio, just south of Rome, and on the city's Ciampino Airport. According to reconnaissance photos, the military targets were hit hard, though only one holy site suffered damage, the Basilica of San Lorenzo. For Roosevelt, approving a raid so near the Eternal City was not arrived at lightly. Rome held the history and treasures of Western civilization, and to millions of Catholics worldwide, the Vatican was sacred. Roosevelt's often breezy manner, however, concealed the grit within. In the end the president accepted General Marshall's reasoning, who "considered the blood of the present to completely outweigh the desire to preserve the historical treasures of antiquity." FDR further defended the raid, telling reporters four days afterward that the Germans had destroyed some 4,000 churches, hospitals, and libraries in Britain. Yet he "did not believe in destruction merely for retaliation . . . but destruction for saving the lives of our men in a great war."

Likely Italy's strongman, Benito Mussolini, suffered the greatest damage from the raid. That very day, the Italian dictator had flown to Rimini, a seaside resort on the Adriatic, to meet with Adolf Hitler. After massive reverses in North Africa and the threat of defeat on Italian soil, Mussolini expected Hitler to understand why Italy could not continue in the war. Instead of sympathy, he was treated to one of Hitler's tirades. No inch of ground was to be given up "so that Sicily may become for the enemy what Stalingrad was for us." On the flight back to Rome, a despondent Mussolini flew through the sooty plumes arising from the twisted, smoking wreckage of the Rome rail yards.

The pope requested a ban on bombing the holy city and the Allies temporarily suspended the raids. But when FDR received a request from the Allied Combined Chiefs of Staff "to revoke, repeat, revoke, the prohibition and again authorize General Eisenhower to bomb Rome," he wrote boldly across the bottom, "I approve heartily sending the directive to Eisenhower." Within three weeks, 274 more bombers struck Rome's rail marshaling yards.

The Vatican sought terms from the Allies to have Rome declared an open city, which meant under international law that it would not be defended, while the opposing armies would agree not to attack it. Churchill scotched the idea. "What will the Russians say," he asked FDR in an August 4 message. "It would appear that we . . . had abandoned the principle of unconditional surrender." Further, "we hope that in a few months Rome will be in our hands and we shall need its facilities for the northward advance."

Eighteen days into the invasion of Sicily, FDR went on the air to arouse among the American people a sense of involvement in the war effort. Civilians might grumble about gas rationing, he said, but "I think the personal convenience of the individual . . . back home in the United States will appear somewhat less important when I tell you" about the invasion of Sicily. He then gave a surprisingly frank inventory of the number of ships, men, guns, and tanks engaged in Husky, with a subtext intended to overwhelm the Germans by pure numbers.

In late July, FDR retreated to the tranquillity of Shangri-La in the rolling Maryland Catoctin Mountains to huddle with Sam Rosenman and Robert Sherwood over a speech dealing with domestic problems that persisted even in wartime. Congress was threatening to abolish a favorite Roosevelt initiative, the National Resources Planning Board. The word "planning" in the lexicon of congressional conservatives smacked of communism. As FDR and his colleagues wrestled over language to save the board, the president took a call from his press secretary, Steve Early, back in Washington. Early had extraordinary news. Radio Rome was reporting that Mussolini had fallen. On July 25, Mussolini had gone to the villa of the Italian king, Victor Emmanuel III, to confess his country's plight. The monarch greeted Il Duce, who was in full military regalia wearing a field marshal's uniform. Victor Emmanuel told the dictator, with as much sympathy as he could muster, "At this moment you are the most hated man in Italy." The king pointed out that the pillar of Mussolini's support, the Fascist Grand Council, had by 19 to 8 voted to oust Il Duce. He explained that he was calling upon a former chief of staff and long-standing Mussolini opponent, Marshal Pietro Badoglio, to head a new government. Mussolini was then taken away under guard two days later and packed off to the tiny island of Ponza under house arrest. One of Churchill's arguments for Husky, that it could presage Italy's removal from the war, began to appear prophetic. Yet Badoglio's first public utterance was disappointing. The new leader told the Italian people, "The war continues. . . . Italy keeps faith to its pledged word." Keener observers, however, read the underlying intent of the general's words. The new minister was saying what he believed he had to say in order to fend off a harsh seizure of his country by a vengeful Hitler.

FDR cabled Churchill in the wake of Mussolini's fall that he favored "good treatment of the Italian people." He sent Eisenhower a text that he should broadcast, saying, "We commend the Italian people for ridding themselves of Mussolini, the man who involved them in a war as the tool of Hitler." The Allies came as "liberators," the message continued, and "our occupation will be mild." For American public consumption, however, FDR raised a clenched fist against the nation that had supinely followed Hitler in declaring war on the United States. During his July 28 speech defending the National Resources Planning Board, he departed from the text to say, "Our terms to Italy are still the same as our terms to Germany and Japan—unconditional surrender. We will have no truck with Fascism. . . . We will permit no vestige of Fascism to remain."

A DEMOLISHED BRIDGE SPANNING a deep ravine halted Montgomery with the prize of Messina only two miles from his grasp. Instead, at 10:25 A.M. on August 17, a triumphant George Patton stood in his command car surveying the port city that he had reached first. America now had what it craved, a soldier in the heroic mold. "Gen. Patton Waded Ashore to Battle," read a *New York Times* headline. The *Los Angeles Evening Herald and Express* described Patton jumping into the surf from a landing craft and personally taking command, "turning the tide in the fiercest fighting." An NBC correspondent described Patton as "a combination of Buck Rogers, the Green Hornet and the Man from Mars. . . . He has enough dash and dynamite to make a Hollywood adventure hero look like a drugstore cowboy." Patton made the covers of *Time*, *Newsweek*, and *Life*. He was now "Old Blood and Guts," a metaphor eliciting mixed interpretations among the men under him. FDR, who had been haunting the Map Room during the fighting, was overjoyed when an aide delivered a dog-eared, sweat-stained field map of the Sicilian front sent by Patton, with a bold crayon arrow pointing to Palermo. FDR responded with a cable telling Patton that after the war he was going to make him "The Marquis of Mt. Etna." Of Montgomery, FDR said privately, "Monty never starts until he's got all the guns and all the men he needs . . . Patton is just the opposite, reckless, quick. . . . I think it works out well to have one cautious and one reckless fellow operating on the same objective."

Apart from conquering Sicily, Husky fell short. A major objective, trapping the Axis force on the island, failed. Over 102,000 German and Italian troops with much of their equipment slipped across the Strait of Messina. The cost to the Allies in thirty-eight days of fighting had been dear, 5,187 killed together with another 22,536 wounded, captured, or missing without an inch of mainland Europe yet taken. The Germans had lost 10,000 killed or captured. The Italians, their hearts never in the fight as Germany's ally, surrendered in droves, with over 100,000 marched into captivity.

HAP ARNOLD, THE AIR CHIEF, suffered from what he brushed aside as a minor cardiac condition. Nevertheless, the twelve-hour days and seven-day weeks began to exact their toll, and in May 1943, Arnold suffered a serious heart attack. He sent a note to General Marshall apologizing that "this is one hell of a time to have this happen." Referring to his pulse, he added, "My engine started turning over at 160 when it should have been doing 74 to 76." Marshall begged Arnold to slow down and take time off. "It is vastly important to you and it certainly is

FDR, in leg braces, waits for the secretary of war, Henry Stimson, to pull a lottery number for the nation's first peacetime draft. Stimson is blindfolded with a strip of linen from a chair used at the signing of the Declaration of Independence. As FDR called out "one-fifty-eight!" a mother screamed. *FDR Presidential Library*

In August 1941, FDR and Prime Minister Winston Churchill meet in Argentia, Newfoundland, for the first time as wartime leaders. FDR is supported by his son Major Elliott Roosevelt. Ensign Franklin Jr. is at far left. Churchill left the conference believing Roosevelt "would wage war but not declare it." *FDR Presidential Library*

Roosevelt and Churchill (top center) attend a Sunday service at Argentia aboard HMS *Duke of York* with American and British sailors intermixed to symbolize Anglo-American solidarity. Amid the hymn singing, Churchill declared, "It was a great hour to live." *FDR Presidential Library*

Army chief George C. Marshall was FDR's stout oak throughout the war. The general favored a thrust across the English Channel. FDR, however, sided with Churchill on first invading North Africa, Sicily, and the Italian mainland. Later, Marshall manfully accepted FDR's decision to give General Dwight Eisenhower command of Overlord. *George C. Marshall Research Library*

FDR made Admiral Ernest King the most powerful leader in U.S. naval history and joked that the proud, vain, cantankerous King shaved himself with a blowtorch. King saw the Pacific as the Navy's battlefield, and argued for parity with Europe. *National Archives*

In an October 1941 speech, FDR claimed to have a map showing that Hitler intended to divide "South America into five vassal states." As revealed in the inscription, the map, planted by British intelligence, was actually of German commercial airline routes. *FDR Presidential Library*

Ever-smiling General Henry H. "Hap" Arnold (right) with George Marshall. Arnold overcame a fear of flying and a stint in FDR's doghouse to turn an air corps of rattletrap planes into a force of 80,000 aircraft and 2.4 million men by the war's end.
FDR Presidential Library

The U.S. fleet aflame after the surprise Japanese attack on Pearl Harbor. No intercepted Japanese message mentioned the American base, though, shortly beforehand, FDR warned that "we are likely to be attacked" somewhere. After nine official investigations, arguments still persist that the president had prior knowledge of the attack.
FDR Presidential Library

After vowing in his Day of Infamy speech that "the American people in their righteous might will win through to absolute victory," FDR signs the declaration of war that launched the United States into World War II, which would cost more than 400,000 American lives. *FDR Presidential Library*

In his fireside chats, the president used radio to talk to the American people about everything from the need for shared sacrifice to Nazi perfidy, and urged people to follow the war's progress with him on maps. The chats became a national ritual, as tens of millions tuned in. *FDR Presidential Library*

FDR glances casually at his notes as he prepares to drop a bombshell at the 1943 Casablanca press conference: a call for unconditional surrender by the Axis powers, terms that did not meet with universal support among his allies. *FDR Presidential Library*

FDR engineered a frosty handshake between competing French generals Henri Giraud and Charles de Gaulle at Casablanca. The president could never stomach de Gaulle's arrogance or his assumption that he led France. Roosevelt was willing, he said, to see de Gaulle made "president, or emperor, or king" of the French, but not to have him "foisted on them by outside powers." *FDR Presidential Library*

FDR with Eisenhower during a quick visit to recently conquered Sicily. Roosevelt chose Ike over the expected Marshall to command the liberation of Europe, explaining, "Eisenhower is the best politician of the military men . . . a natural leader who can convince men to follow him." *FDR Presidential Library*

A scene to be repeated around the globe: an American amphibious landing. In this photo, GIs storm FDR's first choice for engaging the German enemy, French colonial North Africa. *FDR Presidential Library*

Secretary of War Stimson had to cajole FDR into paying attention to intercepted messages from the pro-Nazi Japanese ambassador to Germany, Hiroshi Oshima. The ambassador's dispatches, decoded by American cryptanalysts, revealed Hitler's innermost thinking. *National Archives*

After slapping two shell-shocked soldiers in Sicily, George Patton faces the galling order to apologize to all divisions of the Seventh Army. He never believed he had done anything wrong, noting privately, "It is rather a commentary on justice when an Army commander has to soft-soap a skulker." *Eisenhower Presidential Library*

FDR had to pressure Navy chief Ernest King to adopt the convoy system. Thanks in no small measure to this means of protection, not one of the transport vessels that carried nearly 2 million men across the Atlantic was lost, including the *Queen Elizabeth*, seen here.   *National Archives*

General Mark Clark commanded American forces in Italy, though he initially thought the campaign a mistake. An admiring FDR flew to Sicily and had Clark yanked from the front to be decorated. Clark questioned but did not disapprove bombing Montecassino. *Library of Congress*

Omar Bradley, dubbed "the GIs' general," was shocked when FDR casually revealed to him the secret of the atom bomb while most senior officers were still in the dark. During the war, Bradley went from being Patton's subordinate to being his superior. *Library of Congress*

Eisenhower in a rare moment of ease. He rose in two years from obscure Army colonel to being hailed as the liberator of Europe, springboard of his ascent to the U.S. presidency. *Eisenhower Presidential Library*

Kay Summersby with Eisenhower's dog, Telek. She served as the general's driver and companion throughout much of the war. The intimacy of the relationship stirred speculation. But as one fellow officer put it, "Leave Kay and Ike alone. She's helping him win the war." *Eisenhower Presidential Library*

The longhand message that Eisenhower wrote and tucked into his wallet should D-Day miscarry: "Our landings in the Cherbourg-Havre area have failed to gain a satisfactory foothold and I have withdrawn the troops." Any blame, he said, was his alone. *Eisenhower Presidential Library*

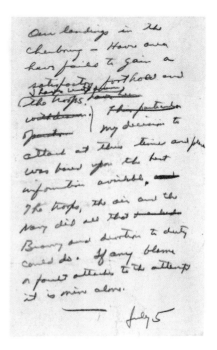

General Omar Bradley (right), commander of ground forces, and Arnold, the air chief, stroll at Normandy shortly after D-Day. Control of the skies was indispensable to keeping down casualties in an invasion that 90 percent of junior officers did not expect to survive. *National Archives*

Eisenhower's most difficult subordinate, Field Marshal Bernard Law Montgomery, to whom Ike nevertheless gave command of half the Allied expeditionary force in Western Europe. "Monty" was brilliant but insufferable. A fellow Briton described him as a "terrier who might bite at any moment." *Library of Congress*

The air war debate: military target bombing or population bombing? FDR supported the former, but in the end, both were carried out. Here, dazed, terrified civilians are seen after one of the Allied raids that systematically reduced German cities to rubble. *ullstein bild/The Granger Collection, New York*

The resilient B-17, backbone of the U.S. bomber force. This one made it back to England after attacking Cologne, Germany. More than 12,700 "Flying Fortresses" were built during the war. *National Museum of the U.S. Air Force*

Roosevelt's heart was always with China. He sent cantankerous "Vinegar Joe" Stilwell, no fan of FDR's, to put spine into Chiang Kai-shek's massive but battle-averse army, with scant success. *Library of Congress*

Well into the war, the news media were barred from showing American dead. FDR reversed the policy, and in September 1943 the public was sobered by this *Life* magazine photo of three dead GIs on a New Guinea beach. *Getty Images*

At Honolulu in July 1944, Admiral Chester Nimitz explains to FDR that the Navy could bypass the Philippines and strangle Japan into surrender without an invasion. General Douglas MacArthur (left) argued for liberating the Philippines first, even warning the president privately that failure to do so would threaten FDR's reelection chances in 1944. *National Archives*

FDR tours military hospitals in Hawaii with Nimitz and MacArthur. Visiting a ward of amputees, Roosevelt allowed the men to see his own disability. During the tour, Nimitz was surprised to hear the egocentric general address the president as "Franklin." *FDR Presidential Library*

FDR's decision not to bypass the Philippines enabled MacArthur to fulfill his promise to the Filipinos, "I shall return." The price was steep: more than 100,000 civilians died in the course of liberation.   *National Archives*

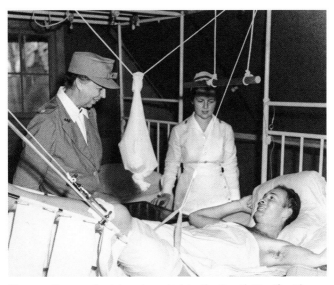

Eleanor Roosevelt visits a hospital in the South Pacific. She was initially regarded by senior officers as a meddlesome do-gooder. But by the time she left, Admiral William Halsey admitted, "I was ashamed of my original surliness." He described her evident concern for the wounded as "a sight I will never forget."   *FDR Presidential Library*

Photographers position themselves to take the iconic photo of FDR, Winston Churchill, and Joseph Stalin at Yalta in 1945. For years the debate would persist: was Roosevelt taken in or a realist in dealing with the Soviet Union? *National Archives*

During the Yalta conference, Soviet "waiters" were largely secret police operatives. Here, chambermaids tend to the bedrooms where Allied staff were quartered. All the rooms were bugged. *FDR Presidential Library*

Jewish and refugee groups pleaded with FDR to bomb concentration camps and the railways leading to them. He resisted, saying victory would end the extermination. Here, Jewish women are herded past ogling German troops at a camp in Poland. *U.S. Holocaust Museum*

A Nazi roundup of Jews from the Warsaw ghetto, most of whom would perish in the gas chambers. *National Archives*

Jewish children held for medical experiments at Auschwitz. *National Archives*

FDR in a rare group shot with his military chiefs and key advisors. The president is seated between General Marshall and Admiral King; second row, left to right: Harry Hopkins; General Hap Arnold; General Brehon Somervell, the logistics chief; and W. Averell Harriman. *FDR Presidential Library*

Albert Einstein's description of the power of an atomic weapon spurred FDR to launch the Manhattan Project to build a bomb. Pictured at the test site: left, J. Robert Oppenheimer, the physics genius behind the project; right, General Leslie Groves, the project's relentless director. *Library of Congress*

Two days after his death, Franklin Roosevelt's funeral cortege passes in review through Washington. George Marshall's wife, Katherine, remembered that a "complete silence spread like a pall over the city, broken only by the funeral dirge and the sobs of people." *Library of Congress*

to me, and to the Air Force that you make a full recovery," he said, ending the letter with a rare "Affectionately."

Unfazed, Arnold was back in the White House that summer eager to see FDR. The president expected that Arnold wanted to see him about FDR's idée fixe ever since Pearl Harbor, bombing Japan, and not simply another symbolic pinprick like Doolittle's raid of April 1942. Japan was not what Arnold had in mind. Oil was the life's blood of Germany's war-making machine. Sixty percent of it came from the rich fields of Germany's ally Romania, with forty refineries concentrated around the small town of Ploesti just north of Bucharest, the first place where oil had been commercially refined in 1867. The gasoline that fueled Luftwaffe aircraft, ships, tanks, trucks, anything with an engine, depended significantly on Ploesti's output. A successful blow against the refineries, Arnold maintained, was tantamount to slashing Germany's aorta. FDR was delighted to have Arnold back, hearing again the man's colorful presentations accompanied by hands mimicking the swooping dives of an airplane. Still, Roosevelt, while never allowing his own handicap to limit his performance, was unsure about a man with a dicey heart continuing to run the Air Forces. He agreed to see Arnold's physician, Dr. Russell V. Lee, and put the key question to him directly. "If he continues as commanding general, is it likely to endanger his life?" Roosevelt asked. Lee answered that yes, it might. But Arnold had told his doctor in advance to remind the president "that whenever his combat crews go on missions they endanger their lives. He sees no reason why he shouldn't do so." Roosevelt liked the feistiness and Arnold kept his job.

The Ploesti raid that Arnold proposed would not be the first against the Romanian oil nexus. The previous June a handful of B-24s had taken off from an RAF strip in Fayed, Egypt. Twelve planes made it to the target, their few bombs like insect bites against the massive complex. Arnold was now proposing a major strike by B-24 Liberators also flying out of North Africa. The air armada struck Ploesti on August 1, 1943. Subsequent aerial reconnaissance estimated that 40 percent of Ploesti's refining capacity had been knocked out. Repairs, however, were discouragingly swift, carried out mostly by conscript and slave labor. In an after-action assessment, the Allies' Enemy Oil Committee reported "no curtailment of overall product output." Within weeks the refineries were pumping out more fuel than before the raid. Of 178 planes that began the assault, fifty did not return. Three hundred and ten fliers were dead, and another 108 in enemy hands. Five Ploesti airmen were awarded the Medal of Honor, three posthumously. As one pilot described that day, "the antiaircraft defenses were literally throwing up a curtain of steel. . . . And we were headed straight into it."

Allied bombing policy had been agreed upon in the Pointblank Directive adopted some seven weeks before Ploesti. Pointblank appeared to represent a victory for the American view of aerial warfare by ranking attacks on specific targets first, and raids to demoralize enemy civilians second. But Pointblank was so porous in its language that air strategists read into it whatever they wanted, as exemplified by four raids conducted around the time of Ploesti. Between July 24 and August 2, the RAF, with minor American participation, sent 1,205 planes loaded with incendiaries against the German port city of Hamburg. So fierce were the resulting fires that they consumed oxygen, sucking in more air, and spinning winds of hurricane force. The air war had produced a new phenomenon, the firestorm, with temperatures in the vortex reaching 1,500 degrees. The man-made gale sent burning debris spreading fires throughout Hamburg. Deprived of air, people on the streets and in shelters suffocated. So scorched were the corpses that identification was usually impossible and casualties uncountable, though estimates ranged from 30,000 to 50,000 dead. Over 800,000 people were left homeless. During a press conference when a reporter questioned the president about the significance of air warfare on this scale, FDR answered, "Hitler built walls around his Fortress Europe; but he forgot to put a roof on it."

Sixteen days after Ploesti, the U.S. Air Force made coordinated raids to sever two more enemy arteries, the first against Regensburg where factories were turning out the vaunted Messerschmitt 109, the second against plants in Schweinfurt that manufactured ball bearings, needed by virtually every piece of German equipment that moved. At

1:30 A.M., at airfields all across southern England, crews were rousted from their bunks and began pulling on flying gear. They breakfasted on real eggs, not the chalky powdered version, along with heaps of bacon, a comparative feast that the men mordantly referred to as the Last Supper. By 5:30 A.M., the fliers, after their briefing, hoisted themselves into 376 B-17s that took off and gathered in formation like swarms of locusts. Three hundred miles from Regensburg, Thunderbolt fighter escorts, their fuel limit reached, turned back, leaving the lumbering B-17s prey to German fighters, which soon materialized out of the sun. By the time the Fortresses released their bomb loads over the two cities and returned to England, nearly twelve hours had passed. Fifty-nine bombers failed to return. At ten men per crew that meant that 590 men, young, healthy, and alive that morning, were either dead or in German hands. The B-17s that did return demonstrated the plane's remarkable survivability. Hap Arnold, in England watching bombers limp back from a raid, described one shot-up B-17: "One tail flipper was gone: in the right wing was a hole as big as a bushel basket; there were holes in the fuselage from stem to stern . . . one engine had been blown from the wing." One hundred of the bombers that did make it back were too battered ever to fly again. These, added to the fifty-nine shot down, totaled a seemingly unsustainable 42 percent loss. In the calculus of war, however, in which blood is measured against results, air advocates found the price acceptable. On October 14, 1943, Schweinfurt was struck again, by 291 Flying Fortresses, running up against fierce resistance by German fighters and antiaircraft batteries, the greatest air duel of the war thus far. Sixty bombers failed to return. With ten men per crew, the loss meant that 600 fliers perished in flames or had been taken prisoner in what came to be called "Black Thursday." Over $20 million worth of precision bombing equipment vanished. Hap Arnold's staff sent him graphs projecting that the average B-17 in the Eighth Air Force would last 161 combat days, or twenty-one missions.

Casualties, such as those taken over Schweinfurt, alarmed Americans at home. Asked at a press conference about the seemingly unsustainable losses, the president was noncommittal and left the answer to

Hap Arnold. During a speech in Philadelphia before the Poor Richard Club, celebrating the birth of Benjamin Franklin, Arnold compared the war in the skies to the war on the ground. His planes were not involved simply in bombing raids, he maintained, but in "a battle between large armies, a major campaign," the equivalent of invading Germany "with almost a division of soldiers." He went on, "How long would it take and what would it cost to fight our way 500 miles overland into these bitterly defended German cities?" His planes did so, he pointed out, "in less time than you would need to travel from Washington to Boston by a good train."

The air attacks benumbing German soldiers occupying France were matched by a rain of death on their families at home from the night-and-day Allied bombing. The endless pounding of the cities was forcing German strategists to make a devilish choice. They could either concentrate the bulk of their airpower on the Russian and Italian battle fronts or employ it to protect their cities. They lacked the manpower or planes to do both fully. Defense of the homeland won out. Much of the Luftwaffe, instead of supporting the army in the field, was kept in Germany defending the skies over Berlin, Düsseldorf, Munich, Regensburg, and dozens more on the Allied target list. Over a million men who could have been sent to fight off the invaders were tied down manning 31,000 antiaircraft guns. Teenaged boys and girls, *flakhelfer*, or flak helpers, were conscripted to man the guns as well.

Raids that left German cities in smoking ruins with charred bodies to be counted in the tens of thousands prompted Hitler on December 22, 1943, to raise the threat of retaliation against downed Allied airmen. The German Foreign Office issued a warning that military courts "will soon have to deal with British and American prisoners who are guilty of a serious breach of international law." General Marshall alerted the pesident. "As the effects of the bombing grow more serious," he told FDR, "desperate measures would probably be employed to discourage further attacks. The recently announced intent of the Germans to try captive American and British airmen is concrete evidence of such intention." He asked FDR for guidance. Roosevelt was determined to make sure that the United States held the moral high ground. "In regard to German reprisals against airmen," he told Marshall, he did not want to threaten in advance but would strike back "the minute the Germans start anything. I think the American public would back this up."

Success in crippling German industry from the air was fleeting at best. Though the second bloody raid on Schweinfurt initially cut ball bearing production by two thirds, the Germans subsequently dispersed manufacturing to concealed underground plants, upped purchases from neutral Sweden and Switzerland, and quickly recouped their losses. The horrific fire bombings of Hamburg in July 1943, damaged the city's aircraft engine and U-boat yards. Yet within months, 80 percent of production had been restored. Still, Hap Arnold's faith remained unshaken that the enemy could be defeated, and far more cheaply, by his fliers. To test his thesis, he asked leading historians, including Carl Becker of Cornell University, Henry Steele Commager of Columbia, and Dumas Malone of Harvard, to review the evidence and evaluate the decisiveness of airpower. The response was hardly encouraging to Arnold. The historians concluded, "There is no substantial evidence that Germany can be bombed out of the War."

ON AUGUST 12, 1943, FDR was relaxing at Hyde Park awaiting a now frequent guest, Winston Churchill, who had just made a dash across the Atlantic aboard the *Queen Mary*. On the prime minister's arrival, FDR treated him to a down-home taste of America, handing him a ten gallon Stetson that Churchill happily donned. They picnicked on hot dogs at Eleanor's cottage, Val-Kill, where Daisy Suckley observed that Churchill "adored the President, loves him, defers to him, leans on him." Secretary of War Stimson had managed an earlier meeting with FDR and warned him that the prime minister was still lukewarm about invading France. "The shadows of Passchendaele and Dunkerque hang too heavily over" the British, Stimson observed. "They were giving it [Bolero] only lip service." As proof, Churchill was now dangling the idea of invading Norway as preferable to a head-on collision in France, which even his own staff dismissed as foolhardy.

On a drizzly August 17, the two leaders boarded the president's train for a conference in Quebec City designated Quadrant. Their arrival had been preceded by a gathering of their military chiefs at the Citadelle, the star-shaped fortress, described as "The Gibraltar of the Americas," that overlooked the St. Lawrence River. Here the chiefs resumed a running quarrel. The British, reflecting Churchill's lack of enthusiasm for a cross-Channel invasion, and having won the two prior arguments over North Africa and Sicily, were continuing to press for the invasion of the Italian mainland. The disgusted U.S. chiefs wondered when, if ever, Western Europe was to be pierced. FDR's military chief of staff, Admiral Leahy, putting a polite patina on the debate, noted, "A difference of opinion was apparent from the outset as to the value of the Italian campaign toward our common war effort against Germany. General Marshall was very positive in his attitude against a Mediterranean commitment." An irascible Ernie King showed no such restraint. He accused the British of deliberately undermining Overlord. As Leahy described King's outburst, the admiral used "very undiplomatic language, to use a mild term."

While their subordinates wrangled, the president and prime minister entertained themselves, picnicking and fishing in Laurentide Park forty miles from the city, accompanied by Harry Hopkins, the prime minister's wife, Clemmie, and his daughter Mary. For the moment the principals were unfurrowed by care. So serene was the mood that Hopkins, during one conversation, fell asleep. But when they returned to the Citadelle, the prime minister embarked on a fresh offensive. He had been chafing for months over an added irritation, America's growing domination of the quest for an atomic bomb. All along, the British had considered themselves the leaders in applied nuclear research, with the Americans serving as junior partners. But by now the major effort was taking place deep within the United States at Los Alamos, and funded by American billions. The security-obsessed General Leslie Groves, along with the physicist James Conant, who had FDR's trust, wanted the British kept out of the project's inner sanctum. In their view, the Britons should stay home and limit themselves to theoretical research while the Americans invented a bomb. When Churchill discovered that Roosevelt supported this limited partnership, he exploded. Well before Quebec, on February 16, 1943, he had risen from a sickbed to fire off a message to the one American he trusted implicitly, Hopkins, in which he charged, "There is no question of breach of agreement." Hopkins, thereafter, lectured FDR that he had indeed "made a firm commitment to Churchill" to share in the development of an A-bomb.

At Quebec, Churchill began pressing Roosevelt for a full partnership in Tube Alloys, the cover name adopted for the atomic enterprise. After closeting privately with FDR, the prime minister emerged waving a Roosevelt rarity, a written agreement signed by the president and himself "to bring the Tube Alloys project to fruition at the earliest moment. . . . This may be speedily achieved if all available British and American brains and resources are pooled." Churchill acknowledged the security advantages of having the principal work continue in the American hinterland. However, he won a concession from FDR to allow British scientists to work alongside Americans in the New Mexico vastness. Among the first to arrive was a slight, high-domed, bespectacled, reclusive thirty-one-year-old bachelor named Klaus Emil Julius Fuchs, a German-born scientist living in England, an expert on uranium-235. Unknown to the British, Fuchs was a communist and a Soviet spy, who, thanks to the deal Churchill had engineered, simply walked through the presumably impenetrable security barrier that Leslie Groves had erected to shield the Manhattan Project.

Upon obtaining a restored role in Tube Alloys, Churchill withdrew his latest reservations about Overlord. Harry Stimson described the prime minister as "magnificent in reconciliation as he was stubborn and eloquent in opposition."

✴

GENERAL SIR ALAN BROOKE had been in a jaunty mood thus far at Quebec. Just a month earlier, Churchill had told Brooke to stop by to see him before the war cabinet met. As Brooke later remembered their conversation, "PM called me in to tell me that he had been wanting to let me know during the last few days that he wanted me to take Supreme Command of operations from this country across the Channel when the time was suitable." Churchill repeated the offer to Brooke at a conversation following a dinner party given for the king at 10 Downing Street. Brooke, it appeared, had nailed down the prized Allied command of the war. Leading Overlord "would be the perfect climax to all my struggles . . . to find myself in command of all allied forces destined for this liberation." He believed he had earned it, loyally serving an arbitrary prime minister who "took a year off my life." The prospect of returning to France as a victor was particularly satisfying, since three years earlier his II Corps had been driven out in the retreat from Dunkirk.

All along Churchill and Roosevelt had agreed that the command of Overlord should go to the country with the most troops committed, which initially appeared to be Britain. But as GIs poured into England in a torrent, Churchill conceded that the Americans would be providing the bulk of the men. On August 15, in Quebec, Churchill asked Brooke to join him for a stroll along the terrace of the Citadelle, where, as the general remembered, they looked "down on that wonderful view of the St. Lawrence River and the fateful scene of Wolfe's battle for the heights of Quebec" in 1759. Churchill offhandedly delivered the news: an American, not Brooke, would lead Overlord. "He asked me how I felt about it, and I told him that I could not feel otherwise than disappointment." What shook Brooke most was that "not for one moment did he realize what this meant to me. He offered no sympathy, no regrets for having to change his mind, and dealt with the matter as if it were of minor importance." Churchill "then said that Eisenhower would replace Marshall" as U.S. Army chief of staff, and he assumed that FDR would give Overlord to General Marshall. The choice was especially galling to Brooke, who had said of Marshall, "In strategy I doubt if he can even see the end of his nose."

Content that Churchill now seemed solidly committed to Overlord, FDR returned to Washington while the prime minister stayed in Quebec to do some fishing. In a lighthearted mood, FDR telegraphed

"Colonel Warden," a pseudonym Churchill occasionally used, accusing him of "teasing the trout" and challenging the prime minister's claim that he had caught a five-pounder. "I shall require sworn verification," he wrote. Refreshed from Quebec, Churchill returned once more to the White House, where the staff reacted to the return of their exacting guest with trepidation. The president too faced the prospect of Churchill's return warily. During his previous visit, FDR confided to Frances Perkins, "he gets bright ideas in the middle of the night and comes puttering down to my bedroom. They are probably good ideas. But I need my sleep." The two men stayed together for four more days before FDR found a reason to flee to the tranquillity of Hyde Park, but Churchill soon followed for two more days.

WHILE VICTORY IN NORTH AFRICA, the swift conquest of Sicily, the massive raids over German cities captured front-page headlines, fighting and dying went on in the Pacific in places whose names mystified Americans. Laconic Army bulletins reported in mid-1943 "small American force is sent to Vella La Vella to examine the possibility of major landings thus bypassing Kolombangara"; "Americans complete the capture of Munda and its airfield"; "The last Japanese resistance at Bairoko is wiped out." In one of the few items that did resonate at home, *The New York Times* reported on August 20, 1943, that a Japanese destroyer had sliced in half a PT boat skippered by Lieutenant (j.g.) John F. Kennedy, called "Shafty" by his mates, the son of the former American ambassador to Great Britain.

Eleanor Roosevelt wanted the troops on these Pacific specks to know that they were not forgotten. In the summer of 1943, she persuaded Franklin to allow her to tour the South Pacific. She was not greeted with open arms. Admiral William "Bull" Halsey complained, "Among an area commander's worst problems are the politicians, admirals, generals, 'special' correspondents and 'do-gooders' who present themselves in the assurance that their visit is a 'morale factor.' . . . Mrs. Roosevelt I classed as a do-gooder, and I dreaded her arrival."

On reaching the island of New Caledonia, clad in a blue-gray Red

Cross summer uniform rumpled by her long journey, Eleanor presented Halsey with a letter from her husband. "She is especially anxious to see Guadalcanal," FDR had written, "and at this moment, it looks like a pretty safe place to visit." "That set me back on my heels," Halsey remembered. "I told her rather curtly, 'Guadalcanal is no place for you, Ma'am.'" He warned, "I need every fighter plane I can put my hands on. If you fly to Guadalcanal, I'll have to provide a fighter escort for you and I haven't got one to spare." He was surprised by the good grace with which she accepted the refusal. Halsey thereafter laid out a sheltered schedule, putting Eleanor up first in a Quonset hut jocularly called the Wicky-Wacky Lodge. He arranged one dinner for her, and MacArthur allowed his wife, Jean, to host another, at which visitors were urged to remove their "MacArthur for President" buttons.

The first lady persisted in wanting to meet the men actually fighting the war. She swung into a feverish twelve-hour-day schedule of visits to military hospitals. An impressed Halsey commented, "When I say she inspected those hospitals, I don't mean that she shook hands with the chief medical officer, glanced into a sun parlor and left. I mean that she went into every ward, stopped at every bed, and spoke to every patient. What was his name? How did he feel? Was there anything he needed? Could she take a message home for Mom?" Halsey finally relented and arranged for the first lady to visit Guadalcanal.

By the time of the first lady's departure, after covering 23,000 miles and visiting nineteen islands, Halsey admitted, "I was ashamed of my original surliness." One image stuck in his memory. After Eleanor had visited severely maimed men in a hospital, one youthful GI noted, "None of us had never seen in over a year an American mother." "It was a sight I will never forget," Halsey recalled.

✳

AFTER THE PRESIDENT AND CHURCHILL had returned to the White House from Quebec, General Marshall called to report that Operation Avalanche, the code name for the invasion of Italy, had begun. American and British troops had gone ashore at Salerno, some thirty miles southeast of Naples. For Churchill, the moment was sweet. At times he had feared that the American generals might carry the day, turning FDR against the invasion that he so fiercely wanted. The prime minister's compass remained fixed: focus on the Mediterranean while dithering on France.

On the eve of the invasion and in keeping with FDR's desire to shatter the bond between the Axis powers, two Americans had embarked on a mission, the stuff of spy thrillers. A ruggedly handsome forty-two-year-old West Pointer and linguist, General Maxwell Taylor, aided by Colonel William T. Gardiner, slipped into the Italian resort town of Gaeta, forty miles north of Naples. The two men wore their uniforms to avoid the traditional fate of spies caught in civilian clothes, but had stuffed their overseas caps into their trench coats to be less conspicuous. Previously, anti-Nazi Italians had asked for an Allied air drop to seize Rome before the Germans took the capital. Eisenhower had assented and had a paratroop force standing by. Maxwell's job was to find out if the Italians could guarantee a relatively safe drop zone. In Gaeta, the two Americans were met by sympathetic Italian officers, bundled into a Navy limousine in the dark of night, and smuggled into Rome, where they rendezvoused secretly with Marshal Badoglio at his villa. They found the Italian leader exhausted and edgy as he tried to juggle pressure from the Allies to take his country out of the war against the threat of a powerful and angered German army seizing Italy if he did drop out. Badoglio wanly confessed that he could not assure the success of an airborne assault, since German troops were already moving on the city. Taylor managed, through a prearranged signal, to get word back to Eisenhower. "Badoglio has gummed up the works." Ike announced upon receiving Taylor's update, "We've just had to call off [the] air drop on Rome." The two disappointed agents were spirited to an Italian airfield outside Rome, where a Savoia-Marchetti bomber was waiting, its three motors already revved up to fly them to safety. Finally, Marshal Badoglio did take Italy out of the war. At 6:30 P.M. on September 8, he went on the air to announce Italy's surrender to the Allies, euphemistically described as an "armistice" to assuage Italy's pride. For the Italians, the invasion represented a triple ignominy. They had been beaten in North Africa, then in Sicily, and now had surrendered unconditionally.

Mark Clark, earlier given command of the Fifth Army and promoted to lieutenant general, had won the plum assignment of leading Avalanche. Clark was no shrinking violet. While rating him one of the best generals in the Army, Eisenhower observed, "it seemed that he was becoming a bit consumed with a desire to push himself." Upon receiving word that his competitor had landed Avalanche, George Patton recorded in his diary, "it was a shock."

Six hours after Badoglio's announcement the night sky above the Salerno beaches exploded in a roar pierced by showers of yellow-red shells as Allied warships commenced their barrage. Higgins boats pushed off from the transports and began delivering troops to the shore, Americans to the right and British troops to the left. The Wehrmacht proved unexpectedly prepared, with one panzer division already in place and reinforcements rushed in from the south, a counterattack that threatened to push Clark's army back into the sea. Churchill, while at Hyde Park, and reflecting upon a past White House visit when he had had to tell Roosevelt of the fall of Tobruk, said this time, "These things always seem to happen when I am with the President."

The day after the invasion, the president and the prime minister issued a joint appeal to the Italian people. "Hitler, through his accomplice, Mussolini, has brought Italy to the verge of ruin. He has driven the Italians into disastrous campaigns in the sands of Egypt and the snows of Russia. . . . Now is the time for every Italian to strike his blow." Their ordeal would be brief, they were assured, since Germany's seizure of their homeland "will not last long." Clark managed to hold on to the beaches, and within eight days, on October 1, the Fifth Army captured Naples, the city still choking from the smoke of the Germans' retreating gesture, blowing up the port, architectural treasures, and museums.

Though Italy was now invaded, no grand strategy existed as to how long and how far up the Italian boot the campaign should continue. Churchill had cautioned his military chiefs not to "crawl up the leg of

Italy like a harvest bug, but strike boldly at the knee," by which he meant take Rome. The actual invasion had taken place at about mid-calf. Roosevelt, with one eye cocked toward Overlord, told Henry Stimson that "he was not insisting on going further than Rome," only far enough north to establish airbases at Foggia, which would allow Allied bombers to strike deep inside Germany.

The invasion of Italy threw several truths into bold relief. First, Marshall's contention that Italy would set back preparations for Overlord proved prescient. An additional 60,000 troops previously destined for the cross-Channel operation were diverted to Italy. Second, the Italian campaign did not end according to American expectations with the acquisition of airfields in the south. Despite Roosevelt's and Marshall's desire to limit the Italian campaign, Churchill again had his way and the Allies began to inch up the peninsula. Finally, the invasion proved Churchill to be a prophet for the moment. Much to the Americans' surprise, Hitler chose to make a fight for Italy, and as the prime minister had predicted, he shifted divisions from France, the Balkans, even from the Russian Front to Italy. When Allied troops first went ashore at Salerno, the Germans had eighteen divisions in Italy. Within six weeks, they numbered twenty-five. Churchill commented, "It is true, I suppose, that the Americans consider we have led them up the garden path in the Mediterranean, but what a beautiful path it has proved to be. They have picked peaches here, nectarines there. How grateful they should be."

Stalin sent five generals to Clark's headquarters to assess how much more relief the Italian campaign might provide his front. While the Russians consumed copious quantities of vodka, which they had brought by the caseful, the leader of the delegation, a General Vasilieff, told Clark, "We want to see what the Americans are like in action against the Huns." Clark was only too happy to oblige and arranged for his visitors to be taken by mule up a twisting mountain trail where American troops were undergoing pinpoint artillery, mortar, and machine-gun fire. On the Russians' return, Clark had a fine dinner ready for them during which Vasilieff complained that the purpose of the trip had been misconstrued. "What we're interested in is logistics," he said. "We want to see how your rear elements are organized and how your supply problems are handled." He added, "We can die for Mother Russia any day in Russia. Why should we die in Italy?"

Mussolini had been deposed, but technically the Badoglio government was still allied with Germany. FDR's hope was that Italy, beyond surrendering, would switch sides and go to war against Hitler. On October 13, 1943, Italy did declare war on its former Axis partner. FDR, still incensed over Mussolini's kowtowing to Hitler and declaring war on America, refused to consider Italy as a full ally but merely a "co-belligerent." By then, it mattered little. In the course of Badoglio's fence-sitting, the Germans had disarmed tens of thousands of Italian troops, a vast number of whom were shipped to Germany as laborers and to an uncertain future.

CHAPTER 16

---★---

From Tarawa to Tehran

IN THE FALL OF 1943, ELMER DAVIS ASKED TO SEE THE PRESIDENT. Davis, eight years younger than FDR, resembled a natty college professor, bow-tied, horn-rimmed glasses, handsome in a studious way. He had gone from newspapering to become a popular CBS commentator with a reputation for integrity and clarity expressed in a comforting Hoosier accent. FDR had recruited Davis to head the new Office of War Information, in effect making him the country's propaganda czar. Davis was guided by a credo: this was a people's war and Americans "had a right to be truthfully informed." It was Davis, with his unbending rectitude, that Roosevelt had deliberately avoided when the official wanted to release the facts about the loss of the carrier *Lexington*.

Administration policy thus far had been to shield the American people from war's harshest truth by barring newspapers and newsreels from showing images of U.S. battle dead. Davis had come to the White House to urge FDR to reverse that policy. For one thing, he claimed, baring the realities of combat would point up the pettiness of civilians who complained about gas rationing while others were dying. The public had in fact grown complacent as the country neared the third year of war, evident in the decline in war bond sales. Davis had found an ally in George Marshall, who also believed that the country needed to face "the dangers and horrors of war." During FDR's 1918 visit to the Western Front he had witnessed the aftermath of battle. As he said in his Chautauqua speech during the 1940 election campaign, "I have seen the dead in the mud." But how the present home front would react to images of the dead was uncertain. Persuaded by Davis and Marshall, FDR finally reasoned, with bloody campaigns yet to be fought, that Americans would have to become accustomed to the true face of war.

Months before Davis had gone to see FDR, a photographer for *Life* magazine, George Strock, had taken a picture at Buna Beach in New Guinea of three Americans lying dead before a gutted landing craft, their bodies half buried in sand as the surf washed over them. Under censorship then in effect, the magazine was forbidden from publishing the photo. But with the change of policy, there appeared in the September 20, 1943, issue of *Life* Strock's graphic image. Alongside, the magazine ran a full-page editorial explaining, "the reason we print it now is that last week President Roosevelt and Elmer Davis . . . decided that the American people ought to be able to see their own boys as they fall in battle." After that breakthrough, public relations officers in the military began collecting photos of what they called the "Chamber of Horrors," selecting the least grisly for release to the media. Certain restrictions continued. The faces of victims were not to be shown, nor their unit insignia. The effect on the public of seeing these images was mixed. War Bond sales went up, but enlistments went down.

A CAMPAIGN ON AN OBSCURE Pacific atoll was about to unfold that would add measurably to the stock of disturbing wartime images. Tarawa was part of the Gilbert Islands chain 2,400 miles west of Hawaii, one of several archipelagos laced across the Pacific leading toward Japan. Tarawa stood in the path that Admiral Nimitz, as commander of the Central Pacific, intended to follow, attacking some islands, bypassing others, until Japan came within striking distance. On November 20, a fleet, the greatest assembled to date in the Pacific, nineteen aircraft carriers, twenty-four battleships and cruisers, sixty-six destroyers, and thirty-six transports carrying 35,000 men spread over fifty square miles, bore down on Tarawa. The first objective was Betio, an islet part of the Tarawa Atoll about the size of New York's Central Park. Betio was flat and featureless, seeming to offer little cover for defenders. A three-hour naval bombardment laid down before troops went ashore reduced the landscape to shell holes and rubble. That anything or anyone could have survived this pounding seemed unlikely to the first Marines crowding into the landing craft. But as the boats approached the beaches, Japanese defenders, 4,600 in strength, crawled out of shelters to man hundreds of blockhouses and pillboxes still surviving under five-foot slabs of concrete reinforced by steel rails. The landing craft failed to clear a jagged coral reef and ground to a halt, leaving the first wave to wade ashore in chest-high water while Japanese guns raked them until the surf turned red with blood. Recovering momentum depended on a new amphibian, the amphtrac, a hybrid equipped with tractor treads that could climb over the jagged teeth of the reef and perform as a tank once ashore. But the plodding crossbreed presented an easy target to Japanese guns, who destroyed 90 of 125 amphtracs heading for the shore. Nevertheless, by nightfall, nearly 5,000 Marines had landed.

Fighting for Tarawa went on for four days. Japanese troops screaming "Banzai" flung themselves against the Marines in heedless charges that left the dead in heaps. Casualties on the first day at Tarawa marked the bloodiest in Marine Corps history. Before the atoll was taken, 978 Marines were killed outright or died of wounds, far deadlier proportionately than the rate of loss in six months of fighting on Guadalcanal. Ninety-seven percent of the Japanese garrison died, including Admiral Keiji Shibazaki, the island's commander. Tarawa reeked for days from the stench of nearly 5,500 dead bodies from both sides. Only seventeen Japanese surrendered, a foretaste of the fanaticism that awaited Americans in the remaining Pacific war. Marine Corps General Holland "Howlin' Mad" Smith, who commanded at Tarawa, was later asked if the struggle had been worth it. His answer was "an unqualified no. From the very beginning the decision of the Joint Chiefs to seize Tarawa was a mistake." The chiefs "should have let Tarawa wither on the vine." Other strategists, however, maintained that Tarawa was essential, a door to be kicked in on the way to Japan. Further, the island provided the equivalent of on-the-job training in the future amphibious operations that would mark the Pacific fighting.

Norman Hatch, leading a Marine Corps movie unit, shot 3,700 feet of film on Tarawa, which, to his surprise, the Navy released to theaters. The horrific sights, even in heavily edited form, produced anguished cries from families wanting to know why a son, a husband, a brother, had died to take a speck of coral in a place none had ever heard of. Robert Sherrod, a *Time-Life* correspondent who had covered Tarawa, subsequently found himself back in Washington attending a presidential press conference after which FDR called him aside. Roosevelt wanted to know why the battleships had not leveled the island before the Marines went ashore. Sherrod explained how the cunning Japanese defenses had withstood everything. FDR then commented that the film shot by Norman Hatch was "pretty raw, pretty rugged." Sherrod replied, yes, "that's the way it is out there." Subsequently, the correspondent asked the head of public relations for the Marine Corps the impact of the film's release. The officer answered, "Enlistments fell off 35%."

EARLY IN NOVEMBER, FDR, always susceptible to respiratory ailments, recorded in his diary while aboard the presidential yacht *Potomac*, "It's a lovely day, but cold." Still, any prospect of adventure at sea buoyed his spirits. The *Potomac* drew alongside the USS *Iowa*, the largest, newest battleship in the U.S. fleet, his yacht dwarfed by the ship's length of three football fields, its turrets sprouting nine 16-inch guns and its crew the size of a small city, 2,600 officers and men. Sailors along the rails gawked in disbelief as the president of the United States was wheeled up a special ramp to the quarterdeck. As the bosun's whistle piped him aboard, FDR and the ship's captain exchanged broad grins. Roosevelt's former naval aide, Captain John McCrea, had finally extricated himself from the White House and achieved what every career Navy officer hungered for, command at sea. Behind the president trailed Marshall, King, Arnold, Watson, Hopkins, and Admiral Wilson Brown, McCrea's successor at the White House. Captain McCrea had been alerted about FDR's special requirements. He was to vacate the captain's cabin, which was easier for FDR to reach than the more spacious admiral's cabin. He was to have a square-shaped tub installed that would enable the president to use his well-muscled arms to hoist himself out of the bath. The president's security chief, Mike Reilly, made a last-minute review of the checklist used for long journeys, which began, "A supply of money," since the president never carried any in his own pockets. Other indispensables included cases of Saratoga mineral water, wooden matches, which FDR insisted on for lighting his Camels, and slapstick movies, leggy musicals, and films starring Walter Huston, FDR's favorite actor. Reilly had also gathered a small library of whodunits to place alongside the president's bunk. Again, FDR had brought his son, Colonel Elliott Roosevelt, with him, and this time, his daughter, Anna, and her husband, Major John Boettiger, to attend the first meeting of the war's three Allied leaders. His wife, Eleanor, still waited for such an invitation.

On Friday, November 12, the *Iowa* anchored temporarily in Hampton Roads to refuel. The president summoned McCrea and told him, "John, I am sailor enough to share the sailor's superstition that Friday is an unlucky day. Do you suppose you could delay getting under way until Saturday?" McCrea agreed and six minutes past midnight a massive chain hauled the Iowa's anchor from the mud of the bottom.

FDR's itinerary called first for a meeting in Cairo with Churchill and Chiang Kai-shek to map out future strategy for the Pacific war and, more to the point from FDR's perspective, to light a fire under the combat-averse generalissimo. Roosevelt and Churchill would then proceed to Tehran, Iran, to join with Joseph Stalin principally to work out a coordinated approach to Overlord. The first evening out, FDR gathered his staff in his quarters and temporarily suspended Navy General Order No. 99. He had been assistant secretary of the navy in 1914, when his boss, the puritanical navy secretary, Josephus Daniels, had banished alcohol from naval vessels. Roosevelt had not thought much of the idea then and this night aboard the *Iowa* had the stewards serve drinks to his guests. Afterward, Admiral King, his tongue loosened and in a garrulous mood, followed McCrea to his cabin and took the only chair available while McCrea leaned against a bunk. "The trouble is," he told McCrea, "you have one outstanding weakness."

322   ROOSEVELT'S CENTURIONS

What was that? McCrea wanted to know. "Your big weakness, McCrea, is that you are not a son of a bitch. And a good officer has to be a son of a bitch." McCrea paused before speaking. "I must say I have never heard anyone refer to you as a son of a bitch." With that, "King stomped out of my cabin," McCrea recalled, "knowing full well I was lying."

The *Iowa* was two days into the voyage, screened by three U.S. destroyers, when Reilly wheeled the president on deck to witness a spectacle that McCrea had arranged. A voice over the ship's loudspeakers called the crew to general quarters, placing the *Iowa* in battle readiness. The ship's 40- and 20-millimeter antiaircraft guns began banging away at balloon targets floating overhead, punctuated by deafening blasts from the 5-inch gun batteries. The president had been given cotton to plug his ears against the racket. As McCrea later reconstructed what happened next, a frantic voice rang out over the Talk Between Ships circuit, the TBS, shouting, "Lion! Lion!," the *Iowa*'s code name. "Torpedo headed your way." A crewman two decks above the president shouted down, "This ain't no drill. It's the real thing! The real thing!" McCrea instinctively turned the *Iowa* parallel to the now visible wake of the torpedo to offer the narrowest target. In mid-turn McCrea heard "a tremendous explosion off our starboard quarter." He turned, white-faced, to his executive officer, Commander Thomas Casey, and asked, "Tom, do you think we've been hit?" Casey answered, "I think we would have felt it much more if we did." Admiral King raced on deck and demanded of McCrea to know what the hell was going on.

As it turned out, a torpedo aboard one of the escorts, the destroyer *W. D. Porter,* had fired accidentally. The destroyer captain explained, unconvincingly, that high seas must have broken the torpedo's restraints and off it went. McCrea later concluded that the explosion he had heard was caused when the *Iowa,* turning at high speed, created enough turbulence to trigger the oncoming torpedo's firing mechanism. Apart from witnessing the commotion on deck, the president, his ears plugged, was unaware of the threat. A chastened Admiral King explained the mishap to him and said that the *Porter*'s skipper would be relieved of command on the spot. An unflustered FDR vetoed King's intention. As Harry Hopkins later remembered the five anxious minutes, "Can you imagine our own escort torpedoing an American battleship—the newest and the largest, with the President of the United States on board!" The *Iowa* was at sea seven days, during which time FDR watched the movies and noted in his diary, "I revel in an old pair of trousers and a fishing shirt." On the morning of November 20, the ship steamed into Oran, Algeria, the largest vessel ever to enter the port. Leaning over the rails, crewmen watched the president loaded onto a breeches buoy, a fragile seat suspended on ropes alongside the battleship. As one sailor recorded the moment, "It was a very dramatic sight to see this single lonely figure lowered into a rowboat."

The president tarried briefly in Oran before boarding a Douglas C-54 transport, irreverently dubbed by FDR the *Sacred Cow,* for a turbulent 653-mile flight along the North African coast to Tunis. On deplaning, Roosevelt was bundled into an Army automobile from which he could look out on burned-out aircraft and tanks, blown-up ammunition dumps, tank traps, and still uncleared minefields, testimony to the fighting that had gone on six months before. A flight of American bombers passed overhead returning from a mission, its V formation punctuated by blank spaces marking planes that had not made it back. The motorcade passed by what seemed a scene out of the Bible, donkeys and shuffling Arabs in flowing white robes and red headdresses, unaware of the president's presence. As the vehicles passed through ancient Carthage, FDR ordered his car stopped while he gazed at the ruins of a long-ago war. He eventually arrived at a villa, known coincidentally as the White House, on the shore of the Gulf of Tunis. He learned to his amusement that the residence, now commandeered by Eisenhower, had been the headquarters of the Wehrmacht commander before the Germans were driven from Tunisia. That afternoon, an Air Force colonel, E. D. Cook, came by the villa and presented a delighted Roosevelt with a jagged piece of fuselage from a downed German bomber.

The president spent much of the afternoon working his way through official papers followed by a visit from Ike's aide, Commander Butcher. "He spoke of his pleasure at being away from Washington," Butcher recalled of the visit, "where he described backbiting" among the military "as rampant." FDR decided to stay another day in Tunis before departing for Cairo in order to have Eisenhower take him on a tour of the Tunisian battlefields. Ike arrived at the villa in an olive drab Cadillac, which FDR happily noted was driven by Kay Summersby, the same attractive woman he had met some ten months before during the Casablanca conference. Eisenhower had brought along his dog, Telek, a Scottie like FDR's Fala, whom the president nuzzled with evident pleasure. As the sedan got under way, eight MPs on motorcycles roared down the road, sending bystanders scattering while Eisenhower pointed out battlefield landmarks. FDR asked Ike if the plain they were passing through might have been the site of the ancient Battle of Zama, since, he remarked, the Carthaginians were known to employ elephants in war, which performed best on flat terrain. He pointed to a tree-shaded spot and said to Summersby, "That's an awfully nice place. Could you pull up there, child, for our little picnic?" The president motioned her to the backseat saying, "Won't you come back here and have lunch with a dull old man?" As an aide served chicken sandwiches and chilled white wine through the open door, the president began questioning Eisenhower about the expedient deal with Darlan, the merits of de Gaulle versus Giraud, the concern he had felt after the setback at Kasserine, and the outlook for Italy. He admitted to having disputes with Churchill but concluded, "No one could have a better or sturdier ally than that old Tory!"

As they resumed the drive, Roosevelt casually raised the subject of Overlord, principally who should command the operation. He confessed that he hated the idea of having Marshall leave Washington. "Ike, you and I know who was chief of staff during the last years of the Civil War but practically no one else knows, although the names of the field generals—Grant, of course, and Lee, and Jackson, Sherman, Sheridan and others—every schoolboy knows them. I hate to think that 50 years from now practically nobody will know who George Marshall was. That is one of the reasons why I want George to have the big command—he is entitled to establish his place in history as a great general." He then outlined his intention to bring Ike back to Washington to take over Marshall's post and serve as acting Army chief of staff.

The prospect was not pleasing to Eisenhower, who had, during his service in the War Plans Division, sought to escape desk duty to become a fighting general. Before the conversation ended Roosevelt added, "But it is dangerous to monkey with a winning team." "I answered nothing," Ike remembered of the moment, "but to state that I would do my best wherever the government might find use for me." Though the president's tone throughout the afternoon had been casual, Summersby had a sense that FDR was measuring Ike.

ON THE EVENING OF NOVEMBER 21, a transport plane with a seat adapted for the president's condition began the 1,305-mile flight from Tunis to Cairo. On awakening the following morning, FDR gazed out of the porthole expectantly. He had told the pilot to approach the city from the south so that he could see the Nile, the pyramids, and "My Friend the Sphinx." By noon he was installed in a grand suite in Mena offering a splendid view of the pyramids. He had invited Chiang Kai-shek to Cairo along with Vinegar Joe Stilwell. Chiang was accompanied by his wife, Mayling. Elliott Roosevelt has left a vivid portrait of the lady. At a cocktail party hosted by the Chinese delegation, Madame Chiang motioned to him to sit by her. "Resting her hand firmly on my knee," Elliott recalled, she proceeded to make him "the center of her universe," even urging him to settle in China where she said fortunes could be made in ranching. Initially, young Roosevelt was captivated, as she flashed a glimpse of well-shaped calf through the slit in her black satin dress, "but there was a hard brightness in her manner that was not compatible with complete sincerity," Elliott concluded.

Churchill had a realistic view of Roosevelt's high hopes for Chiang. "The accepted belief in American circles was that he would be the head of the fourth great power in the world after the victory had been won," he observed, not a conviction the prime minister shared. Stilwell himself was puzzled at being summoned. Just a month before, the president had called in Henry Stimson and conceded that the marriage of the general and the generalissimo was incompatible. Further, the president had found Stilwell's acidic manner unattractive when Vinegar

Joe and Claire Chennault clashed in Washington during Trident. At one point, Stilwell had written in his diary, "FDR doesn't like me to call Chiang Peanut." When Stilwell insisted to George Marshall that he had never used the term in public, Marshall replied, "My God, you have never lied. Don't now." The "Peanut" tag revealed Stilwell's penchant for derisive nicknames. In his diary he referred to the crippled president as "Rubber Legs." FDR too coined nicknames, but they lacked Stilwell's meanness; "Henry the Morgue" for the treasury secretary, "Fannie the Perk" for his labor secretary, and "Henry the Stimp" for the secretary of war.

Before coming to Cairo, FDR had assigned Stimson an unpleasant task, which the secretary of war passed to Marshall. The general was to deliver the coup de grâce to Vinegar Joe. He drafted a cable addressed "Marshall to Stilwell Only." "It has been decided in view of the attitude of the generalissimo," he wrote, that "it will be necessary to replace you in your present position in the Far East." But before the cable could be sent, Vinegar Joe telegraphed that the capricious Chiang had changed his mind and "flopped over to Stilwell." Here in Cairo with Chiang present, Stilwell set his priority to win the president's support for the goal that had thus far eluded him, clearing the Japanese from Burma so that aid could pass from India to Chinese forces. On November 23, the two Allied leaders and their supporting casts met in an opulent conference room in the Mena House Hotel. In the presence of Churchill, Chiang, his wife, and several Chinese generals, Roosevelt asked Admiral Lord Louis Mountbatten, the suave, handsome Southeast Asia commander and a cousin to George VI, to assess the situation in his theater. Mountbatten gave an upbeat briefing assuring all that the Japanese could be driven from Burma completely. Afterward, General Sir Alan Brooke presided over a meeting of only the service chiefs and the presumed cream of the Chinese military. Brooke asked one of them what he thought of the plans Mountbatten had advanced. The man stared blankly and said not a word. Brooke hastily adjourned the meeting and on the way out whispered to Marshall, "a waste of time," adding that Chiang possessed "no grasp of the war," other than fleecing his Western allies. The following day, the president took Hap Arnold on a visit to the Sphinx and got an earful on Chiang. Arnold wrote at the end of the day, "we talked over the air problem and what I could give the Generalissimo. Each time I said I could increase their tonnage over the Hump to 8,000 tons, [Chiang] would reply, 'I am not satisfied. I must have 10,000 tons.' If I said I will build the lift up to 10,000, the Generalissimo would say, 'not enough. I want 12,000.'" Hap advised the president, "don't take the demands of the Generalissimo too serious." The Chinese leader was confirming the journalist Theodore White's judgment that Chiang "was not only useless to us . . . but useless to his own people, which was more important." Joe Stilwell, however, left Cairo believing that his position in China had been solidified.

Despite the dispiriting performance of Chiang, FDR stuck to his conviction that China could be salvaged. When Stilwell's political advisor, the career diplomat John Paton Davies, asked the president what he would do if Chiang fell, Roosevelt replied that he would have to support whoever succeeded him.

ON THE EVENING OF NOVEMBER 23, Churchill invited George Marshall to dinner in the prime minister's suite in Mena House, just the two of them. He immediately turned on his power to charm and entertain, quoting for Marshall swaths of speeches by his long-ago predecessor William Pitt the Elder. Dinner over, he invited Marshall to join him in a walk through the hotel gardens as the night cooled rapidly and the Pyramids stood silhouetted in the distance. To Marshall's discomfort, Churchill began to enumerate the merits of landing troops on the island of Rhodes, south of Turkey. That move, he claimed, could bring the Turks into the war on the Allied side. Further, it would keep British troops gainfully occupied until Overlord could begin. Afterward, the two men returned to the prime minister's quarters, with Churchill still talking a blue streak. At two o'clock in the morning, he woke his military chiefs from their beds and ordered them to come at once. Marshall, sensing that he was about to be outnumbered as Churchill pursued his latest Mediterranean fancy, summoned Eisenhower. As the room filled, Churchill, now flush with brandy, grew "hotter and hotter," as Marshall remembered, arguing for Rhodes until the general could take no more. "God forbid," he rose and said with unaccustomed vehemence, "not one American soldier is going to die on that god damned beach!" British jaws dropped. One did not speak to Winston Churchill in that way. But none protested. Marshall had only spoken what they were thinking. Rhodes was a dead issue.

ON NOVEMBER 25, FDR wanted to celebrate an old-fashioned Thanksgiving with all the fixings. He invited nineteen American and British guests to the Cairo residence of the U.S. ambassador, where two huge turkeys were set before him. He proceeded to carve them with a dexterity that prompted Churchill to comment, "He had calculated to a nicety," so that in the end only two skeletons remained. A smiling Harry Hopkins went to fetch an ancient phonograph and records he had managed to turn up of Harry James, Glenn Miller, and Benny Goodman. Churchill's daughter Sarah, a budding actress and the only woman present, found herself much in demand on a hastily improvised dance floor. Suddenly, Churchill popped up, cigar still in place, and approached FDR's affable military aide, Pa Watson, bowed, and the two began to fox-trot. FDR laughed uproariously, and at the end of the day Churchill wrote, "For a couple of hours we cast care aside. I had never seen the President more gay."

FDR's CUSTOMARY APLOMB underwent a severe test in Cairo when a cable arrived from Elmer Davis's Office of War Information. Drew Pearson, the syndicated columnist and radio commentator, the president was informed, had dropped a bombshell. Roosevelt despised Pearson, once saying, "It is a pity that anyone anywhere believes anything he writes." But Pearson's radio broadcast of November 21 had the disturbing quality of being true. Pearson had uncovered a story that had been suppressed for over three months and decided to run with it.

On August 3, 1943, in the heat of the Sicily campaign, George Patton's command car screeched to a halt before the 15th Evacuation Hospital near the town of Nicosia. Patton jumped out and began moving among the cots talking in fatherly tones to the wounded GIs, one of whom he later described as having "the top of his head blown off." He then glimpsed a private sitting on the edge of his bed, Charles H. Kuhl of the First Division, who had been admitted to the hospital for "psycho-neurosis anxiety state—moderate severe." Seeing no visible evidence of injury, Patton demanded to know why Kuhl had been hospitalized. "I guess I can't take it," the soldier answered. Patton, his face beet-red, began shrieking at the trembling soldier, calling him a yellow coward. Seizing Kuhl by the collar, he slapped him and propelled him from the tent with a stout kick in his backside.

One week later, on August 10, Patton arrived at the 93rd Evacuation Hospital to find another apparently unwounded soldier, Private Paul G. Bennett, an artilleryman from South Carolina, shaking uncontrollably. Patton again demanded to know why he was in the hospital. "It's my nerves," Bennett answered. "I can hear the shells come over, but I can't hear them burst." Patton howled, "Your nerves, hell! You are just a god damned coward." He slapped Bennett once, started to leave, then wheeled around and hit him again with enough force to send the man's helmet liner flying into another tent.

Medical officers familiar with the two incidents reported Patton's behavior to Eisenhower. Ike had to ask himself if he could afford to bench George Patton as he sought to balance military prowess against unconscionable conduct. Ike warned him that his outbursts raised "serious doubt in my mind as to your future usefulness." In the end, however, Ike relented. "It is not my present intention to initiate any formal investigation," he wrote Patton. "There is no record of the attached report or my letter to you except in my own secret files. I expect your answer to be sent to me personally and secretly." In short, no official trace of the slapping incidents was to exist.

However, word of Patton's behavior inevitably reached war correspondents in the theater and three of them, Demaree Bess of *The Saturday Evening Post,* Quentin Reynolds of *Collier's,* and Merrill Mueller of NBC, came to see Ike and confronted him with the facts. They urged that Patton be relieved of command. Reynolds observed that there were at least 50,000 American soldiers in Sicily "who would shoot Patton if they had the chance." Eisenhower replied that he had reprimanded Patton severely but, defects aside, the man's brilliance and dash were vital to the Allied cause and would be lost if the public learned of his offense. Ike told the correspondents that he would not censor the story, but left it up to them whether to report it or not. More out of regard for Eisenhower than sympathy for Patton, they sat on the story. Ike concluded, however, that Patton could not merely walk away from his transgressions. He owed the aggrieved soldiers a public apology and dispatched a deputy, Major General John Porter Lucas, to fly to Palermo on August 21 to deliver Patton the galling verdict. Thereafter, Patton journeyed to all divisions of the Seventh Army, where he uttered an elliptical act of contrition before thousands of GIs, some stony-faced, many not sure what Old Blood and Guts was talking about, while pranksters in the rear ranks of the Ninth Division sent inflated condoms wafting in the breeze. In his heart of hearts, Patton had no doubt that his actions were justified. As he wrote in his diary, "It is rather a commentary on justice when an Army commander has to soft-soap a skulker to placate the timidity of those above."

That was where matters stood for the next three months until Drew Pearson's story broke. The press thereafter had a field day. *Time* magazine reported servicemen stationed in the Pentagon singing, "Pistol Packing Patton Laid That Private Down." Meeting with reporters, FDR, however, had nothing but praise for Patton's performance in Sicily, and made no mention of the slapping incident. When asked specifically about it, he replied, "if you want to write a piece, stick in there the story of a former President who had a good deal of trouble finding a successful commander for the Armies of the United States. And one of them turned up one day and he was very successful. And some very good citizens went to the President and protested: 'you can't keep him. He drinks.' 'It must be a good brand of liquor' was the answer." FDR had garbled the legend of Lincoln's dismissing complaints about General Ulysses Grant's drinking, but his point was clear. General George Patton had no problem with his commander in chief. FDR sent a personal message to him, saying, "Don't let anything that SOB Pearson

said bother you." His opponents would forever condemn FDR as a political weathervane bending to whatever the prevailing winds. Nothing
refutes the charge as emphatically as his handling of two unrelated incidents. The popular course would have been to join the cry for Patton's hide. He did not. Similarly, in 1942, as Eisenhower's Darlan deal
made humanitarians gag, he took the lonely position of sticking by the
beleaguered Ike.

The most interesting interpretation of Patton's bizarre behavior
has been offered by Martin Blumenson, editor of the general's papers.
"Part of this was perhaps due to the injuries and hard knocks he sustained during his hyperactive and accident-prone life. Some physicians
suspected that he suffered from a subdural haematoma."

THE MARATHON JOURNEY UPON which FDR had embarked on the *Iowa*
had as its ultimate objective an encounter the president had sought
since the United States and the Soviet Union had found themselves
allied in the war against Hitler, a face-to-face meeting with Joseph Stalin. On November 27, Roosevelt was taken aboard the *Sacred Cow* for a
1,130-mile flight to Tehran, where he, Churchill, and Stalin were to
meet. The Iranian capital had been agreed upon because Stalin claimed
that he could not be far from the front and had to "maintain constant
direction of the important military operations now in progress." Westerners familiar with the paranoid politics of Moscow suggested that
Stalin's real reason was that he dared not release the levers of control
even temporarily. Thus it was that FDR, an invalid for whom travel
meant pain, journeyed halfway around the world to meet a man in
robust health who had nearly ten more years to live.

Prior to the conference, Roosevelt had confidently told Churchill,
"I know you will not mind my being brutally frank, when I tell you that
I think I can personally handle Stalin better than either your Foreign
Office or my State Department. Stalin hates the guts of all your top
people. He thinks he likes me better and I hope he will continue to do
so." Roosevelt's belief that he could sweet-talk Stalin was rose-colored.
The man whom FDR hoped to win over with reasonableness had dur-

ing the purges of the 1930s ordered the deaths of Leon Trotsky, founder of the Red Army, all of Lenin's Politburo, a quarter of senior Soviet military officers, 1,108 of the 1,966 delegates to the 17th Party Congress, 90 percent of Soviet ambassadors, and two secret police chiefs, Genrikh Yagoda and Nikolai Yezhov, who had produced the trumped-up evidence that doomed so many of these people. It was as if an American president, upon taking power, plotted the deaths of most senators and congressmen, most of the generals, American ambassadors to nine out of ten countries, his political opponents, and potential rivals within his own party.

At 3 P.M. in the afternoon of November 27, the president's plane touched down beneath the 19,000-foot massif of the Elburz Mountains outside Tehran, the airport ringed with Soviet security forces. Initially, the president chose to stay at the American legation, but after one night there, an alarmed Averell Harriman arrived while FDR was breakfasting on White House china and silver flown in on the *Sacred Cow*. The ambassador had an urgent message from Stalin, he explained. The Soviet leader feared threats of assassination and wanted the president to move into the Soviet embassy. The switch produced a rare adventure for the disabled FDR. On Sunday afternoon, Mike Reilly surreptitiously hustled the president into a nondescript Army staff car for a mad dash through Tehran's back streets, alleys, and dirt roads for the two-mile trip to the Soviet compound. Roosevelt, despite the fearful jostling, beamed throughout the ride.

Stalin had arranged for Roosevelt to occupy the only structure in the Soviet embassy complex with central heating, while he himself stayed in a more modest villa. The moment for which FDR had waited two years finally arrived when Stalin came to see him. The president saw a compact, five-foot-four figure, with a formidable mustache, thick dark hair brushed straight back, his face pockmarked, his perfunctory smile revealing discolored, broken teeth from a poor childhood diet. Most striking were the penetrating, yellowish eyes. He wore a plain brown uniform with a lone medal, a gold star suspended from a red and gold ribbon, the Order of Lenin. His pants were tucked into highly polished boots. FDR later described the Soviet leader to Daisy Suckley.

"Stalin came to call on me. Of course, I did not get up when he came into the room. We shook hands and he sat down, and I caught him looking curiously at my legs." At one point Stalin turned to his interpreter, V. N. Pavlov, and said, "Tell the President that I now understand what it has meant for him to make the effort to come on such a long journey. Tell him that the next time I will come to him."

Within the hour, Roosevelt, Stalin, and Churchill held their first full meeting in a conference room at the Russian embassy. Roosevelt presided informally, though a circular oaken table ten feet in diameter had been specifically constructed so that no one would command the head of the table. The president quickly raised one of his motivations for coming to Tehran, to persuade Stalin to join the war against Japan. Given the protracted and bitter struggle expected against the Japanese, his intent was understandable, but probably naive. The Soviet Union needed no persuasion to enter that conflict since it would offer the golden opportunity for Russia to recover territory lost to Japan in the 1905 war and to extend its influence into the Pacific. The only question for Stalin was when he could do so risk-free. For the moment, he played the matter coolly, promising to come into the Asian war, but not until Germany was defeated.

FDR next suggested that the Western Allies might cross the Adriatic, join forces with Josip Broz Tito's Yugoslav partisans, push north into Romania, and effect a juncture with the Red Army moving east from the Odessa region. Churchill looked surprised, but delighted. This was just the sort of lunge at Europe's underbelly that he had been proposing all along. Marshall looked aghast. Harry Hopkins passed a note to Admiral King seated near him, asking, "who's promoting that Adriatic business?" King wrote back on Hopkins's note, "As far as I know, it is his own idea," born apparently in the same opaque mind that had spawned the destroyer deal, Lend-Lease, and other Roosevelt surprises. Stalin showed no interest in an operation that would intrude Western power closer to the Soviet Union. Even the Italian campaign struck him as sterile. He cited a czarist general, Aleksandr Suvorov, who had rejected the spiny Italian peninsula as an invasion route into Germany 144 years before. He asked how many Allied divisions were already tied down in Italy, adding that he saw little point in pushing further north. Churchill was immediately on guard. Failure to capture Rome, he protested, would signal a major Allied defeat. Stalin waved Rome aside. "We Russians believe that the best result would be yielded by a blow at the enemy in northern or northwestern France," Stalin countered. "Germany's weakest spot was France." To that end, he proposed a companion maneuver to Overlord. The Western Allies should forget about Rome and instead invade the south of France two months in advance of the cross-Channel invasion, thus forcing the Germans to divert divisions that could oppose Overlord. Roosevelt hedged. He wanted nothing further to distract from the cross-Channel invasion, but chose to indulge Stalin, suggesting that planners be put to work immediately to thrash out the operation the Soviet leader had proposed.

That evening, FDR invited Stalin, Churchill, and key staff to his rooms for dinner. He began with his proud custom of personally mixing drinks for his guests. He prepared a martini for Stalin with a generous dollop of Vermouth. Stalin sipped politely, pushed the glass aside, then shifted to vodka. Cocktails were followed by a dinner of steak, baked potatoes, and string beans served by Navy Filipino stewards. Stalin turned the conversation to the postwar period, warning Roosevelt and Churchill that they had to be tougher on Germany. The Teutonic militarist streak, he insisted, would be hard to uproot because the Germans were conditioned to blind obedience. He launched into a story of a visit he had made to Leipzig thirty-six years before when he watched hundreds of Germans at a railroad station miss a meeting because no official was there to punch their tickets. He had qualms about unconditional surrender, not in principle, he said, but because it failed to set out specific terms. Averell Harriman, among the guests, recalled Stalin's reasoning. "He felt that to leave the principle of unconditional surrender unclarified merely served to unite the German people," whereas "specific terms, no matter how harsh, would tell the Germans what to expect, and hasten the day of German capitulation." Roosevelt found Stalin's carping about unconditional surrender particularly irksome. He had forced through the demand in the first place to assure him that his Western Allies would never cut a separate deal with Hitler and leave Russia in the lurch. The president was about to speak when, as one guest remembered, "suddenly, in the flick of an eye, he turned green and great drops of sweat began to bead off his face; he put a shaky hand to his forehead" and complained of severe pain in his stomach. Roosevelt was in Soviet diplomatic territory where many of the Russians surrounding him, however thinly disguised, were agents of the secret police serving a dictator who had unblinkingly ordered the deaths of thousands. An alarmed Harry Hopkins ordered the stewards to wheel FDR to his bedroom and summoned Admiral McIntire. The physician disappeared into the room and emerged minutes later smiling. The president, he announced, had suffered only a bout of indigestion.

By day's end, Stalin had etched his impression on the Westerners. He wasted no word or gesture, Harry Hopkins noted. "It was like talking to a perfectly co-ordinated machine. . . . He laughs often enough, but it's a short laugh, somewhat sardonic." Hap Arnold was struck by Stalin's "knowledge of our planes. He knew details of their performance, their characteristics, their armaments and their armor much better than many of the senior officers in our own air force." Harriman, who had the closest personal exposure to Stalin, found him "the most inscrutable and contradictory character I have ever known." Yet he rated Stalin "in some ways the most effective of the war leaders. At the same time he was, of course, a murderous tyrant." Surprisingly, the only figure toward whom Stalin displayed a spark of real warmth was the stolid George Marshall. "In regard to me," Marshall later noted, "he made sort of semi-affectionate gestures. When we were in opposition, he would stand with his hand on my shoulder," a liberty no one ever hazarded with Marshall. Raising the subject of Overlord, Stalin lectured the chief of the American Army on "how to make a landing using the Volga River as one of the Russian rivers as an example of how you do it." In a postmortem with colleagues, Marshall described Stalin as a "rough SOB." Those who had sat near the man during the day watched as Stalin chain-smoked and doodled rather skillful wolf heads on a blank pad, eagerly eyed as souvenirs.

After the first day's debate, General Sir Alan Brooke, who would subsequently be elevated to field marshal, had come to regard Stalin's eagerness for the cross-Channel assault with a jaundiced eye. To Brooke, Stalin's passion for Overlord was a tactic to bog down the British and Americans on the French coast, thus leaving the rest of Europe open for a Soviet sweep. He wrote in his diary that night, noting FDR's solicitousness toward Russia's ruler, "The conference is over when it has only just begun. Stalin has got their President in his pocket."

On the morning of November 29, before the second plenary session opened, Marshall and Brooke met with Marshal Kliment Voroshilov. The marshal, an incompetent political crony of Stalin's who had almost lost Leningrad to the Germans, explained to them how to fight. As comrade Stalin had pointed out, he reminded them, the Russians showed great ingenuity in driving the Germans back over great rivers like the Volga. Why were the Allies dragging their feet on Overlord when the English Channel was no more than a river? Marshall pointed out that the currents of the Channel could be treacherous. "Withdrawal behind a river is a failure," he told Voroshilov, "but failure from the sea is a catastrophe."

At 2:45 that afternoon, still before the plenary session, Roosevelt asked to see Stalin privately, bringing along only Charles "Chip" Bohlen as interpreter and excluding Churchill. Earlier, Elliott Roosevelt had urged his father to press the Russians to allow American planes to use Soviet airfields, which would make shuttle bombing possible. FDR took up the cause with Stalin and pointed out that destruction of Germany could be stepped up significantly if American aircraft, upon landing in Russia, could refuel, reload, and bomb again on the way back to their bases instead of returning empty as they presently did. Stalin was cautious. He did not rule out the possibility, he said, but it would require more study.

At 4 P.M. when the full session got under way, Stalin raised the question uppermost in his mind. Who would command Overlord? he demanded to know. Unless a commander was handed the assignment, all else was "just so much talk." That had yet to be decided, FDR responded. He leaned over to Admiral Leahy and whispered, "That old

Bolshevik is trying to force me to give him the name of our supreme commander. I can't just tell him because I have not made up my mind." George Marshall, his fate so intertwined with Roosevelt's decision, remained inscrutable. The president reminded Stalin that a high-level officer, General Morgan, heading a staff of 3,000, was already immersed in planning the invasion. Churchill chimed in that an American would lead Overlord, and that his name would be announced in a fortnight.

That evening Stalin hosted a dinner, his appearance on his arrival creating a stir. Gone was the simple soldier's garb. Lord Moran described his new dress, "a mustard-colored uniform that looks as if it has not been worn before. . . . It looks, too, as if the tailor has put a shelf on each shoulder, and on it has dumped a lot of gold lace. . . . All this is crowned by a dreadful hat, smothered with gold braid." During the course of a dinner of borscht and fish, generously washed down with wine and vodka, Stalin began needling Churchill. After the prime minister raised a toast to "Stalin the great," Stalin responded, "You are pro-German." The prime minister retorted, "the devil is a communist and God is a conservative." Standing up and waving his glass, Stalin spoke again of the need to root out German militarism once and for all. "At least fifty thousand—and perhaps a hundred thousand—of the German command must be physically liquidated." He raised his glass higher. "I drink to our unity in killing them as quickly as we capture them. All of them. There must be at least 50,000." Churchill protested, "The British people will never stand for such mass murder. I would rather be taken out in the garden, here and now, and be shot myself than sully my country's honor by such infamy." Alarmed by the mounting ill humor, FDR tried to defuse it with a jest. Could they compromise at "say, forty-nine thousand, five hundred"? he asked. Stalin, whether prolonging the repartee, or serious, polled the table, asking each person how many Germans should be shot. Observing Stalin's performance, Hap Arnold was reminded of a description of Russia that Churchill had once given him: "Russia is like an amoral crocodile, lurking in the depths, waiting for whatever prey may come its way." Soon thereafter, the boozy evening ended.

The next day, November 30, FDR stepped up his campaign to woo

Stalin. As he later described his method to Frances Perkins, Stalin "was correct, stiff, solemn, not smiling, nothing human to get hold of. . . . I had to cut through this icy surface so that later I could talk by telephone or letter in a personal way." He continued, "On my way up to the conference room . . . we caught up with Winston and I had just a moment to say to him, 'Winston, I hope you won't be sore at me for what I am going to do.'" Churchill merely grunted. When the session began, FDR began speaking jocularly to Stalin. "Still no smile," he told Perkins. "Then I said, lifting my hand up to cover a whisper, 'Winston is cranky this morning, he got up on the wrong side of the bed.' A smile passed over Stalin's eyes. . . . As soon as I sat down at the conference table, I began to tease Churchill about his Britishness, about John Bull, about his cigars, about his habits. It began to register with Stalin. Winston got red and scowled. . . . Finally Stalin broke out into a deep, hearty guffaw. . . . It was then that I called him 'Uncle Joe.' . . . He came over and shook my hand. From that time on our relations were personal. . . . We talked like men and brothers." FDR may have exaggerated his seduction of Stalin to Frances Perkins, but he did want Stalin to believe that he and Churchill were not a palsy twosome scheming behind "Uncle Joe's" back. Perkins probably reported accurately what FDR told her, but no other participant, including Churchill, ever confirmed Roosevelt's account.

Prior to the third plenary session, Roosevelt and Churchill had ordered their military chiefs to answer one of Stalin's demands, a fixed date for Overlord. They confirmed May 1, 1944. The knowledge put Stalin in a conciliatory mood as he smiled on his fellow leaders. As Churchill recollected the moment, "he pledged that the Red Army would launch simultaneously with OVERLORD large scale offensives in a number of places for the purpose of pinning down German forces and preventing the transfer of German troops to the west." Stalin became effusive, coaching his allies on how to fool the Germans. The Red Army had misled the enemy on its strength and positions by deploying dummy tanks, aircraft, fake airfields, and misleading radio transmissions, a deception not lost on the Western leaders as planning for Overlord went forward.

The third meeting coincided with Churchill's sixty-ninth birthday. The prime minister admitted that he would not mind a grand affair, which the Russians agreed to host in their embassy. The room glittered with crystal, the silver shone in the candlelight, and the table groaned under endless courses of meat, fish, and fowl. Roosevelt sat on Churchill's right and Stalin on his left, the two dressed in black tie, while Stalin wore the bemedaled uniform. As Churchill later described the evening, "Together we controlled practically all the naval and three-quarters of the air forces in the world, and could direct armies of nearly twenty millions of men." Glasses were not left empty and "the champagne consumed would float a battleship," Major Boettiger observed. Churchill joked that, given the spectrum of British politics, his people might consider him "pink." "That is an indication of improved health," Stalin jibed. FDR, exhausted but exhilarated, finally got to bed after 2 A.M.

The conferees met again after lunch the next afternoon to address a final question, Poland's postwar borders. Stalin argued for a frontier between Russia and Poland that essentially legitimatized the chunk of Poland that Russia had stolen under its 1939 pact with Germany. Anthony Eden, Britain's foreign secretary, referred to this border as the "Ribbentrop-Molotov" line. In exchange for the loss of the Polish territory, Stalin offered to move the Polish border west to take in a significant swath of Germany. Churchill sought to put the best face on Stalin's scheme. "I suggested that the value of the German land was much greater than the Pripet Marshes," he replied. "It was industrial and it would make a much better Poland." Assuming that Russian armies would eventually capture the briefly independent Baltic states of Latvia, Estonia, and Lithuania, long part of czarist Russia, Roosevelt decided that a fight to restore their liberty, once occupied, would be pointless. Toward the end of the session, he introduced the idea of dismembering postwar Germany into the five independent states that had existed before Otto von Bismarck, the German chancellor, welded them into one nation. Stalin happily embraced this emasculation of his formidable enemy. The exact partitioning was left to be worked out in subsequent discussions by working staff.

That evening, as he prepared to leave, FDR asked for a list of servants to whom he should present the small gifts he had brought to Tehran. As soon as the gifts were distributed, most of these "servants" reappeared in Soviet military uniforms. Harry Hopkins noted, the domestic staff "who made the President's bed and cleaned his room were all members of the highly efficient OGPU [secret police] and expressive bulges were plainly discernible in the hip pockets under their white coats." Every room that the Americans and British occupied at Tehran had been bugged.

FDR spent the last night at an American base at Amirabad, outside Tehran, in a frigid room buried under heaps of blankets, and on the next morning reboarded the *Sacred Cow* to return to Cairo.

AN ARMY POST IS A SMALL TOWN, and even before the Tehran conference, George Marshall's neighbors at Fort Myer were curious about the activity at Quarters Number One, where the general's wife, Katherine, was seen supervising the loading of furniture into an old trailer she had just bought. She was moving their furnishings from Fort Myer to their home in Leesburg, as she put it, "surreptitiously." She had begun the move because "The rumors grew more insistent that General Marshall was to be named commander-in-chief of the Allied forces in the next invasion," and the Marshalls could expect to transfer to London. On October 1, 1943, *The New York Times* front-page headline reported, "Chief of Staff Will Head Allied Forces in Britain." That FDR would appoint his Army chief to command Overlord was a foregone conclusion. Henry Stimson, secretary of war, averred, "I believe that Marshall's command of OVERLORD is imperative for its success." Harry Hopkins believed, "Marshall should have commanded all the Allied forces, other than the Russians, attacking the Fortress of Germany." FDR himself told Churchill, "I believe General Marshall is the man who can do the job and should at once assume operational control of our forces in the war against Germany." Marshall himself, however discreetly, wanted the post. When, in a private conversation, Stimson kept pressing him to say what he really hoped for, Marshall answered, "Any soldier would prefer a field command." In late September, Roosevelt had told Marshall outright that he would command Overlord and that Eisenhower would replace him in Washington as acting chief of staff, though he had yet to make a public announcement. Curiously, Roosevelt had dodged naming his choice when Stalin had insisted on knowing at Tehran. Support for Marshall, however, was not unanimous, even among his staunchest admirers. His JCS confreres, Leahy, Arnold, and King, all resisted his appointment, the Navy chief giving the reason, "We have the winning combination here in Washington. Why break it up?" An ailing General Pershing, whom FDR venerated, wrote to the president from Walter Reed Hospital, "To transfer [Marshall] to a tactical command in a limited area, no matter how seemingly important, is to deprive ourselves of the benefit of his outstanding strategical ability and experience. . . . It would be a fundamental and very grave error in our military policy." After mulling over Pershing's advice, FDR wrote back, "You are absolutely right about George Marshall—and yet, I think you are wrong too. . . . I think it is only a fair thing to give George a chance in the field. . . . The best way that I can express it is to tell you that I want George to be the Pershing of the second World War—and he can not be that if we keep him here."

During Tehran, Roosevelt had promised Stalin an early answer on who would command Overlord. Churchill had said that the choice would be revealed within two weeks. On Thursday, December 2, the *Sacred Cow* came within sight of the pyramids and the president set his watch back to "Zone Minus Two," Cairo time. On landing, he was installed in the American ambassador's villa in the Mena district. After a nap, he agreed to see an impatient Joe Stilwell, who had remained in Cairo after Chiang Kai-shek left. Before Vinegar Joe could speak, the president began recounting his family's long connection to China. "My grandfather went out there to Swatow and Canton, in 1829," he mused. "He did what was every American's ambition—he made a million dollars." Then, laughing uproariously, he added that his grandfather had returned to the States and put his money into western railroads, "and in eight years he lost every dollar!" Stilwell, still immune to the Roosevelt charm, was eager to win FDR's support for his long-standing objective, to have an Anglo-American force drive the Japanese out of Burma and thus keep open a supply artery between India and China. "I've been stubborn as a mule," FDR explained, but "the British just won't do the operation." This was the message that Stilwell would have to bring back to Chiang Kai-shek, who would interpret it not as Roosevelt's answer, but as Stilwell's impotence.

Joe Stilwell had left Cairo believing that his position in China had been restored. Once back in the country, he wrote in his diary, "First time in history. G-mo gave me full command of . . . troops without strings. . . . A month or so ago I was to be fired and now he gives me a blank check." So harmonious did the new situation appear that Stilwell wrote his wife that he dared to take a vacation. "I've heard from Peanut that I can get away. . . . I'll spend Christmas with the Confucianists in the jungle. 'Jingle Bells, Jingle Bells, jingle all the way. Oh what fun it is to ride in a jeep on Christmas Day!'"

ON SUNDAY MORNING, DECEMBER 5, the president invited George Marshall to lunch at the villa in Cairo, just the two of them. They sat before a wide window opening onto a view of the pyramids as the president began one of his zigzagging monologues. "After a great deal of beating around the bush," as Marshall remembered, FDR came to the point. He asked "just what I wanted to do regarding command of Overlord. It was up to me." The stratagem, leaving the decision in Marshall's hands, was pure Roosevelt, since he knew his man. Whatever lay in his heart, the congenitally modest Marshall would not ask outright for the command. Instead, "in as convincing language as I could," Marshall recalled of this turning point in his life, "I wanted him to feel free to act in whatever way he felt was to the best interests of his country and to his satisfaction. . . . I would cheerfully go whatever way he wanted me to go." Roosevelt then nodded that the conversation was ended. As Marshall rose to leave, Roosevelt said, "Well, I didn't feel that I could sleep at ease if you were out of Washington." Marshall now knew, "I would not command in Europe." He accepted the news with grace. But as Robert Sherwood put it, "Never had he wanted anything in his career as to end it in the field in command of the decisive trans-channel invasion which he had first proposed and for which he had been fighting with unflagging determination ever since he and Hopkins had travelled together to London in April, 1942." FDR had one last request. He asked Marshall to write out a longhand note to be transmitted in the president's name to Marshal Stalin. It read, "The appointment of General Eisenhower to command the Overlord operation has been decided upon." Marshall suggested that the president add the word "immediate" before "appointment." Two days later, Marshall sent a copy of the original text to Ike with a note at the bottom reading, "Dear Eisenhower, I thought you might like to have this as a memento. It was written by me very hurriedly as the final meeting broke up yesterday, the President signing it immediately." Eisenhower kept the note and later called it "one of my most cherished mementos of World War II."

The president informed Mike Reilly that he wanted to make a trip, the sort of spur-of-the-moment notion that gave the security chief fits. He wanted to hop over to Sicily, he said, to pin medals on American soldiers who had fought heroically in the Italian campaign. Eisenhower received word to fly from his headquarters in Algiers to Cairo and join the president. When Ike arrived, the president waved him to a waiting limo. Once they were seated in the back, a grinning FDR said, "Well, Ike, you are going to command Overlord."

AT 2 P.M. ON DECEMBER 8, the president's plane approached Castelvetrano airfield, fifty miles southwest of Palermo, beneath an escort of twelve P-38s. Waiting on the runway were Generals Patton and Clark, the latter yanked from the Italian winter line for the meeting and still wearing battle fatigues. The plane rolled to a stop before files of sharply turned out infantrymen who braced to attention as a band played "Hail to the Chief." Out of the aircraft stepped Eisenhower, Admiral Leahy, and Harry Hopkins. Finally, Franklin Roosevelt, his fedora brim upturned against a bright sun, was lowered to the ground and taken to

a jeep, from which he leaned out and pinned the Distinguished Service Cross on six officers who had fought bravely at Salerno, including Mark Clark. Patton, ever hungry for attention, especially when out of the spotlight, was relieved when the president took his hand and held it warmly, promising, "You will have an Army command in the great Normandy operation," thus confirming the war's greatest secret, where the cross-Channel invasion would take place.

By the morning of December 17, FDR's 17,442-mile odyssey, Cairo to Tehran to Cairo, ended with his return to Washington, while Mrs. Marshall's little trailer returned the chief of staff's furniture to Fort Myer. The certainty among Churchill, Stimson, Hopkins, Stalin, and Marshall himself that the general would command the invasion had somehow been derailed in the curves of FDR's mind. No confidant, however close, had been consulted in advance. As Vice President Henry Wallace once observed, the only certainty in dealing with Franklin Roosevelt was uncertainty.

After he had made his choice, FDR told Henry Stimson that Marshall "perhaps really preferred to remain as chief of staff," a rationalization of stunning magnitude. Averell Harriman, one of those most surprised by Roosevelt's decision, noted, "I had seen a good deal of Eisenhower in London and I liked him. But compared to Marshall, Eisenhower seemed to me inexperienced and personally insecure." Doubtless, Roosevelt was sincere in saying that he would have felt uneasy without having Marshall at his right hand. Along with the general's oaklike support and military judgment, it was Marshall who could do what Roosevelt could not do so readily, win congressional concurrence for FDR's military policies. Others speculated that had FDR made Eisenhower Army chief of staff, while Marshall went to Europe, the switch would have amounted to a demotion for Marshall since Ike would have become Marshall's de jure superior. Keeping Marshall in Washington solved another dilemma for FDR. For all Douglas MacArthur's overbearing egotism, Roosevelt counted on the man in the Pacific. If Eisenhower had become chief of staff, it would have placed MacArthur in the intolerable position of taking orders from the man he had once regarded as his clerk. Another attempt to explain FDR's choice posited that Roosevelt feared damaging relations with Churchill. Marshall was one American who had stood up against the prime minister on North Africa, Sicily, Italy, and most recently had had the audacity to blow up at the prime minister over his scheme for an invasion of Rhodes. Churchill was an ally whom Roosevelt was so determined to keep happy that he once had an Air Force plane fly the prime minister a Christmas tree cut from his Hyde Park stands. Roosevelt himself gave perhaps the most candid explanation for the switch from Marshall to Eisenhower. A politician to his fingertips, FDR had spent his public life juggling competing people and power centers. What he had seen in Eisenhower was a capacity to unify in a common effort political leaders from independent nations, egotistical commanders from foreign armies, and ambitious generals within America's own military. His Marine Corps son, Jimmy, asked his father how he had arrived at choosing Ike. "Eisenhower is the best politician of the military men," FDR responded. "He is a natural leader who can convince men to follow him and that was what we need in this position more than any other quality." What might have happened had Marshall told FDR in Cairo that he did want to command Overlord? Franklin Roosevelt's affability cloaked a will of iron. He would have probably played on Marshall's acute devotion to duty and insisted that he could not run the war without him at his side.

CHAPTER 17

★

D-Day

Kay Summersby claimed in her memoirs that before FDR chose Eisenhower, Ike had confessed, "in hush-hush tones to me," his ambition to lead Overlord. By now the relationship between Ike and his driver had become the stuff of officer club gossip. Everett Hughes, a brigadier general of artillery, after a talk with Ike wrote in his diary, "Discussed Kay. . . . I don't know whether Ike is alibi-ing or not. Says he wants to hold her hand, accompanies her to her house, doesn't sleep with her. He doth protest too much, especially in view of the gal's reputation in London." Kay in her account quoted Eisenhower saying "I'm very out of practice in love," and hinted that Ike had difficulty consummating a romance. To assuage Mamie's suspicions back home, Ike wrote her that he was "an old duffer," and had no emotional attachments. Anything that Summersby says about the relationship has to be judged against two books she wrote at different times. The first, entitled *Eisenhower Was My Boss,* published three years after the war when Eisenhower was still alive, is a fairly decorous account of their association with no mention of an affair. The other, *Past Forgetting: My Love Affair with Dwight D. Eisenhower,* was published in 1976, seven years after Ike's death, in which she claims repeatedly that the two were in love, quoting Eisenhower as saying on one occasion, "Goddamit, can't you tell I'm crazy about you." The second book was written with a ghostwriter when Summersby was flat broke and dying of cancer.

George Marshall was a stickler regarding marital fidelity. Upon hearing rumors that an officer posted overseas might be involved with his secretary, he immediately ordered the woman sent home. Marshall's concern over Eisenhower's speculated involvement with Summersby likely explains an otherwise puzzling order that he made. He sent Ike back to Washington soon after he had been named supreme commander in Europe. Eisenhower protested, but Marshall insisted. "You will be under terrific strain from now on. . . . It is of vast importance that you be fresh mentally and you certainly will not be if you go straight from one giant problem to another." He added, "Now come on home and see your wife and trust somebody else for 20 minutes in England."

Ike and Mamie were reunited after a year-and-a-half separation in Washington's Wardman Park Hotel where she had taken an apartment. She found him visibly older, hair turning gray, thicker across the middle, and chain-smoking. Tension between them was palpable. Ike appeared distant and preoccupied. Mamie, aware of the talk about Summersby, was peevish and touchy. Marshall had made arrangements for the couple to be alone in a cottage at the posh Greenbrier Hotel resort in White Sulphur Springs, West Virginia, now converted into an Army convalescent hospital. But the Eisenhowers traveled first through a raging snowstorm to West Point to visit their son, John, scheduled to graduate in June. Afterward, the cadet noted that his father's "no-nonsense life of the past eighteen months had sharpened his manner somewhat." By the sixth of January, the Eisenhowers were installed in the cottage at the Greenbrier. Ike, still troubled that he had missed his father's funeral two years before, interrupted the reunion with Mamie to make a rush visit to his eighty-one-year-old mother in Manhattan, Kansas. He traveled incognito, since, as he explained to Marshall, "I still have some fear that any knowledge of my going to visit my mother later may work adversely against the war effort," since millions of men would not see their families until after the war ended and some never again. The following day, he returned to White Sulphur Springs. Reportedly, more than once during the stay he referred to Mamie as Kay.

Upon his return to Washington, Eisenhower plunged into a heavy schedule of meetings, lunches, and dinners with congressional leaders, civilian officials, and service chiefs, arranged by Marshall as if to lend an aura of necessity to Ike's unexpected visit. Marshall further asked FDR to see Ike. Eisenhower went to the White House on three occasions during this period, struck each time by its shabbiness as if the place had yet to recover from the Great Depression and wartime paint shortages. On the final visit, January 12, he found FDR in his bedroom propped up in a mahogany four-poster wearing a rumpled gray bathrobe, tired, sniffling, still recovering from a bronchial ailment picked up in Tehran. He gestured for Eisenhower to sit down and began reciting a reverie of his youthful bicycle trips and hikes through the Rhineland, adding proudly that he had mastered some German. When he got around to substance, he raised the issue of postwar occupation zones. Allied planners had already worked out preliminary sectors, with the British getting northwestern Germany and the Americans getting the southwest. Everything to the east, comprising 40 percent of Germany's landmass and 36 percent of the population, would go to the Russians. FDR told Eisenhower that he did not like the arrangement. He preferred the British zone, "so the troops could be supplied through the northern ports of Hamburg and Bremen . . . not be dependent upon the French for supply lines," a reflection of his continuing animus toward de Gaulle. He "kept me by his bedside for more than an hour as we discussed hundreds of details of past and future operations," Ike remembered. "As always, he amazed me with his intimate knowledge of world geography. The most obscure places in faraway countries were always accurately placed on his mental map." Ike was again struck by what he had observed during earlier encounters, that FDR was "almost an egomaniac in his belief in his own wisdom."

Eisenhower asked if the president remembered Kay Summersby, who had chauffeured him on the tour of the battlefields at Carthage. Roosevelt indeed remembered her, having once commented to his son Elliott about her attractiveness. Ike asked FDR if he would sign a photo for Kay taken during this tour, which the president did with a warm inscription. The visit over, Eisenhower rose, and as he left, the president called out "*Adiós*" and wished him Godspeed.

The following day, Ike said goodbye to Mamie and flew back to London, the real purpose of his visit unclear except in the mind of

George Marshall. What seems apparent is that the Army chief feared, if an Ike-Kay romance should be confirmed and become known, this revelation would diminish Eisenhower's stature as supreme European commander and tarnish his public image as a stainless hero; thus Marshall's attempt to reinvigorate the Eisenhower marriage. Eisenhower upon his return immediately became enmeshed in the harsh, masculine world of war making and, as he put it, "leading a rather lonely life" and craving "feminine companionship." His wife was older and frail. Kay Summersby was young, vital, and, most important, at his side. FDR, who at the time was enjoying frequent visits at the White House from Lucy Mercer Rutherfurd, could understand Ike's need. His own attachment to Lucy had never flagged long after their World War I love affair. The adoring Rutherfurd gave the president what his crusading, globe-trotting wife could not, a respite from his crushing burdens. Summersby provided much the same refreshing diversion for Eisenhower. As a fellow general concluded, "Leave Kay and Ike alone. She's helping him win the war."

CHURCHILL'S PERCEPTION OF ITALY AND THE Balkans as Europe's "soft underbelly" proved cruelly fallacious. The grinding slog up the Italian boot by the American Fifth and British Eighth Armies was more like attacking the hide of a crocodile. By the end of 1943, the Germans had stalled the Allies at the Gustav Line, a belt of concrete bunkers, artillery emplacements, machine-gun nests, and minefields that ran from Italy's west to east coasts anchored in the rugged Apennine Mountains near the town of Cassino, with its commanding Benedictine abbey founded by St. Benedict over 1,400 years before. In December 1943, before Eisenhower had gone home to spend time with his wife he faced Churchill on Christmas Day in Tunis, who was pressing for a new Italian adventure. The prime minister had returned from inspecting the Italian front, convinced by General Sir Harold Alexander, heading British forces there, that head-on attacks alone would not break the stalemate. The answer was an end run, circumventing the Gustav Line through an amphibious landing on Italy's west coast somewhere on the

Tyrrhenian Sea between Terracina and Rome. Churchill and Alexander recommended a seaside resort town thirty-five miles southwest of the capital called Anzio where Romans had frolicked since ancient times. Without circumventing the Gustav Line at Anzio, Churchill insisted, with a degree of hyperbole, "we must expect the ruin of the Mediterranean campaign of 1944." President Roosevelt tentatively agreed but awaited the advice of his senior advisors. Eisenhower wondered if "we should content ourselves with minor well-prepared attacks in the mountains with limited economy in men and resources," instead of risking another major front. In the end he concluded that he should not exercise authority over the Anzio decision since the British field marshal, Sir Henry Maitland Wilson, was taking over as Allied commander in the Mediterranean theater while Ike became supreme allied commander. Nevertheless, Eisenhower recognized that Anzio, if embarked upon, would slow preparations for Overlord, since "launching the attack would require a delay in the planned schedule for shipping certain landing craft to England." Churchill did, in fact, ask Roosevelt to allow ships destined for Overlord to be kept in Italian waters to carry out Operation Shingle, as the Anzio assault was code-named. In the end, Roosevelt went along with Shingle, despite his misgivings about sinking deeper into Italy.

On January 22, 1944, 36,000 American and British troops made an essentially unopposed landing at Anzio. The initial assault cost thirteen dead, ninety-seven wounded, and forty-four missing. Success now depended on racing toward Rome and trapping the Germans before they had time to occupy the mountains that ringed the Anzio beaches. But Major John P. Lucas, commanding the American force, let the moment slip by. He delayed a few crucial days under orders from his Fifth Army commander, Mark Clark, to dig in and consolidate his position. Given this gift of time, the wily Field Marshal Albert Kesselring, Hitler's commander of German forces in Italy, not only rushed in reinforcements to lock in the invaders but went on the offensive as Hitler ordered Kesselring to "lance the abscess south of Rome." Instead of dashing toward the capital, the Allies were stalled at Anzio inside a perimeter as German batteries from surrounding hillsides lowered their antiaircraft guns and raked the poorly protected Allied troops below. The Germans next rolled in giant 240-mm railroad guns, the most fearsome of them dubbed by pummeled Allied troops "Anzio Annie." The campaign's champion, Winston Churchill, ruefully admitted, "I thought we were throwing a wildcat onto the beach to rip the bowels out of the Boche. Instead we have a stranded whale."

The Allied forces facing the Gustav Line were supposed to launch an attack coordinated with the Anzio invasion to split the German forces in half. But before them loomed the massive Benedictine monastery at Cassino. General Sir Bernard Freyberg, commanding New Zealand troops, was convinced that the Germans had fortified the abbey. He wanted Montecassino bombed as a target of "military necessity." He warned that "any higher commander who refused to authorize the bombing would have to be prepared to take the responsibility for the failure of the attack." Freyberg, decorated in World War I with the Victoria Cross, Britain's highest military honor, was a voice to be heeded. Mark Clark felt compelled to approve the air strike, though earlier he had said, "If the New Zealand commander of the New Zealand Corps were an American commander, he [Clark] would give specific instructions that it should not be bombed." Freyberg initially asked for a modest thirty-six plane raid, though he proposed obliterating the monastery.

On the morning of February 15, Clark heard a roar above his headquarters as a fleet grown to 255 Allied bombers descended on Montecassino. When the planes finished dropping their 500- and 1,000-pound bombs, an artillery barrage began. One general gazing from an observation post exclaimed, "That's beautiful! Oh, that's beautiful!" By the end of the day, one of the holiest sites in Christendom lay in ruins. Clark subsequently admitted that no German soldier had ever set foot inside the abbey "other than to take care of the sick or to sightsee."

Not until May 25 did the U.S. II Corps driving up the coast above the Gustav Line link up with the Anzio enclave, almost four months to the day after the ill-starred enterprise had begun. By then, Lucas, saddled with the charge of poor generalship, had been relieved and sent home. Later in the Italian campaign when Clark's troops moved north within sight of the Leaning Tower of Pisa, he left the tower unthreatened.

The joining of the Cassino and Anzio forces was to have consequences for the Marshall family. The general was fond of all three of his stepchildren, particularly Allen Brown, with whom he kept up an almost weekly correspondence. When Allen began training for a commission as a second lieutenant, Marshall hesitated to show him favoritism, yet he asked Allen what division he preferred so that "I may be able quietly to arrange it for you." On May 29, Katherine Marshall was puttering around her garden in the warmth of early spring, "with a song in my heart," she remembered, when her husband came home only an hour after leaving for his office in the Pentagon. In recent weeks he had been totally absorbed in Overlord, and his return puzzled her. She left her gardening tools and followed him into the house. Marshall closed the door behind them and told her what he had just learned at the War Department. Allen, serving in Italy, had been leading a tank platoon near Velletri in the march on Rome. He had opened the hatch and raised his binoculars for a view of the terrain when he was killed instantly by a single shot from a sniper. "A blessed numbness comes to one at a time like this," she remembered at this staggering news.

Nearly four months before Allen Brown's death, Harry Hopkins had gone to Florida to restore his failing body when he received a telegram from the president. "I am terribly distressed to have to tell you that Stephen was killed in action at Kwajalein," FDR informed Hopkins of his son, then serving in the Marshall Islands. "We have no details as yet other than that he was buried at sea. . . . I am confident that when we get details we will be even prouder of him than ever. I am thinking of you much. FDR." Soon after, Hopkins received a scroll from Winston Churchill lettered like a medieval manuscript. Churchill entitled the scroll, "Stephen Peter Hopkins Age 18," and quoted Shakespeare's *Macbeth*:

> *Your son, my lord, has paid a soldier's debt:*
> *He only liv'd but till he was a man;*
> *. . . But like a man he died.*

✱

FACED WITH CHURCHILL'S TEPID acceptance of Overlord, FDR exasperatedly told the Joint Chiefs at one point, "We can, if necessary, carry out the project ourselves," while the British could "make the necessary bases in England available to us." Even one month before the invasion date, Churchill was still temporizing. After he had met with dominion prime ministers one participant summed up the prime minister's confidential remarks. "He would have been in favor of rolling up Europe from the southeast and joining hands with the Russians, but it had proved impossible to persuade the United States to this view." In the House of Commons, Churchill raised the ghosts of men who perished in the slaughterhouses of the Somme and Passchendaele. Casting his eye over the chamber, he spoke of "the faces that are not there." He told Eisenhower, "When I think of the beaches of Normandy choked with the flower of American and British youth, and when in my mind's eye, I see the tide's running red with their blood, I have my doubts." His fears were not baseless. His commanders reported that 90 percent of junior officers did not expect to survive Overlord, about the same death rate that subalterns had experienced on the Western Front a generation earlier. On one occasion, he demanded to know from Eisenhower and other officers present when William the Conqueror had crossed the English Channel. General Sir Hastings Ismay, Churchill's liaison with the military branches, said, "1066." Churchill pounded the table, and roared, "Dammit, everybody knows it was 1066!" but when in 1066? Would the answer offer a clue to the best season to strike? Eventually Churchill got his answer. William crossed the Channel on September 28.

While FDR and his chiefs had allowed themselves to be detoured into North Africa, then Sicily, then Italy, costing two years by 1944, the momentum for Overlord was now unstoppable. The British Isles had begun to groan under an American logistics avalanche. Two million U.S. troops were pouring into an island nation about the size of Colorado. Kay Summersby described the inundation of Americans meandering through Piccadilly Circus amid soldiers from a dozen nations:

"overwhelming all others by sheer weight of numbers were the Yanks, hands in pockets, leaning against the walls, flirting with anyone in a skirt . . . or just plain loafing with all the careful, superb nonchalance of the American with time on his hands." The riptide of ships, men, armaments, and supplies was by now flowing into England virtually unimpeded. The U-boats that Churchill once feared would strangle England had been defeated by destroyers, and planes equipped with radar, searchlights, and depth charges guided to wolf packs by decoded German naval signals through the cryptographic triumph, Ultra. Over one four-month period, 3,546 merchant ships crossed the Atlantic without one being sunk. In May 1943, Admiral Dönitz had given up the fight and called his U-boats home after losses became insupportable and life expectancy for the crews shrank to 100 days.

FDR kept pressing Marshall to tell him the strength of the invading force. "You asked the other day the number of divisions," Marshall reported back. Twenty-one divisions were already in the United Kingdom backed by another forty-one in the United States. For every man carrying a rifle onto the beaches, fifteen would be in the rear in supporting roles. Some 4,500 cooks alone had to be trained to feed this multitude. Along with the masses of men, 7,860 bombers and other aircraft spilled over 109 airfields, most in the south of England. Overlord would thrust the most formidable invading force ever assembled, 156,000 men and 20,000 vehicles from tanks to jeeps, against the Atlantic Wall, the strongest defense that Hitler's engineers could devise, a concrete and steel vertebrae of bunkers, pillboxes, artillery, sea mines, land mines, and tank traps girding the entire northeastern coast of France. The initial 73,000 Americans in the assault would within two weeks swell to twice the number of men in the entire U.S. Army in 1939. Transports from ports along England's southerly coast would deliver troops to five Normandy beaches, running from west to east, with the Americans at Utah Beach near La Madeleine on the Cotentin Peninsula below Cherbourg and Omaha Beach near Vierville. The British would embark at Gold Beach near Arromanches, the Canadians at Juno Beach near La Rivière, and the British again at Sword Beach near Lion-sur-Mer. To sustain the element of surprise, major French ports were initially to be bypassed.

On the night before the amphibious landings, the 82nd and the 101st Airborne Divisions were to parachute inland accompanied by glider-borne troops to cut off German access to the beachheads.

Preparations were meticulous. Geologists, some old for the job, were slipped ashore from rubber dinghies onto the Normandy coast. They "crawled half a mile on their bellies on the beach with special instruments taking samples and charting the position of the soft clay," to determine if the landing sites could support tanks and other vehicles that weighed tons, one participant reported. A young British navy lieutenant showed Eisenhower a glass tube filled with what looked like impacted dirt and explained that it had been lifted from Omaha Beach, adding, "You can see by the core . . . there is little danger of your trucks bogging down."

Along the English coast, massive blocks of hollow concrete, almost the size of a battleship and code-named Mulberries, had been constructed. The Mulberries were to be towed near the invasion beaches and sunk in place along with obsolete vessels to create an artificial harbor that would hold back the rough seas and allow transports to come inside and safely unload men and matériel of war. Part of the plan had grown out of a Churchill visit to Hyde Park. FDR had taken him along the Hudson River to a stretch where World War I vessels lay mothballed. "By George," Churchill exclaimed, "we could take the ships . . . and sink them offshore to protect the landings." FDR had by now heard numerous Churchill brainstorms. "He has a hundred a day and about four of them are good," the president concluded.

The relations between the two men, though dominated by matters of deadly consequence, occasionally prompted moments of frivolity. A movement for "Basic English" had begun to take hold, the compression of language into simple phrases that foreigners could easily master. FDR wrote, "My dear Mr. Prime Minister . . . I wonder what the course of history would have been if in May 1940 you had been able to offer the British people only 'blood, eye water, and face water,' which I understand is the best Basic English can do with five famous words."

In the end, all the Allied planning lay hostage to the vagaries of nature. The waters of the English Channel could turn treacherous overnight. Twice a day the tides on the Normandy beaches rose and fell the height of a two-story building. Engineers calculated that under cover of darkness and before the tide rose too high, demolition teams had half an hour to blow up obstructions along the beaches and clear a path for the landing craft. When was the best hour to put the men ashore? Tide too high and the landing craft could be speared by thousands of underwater pikes the Germans had driven into the bottom called "Rommel's asparagus," named for the field marshal charged with making the coast impregnable. Tide too low and infantrymen, bent under sixty-pound packs, would have to trod a quarter of a mile over open beach, defenseless against German fire. H-Hour had to be timed to take place just after the demolition teams had done their work.

A FEARSOME THREAT TO INVASION, poison gas, had as yet not been used in the European war, except by the Nazis against Jews in extermination camps. FDR, from his service as assistant secretary of the navy during World War I, remembered the terror this weapon generated in that conflict. Germany had introduced gas warfare in 1915 and the Allies adapted swiftly and retaliated in kind. Hitler had ended the war in a hospital recovering from a gas attack. Well before D-Day, the president advised Americans, "Regarding gas, evidence that the Axis powers are making significant preparations indicative of such an intention is being reported with increasing frequency. Acts of this nature against any one of the United Nations will be regarded as having been committed against the United States. . . . Any use of gas by any Axis power, therefore, will immediately be followed by the fullest possible retaliation." Toward this end the U.S. Army's chemical warfare service had piled up huge stocks of phosgene, mustard gas, and other chemical killers.

ROOSEVELT WAS HARDLY A MILITARY meddler on the scale of Winston Churchill, yet he had a healthy respect for his own judgments. During World War I, he had persuaded his socialite friends to organize their yachts into a volunteer civilian patrol. During the D-Day planning, he called in Admiral King and similarly recommended rounding up small craft, even lifeboats, from across the East Coast to form an auxiliary flotilla. Anyone but the president advancing such a scheme would have felt King's blistering scorn. Instead, the admiral hoped that the idea would wither from neglect. But FDR kept asking him what he was doing to advance his idea. Enduring King's endless excuses—lack of trained crews, problems getting the boats to England, adding to congestion in the Channel—the president complained to Admiral Leahy, "I rather expected King would answer as he did. . . . I should hate to be accused of not doing all we can in case of a lot of drowning people floating around in the Channel."

Roosevelt injected himself into Henry Morgenthau's responsibility for printing invasion currency. The initial design of the bills carried the words "La République Française" on one side and a tricolor flag on the other with the words, "Liberté, Egalité, Fraternité." Morgenthau brought the design to FDR for approval, noting that the Departments of State, War, and Navy had already approved. Roosevelt's response jarred the treasury secretary. He did not want the word "République" used, only "La France," because the form of the future French government was yet to be determined. When Morgenthau asked what he expected that government might be, Roosevelt answered, "My guess is that it will be headed by a mandarin." The rejection of Morgenthau's design had little to do with words printed on currency. FDR was concerned that the emergent mandarin would be Charles de Gaulle. By now the proud French Committee of National Liberation had amassed a respectable military force, with resistance fighters alone inside France estimated at 175,000. To de Gaulle, the FCNL *was* the provisional government of France, a conclusion not embraced by the president. As for the reverse side of the bills, FDR said, "I would put in the middle, in color, the French flag, supported by the American flag and the British flag on either side." The French, especially de Gaulle, were not to forget who was making the sacrifice to regain France's freedom.

Roosevelt complained to Marshall that he resented news stories charging, "I am anti de Gaulle . . . that say I hate him, etc. etc. . . . I am perfectly willing to have de Gaulle made president, or emperor, or king." But he had to be selected by the French people. FDR was not going to have the man "foisted on them by outside powers." Churchill too regarded the lofty, touchy Frenchman as a pain. "We call him Joan of Arc," he famously uttered, "and we are looking for some bishops to burn him." When the president learned that Eisenhower regarded de Gaulle as the only leader the French people respected, he retorted, "I wonder how he knows this because nobody else knows anything." As Overlord approached, the American and British leaders decided that de Gaulle, the Allies' stepchild, was to be kept in his Algiers headquarters, not flown to London until twenty-four hours before D-Day and then only to deliver a radio message to hearten the French people that liberation was at hand. Even then, he was to be misled and told that the assault on Normandy was merely a diversion.

EISENHOWER'S VISION OF THE ROLE of airpower in Overlord was to render the Germans immobile by bombing rail yards. These targets were located in or near French cities and, inescapably, civilians would die. Churchill came out of a cabinet meeting shaken after hearing estimates that the raids would kill 10,000 men, women, and children. FDR received a cable from the worried prime minister saying, "I am personally by no means convinced that this is the best way to use our air forces." In an April 5 response, Eisenhower countered, "the bombing of these centers will increase our chances for success in the critical battle. . . . I do not see how we can fail to proceed with the program." Roosevelt backed Eisenhower. In the weeks prior to Overlord, Eisenhower ordered that clandestine messages be radioed to the French resistance guiding the populace as to how to conduct themselves during the invasion: "Do not let the Germans entice you onto the road," as this would only block Allied troop movements. "Avoid windows. Cellars, quarries and trenches are the best protection against bombardments."

✶

In November 1943, at Tehran, Roosevelt and Churchill had concluded that Overlord required "a cover plan to mystify and mislead the enemy regarding these operations." Churchill described this deception in his memorable phrase, "Truth is so precious that she should always be attended by a bodyguard of lies." Beneath the pavements of Westminster, in the prime minister's wartime command post, under four feet of concrete ribbed by London tramway rails, the charade was begun by a faceless entity called the London Controlling Section. The enemy was to be misled in two directions. Operation Bodyguard would seek to confuse the Germans as to where, even in which country, the invasion might take place. Fortitude was designed to lead them into believing that the invasion would occur at the most logical point, the narrow twenty-mile strait of the English Channel separating Dover and Calais.

The star actor in this performance was to be George Patton. At one time, Eisenhower had been full of admiration for his onetime superior. During the run-up to Torch he wrote Patton, "I will have to battle with my diffidence over requesting the services of a man so much senior and so much more able than myself." But by the time preparations for Overlord were under way, the deference had faded. Eisenhower found himself in a quandary. He was the coach of a team with a player who broke all the training rules, yet won games. Supreme Allied planners worked out a compromise for handling Patton. Under Operation Fortitude, he was given command of the First U.S. Army Group, FUSAG, an impressive force of over 100,000 men that began gathering in the southeast corner of England opposite the Pas-de-Calais equipped with hundreds of tanks, caissons, and trucks. The force, however, was pure fiction, the troops existing only on paper, the vehicles rubber dummies, conceived by a British stage designer. Phony FUSAG radio traffic, transmitted in easily broken ciphers, crowded the airwaves, misleading German code breakers about the movements of Patton's imaginary divisions. The combative general was eventually to have an authentic command, the Third Army, which was training in the States but not to be committed until after the invasion was well under way. In the meantime, the actor played his role with flair. Patton toured England under lax secrecy, making fire-and-brimstone speeches to authentic units under command of his rival, Omar Bradley. On one such occasion, he warned the troops, "A man must be alert all the time if he expects to stay alive. If not, some German son of a bitch will sneak up behind him and beat him to death with a sock full of shit." After the GIs had defeated the Germans, he added, they would head for the Pacific to lick those "purple pissin' Japs!" Kay Summersby, a keen Patton observer, was struck by the duality of the man's character. "When he shook hands and bowed, everything was there but a continental kiss of the hand," she noted. "There was no hint of the expected American backslap or the wolfish eye."

Yet once again Patton undid himself. The ladies of Knutsford invited him to attend the opening of a club they had established to entertain American servicemen. He arrived resplendent in a uniform that, counting shoulder, collar, and cap insignia, totaled fifteen stars. Mrs. Constantine Smith, founder of the group, rose and said conspiratorially, "I now have the pleasure of introducing someone who really is not supposed to be here. . . . His presence was not to be disclosed." Patton got up before some fifty people, under the impression that no press were present. He praised the hospitality of the British toward American GIs, adding, "The sooner our soldiers write home and say how lovely the English ladies are, the sooner American dames will get jealous and force the war to a successful conclusion." The remark was greeted with laughter. What he said next would later be subject to differing accounts. What Patton recalled saying was "Since it is the evident destiny of the British and Americans, and, of course, the Russians, to rule the world, the better we know each other, the better the job we'll do." The British press got hold of his remarks but made no mention of the Russians, leaving the impression that Patton was saying that the United States and Britain would rule the postwar world. When the story broke in the United States his behavior again ignited a firestorm. Congressman Karl Mundt declared in the House of Representatives that besides slapping GIs, Patton had "succeeded in slapping the face of everyone of the United Nations except Great Britain." *The Washington Post* editorialized, "General Patton has progressed from simple assault on individuals to collective assault on entire nationalities."

Eisenhower cabled Marshall, "On all the evidence now available, I will relieve him from command and send him home unless some new and unforeseen information should be developed in the case." Ike considered demoting Patton from lieutenant general to his Regular Army rank, colonel. Before firing him, he gave the man one last chance to explain himself. Three days after Knutsford, a contrite Patton appeared at Ike's office. "George, you have gotten yourself into a very serious fix," Eisenhower began. As he continued to dress him down, Patton interrupted, "your job is more important than mine, so if in trying to save me, you are hurting yourself, throw me out." If, however, he was to be reduced to colonel, he asked for command of a regiment in the coming invasion rather than being sent home in disgrace. Eisenhower said that he had not yet decided. According to Eisenhower's account, Patton "put his head on my shoulder . . . and this caused his helmet to fall off—a gleaming helmet I sometimes thought he wore while in bed." The bouncing headgear came to a stop in a corner, where Patton picked it up and asked permission to return to his post. Eisenhower mulled over his decision for four days and finally sent Patton an "Eyes Only" message that read, "I am once more taking the responsibility of retaining you in command, in spite of damaging repercussions resulting from a personal indiscretion. I do this solely because of my faith in you as a battle leader and from no other motives." The coach needed his wayward player.

FROM AN UNLIKELY WARREN of cubicles in a former girls school in Arlington, Virginia, the president and the chiefs enjoyed an extraordinary view into what Hitler thought about the expected invasion. Hiroshi Oshima, the Japanese ambassador in Berlin, continued to enjoy Hitler's favor and faithfully reported his conversations with the führer back to the Tokyo Foreign Office. Through Magic, the code breakers in Arlington made Oshima's cables available to the president at almost the same time they reached the Foreign Office. Marshall, however, believed that FDR failed to appreciate this priceless opportunity. "I have learned that you seldom see the Army summaries of 'MAGIC material,'" he once scolded the president. In an October 1943 intercept, Oshima reported a conversation with Hitler that took place in the *Wolfsschanze,* the Wolf's Lair, in East Prussia, during which the führer said, "I am inclined to believe that the Allies would land in the Balkans," a surmise designed to gladden the hearts of the Bodyguard dissemblers. In another intercepted jewel, Hitler told Oshima, "No matter when or at what point it comes, I have made adequate preparations for meeting it. In Finland we have seven divisions, in Norway twelve, in Denmark six, in France including Belgium and the low countries sixty-two. . . . But how vast is that sea coast! It would be utterly impossible for me to prevent some sort of landing somewhere or other. But all they can do is establish a bridgehead. I will stop, absolutely, any second front in the real sense of the word." Hitler's confidences to Oshima also confirmed a long-expected threat. "Then too there is that revenge against England. We are going to do it principally with rocket guns. Everything is now ready. . . . We are really going to do something to the British Isles." On May 28, just nine days before the latest invasion date, the ambassador asked Hitler, "I wonder what ideas you have on how the second front will be carried out?" Hitler answered, "Well, as for me, judging from relatively ominous portents, I think that diversionary operations will take place against Norway, Denmark, the southern part of Western France and the coasts of the French Mediterranean—various places. After that, after they have established bridgeheads on the Norman and Brittany peninsulas and seeing how the prospects appear, they will come forward with the establishment of an all-out second front in the area of the Strait of Dover." Fortitude too was working. Oshima further reported to Tokyo speculation in Germany as to the invasion date: "most indications point to this action around the last of May." Thus FDR and his military staff had it from Hitler's mouth. In expecting the invasion to occur across the narrow strait between Dover and Calais, the führer had it wrong. On the expected date, however, he was chillingly close.

By citing the French Mediterranean coast as one possible invasion site, Hitler had stumbled on to a long simmering Allied controversy. At Tehran, Roosevelt had gratefully heard Stalin praise a Western Allied plan for complementing Overlord with a parallel invasion of the south of France. An operation code-named Anvil had been chosen for a landing in the Toulon-Marseille port area. If the operation worked, German resistance to Overlord would be weakened by the necessity of sending troops south to the Mediterranean. The German army in France would be trapped in a gigantic pincer movement, with the upper jaw, Overlord, crushing the enemy from Normandy, and the lower jaw, Anvil, closing in from the Riviera. The twin assaults were to begin simultaneously. From the outset, Churchill never warmed to Anvil. His aversion fit with his geopolitical template. Any campaign aimed westward was unwise. And anything eastward toward the Soviet Union was desirable. While Marshall was ready to halt operations in Italy at any time, Churchill believed, rather than diverting forces to southern France, that the Italian campaign must be sustained so that the Allies could drive north and beat the Russians to Vienna. To that end he proposed invading Istria, the peninsula jutting into the Adriatic between Italy and Croatia, which had been ceded to Italy after World War I and was now inhabited by Italians, Croatians, and Slovenians. Istria would open the door, he claimed, into the Balkans—Hungary, Romania, and Bulgaria—before these prizes could fall to the Russians. Upon learning of Churchill's latest inspiration, Roosevelt replied, "I cannot agree." With an eye to the 1944 presidential election, he warned, "I would never survive even a small setback in Overlord if it were known that fairly large forces had been diverted to the Balkans."

Mark Clark, his own destiny and prestige tied up in Italy, agreed with Churchill and railed against Anvil. Stalin, he said, "was one of the strongest boosters of the invasion of southern France. He knew exactly what he wanted. . . . And what he wanted most was to keep us out of the Balkans, which he had staked out for the Red Army. If we switched our strength from Italy to France, it was obvious to Stalin, or to anyone else, that we would be turning away from Central Europe." Clark was out of step with Marshall, Eisenhower, and, most of all, his commander in chief. To Roosevelt, Anvil had become a pledge to Stalin. According to minutes of a JCS meeting held on February 21, 1944, he said, "We are committed to a third power," and that he, the president, did "not feel we have any right to abandon this commitment for Anvil without taking up the matter with that third power." The Anvil debate raged on, with Churchill insisting that the operation would not work because a drive up the Rhône Valley from the south of France could easily be blocked "by a small German force." FDR countered that the difficulties of breaking into the Balkans "would seem far to exceed those pictured by you in the Rhône Valley." Churchill came back with a quote from the Bible to prophesy the price of relaxing the fight in Italy: "For if the trumpet gives an uncertain sound, who shall prepare himself to the battle." FDR held fast, leading Churchill to register his distaste for Anvil by having the name changed to Dragoon, since he was being dragged into acquiescence.

Meanwhile, the Russians had provided an intelligence boon to Overlord's planners. During fighting on the Russian Front, the Red Army had captured the files of the Wehrmacht's 320th Infantry Division. This division was among those that had repelled the Dieppe incursion in 1942 and turned it into a catastrophe. After that clash, intelligence officers of the 320th compiled a critique of all the blunders the Allies had committed. Upon seizing a copy of this document, the Russians sent it to the D-Day staff, a virtual how-not-to manual for conducting the invasion.

IN STANDING FAST ON UNCONDITIONAL SURRENDER, FDR appeared at times to be standing alone. Stalin had already expressed misgivings about the president's terms. Churchill had been tepid all along. The Joint Chiefs urged FDR to restate his position in language less threatening to the German people. Two cabinet secretaries, Stimson and Hull, went to FDR and urged him to modify his stance, citing intelligence reports that enemy propagandists were using unconditional surrender to stiffen German spines. Roosevelt preferred the interpretation of Stimson's subordinate, assistant secretary of war John McCloy, who maintained that it was not unconditional surrender that kept the Germans fighting, "but fear of the Red Army" after the atrocities the Nazis had committed in Russia. Roosevelt's stubborn Dutch jaw remained fixed. He told Admiral Leahy, "Please note that I am not willing at this time to say that we do not intend to destroy the German nation," and, therefore, total surrender must be the standard as long as Germany remained a militaristic culture. The Germans would be more mollified by good example, he believed, than by words. In a memorandum to Hull dated January 17, 1944, he went back to the Civil War for a parallel. "Lee wanted to talk about all kinds of conditions," he said. "Grant said that Lee must put his confidence in [Grant's] fairness. Then Lee surrendered." Roosevelt recalled Grant's magnanimity in allowing Lee's army to keep its horses, "since they would be needed in the spring plowing." He ended, "A few little incidents like the above will have more effect on the Germans than lots of conversation between the Russians, British and ourselves trying to define 'unconditional surrender.'"

EISENHOWER HAD SET June 5 for the invasion date, counting on a favorable conjunction of tides, moonlight, wind, and weather. The troops had been issued gas masks, seasick pills, vomit bags, invasion currency, maps, French phrase books, and told to get their family allotments in order. Service troops, mostly black, were loading over 300,000 gallons of fresh water into the holds of cargo ships, enough to sustain the men for the first three days. They further hauled 800,000 pints of plasma, 600,000 doses of penicillin, and 100,000 pounds of sulfa drugs aboard fifteen hospital ships. Eight thousand physicians in combat fatigues came aboard to deal with casualties. The English countryside appeared to be in motion as an endless flow of trucks snaked through once placid villages hauling munitions to camouflaged dumps around the ports of Portsmouth, Plymouth, Portland, and Southampton. British families who had hoped to celebrate the Whitsun holiday weekend were warned to stay home since roads might be blocked and trains canceled without notice. For three days and nights, vehicles loaded with sleepy GIs rumbled toward embarkation ports. On their arrival they boarded gray transports, part of the mightiest armada ever assembled. Over 7,000 battleships, destroyers, cargo ships, and small landing craft bobbed in rough waters along the English coast under gunmetal gray skies that did not augur well for the scheduled invasion date. Once at sea, this armada would stretch over 100 miles in length and five miles deep. All the troops were aboard by June 3. Two years before, the president had been persuaded by Churchill to postpone the invasion of Europe, because American GIs were too green to take on the Wehrmacht. Yet of the five American divisions scheduled to go ashore on D-Day, three had never experienced combat. Even battle-tested divisions included thousands of replacements facing their first test of fire. All told over 60 percent of the Americans had never faced the enemy as they waited for H-Hour.

OVERLORD COULD NOT SUCCEED if the ships clogging the English Channel laden with men and arms were vulnerable to attacks from the air, or if rail lines and roads could speed enemy troops to wherever Allied forces landed, or if German industries and oilfields could continue to pump life into the Nazi war machine. Removing these threats to Overlord fell to Hap Arnold's U.S. Air Forces and the RAF. Though at first overshadowed by the British, the Americans had begun to feel their growing muscularity as the Air Forces swelled from 101,227 personnel at the time of Pearl Harbor to a present 2,385,000. How best to employ Allied airpower presented a still unresolved debate between proponents of saturation bombing of cities and champions of hitting strictly military targets, the latter course preached and practiced, however unevenly, by Arnold's fliers.

Within the school supporting target bombing a further split existed, something of a chicken-and-egg conundrum, the oil strategy versus the transportation strategy. General Carl "Tooey" Spaatz, now commanding the U.S. Strategic Air Forces out of England and charged with air operations for the invasion, believed that if the Allies attacked oilfields and refineries, the German war machine would literally run out of gas. An unlikely British air war expert, a former professor of anatomy, Solly Zuckerman, took a different tack. Zuckerman had studied the impact of raids on Rome's marshaling yards and concluded that destroying railroad junctions could best immobilize the enemy. Eisenhower became a convert to Zuckerman's vision. In actual practice, all strategies were being pursued simultaneously. Under Bomber Harris's brute approach, German cities and towns were being leveled at the rate of two per month. At the same time, the U.S. Air Force sought to sever the arteries of war production by pinpoint attacks on rail yards and arms industries such as ball bearings.

Eisenhower and his commanders faced the immediate necessity of clearing the way for Overlord's success by pounding the enemy's defenses from the sky. On May 22, 1944, *The New York Times* reported, "In the greatest mass air attack of the war the Allies hurled 6,000 Britain-based planes at Hitler's Atlantic Wall defenses yesterday and blasted a 150-mile strip from Brittany to Belgium." Targets struck included "Nineteen rail junctions . . . and many other installations." Enemy fighter opposition against this aerial juggernaut was weak, scoring few kills. In the six months preceding D-Day, a puny thirty-two German flights had made it to England. Luftwaffe strength was now significantly tied up over Germany; the skies over the Normandy beaches appeared safe. Solly Zuckerman's rail interdiction approach, which Eisenhower supported, was under way.

BY THURSDAY, JUNE 1, Eisenhower had moved his headquarters from Bushy Park to Southwick House, a white-colonnaded mansion near the Channel and currently the base for Admiral Sir Bertram Ramsay, the invasion's naval commander. For his personal quarters Ike passed up the stately home and had an aide drop his kit and a stack of western novels in a spartan trailer parked nearby. He was now wearing the "Eisenhower jacket" that had become his trademark, ending at the waist, more comfortable than a full-length coat, the style borrowed from one Montgomery had devised. Ike called his first briefing of senior staff, including Montgomery, who would command ground forces on D-Day; Admiral Ramsay; Air Chief Marshal Sir Trafford Leigh-Mallory; Air Chief Marshal Sir Arthur Tedder, the deputy commander for air; and General "Beetle" Smith, Eisenhower's chief of staff and informal enforcer. They settled into the senior officers mess, tables pushed out of the way, comfortable couches and armchairs arranged around Eisenhower. As they chatted with the easy confidence of men of importance, a tall, trim officer in RAF blue entered, a man whom Eisenhower described as a "dour but canny Scot." In this room, filled with gold braid, a mere group captain, James M. Stagg, the invasion meteorologist, was at this moment the pivotal figure. Stagg must answer the paramount question: did the weather for the morning of June 5 favor an invasion? As Stagg turned to his charts, an officer went to a window and pushed aside the blackout curtain, revealing a sky that looked blue and promising. Stagg, however, was thinking beyond the immediate. He was being asked to predict weather over the next four days, though no meteorologist "could agree on the likely weather even for the next 24 hours," he recalled of his dilemma. The group met again for Stagg's updated forecast at 9:30 P.M. on Friday, June 2, and the good weather appeared to be holding. Yet the frowning meteorologist, described by one participant as "six foot two of gloom," had reports in hand from weather stations monitoring the Atlantic warning that a depression stretching from Newfoundland to Scotland was moving southeast in the direction of the invasion beaches. Force 4 to 5 winds could be expected and a cloud cover of a scant 500 feet. He concluded that June 5 was "full of menace." For Eisenhower, time was running out. The troops were already aboard transports in ports along England's Channel coast. If the fleet could not sail on June 5, suitable weather might not arrive for two more weeks. Eisenhower called a middle-of-the-night session at 4:15 A.M. on Sunday, June 4. The chiefs gathered groggily in the mess room with the sky still black. Ike's large, powerful hands rested on the table before him, his words punctuated with jabs and gestures. The mobile face presented a map of his moods, registering anger, annoyance, puzzlement, and occasionally satisfaction. His speech was a soldier's, laced with profanity but not obscenity. Stagg arrived and continued to forecast rough weather. Eisenhower reluctantly postponed the June 5 invasion date. Elements of the flotilla had already departed and were ordered to return to port.

Ike wrote in his diary, "Probably no one who does not bear the specific and direct responsibility of making the final decision as to what to do can understand the intensity of these burdens." The delay added to his stress. For months the supreme commander had pushed himself mercilessly, working all hours, forcing himself up early seven days a week. The pace took its toll. He suffered bouts of colitis, intestinal blockage, bursitis, back pain, and respiratory infections, and he continued to smoke compulsively, now up to four packs a day. He had stolen whatever relaxation he could at his Telegraph Cottage headquarters outside London, dressed in baggy pants, a battered leather jacket, worn straw slippers dating from his days in the Philippines, playing bridge with Summersby as his frequent partner, and reading westerns, of which she observed, "I think they're frightful." He defended his taste saying, "I don't have to think." Only the most headcracking decisions reached his desk, the simpler issues settled by subordinates beforehand. Winston Churchill, at one point, had insisted that he be allowed to go ashore with the troops on D-Day. Eisenhower braced himself for the prime minister's mulishness and turned Churchill down. He had to deal with the proud Charles de Gaulle, who, unaware of the bit part to which he had been assigned, expected a substantial role in Overlord, since it was his country that was to be liberated.

Eisenhower and the chiefs met again in the mess room at Southwick House at 9:30 Sunday evening, June 4, awaiting Stagg's latest forecast. The room grew still as the phlegmatic Scot entered. The meteorologist's pessimism thus far seemed justified as rains lashed the mansion and shook the windowpanes. Trees outside swayed in howling winds. Yet Stagg predicted a sliver of light. A break in the weather could be expected for the morning of June 6. The rain soon would stop, to be followed by an interlude of thirty-six hours of relatively fair weather and moderate winds. A roomful of middle-aged men broke into cheers like jubilant schoolboys. Eisenhower asked, "just how long can you hang this operation on the end of a limb and let it hang there?"

Surveying the room, hearing no response, he said, "O.K., let's go." A man who had been an obscure Army colonel just two years before had made a decision that would shape the century. The meeting had lasted fifteen minutes.

That same Sunday, on the other side of the Channel, the chief German meteorologist, Major Heinz Lettau, advised his superiors that invasion for the next several days was implausible because of the storm sweeping in from the Atlantic. So rough were the waters that German naval patrols and minelayers temporarily suspended operations. Wehrmacht officers, given the breather, granted their men short leaves. Rommel seized the respite to leave France to deliver a birthday present, a pair of Parisian shoes, to his wife, Lucie-Maria, at their home in the fairy-tale village of Herrlingen.

ON THE PREVIOUS FRIDAY, June 2, FDR had rounded up his daughter, Anna, her husband, Major John Boettiger, the faithful Daisy Suckley, and secretary Grace Tully to accompany him to Pa Watson's Kenwood, a handsome estate near Monticello, Virginia, on land once owned by Thomas Jefferson. Watson, one of the few men FDR trusted to hold him upright on public occasions, had a soothing effect on a president on tenterhooks as D-Day approached. Pa had built a guest cottage especially for FDR, but Roosevelt preferred the conviviality of the Watsons' main house and was given the master bedroom. After breakfast on Saturday morning, the usual soft-boiled eggs, bacon, orange juice, toast, and coffee, FDR gathered his circle and sought suggestions for a statement suitable to make when Americans learned that Overlord had begun. Anna and John suggested a prayer. The president called in Grace Tully and dictated a first draft. She watched the president's hands shake as he searched his family's Book of Common Prayer for inspiration. By Sunday, Tully had typed a final version, which Roosevelt practiced aloud with appropriate pauses and gestures. FDR left the Watson home and returned to the White House on Monday morning, June 5. He played with his Scottie, Fala, and watched his grandson, Johnny Boettiger, perform somersaults on a well-worn sofa. Grace Tully, however, noted the president's ashen color and still trembling hands. "The Boss was keeping up a pretense of normal activity," she recalled of the day, "but every movement . . . reflected the tightly contained state of his nerves."

That night he had himself wheeled into the Diplomatic Reception Room to deliver a fireside chat to the American people. Ordinarily, the news he planned to announce, that Rome had fallen to the Allies, would have given him immense satisfaction. But compared to what weighed on his mind, Rome had become a sideshow. The city's conquest had taken four and a half months. General Mark Clark stood on Capitoline Hill, facing reporters, beaming over his triumph. He had initially set two objectives, first "that the 5th Army was going to capture Rome before the British." The victory, however, had to be shared with the British Eighth Army as the Stars and Stripes and Union Jack were raised simultaneously over the city's heart. Clark's second objective had been to take the Eternal City before his triumph could be overshadowed by Overlord. After delivering the fireside chat, FDR invited Eleanor, Anna, Major Boettiger, and Daisy Suckley to join him for a movie in a makeshift theater set up in the colonnade between the White House and the East Wing. This evening, instead of one of his favorites, a comedy or a musical, they watched recent newsreels in brittle silence. At five past eleven he retired to his bedroom, bringing Eleanor and Daisy with him. He sipped at a glass of orange juice and announced that he had a secret to share. Within hours Allied troops would land on the beaches of Normandy. Sensing the anxiety that his revelation caused, he began making lame jokes about what he would do to Hitler once he was caught. He mused aloud, "I wonder how [Russell] Linaka will come out," referring to a former Hyde Park employee who had worked on FDR's tree farm and was now aboard a D-Day landing craft.

FROM MID-CHANNEL, Omar Bradley, Ike's choice to lead the First Army on D-Day, gazed out from the USS *Augusta* at skies so black that at times the ship's foremast disappeared. The deck glistened from a steady drizzle. A canvas curtain sheltering a makeshift war room on the bridge flapped wildly in the wind. Bradley turned to an aide, saying, "Ike has the forecasters and he undoubtedly knows what he's doing, but by golly, the weather certainly looks lousy here." The night had yet to lift as tens of thousands of men began scrambling down rope ladders draped over the sides of the transports into the Higgins boats bobbing below. The journey to the beaches would cover eleven miles and last two hours, with the landing craft heaving and dipping in five-foot swells, their flat bottoms soon awash in vomit, which seasick soldiers struggled to bail out with their helmets. As dawn began to reveal the faint outlines of the Normandy shore, 16-inch guns from six battleships and cruisers unleashed a bombardment so deafening that it became one continuous roar obliterating every other sound. A new amphibian invention, tanks that could supposedly float, spilled from LSTs, most starting to sink immediately, as crewmen clambered through the turrets in the twenty seconds before the tank went under. In this ill-conceived enterprise, twenty-seven out of thirty-three amphibious vehicles sank. Five thousand yards from the shore, the landing craft came within the range of German batteries.

At 6:40 A.M. the order sounded along the ragged lines of Higgins boats closing on the beach, "Down ramps!" A lieutenant led the way from each boat, followed by six riflemen fanning out, and the rest of the men behind them. The moment was one that Shakespeare caught in *Henry V*, at Agincourt—"He that outlives this day and comes safe home, will stand a-tip-toe when this day is named"—though few of the frightened, soaking men stepping into the cold surf were likely thinking this sentiment. Machine-gun rounds hammered against the landing craft and made a thudding sound as they struck human flesh. German shells exploded, tearing men to pieces. The waters of Omaha Beach began to darken with a red froth.

Eisenhower had prepared two radio addresses beforehand, one in the event of a successful landing, which proclaimed, "The eyes of the world are upon you. The hopes and prayers of liberty loving people everywhere march with you." The other message said, "Our landings in the Cherbourg-Havre have failed to gain a satisfactory foothold and I have withdrawn the troops. . . . If any blame or fault attaches to the attempt it is mine alone." The success message had been drafted by Ike's staff. The failure message he had written in his own hand and tucked into his wallet. As General Bradley scanned early reports from Omaha Beach, Eisenhower's second message appeared the more relevant. "I reluctantly contemplated the diversion of Omaha follow-up forces to Utah and the British beaches," he later admitted. Through heroic exertions, in one case 200 men scaled the perpendicular cliffs at Pointe-du-Hoc on ropes and ladders as German defenders fired straight down on them, the Omaha toehold held. By nightfall, 132,450 American men and their allies were in Normandy.

THE PRESIDENT HAD BEEN STIRRED from a fitful sleep at 3 A.M. by a call from Marshall. The troops, he reported, had landed. FDR called to his valet, Prettyman, to bring him his faded cardigan and to prop him up in bed. He badgered Louise Hackmeister, the chief White House telephone operator, to tell officials at the Pentagon to update him constantly on the invasion's progress. As radio broadcasts confirmed the landings, cities across the country sounded with church bells and factory whistles. Americans began pouring into churches and synagogues. The president went on the radio that night to deliver the prayer he had written at Pa Watson's home. "Almighty God: our sons, pride of our Nation, this day have set upon a mighty endeavor, a struggle to preserve our Republic, our religion and our civilization, and to set free a suffering humanity," it began. "Some will never return," he continued. "Embrace these, Father, and receive them, thy heroic servants, into thy kingdom."

Joseph Stalin's assessment of Overlord elated FDR. Noting that both Napoleon and Hitler had failed to cross the Channel, the Soviet leader said, "the history of warfare knows no other like undertaking from the point of view of its scale, its vast conception and its masterly execution." And as promised, on June 22, sixteen days after D-Day, the Russians launched Operation Bagration, a 2.3 million man offensive in the east.

Bodyguard and Fortitude proved unqualified successes. The Germans completely misread the time and place of the invasion. Three days after D-Day, Field Marshal Gerd von Rundstedt begged Hitler to send the First SS Panzer Division to Normandy. But Hitler, swallowing the deception whole, instead sent the division to join the 15th German Army to repel the still anticipated assault across the Pas-de-Calais. The puzzled chief of German intelligence in the west, Alexis Baron von Roenne, reported of FUSAG, Patton's paper divisions, "not a single unit of the 1st United States Army Group which comprises around 25 large formations . . . has so far been committed." Not until almost two months after D-Day, on August 3, did Hitler accept that he had been duped and sent the idle 15th Army to the front. By then, well over a million Allied troops were in France, including George Patton, now leading an authentic force, the Third Army. However brilliant Bodyguard and Fortitude had proven, Mother Nature had provided Overlord's greatest deception, the brief patch of relative calm on June 6 that the Germans had overlooked while believing that no one would attempt to invade over a tempest-tossed Channel.

Casualties proved well below expectations, particularly Churchill's dread vision of a Channel choked with corpses. A meticulous recent analysis by the U.S. National D-Day Memorial Foundation places American losses at 2,499 dead, most on Omaha Beach, with another 1,915 Allied losses, for a total of 4,414 killed in action. Statistics, however, miss the cold fact that for each of the dead the casualty rate was 100 percent.

STALIN'S FULFILLED PROMISE TO SUPPORT D-Day with a parallel Soviet offensive was an exception to the narrow Soviet idea of partnership. FDR, however, was willing to meet the Soviet dictator more than halfway. As early as the summer of 1942, he had told Marshall, "I wish you would explore the merits and possibilities of our putting an American force on the Caucasian front to fight with the Russian armies." He told Hap Arnold, "I understand that we are giving something like 150 P-39s to the British each month. Would it not be possible to postpone the

British allotment and give the Russians those 150 planes each month for a few months?"

The president understandably expected reciprocity from the Russians in pursuit of what he regarded as a common cause. Reaction to American requests to use Russian airfields illustrated how wide the gap was between U.S. accommodation and the Soviet concept of cooperation. The first instance had occurred in the summer of 1943 as the U.S. Air Forces planned the raid against the Ploesti oil installations in Romania. FDR had dispatched Marshall to see Maxim Litvinov, the old Bolshevik ambassador to the United States, asking permission for U.S. bombers to land in southern Russia after the long, perilous Ploesti mission. The Kremlin dithered for so long before responding that its assent was useless by the time it arrived. On the next occasion, at Tehran in the fall of 1943, FDR at his son Elliott's urging asked Stalin to allow U.S. planes to land on the Russian fields after bombing Germany. Stalin put him off, saying that the issue required further study. By 1944, when bomber runs over Germany had become as regular as mail deliveries, American air officials again approached the Russians asking permission to set up a shuttle bombing arrangement. Shuttle raids, they averred, would not only double bombing results, but would conserve fuel and save the lives of crewmen aboard planes too badly shot up to make it back to their bases in England and Italy. Roosevelt instructed his ambassador to the Soviet Union, Averell Harriman, to sound out Stalin about the idea. On February 2, 1944, Harriman managed an appointment with the Soviet leader during which he explained that "Daylight bombing can penetrate more deeply into Germany if American bombers from the United Kingdom . . . are permitted to land regularly in the Soviet Union." On this occasion, as before, Harriman was amazed by Stalin's "grasp of detail." He cross-examined the ambassador "about the octane rating of the fuel needed for the American bombers, about air-to-ground communications and the language barrier to be overcome, if American pilots and Russian air controllers were to work together." Harriman happily reported back to Roosevelt that Stalin had "agreed to provide facilities for shuttle bombing on Soviet airfields for 150 to 200 U.S. bombers as a starter." Harriman also queried Stalin about using Soviet airbases in the Far East "after Russia enters the war against Japan." This concession was beyond what Stalin was willing to do. "He could not afford to provoke an incident now," Harriman reported back to FDR.

With Stalin's approval won for the shuttle plan, American and Soviet officials began to work out the logistics. The Russians proved hard bargainers. The U.S. Air Forces asked to send 2,100 American ground personnel to work at the airfields around Poltava in Ukraine. The Russians approved half. They further expected to exercise veto power over German targets the Americans selected for their return flights. U.S. fliers wanted to take reconnaissance photos of the raids; the Russians rejected having foreigners with high-power cameras traipsing around the Soviet Union. Additionally, the Russians expected to be given the Norden bombsight for their planes, the device so zealously guarded by the United States. General John Deane, heading the U.S. military mission in Moscow, reported that the Soviet "General Staff, the NKVD, the foreign office and party leaders did their utmost to sabotage the venture to which they had reluctantly approved." The shuttle enterprise received a code name, either coincidental or ironic, of Operation Frantic.

On June 2, 1944, Ambassador Harriman, and his daughter Kathleen, stood under clear skies at Poltava, eagerly scanning the horizon. Finally, seventy-three specks appeared, the first planes returning from a mission led by the Allied air chief for the entire Mediterranean, General Ira Eaker. The planes had flown from airfields near Naples, bombed German targets at Debrecen, Hungary, then headed east, becoming the first American bombers allowed to land on Soviet soil. As Kathleen Harriman remembered the moment, the Soviet officer in charge of the joint operation, Major General A. R. Perminov, "bubbled over with joy and threw his arms around Ave to kiss him," a gesture that startled the undemonstrative Harriman. That evening the fliers were honored with a concert followed by a banquet where the vodka and champagne flowed without stint. Kathleen, carried away by the camaraderie, wrote home, "Dammit, we all can do a job of work together." But the euphoria did not last. "For a while, the Russians were glad to have us," Hap Arnold remembered. "They permitted their people to come around and talk with our soldiers and officers, see what we were doing, and how we were doing it. . . . But when our radios and magazines—*Life, Time, The Saturday Evening Post, Collier's, Look, PM* and such periodicals—started coming into our various squad rooms, dayrooms and clubs, and their people had an opportunity to see the kind of life we lived in the United States, apparently the Russian leaders didn't like it. Orders were given that there would be no more fraternization between the Russians and the Americans at the shuttle bombing bases."

As Allied bombers flattened one German city after another, Hitler confided to Ambassador Oshima that his scientists were mastering super-weapons that would yet turn the tide to German victory. The first was the V-1, "Vengeance Weapon Number 1," a small, pilotless aircraft with a stubby fuselage and short wings guided by a gyropilot. The V-1, on impact, could deliver a 1,870-pound warhead. Hitler predicted that "London would be leveled to the ground and Britain forced to capitulate after V-1s began smashing the city." Simultaneously German scientists were developing the even deadlier V-2, a liquid-fueled rocket capable of reaching supersonic speeds that rendered it undetectable and invulnerable before it plunged to earth, exploding its 2,000-pound warhead. Fortuitously, the British had been alerted as early as March 22, 1943, of German rocketry progress when two Afrika Korps generals captured in North Africa were overheard in their bugged cells boasting of the wonder weapons to come. The secret work was being conducted principally at Peenemünde, a thumb of land jutting into the Baltic Sea. On the night of August 17–18, 1943, 600 RAF bombers struck Peenemünde, killing 120 scientists and 600 conscripted foreign workers. The attack set the program back for months but did not kill it.

On October 14, 1943, George Earle, a wealthy former governor of Pennsylvania and political crony of FDR's, a part-time spy and full-time playboy, reported from Istanbul that Turkish sources had informed him that a "Devastating robot land torpedo plane attack on England will surely take place this month from Northern France and

Belgium." Earle followed with another cable warning that, after the predicted rocket blitz against England, "stratospheric attacks on America will follow." Lending credence to Earle's prediction was a broken Oshima dispatch informing Tokyo that Luftwaffe engineers were developing the Me 264, a bomber capable of reaching New York. Eleven days after Earle's first warning a Map Room duty officer brought FDR a cable from Winston Churchill reporting that "during the last six months, evidence has continued to accumulate from many sources that the Germans are preparing an attack on England, particularly London, by means of very long-range rockets which may conceivably weigh sixty tons and carry an explosive charge of ten to twenty tons."

The first unmanned V-1s struck England just a week after D-Day, jarring Britons grown complacent that the horrors of the Blitz lay behind them. *The New York Times* of June 17 described what looked like a "new toy" that flew "at about one thousand feet and gives a tell tale glow from its tail. Its engines, which have an ominous, sputtering throb, die out a few seconds before the whole mass plunges to earth and explodes with a terrific lateral blast." In all, over 8,000 V-1s were fired, of which 2,450 struck their targets, killing 6,000 British civilians. An outraged Churchill proposed retaliating with poison gas. But his air chief, Marshal Arthur Tedder, opposed the move. Eisenhower too, fearing a horrendous cycle of measure and countermeasure, concluded, "I am opposed to retaliation as a method of stopping this business—at least until every other thing has been tried and failed." Roosevelt sided with Ike against Churchill. The V-1s were slow and noisy enough to spot so that fighters and antiaircraft guns could dispatch them with relative ease. But the ballistic V-2s fired from hidden launch sites were too fast to be seen or repelled before reaching London and other target cities. When they crashed noiselessly to earth, death came randomly and without warning.

The American Air Forces in England did come up with Operation Aphrodite, a countermeasure to be directed at rocket-launching sites. Aging bombers, called "Weary Willies," were crammed with 10,000 pounds of explosives. A two-man crew would take off and bail out just as another bomber took over via remote control and guided the Weary

Willie to its target, in effect, an early guided missile. A handsome twenty-nine-year-old American Navy flier, Lieutenant Joseph P. Kennedy Jr., with his tour of duty already completed, volunteered for an Aphrodite mission, some friends believed to surpass the heroism and press attention won by his younger brother Jack, who had rescued the crew of his PT boat in the South Pacific. On August 12, 1944, Joe Jr. and Wilford J. Willy, a Texas father of three, took off in a PBY-1 Liberator from Fersfield aerodrome in southern England, the target a V-1 launch site on the French coast. Before the two men could bail out, the plane blew up, taking the life of the son of the former U.S. ambassador to Great Britain and brother of the future president. The cause of the failure was never determined and the bodies never recovered. Joe Kennedy, devastated by the loss of the son he was grooming for the presidency, later referred to FDR as "that crippled son of a bitch that killed my son Joe."

Late in 1944, George Earle warned that along with the V-1s and V-2s, the Germans were about to launch the V-3, a missile capable of striking the U.S. East Coast. FDR confided to Daisy Suckley that according to a reliable source, the Germans had a weapon capable of killing by concussion everyone within a mile. He was worried, he said, over the laxity of U.S. coastal defenses. Daisy afterward recorded in her diary, "he feared that in the next war the side which first uses these new explosives will undoubtedly win." FDR advised Admiral Leahy that Earle may have been retailing a rumor, but the leader who had been blindsided at Pearl Harbor was not about to risk another debacle. He instructed Leahy that "every precaution should be taken." On December 7, three years after the Hawaii attack, Leahy ordered coastal, land, and sea commanders to place the entire East Coast on alert in preparation for a possible attack in the next thirty days. The new commander in chief of the Atlantic Fleet, Admiral Jonas H. Ingram, predicted that such an assault was not only "possible but probable." Meeting with reporters in the wardroom of his flagship, Ingram advised, "The thing to do is not to get excited about it . . . think what it would mean to Dr. Goebbels at this stage of the war to announce that 'today we have destroyed New York.'"

✳

"BILL DONOVAN IS ALSO AN OLD FRIEND OF MINE," FDR liked to say of William J. "Wild Bill" Donovan. "We were in law school together." Though there were only twenty-one members in the Columbia Law School class of 1907, Donovan, a Republican political foe, never acknowledged Roosevelt's claim of intimacy. He had been born in Buffalo, New York, the son of devout Irish Catholics, became a star quarterback at Columbia, and later an authentic World War I hero. Donovan joined the 69th Regiment, the fabled Fighting 69th, as a battalion commander, and on October 14, 1918, during the Meuse-Argonne Offensive, waving his pistol overhead, led his men into withering machine-gun fire where they fell thickly around him. Pressing on, Donovan was finally hit himself. Though bleeding profusely, he refused to leave the field, directing his troops while lying on the ground before being carted off on a blanket five hours later. His bravery that day won him the Medal of Honor. Several origins exist for the nickname "Wild Bill," including a story that after witnessing his fearlessness, one of his men exclaimed, "Wild Bill is a son of a bitch, but he's a game one." After the war Donovan became a hugely successful Wall Street lawyer and in 1932 ran unsuccessfully as the Republican candidate for governor of New York on an anti–New Deal platform. Donovan was fifty-seven when he came into FDR's view, sponsored by the navy secretary, Republican Frank Knox. Knox and Henry Stimson had been recruited by Roosevelt to give a bipartisan character to his wartime cabinet, which had led to Stimson's being drummed out of the Republican Party. Knox now urged FDR to bring Donovan into his administration, another GOP member and a war hero to boot. FDR in effect made a test run. He sent Donovan to Europe in 1940 to gauge Britain's chances of survival as she stood alone against Hitler and threatened with imminent invasion. Upon his arrival, Donovan, carrying FDR's imprimatur, was courted ardently, given credit by Englishmen for engineering the destroyer deal, and on his fifty-eighth birthday treated to a feast in food-short Britain of lobster, pheasant, turtle soup, and three bottles of Moselle wine. Churchill invited Donovan to a lunch at 10 Downing Street during which he mentioned that at this very moment RAF bombers were striking the German city of Mannheim. The message was not lost on Donovan. The British could not only take it, they could dish it out. Back at the White House, he reported Britain's pugnacity, and FDR liked what he heard.

While in England, Donovan had met with Admiral John H. Godfrey, director of British naval intelligence, and other members of the secret service from whom he caught the espionage bug. For their part, the British saw in Donovan a plucky Yank who might prove a useful ally in drawing the United States into the war. Godfrey began angling to promote Donovan as chief of American intelligence, traveling to the United States with another intelligence officer, Ian Fleming, later creator of James Bond, to lobby for Donovan. Roosevelt invited Godfrey to the White House for dinner and promised him an hour alone afterward. In June 1941, coached by Godfrey and Fleming, Donovan made his move. He presented the president with a proposal that began, "Strategy, without information upon which it can rely, is helpless. Likewise, information is useless unless it is intelligently directed to the strategic purpose." The solution, he went on, was to establish a "Service of Strategic Information." Donovan had a subsequent session with FDR during which the president, to Donovan's bafflement, rambled on irrelevantly for a full hour, but said little about having him enter the administration. Political differences apart, their temperaments were remarkably alike. Bill Donovan was charismatic, irrepressible, optimistic, stout-hearted, and possessed of an imagination that popped with ideas, much like FDR. On July 11, 1941, the president appointed Donovan to the unrevealing position of "Coordinator of Information," the news receiving a third of a column on page five of *The New York Times*. This inconspicuous beginning marked the birth of America's first intelligence service, the progenitor of the Central Intelligence Agency. Army intelligence officers greeted Donovan's appointment like wolves spotting a lamb and balked at commissioning the old war hero a major general, as Roosevelt wanted. Wild Bill was initially allowed only to use the honorific "Colonel," his World War I rank.

Donovan demonstrated immediate skill as an empire builder, a man who, as one observer put it, could "see an acorn and envision an oak." Dumpy-looking, an indifferent dresser, unprepossessing until he spoke, he nevertheless radiated a quiet magnetism. As James Angleton, an early Donovan recruit, described his chief, "He would grasp a man's hand, fix you with those blue eyes, and say, softly, 'I'm counting on you.' And people believed him." Within a year Donovan managed to have his agency rechristened from the bland COI to the mysterious Office of Strategic Services, the OSS. He built the organization from zero to an eventual 17,000 members in short order, recruiting college presidents, professors, linguists, film directors, chemists, physicians, journalists, actors, linguists, counterfeiters, anyone with a skill that could produce intelligence, ranging from academics digesting scientific monographs to shadowy figures who knew how to blow a safe. The roster included Arthur Goldberg, a future Supreme Court justice; Arthur Schlesinger Jr., a future Pulitzer Prize–winning historian; Archibald MacLeish, distinguished poet; John Ford, Oscar-winning movie director; Sterling Hayden, film star; Gene Fodor, travel writer; Julia Child, future television chef; and three future directors of Central Intelligence, Richard Helms, William Colby, and William J. Casey. Ford once described his chief as "the sort of guy who thought nothing of parachuting into France, blowing up a bridge, pissing in *Luftwaffe* gas tanks, then dancing on the roof of the St. Regis Hotel with a German spy." Eventually, Donovan was promoted to general, and by the time of D-Day he had compiled a spotty performance record, reflecting the man's wild fancies. OSS schemes ranged from the crackpot—attempting to slip female hormones into Hitler's vegetarian diet, causing his mustache to fall out, his breasts to swell, and his voice to rise—to infiltrating 523 agents into France prior to D-Day to collect intelligence, arm the resistance, and carry out sabotage. By the fall of 1944, the OSS was running agents with forged identities into Germany proper, a feat that British intelligence had dismissed as improbable.

Donovan had cultivated a relationship with Grace Tully, enabling him to get his intelligence to the president's desk. On July 12, 1944, Allen Dulles, Donovan's man in Bern in neutral Switzerland, cabled a cryptic but intriguing speculation. "There is a possibility," Dulles reported, "that a dramatic event may take place up north if Breakers courier can be trusted." Breakers was the code name given a half-blind, hulking six-foot-four agent of the Abwehr, posted to Zurich, Hans Bernd Gisevius, a secret anti-Nazi working with the OSS. This message was followed by a darker hint of cracks within the Third Reich. "Those opposed to the Nazis realize . . . that the next few weeks may be their last chance to show that they are willing to take some risks in making the first move to clean up their own house." Donovan put the issue squarely before the president, saying, "We must judge whether the encouragement of any effort towards a revolution in Germany will, at this juncture, help to save thousands of lives of Allied soldiers." Yet, another intelligence estimate informed the president, "A revolution is not to be expected; the people are too apathetic and too closely supervised by the police. . . . The opposition are not in any position to take such a step." The nation's fledgling spy chief was thus sending mixed signals on the most explosive event in Germany since the Nazis had come to power. On July 20, 1944, Colonel Claus Schenk von Stauffenberg, missing an eye, his right hand, and two fingers on his left hand, had attempted to assassinate Hitler in his Wolfsschanze headquarters in East Prussia. While initial reporting was sketchy and speculative, FDR had a direct pipeline into the plot provided by the unwitting Ambassador Hiroshi Oshima. Immediately after the assassination attempt, Oshima had a conversation with the German foreign minister, Joachim von Ribbentrop, which he relayed to Tokyo and that Magic soon made available to the White House. "Colonel Stauffenberg entered a meeting which was in progress in order to make a report to Chancellor Hitler," Oshima cabled. "After he [Stauffenberg] had placed a bag in which the bomb had been put upon the floor about two meters from where Chancellor Hitler was, he said that he had other business and left the room. . . . The bomb exploded with tremendous force after the lapse of about five minutes. . . . What was really mysterious was the fact that the Chancellor, who was nearest to the bomb when it exploded was unhurt with the exception that his clothes were torn to pieces by the blast and he sustained a few burns." Before the day was out, Stauffenberg and fellow conspirators were shot, inaugurating a Gestapo bloodbath in which an estimated 4,000 suspects, however remotely connected to the plot, were executed or driven to suicide.

Roosevelt let a week pass before, under constant press questioning, he said anything publicly about the attempted assassination. "I don't think I know anything more about it than you do," he said with a straight face. But he made one thing clear. Had the conspirators succeeded and expected to negotiate, Roosevelt's terms remained fixed: unconditional surrender. "Practically every German denies the fact that they surrendered in the last war," he told the reporters. "But this time they are going to know it."

AFTER THE FALL OF ROME, FDR had signaled his doubt about the necessity of advancing further in Italy. "From a strictly military standpoint," he said, "we had long ago accomplished certain of the main objectives of our Italian campaign. . . . Control of the major islands— control of the sea lanes of the Mediterranean to shorten our combat and supply lines, and the capture of the airports of Foggia, south of Rome." Marshall was of a like mind. While the Anzio beachhead was still under threat, he had told Eisenhower, "I see no great purpose to be achieved in Italy aside from maintaining pressure on the enemy to prevent the transfer of his forces to your front." Churchill, however, remained unsated and wanted to keep pressing up the peninsula. Knowing Roosevelt's determination to keep Stalin happy, he maintained that Italy was tying down at least twenty Nazi divisions that might otherwise be fighting in Russia. According to Churchill's arithmetic, Germany also kept divisions in the Balkans to block an Allied strike launched from Italy. Thus the Italian Front was tying up a total of forty enemy divisions. "I called it the Third Front," he said. In his book *Great Mistakes of the War*, the astute military analyst Hanson Baldwin asked "who diverted whom?" since, by August 1944, tens of thousands of Americans were pinned down in the Mediterranean theater, many of whom could have joined in the Normandy campaign in the drive toward Germany's heart. Italy, on the other hand, never absorbed more than a tenth of the Wehrmacht's strength.

If Italy was a blunder, it was proving a bloody misstep. On the morning of D-Day, FDR queried Marshall about the latest casualties in Italy. Marshall's figures revealed that in just the three weeks before Rome fell, 2,129 men of Clark's Fifth Army had been killed, including Allen Brown, along with 2,500 Britons and commonwealth troops. The price for Anzio was 2,800 American dead along with 11,000 wounded. The British lost 1,600 killed and 7,000 wounded for a total Allied loss of 22,400 men. Anzio proved practically a casualty tie, with 27,500 Germans killed, wounded, captured, or missing. Which raises the question as to why Hitler held on so doggedly to what Mark Clark referred to as the "forgotten front." According to the military historian John Keegan, "Hitler valued Italy because its loss would be a blow to his prestige," and, partially vindicating Churchill's position, "because it offered flank protection to the Balkans." Still, as Hanson Baldwin summed up the Italian campaign, "All roads led to Rome, but Rome led nowhere."

FDR, so caustic toward Charles de Gaulle, decided at long last to stroke the Frenchman's considerable ego. An elated de Gaulle, whose Free French Forces now numbered upward of 400,000 resistance and uniformed fighters, was invited to the White House where he arrived on July 6, one month after D-Day. His visit fulfilled the prejudices of at least one of his detractors, Bill Hassett, FDR's correspondence secretary. Hassett wrote that the man "stepped from the automobile with an air of arrogance bordering on downright insolence, his Cyrano de Bergerac nose high in the air." Roosevelt, however, was charm itself toward de Gaulle. Wooing a visitor, even one whom he disdained, came as natural to FDR as breathing. He also had a motive. He wanted to use the occasion to have de Gaulle coordinate actions of the French resistance with the movement of Allied troops across France. The president arranged the grand tour for the French leader. "I did not fail to salute the Tomb of the Unknown Soldier," de Gaulle wrote in his memoirs. He visited Arlington Cemetery and called upon General Pershing. He paid "homage to the memory of George Washington, I made a pilgrimage to Mount Vernon." The following evening, FDR hosted a state dinner for de Gaulle befitting a man likely to become head of state. What the French leader could not know was that FDR had rushed through the dinner to await an 8:45 P.M. visit to his study from Lucy Mercer Rutherfurd. The president managed one final meeting with de Gaulle the following Saturday afternoon and then had himself driven to 2238 Q Street where Lucy was staying with her sister, Violetta, and brought her back to the White House for a dinner arranged, at his request, by his daughter, Anna. Her connivance plagued Anna with guilt since she knew that her unsuspecting mother was away celebrating the desegregation of buses on military bases. However, she was increasingly aware of the steady decline in her father's health and could not deny him the company of the woman he loved and who so visibly lifted his spirits.

CHAPTER 18

MacArthur Versus King: FDR's Decision

AFTER THE DE GAULLE VISIT, THE PRESIDENT DIRECTED GENERAL Marshall to have Douglas MacArthur, then at his headquarters in Brisbane, to "Arrange your plans so as to arrive in Honolulu July 26." Though Marshall did not explain why or with whom he was to meet, MacArthur "felt reasonably certain it was President Roosevelt." The tug-of-war between Admirals King and Nimitz on one side and MacArthur on the other over the best ways to fight the Pacific war had dragged on inconclusively. Three months before MacArthur had received his summons, the Joint Chiefs of Staff considered redrawing the lines of command in the Pacific so that the Navy would take over MacArthur's authority for the Admiralty Islands just north of New Guinea. MacArthur, upon learning of the proposed shearing of his fiefdom, sent an objection that startled FDR. He intimated that if Roosevelt ruled in favor of the Navy, he just might resign his command. The JCS backed off and the controversy over Pacific strategy went on.

This was to be a politically charged year for FDR since it was conceded that he would run for a fourth term in 1944. Those who sought to penetrate the impenetrable FDR mind pondered whether he was calling the meeting in Honolulu for strategic or political reasons, or both. The president's presence at Pearl Harbor, reported by the press, filmed and photographed as he conferred with the nation's storybook general and the naval paragon, Chester Nimitz, would project a powerful image of FDR as commander in chief as the election neared. To Roosevelt, the title meant more than a constitutional honorific. He had once dispatched Bill Leahy to advise Ernest King to stop using the title, though King was in fact the Navy's commander in chief. He was to stick to commander of the U.S. Fleet, leaving Roosevelt sole use of the term designating the nation's highest military figure. Beyond political advantage to be gained at Honolulu, Roosevelt had to resolve the Pacific strategy debate. MacArthur favored a drive northward from New Guinea, leading to reconquest of the Philippines. King and Nimitz wanted to move westward across the Central Pacific, taking certain islands while leaving others to rot, until Japan was within reach. At its rosiest, the King-Nimitz position posited that Japan could be strangled economically and forced to submit without an invasion.

Upon receiving Marshall's order, MacArthur boarded his customized B-17 and headed for the Hawaiian Islands. The plane was christened the *Bataan*, suggesting that every time he boarded it he was making a symbolic return to the Philippines. He was ill-tempered during the trip, pacing up and down the aisle complaining about "The humiliation of forcing me to leave my command to fly to Honolulu for a political picture-taking junket!" His complaint contained a trace of hypocrisy. Just one week before, he had asked permission to come to Washington "to present fully my views" on the conduct of the Pacific campaign. Now Roosevelt was coming halfway around the world to meet him. While MacArthur's pique might be seen as another expression of the "great man" complex, his suspicions about FDR's political motivation did not lack credibility. For the first time, the president was going into a war zone leaving behind his key military advisors, Marshall, King, and Arnold. He brought with him only Admiral Leahy; Pa Watson; his confidant, Judge Sam Rosenman; his naval aide, Admiral Brown; his physician, Admiral McIntire; and a new figure in the Roosevelt retinue, Commander Howard Bruenn, chief cardiologist at the Bethesda Naval Hospital. Bruenn had exhaustingly examined FDR, discovering that the president suffered from hardening of the arteries, a failing left ventricle, and stratospheric blood pressure with readings as high as 218 over 120. McIntire had quietly brought Bruenn into the White House with Franklin Roosevelt as his sole patient.

On the night of July 13, FDR boarded the *Ferdinand Magellan*, making a quick visit the next day to Hyde Park to see how the Roosevelt Library was progressing. Moving on to Chicago, he left the train briefly to huddle with party stalwarts in the city where Democrats were holding their national nominating convention. He proceeded on to San Diego, arriving on July 20, where he received the less than astonishing news that he had been nominated unanimously.

The crewmen of the heavy cruiser *Baltimore* watched with curiosity as a ramp was constructed from the pier to the ship's main deck. On July 21, a feisty Scottie came aboard, which ignited a wildfire of rumor. The feverish activity was soon explained when the men saw their president wheeled up the ramp. He arrived without fanfare, since he had dispensed with the customary honors upon boarding a man-of-war. So avid were the sailors for a lock of Fala's fur that Sam Rosenman had to step in before "the poor dog was in danger of being completely shorn." Still heeding nautical superstition that it was unlucky to start a voyage on a Friday, FDR asked the ship's captain to delay their departure until one minute after midnight. The *Baltimore* set a course for Pearl Harbor shielded by six destroyers and near total air cover. The cruiser, to FDR's delight, sailed under combat conditions, darkened ship from sunset to sunrise, with frequent lifeboat drills and following a zigzag course that delivered the presidential party to its destination on the afternoon of Wednesday, July 26. "We assumed . . . that our expected arrival had been kept secret," Rosenman later wrote. Instead, sailors in dress whites manned the rails of every vessel in the harbor. A crowd of civilians that Rosenman estimated at "two acres" cheered the president. A trim, chiseled-featured, silver-haired Chester Nimitz bounded up the gangway and gave the president a crisp salute. The president greeted Nimitz warmly, then looked about and asked, "Where's Douglas?"

MacArthur had arrived an hour before where Nimitz had waited to greet him on the tarmac as the *Bataan* touched down at Hickam Field. Having flown through four time zones over the past thirty-six hours, the general descended the stairway, unshaven, unwashed, rumpled, sleepless, an unkempt MacArthur that the world was rarely permitted to see. After shaking the hand of the man who was, in effect, his rival,

MacArthur had himself driven to Fort Shafter to a mansion with a breathtaking view of the harbor, and manned by eager servants, the residence of Lieutenant General Robert C. Richardson Jr., an old comrade from the Philippines. MacArthur announced that before going anywhere he intended to take a leisurely bath.

In the meantime, a restless FDR waited, making small talk with officers aboard the cruiser. Finally, he announced that he was going ashore. Just as he spoke, according to Rosenman, "a terrific automobile siren was heard, and there raced onto the dock and screeched to a stop a motorcycle escort and the longest open car I have ever seen." The flaming red vehicle belonged to the Honolulu fire chief. Alone in the backseat sat an immaculate Douglas MacArthur, puffing a corncob pipe, wearing a leather flying jacket, Ray-Bans, and his trademark battered cap with the gold-encrusted visor, "scrambled eggs" to the irreverent. As he stepped from the car the crowd cheered wildly. MacArthur strode halfway up the ship's gangway, turned, and waved, igniting another round of applause. He stepped onto the deck facing the man in the wheelchair whom he had not seen for nine years. "When I last saw you, I was your chief of staff," MacArthur said, shaking the president's hand. After waiting for an hour for MacArthur to appear, the president responded with only the faintest trace of vexation, "Hello, Douglas, what are you doing with that leather jacket on? It's darned hot today." MacArthur answered, "Well, Mr. President, I've just landed from Australia," and pointing skyward he added, "It's cold up there." Roosevelt insisted on having photos taken and told MacArthur that he planned to tour military installations the next day and wanted the general and Nimitz along with him. MacArthur returned to Fort Shafter while the president was taken to a sumptuous cream-colored, three-story residence on Waikiki Beach, 2709 Kalakaua Avenue, its gardens a riot of flowering trees, shrubs, and gently lilting royal palms. The home, once belonging to Christopher Holmes, a hard-drinking millionaire and a recent suicide, was now a rest center for fatigued naval aviators.

The next morning, Roosevelt, MacArthur, Nimitz, and Admiral Leahy boarded the fire chief's convertible for the tour. Roosevelt put himself in the backseat, Nimitz on one side and MacArthur on the other, the latter more convinced than ever that he had become a prop in a political spectacle. As the car moved through jammed streets, cheering throngs lined the route, many according to Admiral Leahy "patently of Japanese extraction . . . their demonstrations were equal to those of the Hawaiians and continental Americans." During a six-hour odyssey, Roosevelt and MacArthur monopolized the conversation. To MacArthur's puzzlement, FDR talked "of everything but the war—of our old carefree days when life was simpler and gentler, of many things that had disappeared in the mist of time." A surprised Nimitz noticed that MacArthur addressed the president as "Franklin." The tour ended with Roosevelt tired but pleased. To MacArthur, FDR had changed shockingly in the years since he last saw him. Gone was the sturdy, muscled torso, the full, handsome face. The man he saw now was gaunt, jowls slack, face gray, hands trembling. Later, upon his return to Australia, MacArthur would tell his wife, "He is just the shell of the man I knew." To one of his officers he remarked, "the mark of death is on him. In six months he'll be in his grave."

That evening in Honolulu, Roosevelt gathered MacArthur, Nimitz, and Leahy in a secluded room at the Holmes villa. A map of the Pacific covered one wall practically from floor to ceiling. The president, from his wheelchair, jabbed at the map with a long bamboo pointer and, turning to MacArthur, said, "Well, Douglas, where do we go from here?" FDR then pointed to Nimitz, who was to speak first. Spread before the admiral were studies in thick ring binders, maps, and graphs all prepared by his staff. The table before MacArthur was bare. Nimitz began speaking in a deliberate, dispassionate tone. Though he endorsed the case he was about to present, he spoke as Ernie King's proxy, reflecting the views of his uninvited superior who had briefed him earlier on exactly what to say. King believed, without question, that the Navy could sweep across the Pacific, take Formosa (Taiwan today), lying only 700 miles from Japan, then seize Iwo Jima and Okinawa, the latter only 375 miles from the Japanese homeland. Nimitz maintained that the Navy could do so because his ships had grown into a mobile military front capable of putting 1,000 aircraft and twelve divisions ashore. He could interdict sea lanes, thus frustrating Japanese attempts to shift their troops. His approach would create a blockade depriving Japan of the vital oil, rubber, and tin that it had been sucking out of its conquered territories. In short, the enemy could be forced to its knees without a bloody invasion. The MacArthur approach, on the other hand, invading the Philippines, if worth doing at all, could only serve a narrow tactical purpose, providing airfields on Luzon from which to bomb Formosa. Nimitz spoke for two hours, presenting a solidly documented, well-argued thesis.

Now it was MacArthur's turn. Rising, armed only with the bamboo pointer, he began to dismantle Nimitz's case. Most dangerous, he said, was that the King-Nimitz plan would strip his armies to the bone. "All of my American forces, except for a token group of two divisions and a few air squadrons, were to be transferred to the command of Admiral Nimitz," he warned. Occupying Luzon, the largest, northernmost Philippine island, offered a far better way to cut Japan's lifeline than flitting from island to island. "If I could secure the Philippines, it would enable us to clamp an air and naval blockade on the flow of all supplies from the south to Japan, and thus, by paralyzing her industries, force her to early capitulation." Though unspoken, the Philippines approach could also rescue MacArthur from ending up with a middling war. At this point, he was largely occupied directing the fighting in northern New Guinea. Without retaking the Philippines, he could find his war record consisting of one major victory over a barely remembered island.

He then rolled out his emotional clincher. Since the Philippines were American territory, how could the country justify liberating the Chinese on Formosa while abandoning seventeen million Filipinos and tens of thousands of American and Allied POWs currently suffering in Japanese captivity? He had vowed to the Filipinos that he would return, which he regarded as a solemn promise incumbent not only on him, but on the United States as well. Marshall had anticipated this tactic and had warned MacArthur before the conference, "We must not allow our personal feeling . . . to override our objective which is the early conclusion of the war with Japan. In my view, 'by-passing' is in no way synonymous with 'abandonment.'" If the King-Nimitz proponents intended to paint MacArthur as placing his ego above the larger objective, he had a ready response. Admiral King, he said, "apparently felt that the only way to remove the blot on the Navy disaster at Pearl Harbor was to have the Navy command a great victory over Japan," a motivation not so different from his case that liberating the Philippines would also vanquish the enemy.

Nimitz had spoken well, backed by impressive evidence supporting his position. MacArthur had spoken eloquently without glancing at a note, seeming to have the entire case in his head and heart. By all accounts, FDR conducted the debate with a judge's impartiality—though in remarks made in a fireside chat several weeks before he seemed to support island hopping, saying, "We have cut off from a return to the homeland tens of thousands of beleaguered Japanese troops who now face starvation or ultimate surrender." MacArthur pleaded for ten minutes alone with the president, who agreed. No record was kept, but according to MacArthur, he told FDR, "If your decision be to bypass the Philippines and leave its millions of wards of the United States and thousands of American internees and prisoners of war to continue to languish in their agony and despair—I dare to say that the American people would be so aroused that they would register most complete resentment against you at the polls this fall." At the end MacArthur left believing that he had carried the day. According to his account the president had agreed, "We will not bypass the Philippines." After the session, Roosevelt took the elevator to the third floor bedroom and called for his physician, Admiral McIntire. "Give me an aspirin before I go to bed," he said. He paused for a moment, then added, "In fact, give me another aspirin to take in the morning. In all my life, nobody has ever talked to me the way MacArthur did."

We have only MacArthur's word that FDR acquiesced, and the general's actions the next morning suggest that he was still unsure, since he again began pressing for liberation of the Philippines. Roosevelt was all too aware of the bloody potential of invading the islands. Fresh in his mind was the recent, bitter struggle for Saipan in the Marianas chain. On June 15, two Marine divisions, under hot-tempered General Holland "Howlin' Mad" Smith, later supported by Army infantry, poured onto beaches defended by 30,000 Japanese. Saipan was eventually taken in three weeks after a final suicide charge left the Japanese heaped in the thousands before American positions. During the battle, Marines and GIs had watched in horror as Japanese civilians flung themselves to their death over cliffs onto the rocks below rather than face their fear of conquest. Along with the staggering death toll among the Japanese, the Saipan campaign had cost 15,000 American casualties. And now MacArthur was arguing for another major invasion that King and Nimitz regarded as useless against nearly a half million Japanese. "But Douglas," FDR protested, "to take Luzon would demand heavier losses than we can stand." MacArthur answered, "Mr. President, my losses would not be heavy, any more than they have been in the past." The days of the "frontal attack should be over," he claimed. "Modern weapons are too deadly, and frontal assault is only for mediocre commanders." He did not explain how he expected to escape frontal assaults against stoutly defended Luzon.

The arguments volleyed back and forth, until the party broke for lunch. A fidgety MacArthur was impatient to leave, but FDR wanted the two seen together one more time. He dragooned MacArthur into a final automobile tour, including a stop at a military hospital. During this visit, FDR insisted on being wheeled through a ward of amputees. As Sam Rosenman remembered the day, "He wanted to display himself and his useless legs to these boys who would have to face the same bitterness. This crippled man in the little wheelchair wanted to show them that it was possible to rise above such physical handicaps." The visit was a rare instance in which Roosevelt allowed attention to be drawn to his disability. On only one other recorded occasion had he done so. In 1936, when invited to dedicate a building at Washington's historically black Howard University, the school's president asked FDR if he would display his infirmity because his students had, in a sense, been crippled by racism. FDR obliged. He allowed himself to be lifted from his chair and then, braces locked, made his slow, painful way to the speaker's platform.

As the president and MacArthur settled back in the car after the hospital tour, MacArthur caught FDR off guard, asking him about his reelection opponent. "What chance do you think [New York governor

Thomas E.] Dewey has?" MacArthur asked. MacArthur's own presidential ambitions were scarcely concealed. Earlier that year, as the Republicans looked over candidates to face Roosevelt, MacArthur had written to Senator Arthur Vandenberg that he would not campaign for the nomination, but would respond to a popular draft. For a serving officer to oppose his commander in chief in wartime was brazen, even by MacArthur's standards. In doing so, he was biting the hand that fed him. In 1933, upon becoming president, Roosevelt could have dumped MacArthur as chief of staff. Instead, he kept him on for another year. Later, FDR rescued MacArthur, then a field marshal in the Philippine army, from oblivion and brought him back to serious soldiering, making him commander of American forces in the islands. Roosevelt made no rebuke when MacArthur was caught flat-footed and lost his Philippine B-17s hours after Pearl Harbor. As Bill Hassett noted, "MacArthur seems to have forgotten his losses in the Japanese surprise attack on Manila despite the fact that Admiral Kimmel and General Short faced court martial on charges of laxity at Pearl Harbor." Further, when in the face of rapid Japanese advances in 1942, MacArthur, with Quezon, had been willing to abandon the Philippines, it was Roosevelt who delivered an emphatic "No." Instead, he arranged to have MacArthur rescued and made him commander of the Southwest Pacific theater. But MacArthur, encased in a cocoon of self-centeredness, let none of this generosity temper his political behavior. Undeniably, MacArthur generated a near hypnotic charisma not only within his coterie but among the American public. Yet his behavior toward the president was inexcusable.

When Roosevelt finally answered MacArthur's question about Dewey's prospects, the president said at first that he had no time for such matters. Then, breaking into a broad grin, he said, "I'll beat the son of a bitch in Albany if it's the last thing I do." He offered one caveat. "If the war with Germany ends before the election," he said, "I will not be re-elected." He had confided to Daisy Suckley that he was already "planning his life after he leaves the White House. . . . He will write and make a lot of money that way." MacArthur finally managed to get away from Honolulu, but not before Roosevelt had one last chance to twist the lion's tail. Noticing that MacArthur's fly was unzipped, he whispered to a photographer, "Quick, get a shot of it." MacArthur, responding with an expression of utter contempt, hastily crossed his legs.

The following morning, the president was asked by a reporter, "At your conference at Casablanca you gave us a very fine phrase, about unconditional surrender. Are we going to make that our goal out here in the Pacific?" Confident in his knowledge of history, the president repeated his version that when in 1865 General Robert E. Lee was driven into a corner at Richmond, "His Army was practically starving . . . his arms were practically expended. So he went under a flag of truce, to Grant. . . . He asked Grant for his terms of surrender. Grant said, 'Unconditional surrender.'" In FDR's telling, Lee surrendered his sword to Grant, and the victor magnanimously told the defeated leader to keep it and his horses as well so that his soldiers could "do the spring plowing," a magnanimous gesture. As for Japan, he was sticking by unconditional surrender for them. "We are human beings—normal thinking human beings." The enemy must surrender totally and then, as in the case of Grant and Lee, there would be time for humanitarian conduct.

At the tail end of the conference, an FBI agent, upon seeing the president, had filed a report back to Washington commenting on FDR's wan appearance. An outraged Admiral Leahy wired Harry Hopkins, noting that the president had just put in a thirteen-hour day and closed, "Tell FBI Hoover that this agent here should be disciplined for making a false report." From Hawaii the president sailed north for a morale-boosting visit to possibly the most forlorn outpost where GIs served, the Aleutian Islands. "I like your climate," he said upon his arrival. "Thousands upon thousands of people would give anything in the world to swap places with you people." The remark met with uproarious laughter.

TWELVE DAYS AFTER THEIR MEETING FDR sent MacArthur a radiogram while returning home aboard the *Baltimore* seeming to confirm the general's triumph in the Honolulu debate. "You have been doing a really magnificent job against what were great difficulties," Roosevelt told him. "As soon as I get back, I will push on that plan." He closed, "Someday there will be a flag-raising in Manila—and without a question I want you to do it." MacArthur wrote back, "It is my considered professional opinion that the re-conquest of the Philippines is the essential strategic prerequisite in the prosecution of the Pacific War." Beyond strategy, he repeated the stand he had taken at Honolulu that the United States had a moral obligation to reverse the "enslavement of a loyal people who were dependent on us." When MacArthur returned to Australia he announced to his staff, "the President has accepted my recommendations and approved the Philippine plan." Nevertheless, Roosevelt's performance as referee in the Formosa-Luzon debate had actually resulted in a split decision. As MacArthur wished, the Philippines were not to be abandoned and Formosa was to be dropped. But what the Navy wanted, continued island hopping across the Central Pacific with Iwo Jima and Okinawa next, was also endorsed by FDR. The president wanted to pursue both routes to Japan's defeat, especially since the work of the atomic scientists at Los Alamos offered no guarantee of success. FDR's decision to leave his key military advisors behind when he went to Honolulu suggests that he had already made up his mind on the two-pronged strategy before he ever boarded the *Baltimore.*

CHAPTER 19

⸻ ★ ⸻

Europe: Broad Axe Versus the Spear

WHILE THE INITIAL LANDINGS ON THE NORMANDY BEACHES HAD been spectacularly successful, German resistance quickly stiffened. Caen, just ten miles inland, was supposed to be taken on the first day. Forty-four days later, the British were still fighting for the city. By mid-June the Allies had expected to take Falaise, less than twenty-five miles from Caen, but a strong German defense stalled the drive. The Allies found themselves stymied by an unforeseen enemy. George Marshall after the war revealed that Army intelligence "didn't tell me about hedgerows until it was so late we had to pay in blood for our lack of knowledge." He then warned his interviewer, "Don't print that!" French peasants had created these hedgerows, called *bocage,* from time immemorial to mark off the boundaries of farmlands. The earthen barriers, heaped up to six feet high, were topped by beech and chestnut trees, their intertwining roots forming a near impenetrable barrier and providing ideal defensive positions for the Germans.

The stubborn, costly German resistance in Normandy made it all the more likely that Dragoon, the invasion of the south of France, might have diverted and diluted the strength of this opposition. D-Day had come and gone, however, and still not a single Allied soldier had set foot on France's Mediterranean coast. The delay was countenanced by if not directly attributable to Churchill's foot-dragging, illustrated by his ill-conceived hope to invade Istria as an alternative in order to open a gateway into the Balkans and Austria. The Americans saw his notions as jabs, while they sought a knockout punch against Germany through France. The prime minister had begun stalling on Dragoon even after a date had been set. In July 1944, while Roosevelt sailed aboard the *Baltimore* en route to the Aleutians, enjoying movies and playing poker, he was handed a message from the ship's radio shack. Churchill alerted him to expect within hours a communication that "I have prepared with my own hands" on Dragoon. Roosevelt thereafter received one of the lengthiest cables ever from the prime minister, nearly 2,000 words. Its gist was that Dragoon, by siphoning troops to the French Riviera, "would ruin all hopes of a major victory in Italy. . . . Having broken up the fine Allied army which is advancing so rapidly through the peninsula." Roosevelt, however, saw Dragoon as an obliga-tion. He responded the next day, "I am mindful of our agreement with Stalin as to an operation in the south of France and his frequently ex-pressed views favoring such an operation." He brushed aside Churchill's prediction that Dragoon meant "ruin" in Italy. "My interest and hopes center on defeating the Germans in front of Eisenhower and driving into Germany rather than limiting this action for the purpose of stag-ing a full major effort in Italy. . . . I always think of my geometry— a straight line is the shortest distance between two points." FDR cited another supporter. "I am impressed," he added, "by Eisenhower's state-ment that Anvil [Roosevelt's still preferred code name] is of transcen-dent importance." Without the diversion, Eisenhower saw the Allied forces facing a drawn-out campaign across France with some 500 miles of his southern flank exposed to German harassment. Further, a linkup of Allied forces from the north and south would give the Allies the in-valuable port of Marseille. Roosevelt closed, "My dear friend, I beg you let us go ahead with the plan."

Roosevelt's rejection of Churchill's arguments provoked one of their bitterest exchanges. The prime minister charged that proceeding with Dragoon represented "the first major strategic and political error for which we two have to be responsible." He distrusted Stalin's sup-port of the operation, saying, "On a long-term political view, he might prefer that the British and Americans should do their share in France and that east, middle and southern Europe should fall naturally into his control." Privately he was more caustic. When his personal physician,

Lord Moran, came to the prime minister's bedroom to check on his patient, Churchill exploded, "Good God, can't you see that the Russians are spreading across Europe like a tide." In a final verdict, he branded Dragoon "sheer folly." He attempted one last stand, summoning Eisenhower for a marathon monologue that ended with his threat to go to the king and "lay down the mantle of my high office," should he fail to derail Dragoon. In the end, he yielded, accepting that the Americans were adamant. The United States by now clearly had become the senior partner in the Western Alliance, its industry an arms cornucopia, its manpower apparently inexhaustible. By July 4, Army public relations officers trumpeted that less than one month after D-Day, the planned one million American troops had arrived in France. Meanwhile war-weary Britain was stretched to the limit in men and matériel. On August 10, Churchill reluctantly ordered the British chiefs of staff to cooperate on Dragoon. On August 15, Allied forces landed between Toulon and Cannes, two months too late to perform the originally intended pincer movement. Churchill had chosen to ride with one of the destroyers in the invasion flotilla, scanning the beaches with his binoculars, his expression registering little enthusiasm. Later, writing in his wartime history, *Triumph and Tragedy*, Churchill lamented that a major opportunity had been lost by the invasion of southern France. Dragoon had cost the Allies a golden opportunity to reach Vienna before the Russians, "with all that might have followed there from."

The ease of the landing in the south of France questions again the wisdom of America's entering the European war via North Africa. Given almost a year and a half more to strengthen their defenses in the south of France, the Germans had offered only feeble resistance to Dragoon and inflicted only 183 initial casualties. The advantages of invading southern France in 1942, instead of the long, costly 1,100-mile trek across Morocco, Algeria, and Tunisia, seems increasingly a plausible scenario.

As inflammatory as the Dragoon debate had been, it was overshadowed by an even sharper controversy. Eisenhower favored a European campaign to be fought on a wide front versus Montgomery's case for a single narrow drive, their differences simplified as the broad axe versus the spear. Eisenhower believed that the Allies should bring all their forces up to the Rhine more or less simultaneously, then execute a two-pronged attack, one from the Aachen area in the north and the other through a gap at Metz in the south, the two forces joining to snare Germany's industrial base in a noose. "This would mean the end of the war in Europe," in Eisenhower's view. Montgomery, though Eisenhower's subordinate, was unabashed in pushing his opposing concept. He noted that Ike's broad axe front was three and a half times wider than his proposed spear point. He scoffed at "aggressive action on the part of everyone at all times," as "unsustainable" logistically. He sent a message to Ike claiming, "one really powerful and full-blooded thrust toward Berlin is likely to get there and thus end the German war" by Christmas 1944. Monty had it backward, Ike countered. The spear point would prove the more unsustainable because supplies could not keep pace with a headlong advance. Eisenhower summed up Monty's idea as "crazy."

In the meantime, France had yet to be conquered. After clawing through the *bocage* country well behind schedule, the Americans, on July 3, began a breakout from the Cotentin Peninsula at Saint-Lô, the way paved by a murderous bomber attack that a panzer commander said left 70 percent of his men "dead, wounded, crazed, or numbed." British and Canadian troops moving from the north and Americans moving up from the south could now seal off over 110,000 German troops in what came to be called the Falaise Pocket. Allied strategists believed that springing this trap would defeat Germany by the end of 1944. George Patton, now in France commanding the Third Army, wanted his part. Since Sicily he had undergone a reversal of roles with his former subordinate, Omar Bradley. Eisenhower had chosen Bradley as commander of the 12th Army Group, in which Patton's Third Army became a component.

The Canadians were stalled, leaving the Germans a fifteen-mile-wide escape hatch from the Falaise Pocket. Patton begged Bradley to let him move up from the south to seal the gap. Bradley refused, fearing that the Canadians and Patton's army would collide and that they would begin shooting at each other. Bradley instead ordered Patton to halt before the Seine River. His irrepressible subordinate crowed in reply that he was already at the Seine and had "pissed in the river that morning. . . . What would [Bradley] want him to do, pull back?" In the view of historian Martin Blumenson, Bradley was "troubled by doubt, he made instant decisions, then second-guessed himself." Still, to Ernie Pyle, the GIs' favorite journalist, "There isn't a correspondent over here, or soldier, or officer I ever heard of who hasn't complete and utter faith in General Bradley. . . . He is so modest and sincere that he probably will not get his proper credit, except in military text-books."

Much of the German army, 50,000 battle-hardened Wehrmacht troops, did escape the Falaise Pocket, but at an exorbitant price, 10,000 dead, 50,000 prisoners, and almost all equipment lost. So blood-soaked was the battlefield that upon inspecting it Eisenhower wrote, "It was literally possible to walk for hundreds of yards at a time, stepping on nothing but dead and decaying flesh."

By now, Patton's past sins were largely forgiven as he became the darling of the press. "He's colorful, fabulous. He's dynamite," a United Press radio correspondent exulted. "No wonder the brass hats don't like Lieutenant General George Patton." The soldier was in his element. Driving along an unbroken stretch of bodies and smashed equipment, he turned to an aide and said, "Compared to war, all other forms of human endeavor shrink to insignificance. God how I love it."

PARIS, LYING IN THE PATH OF THE ADVANCING ALLIES, presented a dilemma to Eisenhower. The capital's shocking fall in 1940 seemed a testament to Germany's invincibility. Its liberation now would signal the Third Reich's vulnerability. Eisenhower prided himself, whenever possible, on placing military above political considerations. He was most concerned as the Allies neared Paris with conserving "every ounce of fuel and ammunition for combat operations," rather than staging a victory parade down the Champs-Elysées. He hoped instead to surround Paris, cut off the German garrison, and await its surrender.

Events forced his hand. French resistance fighters heeded the message of the Allied propaganda station, Radio France, urging, "It is the duty of all Frenchmen to participate in the fight against the Germans." On August 19, guerrilla attacks broke out across the city, as impromptu outfits seized police stations, municipal buildings, government ministries, and newspaper offices. Their leaders begged Eisenhower to allow General Philippe Leclerc, commanding the French Second Armored Division under de Gaulle, to march into Paris and thus restore France's honor. Ike agreed to grant the French a role in freeing their capital, but American and British units had to take part too. The liberation of France must be seen as an Allied enterprise. General Dietrich von Choltitz, the German commander of Paris, received an order direct from Hitler, "Paris must not fall into the hands of the enemy except as a field of ruin." The führer kept dogging the general, demanding to know, "Is Paris burning?" To civilization's everlasting gratitude, Choltitz chose to ignore the command and instead, on August 24, surrendered the French capital.

Franklin Roosevelt marked the liberation of Paris at a tea on the South Portico of the White House, with his daughter, Anna, Lucy Rutherfurd, Lucy's daughter Barbara, and her stepson, John. Secretary Stimson, who had just come from seeing the president, remarked that he was "in better physical form than I expected." FDR happily described for his guests tens of thousands of Parisians pouring into the boulevards offering wine, flowers, and kisses to their liberators. For Roosevelt, the victory had only one drawback. On the day of liberation, Charles de Gaulle was greeted by madly cheering throngs at the office of the prefect of the Seine. One official shouted out that, with the capital free, de Gaulle should proclaim the rebirth of the republic. "The Republic has never ceased," he answered. The Vichy interregnum had been a sham. "I myself am the President of the government of the Republic," he said. "Why should I proclaim it now?" With their ring of Louis XIV's "*L'État, c'est moi*" ("I am the state") de Gaulle's words struck the imperious note that raised Roosevelt's hackles. In the end, however, FDR and Churchill bowed to the inevitable. No Frenchman remotely matched de Gaulle's stature in France. Two months after the liberation of Paris, the United States, Great Britain, and the Soviet Union recognized him as the provisional French head of state.

THE ORIGINAL BATTLE PLAN HAD ANTICIPATED THAT by D-Day+70 the Allied armies would need supplies to take them up to the River Seine. But by D-Day+90 the armies had raced 150 miles beyond the Seine, and port facilities and transports, "stretched to the limit" as Ike put it, could not keep up with the whirlwind advance. With the front moving so quickly, the moment had come to resolve the question of the broad axe versus the spear point to bring the war to an end. Upon the right decision depended the lives of tens of thousands of soldiers and civilians on all sides, an end to brutal Nazi occupation, and a halt to the extermination of the Jews. Early in September, Montgomery asked Eisenhower to come to his headquarters to resolve the issue. Ike had recently twisted his leg in an accident and could barely walk. Still he regarded stroking Montgomery's ego as necessary and agreed to come to his subordinate. They met inside Ike's plane at an airfield near Montgomery's headquarters. The field marshal began by brandishing a fistful of messages signed by Ike. He demanded to know if Eisenhower had really written them. When Ike answered "Yes," Montgomery responded, "Well, they're balls, sheer balls, rubbish." Eisenhower checked his temper, put a hand on Montgomery's knee, and said, "Steady, Monty. You can't speak to me like that. I'm your boss." For the moment, Montgomery accepted that "my arguments were of no avail. The broad front strategy was to be adopted."

On September 11, near the town of Sombernon, tanks from Patton's Third Army linked up with the U.S. Seventh Army and the French II Corps, the latter forces having been part of the 190,000 men put ashore during Operation Dragoon. As for the strategy of splitting the Germans in France, the protracted wrangling between proponents and opponents had delayed the operation too long to matter. The bulk of the German army, though in retreat, remained intact and still fighting.

ONE LIGHT MOMENT RELIEVED THE CONSTANT PRESSURE on Eisenhower. Kay Summersby wanted to join the American Women's Army Corps. Ike put in a request through channels, which Colonel Oveta Culp Hobby, the WAC commander, blocked. Marshall's assistant chief of staff, Major General M. G. White, sent Ike a memorandum on Marshall's behalf, pointing out that WACs had to be American citizens and that breaking this rule and giving Kay a direct commission would be "embarrassing, not only to me, but to the chief of staff and you." In the end, White left the decision to Eisenhower's discretion, saying that if commissioning the woman meant that much, he would consider a waiver. Marshall cleared the way, writing Colonel Hobby that he "never felt like telling a man who was responsible for winning a war not to do little things that he thought would help him win the war." As Kay Summersby later described her triumph, "General Ike pinned gold bars on my shoulders. . . . I went back to work. Second Lieutenant Summersby, Army of the United States."

THE REVERSAL OF FORTUNE FOR THE RED ARMY from the time of the German invasion in June 1941 until 1944 had been extraordinary. Initially caught flat-footed by the betrayal of Russia's erstwhile ally, the Russians suffered devastating early defeats. Whole divisions surrendered, with over 3,300,000 taken prisoner in the first five months. By December, the Germans were north of Moscow within sight of the Kremlin ramparts and had begun the siege of Leningrad. The Soviet government fled east to Kuibyshev. Possessed, however, of inexhaustible reserves of manpower and a fight-to-the-death grit, the Russians began to reverse the tide. After seventeen months of brutality unmatched in modern warfare, in battles seesawing across the vast steppes of the Soviet Union, the Germans suffered their signal defeat at Stalingrad on February 2, 1943. Afterward, the Russians shattered the myth of the German superman, parading thousands of ragged prisoners of war, including twenty-one generals, through the streets of Moscow as crowds glared, silently punctured by an occasional mocking "Sieg Heil." There followed the greatest conflict yet staged in the war, the Battle of

Kursk, beginning on July 5, 1943, with over two million men, 6,000 tanks, and 4,000 aircraft engaged on both sides. A week later, Hitler resigned himself to defeat and ordered the battle broken off. Fierce fighting continued, the cruelty and bloodshed dwarfing the fighting on the Western Front.

A year later, in late July 1944, the Russians reached the Vistula River, with Warsaw looming on the opposite bank and the German border only 100 miles distant. The Red Army, it was expected, would cross the river and liberate the Polish capital. Within Warsaw, suffering its fifth year of a hard-handed Nazi occupation, a resistance army had been quietly building, nearly 40,000 Poles meagerly supplied with arms and medicine, called the Home Army, under the command of General Tadeusz Bor-Komorowski, a Polish count, code-named "Bor." On the evening of July 29, Poles listened to a clandestine broadcast out of Moscow by Radio Kosciuszko, named for the eighteenth-century Polish hero General Tadeusz Kosciuszko, the station claiming to represent the "Union of Polish Patriots." A voice announced that "the hour for action is now" and urged "direct active struggle in the streets of Warsaw. . . . Poles, to arms! There is not a moment to lose." The broadcast could not have been made without authorization of the Soviet government, and consequently, the next day, General Bor ordered the start of the uprising. The moment seemed ideal, a fight from within by the Poles and a fight from without by the advancing Soviet armies. But, as mysteriously as it had come on, the voice of Radio Kosciuszko fell silent. Not a sign of movement could be detected among the Russians massed across the Vistula. The Polish prime minister–in–exile, Stanislaw Mikolajczyk, hurried to Moscow to plead with Stalin to support Bor's insurrection and came away thinking he had received the Soviet leader's promise. Stalin, however, reneged. As Ambassador Averell Harriman described the situation, Stalin "refused to help. Nor would he permit the British or ourselves to resupply [the Poles]." To the Soviet leader, the wrong Poles had risen up. Three months before, he had broken off relations with the London-based Polish government-in-exile, charging that its leaders had conducted a campaign of "calumny against the Soviet Union" by rejecting Moscow's false contention that the Katyn Massacre had been carried out by "the German Fascists," not by Russia. He dismissed the London Poles as "pro-Hitler brawlers." Stalin had his own surrogate, the "Lublin Poles," sponsored by Moscow and set up in the recently conquered city of Lublin.

After another conversation with the Soviet leader, Harriman reported to FDR Stalin's rationale for the inaction along the Vistula. The Soviet leader told Harriman, "it had proved impossible to get tanks across the Vistula"—this from the most powerful tank army in the war, the victors in the titanic clash of tanks at the Battle of Kursk. Stalin told Harriman that when he had allowed Polish battalions, equipped by the Russians, to cross the river, "These had suffered heavy losses" and proved to be more bother than they were worth. A frustrated Harriman now told FDR that Stalin "wanted it understood that the Poles had risen up on their own and if the Germans had disposed of them, that was not his responsibility. I'm convinced that he was not the slightest bit distressed to see them killed off." The German reprisal against the uprising had in fact been swift, with 2,500 poorly armed insurgents killed on the first day. Two weeks into the insurrection, Stalin ducked another meeting requested by Harriman, who was still pleading for relief for the Poles. The ambassador then went to the foreign minister, Molotov, begging him for permission to allow American aircraft to drop arms to Bor's Home Army and then land on Soviet airfields. Molotov turned him down, saying that the Warsaw uprising was purely "an adventuristic affair to which the Soviet government could not lend its hand." FDR and Churchill then sent a joint plea to Stalin, "We hope that you will drop immediate supplies and ammunition to the patriot Poles of Warsaw, or you will agree to help our planes in doing it quickly." Stalin turned them down, branding the resistance army a "handful of power seeking criminals." The British made a few ineffectual attempts to supply Bor's fighters, flying 700 miles from bases in Italy, while Russian airbases stood only 100 miles away. On August 15, Roosevelt received an even more disturbing "eyes only" cable from Harriman. "For the first time since coming to Moscow," the ambassador reported, "I am gravely concerned by the attitude of the Soviet government in its refusal to permit us to assist the Poles in Warsaw, as well as its own policy of apparent inactivity." The Soviet government's decision, he concluded, was "based on ruthless political considerations." Still Roosevelt clung to his conviction that the Soviet Union, bearing so disproportionate a share of the fighting, must not be provoked. On August 26, he wrote to the American ambassador in London, "I do not believe it would be good for our long range general war prospects to make a further endeavor to induce Stalin to reverse his present attitude in regard to the use of Soviet airfields to assist Warsaw."

On September 18, the Red Air Force finally dropped token supplies to the Home Army and allowed U.S. Air Force bombers to make drops to the Poles, but from such high altitudes that most of the arms landed in German hands. The help was far too little and far too late. On October 2, after a heroic sixty-two-day struggle, out of ammunition, food, and medicine, the Home Army surrendered, while the Red Army sat on its hands. Fifteen thousand Home Army fighters had been killed and 250,000 civilians lay dead or wounded. Not for another three months did the Russians enter the wrecked ghost of Warsaw. Stalin continued to claim that his army could not have taken the city earlier because it had outrun its lines of supply and lacked boats or bridges to cross the Vistula. Had the Lublin rather than the London-supported Poles risen up against the Germans, Stalin would doubtless have been more vigorous in coming to Warsaw's rescue.

WHILE THE POLES' ORDEAL WAS STILL UNDER WAY, FDR arrived on September 11, 1944, in Quebec with his military team for his seventh wartime meeting with Churchill. On a gloriously sunny morning with just the faintest intimation of fall in the air, FDR was wheeled from his train at Wolfe's Cove Station in Quebec and seated in an open black touring car. Within minutes the dumpy figure of Winston Churchill, in his favored blue jacket and nautical cap, wielding a cane, clenching a cigar, emerged from another train. The two men grinned at each other and shook hands while a crowd cheered. Churchill entered FDR's car and the motorcade began snaking its way up a steep hillside to the Citadel. The second Quebec conference, code-named Octagon, was to determine Britain's role in the war against Japan. Churchill was eager to join in that battle in order to restore a globe in which the sun never set on the British Empire. As the old imperialist explained in his memoirs, "We had to regain on the field of battle our rightful possessions in the Far East." At the first plenary session, on the thirteenth, held within the stout walls of the fortress, Churchill explained how the British navy, largely idle at this point, could help the American fleet win the Pacific war. He was even prepared, he said, to have His Majesty's ships serve under a supreme American commander. Admiral King glowered. The Pacific Ocean, in his view, was the American Navy's battlefield. He had taken that position against Douglas MacArthur; he was not eager to give it up to the British navy. Churchill pressed his point. "The offer has been made," he said. "Is it accepted?" Roosevelt, nodding toward King, answered, "It is." The admiral refused to take the bait and said only that he would study the issue. The next morning, after reviewing a portable version of the White House Map Room, FDR met again with Churchill, who raised the question of the British navy's part in the Pacific. King answered irascibly that the president's apparent concurrence the day before had been misconstrued. He turned to Marshall for support and, not getting it, spoke harshly about a lack of loyalty among the American chiefs. Admiral Leahy cleared his throat and said quietly, "I don't think we should wash our linen in public." The issue of Britain's naval role in the Pacific was left unresolved.

Though at this point Russia was not at war with Japan, Stalin had also been invited to Quebec to take part in forming future Pacific strategy. He had not accepted, he said, because he must continue his personal direction of the Soviet armies from Russia. However, he concluded, he would be willing to discuss his country's position on Japan once Germany was vanquished, which lifted Roosevelt's expectation that Russia could be drawn into the Pacific war.

Churchill would not let Octagon pass without flogging a pet theme. At the session on the thirteenth he explained that "he had always been attracted by a right handed movement with the purpose of giving Germany a stab in the armpit." Notes taken at the Quebec conference record him as saying, "Our objective should be Vienna," before the

Russians beat the West to it. He again spoke of "an operation for the capture of Istria, which would include the occupation of Trieste and Fiume," a venture that he had been promoting since before D-Day. Churchill had earlier tried to sell the Balkans to Eisenhower, not as a geopolitical move, he said, but as sound military strategy. Ike was having none of it. In his own history of the war, *Crusade in Europe*, he wrote, "if the President and the Prime Minister should decide that it was worthwhile to prolong the War, thereby increasing its cost in men and money, then I would instantly adjust my plans accordingly. But I did insist that as long as [Churchill] argued the matter on military grounds alone I could not concede validity to his arguments." Lord Moran, his physician, wrote in his diary at the time of Octagon, "Winston never talks of Hitler these days. He is always harping on the dangers of Communism. He dreams of the Red Army spreading like a cancer from one country to another. It has become an obsession and he seems to think of little else."

On the last evening at Quebec, the president hosted a farewell dinner at which Lord Moran, studying the president's haggard aspect, observed, "You could have put your fist between his neck and his collar." FDR, nevertheless in good spirits, launched into a Civil War story about the Battle of Antietam "in 1863." Churchill, his glasses perched on the end of his nose, appeared to be engrossed in reading a telegram from Stalin, and muttered without looking up, "It was 1862." Roosevelt conceded.

EISENHOWER AND MONTGOMERY CONTINUED at loggerheads in the debate over the broad axe versus the spear point. The fair-minded Ike wrote Monty, "Never at any time have I implied that I was considering an advance into Germany with all armies moving abreast." Further, he was ready to consider Montgomery's latest proposal, code-named Market Garden, an operation that the cocky field marshal described as a "left hook" that would open the way to Berlin and end the war in 1944. Market Garden, he claimed, was the same kind of knockout punch that he had delivered to win the victory at El Alamein in 1942.

"After all," he claimed, "I know something about that sort of thing." Montgomery's idea was to drop paratroopers who would then seize a series of bridges that crossed rivers and canals in Holland before the enemy could blow them up, thus opening up a sixty-five-mile-long corridor into Germany. The final bridge to be taken spanned the Rhine at Arnhem. Eisenhower felt pressured by Marshall, who favored airborne assaults, and General Arnold, ever seeking victories from the skies, to approve Market Garden. The operation began promisingly on September 17, 1944, with the U.S. 82nd Airborne Division taking bridges near Eindhoven on the first day. The U.S. 101st Airborne Division also accomplished its objectives, securing bridges over the River Maas. But the British First Airborne Division, assigned to seize the final bridge at Arnhem, had the bad luck to jump into a sector occupied by a battle-hardened SS panzer division resting after fighting on the Russian Front. The British paratroopers managed at first to take, but then lost, the northern end of the bridge. As portrayed in the later book and film, Arnhem proved "A Bridge Too Far." Eight days after Market Garden began, the mauled British paratroopers began to evacuate. Of 10,000 men who had landed around Arnhem, 1,100 were dead and 6,400 taken prisoner. Market Garden was the largest airborne operation ever attempted to date, its total British and American casualties exceeding those of D-Day. Montgomery attributed the defeat to bad weather and maintained in his memoirs that the operation had been "ninety percent successful," which the outcome surely belied.

TO THE SOUTH OF MONTGOMERY, George Patton continued to burnish his legend. Early in September, he had gone with Omar Bradley to meet Eisenhower in the World War I charnel house of Verdun. Give him enough gas and supplies, he assured them, and "we could push on to the German frontier and rupture that goddamned Siegfried Line." Instead, Patton's headlong drive literally ran out of gas. The failure was not his, Patton complained, "We got no gas, to suit Monty. The [British] First Army must get most of it." Patton was not to be thwarted for long. In October, Marshall was scheduled to visit the Third Army and Patton wanted to present him the city of Metz, 100 miles west of the Rhine, as a trophy. He told his subordinate, General Walton H. Walker, that Metz must be captured, "if it took every man in XX Corps." The advance was slowed by rains so torrential and mud so deep that, as described by historian Max Hastings, "condoms became a universal prophylactic not for sexual activity but for protecting rifle barrels, gun sights, and radio and telephone mouthpieces." By November 18, Patton's men were in Metz.

Along with his bullying and braggadocio, Patton had a fingertip feel for the GIs' psyche. When a town was taken, he left the brothels open, believing that without them, "our troops will simply produce a flood of illicit prostitution which will be more difficult to control and which will cause greater infection." When penicillin became available, Patton suggested that it be distributed to bordellos to keep the prostitutes clean for his soldiers. Eisenhower shot back, "absolutely unacceptable." When he received an order prohibiting fraternization with women as the Army neared the German border, Patton responded, "tell the men of the Third Army that as long as they keep their helmets on, they are not fraternizing."

ALAN BROOKE HAD YET TO RECOVER FROM the blow he suffered when Churchill acceded to FDR's wish that Eisenhower be appointed supreme commander in Europe. Brooke rated Ike a poor tactician and noted in his diary, "It is highly improbable that we should cross over [the Rhine] before the end of the year." He had an explanation for Ike's alleged laggard leadership: Eisenhower "is detached and by himself with his lady chauffeur on the golf links at Rheims." Nevertheless, a signal victory, perhaps not over the Rhine but near enough, did occur well before the end of the year. On October 21, in a moment rich in symbolism, Aachen, thirty miles west of the Rhine, became the first German city to fall to the Allies. In its cathedral, thirty kings and twelve queens of Germany had been crowned. Charlemagne was said to have been born there. In Hitler's rendering of history, Charlemagne's Holy Roman Empire was the First Reich, Bismarck's united Germany the second, and Hitler's Nazi state the Third Reich. As GIs made contact with German civilians, news photos of them smiling and posing with the enemy angered FDR. He called in Marshall and warned, "These photographs are considered objectionable by a number of our people." He wanted Eisenhower ordered "to discourage fraternizing by our troops with the inhabitants of Germany and that publication of such photographs be effectively prohibited."

WITH GERMANY PENETRATED AND CONTINUING TO FALL BACK, the rumor among GIs was "Home by Christmas." Britain, with fears of a Nazi invasion long past, dismantled its Home Guard. The war all but won, Roosevelt's thoughts turned to the kind of Germany he wanted to see after its defeat. As early as August 19, 1944, Henry Morgenthau, seething over the fate of Jews in Europe, had spoken to FDR about how to treat postwar Germany. No one, Morgenthau pointed out, was facing up to the near genetic militarism of the German people. Roosevelt's reaction heartened him. "We've got to be tough with Germany," FDR responded, "and I mean the German people, not just the Nazis. We either have to castrate the German people or you have got to treat them in such a manner so they can't go on reproducing people who want to continue as they have in the past." He told Henry Stimson, "The prisoners of 17, 18, 20 [years old] that we're capturing now . . . are even worse than prisoners of 40 or 45. And therefore, as long as these young men have anything to say about it, the peril of Nazism will always be before us." Roosevelt's convictions about the German character reflected his awareness that within the span of sixty-nine years, Germany had instigated three wars, the first against France in 1870, then World War I, and now World War II. Encouraged by Roosevelt's apparent agreement, Morgenthau had his Treasury Department draft a policy for breaking up postwar Germany into small states to be inhabited by peasants and laborers. Germany's production of arms was to be outlawed and its aircraft confiscated. Farmers and workers did not need cannons and airplanes.

Henry Stimson first read the proposal while being driven to his office and shuddered at what Morgenthau was promoting. He questioned whether "a nation of seventy million, educated, efficient and imaginative people can be kept within bounds on such a low level of subsistence." What he saw in Morgenthau's plan was not reason but Jewish vengeance. On September 6, Roosevelt brought Stimson, Secretary of State Cordell Hull, and Morgenthau into his study to thrash out their differences. As Morgenthau recorded the president's remarks in his diary, "he was thinking of Dutchess County and how it was in 1810, and how the people lived in homespun wool. He went back to when he was a boy. . . . There is no reason why Germany couldn't go back to 1810, where they would be perfectly comfortable." Paraphrasing the nineteenth-century essayist Charles Lamb, Stimson argued that they should not burn down the house "for the purpose of getting a meal of a roast pig."

During the Octagon meeting in Quebec, FDR appeared to have won agreement for Morgenthau's policy. He and Churchill signed a memorandum stating that "the industries referred to in the Ruhr and the Saar would therefore be necessarily put out of action and closed down . . . looking forward to converting Germany into a country primarily agricultural and pastoral in its character." On September 21, Morgenthau's plan leaked to the press, and support began to unravel. *The New York Times, Wall Street Journal,* and *Washington Post* reported on the infighting the proposal had provoked within the Roosevelt administration. A Drew Pearson column presented an uncomfortably close inside account of Stimson's and other officials' fierce opposition. General Marshall went to the Treasury Department and told Morgenthau that his plan was stiffening enemy resistance. "We have got loudspeakers on the German lines telling them to surrender," he informed him, "and this doesn't help one bit." Nazi propaganda minister Goebbels leaped gleefully onto Morgenthau's scheme, asking the German people which they preferred, defiance or serfdom?

With the 1944 presidential election just weeks away, FDR's Republican challenger, New York Governor Dewey, began warning Americans that their sons were going to die because Franklin Roosevelt insisted on returning Germany to the Dark Ages. The effect of Morgenthau's extreme policy on the enemy's will to fight, Dewey claimed, was the equivalent of "ten fresh German divisions." On October 3, Stimson was invited to have lunch at the White House. He found FDR looking fatigued and unwell. "He had no intention of turning Germany into an agrarian state," Stimson remembered the president telling him. Then, turning 180 degrees, FDR brightened and said, "Henry Morgenthau pulled a boner!"

CHAPTER 20

※

Stilwell Leaves China,
MacArthur Returns to the Philippines

By THE FALL OF 1944, FDR FOUND HIS VISITS TO THE MAP ROOM heartening, except for one blot. Bold arrows traced the Allied advance across France and into Germany. MacArthur was preparing to invade the Philippines. B-29 bombers were poised to burn out Japanese cities. But in China, to the president's puzzlement, the arrows were reversed. The United States had spent untold millions and invested over two and a half years to build airbases in China. Yet with Japanese forces falling back almost everywhere else, they were, as General Marshall pointed out, "overrunning eastern China and rapidly eliminating the air fields of the Fourteenth Air Force," created by the maverick general Claire Chennault.

At last, after long indulging illusions of China as a "great power," the scales began to fall from FDR's eyes. Most recently, he had authorized enough arms and supplies to equip eleven Chinese divisions, known as the Yoke Forces, to take on a second-rate Japanese division in Yunnan Province. A trip to the Map Room in April 1944 revealed that instead of attacking the outnumbered Japanese force, Yoke was sitting on its hands, with Chiang Kai-shek declaring that an offensive at this time was "impossible." Neither could the Chinese army protect construction of a linkup between the Ledo Road and the old Burma Road, which would have completed a vital supply artery from India to China, a project on which General Joe Stilwell had spent over two years. On

April 3, 1944, FDR fired off a radiogram to the generalissimo harsher than any he had ever addressed to a foreign leader. "It is inconceivable to me that your Yoke Forces, with their American equipment, would be unable to advance against the Japanese 56th Division in its present depleted strength," he said. "Your advance to the west can not help but succeed." He ended with, "I do hope you can act." Chiang made no reply. Messages intended for him were often intercepted by the Chinese embassy in Washington or by his wife in China and suppressed to shield the generalissimo from unpleasantness.

FDR had sent Vinegar Joe Stilwell to China in February 1942 to stiffen Chiang's will. At the root of Stilwell's inability to do so lay two opposing views of his role. He assumed that he had been given genuine authority as chief of staff to the generalissimo. Chiang saw it differently. To him, America was the quartermaster corps and Stilwell the supply sergeant, expected to deliver, as Henry Stimson put it, "clouds of war planes and swarms of tanks, insisting to the Western World that America must help her faithful ally. But they would not help themselves." From his vantage point Chiang's stance made sense. He assumed that the United States would defeat Japan whether his armies fought or not. Consequently, his primary objective was to stave off his real enemy, the Chinese communists. "He hates the Reds and will not take any chances of giving them a toehold in the government," Stilwell wrote in his diary. "The result is that each side watches the other and neither gives a damn about the war." He then added, with prescience, "If this condition persists, China will have civil war immediately after Japan is out." He told an astonished Theodore White, *Time* magazine's correspondent, that the trouble with the Chinese was simple: "They are allied to an ignorant, illiterate, superstitious, peasant son of a bitch."

Sensing that the communists possessed more fight than Chiang's Nationalists, FDR sought to foster cooperation between the generalissimo and the Reds' leader, Mao Zedong. The communists controlled a large swath of northwest China, a sector where Chiang kept 200,000 men tied up, as he claimed, to protect Mao's borders from the Japanese. Roosevelt thought that he had found an angle for testing Chiang's willingness to cooperate with the communists. Mao's territory, running alongside Japanese positions, could provide American Army observers with an ideal vantage point for gathering intelligence. On February 9, 1944, Roosevelt sent Chiang a message, stating, "It appears to be of very great advisability that an American observers' mission be immediately dispatched to North Shensi and Shansi Provinces," two territories under Mao's control, "and such other parts of North China as may be necessary." The president ended, "May I have your support and co-operation in this enterprise?" Chiang did not reply for almost two weeks. When he did, he said that of course he was ready to support a mission to collect intelligence in the north, but only in "areas where the political authority of the national government extends or wherever our army is stationed." In other words, he wanted no American contact with the communists.

Joe Stilwell was a staunch anti–New Deal conservative and hardly a communist sympathizer. Nevertheless, he was ready to take his allies wherever he could find them. He told Chiang that he would distribute Lend-Lease aid to anybody who would fight the Japanese, including the Reds. He considered flying to Mao's territory himself to arrange for troops to fight under his command. This possibility was more than Chiang could stomach. The two men by now had reached stasis. Stilwell hated and disrespected "the peanut." Chiang hated and dismissed Stilwell as a tool to supply his wants. Vinegar Joe wrote a private appraisal of China's plight: "We were fighting Germany to tear down the Nazi system—one party government supported by the Gestapo and headed by an unbalanced man with little education." How different was the situation in China, with one-party rule, the Kuomintang, running the country, a Chinese Gestapo, under Tai Li, and a government "headed by an unbalanced man with little education"?

George Marshall appreciated Stilwell's predicament. On the Fourth of July 1944, he entered the Pentagon, largely quiet on a holiday, to write an appraisal that he intended to present to the Joint Chiefs. "The Chinese ground forces in China, in their present state of discipline, training, and equipment and under their present leadership, are impotent," he wrote. "The Japanese forces can, in effect, move virtually unopposed." He radioed Stilwell asking if there was any hope of staving off defeat. Stilwell answered, yes, but only if FDR could persuade Chiang to give him real command over Chinese forces. Marshall then came to see the president on July 7 with a JCS-approved draft to send to Chiang. The chiefs advised FDR to demand that Chiang place Stilwell "directly under you in command of all Chinese and American forces." The proposed message went on, "The extremely serious situation which results from Japanese advances in central China, which threaten not only your government but all that the U.S. Army has been building up in China leads me to the conclusion that drastic measures must be taken immediately if the situation is to be saved." Roosevelt added a conciliatory touch before approving the cable, adding, "I am fully aware of your feelings regarding General Stilwell. Nevertheless, I think he has now clearly demonstrated his farsighted judgment, his skill in organization and training and above all in fighting your Chinese forces."

Over two months passed, Japanese advances continued, more airfields fell to the enemy, and still Chiang failed to act. FDR's next communication to him dropped completely the obliging tone and adopted the hectoring voice of a Hyde Park squire dressing down a wayward gamekeeper. "I have urged time and again in recent months that you take drastic action to resist the disaster which has been moving closer to China. Now, when you have not yet placed General Stilwell in command of all forces in China, we are faced with the loss of critical areas in East China, with possible catastrophic consequences." Further, he reminded Chiang that the Ledo–Burma Road was still unfinished. The rebuke went on for 600 words and in the closing line FDR warned again that China was lost unless Chiang placed "General Stilwell in unrestricted command of all your forces. On doing so depended the efforts of the United States to maintain and increase our aid to you." No chance was to be taken this time that his underlings should shield the generalissimo. Stilwell himself was to hand the message to Chiang Kai-shek personally.

Marshall had forewarned Stilwell against irritating Chiang. But restraint was not in Vinegar Joe's makeup. The message in hand, he strode into the generalissimo's country retreat in Huang Shan. He has left a vivid account of what happened next: "I handed this bundle of paprika to the Peanut and then sank back with a sigh. The harpoon hit the little bugger right in the solar plexus and went right through him. It was a clean hit, but beyond turning green, and losing the power of speech, he did not bat an eye . . . and sat in silence, jiggling one foot." Chiang subsequently replied to the president that giving Stilwell so much power would incite mutiny in the Chinese army. As Stilwell paraphrased Chiang's answer in his diary, it was "Throw out General Stilwell. He's a non-cooperative s.o.b. He has broken his promises. General Stilwell has more power in China than I have. Etc., etc." Stilwell's promotion in 1944 to four-star general, a distinction shared only by Marshall, Eisenhower, MacArthur, and Arnold, seemed hollow given his impotency as a figure of military consequence in China.

To George Marshall the sinkhole that Chiang oversaw affected the war effort well beyond China's borders. He told Roosevelt that the aid squandered on China "has been done at a heavy cost to our effort in other theaters. . . . We have not been able to meet General MacArthur's urgent requirements for air transport. General Wilson in Italy has not had the transport planes he needed," he said, referring to the massive Field Marshal Henry Maitland "Jumbo" Wilson, the Mediterranean theater commander. Most critically, Eisenhower needed more airpower "to secure the Rhine crossings . . . which involves the lives of American soldiers." The aid given China, if available in other theaters, "would undoubtedly . . . [have] shortened operations in those areas." Secretary Stimson noted in his diary that supporting China was "bleeding us white in transport planes." Teddy White wrote that China had absorbed "so much American air-freight capacity that now there wasn't enough to settle the dispute between Patton and Montgomery," which otherwise "might have finished off the war against Germany in the fall of 1944."

China had FDR in a bind. The president knew that Marshall and the impolitic Stilwell were right about Chiang. But he faced reelection in November 1944 and the China lobby wielded political power in the United States. He must not have it appear that he was abandoning the generalissimo, a leader portrayed to the American people as a valiant soldier and statesman. Above all, he could not have it seem that China had been a profitless investment. In October 1944, he sent a special envoy to China to iron out the mess, Brigadier General Patrick Hurley, a Republican secretary of war under Herbert Hoover. Hurley subsequently cautioned that if FDR backed Stilwell over the Chinese leader, "you will lose Chiang and possibly you will lose China too." In an October entry Stilwell wrote in his diary, referring to FDR, "If Old Softy gives in on this, as he apparently has, the Peanut will be out of control from now on. . . . My conscience is clear. I have carried out my orders. I have no regrets. Except to see the U.S.A. sold down the river."

That fall, Chiang gathered his Kuomintang Party leaders and assured them that he would never relinquish control of the army to a foreigner, particularly the rude and presumptuous Joseph Stilwell. Sixteen days later, Marshall informed Stilwell that the president had made a decision. He was booting Joe out of China. "You will be ordered home," Marshall wrote. No public announcement was to be made of his dismissal and Stilwell himself was to "make no comment." As Vinegar Joe was packing, a low-level Chinese bureaucrat came to his residence bearing China's highest decoration for a foreigner, "the Special Grand Cordon of the Blue Sky and White Sun." As Teddy White later reported the moment, "Stilwell told his aide to tell the generalissimo's aide to shove it."

Henry Stimson accepted that Stilwell had "never really made his number with the President." When Vinegar Joe returned to Washington, neither the secretary of war nor Marshall, the two men who had originally consigned him to his fate, were on hand to greet him, only two obscure officers, who reminded Stilwell again to keep his mouth shut. Pestered by reporters who wanted to know what had happened between Chiang and Stilwell, an impatient FDR brushed the question aside, saying only, "just a case of personalities." What he could not say was that the United States had poured over $380 million in Lend-Lease aid to China, equivalent to $5 billion currently, and had nothing to show for it.

✶

MacArthur had left Hawaii in July 1944 assuming that he had the president's blessing for a Philippine campaign. Two months later, during the second Quebec conference, FDR took a moment to reassure the general. "The situation is just as we left it at Hawaii though there seem to be efforts to do a little bypassing which you do not like," he cabled, referring to King's and Nimitz's preference to skip the Philippine venture. "I still have the situation in hand," he told MacArthur. "Take care of yourself and give my warmest regards to your wife and youngster." Three days later, on September 18, Chester Nimitz, bowing to the inevitable, told a convention of the American Legion that MacArthur would command the campaign to reconquer the Philippines.

On October 16, MacArthur boarded the cruiser *Nashville,* sailing from Hollandia in New Guinea, to fulfill his pledge to the Philippine people. Gazing out from the ship's bridge, he surveyed the power at his command, "Ships to the front, to the rear, to the left, and to the right as far as the eye could see," twenty aircraft carriers, twelve battleships, as well as cruisers and destroyers, the greatest armada ever assembled in the Pacific. Troop transports crammed with 175,000 men exceeded the invasion force at Normandy. Compared to the 1,200 miles that this fleet was zigzagging through the South Pacific to reach MacArthur's first objective, Leyte, Overlord's crossing of the English Channel had been an overnight cruise. MacArthur had long complained about the short shrift given the Pacific theater. By now, however, the number of ground, naval, and air forces in the Pacific totaled 1,878,000 men compared to 1,810,000 Americans in Europe under Eisenhower.

Leyte was the third-largest island in the Philippine archipelago, 115 miles long, 40 miles at its widest, selected by MacArthur because its airfields could provide cover for his principal objective, the liberation of Luzon, site of his stinging defeats at Manila, Bataan, and Corregidor. On the night of October 19, he retreated to his quarters aboard the *Nashville* and wrote FDR a four-page letter in his bold script. At the top he entered, "Philippine Islands" and dated it for the next day. Early the next morning he was jolted awake by an unceasing roar as the battleships and cruisers laid down a barrage to level the Japanese defenses on Leyte, the huge guns' recoil rocking the cruiser back and forth. MacArthur remembered, "the smoke from the burning palm trees was in our nostrils." The first wave went ashore at 10 A.M. Three hours later, MacArthur clambered into an LCM, a medium-sized landing craft, with a handful of staff and four war correspondents, the corncob pipe jutting between his teeth. In his pants pocket he carried his father's old two-shot Derringer. He placed himself just ahead of the helmsman, his expression unchanging during the two-mile trip to Red Beach. When within fifty yards, he ordered the ramp dropped and stepped into the surf up to his knees. One reporter carrying a camera had jumped ahead of MacArthur and took a shot of him striding ashore. After two and a half years, Douglas MacArthur had again set foot on the Philippines. The rattle of machine guns, the crump of mortars, and the whine of American dive-bombers still sounded just 300 yards ahead. A cloudburst suddenly drenched the beach as Army signalmen set up a portable transmitter from which MacArthur intended to send a message to the *Nashville*, which would then be relayed all across the Philippines. Soaking wet, he was handed a large, heavy microphone and started to speak. "People of the Philippines," he began, his hand shaking and voice tremulous, "I have returned . . . our forces stand again on Philippine soil." As he continued, his voice grew stronger and reached its rich baritone. "Rally to me. Let the indomitable spirit of Bataan and Corregidor lead on," he urged. "For your homes and hearth, strike! For future generations of your sons and daughters, strike! In the name of your sacred dead, strike!"

After finishing the broadcast, MacArthur walked to the nearest command post as Japanese mortar rounds exploded nearby, displaying the same contempt for danger that he had shown in World War I. At the CP, he handed a signalman the letter that he had written to FDR the night before aboard ship. The exercise was pure theater since MacArthur was suggesting that he was writing it under fire. "Please excuse the scribble but at the moment I am in the combat line with no facilities except this field message pad," it began. He described his message as "the first letter from the freed Philippines" and hoped the president might add the stamp to his collection. He went on to reaffirm the advantages he saw in the Philippine campaign, "it will pierce the center of [Japan's] defensive line extending along the coast of Asia from the Japanese homeland to the tip of Singapore" thus cutting the enemy forces in two. Furthermore, he was not overlooking the merits of the bypassing strategy. He intended to leave Japanese garrisons on the southern half of the Philippine Islands to wither, "which will result in the saving of possibly 50,000 American casualties." His letter closed proposing a bold stroke. As soon as the islands were liberated, he urged that the president grant them immediate independence. "Such a step," he predicted, would honor "the United States for a thousand years."

Later, when MacArthur saw a print of the photo of himself wading ashore, its drama struck him. The next day he decided to give the scene wider dissemination by restaging the landing in front of a batch of cameramen and photographers. GIs watching the spectacle for the first time assumed that MacArthur was hunting for glory from a safe remove, reigniting the image of "Dugout Doug." Immediately upon receiving word that the Leyte landing had succeeded, FDR dashed off an homage to its leader. "I know well what this means to you," he wrote MacArthur. "I know what it cost you to obey my order that you leave Corregidor in February 1942 and proceed to Australia." To the American people, Roosevelt announced, "We have landed in the Philippines to redeem the pledge we made over two years ago." He added, "We promised to return. We have returned." To Roosevelt the return was "We." To MacArthur, it had been "I."

As MacArthur's troops poured onto Leyte, a titanic naval battle began offshore in the Leyte Gulf. The Japanese navy was attempting a last bid to engage the Americans in a decisive showdown by converging two huge task forces in the gulf, including a pair of leviathans, the

Musashi and the *Yamato*, the world's largest battleships. The plan was to trap the American fleet between a force sailing south from the San Bernardino Strait and another sailing north through the Surigao Strait, stranding the invasion army on the beach unsupported. U.S. submarines spotted the south-moving force under Admiral Takeo Kurita and soon after the north-moving force under Admiral Shoji Nishimura. The battle raged for three days with the Japanese mauled between elements of Admiral Bull Halsey's Third Fleet and Admiral Thomas C. Kincaid's Seventh Fleet. Nineteen torpedoes and seventeen bomber strikes ripped apart the *Musashi*, which went down with over 1,250 of her crew. Admiral Nishimura died in the battle. Admiral Kurita's flagship went down and the admiral had to be fished from the sea and hauled aboard the *Yamato*, which then slunk off. All told, three battleships, nine heavy and light cruisers, and four carriers were destroyed, leaving only three carriers afloat in Japan's once mighty fleet. When the smoke cleared, more major Japanese warships engaged at Leyte were on the ocean's bottom than on the surface and over 14,000 men died. The U.S. Navy lost one carrier, the *Princeton*, and suffered sinking and damage to several other vessels, but nothing remotely comparable to Japan's disaster. American battle deaths totaled 475. Leyte Gulf was to be the last great surface battle in naval history and the last gasp for the once awesome Japanese fleet. On October 25, a jubilant FDR summoned reporters to the Oval Office and repeated to them what Bull Halsey had said of Leyte Gulf, "The Japanese Navy has been beaten and routed and broken by the Third and Seventh fleets."

Despite suffering a near mortal blow, the Japanese did introduce one tactic in the Leyte Gulf that terrified crews aboard American ships. On October 25, a wing of five Japanese Zero fighters circled above the U.S. fleet each carrying a 500-pound bomb in its rack. Admiral Kincaid, who witnessed the maneuver, described how, as the formation approached the ship, one plane dropped behind as if experiencing engine trouble. As the ships' batteries concentrated fire on the main body of aircraft, the laggard plane, with its heavy payload, deliberately crashed into the target vessel. The Japanese called such suicide missions "kamikaze," divine wind, named for the typhoons that had driven

Mongol invaders away from Japan six hundred years before. A rear admiral, Masafumi Arima, had first volunteered to test the tactic. While the kamikaze raids were not decisive at Leyte, they did sink four escort carriers and seriously damaged three more, their suicidal fanaticism as chilling as their destructiveness. The introduction of kamikaze attacks underscored two points about the war in the Pacific: the Japanese had become desperate, but they would, nevertheless, fight to the death.

AMERICANS HAVE HISTORICALLY BEEN DRAWN to the man on horseback. Witness the ascent to the White House of twelve men who had been generals, including George Washington, William Henry Harrison, Andrew Jackson, and Ulysses Grant. World War II would continue the predilection. Nearly a year before Leyte, in November 1943, a Democratic senator, Edwin C. Johnson of Colorado, concerned about FDR's ability to stay in power, issued a statement declaring, "The New Deal is through," and closing, "In this grave crisis, the Democratic Party owes it to the American people to draft General Marshall for president." Johnson acknowledged that he was proposing a long shot, "but no patriotic American from George Washington down can refuse such a call." Marshall's image was burnished further when *Time* named him "Man of the Year," describing the chief of the Army as "the closest thing to 'the indispensable man.'"

A horrified Marshall sent Henry Stimson a batch of newspaper clippings generated by Johnson's move with a covering note. He asked the secretary of war to say something at his next press conference along the lines of, "I regret very much the recent references to General Marshall of a political nature. . . . I know they are embarrassing to General Marshall and furthermore, I feel that they make his present task more difficult. . . . He will never allow himself to be considered as a possible presidential candidate." Stimson obliged. In her memoirs, Marshall's wife spoke of the stock rebuttal adopted by the general's close associates to knock down presidential speculation: "General Marshall would no more think of lending himself to such a proposition than he would resign his post in the midst of battle."

At roughly the same time, presidential speculation rose over another wartime paragon. Dwight Eisenhower received a letter from an old comrade, General George Van Horn Moseley, reporting what the popular radio commentator Walter Winchell was saying: "If the Republicans ran MacArthur as president, Mr. Roosevelt would take [Eisenhower] on as his running mate." Ike wrote back to Moseley, "When Mr. Winchell brought up such a subject, he was, to say the least, badly misinformed. . . . I can scarcely imagine anyone in the United States less qualified than I for any type of political work." However, Edward J. Price, who had served years before as a corporal under Eisenhower in the nascent tank corps, continued the drumbeat for Ike. Price had since become a successful business executive and headed a veterans organization called the World War I Tank Corps Association. In October 1943, Ike showed his confidant, Harry Butcher, a clipping from *The Washington Post,* mailed to him by a friend, George Allen, announcing that Tank Corps Post No. 715 of the American Legion in New York City had passed a resolution endorsing Eisenhower for president. As Butcher recalled Eisenhower's reaction, "He was exasperated. He quickly wrote in pencil on George's letter, which he asked me to stick in an envelope and mail, 'Baloney! Why can't a simple soldier be left alone to carry out his orders?'"

The U.S. ambassador to the Soviet Union, Averell Harriman, remembered a more politically ambitious Eisenhower. He had gone to the European theater in order to assure Stalin that his Western Allies were putting up a serious fight. There he spoke with Eisenhower and wrote in his memoirs, "That night we had a long talk and Eisenhower for the first time mentioned his presidential aspirations. . . . He said that some of his friends had come to him and said that he ought to be president." Harriman found Eisenhower ambivalent about the prospect, "torn between becoming President and playing the role of elder statesman after the War." Harriman then rendered his private judgment. He liked Ike personally, he said, but "I did not feel that he was qualified to be President."

Douglas MacArthur never saw himself simply as an Army officer following orders. In the spring of 1943, bypassing channels including his superior, George Marshall, MacArthur asked a British liaison officer to get word to Winston Churchill offering his advice for conducting the war in Europe. MacArthur wanted Churchill to know that he too viewed the cross-Channel strategy as ill conceived. Instead, he urged throwing "all the resources of America and Great Britain on the Russian front." Churchill, upon seeing this proposal, told his representative to the American chiefs, General Sir Hastings Ismay, "the General's ideas about the European theatre are singularly untroubled by considerations of transport and distance." No evidence exists that FDR was ever informed of this interchange between MacArthur and a foreign head of state. Another British officer to whom MacArthur spoke with heedless candor was Lieutenant Colonel Gerald Wilkinson. He invited Wilkinson to his well-appointed quarters in Brisbane, where he claimed that Roosevelt was out to get him. Stunned, Wilkinson was initially skeptical. But MacArthur pressed his case, insisting that FDR might well pull it off. Wilkinson, evidently persuaded, recorded in his journal, "FDR will find some pretext to relieve MacArthur altogether of his command." MacArthur's paranoidal accusation that FDR wanted his scalp flew in the face of all the president had done for him. With the presidential election still over a year away, MacArthur had unburdened himself to one of his corps commanders, Lieutenant General Robert Eichelberger, who subsequently wrote in his diary, "My chief talked of the Republican nomination—I can see that he expects to get it." Eichelberger then added, with the hero worship commonplace among MacArthur subordinates, "And I sort of think so too." During a lunch with officers of I Corps, MacArthur held forth for an hour on the executive responsibilities of the presidency.

After the July conference in Honolulu, the president had told MacArthur that he would trounce his Republican opponent, Tom Dewey, except for one condition. He had been given an advance peek at an Elmo Roper poll in which respondents were asked, "If the war is over by election day, would you favor or oppose the re-election of Roosevelt?" Almost 60 percent said "opposed." But if the war were still on, nearly two thirds favored his reelection. The results produced a Roosevelt campaign theme: you did not change horses in midstream or a leader in wartime.

MacArthur had long let his barely concealed hatred of the president and his own egotism blind him to Roosevelt's political buoyancy. As far back as FDR's campaign for a second term in 1936, when both MacArthur and Eisenhower were serving in the Philippines, the general loudly predicted that Roosevelt would go down in defeat. Ike counseled him to tone down his open preference. For his pains Ike received a tongue-lashing from MacArthur, who rebuked him for being "fearful and small-minded." When Roosevelt went on to score a spectacular victory, winning every state but Vermont and Maine, Eisenhower noted gleefully in his diary, "Boy, did the general back pedal rapidly. . . . And took back what he had said at first." Ike also described MacArthur's fear that Roy Howard, publisher of the Scripps Howard newspapers and privy to MacArthur's Roosevelt animus, might "tell on him in Washington."

"MacArthur for President" movements began springing up across the country. His name appeared on the ballot for primaries in two states, Wisconsin and Illinois. In Illinois, a supporter, as if testing his seriousness, sent MacArthur a certificate that if signed would have removed him from the balloting. He let his name stand. Three of MacArthur's top aides, Generals Richard Sutherland, George C. Kenney, and Charles Willoughby, took advantage of a trip to Washington to meet with Senator Vandenberg and extolled their chief's qualities to the heavens. When the issue arose as to the legality of a serving officer running for president, Vandenberg publicly defended MacArthur's right to do so. MacArthur wrote back, "I am most grateful to you for your complete attitude of friendship. I want you to know the absolute confidence I feel in your experienced and wise mentorship." The general began quietly devising a nomination strategy for 1944, inviting wealthy backers to his cause.

While public opinion polls showed high esteem for MacArthur the general, little support emerged for MacArthur the candidate. Still, hope died hard. The MacArthur movement largely benefited from the "hate Roosevelt" crowd, and a conservative freshman congressman and Lions Club leader, Dr. Arthur Miller of Nebraska, took up the gauntlet. The year before the election, he wrote MacArthur that, "unless this New Deal can be stopped, our American way of life is doomed forever." MacArthur replied to Miller, "I do unreservedly agree with the complete wisdom and statesmanship of your comments." Encouraged, Miller wrote the general again, in early 1944, maintaining that MacArthur was the one man who could "destroy this monstrosity." MacArthur replied again, praising the congressman for his "scholarly" letter and adding that his views would "arouse the consideration of every true patriot." On April 13, 1944, heartened by MacArthur's replies, Miller took it upon himself to release to the press the four letters between him and the general, believing that they documented his hero's readiness to take up the Republican mantle.

FDR revealed how he felt about MacArthur as a prospective rival in an encounter between himself and a MacArthur subordinate, Major General George Kenney, a straight-talking, feisty commander of the Fifth Air Force. Kenney had been dispatched by MacArthur to lobby the War Department for more planes for the Southwest Pacific. Learning that the general was in town, FDR invited him to the White House, where he impressed Kenney with his grasp of air warfare. Then, out of the blue, FDR asked Kenney if Douglas MacArthur was going to run for president in 1944. Kenney answered loyally, "General MacArthur has one ambition, and that is to ride down the Ginza at the head of the parade when we enter Tokyo." After the Kenney visit, as if taking out an insurance policy, Roosevelt instructed Henry Stimson to remind reporters that under Army regulations a career officer could not run for office unless he had held that office before going on active duty. Roosevelt further directed his naval aide to provide him with copies of a report that should deflate the idea that MacArthur walked on water. In it, MacArthur had written just before Pearl Harbor that he could defeat any attempt by the Japanese to take the Philippines.

In the meantime, Dr. Miller's release of his correspondence with MacArthur stirred intense press speculation. *The New York Times* reported that the letters "were generally construed to mean that General

MacArthur would be a receptive candidate for the presidential nomination on an anti-Administration platform." Senator Vandenberg recognized Miller's release of the letters as a political "boner," probably sinking a MacArthur presidential bid. The general, as if fearing his responses to Miller might risk his dismissal from the Army for insubordination, rounded up reporters three days after the release, claiming that the letters "were never intended for publication." He then added disingenuously, "I entirely repudiate the sinister interpretation that they were intended as criticism of any political philosophy or any personages in office." Vandenberg warned that this response failed sufficiently to remove from MacArthur the taint of a soldier's disloyalty. Consequently, on April 30, MacArthur beat a Shermanesque retreat. "I request that no action be taken that would link my name in any way with the nomination. I do not covet it nor would I accept it," he insisted. Roosevelt need not have concerned himself with facing Douglas MacArthur that November. The Republican convention held in June nominated Tom Dewey as its candidate. Dewey received 1,056 delegate votes. Douglas MacArthur received one. In his reminiscences, published after the war, the general admitted that Roosevelt had told him, after the Bonus Marchers controversy, "I think you are our best general, but I believe you would be our worst politician."

As the 1944 presidential election approached, the Dewey team thought it had uncovered a flagrant example of Roosevelt's highhandedness. They charged that the president had dispatched a Navy destroyer to bring his dog, Fala, back from the Aleutian Islands. On September 23, Roosevelt spoke at a national convention of the Teamsters union, and gave the Republicans a taste of the consummate performer they faced. With a mischievous smile, he began, "These Republican leaders have not been content with attacks on me, or my wife, or on my sons. No, not content with that, they now include my little dog, Fala. Well, of course, I don't resent attacks, and my family doesn't resent attacks, but Fala *does* resent them. You know, Fala is Scotch, and being a Scottie, as soon as he learned that the Republican fiction writers in Congress and out had concocted a story that I had left him behind on the Aleutian Islands and had sent a destroyer back to find him—at a cost to the taxpayers of two or three, or eight or twenty million dollars—his Scotch soul was furious. He has not been the same dog since." Laughter erupted throughout the convention hall and soon spread all across a nation of dog lovers, leaving Dewey's operatives looking small and mean-spirited.

Within days, however, a serious threat to FDR did arise. James V. Forrestal, whom FDR had named secretary of the navy after the April 1944 death of Frank Knox, wrote a longhand note to the president. "Information has come to me," Forrestal reported, "that Dewey's first speech will deal with Pearl Harbor." And it would drop a bombshell. An anti–New Deal Army officer had leaked information to the Republican camp that, prior to the sneak attack, Magic was breaking the Japanese diplomatic code. Therefore, the reasoning ran, Roosevelt must have known what was coming and deliberately did nothing. He was, in short, guilty of treason.

George Marshall abhorred the intrusion of politics into the conduct of the war. But upon learning of Dewey's expected speech, he saw a political issue turning into a military catastrophe. If FDR was publicly attacked on grounds that, through Magic decryptions, he had prior knowledge of Japanese intentions, America's most priceless espionage triumph would be exposed and the Japanese would change their codes. Marshall summoned Colonel Carter Clarke, who managed intelligence collection, particularly decrypts relating to Magic. He handed Clarke a letter marked in capitals and underlined, "For Mr. Dewey's eyes only." Marshall began with an apology, "I should much have preferred to talk to you in person, but I could not devise a method that would not be subject to press and radio reactions as to why the chief of staff of the Army would be seeking an interview with you at this particular moment." He further underscored that the president had no "intimation *whatever* that such a letter was addressed to you."

Colonel Clarke, in civilian dress, caught up with the Republican candidate in a Tulsa, Oklahoma, hotel suite, where he handed Dewey the Marshall letter, which he had previously placed in an envelope stamped in red, "Top Secret." Marshall wrote that Dewey should read only the first paragraph, and unless he would agree not to divulge the letter's full contents to anyone else, he should read no further. Marshall's condition made Dewey suspicious, a trick to rob him of a winning campaign issue. He refused to accept the general's terms. Clarke returned and reported Dewey's reaction, whereupon Marshall rewrote the letter to make it more convincing. Clarke went again to see the Republican candidate, now in the gingerbread Victorian governor's mansion in Albany. The amended version revealed that the Battle of the Coral Sea and the epic victory at Midway were "based on deciphered messages and therefore our few ships were in the right place at the right time." Marshall described the prized window into Nazi Germany's intentions provided by the intercepted and decoded messages that Ambassador Oshima sent from Berlin to the Tokyo Foreign Office. The general spoke of the calamitous outcome of a bungled OSS break into Japan's embassy in Lisbon, which led the Japanese to change their military attaché code. In sum, he sought to demonstrate that Magic contributed "greatly to the victory and tremendously to the saving in American lives."

Tom Dewey found it hard to accept Marshall's avowal that he had acted without FDR's knowledge. He suspected that Roosevelt was having Marshall do his dirty work. The governor further found it inconceivable that the Japanese had failed to discover the gaping hole in their security. "Why in hell haven't they changed [the codes] especially after what happened at Midway and the Coral Sea?" he demanded of Clarke. The GOP candidate's skepticism was understandable. With the headline "Navy Had Word of Jap Plan to Strike at Sea," the *Chicago Tribune* had made it obvious that the Midway victory had been won by breaking Japanese ciphers. Tom Dewey, a patriot at heart and aware of Marshall's stature as a man of probity, decided to question the general personally. He phoned Marshall and was moved by his rocklike integrity. After their conversation, Magic remained secret and guilt for Pearl Harbor disappeared as a campaign issue.

FDR's FAILING HEALTH HAD BECOME ALL too evident to his inner circle. His energy flagged and an unexplained recent loss of thirty pounds had left his clothes sagging. Edward Stettinius, who had replaced the ailing Cordell Hull as secretary of state, noted that "a few of Roosevelt's most trusted supporters had made an agreement among themselves to call on the President in a body, to beg him not to run for a fourth term." Roosevelt wrote to an old friend, Hamilton Holt, president of Rollins College, explaining how he had hated to have to run for a third term. "It would be a mistake, of course, to establish it as a tradition," he said. But as for a fourth term at this point in the war, "I think I can well plead extenuating circumstances." He told another friend, "I have as little right to withdraw as a soldier has to leave his post in the line." In the end the supporters who had intended to urge the president not to run lost their nerve. None wanted to bell the cat.

Given his health, FDR plunged into the campaign with surprising vigor. On October 21, during a cold, heavy rain over a million people lined a fifty-one-mile route through four of New York City's five boroughs, cheering a smiling, hatless FDR waving from an open touring car. New York with its forty-seven electoral votes was crucial and, against the advice of advisors to cancel, Roosevelt had dismissed the ugly weather and went ahead. He saw in braving the storm an opportunity to demonstrate his fitness to stay in office. Under his suit he wore long underwear and his legs were warmed by a heater in the backseat. Halfway through the journey, the motorcade stopped, and the president, soaked to the skin, was taken inside a building, given a shot of whiskey and a dry suit, and resumed his odyssey.

Though Tom Dewey had kept the secret of Magic, he nevertheless did make FDR's conduct of the war an issue on other grounds, accusing the president of holding back support for MacArthur in the Pacific. His timing, however, proved luckless. He leveled the charge just as MacArthur was invading Leyte, which allowed FDR to exclaim at a speech in Philadelphia, "speaking of the glorious operation in the Philippines, I wonder whatever became of the suggestion made a few weeks ago that I had failed for political reasons to send enough forces or supplies to General MacArthur?"

On election day, as was his custom, Roosevelt sat in the dining room at Hyde Park with a clutch of sharpened pencils and a notepad while his daughter, Anna, her husband, John, and Bill Hassett delivered election returns from a clacking teleprinter. When the outcome became certain, the president went outside, "full of fight," as Daisy Suckley recalled, to watch a torchlight parade. He had beaten Dewey by over three million votes and 432 electoral votes against 99 for his opponent.

Dwight Eisenhower had once confessed to Harry Hopkins that, coming from a Republican family, he "had voted against Roosevelt" during his first three presidential campaigns. This time, however, Ike had voted for FDR but chose a circuitous route to make his support known to the winner. He explained to Marshall that he found it inappropriate for him to send a congratulatory message to Roosevelt on his victory. But the chief of staff might, if he chose, "let him know, informally, of my satisfaction that our War leadership is permitted to continue uninterruptedly to the completion of its task."

CHAPTER 21

From the Home Front to Yalta

MUCH OF THE CONVERSATION AT SENIOR OFFICERS CLUBS IN DECEM-
ber 1944 dealt with a debate under way in Congress: should five-star
rank be created for meritorious four-star generals and admirals? Ernest
King became an avid lobbyist and sought to enlist Marshall in support
of the bill. They should advise the president, King said, to "recognize
the fact that there is a need to prepare for ranks higher than that of
Admiral and General." "I didn't want any promotion at all," Marshall
commented on the issue. "I thought it was much better that I personally shouldn't be beholden to . . . Congress except for their fair treatment." The legislators, after heated discussion, finally enacted five-star
rank on December 11, which the president swiftly approved. Thereafter ensued a lively discussion as to what to call the new rank. FDR
liked "Chief General" and "Chief Admiral," but the designations finally
agreed on were "General of the Army" and "Fleet Admiral." Roosevelt
then conferred the rank upon Marshall, MacArthur, Eisenhower,
Arnold, King, Leahy, and Nimitz. The new grade raised them to the
equivalent of field marshal and admiral of the fleet in the British military. Eisenhower, who had once spent sixteen years as a major and was
a brigadier general at the time of Pearl Harbor, had risen in less than
four years to the highest rank the American military offered.

✯

ON A SLEEPY SUNDAY MORNING six days after the promotion issue had
been settled, the Map Room duty officer delivered to the president

Communiqué 253 from Eisenhower's Supreme Headquarters. "Allied Forces yesterday repulsed a number of counterattacks," it read tersely. On the same day, *The New York Times* reported, "The Germans took the offensive today on much of the American First Army front.... These counter-attacks were checked everywhere, usually after hours of severe fighting, and they cost the enemy heavy casualties." The *Times* story appeared on page 19. Apart from these clashes and a drive by Patton's Third Army in the southern sector, the bulk of Allied forces in Western Europe were essentially idle, "getting ready," as General Marshall put it, "to launch another attack towards the Ruhr River." The major story that day focused on MacArthur's Philippines campaign, the *Times* front-page headline reading, "Americans Capture Airfield on Mindoro as San Jose Is Won."

George Marshall had instructed Eisenhower that the objective in Europe was "completing the defeat of Germany by 1 January." With the war's end in sight, Army postal officials began arranging to return Christmas presents mailed to GIs back to the United States. Ike had made a £5 bet with Montgomery that the war would be won by Christmas. As the deadline approached, he reminded Monty, "I still have nine days," and he would not pay up "until that day." Montgomery, assured by his intelligence chief that the German army was "fighting a defensive campaign on all fronts . . . and cannot stage major offensive operations," informed Eisenhower that he would "like to hop over to England" and spend Christmas with his son. Eisenhower concurred, adding, "I envy you."

That Germany could go on the offense again seemed far-fetched. A captured German soldier's diary read, "The men are done. . . . Poor Germany! Everybody is under the impression that he is selling his life cheaply." Two years of around-the-clock bombing had reduced sixty-one German cities to a shambles. Seventy-five percent of Hamburg, Cologne, and Essen lay in ruins, and 7.5 million Germans were homeless. The raids were not without cost, but the American Air Forces proved willing to absorb terrible punishment if the results appeared commensurate. Fifty-six Flying Fortresses were expended in a single raid against oil refineries in the Leipzig area.

Despite good news, the president feared that the American people had become complacent. Roosevelt, whose life had once seemed infinitely rosy, had ever since the blow of polio maintained a healthy regard for the caprices of fate. He dictated a letter to Grace Tully to be sent to heads of all government agencies warning, "public statements by responsible military and civilian officials at home and abroad indicating an early termination of the war tend to curtail production of essential war materials."

One voice vigorously rejected the specter of imminent German defeat, that of *Obersten Befehlshaber der Deutschen Wehrmacht,* the commander in chief of all German armed forces, Adolf Hitler. In September 1944, Hitler gathered his operations staff at the Wolf's Lair in East Prussia, telling them, "I have made a momentous decision. I shall go over to the offensive ... out of the Ardennes." His objective was to break through a thinly held sector of the Allied line known as the "ghost front," split Montgomery's 21st Army Group in the north from Omar Bradley's 12th Army Group to the south, drive to the English Channel, and seize the Belgian port of Antwerp, so critical to the Allies. If successful, Hitler believed, *Wacht am Rhein,* Watch on the Rhine, as the operation was named, would force the Western Allies to make a separate peace and free up the full might of the German armies to defeat Russia. Hitler brushed aside Roosevelt's avowal to fight until unconditional surrender had been achieved. A reeling Western Alliance, he reasoned, would have no choice but to negotiate. Hitler chose two of Germany's finest soldiers to lead the offensive, Field Marshal Gerd von Rundstedt, whose panzers had spearheaded the Nazi conquest of France four years before, and Field Marshal Walther Model, who had carved out a formidable reputation fighting the Russians.

Planning for *Wacht am Rhein* was thorough. Weather stations set up on ice floes near the Arctic reported that bad weather in mid-December would ground Allied planes and thus conceal German movements. A Hitler favorite, the flamboyant Otto Skorzeny, who had snatched the deposed Mussolini from his captors in Italy, began to comb German units for soldiers who could speak colloquial American English to carry out Operation Greif. These men were given American uniforms and dog tags taken from dead GIs and POWs. Their mission was to slip through the American lines, seize two key bridges over the Meuse River, switch signposts along the way, give American units erroneous directions, and generally sow confusion.

On December 12, Hitler gathered his generals near Ziegenberg Castle in Germany, 200 miles from the point where the attack was to begin. He had rejected the castle as too ornate a site for the soldierly task at hand. A camouflaged underground bunker nearby was safer and hidden from air reconnaissance. Hitler described the Allies as a mongrelized pack and said, "If we can deliver a few more heavy blows, then this artificially bolstered common front may suddenly collapse with a gigantic clap of thunder." Over 200,000 German troops, 600 tanks, and 1,900 field guns, observing total radio silence, had been massed in the rugged, thickly forested Ardennes. On December 16, Hitler launched *Wacht am Rhein*.

THE PREVIOUS OCTOBER, General Marshall had taken a tour through the Ardennes, retracing his footsteps during World War I. He concluded that a major offensive in this sector made no sense given Germany's continuing retreat. Fuel shortages alone, caused by Allied bombing of oil installations, made it unlikely that Germany could achieve enough mobility to go on the offensive. Nevertheless, there were signs of an enemy mobilization. Before the bad weather shut down air reconnaissance, Allied planes had spotted a steady flow of men and equipment crossing the Rhine, headed west. On December 10, Colonel Monk Dickson, First Army's intelligence chief, released Estimate 37. "It is plain," Dickson reported, "that [the enemy's] strategy in defense of the Reich is based on the exhaustion of our offensive to be followed by an all-out counterattack." But Dickson predicted that the Germans would strike over fifty miles from the Ardennes. On the morning of December 16, George Patton's intelligence officer, Colonel Oscar Koch, informed his superior that the Germans had imposed radio silence, and they knew what that usually meant. "I believe the Germans are going to launch an attack," he said, "probably at Luxembourg." Neither Patton nor Eisenhower nor other Allied leaders, given the information in hand, doubted that the enemy was on the move. They assumed, however, that the movement meant only that the Wehrmacht was girding up, not to go on the offensive, but to repel an expected Allied drive into the Ruhr, the seat of German industrial strength.

On December 16, Eisenhower summoned Omar Bradley to meet him at Versailles. Heavy losses in the previous months' fighting along the Western Front had left gaping holes in several divisions and replacements had to be found, especially after the War Department turned down Ike's request for 100,000 Marines. He and Bradley talked of stripping the rear echelons of all but the most indispensable personnel. Still, they discounted an immediate threat and took time to attend a wedding and a reception where they consumed oysters and other delicacies. Much of the conversation at the party centered on the fate of the band leader Glenn Miller, whose plane had gone missing after a flight over the English Channel in the same bad weather that had shut down Allied aerial reconnaissance.

Earlier that morning, Wehrmacht officers spread over a fifty-mile front were checking their watches. They had just delivered Field Marshal von Rundstedt's Order of the Day to their men: "Soldiers of the west front: Your great hour has struck . . . to achieve the superhuman for our fatherland and our Fuehrer." The Ardennes was blanketed in snow and the roads slick with ice. Fog clung to the ground, and clouds hung low from the sky, creating perfect conditions for a sneak attack. At 5:30 A.M., whistles shrieked, setting in motion the tramp of hobnailed boots and the creaking of tank treads. Four armies roared through the forest, quickly tearing a forty-mile hole in flimsy Allied defenses at a point where the Belgian, French, and Luxembourg borders converged. Absorbing the brunt of this blow was an undermanned front of 80,000 Americans, presumed safe from combat, men who had never heard an enemy shot fired, along with weary combat veterans pulled out of the line for a rest. Fast-moving German tanks and infantry drove a roughly triangular bulge into the American lines fifty-three miles deep, giving the battle its eventual name. The enemy quickly engulfed one untried unit, the 106th "Golden Lion" Division, inflicting 8,663 casualties, including nearly 7,000 men captured.

ON DECEMBER 19, three days since the launching of *Wacht am Rhein*, FDR returned to the White House from a three-week respite at Warm Springs. He went immediately to the Map Room, where he watched grim-faced officers moving red pins forward to mark the German advance and green pins back to mark the American retreat on the Western Front. Secretary of War Henry Stimson, who brought FDR updates from the War Department, noted in his diary that Roosevelt remained cool: "He doesn't seem to be too much discouraged."

AT 11 A.M. ON DECEMBER 19, an armor-plated Army sedan, shielded by military police in jeeps manning machine guns, pulled up before an old stone French barracks in Verdun. Eisenhower and his deputy, Beetle Smith, stepped out and went to the second floor. A potbellied stove struggled to repel the damp, penetrating cold. Outside, GIs huddled in long olive drab overcoats in bitter temperatures that would ultimately send 17,000 of them to the rear for frostbite. Drivers of vehicles started their motors every half hour to keep the oil from freezing. Eisenhower found Omar Bradley hunched silently and George Patton pacing like a caged lion. Ike immediately sought to set the tone. Scanning the grim visages, he ordered, "There will be only cheerful faces at this table." The situation, he said, was one of "opportunity, and not of disaster." As they huddled over maps, Patton, drawing his finger along the Meuse River, said, "Hell, let's have the guts to let the bastards go all the way to Paris. Then we'll really cut 'em off and chew 'em up." Patton's Third Army at this point was some forty miles south of the German attack. Patton was intemperate, a blowhard, and a frequent embarrassment to Eisenhower. Yet Ike knew why he tolerated the man. He turned to Patton, asking how long, under Bradley's supervision of course, it would take him to turn his eastward-facing army 90 degrees and head north to relieve the beleaguered Belgian city of Bastogne, crossroads of six crit-

ical intersecting roads, and faced with imminent encirclement. Patton told a skeptical Eisenhower that he could do it within forty-eight hours. Then, turning toward his superior and waving a cigar, Patton crowed, "Brad, this time the Kraut's stuck his head in the meat grinder. And this time I've got hold of the handle."

DURING THE BATTLE OF THE BULGE, American soldiers were introduced to the way the Germans waged war on the Russian Front. Nearly 150 GI POWs were marched into a field near Malmédy in Belgium and machine-gunned by men of a panzer unit commanded by Lieutenant Joachim Peiper with few escaping. Peiper had won his reputation on the Eastern Front where he reportedly captured villages, shot the inhabitants, and razed their homes to the ground. When Secretary Stimson brought the news to the White House of what came to be called the Malmédy Massacre, FDR thought for a moment, then responded, "Well, it will only serve to make our troops feel toward the Germans as they have already learned to feel about the Japs."

Skorzeny's faux Americans of Operation Greif stirred considerable havoc behind the lines, which forced American military police to set up numerous checkpoints where GIs were stopped and asked to name Mickey Mouse's girlfriend, who won the last World Series, or the first names of movie stars. An impatient Omar Bradley, held up at a checkpoint, was asked the capital of Illinois. "Springfield," he answered. No, the MP insisted incorrectly, it was Chicago.

Aware that the Germans had shifted divisions from the Russian Front to the Ardennes, Roosevelt heeded Eisenhower's request to ask Stalin if he might send a representative to Moscow to find out if "it is the Russian intention to launch a major offensive in the course of this or next month." Marshall saw the request as an acid test. He told Henry Stimson that if the Russians refused to help and the German offensive succeeded, the American people would have to "decide whether they wanted to go on with the war enough to raise the new armies which would be necessary to do it." Stalin craftily replied that he was willing to help, but expected a quid pro quo. He wanted more access to secret Western intelligence "that will be of mutual benefit."

Patton validated his seeming boast. On December 26, the trapped men of the 101st Airborne heard gunfire from outside their Bastogne perimeter. Near five that afternoon, Patton's Fourth Armored Division, after breaking through the German vise around the city, ended the siege. Brigadier General Anthony McAuliffe, who had won a measure of immortality by answering a German commander's earlier demand that he surrender with the single word "Nuts," rushed to meet his tanker saviors. "I'm mighty glad to see you," he greeted them. Once again Patton was the hero of the hour, enshrined again by the press. Still the fight raged on and as casualties mounted, American dead in the Bulge would eventually surmount 19,000. An alarmed FDR called in Leslie Groves, now a major general heading the Manhattan Project. The president, with Henry Stimson present, studied this jowly, cold-eyed, bulldog figure and said that as soon as an atom bomb could be ready, he wanted it dropped on Germany. The usually unflappable Groves looked for once nonplussed. A workable bomb, he answered, was months away.

Patton had argued all along for striking hard at the base of the German salient, but Eisenhower and Bradley, more cautious, were content with wearing down the bulge to its nub. Nevertheless, the forward motion of the Wehrmacht had been spent. On January 7, Hitler ordered his troops withdrawn from the Ardennes. As a German lieutenant, Rolf-Helmut Schröder of the 18th Volksgrenadiers, put it, "That's it—we've lost the war."

✳

THE FREEDOMS FOR WHICH AMERICAN troops were fighting and dying abroad had yet to fully penetrate their own society. Lena Horne, the beautiful, silken-voiced black singer, journeyed to Fort Riley, Kansas, to entertain the troops where she found that only white soldiers were allowed to attend her first show. In the era of segregation, she nevertheless accepted that situation, and the next day was to entertain black soldiers. At the second performance, to her puzzlement, the first rows of the theater were occupied by whites with blacks sitting behind them. Asking who they were, she was told they were German prisoners of war. She started to sing, but this slap at black GIs was more than she could bear and she stormed off the stage in a rage.

The bigotry in the military that Horne had run up against ran deep. A black corporal, Rupert Trimmingham, wrote to *Yank*, the GI magazine, "Here is a question that each Negro soldier is asking. What is the Negro soldier fighting for?" He recounted how, while traveling in the South, he and eight black soldiers were told by the lunchroom manager at a Texas railroad station to go around to the back of the kitchen if they expected to be served. As they did so, Trimmingham remembered, "About two dozen German prisoners of war . . . came to the lunchroom, sat at the tables, had their meals served, talked, smoked, in fact had quite a swell time. . . . If we are to die for our country, then why does the government allow such things to go on?"

George Marshall, who had come to appreciate the inequities black troops faced, attempted to alter racial attitudes. He approved the printing of 55,000 copies of a pamphlet written by the distinguished Columbia University anthropologists Ruth Benedict and Gene Weltfish entitled *The Races of Mankind,* to be used in basic training orientation. Its purpose, as described in *The New York Times,* was "to promote tolerance by teaching the fundamental unity of races and contending that economic differences were largely responsible for racial differences." Discovery of the Army's intention brought howls from conservative members of Congress. Representative Andrew May of Kentucky, still chairman of the House Military Affairs Committee, was incensed by a survey cited in Benedict's pamphlet stating that "the average Negro in New York, Massachusetts and Connecticut ranked on an intellectual level with the average white man in . . . Kentucky and Arkansas and Mississippi." The War Department dropped this minimal experiment in racial tolerance.

FDR received a memorandum from his navy secretary, James Forrestal, proposing a program for commissioning ten black women as

Navy officers in the WAVES who would then serve as a cadre for an all-black unit. Forrestal took pains to make clear that living quarters "will not ordinarily be shared with white women." Further, "Negro women will be detailed . . . preferably to stations where there are already Negro men." Though Mark Clark labeled black soldiers "the worst in Europe," an officer in Clark's Fifth Army commented that he was so strapped that he "would have settled for an orangutan." The pope requested that black GIs, risking their lives to liberate his country, be kept out of Rome.

Major General Edward M. Almond, a southern VMI graduate, commanded the black 92nd Infantry Division and was clear in his contempt. White officers commanded these men, since Almond believed that leadership and discipline were "characteristics that are abnormal to the race." His best officers, he said, were southerners, since they knew how to treat blacks. Almond ran his training camp like a plantation overseer. Upon addressing black soldiers being sent to the war zone, he told them, "I did not send for you. Your Negro newspapers, Negro politicians and white friends have insisted on your seeing combat." If that was what blacks wanted, he promised, "I shall see that you get combat and your share of casualties," a promise he kept by sending blacks into battlegrounds in Italy so perilous that the troops saw themselves as cannon fodder. In the face of such raw bigotry a surprising number of blacks managed to maintain a healthy outlook. "America wasn't perfect but it still was the best country in the world and it was being threatened by dangerous racist regimes that were a threat to my own people," wrote Vernon Baker, a black GI. Faced with flagrant injustice, Baker bolstered himself, saying, "I tried not to let this get to me. I focused on being a soldier and surviving."

George Patton was notified that a black armored unit, the 761st, was to be assigned to his Third Army. Upon the tankers' arrival, Patton, helmet gleaming, ivory-handled pistols strapped to his hips, adopting his war face, clambered onto a half-track, and told the men, "I don't care what color you are as long as you go up there and kill those Kraut sons of bitches." As he prepared to jump off, he said, "Damn you, don't let me down." The 761st went into action in Patton's drive for Metz and proved itself, in the judgment of its white officers, the equal of any white tankers.

The dashing service, the Air Forces, posed a formidable obstacle to would-be black fliers. One of Hap Arnold's generals advised him, "the Negro type has not the proper reflexes to make a first class fighter pilot." Nonetheless, spurred by black leaders and supported by Marshall, Hap Arnold permitted formation of an all-black pursuit squadron to be trained in Tuskegee, Alabama. Creation of the unit was, however, a hollow gesture to civil rights activists, since the blacks were never intended to fly in combat. Necessity broke the color barrier. A black captain and West Point graduate, Benjamin O. Davis Jr., son of the Army's first black general, was assigned to form the all-black 332nd Fighter Group. Davis, no stranger to prejudice, had endured four years at West Point during which time not a single cadet ever spoke a word to him. The black fliers became known as the Tuskegee Airmen, and flew P-51 Mustangs in the Sicily and Italy campaigns. They escorted bombers in the murderous raids on the Ploesti oilfields witnessing horrors so appalling that men vomited in their oxygen masks. Tuskegee Airmen protected planes striking deep inside Austria and Germany, and in 200 missions are believed never to have lost a bomber to German fighters. One hundred black fliers earned the Distinguished Flying Cross. Yet, in 1945, when a group of Tuskegee Airmen tried to enter an all-white officers club at Freeman Field in Indiana, they were arrested and thrown into prison for ten days until Marshall ordered their release.

Eleanor Roosevelt abhorred the bigotry. From the war's outset she had bombarded Marshall with appeals to do more for blacks. At her insistence, the War Department took a modest step, banning segregated recreational facilities such as baseball diamonds, basketball courts, and bowling alleys on military bases. When it appeared that the Tuskegee Airmen would never be allowed to leave the country, she had pressured Henry Stimson to let them fly in combat. She fought successfully to end segregation aboard buses on military bases, an early civil rights victory that presaged Rosa Parks's refusal to sit in the back of a bus over ten years later, ending segregation of public transportation. FDR, however, continued to lag behind his first lady on human rights. On February 5, 1944, he agreed to hold a White House press conference with black newspaper publishers where one journalist, Ira Lewis of the *Pittsburgh Courier,* charged that black soldiers "haven't been treated right by civilian police and by the M.P.s. We know of instances where soldiers on furlough have come home and taken off their uniform, on account of intimidation." Such an injustice, he said to the president, "is your responsibility . . . you alone can correct that." Roosevelt answered that his administration was dealing with the situation, but, "The trouble lies fundamentally in the attitude of certain white people—officers down the line who haven't got much more education, many of them, than the colored troops. . . . And, well, you know the kind of person it is. We all do." His response was hardly a ringing call for racial equality. The different pace between husband and wife on the issue of race can be explained by the fact that Eleanor Roosevelt did not have to contend with southern Democrat chairmen in the Congress upon whom FDR depended to enact his liberal agenda and to appropriate funds for the kind of war he wanted to fight.

ABSENT ANY PROOF THAT THEY POSED a threat to the country, 120,000 persons of Japanese ancestry, nevertheless, remained locked in relocation camps. By January 1943, Roosevelt softened to the extent of allowing men in these camps to enlist, which they did in droves. Marshall recalled in his reminiscences, "We had a [Japanese] battalion in Hawaii. Our commander out there . . . urged that we use those fellows." Recognizing the suspicion, however unfounded, that these soldiers might prove disloyal if sent to fight against the Japanese, Marshall "offered them . . . to commanders in Europe and . . . as I recall, Eisenhower's staff declined them." But in Italy, Mark Clark, despite his earlier disdain for black troops, responded, "We will take anybody that will fight."

The Hawaiian enlistees, mustered as the 100th Infantry Battalion, eventually joined with mainland Japanese volunteers, and together they formed the 442nd Regimental Combat Team. The regiment fought at Salerno, Anzio, Montecassino, and eventually Eisenhower accepted them in France. Its casualties began to approach 60 percent. Public opinion began to shift as the 442nd won a reputation as the "Christmas tree" regiment because of the number of decorations awarded, including 21 Medals of Honor, 5,200 Bronze Stars, 18,000 individual citations, and 9,486 Purple Hearts. In the meantime, their families remained imprisoned in some of America's harshest wastelands, hemmed in by barbed wire, watched over from towers mounted with machine guns, and guarded by GIs bearing fixed bayonets.

As manpower needs continued to rise, fear of Japanese disloyalty was suspended, partially at least, and FDR approved drafting men from the camps. Of the Japanese called up most went willingly. Others protested, of whom nearly 300 were sentenced to prison terms of three years. The president remained wary of the interned Japanese. After relocation had been in force for over two years, he told Secretary of State Stettinius, "The more I think of this problem of suddenly ending the order excluding Japanese Americans from the West Coast the more I think it would be a mistake to do anything drastic or sudden." Voices of reason, notably Eleanor Roosevelt, Harold Ickes, the secretary of the interior, and former Secretary of State Cordell Hull, began to break down the president's resistance. By the fall of 1944, 20,000 internees were being released every month. By December, FDR began allowing all Japanese Americans to return to the West Coast.

The American Civil Liberties Union branded the internment of the Japanese "the worst single wholesale violation of civil rights of American citizens in our history," and Executive Order 9066 remains an ineradicable stain on Franklin Roosevelt's legacy as a humanitarian. Three causes may explain this departure from his liberal political conscience. First, the treachery of the Japanese in wreaking death and destruction on the American fleet in a sneak attack on Pearl Harbor had dealt a blow to Roosevelt's pride as defender of the nation, and his outrage colored his view of all Japanese. Secondly, Roosevelt, ever the politician, yielded to pressure that he must do something to assuage the fears of Americans over the presence in their midst of people, whether citizens or not, whose skin and eyes looked like the enemy's. Finally,

FDR had been convinced ever since the fall of France, the Netherlands, Belgium, Norway, and Denmark that only disloyalty and subversion from within could have explained their swift collapse. He wanted to take no chance that the same could happen in America. Not until forty-six years after they had first been incarcerated did the Japanese families receive an apology and modest restitution from the U.S. government.

As casualties mounted, the immediate need continued to put more men in uniform, reviving a thorny issue between parents and draft boards. The boards had possessed the authority since early 1942 to draft eighteen-year-olds, and by 1943, teenagers were being drafted, which Paul V. McNutt, chairman of the War Manpower Commission, described as "scraping the bottom of the barrel." As ever during wars, the impact of military service fell unfairly. General Marshall, driving one day in civilian dress, offered a lift to a twenty-five-year-old antiaircraft crewman in suburban Alexandria, Virginia. He was appalled to find that the soldier had already spent two years safely in Washington. "We are holding here for practically the duration of the war young men who ought to be overseas," he told his personnel chief. Marshall was particularly incensed by the special treatment given athletes. He was outraged to learn of a big league catcher who had escaped active duty "because he had a couple of fingers broken. . . . It is ridiculous from my point of view to place on limited service a man who can catch, with his broken fingers, a fast ball." A catcher could certainly "handle a machine gun." He knew of numerous cases, he noted, of older men, "with a half dozen serious complaints," who had been drafted. "To find great athletes, football and baseball, exempted is not to be tolerated." He dashed off a directive to his personnel staff, "I don't want any damn nonsense about this thing." FDR, with four sons in uniform, took a special interest in the treatment of the well-born young men of his class. One day, out of the blue, he handed Frank Knox a list of Navy officers fighting their war behind Washington desks. The list read like the *Social Register:* Clarence Douglas Dillon, Ernest DuPont Jr., Leonard K. Firestone, Henry S. Morgan, Robert Sarnoff among them. Knox looked into the matter and reported back, "several of them have already been ordered to sea." FDR shot back, "why not order them all to sea."

★

EAGER TO HAVE AMERICANS UNDERSTAND the necessity for wartime sacrifices, FDR was much impressed by a British morale-boosting success. He wrote Churchill on March 17, 1943, complimenting the prime minister on a new British documentary, *Desert Victory*. He found it "about the best thing that has been done about the war on either side." He assured Churchill that the film "will be in the picture houses. Great good will be done." He arranged to have *Desert Victory* shown to the White House staff. He wanted it to run in defense plants. He chose first the Christie plant in Rahway, New Jersey, where the M-IV tank was manufactured, since its workers appeared in the film. He prized the opinion of the British and was shocked to read the results of a Gallup poll conducted in their country at the same time that he was singing the praises of *Desert Victory*. After giving the British navy fifty destroyers, after launching Lend-Lease before the United States had entered the war, after waging an undeclared war against the Nazis in the Atlantic, after American divisions had fought alongside the British in North Africa and Europe, he saw that Britons, when asked what country had made the greatest contribution to winning the war, ranked the United States last. Fifty percent chose Russia, 42 percent Britain, 5 percent China, and 3 percent the United States.

One element vital to home front morale, in FDR's view, was to keep hostility toward the enemy at a high pitch, lest Americans become complacent. He was furious when late in 1943 the Congress sent for his approval Joint Resolution 59 proclaiming December 7 "Armed Services Honor Day." "I consider the commemoration of the day fixed in the measure to be singularly inappropriate. December 7," he said, "two years ago, is a day that is remembered in this country as one of infamy." He vetoed the resolution.

A threat to morale rose from an unlikely source, music. Ever since 1942, a former cornet player, James Caesar Petrillo, scrappy president of the American Federation of Musicians, called his members out on strike to protest the failure of recording companies to pay royalties on copyrighted music. The strike had continued for twenty-six months and radio listeners were tired of hearing "I Dream of Jeanie with the Light Brown Hair" and other old refrains out of copyright. In March 1944 the War Production Board ordered Petrillo to send his musicians back to work. He thumbed his nose at the order. FDR intervened, appealing to the union leader's patriotic impulses and pleading that music was essential to home front morale. For once, FDR's blandishments failed. "We're not a war industry," Petrillo countered. The strike did not end entirely until November 11, 1944.

WHILE HIS SON JOHN WAS STILL at West Point, Eisenhower had written him, "I hope that no matter what happens you will get no foolish ideas about trying to resign . . . in order to get into more active service. As a cadet you have a very definite responsibility . . . on active duty, you would be just another second lieutenant." Young Eisenhower stayed on and graduated from the academy in 1944. He then spent a short leave at his father's headquarters. When it was over, Eisenhower arranged to have John flown back to the States aboard a B-17 to take up his duties at Fort Benning accompanied by staff aides and Kay Summersby. On their arrival, the passengers went their separate ways and Kay journeyed to Washington to call on Ike's wife, Mamie, at the residential Wardman Park Hotel. Mamie "greeted me at the door with a welcome, tinkling, orange-filled Old Fashioned," Kay remembered. Touring the capital, Summersby was astonished by the plenty in a country in the midst of war compared to the shortages and drabness in her own land. Kay was now an officer in the Women's Army Corps, proud to wear the uniform. Though most Americans showed her kindness, "Some of the Army wives I met this time left a bad taste in my memory," she recalled. "I was hurt, then angered at the slander of WACs overseas. . . . Some of the most social Army wives made it clear—crystal clear—they regarded any uniformed female overseas as a mere 'camp follower.'" She studied "these Washington wives in their smart frocks, nibbling luxurious foods, making cocktail talk, safe in one of the world's few unbombed cities," and thought of her fellow WACs, "working long and thankless hours overseas, often living in tents or buggy barracks. . . . I thought of Red Cross girls who got up before dawn to drive their Clubmobiles onto isolated airfields, distributing coffee, doughnuts and good American cheer to airmen taking off for possible death over Europe. I thought of the mutilated men I'd seen in hospitals, of the American nurses who worked day after day with those wounded." These well-fed, well-dressed, well-coiffed women who lumped "all overseas service women into one dirty group" were guilty of "woman's cruelest weapon against woman: moral slander."

TWO POINTS MAY BE CITED when Germany lost the war. The earliest occurred in 1941 when, ironically, the Reich appeared at its zenith. Though not apparent after early easy Nazi victories, the invasion of the Soviet Union laid the lid on Germany's coffin. Secondly, Hitler's declaration of war against the United States after Pearl Harbor nailed the lid down. Beaten in North Africa, losing in Sicily, retreating in Italy, driven across France, defeated at Stalingrad, invaded from east and west, suffering horrendous battle casualties, its cities in ruins, with civilians doomed to die in the hundreds of thousands, the baffling question persisted, why did Germany fight on? After June 6, 1944, and probably well before, every life lost, on both sides, was sacrificed needlessly.

During the First World War, after a do-or-die 1918 spring offensive failed and with its manpower depleted, the Germans surrendered on November 11 before a single yard of their nation had been taken or a home destroyed. The loss of life on both sides ended overnight. The World War II German generals were not a clutch of fools and read the signs of defeat as unmistakable. Field Marshal Rommel's Atlantic Wall, designed to hurl the Allies back into the sea from the Normandy beaches, had collapsed. His superior, Field Marshal von Rundstedt, commander in chief west, who had gone in and out of Hitler's mercurial favor, was beaten in the Battle of the Bulge. After the Bulge the Western allies occupied the first major German city, Aachen, and had driven to the Rhine. Marshal Georgi Zhukov's Red Army was on the Oder River, less than fifty miles from Berlin. From June to September 1944, Germany paid a terrible price for fighting on, with well over one million men dead, seriously wounded, or taken prisoner. Even before these defeats, on June 29, 1944, Rommel and von Rundstedt had decided to confront Hitler at the Berghof, his mountaintop retreat near Berchtesgaden. As they wound through the rubble of shattered cities, they agreed that the only sensible recourse was to make peace. "The war must be ended immediately," Rommel said. "I shall tell the Führer so, clearly and unequivocally."

Hitler had gathered his chief lieutenants in a room offering breathtaking views of the Bavarian Alps. Along with Rommel and Rundstedt were Field Marshals Göring and Wilhelm Keitel, General Alfred Jodl, and the navy chief, Admiral Karl Dönitz. When called on to speak, Rommel had said, "The whole world stands against Germany." As he began to explain the hopelessness of the situation, the führer cut him off in mid-sentence. Adolf Hitler was not a man swayed by cold logic but possessed unshakable faith in his own intuition. He began shrieking at Rommel. He was not there to give political advice, only to assess the military situation. Hitler's hands swept across a map spread across a table and spoke of thousands of new fighters joining the Luftwaffe, the navy blocking further invasion routes, and V-2s raining destruction on England. The tide was about to turn, he predicted. When Rommel made one last stab at reason, Hitler ordered him out of the room. Afterward, the field marshal glumly told a fellow officer, "I know that man. . . . He will fight, without the least regard for the German people, until there isn't a house left standing in Germany." Rommel, for all the adulation he enjoyed as Germany's stainless war hero, was remotely connected to the July 20 plot to kill Hitler and was later pressured to take a vial of poison to protect his family from reprisal.

Not a few Allied leaders cited Roosevelt's insistence on unconditional surrender as the reason Germany refused to quit. Allen Dulles, the OSS chief in Bern, Switzerland, reported, "Goebbels has twisted the slogan of unconditional surrender and made the people feel that the slogan means unconditional annihilation." Hitler, however, in private conversation with his inner circle acknowledged the real reason he would not capitulate. "Nobody will make peace with me," conditionally or unconditionally, he said. Goebbels was even more revealing in his diary when he wrote that the Nazi leadership "realizes what is in store for us if we show any weakness in this war. On the Jewish question especially, we have taken a position from which there is no escape." As Germany retreated, the enormity of the Nazi crimes that Goebbels spoke of became apparent. In July 1944, the Russians reached Majdanek, a concentration camp near the Polish city of Lublin, and found gas chambers and crematoria, huge piles of shoes, bales of hair, and machines for grinding human bones into fertilizer. Over 80,000 people had died in this camp alone, a fraction of the total savagery committed in pursuit of the Final Solution. Fearing their fate, Nazi diehards successfully exploited unconditional surrender as a rationale that the German people would accept for continuing the war. Which they did, continuing to do their jobs, obey their masters, and to the extent that chaos permitted, go about their daily lives despite constant bombing, unremitting bad news from every front, and casualties that touched almost every family. Rather than anticipating the end of the war, three million home guards, old men and boys, were training and expected to defend Germany to the death. Allen Dulles reported from his perch bordering the Reich that he had seen "no evidence that the German morale has been greatly affected by recent bombings. . . . There are in Germany millions of discouraged, disillusioned, bewildered, but stubbornly obedient people who see no alternative other than to continue their struggle." Astonishingly, German war production, under the organizational genius of Albert Speer, reached its peak in the fall of 1944 even as generals like Rommel and Hasso von Manteuffel were trying to salvage their country from ruin.

No one understood the Nazi game more clearly than Winston Churchill. In September 1944, in a break from the second Quebec conference, he had gone with FDR to Hyde Park where, in the Snuggery, he showed the president a statement that he wanted to send to Stalin. "At the present time, Hitler and his leading associates know that their fate will be sealed when the German army and people cease to resist," he wrote. "It therefore costs them nothing to go on giving orders to fight to the last man, die in the last ditch, etc., as long as they can persuade the German people to do this . . . they represent themselves and the German people as sharing the same fate." Churchill was suggesting that the Allies publish a list of the top Nazis, so that "the mass of the German people will infer rightly that there is a difference between these major criminals and themselves," thus removing their fear of what unconditional surrender might cost them. After discussing the merits, FDR decided against drawing such a distinction between the people and their leadership. For one reason, Roosevelt knew that, with victory won, Stalin intended to seize "several million Nazi youth, Gestapo, and so forth, for prolonged work of reparation" in the Soviet Union. FDR did not object to this plan, given the scale of atrocities and willful destruction perpetrated against Russia. But telling the German people they had no responsibility for the crimes of their regime and then sanctioning the deportation of millions of them could render the Allied cause hypocritical before the world, cruel and vengeful rather than just. Best to drop Churchill's suggestion.

Those who argued that unconditional surrender kept the Allies from negotiating an end to the war tend to ignore the fact that when an opportunity did arise, nothing happened. When anti-Hitler Germans attempted to assassinate Hitler and topple the Nazi regime in the 20th of July plot, not a single Allied leader in Britain or the United States trusted the plotters sufficiently to lift a finger in support. The Allies held back, not because they insisted on unconditional surrender, but because they believed the plotters would only substitute the belligerence of the Nazis with the belligerence of the German officer class, and the war would go on. Further, after the plot failed, virtually no one was left with whom the Allies could negotiate. Not a scintilla of renewed resistance occurred in Germany after the Gestapo hunted down and executed thousands of people however remotely connected to the plot. Ordinary soldiers suspected of desertion, insubordination, and defeatism were executed, as many as 5,000 every year. Heinrich Himmler, head of the SS, the Gestapo, and the concentration camps, decreed on September 10, 1944, that the families of deserters "will be summarily shot" as well.

Fear of punishment was not necessary to keep most ordinary soldiers fighting. They expected, not without reason, that defeat meant deportation to Siberia, violation of their women, and communist rule over their country. American psychologists polled German POWs and found as late as November 1944, even with the Allies now on German soil, that two thirds of them still supported Adolf Hitler. A poll of eighty-two captured German parachutists showed that forty-seven believed Germany could still win the war, thirty-two of them "certain" of victory.

One powerful argument that Hitler employed to continue resistance was to compare the fate of Germany with that of the West. "We've got everything at stake," he told his people. "If America says, 'We're off, period, we've got no more men for Europe,' nothing happens. New York would still be New York, Chicago would still be Chicago, Detroit would still be Detroit, San Francisco would still be San Francisco. But if we were to say today, 'We've had enough,' we should cease to exist."

And so, with defeat inevitable, Germany would fight on, though every man killed, woman widowed, and child orphaned would be for nothing.

FDR HAD BEEN PRESSING for another meeting of the Big Three since the fall of 1944, to resolve major issues yet to be settled. For one thing, he could not count on the experimental research under way in the New Mexico desert to produce a weapon that would end the war. Therefore, he must persuade Stalin to bring Russia into the campaign in the Pacific. Otherwise, his advisors warned him, Japan might not be defeated until 1946, or 1947, even 1948. Further, how was Germany to be dealt with postwar? What was to be the fate of Poland? Would Stalin join in FDR's dream of creating a United Nations, and on what terms? Roosevelt sought to have the meeting take place in November and wrote Churchill, "I have been thinking about the practicability of

Malta, or Athens or Cyprus. . . . The Mediterranean would be more convenient for all of us." To attend the Tehran conference in 1943, the impaired Roosevelt had traveled 17,442 miles while a robust Stalin had traveled 1,529 miles. The Soviet leader's explanation was that he dared not stay far from the Russian Front. Skeptics suggested that the real reason was that he feared domestic enemies behind his back more than foreign enemies in front of him. For the next summit, FDR believed he could persuade Stalin to join him at a more mutually convenient rendezvous.

FDR's ambassador to Moscow, Averell Harriman, went to Stalin to discuss a suitable site for the next gathering. Harriman suggested that the warmth of the Mediterranean might do him some good. Stalin replied that he had been warned that "any change of climate would have a bad effect." "While Stalin agreed that a meeting was desirable," Harriman cabled the president, "he was afraid his doctors would not allow him to travel." Roosevelt suggested Piraeus, Salonika, or Istanbul, but in the end yielded to Stalin's choice, Yalta on the Black Sea in the Crimea, which would require FDR to travel over 5,000 miles by sea and air versus 456 miles for Stalin coming from Moscow. Roosevelt asked that they meet in February, after Congress returned from its Christmas break and after he had delivered his State of the Union message. In January, Harry Hopkins while in London went to see Churchill and asked about Stalin's choice of Yalta. He relayed to FDR Churchill's reaction: "He says that if we had spent ten years on research we could not have found a worse place in the world than Yalta. . . . He claims it is good for typhus and deadly on lice which thrive in those parts." Churchill further told Hopkins that the only way he could survive there was by "bringing an adequate supply of whiskey."

On the morning of January 23, 1945, the president boarded the heavy cruiser USS *Quincy* at Newport News, Virginia. Among his party were Hopkins, Admiral Leahy, Dr. Bruenn, his cardiologist, former Supreme Court justice James Byrnes, now heading the Office of War Mobilization, and Edward Flynn, a Catholic and former Democratic national chairman, who was expected to bridge the divide between the Kremlin and the Vatican. Mrs. Roosevelt, yet to attend a major conference with her husband, had hoped to be invited this time, but FDR told her, "If you go they will all feel they have to make a great fuss." Instead, he chose to bring his daughter, Anna, now living in the White House as her father's Girl Friday handling a miscellany of duties, from filling his cigarette case to planning state dinners. Marshall and other military leaders traveled separately.

The president spent his days aboard the *Quincy* sunning himself on deck and watching movies, among them, *Our Hearts Were Young and Gay, Hail the Conquering Hero,* and recent newsreels. On February 2, the *Quincy* sailed into Malta, anchoring at the Grand Harbor in Valletta amid rusting hulks of vessels smashed when the Germans had made the island the most bombed spot on earth. From Malta he was to fly to the Crimea and by car to Yalta. To those who had not seen him recently, FDR's appearance came as a shock. Before leaving for Yalta, he had invited his sage friend Bernard Baruch to the White House for last-minute advice. Baruch noticed the president's hands shaking, which FDR explained, unconvincingly, by saying, "I had too many with the boys last night." When the British air chief, Sir Charles Portal, saw FDR, he wrote Pamela Churchill, the prime minister's daughter-in-law, "He is very thin & his face is drawn & deeply lined & he looks weary all the time. . . . he looks as if Truman might be in for a job of work." Usually a long sea voyage revived the president, but this time, another witness noted, "instead of improvement, there had been serious deterioration."

That evening in Malta, Churchill, who had arrived aboard HMS *Orion,* dined with the president aboard the *Quincy.* They were about to enter the cave of the Russian Bear, he reminded FDR, and "we ought to occupy as much of Austria as possible. . . . It was undesirable that no more of Western Europe than desirable should be occupied by the Russians." Later, in the dark of night, FDR traveled to Luqa Airfield outside Valletta and, still in his wheelchair, was hoisted aboard the specially adapted *Sacred Cow.* The entire party, American and British officers, diplomats, strategists, and service personnel, filled twenty-five transports, 700 people in all, making the flight to the Crimea.

Six hours and forty minutes later, the president's plane rolled to a stop on an ice-encrusted runway made of cinder blocks that the Russians had built at Saki Airport in the Crimea. The air was frigid and the president wore his heavy Navy cape draped over his shoulders during a hair-raising drive to Yalta in a massive black Packard equipped with a primitive heater, the automobile given to the Russians under Lend-Lease. A British officer had test-driven the route the week before and reported that two attempts had been turned back by a blizzard. He found the trip, the officer said, a "most terrifying experience." FDR's naval aide, Captain Wilson Brown, describing the president's journey, remembered, "The curves were short and sharp without retaining walls, and jutted out to the very edge of one continuous precipice." Shivering Russian soldiers stood at attention every 100 yards, saluting stiffly as the Packard passed by. Anna, gazing out at stolid peasant faces, remarked, "Look how many are girls." The president, for whom the swaying of a train could be agonizing, tried to catnap in the backseat but was jolted awake by the Packard's swerving and bouncing. He looked out on a spectacle of ruin, charred shells of buildings and blackened tree stumps, burned-out tanks, trucks, and upended railroad cars. The devastation, he told Anna, made him "even more to want to get even with Germany."

A chilled and much shaken presidential party finally arrived at Livadia Palace, two miles south of Yalta, site of the conference. Czar Nicholas II had built the white fifty-room Italianate residence in 1911 as his summer retreat. It had never been intended for winter occupancy. FDR was pleased to learn that, after the Revolution, the Soviets had converted Livadia into a rest home for poor tuberculosis patients. Three weeks before, the palace had been uninhabitable, sacked by the retreating Germans, shorn of all its furnishings, and infested with vermin. Since then the Russians had performed prodigies to bring Livadia back to its former glory, stripping Moscow's Hotel Metropol of its gilded furniture, heavy drapes, and chandeliers. The rehabilitation afforded the opportunity for Sergo Beria, son of Stalin's dread NKVD chief, Lavrenty Beria, to bug the guest rooms, including those of Roosevelt and Churchill.

The president was installed on the first floor in the only suite with a private bath. Czar Nicholas had shared these quarters with his hemophiliac son, Alexis. Harry Hopkins, at FDR's insistence, was installed in a room a few feet away, where the presidential confidant immediately collapsed onto his bed from which he was rarely to emerge except for formal sessions. Marshall was assigned the czarina's rooms in the floor above and Admiral King was given her boudoir, which prompted endless jests. The new occupants were informed that Rasputin, the czarina's Svengali, had climbed a ladder to this room to counsel and comfort her. Other accommodations were less sumptuous: sixteen colonels occupied a single bedroom and the president's daughter was given a small cubicle, "a block to the bath I'm supposed to use." As she passed through a dimly lit corridor a Russian officer groped her.

The conference followed a fixed routine. The American and British military chiefs, led by Marshall and Brooke, would gather in the morning to arrive at a common position before dealing with their Soviet counterparts. At lunch, the foreign ministers met—Eden, Molotov, and Stettinius. Roosevelt, Stalin, and Churchill, with senior staff, were to hold plenary sessions at five in the afternoon in the czar's alabaster ballroom, where counts and princesses had once waltzed. Dinner would follow at 8 P.M.

On February 4, just before the first session was to begin, a security agent wheeled the president to a massive round table in the ballroom. His early arrival was intended to give FDR time to swing himself from his wheelchair onto his seat before others could witness this maneuver. He signaled Hopkins, still deathly pale, to sit directly behind him. Charles "Chip" Bohlen, assistant to the secretary of state, a fluent Russian speaker, sat next to the president to serve as his interpreter. Roosevelt warmly greeted the conferees with an outstretched hand as they filed in. Stalin entered trailed by guards brandishing submachine guns. Stettinius, upon seeing the Soviet dictator for the first time, noticed that "his powerful head and shoulders set on a stocky body, radiated an impression of great strength." No formal arrangement had been made as to who would preside, though the participants deferred to FDR, who slipped into the role with easy authority.

A long, numbing recitation of the current military situation, delivered by handsome Aleksei Antonov, Soviet general of the army, opened the session. The proceedings finally came to life when Stalin raised his head from his doodling and began speaking in an unexpectedly harsh voice. He wanted it understood that his Red Army, though it had attacked to relieve pressure on the Americans during the recent Battle of the Bulge, had been under no obligation to do so. "I mention this only," he said, to show "the spirit of the Soviet leaders, who . . . acted on what they conceived to be their moral duty to their allies." Roosevelt and Churchill fell all over themselves thanking him and saying that they knew they could always count on Russia.

At dinner that evening, whatever privations the Russian people were enduring, the banquet tables sagged under bowls of caviar, smoked fish, venison, and pork, washed down with eight different wines. Throughout dinner toasts were raised to Allied victories. Stettinius caught Stalin watering his drinks. The once virulent anti-Bolshevik, Churchill, raised his glass to "the proletarian masses of the world." Roosevelt spoke of his hopes for a United Nations. Stalin saw the opportunity to note the disparity in representation in the proposed General Assembly. The Soviet Union had not fought this war to share parity with Albania, he pointed out. The massive, ethnically varied USSR deserved more than one seat.

The next day, at the second plenary session, the conferees took up the fate of postwar Germany. Occupation zones for the United States, Britain, and the Soviet Union had been worked out by the European Advisory Commission and ratified at Quebec the previous September. The president and the prime minister suggested giving France a piece of Germany to occupy. Stalin's retort was instantaneous. His nation, for the past three and a half years, had suffered death in the millions, while the French had folded in six weeks. What contribution had France made to victory? he asked. Churchill argued that Britain needed a strong, revived France to keep Germany hemmed in after the war. Privately, he confided to FDR that he needed a strong France as a bulwark against Russia. In the end, the leaders agreed that France would be given an occupation zone, but Stalin insisted that it be carved out of the American and British sectors, not from Russia's.

Stalin raised the matter of reparations. Soviet factories, rolling stock, and raw materials had been demolished in the early stages of the war. The Nazis had ravaged over 3,500 towns and villages, leaving millions homeless. Once victory was in hand, Stalin wanted to rebuild his nation by moving German plants, lock, stock, and barrel, to the Soviet Union, over 80 percent of the Reich's heavy industry. He expected monetary reparations as well. Why, he reasoned, should his countrymen, the victors, end up with a lower standard of living than the Germans, the losers? Roosevelt and Churchill pointed out how futile it had been to exact monetary reparations from Germany after the First World War. The United States wound up lending Germany the money to pay off France and Britain. A final decision on reparations was postponed. Realistically, as the war went on, confiscation would become a question of where the armies stood. Wherever the Russians became occupiers, they took whatever they wanted.

The fate of Poland dominated the third plenary session. The West had its Polish government-in-exile in London. The Soviets had installed their own proxy in the Polish city of Lublin. To Stalin, Lublin was the party of the people, while the London Poles were old-world reactionaries, hostile to communism. Even before Yalta, he had laid out his position: "Whoever occupies a territory also imposes on it its own social system." And by now, the Red Army had overrun most of Poland. Churchill objected to batting Poland back and forth like a political shuttlecock. "It must never be forgotten," he told the conference, that in 1939, "Great Britain had gone to war to protect Poland against German aggression," tactfully omitting that the Russians had been arm in arm with the Nazis in carving up Poland.

As at Tehran, deciding Poland's postwar borders again proved thorny. After the First World War the British foreign secretary, Lord Curzon, had suggested a frontier between Poland and the new Bolshevik regime in Russia that would have given the Soviets a substantial chunk of eastern Poland. When Germany and Russia divided up Poland in 1939, they largely adopted the Curzon Line. At Yalta, Stalin made a forceful argument, his longest to date, that he intended to stick to the line that the British diplomat had drawn over twenty years before. Roosevelt and Churchill went along, but argued that Poland had somehow to be recompensed. If part of Poland was to be given to Russia, then Poland should get a part of Germany. Shrinking the enemy's territory was easily agreed upon. Poland's prewar frontier with Germany was to be moved westward, generally following the Oder-Neisse Line, which would give Poland a huge swath of the Reich only thirty-five miles from Berlin and inhabited by nearly eight million Germans. Churchill agreed at the time, but would one day bitterly regret bowing to an arrangement that considerably enlarged a Poland fated to become communist.

FDR's failing health at Yalta was beyond disguising. His collar drooped around a corded neck. His hands trembled, his lips were purplish, dark pouches sagged beneath his eyes. His fingernails had a bluish tinge. His breathing was shallow and he spilled ashes down his suit as he smoked. Anna seized a free moment to write to her husband, "I have found out through Bruenn (who won't let me tell Ross [McIntire] that I know) that this 'ticker' situation is far more serious than I ever knew." She closed saying, "Better tear off and destroy this paragraph." Yet, when the third plenary session opened on February 7, with the future United Nations on the agenda, FDR came to life. Stalin agreed to participate in the international body, but set his price. Every one of the USSR's fifteen republics, he claimed, should be treated as a sovereign nation deserving its own vote. Churchill was initially receptive, generously comparing the Soviet republics to British commonwealth members such as Canada and Australia. By shrewdly asking for too much in the beginning, Stalin won agreement for two additional seats in the General Assembly, one for Ukraine and the other for White Russia.

On February 8 the conference dealt with the prime issue that had brought FDR to Yalta. During pre-conference preparations, Marshall had urged the president to press for "Russia's entry at as early a date as possible" in the war against Japan. The Manhattan Project could prove to be a $2 billion dud, and without the Russians, the Pacific campaign could drag on for years. Planners estimated that breaking the Japanese in their home islands could require five million American troops, with the prospect of tens of thousands of dead Americans carpeting the beaches of Kyushu and Honshu. D-Day for the invasion had already been set for November 1, 1945. Roosevelt met privately with Stalin in his Lavidia quarters to plea for help in the Pacific. Stalin responded that if he were to engage his country in still another war, he must have something to show for it. The Russians had already presented Harriman with a formidable shopping list: 500 locomotives, 6,000 freight cars, 64 ships, 500 transport planes, and 31,500 trucks, jeeps, and other vehicles in addition to the already massive American aid being provided through Lend-Lease. Further, Stalin wanted back the southern half of the Sakhalin Island, seized by Japan in the Russo-Japanese War forty years before, control over Outer Mongolia and the Kuril Islands, a role in Dairen in Manchuria, and the use of Port Arthur as a Soviet naval base. Stalin reiterated his promise that Russia would break its peace pact with Japan and come into the Pacific war sometime in June 1945 when presumably Germany would have been beaten. Admiral King exulted, "We've just saved two million Americans."

After the day's deliberations, the Russians outdid themselves, hosting a dinner at the Yusupov Palace, the former summer residence of a Russian prince, where it was said Rasputin had been murdered. The evening was leavened by the presence of three young women, FDR's daughter, Anna, Churchill's daughter Sarah, and Kathleen Harriman, whom FDR was delighted to hear had supposedly carried on a torrid romance with Franklin Jr. Forty-five toasts were raised. A genial Stalin lifted his glass and described Churchill as "the bravest government figure in the world," one who had led his country when "England stood alone. . . . I drink to Prime Minister Churchill, my fighting friend and a brave man." Churchill lavished his eloquence, toasting Stalin as "The mighty leader of a mighty nation, which took the full shock of the German war machine, broke its back and drove the tyrants from her soil." Stalin next waved a glass in FDR's direction and praised the president for conceiving Lend-Lease, and noted that "even though his country had not been directly imperiled, he has been the chief forger of the implements that have led to the mobilization of the world against Hitler." A beaming FDR gestured across the room, saluting what he called a "family gathering." The three Allies had joined, he said, in a common objective, to achieve "the possibility of security and well being for every person in the world." Washed away by the sea of *gemütlichkeit* was the fact that their host would have unhesitatingly shot any one of them who threatened his grip on power. Asked by FDR about Lavrenty Beria's role, Stalin replied with a sardonic laugh, "That's my Himmler." The evening ended at 1 A.M. when a tired but contented FDR was wheeled to his quarters. Harriman's daughter Kathleen wrote to her sister Mary in New York that while she had heard frequent comments about FDR's sickly appearance, she found him "absolutely charming, easy to talk to, with a lovely sense of humor."

Sanitary conditions at Yalta began to take a toll. After leaving the dinner, Admiral Leahy complained of "mosquitoes under the table that worked very successfully on my ankles." Churchill called in Lord Moran to treat the tormenting itch on his feet. The doctor marveled that "In this palace, with its gilt furniture, its lashings of caviar, its grand air of luxury," one enemy had proved unconquerable: vermin. Called to treat a sick Foreign Office deputy, Moran found "seven officers in a room . . . spread out on the floor, and bugs in all the bedding. . . . I telephoned the Americans and found they were in trouble too."

The final session opened on February 10, a chilly Saturday. Stalin again raised the issue of reparations, saying that Germany must pay for the agony it had inflicted on his country. Roosevelt had already described the futility of reparations and thought the issue settled. The conferees, however, were about to witness the steel in Stalin, who had chosen the Russian word for his own name. He "rose and gripped the back of his chair with such force that his brown hands went white at the knuckles," Lord Moran remembered. "He spat out his words as if they burnt his mouth. Great stretches of his country had been laid waste, he said, and the peasants put to the sword. Reparations should be paid to the countries that had suffered most. While he was speaking no one moved." Harry Hopkins, who had risen from his sickbed for the final sessions, slipped FDR a note. Since the Russians had given so much at the conference, he urged that the president should support them on this point. Roosevelt nodded, and the reparations issue, instead of dying, was referred to a committee.

A discussion arose over a ticklish and unanticipated issue. More than a million Soviet defectors were serving in the German army and a large number of civilians had fled Russia and were collaborating with the enemy. Stalin considered these people traitors who could not be allowed to grow like an anticommunist cancer outside his control. They must be returned to Russia, he demanded. The initial American position had been to allow expatriates who resisted returning to stay where they were. But the British had no problem with supporting Stalin's demand. In the end, both Western Allies gave in. The mass murder and imprisonment of thousands of alleged "enemies of the people" during the Stalinist show trials of the 1930s should have left little doubt as to the fate of resistant Russians forced to return to the Soviet Union.

At a small farewell dinner that evening, including only the principals, foreign ministers, and interpreters, Stalin addressed the one question that had been on all their minds, but no one dared ask: how could he have aligned himself with the monstrous regime of Adolf Hitler in 1939, especially given the Nazis' visceral hatred of communism and the Soviet Union? The Western Allies must see the pact as it looked to him, Stalin told them. When Britain's Neville Chamberlain signed the Munich agreement with Hitler in 1938, it looked to him as if Russia had been left alone to face Germany. In that disquieting position, he would rather have Hitler as an unnatural ally than as a natural enemy; hence their peace treaty.

On Sunday afternoon, February 11, the de rigueur farewell photo was taken, the principals bundled warmly, the president in his naval cape. The leaders sat down out of deference to Roosevelt's condition, an image that would become iconic for Yalta. Gifts were exchanged, huge tins of caviar and boxes of strong cigars from the Russians; commemorative medals struck by the U.S. Mint given by FDR to his hosts. The conferees had been advised, instead of tips, that Russians who had served them would much prefer cigarettes, candy, and chewing gum. Churchill and Stalin bade farewell to Roosevelt as he and Anna entered the Packard for the eighty-mile drive over twisting mountain roads skirting the Black Sea to the burned-out husk of Sevastopol, where FDR would board the *Quincy* for the trek home. Before leaving the

Crimea, he insisted on a tour of the field at Balaklava where the Light Brigade had been torn to pieces ninety years before.

At the time, Yalta won high marks. While en route home, FDR eagerly read a digest of public reaction radioed from the White House press office. *The New York Times* said editorially that the Yalta results "justify and surpass most of our hopes placed on this fateful meeting." The *New York Herald Tribune* noted, "The conference has produced another great proof of Allied unity." *The Washington Post* exclaimed, "The President is to be congratulated on his part in this all-encompassing achievement." Roosevelt's Republican opponent in 1932, former President Herbert Hoover, said of Yalta, "It will offer great hope to the world."

One event had marred FDR's triumphant return. Pa Watson suffered a stroke aboard the *Quincy.* The president summoned a Catholic Navy chaplain and arranged to have his loyal friend received into the Church, which he knew that Watson had planned to do to please his Catholic wife. "I just thought that Pa would like it," he told the priest. Two days later Watson died. FDR had lost what every burdened leader counts on: someone whose loyalty was unconditional, whose ambitions were subordinated to those of his chief, who possessed the common touch and common sense, a pal as well as an aide. Pa Watson had given FDR all this.

FOR MUCH OF HIS CAREER, Franklin Roosevelt had been denounced as a manipulator, a schemer, a Machiavellian, not always without reason. At heart, however, he remained an idealist willing to employ devious means to achieve desirable ends. Nowhere was his idealism more evident than on the issue of colonialism in the postwar world. In 1943, in Cairo, he told the prime minister, "You have 400 years of acquisitive instinct in your blood." The British, he charged, would take land anywhere, "even if it were only a rock or a sand bar." He warned that "A new period has opened in world history, and you will have to adjust to it."

FDR disapproved of Churchill's actions to bolster the monarchy in

Greece. On another occasion he told the old imperialist, "It would be a grand gesture if the British restored Hong Kong to China." Most aggravating to Churchill, FDR favored removing the jewel from the crown of the British Empire: the president supported independence for India. One of Bill Donovan's OSS analysts wrote what reflected FDR's thinking, that the British "have set themselves up as the master race in India. British rule in India is fascism; there is no dodging that." Roosevelt was particularly determined, when the war ended, that the French as well would not again climb onto the backs of colonial peoples in Indochina. In early 1944, he sent the following guidance to then Secretary of State Cordell Hull. "France has had the country—30 million inhabitants—for nearly 100 years, and the people are worse off than they were at the beginning. . . . France has milked it for 100 years. The people of Indo-China are entitled to something better than that." The loggerheads over colonialism marked most sharply the point at which the common will of the Allies to win the war collided with their divergent goals for shaping the postwar world.

FDR vented his views on colonialism aboard the *Quincy*. To break the voyage's tedium, he had invited to his quarters reporters who covered Yalta. One asked if it were true that Winston Churchill intended to undercut the Atlantic Charter's promise of self-determination for all peoples, including those under colonial rule. "He made a statement the other day," the reporter pointed out, "that it [the charter] was not a rule, just a guide." Roosevelt answered, "The Atlantic Charter is a beautiful idea." Dissatisfied, the reporter pressed on. "Is that Churchill's idea, on all that territory out there, he wants them all back, just the way they were?" "Yes," FDR finally admitted, "he's mid-Victorian on all things like that." The reporter continued, "You would think some of that would be knocked out of him by now." "Dear Old Winston will never learn on that point," FDR concluded. "He has made a specialty on that point." Then raising a finger to his lips, FDR said, "This of course is off the record."

By March 1, the president was back in Washington preparing a report to be delivered to Congress on Yalta. As he reviewed the record, his hopes for a United Nations had advanced with Stalin's agreement on the voting formula. The first session was to be held on April 25 in San Francisco. Agreement had been reached for a supposedly free and democratic Poland with a government representing the political spectrum from left to right. The Western Allies had managed to lift the French from the shame of defeat to a limited partnership by providing them a postwar occupation zone in Germany. Most satisfying to the president, though premature to discuss publicly, he had obtained Stalin's promise to make war against Japan within ninety days of Germany's defeat.

Only thirty-six hours after the president's return from Yalta, he entered the House chamber to address a joint session of Congress. His entrance raised discreet eyebrows. He did not approach the well of the House with his usual lurching semblance of a walk, clutching the arm of a son or aide. He was wheeled down the aisle in the old converted kitchen seat that he had used as a wheelchair for years. He did not stand at the rostrum supported by his braces, but pivoted from the wheelchair and hoisted himself onto an upholstered seat before a table bristling with microphones. The man who customarily behaved as though his impediment did not exist began with an apology. "I hope you will pardon me for the unusual posture of sitting down during the presentation of what I want to say," he began, "but I know that you will realize that it makes it a lot easier for me in not having to carry about ten pounds of steel around on the bottom of my legs, and also because I have just completed a 14,000 mile trip." His labor secretary, Frances Perkins, later wrote, "I remember of the moment, choking up to realize that he was actually saying, 'You see, I'm a crippled man.' . . . It was one of the things that nobody ever said to him or even mentioned in his presence." Roosevelt began, venturing a few light touches. Citing his long journey, he looked in the direction of his peripatetic wife and said, "The Roosevelts are not, as you may suspect, averse to travel," which was greeted by gales of laughter. Referring to his health at Yalta, he said, "I was not ill for a second, until I arrived back in Washington—and there I heard all the rumors which had occurred in my absence." He spoke for an hour, rambling and at times losing his place occasionally in his text. He reiterated his demand for unconditional surrender. "It means," he said, "the end of the Nazi Party and all of its barbaric laws and institutions," and it includes punishment of war criminals. The United Nations, he insisted, would correct the mistakes of the past. "Twenty-five years ago, American fighting men looked to the statesmen of the world to finish the work of peace for which they fought and suffered. We failed them. We cannot fail them again." As he reached his peroration his voice summoned the resonance of the old Roosevelt. Yalta, he said, "ought to spell the end of the system of unilateral action, the exclusive alliances, the spheres of influence, the balances of power, and all the other expedients that have been tried for centuries—and have always failed."

In years to come, foes of Roosevelt would paint Yalta as a shameless surrender to a Soviet tyrant, a giveaway of great swaths of Eastern Europe to the communists. During the Cold War, conservatives would raise the battle cry "No more Yaltas." Critics, many young or unborn at the time of the conference, would later grant themselves the gift of hindsight and condemn Roosevelt's blunders at Yalta, which they would never have committed. The truth, however, was that in 1945 a massive and victorious Red Army, far superior in numbers to the West, already occupied the lands supposedly given away by FDR to the Soviet Union. Nothing short of starting a war against Russia could have budged them. No serious Western leader at the time proposed such a move. As for Roosevelt's concessions to draw the Soviet Union into the war against Japan, only a psychic would have gambled in February 1945 that a bomb, as yet untested, would end the war and make Russia's entrance unnecessary.

Physically, Franklin Roosevelt at Yalta was a dying man, which raises the question of his mental capacity at the time. Was the president able to bring intellectually vigorous leadership to the table? Commander Bruenn, FDR's cardiologist, knew that his patient was suffering from advanced arteriosclerosis. His heart had become enlarged trying to pump blood through ever narrowing vessels. The constricted passageways delivered less nourishment to the brain, especially sugar, which could impair one's ability to think, concentrate, and absorb information. Two British witnesses declared Roosevelt a clueless participant at Yalta. The sharp-eyed, tart-tongued Lord Moran wrote in his journal, "Everyone seemed to agree that the President had gone to bits physically. . . . He intervened very little in the discussions, sitting with his mouth open." Moran concluded, "I doubt from what I have seen, whether he is fit for his job here." Churchill's air chief, Charles Portal, was more damning. Roosevelt "just blathered," he charged. "Honestly, FDR spoke more tripe to the minute than I have ever heard before, sentimental twaddle without a spark of real wit." Others disagreed. Averell Harriman found the president "worn, wasted . . . but alert." To Secretary of State Edward Stettinius, the "President looked better, seemed much calmer and more relaxed" than when the secretary had last seen him. The keen Chip Bohlen, who had to interpret the president's every utterance, and who would later advise seven U.S. presidents and serve as ambassador to the USSR and France, concluded that the president "was lethargic, but when important matters arose, he was mentally sharp. Our leader was ill at Yalta . . . but he was effective." Other Americans who worked closely with FDR at the time concluded, sick, yes, intellectually impaired, no. Evidence of Roosevelt's mental condition at Yalta is contradictory and conclusions depend on whether one is trying to paint him a dupe at the time or, more likely, still a cogent world leader.

CHAPTER 22

---★---

Leveling Japan, Invading Okinawa

MacArthur had launched the invasion of Leyte on October 20, 1944, the first stage in the struggle to liberate all the Philippines. Enemy losses willingly sustained in defending the island provided a harbinger of what lay in store to defeat the Japanese in their homeland. An estimated 48,700 soldiers gave up their lives. Only 798 surrendered. The 16th Division, which had carried out the infamous Bataan Death March in 1942, was wiped out to a man. American losses, while a fraction of the Japanese, were not insignificant; 3,320 men died and 12,000 more were wounded on Leyte. On January 8, 1945, MacArthur began the next phase, the invasion of Luzon, the largest of the Philippines and site of his earlier defeats. He described to his staff the victory parade he anticipated upon retaking Manila with himself at the head wearing his five stars as general of the army, the insignia fashioned by a Filipino silversmith from coins of the Philippines, the Dutch East Indies, and Australia.

The battle for Manila had combined elements of siege and massacre. The Japanese commander of the city, Admiral Sanji Iwabuchi, chose to commit 20,000 troops to a last-ditch stand. His forces barricaded every intersection, mined every street, rounded up civilians in droves and shot them, and repeatedly raped women regardless of age. Patients were tied to their beds and hospitals set afire. MacArthur sought to avoid destruction of his beloved city by barring air strikes. But American artillery pounded Manila into a shambles, block by block, with damage indistinguishable from what would have been wreaked from the air. On February 7, MacArthur, wearing a plain khaki uniform, saluted as the American flag was raised above Santo Tomas Camp, from which 3,700 men, women, and children had been rescued. Though liberated, Manila was a dead, smoke-shrouded husk, with 80 percent of its main residential district leveled, 100 percent of the business center razed, and 75 percent of industry gone. Dry blood caked the gutters where over 100,000 Filipinos died, one in every eight inhabitants. Manila was without electricity, water, or public transportation. When MacArthur reentered the penthouse apartment in the Malacañang Palace hotel that had once been his home, he found priceless furnishings smashed, including a vase the Japanese emperor had given his father in 1905, and the library reduced to a mass of charred volumes. Amid the debris lay a Japanese officer who had killed himself. MacArthur's subordinate, Lieutenant General Robert Eichelberger, whose Eighth Army had carried out much of the Philippines campaign, commented, upon looking out over the sea of destruction, "I understand the big parade has been called off."

The president and the JCS assumed that with Luzon taken MacArthur's ambitions in the Philippines had been sated. Instead, on his own hook, he launched invasions of seven more strategically insignificant islands. FDR and the chiefs accepted that MacArthur had handed them a fait accompli, and made no fuss, retroactively sanctioning the landings and approving three more. At their Pearl Harbor meeting in July 1944, FDR had allowed himself to be persuaded by MacArthur that the Philippine Islands must not be bypassed. Further, MacArthur had promised a relatively bloodless campaign, claiming, "Mr. President, my losses would not be heavy." Liberating the Philippines cost almost 14,000 American lives, hardly the dustup that MacArthur had predicted. Sixteen American divisions had destroyed a force of 450,000 Japanese defenders with less than 4 percent of the enemy surrendering.

Calculating the worth of MacArthur's Philippine venture is elusive. He would argue that beyond redeeming his promise to liberate the Filipinos, the campaign pinned down nearly half a million Japanese who were eventually killed, captured, or cut off. Further, he maintained that his over fifty amphibious landings provided invaluable lessons when the time came to invade Japan's beaches. He had also captured well-placed bases from which troops, after liberating Europe, could be mustered for the assault on Japan. These advantages must be weighed against the likelihood that the Japanese divisions in the Philippines could have been bypassed and the fighting that caused thousands of American casualties and took tens of thousands of Filipino lives in the course of their being liberated need never have happened. As Gerhard Weinberg, distinguished World War II historian, put it, those who questioned MacArthur's Philippine adventure "are likely to have the best of the argument."

GENERAL GEORGE MARSHALL, hardly a malevolent man, had no qualms about using poison gas, especially in the Pacific, where the Japanese were resisting so savagely. MacArthur shared the same view, stating that he could see "no reason why we should not use right now against Japan proper any kind of gas." Newspapers fired up public support for employing these poisons. The *Washington Times-Herald* proclaimed, "We Should Have Used Gas at Tarawa . . . You Can Cook 'Em Better with Gas." Though Franklin Roosevelt's exposure to war had been brief, in his two-month tour of the Western Front in 1918 he had seen enough to develop a repugnance for gas warfare. "I state categorically," he affirmed, now that he was president, "we shall under no circumstances resort to the use of such weapons unless they are first used by our enemies." Early in 1945, as plans for further Pacific invasions went forward, Marshall, fearing heavy casualties as in every previous confrontation with the Japanese, turned up the pressure on Roosevelt to change his stand. FDR stood firm and the use of gas was never seriously considered.

BY EARLY 1945, THE B-29 BOMBER, the Superfortress, a behemoth built specifically to blast Japan into submission, and on whose development more money was spent than on the Manhattan Project, $3 billion versus $2 billion, had become operational. The first B-29 put down on

Saipan on October 12, 1944, to the wonderment of GIs and Air Forces ground crews. Double the weight of a B-17, carrying twice the bomb load, the largest war plane in the world at that point, with a pressurized cabin that freed fliers from the necessity of wearing clumsy oxygen masks and bulky, heated flying suits, the B-29 was a slick, silver, death-dealing thing of beauty. The reason for which it had been built was realized when B-29s based on Saipan and other islands in the Marianas began flying the demanding 1,500 miles to Japan. The bombers could not expect fighter protection all the way since the P-51 Mustang lacked sufficient fuel for the entire mission. Crews of bombers damaged or running out of gas were condemned to ditch in the sea, with scant hope of survival.

Iwo Jima was a sliver of volcanic ash, the name in Japanese meaning "Sulfur Island." It was under five miles in length, three and a half miles at its widest, and less than a mile wide at its narrowest—in all, eight square miles lost in the vastness of the Pacific. Yet American air strategists eyed Iwo Jima covetously. The island lay less than 800 miles from the Japanese mainland. Iwo Jima could provide emergency landing fields for B-29s in trouble. The distance was short enough that Mustangs could escort bombers on their final leg to the target, and the island could provide airfields for shorter raids against Japan. Finally, Iwo Jima had a psychological attraction. It was essentially part of Japan, administered by the Tokyo prefecture. Thus this speck in the Pacific held an appeal out of all proportion to its size.

At nine on the morning of February 19, 1945, 30,000 men of the V Amphibious Corps, led by General Holland "Howlin' Mad" Smith, began to wade ashore. Thereafter followed an eerily familiar pattern in the Pacific. Days of naval and aerial bombardment had reduced Iwo Jima to a featureless landscape of seared stumps and charred cane fields. The island appeared deserted. Little reason existed to doubt the two-week timetable set for taking this objective. Geologists in the OSS did warn, however, that a loamy, greasy ash comprising the beaches would afford poor traction for armored vehicles or for men digging for shelter. Somehow the OSS analysis was lost. Within a half hour of the landing, 21,000 Japanese defenders began crawling from bombproof shelters into the bunkers honeycombing the island, from which they poured deadly fire onto Marines struggling for a footing in the soft soil. Instead of the scheduled two weeks, the battle for Iwo Jima went on for thirty-six days. When it was over, 6,821 Americans were dead and almost another 25,000 wounded, becoming the Marines' bloodiest battle thus far in the war. As one Navy chaplain noted, "At one time we had 400 or 500 bodies stacked up, awaiting burial." Japanese losses were shocking, not just because of the number of dead, over 20,000, but because only 200 of the enemy allowed themselves to be taken alive.

Shortly after the president's return from Yalta, his valet delivered to him the bulky Sunday edition of *The New York Times*. He, along with millions of Americans, was electrified by what he saw on the front page. Under the headline "Old Glory Goes Up over Iwo" was a perfectly composed wireless photograph of five Marines and a Navy corpsman amid the detritus of war raising the American flag over Iwo Jima's Mount Suribachi. The flagpole leaned at just the right angle; the flag was unfurled as an artist would have painted it. The flag raisers suggested poetry in motion. Actually, the photo was unstaged, spontaneous, a convergence of skill and chance. A diminutive AP photographer, Joe Rosenthal, had scrambled to the top of Suribachi just as a smaller flag was being lowered, to be replaced by one eight feet long and almost five feet wide that had flown over Pearl Harbor. Rosenthal caught the action out of the corner of his eye. As he later explained, "I swung my camera and shot the scene." He was unaware, in that split second, that he had captured one of the indelible images of the war. Rosenthal, unwitting of what he had achieved, next took a shot of cheering Marines standing alongside the flagpole, rifles raised over their heads in triumph, and assumed that this was the picture that the AP would put on the wire.

The White House press secretary, Steve Early, told the president that the flag raising photo had appeared on almost every front page in the land. The country's seventh war bond drive was about to begin in a nation that was growing weary of appeals to patriotic fervor. FDR immediately grasped the morale-boosting possibilities of so potent an image. He informed his treasury secretary, Henry Morgenthau, that he had ordered the six flag raisers brought home to lead the next war bond drive. The campaign turned out to be the most successful, netting $220 million, and Joe Rosenthal won a Pulitzer Prize for his photograph. The image appeared on the first-class three-cent stamp and countless posters. But only three of the flag raisers made it home for the celebration, Marines Rene Gagnon and Ira Hayes and Navy corpsman John Bradley. The other three, Franklin Sousley, Harlon Block, and Michael Strank, were killed in the fighting. To Americans at home, the combat veterans embodied what Admiral Nimitz had proclaimed: "On Iwo Island, uncommon valor was a common virtue," testified to by the twenty-seven Medals of Honor awarded, fourteen posthumously. George Marshall, an Army man grown weary of the heroic image of the Marine Corps, had once said, "I am going to see that the marines never win another war." But James Forrestal, the navy secretary, claimed that the photograph would ensure the Marine Corps' existence for another 500 years. This fleeting instant would be immortalized after the war in a 100-ton bronze re-creation of the flag raising placed near Arlington National Cemetery with figures standing thirty-two feet tall.

Iwo Jima prompted a modest step toward racial equality. The president issued an executive order directing that men volunteering for the Marine Corps were not to be turned away because of their race. Initially, the Corps leadership resisted, claiming that a Negro could never become "a real marine." The president's order stood, however, and at the far end of the Corps' Camp Lejeune in North Carolina, a facility for training black Marines was constructed, including barracks, training areas, medical facilities, movie theaters, and athletic fields, all purported to be equal to white installations, paralleling what southern blacks already knew at home, conditions separate and supposedly equal. Units like the Tuskegee Airmen had tasted combat, but black Marines on Iwo Jima initially experienced what they had encountered in other war zones, relegation to the margins of battle. They unloaded supplies, trucked ammunition up from the beaches, and buried the dead. But as combat losses mounted, they were sent into the fight cheered by exhausted white veterans. The blacks took heavy casualties, bleeding as copiously as their white comrades.

Justifying the Iwo Jima campaign involved the grimmest kind of wartime calculus. By its capture, Japanese planes were denied the island's airfields from which they had been able to harass B-29s en route to Japan. Instead, with the fields now in American hands, escort fighters protected bombers from Saipan, Tinian, and Guam on their last leg to Japan. The island, as planned, also served as a haven for stricken bombers. Nearly 2,400 B-29s made emergency landings on Iwo Jima, sparing their eleven-man crews from near certain death at sea. Finally, in taking the island, the United States acquired a base close to Japan for the forthcoming invasion. All this, however, had been purchased by the lives of over 6,000 men, their loss as devastating to their families as the joy of families whose airmen had been saved by emergency landings on Iwo Jima.

THE REFUGEE HUNGARIAN PHYSICIST LEO SZILARD had first pleaded with Albert Einstein to alert FDR to the destructive potential of an atomic bomb and of the catastrophic consequences should Germany achieve a nuclear weapon first. However, as Szilard saw the work at Los Alamos start to bear fruit, he began to suffer pangs of conscience. He went back to Einstein urging him to write another letter to Roosevelt raising the moral issue of using a weapon of such unimaginable havoc. Einstein agreed, but his letter asked only that FDR see Szilard, and closed, "I do not know the substance of the considerations and recommendations which Dr. Szilard proposes to submit to you." His oblique tone suggests that at this point Einstein had no moral compunction about using the bomb. Alexander Sachs, who had delivered Einstein's initial alert about the power of the atom in 1939, returned to the White House and urged that, "Following a successful test, there should be arranged a rehearsal demonstration" to be witnessed by an international body before the bomb was used against the enemy. Upon Sachs's departure, the president said that he would look into the matter. No record exists, however, that FDR responded to Szilard's or Sachs's appeal.

The qualms that Szilard and like-minded colleagues experienced over dropping the bomb on populated areas raised a fundamental question about weaponry. To the dead and their loved ones, do the means matter? Is there a more humane way to die in war? That conundrum was faced by Curtis LeMay, a burly, square-jawed Air Forces general who resembled a pit bull, with tenacity to match. LeMay was a self-made comer who worked his way through Ohio State in an iron foundry. Dazzled by airplanes since childhood, his flying career began when he earned an Army commission through ROTC. In 1937, he met the love of his life, the B-17. At age thirty, LeMay took part in a demonstration requested by FDR to see if the Flying Fortress could sink a battleship. In the World War II debate over aerial strategy, LeMay became a champion of daylight raids against selected targets, making the case by leading his own missions out of England. By 1944, he found himself in the Pacific in command of all air operations against Japan.

The issue in the debate over how best to defeat Japan was deciding which strategy would produce victory with the lowest cost in American lives. Hap Arnold remained convinced that airpower could win the war. The alternative was the estimated loss of as many as half a million men in a land campaign. Arnold believed that his Air Forces possessed, in the B-29 bomber, the weapon capable of doing the job. He began to lean hard on LeMay to produce better results in raids against Japan, or else, he warned, he would relieve him.

The key to accuracy in hitting a target, LeMay knew, was to fly at the lowest possible altitude. Instead of conventional bombs dropped scattershot from 30,000 feet as was then the tactic, he considered dropping a new type of explosive from an unimaginably low 5,000 feet. The weapon, recently developed by Standard Oil and DuPont, was a thick gasoline gel that stuck to whatever it hit and burned ferociously: napalm. Photo intelligence had revealed to LeMay that 90 percent of Tokyo was constructed of wood and paper, perfect for a napalm attack. He ordered 334 B-29s to be stripped of all guns and ammunition, the weight saved to be used to carry hundreds of small, six-pound cylinders of napalm. On the night of March 9–10, 1945, the Superfortresses took off from Guam, Saipan, and Tinian. With their defenses neutered and the altitude set below a mile, the fliers concluded that they were being sent to their deaths. LeMay's antiaircraft intelligence officers predicted plane losses of 70 percent.

That night in Tokyo, the city's five million inhabitants slept with no hint of what awaited them. Life in the capital was drab and food scarce as shipping losses cut imports to subsistence levels. Pumpkins were now a diet staple, and with meat in short supply, dogs had disappeared from city streets. In order to keep people at their civil defense posts, the military allowed few air raid shelters. The government tried to brighten Tokyo life by distributing sunflowers.

LeMay, in his operations center on Guam, received word that on the outbound leg to Tokyo the bombers had encountered almost no opposition. Still, his concept was so radical that he stayed up all night, fidgeting, pacing, sipping Cokes, and chewing on an ever-present cigar. The lives of over 3,600 airmen depended on his being right. Just after midnight, the B-29s reached Tokyo, swooped low, and for three hours dropped the incendiaries, again facing barely any resistance. With bomb bays empty, the B-29s headed home, leaving an inferno. Panicked by the smoke and heat of thousands of fires, people staggered through the streets seeking relief by plunging into rivers and canals, only to find the water boiling. In a single night, one quarter of the city's buildings and homes were burned to the ground, 267,000 in all. Photo reconnaissance showed sixteen square miles of the city reduced to a charred wasteland, the plain of ruin interrupted only by a few surviving steel beams of a hollowed-out building. Deaths were on so vast a scale as to defy measurement. No estimate, however, was lower than 80,000 and some as high as 120,000. Pilots returning from the mission claimed they could smell burning flesh. LeMay's gamble had produced the greatest loss of human life in a single day in the war, and likely in the long catalogue of human violence. Though prodded by pressure from Arnold, LeMay had conceived and executed the raid on his own hook. Arnold had not been alerted until the day before, past the point of no return. LeMay did not want to be overruled by his chief, and if the mission failed, he intended to assume all blame. Buoyed by success, LeMay next sent B-29s to shower incendiaries over Nagoya, Osaka, and Kobe as Japan began to experience the fate of Germany, the systematic obliteration of its cities, one by one. It still remained in the future to know how a successful atomic bomb might compare in lethality and morality to the holocaust inflicted on Tokyo on March 10, 1945.

A TIRED FDR WAS RESTING at Warm Springs in April 1945 when a signal corpsman brought word of the invasion of Okinawa, code-named Operation Iceberg. Fighting on Iwo Jima still raged as Admiral Nimitz's U.S. Pacific Fleet advanced nearly 600 miles west, forging another link in a chain running across the Central Pacific. Okinawa would put the invaders within 411 miles of the Japanese home islands. The campaign had three objectives: to starve the enemy by blocking merchant shipping from delivering foodstuffs to Japan, to put Japanese cities and military installations within reach not only of long-range Superfortresses but of medium-size bombers, and to seize another staging area for Operation Olympic, the invasion of Japan proper. Nimitz had never been enthusiastic about Okinawa as a stepping-stone, believing that the blockade, if tight enough, could force Japan to its knees without another battle. He viewed Iceberg much as Churchill did Overlord, envisioning beaches choked with the dead.

Okinawa was serpentine in shape, sixty miles long, eighteen miles at its widest, two miles at its narrowest, and ringed by coral. Unlike the lightly populated atolls, steaming jungles, and volcanic ash of other objectives, Okinawa, the largest of the Ryukyu island chain, was a fully developed society of city dwellers and farmers with a population of nearly half a million. The strategy for its conquest was to apply overwhelming force. The invasion fleet departed according to a pinpoint schedule from eleven ports on the U.S. West Coast, Hawaii, and the Philippines, timed to converge simultaneously at a small Pacific island. Soldiers leaning against the rails of the ships looked out on a flotilla disappearing over the horizon: battleships, carriers, destroyers, transports, minesweepers, oilers, tenders, over 1,500 vessels in all, every kind of craft necessary for the mission. The landing force of 150,000 men approximated the armies landing at Normandy. The defenders were estimated at fewer but strongly entrenched. Intelligence estimates projected casualties as high as 85 percent. The plan was to split Okinawa in the middle with two Marine divisions driving north from the invasion beaches into rugged, forested terrain, while two Army divisions headed south across rolling farmland to Okinawa's more densely populated southern tip. D-Day began on April 1, Easter Sunday.

The first 60,000 troops bobbed about in landing craft before receiving the signal to start for the beaches at 8:56 A.M. A young Marine, Eugene Sledge, who had survived the savagery of Peleliu, described Okinawa as "pastoral and handsomely terraced, like a postcard picture of an Oriental landscape . . . a patchwork quilt, with little farms and fields and rice paddies. . . . It was such a beautiful island." In this idyllic setting, future biographer and historian William Manchester, then a twenty-three-year-old Marine, remembered thinking, as the landing craft neared the beach, "My chances of becoming twenty-four were . . . very slight." Again, the initial wave found the landing so quiet that Major General Roy Geiger, commanding the Marine ground force, commented, "Goddam—this is April Fool's Day, all right!" The 110,000-man Japanese garrison employed its classic defense, emerging from bombproof subterranean tunnels into pillboxes and trenches to catch the enemy in an open field of fire. Three costly weeks passed before the Marines subdued the northern half of Okinawa. They then moved south, where the Army divisions were running into a fierce, bloody defense.

Six months before, sailors had stared in disbelief during the invasion of the Philippines as Japanese kamikazes deliberately crashed into their ships. By the time of Okinawa, the enemy had refined these early pinpricks into a far more murderous tactic. In order to survive, the Okinawa invasion force depended on resupply from the flotilla offshore, much as a body demands nourishment. The Japanese sailed the battleship *Yamato*, pride of their navy, and carrying only enough fuel for a one-way trip on a suicide mission. The dreadnought was to shell the American amphibious force at Okinawa, then beach herself while continuing fire support for the island's defenders. The tactic was also to lure American fighters and bombers into attacking the irresistible target. Once these planes were drawn off, the way would be clear for swarms of kamikazes and conventional aircraft to swoop down and destroy the unprotected American ships, cutting off resupply and abandoning Marines and infantrymen on Okinawa to their fate.

To young Americans, instinctively driven by the will to survive, the idea of Japanese initiating their own deaths seemed inconceivable. The kamikaze, however, were not mindless fanatics but for the most part educated youths motivated by deeply ingrained Japanese concepts of virtue, duty, family honor, love of country, and worship of the emperor. As one volunteer wrote his parents, "It is an honor to be able to give up my life in defense of these beautiful things." And give their lives they did. Flying from Kyushu, like plagues of locusts, the kamikazes swept on in waves of as many as 250 old Zeros aiming at a single American ship. In one twenty-four-hour period, April 6–7, over 7,700 Japanese planes, about 1,500 of them kamikaze, attacked the fleet off Okinawa. Defensive fire from American ships and fighter aircraft dotted the sky with fire-red puffs of exploding kamikaze. Still, half of the flying bombs got through, sinking 26 ships, battering another 164, and putting 3 carriers out of action. At Okinawa the U.S. Navy suffered its greatest losses in a single encounter in World War II, with 4,907 men killed, many burned to death by gasoline fires that the kamikazes ignited. The carrier *Bunker Hill*, its deck crammed with 34 fully fueled planes, took two kamikaze hits. In the resulting inferno, 576 men lost their lives. The American public was aghast upon learning that a single suicidal zealot could sink a ship or put a massive carrier out of commission. Admiral Bull Halsey sought to put the threat into perspective. The damage inflicted "at the price of one pilot and one ramshackle plane seems to be a bargain," he noted. But that price was skewed. According to Halsey, "our statistics show that of all the kamikazes attempting to dive on us, about 1 per cent succeeded; the rest either crashed harmlessly or were shot down. The true price therefore becomes 100 pilots and 100 planes," not one. In the end, the proud *Yamato* was sacrificed much like any kamikaze pilot. Without air cover, the monster vessel became an easy mark. Wave upon wave of American planes, 386 in all, pounded the ship, scoring ten torpedo hits, until like a harpooned whale the ship rolled over and sank, carrying most of her 3,300-man crew to their deaths. Only 269 *Yamato* sailors survived.

✶

THUS FAR IN THE PACIFIC, the peculiar organizational hybrid had persisted under which MacArthur commanded both Army *and* naval forces within the Southwest Pacific Area while Nimitz commanded Navy *and* Army units within the Pacific Ocean area. But as the big push neared for the invasion of Japan, FDR discussed with the Joint Chiefs changes to create cleaner lines of authority. On April 5, 1945, MacArthur was given control of all Army forces throughout the Pacific and Nimitz control of all naval units, an action *The New York Times* described as "the most important military command decision since the invasion command for Europe," and one that made clear "there will be no 'Eisenhower'—or Supreme Commander—of the Pacific."

The fighting on Okinawa dragged on for nearly three months. The military casualties that the Japanese were willing to absorb were stupefying, 120,000 dead, including the Japanese commander, General Mitsuru Ushijma, killed by his own hand. Most disturbing and incomprehensible to the Americans during the campaign was the conduct of Okinawan civilians. The island people had been indoctrinated to believe that the invaders would plunder, torture, rape, and in the end murder them. Rather than submit to this fate, many, even mothers clutching babies, flung themselves from steep cliffs to their deaths on the rocky coastline below. Over 12,500 Americans died in taking the island, including General Simon Bolivar Buckner Jr. commanding the 10th Army, killed by an artillery shell. To replace Buckner, George Marshall chose a general whose talents, he believed, had been squandered and whose pride had been bruised in China, Vinegar Joe Stilwell.

Okinawa was a battle of superlatives, the greatest fleet assembled in the Pacific, the largest contest of planes against ships, the highest loss of American vessels in a single battle, the heaviest toll of American battle deaths against the Japanese in a single campaign, the highest

Japanese losses, and, proportionately, the greatest amount of killing in the smallest space in the Pacific war. The ferocity of Okinawa augured chillingly for the invasion of Japan.

HALFWAY AROUND THE WORLD, Hermann Göring, chief of Germany's Luftwaffe, had been impressed by the kamikazes. Three hundred Luftwaffe volunteers were recruited and trained in a ten-day course at a base near Stendal, where they learned how to ram American bombers. The unit was designated *Sonderkommando Elbe,* "Special Unit of the Elbe." While the Okinawa campaign was still in its first week, 143 Me-109s, their radios blaring patriotic music, took off intending to smash into a formation of 1,300 Eighth Air Force bombers. The result was disastrous, but not for the Americans. A wall of fire from American fighter planes and gunners met the *Sonderkommando Elbe* and only twenty-one enemy planes returned. The German zeal for heroic self-immolation cooled instantly.

CHAPTER 23

★

To Take Berlin?

THE CITY WAS CALLED "THE FLORENCE OF THE ELBE," A SEAT OF SAXON kings, settled by the Germans 700 years before and steeped in a medieval past. One hundred miles southeast of Berlin, Dresden rose like a jewel of Baroque and Rococo architecture, its skyline limned by needle-like church spires and onion domes, a cultured town distinguished by its opera house, museums, and art galleries. Graceful arches spanned the River Elbe, which meandered through the city's center. The future American novelist Kurt Vonnegut Jr., a POW during the war, recalled arriving at Dresden in a boxcar and, when the door was opened, glimpsing "the loveliest city that most of the Americans had ever seen." Until 1945, Dresden had largely been spared the bombing raids that were pulverizing other German cities. Two minor attacks had inflicted little damage. Dresden's major industry was the manufacture of precision optical instruments, while the city's military significance consisted almost solely of a railroad marshaling yard through which German troops moved. Allied strategists, however, saw the city differently. General Marshall cited intelligence reports describing Dresden as "a center of a railway network and a great industrial town." Further, it was believed to be "a communication center of major importance through which reinforcements pass to reach the Russian front." The Russians, Marshall knew, wanted the city bombed.

The night of February 13 was one of muted celebration in Dresden. In the old days, Shrove Tuesday, Carnival, was an occasion for unbridled merrymaking. With the Red Army approaching, however, almost every house, the railroad station, the streets were jammed with thousands of refugees, each with a tale of atrocities committed when the Russians had captured their town. Only a bedraggled circus and knots of little girls in fancy dresses suggested carnivals of the past.

At 9:55 P.M. the air raid siren sounded and people began shuffling into shelters. Fourteen minutes later, 796 RAF Lancaster bombers in two waves blanketed Dresden with high explosives and incendiaries. At daylight 300 American B-17s pounded the already reeling city, and the next day another 211 struck. Hundreds of separate fires merged into one firestorm that sucked the oxygen from shelters, stirred hurricane-force winds, and drove the temperature in places to 1,000 degrees Fahrenheit so that even pavements melted. Fire burned out thirteen square miles of the city and the glow could be seen in the sky 200 miles away. German Transocean Radio announced after the raids, "Today we can only speak of what was Dresden in the past tense." In the following days, victims were piled by the tens of thousands in raglike heaps to be burned. How many perished will never be known with precision, particularly given the influx of unregistered refugees. The highest death toll, cited by Nazi propagandists at the time, was 200,000. In recent years, scrupulous research supported by the Dresden city government has put the figure at 25,000.

The Allies, most notably General Harris's Bomber Command, had long since practiced a policy of deliberately attacking population centers. The chief of the U.S. Air Forces, Hap Arnold, and his commander of American Air Forces in Europe, Tooey Spaatz, professedly championed strategic bombing. But when bad weather shrouded targets, the bombers dropped their loads indiscriminately. Further, they joined in RAF missions whose unvarnished objective was to bomb civilians. As Arnold expressed it, area bombing was justified "when the occasion warrants."

By no stretch of the imagination could Dresden be described as militarily significant, especially with the war's end so near. Then why the raid? During the First World War, British Tommies, stalemated in the trenches, would sing, "We're here because we're here because we're here . . ." As Germany sank to its knees, Allied fliers might well have sung, "We bomb because we bomb because we bomb . . ." The most chilling reason for bombing Dresden was simply that the Allies were running out of cities to crumble. Long years afterward, Dresden would become an antiwar rallying cry to prove that the Allies committed crimes equally as heinous as the Nazis. The moral revulsion may explain why, of all the major British wartime leaders, only Bomber Harris failed to be knighted. While the incineration and asphyxiation of thousands of human beings can only be described as horrifying, the question arises, how different was the fate of Dresdeners from that of people in almost every German city of any size, including Berlin, where the week before an estimated 35,000 died in a single night's raid—or Augsburg, Bremen, Cologne, Düsseldorf, Essen, Frankfurt, Hamburg, Karlsruhe, Leipzig, Munich, Regensburg, Schweinfurt, or Wilhelmshaven?

Germany was to know even more ruin from the sky. On February 22, 1945, a week after Dresden, an air armada took off from fields in England, France, Italy, Holland, and Belgium, over 10,000 aircraft destined to hit 200 targets over a quarter of a million square miles of the Reich. The objective was to paralyze Germany by knocking out rail heads, bridges, canals, and, unstated but inevitably, to continue the obliteration of German cities and their inhabitants. No record exists that FDR ever expressed himself specifically on Dresden or other bombed cities. But he did not object to any measure, except for poison gas, that would help defeat the enemy. He told Stimson, "every person in Germany should realize that Germany is a defeated nation."

THE DEBATE OVER THE SPEAR POINT versus the broad axe persisted into 1945. Sir Alan Brooke, now a field marshal, argued with Eisenhower that the Allies lacked enough power to sustain multiple broad-based frontal assaults. The Western armies, Brooke believed, vigorously seconded by Montgomery, should knife across the Rhine and drive to Berlin. Unengaged divisions should remain in place, ready to shield the attacking force from counterattack. Eisenhower himself recognized the risk in attempting too many simultaneous fronts, since, as Clausewitz warned, "Dispersion is one of the greatest crimes in warfare." But Ike,

a pragmatist, believed that commandments, when the situation war-
ranted, were meant to be broken. The broad axe would continue to
strike along a wide front.

ON MARCH 10, 1945, *The New York Times* reported on the front page
what FDR had learned the day before from the Map Room: "Bridge
over Rhine Seized with 10 Minutes to Spare." The river had thus far
presented the last natural barrier to an Allied sweep through the enemy
heartland. The Rhine was turbulent, fast-flowing, spinning with eddies
and whirlpools, over a third of a mile wide at points, and a challenge to
amphibious operations. The Germans had already blown up Rhine
River bridges at Cologne, Coblenz, and Bonn. Spanning the river between Remagen on the west bank and Erpel on the east bank stood
four frowning Gothic towers holding up the Ludendorff Railroad
Bridge. As tankers of the Ninth Armored Division rolled into Remagen, they stared in disbelief. The Ludendorff Bridge was still standing.
The Germans had set four that afternoon as the hour to blow it up. The
time was ten minutes before four. Engineers and infantrymen of A
Company, 27th Armored Infantry Battalion, raced across the bridge,
drove off the defenders, and cut the wires set to detonate explosive
charges under the bridge's supports. Troops and vehicles began pouring across in division strength. Outraged over the defenders' failure to
destroy the bridge, Hitler fired one of his finest soldiers, Field Marshal
von Rundstedt, who only months before had been entrusted with command of the Ardennes offensive. Within ten days, enough time for the
Americans to secure a foothold on the east side of the river, the bridge,
creaking and groaning under the weight of tanks, bombed and strafed
by the Luftwaffe, sank beneath the waters of the Rhine.

ON THE SAME DAY THAT THE NINTH ARMY crossed the Rhine, George
Patton's Fourth Armored Division, just to the south, after a mad sprint
of fifty-five miles in under two days, reached the river near Coblenz.
Another prong of Patton's Third Army pushed toward the city of

Mainz. As one correspondent put it, "Patton's forces seemed to be everywhere at once." On the night of March 22, twelve days after the Ludendorff Bridge had been taken, Patton's men managed to cross the Rhine. The next evening he put through a call to his chief, General Bradley. "Brad," Patton exclaimed, "for God's sake tell the world we're across.... I want the world to know Third Army made it before Monty." The next day Patton led his staff onto a swaying pontoon bridge over the river. Halfway across, he stopped, unzipped his fly, and proceeded to relieve himself in the Rhine while GI cameras recorded the moment. On the opposite bank he dropped to the ground and scooped up German soil into his hands, exclaiming, "Thus William the Conqueror."

Patton had earlier made a diary entry in which he wrote of Eisenhower, "So far in my dealings with him, he has never mentioned in a complimentary way any action that myself or any officer has performed." He noted that the supreme commander "had on his new five stars—a very pretty insignia," while he still had only three. After Patton's sweep across the Rhine, Ike said on their next meeting, "George, you are not only a good general, you are a lucky general, and as you will remember, in a general, Napoleon prized luck above skill." Patton replied, "Well, that is the first compliment you have paid me since we served together." After this encounter Patton told his staff why Ike had finally commended him. "Before long, Ike will be running for President. . . . You think I'm joking. I'm not. Just wait and see."

The assignment of sons of major leaders in wartime posed ticklish questions. Sons of the highly placed did die in the war: Marshall's stepson, Allen Brown, killed in Italy; Harry Hopkins's son, Stephen, killed at age eighteen in the Pacific. The son of General Alexander Patch died while serving in his father's Seventh Army. Patch was so devastated that he seemed for a time incapable of carrying out his duties. That March, Second Lieutenant John Eisenhower had orders to Europe as an infantry platoon leader. To avoid the semi-paralysis that had struck "Sandy" Patch after his son's death, young Eisenhower, to his chagrin, was assigned a staff job that kept him out of combat. The determination, however, in a democracy's citizen army not to show favoritism was strong. In a brazen display of favoritism, Patton, the racing commander who had breached the Rhine, the rescuer of Bastogne, FDR's much-admired scrapper, ordered an action that raised questions about his mental balance, left even his supporters shaking their heads, and stained his name once again. Lieutenant Colonel John Knight Waters, Patton's son-in-law, had been taken prisoner in Tunisia in 1943. Patton was later to deny that he knew with certainty that Johnny Waters was one of the POWs held in a German camp outside Hammelburg, Oflag XIIIB, some forty miles beyond the American front. On March 26, Patton's order was passed along to the commander of his Fourth Armored Division, William Hoge, to cross the Main River and rescue prisoners from the camp. Hoge resisted, but Patton insisted. On the night of March 26, a force of 294 men accompanied by sixteen tanks moved out, meeting little initial resistance. As the tanks smashed through the gates of Oflag XIIIB, 1,291 Americans, including Waters, were momentarily freed. Quickly, the Germans mounted a counterattack during which Waters was near fatally wounded when a sniper shot the lower section of his spinal column. He was recaptured along with hundreds of other POWs. Only a handful of prisoners made it back to the American lines. Of the 294 men who set out on the rescue mission, nine were killed, thirty-two wounded, and sixteen missing in action and presumed dead. Upon learning of Patton's escapade, Omar Bradley commented, "He knew damn well if he asked me for permission, I would have vetoed it. Because it was a foolhardy thing to do."

Ten days later, Patton's army overran Hammelburg, freeing the POWs for good, including Lieutenant Colonel Waters. While eighty ex-POWs awaited medical treatment, Patton had his son-in-law airlifted aboard a Piper Cub to Frankfurt for treatment. He arranged personally to decorate Waters with two silver stars. Waters asked Patton if he knew that he was being held at Oflag XIIIB before ordering the rescue mission. Patton answered, "I didn't know, but thought you might be there." The response was not entirely true. According to one witness, when Hoge resisted Patton's initial order, he was told that "John Waters, Patton's son-in-law, was one of the prisoners." Further, Patton had sent along with the rescue party an aide, Alexander C. Stiller. When asked why he was being included, Stiller answered, "Because I'll recognize Johnny Waters." Patton's Hammelburg folly had been far more serious than the slapping incidents in Sicily. The latter had cost men their pride, but they would return home. Hammelburg had cost men their lives who would never return home. Eisenhower informed George Marshall only that Patton had "sent off a little expedition on a wild goose chase in an effort to liberate some American prisoners." Ike further admitted that Patton had tried to hush up the matter by censoring the press, but "The story has now been released and I hope the newspapers do not make too much of it." Eisenhower closed his report saying, "Patton is a problem child, but he is a great fighting leader." Within weeks of the matter Patton was promoted to full general, four-star rank.

✶

In November 1942, Jan Karski had given FDR a firsthand account of what the Nazis were perpetrating in the concentration camps and had begged the president to intervene. Roosevelt's solution at the time was, "Tell your nation we shall win the War." In 1944, a respected administration figure, John J. McCloy, relayed to the president the appeal of Jewish organizations asking for concrete action to end the extermination. McCloy was a tough-minded forty-nine-year-old World War I veteran and lawyer whom FDR had appointed, with Henry Stimson's sponsorship, as assistant secretary of war. Jewish leaders pleaded with him to persuade Roosevelt that the U.S. Air Forces bomb railheads leading to German concentration camps and even strike the camps themselves to interrupt the machinery of mass death operating within them. Many years later, McCloy, at age ninety-three, in an interview with historian Michael Beschloss, claimed that he had brought the issue before FDR in August 1944, and Roosevelt, in McCloy's telling, rejected the idea, saying it "wouldn't have done any good. . . . Why, the idea! They'll say we bombed these people, and they'll only move it down the road a little way and [we'll] bomb them all the more. . . . I won't have anything to do [with it]."

By the time that McCloy had spoken to the president, the industrialized murder of Jews, Gypsies, and communists at Auschwitz, Bergen-Belsen, Mauthausen, and dozens more camps had been documented beyond dispute. Roosevelt took one modest step, a warning to the Nazis. He had Sam Rosenman draft an admonition released on October 18, 1944. "Germans!" it began, "There are within your midst large numbers of persons in forced-labor battalions and concentration camps." Whether the victims were "Jewish or otherwise," the German populace must "disregard any order from whatever source, or otherwise harm or persecute any of these people. . . . We shall expect to find these people alive and unharmed. Severe penalties will be inflicted upon anyone who is responsible, directly or indirectly, in large measure or small, for their mistreatment."

Jewish appeals to bomb the camps continued, but got nowhere. Eisenhower and Marshall opposed the idea, as did Hap Arnold, whose bombers would have to do the job. Churchill and the British generals showed no enthusiasm, giving a stock answer that attacking the camps would require a diversion of airpower that should be spent solely to bomb Germany into submission. Concentration camp survivors who would have been under those bombs, among them Elie Wiesel, the later Nobel laureate, maintained that the risk was worth the effort. "To see the whole works go up in fire—what revenge!" Wiesel noted. "We were not afraid. And yet, if a bomb had fallen on one block alone it would have claimed hundreds of lives on the spot. We were no longer afraid of death; at any rate, not of that death." Another camp survivor, Viktor Frankl, later a distinguished psychiatrist, claimed that bombing the camps would have given inmates, whose lives already appeared forfeited, the will to survive. Why did FDR and the others reject bombing the camps? A genuine concern not to divert airpower from its major mission? Indifference toward the fate of a historically persecuted people? Lingering doubts over the credibility of reports of atrocities on so vast a scale? The answer is difficult to disentangle from the web of possibilities. Part of the answer lies in FDR's overarching vision of the war. While the president unhesitatingly made global strategic decisions, he was disinclined to second-guess his commanders on tactics.

FDR viewed Nazi bestiality in terms of crimes to be prosecuted after the war. In January 1945, he had told Rosenman "he did not want to see the record of the First World War repeated, where it had taken years before anyone was ever brought to trial." That effort had indeed been a fiasco. A list of 4,900 alleged war criminals had soon been whittled down to 901, then to 12 who were ordered to stand trial in a German court in Leipzig three years after the war. Three defendants simply failed to show up. The others received wrist slap sentences. "This time," Roosevelt told Rosenman, "let's get the trials started quickly and have the procedures worked out in advance. Make the punishment of the guilty swift." He then dispatched Rosenman to London to discuss with the Allies arrangements for trying war criminals.

By the spring of 1945 the reality of mass murder was confirmed firsthand as advancing Allied armies liberated concentration camps. The leading radio broadcaster of the day, Edward R. Murrow, brought into American homes what he witnessed upon the liberation of Buchenwald. "Men and boys reached out to touch me; they were in rags and the remnants of uniforms. Death had already marked many of them. . . . I looked out over that mass of men to the green fields beyond where well-fed Germans were ploughing." In one reeking corner he saw "rows of bodies stacked up like cordwood. They were thin and very white. Some of the bodies were terribly bruised, though there seemed to be little flesh to bruise." After the war, Germans accused of murder in the camps offered the defense that they were compelled to carry out orders or face punishment themselves. The defense was specious. Those who resisted doing the deadliest work were assigned other tasks. Further, the German soldier's pay book stated that unlawful orders need not be obeyed.

FDR was largely right about the effectiveness of bombing the camps. When rail lines bringing victims to extermination camps were struck in the course of routine air raids, the Germans repaired the damage within hours, or failing that, victims were trucked in or marched to their deaths. Nor would these raids have deterred an obsessed Hitler from continuing to pursue the Final Solution, which he did to the very end. From the standpoint of morale and morality, however, FDR was probably mistaken to reject bombing of the camps. How many otherwise doomed lives the raids would have saved or cost is unknowable. Nevertheless, sparing a few planes to attack the camps, while having a negligible effect on the overall air campaign, would have had powerful symbolic significance. Had FDR agreed, he would certainly have burnished his reputation in history's judgment.

PRIOR TO YALTA, HENRY STIMSON had shown FDR a troubling report from Major General John R. Deane, heading the U.S. military mission to Moscow. Deane had dealt with Stalin and Soviet officialdom for a year and confided his disillusionment to the secretary of war. "When the Red Army was back on its heels," he wrote, "it was right for us to give them all possible assistance with no questions asked." But the Soviet victory at Stalingrad and subsequent triumphs had reversed the dynamic. "They are no longer back on their heels; and if there is one thing they have plenty of, it's self-confidence. The situation has changed, but our policy has not. We still meet their requests to the limit of our ability, and they meet ours to the minimum that will keep us sweet." He had been "nauseated," he said, by "banquets featuring endless toasts to American-Russian friendship where the vodka had to go down past the tongues in the cheeks. . . . After the banquets, we send them another thousand airplanes, and they approve a visa that has been hanging fire for months." No Russian official with whom he worked closely had ever invited Deane to his home, apparently fearing the consequences of socializing with a capitalist emissary.

When the Russians conquered Ploesti in Romania, General Ira Eaker, chief of Allied Air Forces in the Mediterranean, asked if he might send a team to assess how effective bombing of the city's refineries had been. He received no answer. After torturous negotiations with the Russians, Ambassador Harriman had won permission for American aircraft to use Soviet airfields to conduct shuttle bombings of Germany during the summer. When Harriman sent the Kremlin a request to arrange for a similar shuttle in the winter, he received no answer. When he requested permission for U.S. trucks to pass through Russia to supply U.S. airbases in China, again the answer was silence. In a report to

FDR, he condemned Russia's "ruthless attitude toward the uprising in Warsaw and their unyielding policy towards Poland." He concluded, "our generous attitude toward them has been misinterpreted as acceptance of their policies and as a sign of weakness. . . . There is every indication that the Soviet Union will become a 'world bully' wherever their interests are involved unless we take issue with the present policy."

By the spring of 1945, the shotgun marriage between East and West began to unravel. The worst breach occurred, not on the Eastern or Western Fronts, but in Italy. Fighting up the Italian boot during the previous twenty months had been dogged, with the Germans absorbing over 27,000 casualties and giving up every mile grudgingly in the face of inevitable defeat. In March an ebullient Wild Bill Donovan briefed FDR on an extraordinary opportunity to end the war in Italy. Donovan had been informed by his man in Bern, Switzerland, Allen Dulles, that Field Marshal Albert Kesselring, the Luftwaffe's former star tactician and now commanding ground forces in Italy, might be receptive to unconditional surrender in his sector. Though loyal to Hitler thus far, the field marshal was no sycophant and possessed an independent streak. Allen Dulles code-named these deliberations Operation Sunrise. The promising contact was broken off when Hitler dispatched his private plane to bring Kesselring to the Western Front as Rundstedt's replacement. The connection, however, was not severed completely. After Kesselring's departure, an SS general in Italy, Karl Wolff, a whole-souled Nazi who had happily dispatched Italian Jews to Auschwitz, offered to continue talking surrender with Dulles.

Upon being briefed by Donovan on the peace feelers, FDR directed Harriman to inform the Russian foreign secretary, Molotov, that a major front might be neutralized. Molotov's reply shocked the president. The foreign minister, following Stalin's orders, demanded that Russian officers be allowed to participate in the negotiations or else the talks must not go forward. On March 24, Roosevelt cabled a top secret appeal to Stalin, explaining that the United States could not ignore a peace tender from the enemy in Italy. "It would be completely unreasonable for me to take any other attitude or to permit any delay which must cause additional and avoidable loss of life in the American forces," he told Stalin. He drew a parallel. When Russian troops had recently trapped German forces at Königsberg and Danzig and forced their surrender, the United States had made no demand to be involved. Henry Stimson was more blunt. He advised FDR that the surrender of the Germans in Italy was "a matter in which Russia has no more business than the United States would have at Stalingrad." Stalin responded to the president with the harshest words yet in their wary partnership. No equivalency could be drawn between Italy and Königsberg-Danzig, Stalin maintained. The enemy in that pocket was surrounded and could not have been shifted elsewhere. But in Italy, "the Germans have already used these negotiations ... in shifting three divisions from northern Italy to the Soviet front." To Stalin, surrender in Italy might mean victory for the Anglo-Americans, but a strengthened enemy facing the Red Army. FDR answered, "I feel that your information about the time of the movements of German troops from Italy is in error." Yes, three divisions had been transferred to the Russian Front, he acknowledged, but "more than two weeks before anybody heard any possibility of surrender" in Italy.

On April 3, Stalin fired off an even more brutal rejoinder to FDR, then at Warm Springs. He charged that Kesselring, in his new western command, "has agreed to open the front and permit Anglo-Americans to advance to the east, and the Anglo-Americans have promised in return to ease for the Germans the peace terms." He was charging, in effect, that despite all Roosevelt's repeated avowals to fight until unconditional surrender, the Western Allies were ready to sell out Russia and make a separate peace with Germany. How was it possible, Stalin wanted to know, that the Germans had left the bridge over the Rhine at Remagen standing, unless they wanted the Americans to get across? "The Germans on the Western Front have in fact ceased the war against England and the United States," he maintained. "At the same time they continue the war against Russia." FDR called in Leahy and Marshall and showed them a draft of what he next intended to tell Stalin: "I cannot avoid a feeling of bitter resentment towards your informers ... whoever they are, for such vile representations of my actions or those of my trusted subordinates." Stalin's reply ratcheted up the acrimony.

Why, he asked, did the Germans "continue to fight savagely with the Russians for some unknown junction, Zemlianitsa in Czechoslovakia which they need as much as a dead man needs poultices, but surrender without resistance such important towns in central Germany as Osnabrück, Mannheim, Kassel. Don't you agree that such a behavior of the Germans is more than strange and incomprehensible?" He went further. He accused General Marshall, in February, of deliberately misleading the Red Army by providing spurious intelligence about a forthcoming attack on Pomerania when, in fact, the Germans attacked south of Budapest. Stalin characterized Marshall's action as "one of the most serious blows of the war." In lodging this charge, Stalin was accusing his allies not simply of bad faith, but of outright treachery. So incredulous was FDR that the Soviet leader could believe such a thing that he instructed Harriman to find out if Stalin had originated these words himself or had they been written by some Kremlin apparatchik. Harriman reported back that the words and the sentiments were Stalin's. A shaken FDR began to express to confidants his growing disillusionment. At a lunch including a longtime labor advisor, the Hungarian-born Anna Rosenberg, he leaned over to her and whispered, "Averell is right. We can't do business with Stalin." He told Anne O'Hare McCormick, a foreign correspondent for *The New York Times,* "that he had fully believed what he said in his report to Congress on the Yalta conference agreements. But he had found that Stalin was not a man of his word." He confessed to another associate that "Stalin has been deceiving me all along." Amid this rancor, Allen Dulles continued to try to move Operation Sunrise forward, which he and his chief, Bill Donovan, believed would mark the crowning achievement of the OSS in the war.

THE CONQUEST OF BERLIN would seem the ultimate expression of Allied victory, an inescapable signal to the German people that the war was lost. FDR strongly wanted the city taken. Well before D-Day, as the Russians advanced from the east, he asserted that "there would definitely be a race for Berlin. . . . We may have to put United States

divisions into Berlin as soon as possible." In sketching out postwar occupation zones, he initially included Berlin in the U.S. sector. Eisenhower at the time shared the same views. In November 1944, a month
before the Bulge, when the advance of the Americans and British across
Western Europe seemed unstoppable, Ike wrote to Montgomery,
"Clearly Berlin is the main prize. . . . There is no doubt whatever, in my
mind, that we should concentrate all our energies and resources on a
rapid thrust to Berlin. . . . Simply stated, it is my desire to move on
Berlin by the most direct and expeditious route, with combined U.S.-
British forces." Winston Churchill had said at one point, "I say quite
frankly that Berlin remains of the highest strategic importance."

In September 1944, the Red Army had been camped outside Warsaw, 300 miles from Berlin. The Western Allies in France were roughly
the same distance away. A race to Berlin at this point seemed a fair
contest. But by March 1945 the situation had altered. The Russians
were on Germany's doorstep. Ike met with reporters on March 2 in his
current headquarters, a former technical school for boys in the French
cathedral city of Rheims, where one correspondent asked, "Who do
you think will get to Berlin first, the Russians or us?" "Well, I think
mileage alone ought to make them do it," he answered. "After all, they
are 33 miles and we are 250." Clearly, Eisenhower's earlier resolve that
Berlin was the main prize had begun to waver. He consulted the sober-
minded Omar Bradley and asked how many casualties Berlin might
cost. Bradley answered 100,000, and added, "a pretty stiff price to pay
for prestige." Bradley's estimate raised the specter of tens of thousands
of telegrams from the adjutant general's office going out to families
across America reading, "The Secretary of War desires me to express
his deep regret that . . ." Another factor figured in Eisenhower's thinking. The Allies had earlier created the European Advisory Commission
to work out occupation zones once Germany was defeated. The lines
drawn were ratified at the Big Three conferences in Tehran and Yalta.
Regardless of where the armies stood at the war's end, the Allies had
agreed to withdraw to their assigned zones, even if it meant giving up
ground taken. Eisenhower, bound by the occupation agreement, found
it indefensible to expend the lives of GIs and Tommies in taking a city

solely for a fleeting moment of glory. He told Marshall, "Through bombings and transfer of governmental offices . . . Berlin itself is no longer a particularly important objective. Its usefulness to the Germans has been largely destroyed and even their government is preparing to move to another area." He told his staff that his mind was made up. He was fighting this war militarily, not politically, and militarily Berlin had no value. If he did not intend to take the capital, he believed that he had an obligation to inform the Russians so that East-West strategies could be coordinated. On March 28 he took the unusual step of communicating directly with Stalin. He asked the chief of the American military mission to Moscow, General Deane, to hand-deliver a message to the Soviet ruler explaining that Berlin did not figure in his strategy. His plan was to push along the Leipzig–Dresden line, almost 100 miles south, "to divide the enemy's remaining forces by joining hands with your forces."

Eisenhower's decision had been influenced by reports coming out of OSS Bern that die-hard Nazis were hewing a "National Redoubt" from the mountain fastness where south Germany bordered western Austria, a stronghold where SS fanatics, sustained by huge stores of buried arms, ammunition, food, and fuel, would fight to the death and, in the assessment of the OSS, extend the war anywhere from another six months to two years. A further assessment from Bern reported that the redoubt could "hold 15–25 divisions composed of SS storm troop detachments" and zealous Hitler Youth. Donovan informed FDR that Swiss newspapers were printing maps showing the outlines of the redoubt. Thus far, Donovan's operation had achieved a mixed record, from silly tricks to gathering intelligence that made Dragoon, the assault on the south of France, "the best briefed invasion of the War." Eisenhower took Donovan's warning seriously. Marshall concurred. The Nazis had already displayed stunning resiliency in the Bulge and, "if the German was permitted to establish the Redoubt," Ike concluded, "he might possibly force us to engage in a long-drawn-out guerrilla type of warfare, or a costly siege." Hitler could "keep alive his desperate hope . . . to be able to secure terms more favorable than unconditional surrender. . . . I decided to give him no opportunity to carry it out." By joining with the Russians south of Berlin, thus splitting Germany in half, Eisenhower reasoned that he could then turn south and stamp out the threat of a National Redoubt.

It would be difficult to conjure more joyous news for Stalin than to learn that Eisenhower did not intend to move on Berlin. Ambassador Harriman reported to Ike Stalin's reaction to his message. Practically parroting Eisenhower's words, Stalin told Harriman that he agreed with Eisenhower that "Berlin has lost its former strategic importance. The Soviet High Command therefore plans to allot secondary forces to its capture." He assured Harriman that the Red Army's major emphasis would be to link up with Eisenhower somewhere in the vicinity of Dresden. In truth his generals were massing 1.25 million Russian troops on the Oder-Neisse front, less than thirty-five miles from Berlin. Five hundred tanks and artillery were crammed along every mile of the front. On April 1, Stalin summoned to his private study in the Kremlin two of his best tacticians, Marshal Georgi Zhukov and Marshal Ivan Konev. He goaded them, falsely claiming that the American and British forces were headed for the German capital. "Who is going to take Berlin," he asked, "are we or are the Allies?" Konev answered, "It is we who shall take Berlin. And we will take it before the Allies."

Churchill and his generals were furious upon discovering that Eisenhower had communicated directly with Stalin. The day that Brooke learned of Ike's action, he wrote in his diary, "he has no business to address Stalin direct, his communication should be through the combined Chiefs of Staff." Two days after Eisenhower's message to Stalin, Churchill sent a long cable to Roosevelt bending over backwards to express "the complete confidence felt by His Majesty's government in General Eisenhower." But, "I say quite frankly that Berlin remains of high strategic importance. Nothing will exert a psychological effect of despair upon all German forces of resistance equal to that of the fall of Berlin." He then expressed his worst fear. If the Russians "take Berlin, will not their impression that they have been the overwhelming contributor to our common victory be unduly printed in their minds, and may this not lead them into a mood which will raise grave and formidable difficulties in the future? I therefore consider that from a political standpoint we should march as far into Germany as possible and that should Berlin be in our grasp, we should certainly take it." By now, Churchill's expedient amity toward the Soviet Union was approaching the vanishing point. Russia "had become," he feared, "a mortal danger to the free world." He told Eisenhower, "I deem it highly important that we should shake hands with the Russians as far to the East as possible."

An ailing Roosevelt, still at Warm Springs, and aware of the casualty estimates for taking Berlin, was disinclined to second-guess Eisenhower. He cabled Churchill that, under Ike's plan, German forces would be "completely broken up," leaving the Allies in a position to "destroy in detail the separated parts of the Nazi Army." Churchill persisted, telephoning Eisenhower and demanding to know why his goal had been changed. He insisted that taking Berlin was not just a political ploy, but militarily essential, since, "Whilst Berlin remains under the German flag, it cannot in my opinion fail to be the most decisive point in Germany." Kay Summersby, upon entering Churchill's message in Eisenhower's office log, noted that it had "upset E. quite a bit." An angered Eisenhower laid it on the line in a message to Marshall. His decision to skip Berlin, he said, was purely military, but if the Combined Chiefs of Staff insisted on a political campaign to take the capital, "I would cheerfully readjust my plans and my thinking so as to carry out such an operation."

Montgomery found Eisenhower's decision to forgo Berlin galling. Not only would this gamecock be denied the capital, now only some seventy miles away from his forces, but he was expected to sit on the sidelines while the Russians took the city. Instead of unleashing him, Ike weakened him, ordering that the U.S. Ninth Army, thus far under Monty's command, be returned to General Bradley, shrinking the field marshal's 21st Army Group almost in half. Churchill lamented that with victory within Monty's grasp, Eisenhower had left his scrappiest fighter "in an almost static condition." A disgusted Montgomery, now reduced to protecting Bradley's northern flank, dismissed the likelihood that Stalin had been straight with Eisenhower. He told Ike, "I consider that Berlin has definite value as an objective and I have no doubt that the Russians think the same; but they will pretend that this is not the case." He further endorsed the conclusion of British intelligence that "the so-called National Redoubt . . . should be dismissed as a factor on which to base strategy." George Patton agreed. When a reporter asked him about the purported fortress in the mountains, he answered, "I think that it is a figment of the imagination. Just a good word." On April 3, Omar Bradley, usually cautious, and despite Eisenhower's decision not to take the German capital, ordered William Simpson's Ninth Army to "exploit any opportunity for seizing a bridgehead over the Elbe and be prepared to advance on Berlin." Patton estimated that Simpson could be in Berlin in forty-eight hours. The Ninth was advancing at breakneck speed and by early April was at Magdeburg, about sixty miles from the capital. At this point Simpson and Marshal Zhukov were roughly the same distance from the bunker where Hitler had gone to ground, with the Russian having a slight edge.

Churchill led FDR to believe that he had capitulated on Berlin. On April 5, he cabled Roosevelt, "I regard the matter as closed and to prove my sincerity I will use one of my very few Latin quotations, 'Amantium irae amoris integratio est.'" FDR immediately asked Leahy to look up the translation, and the admiral came back with, "Lovers' quarrels are an integral part of love." Still, Churchill the old soldier understood that strategic decisions need not be forever. The Russians might be closer to Berlin, "but the Germans were entrenched on the Oder and much hard fighting was to take place before they could force a crossing and resume their advance," he believed. As Allied troops drove more swiftly than expected through crumbling German resistance, he asked Eisenhower to come to London and meet him at 10 Downing Street. Churchill, "upset and even despondent," Eisenhower remembered, kept questioning the supreme commander's decision. Ike told him that, if such were the case, he should appeal to FDR. Otherwise, "I alone had to be the judge of my own responsibilities and decisions." Eisenhower then issued an order that ended the debate. American forces, including Simpson's, were to stop at the Elbe.

Eisenhower's judgment to forgo Berlin has been described by historian Stephen Ambrose as "his most controversial decision of the War." As seen by critics through the rearview mirror of history, Ike and Roosevelt had been suckered into giving up the most glittering prize, one that would have said to the Russians, "Here we draw the line." This retroactive wisdom proved handy for Cold Warriors over the next two generations. Given Eisenhower's situation at the time, did he commit a geopolitical blunder? Could he have agreed to what Churchill was essentially saying: Don't worry about occupation zones. Take all you can, including Berlin, and we'll hold it. At this point the Red Army had three times as many divisions as Eisenhower. The Russians, reeling back to the gates of Moscow in 1941, were now poised to crush what had once been the most vaunted army in the world. Stalin could be expected to bleed as much of his army as necessary to take Berlin and hold on to Russia's conquests, including Poland and the Balkans. According to Soviet records, 81,116 Red Army soldiers were killed taking Berlin while no GI or Tommy died there.

Might the Western Allies, by taking Berlin and refusing to pull back to prearranged occupation zones, have triggered war with the Soviet Union, and could the West have won? Possibly. Had the Anglo-American forces taken Berlin, another victory medal would have been struck, a campaign ribbon awarded, exultant headlines produced, and grand parades held down Unter den Linden with the Stars and Stripes, the Union Jack, and the Tricolore flying overhead. And then, unless a fresh world war was to be risked, all parties would retreat to the agreed-upon occupation zones, which gave the Western Allies part of Berlin 225 miles inside the Russian zone. Eisenhower later described his dilemma. If his armies had taken territory destined for the Soviet zone, and the Russians demanded it back, "I cannot see exactly what the British have in mind for me to do." He reported to the Combined Chiefs of Staff, "We have already had minor incidents due to air contact [with the Russians], which have been magnified and have resulted in recriminations." Eisenhower was referring to five brushes on April 2 in which American planes had been fired upon by Russian aircraft and then returned fire, with no serious damage done to either side. He believed it

critical to "safeguard us against more serious incidents in the future."
Again, to cite Stephen Ambrose, "In thirty years of interviewing GIs . . .
I have not yet heard a single one of them say that he wanted to charge
into Berlin." Eisenhower's decision to forgo the city had been practical,
analytical, cool, and lacking in drama. But it was also the right decision.

CHAPTER 24

———— ★ ————

Death of the Commander in Chief

In the life of his presidency, Franklin Roosevelt, a man who could not take a step unaided, traveled a half million miles, including punishing voyages to Casablanca, Cairo, Tehran, Yalta, and Hawaii. He returned to Hyde Park whenever possible, over two hundred trips in all, his ancestral home providing a refuge where he refreshed his spirits and restored his strength. In the spring of 1945, he had gone home but found no respite in the cold and damp that shrouded the Hudson Valley in that time of year. He slept poorly and finally told Eleanor, "It's no good, I must go to Warm Springs."

On March 30, a Friday, the presidential train pulled into the tiny station serving the resort town. FDR, wearing a dark blue suit, his inevitable fedora turned up at the brim, looking drawn, his head lolling, was lifted by the brawny Mike Reilly into a black sedan with the license plate FDR I. Ordinarily, Roosevelt took pride in his ability to propel himself into the seat. This day Reilly found himself struggling against a deadweight. On the drive to the Little White House, FDR gave a listless wave and a wan smile to townspeople gathered along the route. That night, his faithful assistant and chum, Bill Hassett, wrote in his diary that the president's state this day had filled him "with an overpowering sense of last things." Yet as soon as FDR was settled in, he began to display his remarkable resiliency. Merriman Smith, the United Press reporter, part of a three-man pool covering the trip, while riding horseback, came upon the president sitting before the Little White House. "As I reined in the horse," Smith recalled, the president bowed with mock solemnity and greeted him. "His voice was wonderful and reso-nant," Smith recalled. "It sounded like the Roosevelt of old. In tones that must have been audible blocks away, FDR hailed me with 'Heigh Ho, Silver!'"

FDR had brought with him Daisy Suckley to look after Fala, and a first cousin, Laura "Polly" Delano, both Hudson Valley ladies with whom he could be completely himself and who were attentive to his every whim. Daisy, a faithful diarist, wrote of the president's mood as he entertained guests at Warm Springs, "We can hear the laughter com-ing from the living room," she remembered. Privately FDR dropped a bombshell on the prim, close-mouthed Daisy, a scoop that would have sent reporters rushing pell-mell to the phones. "He says that he can probably resign some time next year when . . . the United Nations is well started," she wrote in her diary. Despite Hassett's efforts to slow him down, FDR bubbled with plans. He told his aide that he would leave Warm Springs on April 19, and then "give a state dinner for the Regent of Iraq" in Washington. On the twentieth he would leave for San Francisco to deliver the principal address at the inauguration of the United Nations. FDR asked Hassett to listen as he read from a rough draft of the speech he intended to make. "The work, my friends, is peace, more than an end of this war," it began, "an end to the begin-ning of all wars. An end forever to this impractical, unrealistic settle-ment of the differences between governments by the mass killing of peoples." He was determined, he said, to deliver finally on Woodrow Wilson's failed pledge to make the First World War "the war to end all wars." Hassett accepted that however strenuous the schedule, his chief intended to go to San Francisco, "come hell or high water."

The war news forwarded to the president daily continued to signal the approaching victory over Germany. Allied troops had entered the Krupp arms plant in the Ruhr, Germany's industrial heartland, and Königsberg, capital of East Prussia, had surrendered to the Red Army. The president began planning what he intended to do when peace came. Prior to leaving for Warm Springs, he had spoken with his labor secretary, Frances Perkins, and told her, "We are going to England. Eleanor and I are going to make a state visit. . . . I told Eleanor to order her clothes and get some fine ones so that she will make a really hand-some appearance." They would stay, he told her, with the king and queen at Buckingham Palace. Churchill had assured the president that the British people would give him "the greatest reception ever accorded to any human being since Lord Nelson made his triumphant return to England." Perkins mentioned the risk of his traveling with the war still on. "Although we were alone in the room," Perkins recalled, "he put his hand to the side of his mouth and whispered, 'The war in Europe will be over by the end of May.'"

Daisy knew that FDR looked forward to the arrival of another guest, Lucy Mercer Rutherfurd, the woman FDR had loved since their romance during World War I while he was serving as assistant secretary of the navy. After Eleanor discovered the affair he admitted that he wanted a divorce and intended to marry Lucy. The dream fell through when FDR's mother, Sara, informed her high-living son that if he left his wife and five children, she would cut him off without a penny; and she controlled the family fortune. One condition that Eleanor extracted for preserving the marriage was a pledge from Franklin never to see Lucy again. The hope for remarriage had ended, but not the feelings between them. Through the dark years, while he struggled against polio, they continued corresponding. FDR entered the White House in 1933, and even during the mad whirl of the first hundred days of the New Deal, when he accepted phone calls only from important figures and immediate family, he always took the calls of "Mrs. Paul Johnson," the cover that Lucy had adopted. Beginning in 1941, she started visiting FDR at the White House during Eleanor's absences, still using the name Mrs. Paul Johnson. After the death of her husband, the socialite Winthrop Rutherfurd, she allowed her visits to be recorded by the White House usher in her own name. Amazingly, nearly thirty years had gone by without Eleanor having the faintest inkling that Franklin had broken his promise to her and that contact between him and Lucy had never ceased. On April 9, so eager was FDR for Lucy's arrival at Warm Springs that he drove eighty-five miles with Daisy and Fala to intercept Lucy's car en route from her home in Aiken, South Carolina. She would not be arriving alone. The president had agreed to let her bring Elizabeth Shoumatoff, a successful Russian émigré society portraitist for whom he would sit. Also with the two women was another émigré Russian, Nicholas Robbins, who was to take photographs of the president to aid the painter.

Though FDR had fled to Warm Springs to unwind, he barely scanted his workload. Harriman sent a cable, relayed by the Army Signal Corps, confessing that he had not yet delivered to Stalin a conciliatory message the president had written to defuse the rancor over Allen Dulles's attempts to win a Nazi surrender in Italy, Operation Sunrise. In it, Roosevelt had gone out of his way to thank Stalin for expressing his views forthrightly during the bitter exchanges. He brushed aside the recent war of words as "a minor misunderstanding." Harriman feared that the tone was all wrong. "I respectfully request that the word 'minor' as a qualification of 'misunderstanding,' be eliminated," he advised the president. "I must confess that the misunderstanding appeared to me to be of a major character and the use of the word 'minor' might well be misinterpreted here." Roosevelt knew all that, but with the war's end so near and his dream of a United Nations, including Soviet membership, so close, he wanted no further acrimony. He called in a secretary and dictated a brusque reply, telling Harriman, "It is my desire to consider the Bern misunderstanding a *minor* incident." Similarly, he received a request from Churchill asking for guidance as to what the prime minister should tell the House of Commons regarding the Soviet Union's truculence over Poland. FDR dictated a reply that began, "I would minimize the general Soviet problem as much as possible because these problems, in one form or another, seem to arise every day and most of them straighten out as in the case of the Bern meeting." He was not blind, he said, to the true face of Stalinist Russia and added, "We must be firm, however, and our course thus far has been correct."

On the evening of Lucy's arrival, FDR invited her, Madame Shoumatoff, Daisy, and Polly Delano into the small wood-paneled combination living and dining room for cocktails. On their drive from Aiken, Shoumatoff had mentioned to Lucy the pictures she had seen of the president in newspapers and that "those photos look ghastly." The artist now studied her subject, his face haggard, his complexion the color of cement, his shoulders thin and slumped. The president had confided to Bill Hassett that he had been losing weight, twenty-five pounds in recent months. Nevertheless, he was in high spirits this night, regaling the women with stories of what had gone on behind the scenes at Yalta. Stalin, at his ease, he said, "was quite a jolly fellow, but I'm convinced he poisoned his wife!" The Soviet leader had given him cases of vodka and caviar, which he promised to serve soon. And then it was off to bed at Dr. Bruenn's insistence. When Bruenn monitored the president's blood pressure, the readings were now astronomical, once reaching 230 over 120. Hassett confided to the doctor, "He is slipping away from us and no earthly power can keep him here." The cardiologist, a staunch Republican who had fallen under his patient's spell, disagreed. "His condition was not hopeless," Bruenn insisted. "He could be saved if measures were adopted to rescue him from certain mental strains and emotional influences." That night Hassett wrote of Bruenn in his diary, "I understood his position—his obligation to save life, not to admit defeat." Still, Hassett concluded, "The Boss is leaving us."

In the afternoons, the president liked to take Lucy on a ride up to Dowdell's Knob, a promontory offering a sweeping vista of the Georgia countryside. The tonic effect of the woman's company on this dog-tired man was obvious to Daisy. She wrote in her diary, after having been taken on one of these drives, "Lucy is so sweet with F—no wonder he loves to have her around. Toward the end of the drive, it began to be chilly and she put her sweater over his knees. . . . She would think of little things which make so much difference."

On April 11, Henry Morgenthau, en route to Florida to see his wife, who had suffered a heart attack, stopped at Warm Springs. The visit afforded another chance to revive his plan for "removing all industry from Germany and simply reducing them to an agricultural population of small landowners." He arrived at 7:30 P.M. and found FDR seated at a card table mixing cocktails, surrounded by his court, his withered legs propped on a stool. "I was terribly shocked when I saw him," Morgenthau later wrote in his diary. "I found that he had aged terrifically and looked very haggard." Still, the president was not in the mood for Morgenthau's weighty concerns. His attention was fixed on preparing the drinks and telling stories. "His hands shook so that he started to knock the glasses over, and I had to hold each glass as he poured the cocktail," Morgenthau recalled. "I noticed that he took two cocktails and then seemed to feel a little bit better. I found his memory bad, and he was constantly confusing names. . . . I have never seen him have so much difficulty transferring himself from his wheelchair to a regular chair, and I was in agony watching him." Yet, Morgenthau noted, the president seemed better after putting away a hearty dinner, veal and noodles and a large waffle topped with ice cream and chocolate syrup. As the Filipino servant, Irineo Esperancilla, cleared away the dishes, FDR began regaling his guests with tales of Eleanor's efforts as a furniture manufacturer during the 1930s to support her worthy causes. He described to Morgenthau his anticipated trip to address the United Nations in San Francisco. "At three o'clock in the afternoon," he said, "I will appear on the stage in my wheelchair, and I will make the speech." He clasped his hands together in prayer. "And then they will applaud me and I will leave and go back on my train, go down to Los Angeles and dump my daughter-in-law, and I will be back in Hyde Park by May first." As the treasury secretary prepared to leave, FDR bid a warm farewell to his longtime Hudson Valley neighbor.

That night the president placed a phone call to his daughter, Anna, and told her how eagerly he was looking forward to the next day. Frank Allcorn, the mayor of Warm Springs, and Ruth Stevens, a salty Warm Springs neighbor, planned a barbecue for him featuring, as Stevens put it, "a goddamned pig that weighed 300 pounds" along with FDR's favorite, Brunswick stew. When he finished the call to Anna, he invited his guests to gather around the fireplace where Madame Shoumatoff held them spellbound with ghost stories recalled from her Russian childhood. Soon after, Dr. Bruenn ordered a protesting FDR to bed. Daisy and Polly went with him. Suckley recorded in her diary a recent routine they had adopted: "I get the gruel and Polly and I take it to him. I sit on the edge of the bed & he puts on an act, he is too weak to raise his head, his hands are weak, he must be fed. So I proceed to feed him with a teaspoon & he loves it!" Remarking on his high spirits that night, she wrote, "The trouble is that just as soon as he gets a little better he feels full of pep and proceeds to use it all up again. It's next to impossible to stop him at just the right moment between his having a happy interesting time, and his getting overtired." The two women gave the president a peck on the forehead and left.

FDR awoke at 8:30 the next morning complaining of a headache and a stiff neck. The valet, Arthur Prettyman, wheeled him into the living room and parked him behind the card table. A waiting Bill Hassett began handing him proclamations, letters, and legislation for his signature. The relationship between the two men had always been easy, suggesting dueling raconteurs. As FDR signed the papers, Hassett spread them over a sofa, a chair back, and a table to let the ink dry, a spectacle that the president referred to as hanging out the laundry. Waving his pen with a flourish, FDR announced, "Here's where I make a law." Hassett could not help notice the once bold signature was now spidery and simply trailed off.

Near noon, Madame Shoumatoff appeared with a tiny palette and brushes for what would be the president's final sitting. The man she had earlier described as looking ghastly surprised her. "I was struck by his exceptionally good color. . . . That gray look had disappeared." Still, she draped his cape over his shoulders to fill out his shrunken frame. At twenty minutes before one, Prettyman set a small bowl of oatmeal, cream, and a green liquid on the card table beside the president. With a grimace, FDR downed the vile-tasting substance, which was supposed to stimulate his appetite. Madame Shoumatoff quickened her brushstrokes to finish FDR's forehead and hairline, knowing that her allotted time was running out. Irineo Esperancilla started setting a table for lunch when Daisy suddenly leaped to her feet. The president's head had slumped to his chest, his arms fell to his side, and his hands were thrashing. "Have you dropped your cigarette?" she asked. The president raised his left hand to the base of his skull where he had felt the stiffness that morning and said, "I have a terrific pain in the back of my head." She raced to the phone and told the operator to track down Dr. Bruenn and have him come to the cottage immediately. Prettyman and Esperancilla tried to lift the president to take him to his bedroom, but found him too heavy. Daisy and Polly helped by taking his legs. A shaken but discreet Lucy Rutherfurd turned to Madame Shoumatoff and said, "We must go." Bill Hassett entered the room and later wrote in his diary what he had seen. "His eyes were closed—mouth open. . . . But the Greek nose and the noble forehead were grand as ever."

Franklin Roosevelt had suffered a massive cerebral hemorrhage. Blood was spilling into the brain, robbing the surrounding vessels of oxygen. Dr. Bruenn pronounced him dead at 3:35 P.M., almost three hours since the initial attack. Bill Hassett's melancholy responsibility was to tell the world that Franklin Roosevelt was dead. A reporter asked who was present at the end. Hassett gave a largely honest answer, with one twist. He said that the president was stricken while his portrait was being painted by a Mr. Nicholas Robbins, Hassett's attempt to minimize speculation over FDR's female companion.

ON THE EVENING OF APRIL 12, Dwight Eisenhower, Omar Bradley, and George Patton were chatting in a small commandeered house near Patton's front. With the battle for Germany all but won they had, as Ike recalled, "sat up late talking of future plans, particularly of the selection of officers and units for early deployment to the Pacific." At midnight, they broke up and headed for bed. Patton explained in his diary what happened next. "I had failed to wind my watch, so I turned on the radio to see if I could get the time. Just as I turned it on, the announcer reported the death of the President." He rushed to Bradley's room and then woke up Eisenhower. The leading American generals in Europe sat down, "depressed and sad," and began considering the impact of the news on prosecution of the war. "We were doubtful," Ike said, "that there was any other individual in America as experienced as he is in dealing with the other political leaders." Reflecting on the obscure former senator from Missouri who was now president, Patton added gloomily, "It seems very unfortunate that in order to secure political preference, people are made Vice Presidents who were never intended . . . by the Lord to be Presidents." Bradley remembered, "from our distance, [Harry] Truman did not appear at all qualified to fill

Roosevelt's large shoes." An ailing Hap Arnold learned of the president's death from his doctor while recovering from a heart attack. "The news was a great shock," Arnold remembered. He recalled how Roosevelt had reprieved him long ago, "when I was in the doghouse. Many times he seemed more like a fellow airman than he did the Commander-in-Chief of all our armed forces and I one of his subalterns in charge of aviation." The statement that Douglas MacArthur issued upon Roosevelt's death began with what appeared a backhanded compliment: "He had greatly matured since our former days in Washington." MacArthur went on more graciously, "His political star had risen to its zenith, but poliomyelitis had struck him painfully. He became the leading liberal of the age. . . . Whatever differences arose between us never had sullied in slightest degree the warmth of my friendship for him."

George Marshall was relaxing on the porch at the chief of staff's Fort Myer residence when Colonel Frank McCarthy, a fellow VMI alumnus and secretary of the general staff, came to report the death of the president. Marshall had McCarthy drive him immediately to the White House where he found Mrs. Roosevelt, red-eyed but composed. She had just sent telegrams to her four sons in service, Marine Colonel James, Navy Lieutenants Franklin Jr. and John, and Brigadier General Elliott Roosevelt in the Air Forces. "Darlings," she wrote, "Pa slept away this afternoon. He did his job to the end as he would want you to do. Bless you. All our love. Mother." She told Marshall that she was preparing to fly to Warm Springs and asked if he would begin to arrange for the presidential funeral. Marshall agreed and next summoned the Joint Chiefs to meet with President Truman to brief him on the status of the war. At this time, Secretary of War Henry Stimson revealed to Truman that a weapon of unimaginable power was being developed in secret in the New Mexico desert.

Averell Harriman learned of the death of the president on April 13, at 3 A.M. Moscow time. Knowing that Stalin was a nocturnal creature, he took the liberty of proceeding to the Kremlin in the middle of the night. After delivering the news of FDR's death to Stalin, he was gratified to see that the Soviet leader appeared genuinely moved. Stalin took Harriman's hand and held it for almost a minute. Then he began to grill Harriman about the facts of FDR's demise. The next day the Soviet dictator sent a message to the U.S. State Department urging an autopsy to find out if the president had been poisoned. In the Soviet Union, powerful figures did not always die of natural causes.

Joseph Goebbels, the Nazi propaganda minister, arrived in Berlin from a trip to find the night sky aglow from the fires of the latest Allied raid, with flames shooting from the once luxurious Adlon Hotel. As he stepped from his limousine, a secretary came running toward him shouting, "Roosevelt is dead!" Goebbels stood transfixed for a moment and then his face broke into a broad smile. "Bring out the champagne," he ordered, "and get me the Führer on the telephone!" A dozen aides hunched behind Goebbels to hear him report to Hitler in the Führerbunker beneath the Reich Chancellery where he had entombed himself for the last three months. "My Führer," Goebbels shouted. "I congratulate you. Roosevelt is dead! It is written in the stars that the second half of April will be the turning point for us. This is Friday, April the thirteenth. It is the turning point." The next day, Hitler, in his daily order to the German army, announced, "Fate has removed the greatest criminal of all time." Germany, he believed, had been rescued.

Through Magic decryption of diplomatic signals, the Map Room quickly knew Japan's reaction to FDR's death, a more reasoned response than that of the Nazis. "Do not make personal attacks on Roosevelt," Japanese officials were instructed. "Do not convey the impression that we are exultant over Roosevelt's death. Avoid observations such as that Roosevelt's death will have an immediate effect on the fighting spirit and war strength of the United States. . . . Lay great stress on such things as the mistakes and discords that will now arise in the anti-Axis camp."

SINCE THE WAR, NEWSPAPERS had carried daily notices reading, "The following are the latest casualties in the military services, including next of kin." The first listing on April 13 read: "Roosevelt, Franklin D. Commander in Chief. Wife, Mrs. Anna Eleanor Roosevelt. The White House."

On Saturday morning, April 14, the train bearing the president's body arrived at Washington's Union Station, the casket draped in an American flag that had to be strapped down to thwart the wind. An honor guard lifted the burden and placed it onto an old artillery caisson. Riders on seven white horses clip-clopping in unison pulled the caisson with a riderless horse, stirrups reversed, trailing behind symbolizing a leader fallen. Marshall's towering sergeant, James Powder, commanded the pallbearers. The route, lined by over 300,000 mourners, wound up Constitution Avenue, turned right at 15th Street, and arrived at the White House. Despite the immense crowds, George Marshall's wife, Katherine, remembered that a "complete silence spread like a pall over the city, broken only by the funeral dirge and the sobs of people." To Sam Rosenman, the crowd's silence reflected "bewilderment, as though having lost the leader to whom they could always turn, they felt uncertain—almost frightened." The indelible image of the nation's grief had been struck earlier in a photo of FDR's body being taken from Warm Springs while Graham Jackson, an accordionist whom the president admired, played "Goin' Home," his eyes shut, his lips trembling, tears rolling down his cheeks.

THE SUN SHONE IN A SKY of cloudless blue and spring flowers had begun to bud as mourners gathered around a small rose garden near the banks of the Hudson River. West Point cadets fired three-volley salutes above a gravesite, the sharp report of the guns making Fala jump and bark. Franklin Roosevelt, at age sixty-three, was laid to rest at Hyde Park, where he had been born.

CONSPICUOUSLY ABSENT FROM the funeral ceremonies was Winston Churchill. Five days after Roosevelt's death the prime minister wound his way through huge crowds around Parliament to deliver a eulogy to his late partner. Roosevelt, he exclaimed, ranked with the immortals of the American presidency, maybe above Washington and Lincoln, since his leadership had benefited the entire world. "What an enviable death was his," he declared. "He had brought his country through the worst of its perils and the heaviest of its toil. Victory had cast its sure and steady beam upon him. . . . He had raised the strength, might, and glory of the great Republic to a height never attained by any nation in history." He made an oblique reference to the point rarely mentioned, the president's disability. "Not one man in ten millions," he noted, "would have attempted to plunge into a life of physical and mental exertion. Not one in a generation would have succeeded . . . in becoming indisputable master of the scene." He described their last meeting at Yalta. "I noticed the President was ailing. His captivating smile, his gay and charming manner had not deserted him, but his face had a transparency of purification and often there was a faraway look in his eyes. . . . I must confess that I had an undefinable sense of fear." The tribute was moving, heartfelt, and touched the audience. Yet, while the severely handicapped Roosevelt had traveled in wartime to Casablanca, Malta, Cairo, Tehran, and Yalta to meet with Churchill, the prime minister chose not to cross the Atlantic to join other heads of state who came to bid Franklin Roosevelt farewell. The reasons why he did not do so have engaged historians ever since. Certain explanations do not do credit to the character of Winston Churchill. Perhaps, some observers conjectured, the presumed affinity between the two men was an expedient illusion. The respected military historian Max Hastings concluded, "It is difficult not to regard the Prime Minister's absence as a reflection of the alienation between himself and the President, which grew grave indeed in the last months of Roosevelt's life." Jon Meacham, in *Franklin and Winston,* has suggested "a more complicated possibility." Could it have been "a prideful moment in which Churchill, after playing the suitor to Roosevelt, wanted himself to be courted. . . . Was Churchill tired of dancing to another man's tune, relieved Roosevelt was dead? Had it all been an act?" Warren Kimball, editor of the Roosevelt-Churchill correspondence, wrote of the prime minister's passing up the perfect opportunity to meet the new president, Harry Truman, and reflected, "Churchill's decision was an attempt to bring the mountain to Mohammed—subtly to shift the focus of the Anglo-American relationship from Washington to London." What did Churchill himself have to say about his failure to come to America? "My first impulse was to fly over to the funeral, and I had already ordered an aeroplane," he wrote in his memoirs. "Lord Halifax telegraphed that both Hopkins and Stettinius were much moved by my thought of possibly coming over, and both agreed with my judgment of the immense effect for good that would be produced. Mr. Truman had asked [Halifax] to say how greatly he would personally value the opportunity of meeting me as early as possible." Churchill told King George VI, "However, so many of your majesty's ministers are out of the country, and the foreign secretary had arranged to go anyhow, and I felt the business next week in Parliament and also the [British] ceremonies connected with the death of Mr. Roosevelt are so important that I should be failing in my duty if I left the House of Commons without my close personal attention." In short, he felt it more suitable to pay homage to Franklin Roosevelt from London than in Washington. Given time to reflect, Churchill later wrote, "In the afterlight, I regret that I did not adopt the new President's suggestion ... there were many points on which personal talks would have been of the greatest value." His words suggest that he regretted the lost chance to meet Truman more than his failure to attend Roosevelt's funeral.

In the end, all Churchill's reasons for not coming to America seem lame, not frank explanations of his inaction, which lies in the unknowable heart of the man. A convincing explanation may be that the prime minister viewed Roosevelt much differently in 1945 than he had in 1941. Earlier, they had been shoulder to shoulder to defeat a common enemy. By 1945, their objectives were poles apart, Churchill's being to restore and maintain the empire, and FDR's to dismantle all empires. The prime minister may well have resented that the leader of the younger, stronger nation wanted to pursue a course that would reduce a once global power to a mere island.

CHURCHILL WAS INSIGHTFUL IN DESCRIBING FDR as the one in a million who could achieve what he did against incalculable odds. Because he never complained, the underestimated dimension of FDR's life was his courage and will in overcoming the crippling affliction that would have broken a lesser man. His closest associates noted, not only the absence of self-pity, but the obliviousness to his disability that he projected, which put others at ease and enabled them to get on with their jobs. Only on the rarest occasions did he ever raise the issue of his impairment. In answering a letter from a friend, Arthur B. Sherman, he once wrote, "There were a good many people who at that time, in 1928, believed—some honestly and some because they wanted to—that I was headed for a tombstone." He went on to describe to Sherman a visit by James Cox, whose vice presidential running mate he had been in the 1920 election. "At that time I was, of course, walking with great difficulty—braces and crutches," FDR wrote. "Jim's eyes filled with tears when he saw me, and I gathered from his conversation that he was dead certain that I had had a stroke and that another one would soon completely remove me." Subsequently, after twice being elected governor of New York, FDR stopped to visit Cox in Dayton, Indiana, and, "His whole attitude," Roosevelt recalled, was "that I could stand the strain of the governorship, but that in all probability, I would be dead in a few months."

THIRTEEN DAYS AFTER THE PRESIDENT'S DEATH, men of the U.S. 69th Division linked up with Red Army soldiers of the 58th Guards Division and shook hands at Torgau on the Elbe River southwest of Berlin. What remained of the Third Reich had been severed in two. The same day, the armies of Marshals Ivan Konev and Georgi Zhukov completed the encirclement of Berlin. Five days later, in the Führerbunker, twenty feet beneath the Berlin sewer system, Adolf Hitler called in his attractive twenty-five-year-old secretary, Traudl Junge, to dictate his last political testament. "I will not fall into the hands of an enemy that requires a new spectacle, exhibited by the Jews to divert its hysterical masses," he said. "My wife and I choose to die in order to escape the shame of overthrow or capitulation." The once vast Nazi empire over which he had ruled, stretching from the gates of Moscow in the east to the English Channel in the west, from Norway in the north to North Africa in the south, had been reduced to a heap of ruin in the heart of Berlin. He then married his ever-loyal mistress, Eva Braun, retreated to a small inner room with her, watched her bite into a cyanide capsule, and then shot himself. He was fifty-six years old. His accomplice Mussolini, the bombastic founder of fascism, had died in ignominy the day before, caught by Italian partisans while huddled in the backseat of a car, his face concealed under a German helmet. Il Duce was summarily shot and his body strung upside down on a beam in a gas station in Milan alongside that of his mistress, Clara Petacci.

TWO HOURS AFTER MIDNIGHT ON MAY 7, in the Boys' Professional and Technical School, Eisenhower's current headquarters, the stiff-backed General Alfred Jodl, Hitler's operations chief, accompanied by Admiral Hans von Friedeburg, entered a makeshift war room where French boys had once played Ping-Pong to sign what Franklin Roosevelt had demanded from the outset, the unconditional surrender of Germany. Eisenhower, though upstairs in the building, left direct dealings with the Nazis to his deputy, Walter Bedell Smith. On the day that the president had died, Eisenhower, Patton, and Bradley had toured the liberated concentration camp of Ohrdruf, where Bradley remembered, "The smell of death overwhelmed us even before we passed through the stockade." Eisenhower wanted no truck with men who had served such a regime. Once the surrender had been signed, he received Jodl briefly, only long enough to warn him that he would "be held responsible if the terms of the surrender are violated." While Ike's staff wrestled with language appropriate to so auspicious an occasion, Eisenhower wrote out the statement he preferred. It read simply, "The mission of this Allied force was fulfilled at 0241 local time, May 7, 1945." The next day another signing took place in Berlin to allow the Soviets to affirm their parity in winning victory. The Germans in Italy had surrendered six days before, which meant that Allen Dulles's zeal to win an earlier peace through Operation Sunrise had proved of negligible significance. Conservatively, between dead, wounded, and missing, the Italian campaign had cost 189,000 Americans, 123,000 British and commonwealth troops, and 434,000 Germans, a total of 746,000 lives lost, maimed, or injured in a campaign of arguable necessity. Total American battle deaths in the European war approached 174,000, another 23,514 were missing in action, many presumed dead, and 485,000 were wounded. Max Hastings has rated "the Wehrmacht the greatest fighting machine the world has ever known," a judgment shared by other military historians. Yet, whatever the reasons, Germany was beaten in North Africa, beaten in Sicily, beaten in Italy, beaten in France, beaten in Russia, beaten at home, and lost the war.

FOR GENERATIONS, FRANKLIN ROOSEVELT would be castigated by his political enemies for knuckling under to Stalin and his regime. His actions, however, were prompted by an awareness that the Soviet military inflicted nearly three quarters of Germany's battle losses while suffering approximately eight million Soviet dead in doing so. This sacrifice, compared to less than 1.5 million deaths for all the Western Allies fighting in Europe, worked out to over five Russians killed for every death among the other forces, a bloody bargain, but one that explains FDR's determination to keep the Soviet Union fighting whatever it took.

The German people's seduction by Hitler cost them horrifically, 3,050,000 dead, of whom 500,000 were civilians, mostly women and children. More Germans died in the last year of the war, with all hope of victory vanished, than in any other year. The pointless battle for Berlin cost Germany some 325,000 military and civilian deaths. Though the Japanese were portrayed as fanatics, it was the Germans who fought until nearly the last building on the last block of the last street in the heart of Berlin had been laid waste. To the end, Hitler maintained his grip on the psyche of a vast majority of Germans who remained convinced that a leader so messianic, so mesmerizing, so supremely confident could still pull it off with secret weapons and brilliant stratagems. He would somehow pluck the nation from the abyss of defeat, and deliver it to victory. Did most Germans look over their shattered homes, contemplate the millions of sons, fathers, and brothers dead in North

Africa's sands, in France's fertile earth, and on the frozen steppes of Russia, and blame Hitler? Apparently not many. They had been propagandized to believe that their suffering was brought on by Anglo-American enemies too obtuse to see that Hitler's struggle should have been their struggle, to halt the march of communism, to replace the weakness and disorder of democracy with the strength and discipline of National Socialism.

In July 2010, sixty-five years after the country's defeat, the military history center of the German armed forces published the last two volumes of *The German Reich and the Second World War*. The center's analysts concluded that Hitler was supported "by sentiments in Germany that remained broadly favorable even after a series of defeats never turned to public resentment." The historians concluded that without Hitler's "suicidal urge," the war might have ended three years earlier, since the führer had been warned by thinking generals as early as 1942 that Germany could not win. Thus, every German life expended from the time of the Red Army's recovery and America's entry into the war alongside Great Britain had been sacrificed in vain.

A year and five months after the defeat of Nazi Germany, on October 16, 1946, ten surviving masters of the Third Reich found guilty of war crimes by the International Military Tribunal mounted a gallows erected in a converted basketball court in Nuremberg prison. An hour before, Hermann Göring had escaped the hangman by taking cyanide. After the defendants were pronounced dead at 2:54 A.M., GIs delivered their bodies to a crematorium in the Munich suburb of Solln. The ashes were unceremoniously dumped into a small stream, the Contwentzbach, and the urns smashed to pieces with axes and stamped flat under boot heels. No trace of the men who had created Nazi Germany was to survive and the movement died along with them, obliterated as certainly as their mortal remains.

ALMOST SIX YEARS HAD PASSED since Albert Einstein had written FDR describing the extraordinary potential of a nuclear chain reaction. Since then 150,000 scientists, technicians, and support staff had labored to bring an atomic bomb into being at a cost of $2 billion, approximately $26 billion in current value. Even senior officers, still in the dark, questioned the unexplained expense. What was this mysterious enterprise? How much was it costing? Wasn't it swallowing up resources better used elsewhere? Pa Watson had cautioned doubters, "The boss wants it, boys." Upon the success of this covert activity hung the fate of millions. A War Department analysis estimated that nearly two million Japanese soldiers defended the home islands, part of an army that had shown a willingness on Tarawa, Saipan, Iwo Jima, and Okinawa to face annihilation before surrendering. Another five million Japanese were serving in China and far-flung Pacific posts, men who could be brought back to protect the homeland. Thousands of kamikaze planes stood poised in Japan to punish an invasion force the moment it hit the beaches. Former President Herbert Hoover was asked to lead an expert panel to forecast the cost for defeating Japan and came up with a range of 500,000 to 1,000,000 combat deaths. At a JCS meeting, Admiral Leahy took a pad and pencil and figured, on the basis of American casualties suffered on Saipan, that the invasion of Japan could cost 268,345 American dead and wounded. MacArthur estimated that Operation Olympic, the invasion's code name, would cost 50,000 dead and wounded within the first thirty days. Estimates of when the war would end ran as late as 1947. The wild card in this hand was whether the Soviet Union would enter the fight against Japan. Would Stalin keep his promise made at Yalta to do so within three months after the defeat of Germany?

ON JULY 16, 1945, Robert Oppenheimer and Major General Leslie Groves crouched at a desolate strip of rock and sand near Alamogordo in southern New Mexico to observe the first attempt in history to release the power of the atom. At 5:30 A.M. a fireball exploded, generating the heat of 10,000 suns. President Truman at the time was at Cecilienhof Palace in the relatively untouched Berlin suburb of Potsdam meeting with Marshal Stalin and Clement Attlee, who had succeeded Winston Churchill after the prime minister had been dumped in British parliamentary elections. Upon receiving the report on Alamogordo, Truman recorded the facts in his diary. The detonation had created a crater nearly a quarter of a mile wide and vaporized the sixty-foot steel tower from which the bomb was detonated. "The explosion was visible for more than 200 miles and audible for 40 miles and more," he wrote. The United States now possessed a weapon that dwarfed by an incalculable magnitude any other means of dealing death that the world had ever devised. Truman approached Stalin, who was standing with his interpreter, and confided that the United States had achieved this weapon. Stalin appeared unsurprised, and understandably so. Soviet spies had penetrated the Manhattan Project and had stolen some 10,000 pages of secret documents. Bomb or no bomb, Truman was taking no chances, and his objective at Potsdam was much the same as Roosevelt's at Yalta, to press Stalin into entering the war against Japan. This time, Stalin agreed to a specific date, which allowed an ecstatic Truman to write his wife, "I've gotten what I came for—Stalin goes to war August 15. . . . I'll say that we'll end the war a year sooner now, and think of the kids who won't be killed."

On July 26, Truman obtained agreement from his Allies to issue the Potsdam Declaration intimating the fate in store for Japan: "The full application of our military power, backed by our resolve, will mean the inevitable and complete destruction of the Japanese armed forces and just as inevitably the utter devastation of the Japanese homeland." The current Japanese prime minister, Kantaro Suzuki, publicly dismissed the declaration as "unworthy of public notice." Privately, however, Suzuki and other realists recognized, with nearly 90 percent of the navy destroyed and with unopposed American B-29s leveling their cities day after day—sixty-six by now—that the war was lost. Suzuki attempted to have the Soviet Union broker a face-saving peace. But Stalin, his eye fixed on recovering the territory lost to Japan in 1905, was uninterested in playing peacemaker. Further, Japan's militarists, who still held the edge in the Supreme War Council, scorned peace overtures and were determined to fight to the death.

The moral question of whether the atom bomb should be employed in a nonlethal demonstration or used deliberately against Japan continued and provoked an internal debate within the Truman administration. "Some wanted it dropped on the Sea of Japan," Marshall noted. "Others wanted to drop it on a rice paddy." Oppenheimer doubted that "any sufficiently startling demonstration could be devised that would convince the Japanese that they ought to throw in the sponge." In the end, logistics decided the issue, since only two atom bombs were believed operational, and none ready in reserve. In mid-July, the JCS sent a puzzling message to MacArthur, Arnold, and Nimitz, who were still in the dark about the bomb. Under no circumstances, they were informed, were relatively undamaged Hiroshima, Kyoto, Niigata, or Nagasaki to be harmed.

In Hiroshima, on the morning of August 6, 1945, commuters boarded their buses to work, housewives went shopping, and children walked to school. At 8:15 a ten-foot cylinder dropped from the belly of a lone B-29 flown by a thirty-year-old Air Forces pilot, Colonel Paul W. Tibbets, the plane named *Enola Gay,* for his mother. The bomb detonated over the Shima Surgical Hospital. Five square miles of Hiroshima evaporated in an instant. At least 70,000 Japanese died from the initial blast. While the bomb weighed 9,000 pounds, its explosive nuclear core could be cupped in two hands. Still Japan did not surrender.

Two days after Hiroshima, the Soviet Union declared war on Japan. Stalin's fulfillment of a now useless promise represented the ultimate in hypocrisy. His sole motive was to recover, at a cheap price, the territory lost to Japan in 1905. The following day, August 9, a second atomic bomb fell, on Nagasaki. Five days later, Emperor Hirohito broke a deadlock in the Supreme War Council between the pro-war and pro-peace factions and ordered the fighting ended. The Japanese people heard the emperor's voice over the radio for the first time telling them that "they must bear the unbearable," though he made no mention of defeat. On August 14, President Truman announced Japan's surrender, setting off celebrations from New York's Times Square to town squares all across America. On September 2, at the formal surrender signing by Japanese officials aboard the USS *Missouri* in Tokyo Bay, the ordinarily grandiloquent Douglas MacArthur ended the ceremony saying simply, "Let us pray that peace be now restored to the world and that God will preserve it always. These proceedings are closed."

Franklin Roosevelt's pledge made the day after Pearl Harbor that "The American people in their righteous might will win through to absolute victory" had been fulfilled. While initially Pearl Harbor meant a humiliating defeat for the United States, in the end the sneak attack proved to be a far greater catastrophe for Japan. With its greatest cities burned to ash, with two million military and civilian dead, with tens of thousands left homeless, dispirited, and hungry, the attack on Pearl Harbor turned out to be an infamy the Japanese inflicted on themselves. The pity was that fate denied FDR as commander in chief from witnessing this moment.

Controversy over the morality of using the atomic bomb to end the war would persist as long as contemporary critics saw the decision through a different lens than the men who made the decision in 1945. While the horror wrought in seconds by the two atomic bombs staggered the imagination, more Japanese died in Curtis LeMay's May 9–10 conventional raid on Tokyo than at either Hiroshima or Nagasaki. More Germans died uselessly in the final year of the war than did Japanese from the atomic bombs. Since Harry Truman made the final decision to drop the bomb, the question arises, would FDR have arrived at the same conclusion? Roosevelt was a humanitarian on social issues but hard as nails as a wartime leader. It was FDR who launched the Manhattan Project in the first place; who asked Leslie Groves if the bomb was ready to use against Germany in the darkest days of the Bulge; who with Churchill made an agreement that the bomb should be used "against the Japanese who should be warned that the bombardment will be repeated until they surrender"; and whose conversations led Henry Stimson to say, "At no time, from 1941 to 1945, did I ever hear it suggested by the President . . . that atomic energy should not be used in the war." On the personal level, in January 1945 FDR had assured his Marine son, who feared he might not survive a bloody invasion against the Japanese, "James, there will be no invasion of Japan. We have something that will end our war with Japan before any invasion ever takes place." There cannot be the slightest doubt that Franklin Roosevelt would have used the atom bomb.

After 2,193 days, the most catastrophic event in human history, costing an estimated 62 million to 78 million military and civilian lives, ended. Numbers on so vast a scale numb rather than shock. What is lost is the personal tragedy behind every impersonal statistic: a youth never granted time to grow old, the mother sending off a son and getting back a folded flag, a wife widowed, children left fatherless, the promising pianist, surgeon, or scientist cut off unfulfilled, the fate of an Anne Frank multiplied by millions. The evils of Nazism, the belligerent imperialism of Japan had to be ended, but at what a price.

CHAPTER 25

* * *

Anatomy of Victory

Franklin Roosevelt's success as a wartime commander in chief must be measured against his performance in three principal roles: Roosevelt the recruiter in chief, charged with selecting military leaders capable of winning a war; Roosevelt the strategist in chief, deciding how, when, and where the war should be fought; and Roosevelt the home front leader, motivating, marshaling, and inspiring a people at war.

Roosevelt as Recruiting Officer

His choice for running the Army was paramount. George C. Marshall had moved into Roosevelt's field of vision early in the New Deal through his energetic involvement of the Army in a pet FDR New Deal initiative, the Civilian Conservation Corps. Marshall's star began its real ascent in 1935, when General John J. Pershing, a man for whom Roosevelt's admiration was unbounded, recommended his World War I aide for promotion to general in a peacetime Army on which few stars fell. Thereafter, Marshall stood out for his independence of mind, however perilous to his career. In 1938, in his first major encounter with the president, FDR asked him what he thought of his ideas for expanding the Air Corps and Marshall disagreed vehemently. People who reflexively nodded "yes" before the persuasiveness and charm of FDR were a dime a dozen. The president found Marshall's backbone a novel and refreshing experience. The following year he named Mar-

shall chief of staff with a near impossible mandate. During the lingering Depression years, when military spending ranked below post office
construction, Marshall was charged with converting an anemic Army
into a military power. By 1945 this Army was second only to the Soviet
Union in size and strength. Marshall had largely achieved the transfor-
mation.

He suffered defeats, particularly at the hands of Winston Churchill
in the battle for FDR's soul on the crucial question of how to win the
European war, with Marshall preaching a direct thrust into Germany's
heart versus Churchill's preference for gnawing at the edges. Marshall
lost to Churchill on North Africa, Sicily, and Italy, all of which he initially resisted. He warned the president that these campaigns could
only delay victory.

Churchill's chief of the Imperial General Staff, Field Marshal Sir
Alan Brooke, was ungenerous in his judgment of Marshall's military
gifts. He liked the man, he said, but dismissed him as not "a great man."
Churchill, however, who often found Marshall trying because of his
reluctance to embrace the prime minister's side shows, invited Marshall to lunch after the war in Europe was won and later told his physician, Lord Moran, "That is the noblest Roman of them all." After the
European victory, Henry Stimson called together the JCS and made an
oblique reference to Marshall's not being chosen for Overlord, calling
him "the commanding general of the greatest field Army in our history." Then, pointing to the general, he added, "I have seen a great
many soldiers in my lifetime and you, sir, are the finest soldier I have
ever known." Averell Harriman, writing in his memoirs about Overlord, said, "I know that General Marshall wanted more than anything
else to command this historic military action, and I have no doubt that
Roosevelt would have appointed him if he had given the slightest indication of his personal desires. But he left the decision entirely to the
President. It was the most selfless thing any man could do." In Harriman's judgment, FDR paid a high price by appointing Eisenhower instead of Marshall. "I still feel, as I felt at the time, that the campaign in
Europe would have been concluded more swiftly if Marshall had been
in command."

Dwight Eisenhower, who did get the supreme command, would be regarded as the liberator of Europe and become president of the United States. Could Marshall, had he commanded Overlord, have followed the same path? Even though Marshall lacked Ike's natural political touch, as a Republican candidate he would probably have beaten Adlai Stevenson, the Democratic candidate whom Eisenhower defeated in 1952. The question remains whether this sober, modest, almost egoless man who went on to become secretary of state and father of the Marshall Plan to rebuild Europe would have been comfortable in the hurly-burly of elective politics. Unfortunately, given the public's ephemeral memory, Marshall's star has faded, while Eisenhower's is fixed in the American firmament. Marshall always resisted FDR's palsy overtures and there was little real affection between the two men. Yet FDR's single wisest appointment in the war was his enlistment of George Catlett Marshall.

JUST AS ROOSEVELT HAD RECOGNIZED Marshall's qualities, the chief of staff displayed his own scent for talent. His feared and famous little black book ignored rank, seniority, or political pull in advancing the careers of officers whom Marshall found promising, the most notable example being Dwight Eisenhower, who rose from an obscure colonel in 1941 to victorious commander of the greatest Western fighting force ever assembled. We see Ike after Pearl Harbor reluctantly tethered to a desk in the War Plans Division, when his name was still unknown and even misspelled. There he drafted the first plan for rebuilding a defense in the Pacific, though from the outset he believed that Europe must be the principal battleground. He stood squarely with Marshall in opposing the back-alley thrust through North Africa, rather than a frontal assault on the continent, and called the day when Torch won out over a cross-Channel invasion the blackest in history.

Eisenhower was not a natural battlefield commander. Montgomery, Bradley, Alexander, and Patton were all better in the field. But having them, he did not have to be a Napoleon himself. While observing Eisenhower in North Africa, Roosevelt, the consummate politician, grasped that Ike was the ablest "political general" in the best sense of the word. He was capable of forging a team from rivals representing half a dozen nations with competing interests, serving at times as a referee pulling apart antagonists and turning them against the enemy rather than against each other. He stood up to Churchill, often angering the prime minister but never losing the man's respect. He was an adroit military psychologist who could juggle the egos of a Patton and a Montgomery. Eisenhower's nastiest trial occurred early when he commanded the invasion of North Africa. In the deal with François Darlan, Ike, then a political tyro, stood accused of being taken in by a French Nazi who was reviled in the American and British press and even by Roosevelt cabinet members like Henry Morgenthau, who asked, if we were supporting a Darlan, what was the war all about? Still, Roosevelt, the realist, recognized a time and place for expediency. He backed Eisenhower, declaring publicly that Ike had done the wise thing by exploiting Darlan to defuse French opposition in North Africa. It was FDR who urged Ike to let the American people know that the Darlan deal had cut North African casualties to one tenth of what had been feared.

Field Marshal Bernard Law Montgomery likely presented the prickliest challenge to Eisenhower's gift for conciliation. If de Gaulle was Churchill's cross, Monty was Eisenhower's. The nonsmoking teetotaler could be insufferable, described by one subordinate as "an efficient little shit," by another as "an intelligent terrier who might bite at any moment." And by still another as "what a headache, what a bore, what a bounder." Still, a battlefield general does not have to be a gentleman, which one of Monty's associates said he was not. Eisenhower was willing to overlook numerous provocations by the hero of Alamein and gamble on military genius over flawed character. Thus he gave Monty command of half the Allied Expeditionary Force, the other half going to Omar Bradley. Montgomery was convinced that if Eisenhower had not stalled him and stripped his 21st Army Group in 1945, he could have won the war earlier, and even have taken Berlin. Monty said of Eisenhower's military aptitude, "I would not class Ike as a great general." His reading of Ike's character, however, reflected a keen grasp of the man. "His real strength lies in his human qualities," Montgomery concluded. "He has the power of drawing the hearts of men towards him as a magnet attracts bits of metal. He merely has to smile at you and you trust him at once. He is the very incarnation of sincerity."

Eisenhower gambled on a deeply flawed soldier, George S. Patton, and stuck by the man even as others clamored for his scalp, particularly after the unconscionable slapping incidents in Sicily. Ike understood that beneath the bluster, Patton was a brilliant field commander and accepted that great generals are not necessarily model human beings, borne out by Patton's performance in turning North Africa around after the debacle at Kasserine, his swift victory in Sicily, his rescue of besieged Bastogne, and his headlong race across Europe. Patton's nadir as a soldier was his decision to send men to die to rescue his son-in-law from a German POW camp.

While Omar Bradley lacked Patton's pyrotechnics, Eisenhower read the two men well enough to conclude that they could make a successful pairing, if Bradley were the superior. He rated him "the best rounded, well balanced senior officer that we have in the service." Bradley had been in charge of the harrowing landings on D-Day and pressed on when it looked as if the invading force at Omaha Beach could be thrown back into the sea. He managed to blunt the German breakthrough during the Bulge well before the enemy achieved its objectives. His feuds with the overweening Montgomery were worrisome but not fatal.

The relationship between Eisenhower and Kay Summersby could not fail to provoke speculation, an American commander at the vortex of history in the world's greatest war keeping at his side an attractive, bright, and charming woman not his wife. On the day that Germany surrendered at Rheims, Kay can be seen standing behind a grinning Ike in news photos capturing the moment. In his history, *Crusade in Europe,* Eisenhower made his only published reference to Kay's existence, listing her along with fifteen other members of his personal staff as "Corresponding Secretary and doubled as a driver." Only in Ike's unpublished papers did he include Kay in a more select list. In a letter to his brother Milton, then president of Kansas State University, who was handling negotiations for a movie about his brother, Ike mentioned "Four individuals that could cover quite accurately all details of my life since leaving Washington." Along with Beetle Smith, Harry Butcher, and a staff member, Ernest Lee, he included "my personal chauffeur and corresponding secretary for two years, Mrs. Kay Summersby." In her first autobiography, Kay exulted that she had risen above "odd job handler" to become an "aide to General of the Army Eisenhower, Supreme Commander Allied Expeditionary Force," but she admits in her second autobiography that the relationship was never consummated. The historian Arthur Schlesinger Jr. said of the relationship between FDR and Lucy Mercer Rutherfurd, "If Lucy in any way helped Franklin Roosevelt sustain the frightful burdens of leadership in the Second World War, the nation has good reason to be grateful to her." The same might be said of Kay Summersby and Eisenhower.

At the war's end, Ike was greeted by ecstatic crowds in London, Paris, New York, and Washington. "Let me tell you what General Eisenhower has meant to us," Churchill told America. "At no time has the principle of alliance between noble races been carried and maintained at so high a pitch. In the name of the British Empire and Commonwealth, I express to you our admiration of the firm, farsighted, and illuminating character of General of the Armies Eisenhower." After Germany's defeat, Eisenhower gathered his staff around him and said presciently, "The success of this occupation can only be judged fifty years from now. If the Germans at that time have a stable, prosperous democracy, then we shall have succeeded."

It is to Franklin Roosevelt's credit that he sensed in Eisenhower that indispensable and undefinable seed of leadership more than in the equally gifted but politically less attuned Marshall. Marshall had discovered Eisenhower but FDR, by giving Ike Overlord, set him on the path of immortality.

THE PRESIDENT HAD RESCUED ERNEST KING from oblivion. By 1939 the irascible admiral was approaching the mandatory retirement age of sixty-four and waiting out his pension while serving on the Navy's obscure General Board. Even in this career dead end, King's restless energy and ability caught the eye of then Secretary of the Navy Charles Edison, who touted King to Roosevelt. FDR, the charmer, spotted in King, the holy terror, what he wanted, a fighter to whom he could entrust the undeclared war in the Atlantic and who would not trouble him too much with the niceties of neutrality. After Pearl Harbor, Roosevelt gave King the whole Navy, first under the revived title Commander in Chief, U.S. Fleet, then folding into that job the old title of Commander of Naval Operations, heretofore the pinnacle of Navy leadership. King became the most powerful figure in the history of the U.S. Navy. Before the war, his branch consisted of some 285,000 men. By the end, under King, it had grown to 3.3 million. By far the launching of ninety-two new aircraft carriers was the most significant advance, signaling the greatest shift in naval warfare since the ancient Greeks had defeated the Persians at the battle of Salamis: the ocean-fighting U.S. Navy yielded priority to an air-fighting Navy. Crediting King alone with this extraordinary growth would be unfair. Again it was the president who recruited people who knew how to marshal the might of U.S. industry in building a powerful Navy, men like Henry J. Kaiser, former yacht builder, who cranked out destroyer escorts and Liberty ships sometimes in days; and the Danish immigrant dynamo William S. Knudsen, former General Motors president, who spent a great part of a $4.3 billion military appropriation on building ships. Andrew Higgins devised the landing craft that bore his name and without which, Eisenhower claimed, "We never could have landed over an open beach." To Ike, Higgins was simply "the man who won the war for us."

In the conference at Honolulu in the summer of 1944, held to determine how best to fight the Pacific war, King both won and lost. He was not present personally, since Roosevelt had left the three service chiefs at home. Beforehand, however, King deputized Nimitz to make his case. Nimitz mounted a brilliant argument for continuing island hopping westward across the Pacific, all the way to Formosa, thus cutting off Japan without a shot being fired or an American life lost in an invasion. MacArthur countered with his contention that America had a debt of honor to liberate the Filipinos. FDR performed an election-year straddle, approving both approaches. By this time, American industrial might could easily support both campaigns. King had scored a split decision.

The differences between King and Nimitz bear examining, one behaving like a schoolyard bully and the other like a schoolyard hero. King feared that Nimitz was too soft, too conciliatory, too gentlemanly in the competition between the military services. He did not give Nimitz his head, frequently dragging the Pacific commander back from his Pearl Harbor headquarters to San Francisco for instruction, admonition, and, rarely, praise. An unofficial duty of the civil Nimitz was to serve as a firewall between King's blowtorch leadership and naval officers who did not deserve to be singed. It was to Nimitz that FDR turned to immediately after the shock of December 7. "Tell Nimitz to get the hell out to Pearl Harbor," he ordered. It was Nimitz who gambled on the predictions of his code breakers and thereby won the Battle of Midway, the turning point in the Pacific war. It was Nimitz's Navy, led by outstanding subordinates Bull Halsey, Raymond Spruance, Marc Mitscher, Richmond Turner, John McCain Jr., and a half dozen others who won the great naval battles, Midway, Philippine Sea, Leyte Gulf, with Coral Sea a mixed result and only Savo Island a defeat. It was Nimitz's forces who mastered the tactics of amphibious invasions, producing victories on Guadalcanal, Tarawa, Saipan, Iwo Jima, Okinawa, and lesser islands while leaving strongly held fortresses like Truk Island impotent. It is difficult to quarrel with Roosevelt's selection of the two admirals who ended the war victoriously in the Pacific, leaving the Japanese navy largely on the ocean's bottom. The Atlantic was swept so clean by the American and British navies that not a single troop transport, carrying nearly two million men to Europe, was lost.

HAP ARNOLD ENTERED THE PRESIDENT's orbit through two sponsors, Harry Hopkins and FDR's son Elliott, the flier and aviation enthusiast. It was young Roosevelt who urged his father to support Arnold's early promotion to brigadier general. Not long after Roosevelt made Arnold chief of the Army Air Corps. The flier preached an aviation philosophy compelling to FDR, that airpower could win a war. Early in his dealings with the president, however, Arnold ran into the steel beneath the genial Roosevelt facade. He learned that FDR banished anyone he felt was not "on board." The general's hopes revived when Roosevelt began talking about plane production in the tens of thousands, and the air chief trampled over bureaucrats to make it happen. Roosevelt raised the prestige of Arnold's branch by renaming the Army Air Corps the more resounding Army Air Forces, and put Hap on the JCS, sitting as an equal alongside Leahy, King, and Marshall, the latter technically Hap's Army superior.

President Roosevelt had set out to create a powerful air force and Hap Arnold took up the mandate zealously with punishing effects on himself, suffering four heart attacks during the war. As Arnold saw it, FDR had handed him aviation's Magna Carta, and with it he took over a starveling force of 20,000 men and a few hundred rattletrap planes in 1938, and in seven years built it to 2.4 million men and 80,000 aircraft, the mightiest air force on earth.

FRANKLIN ROOSEVELT's dealings with Douglas MacArthur offer a case study in forbearance. After becoming president in 1933, FDR kept MacArthur on as Army chief of staff though the general was still in bad odor over his harsh suppression of the Bonus Marchers. Had Roosevelt not brought MacArthur back to active service before Pearl Harbor, he might have been remembered faintly as a general who had held key posts and ended his career, almost laughably, as a field marshal in the Philippine army. FDR overlooked the fact that MacArthur had been caught flat-footed in the Philippines hours after the attack on Pearl Harbor and mismanaged the defense of the Philippines. The president could have abandoned MacArthur, at best to die, or more humiliating, to be captured. Instead, he pulled him out and gave him command of the Southwest Pacific. FDR sided with MacArthur over King and Nimitz in the 1944 Honolulu debate, and allowed the general to retake the Philippines, which could have been bypassed. MacArthur's obsession with liberating the islands was not rooted in sound generalship, but in restoring his pride and punishing the Japanese who had bruised it.

At any one of several junctures Roosevelt could have cut MacArthur off at the knees. He didn't. The question remains why he did not. However egomaniacal MacArthur might be, Roosevelt recognized that the man possessed military brilliance. Being a preening peacock did not disqualify a man from being a gifted commander. The operations that MacArthur conducted were well executed. His success in New Guinea was vital in stopping the early Japanese juggernaut from reaching Australia. He was successful in freeing the Philippines, but at what a cost? MacArthur was capable of stunning pettiness. Marshall once noted, "I would send my compliments to someone under his command . . . and he would wait as much as two months before forwarding." He resented anyone sharing the spotlight and poured scorn on his contemporaries. He charged Eisenhower and his deputies in Europe with making "every mistake that supposedly intelligent men could make." He dismissed as useless, no doubt rightly, the North African campaign.

MacArthur was not without his champions. The eminent British soldier and historian B. H. Liddell Hart proclaimed MacArthur "supreme among the generals. His combination of strong personality, strategic grasp, tactical skill, operative mobility, and vision put him in a class above other Allied commanders in any theatre." Field Marshal Alan Brooke noted in his diary that MacArthur "outshone Marshall, and the other American and British generals, including Montgomery." It should be borne in mind that Brooke's immediate contact with the foregoing generals could be contentious, while his admiring opinion of MacArthur was arrived at from afar. Further, Alan Brooke had been crushed when Overlord went to Eisenhower and not to himself.

MacArthur's greatest gifts would not flower until after the war, when he served as a wise proconsul in democratizing Japan. His high-risk gamble in invading Inchon during the Korean War showed MacArthur at his canniest. But even in Korea, hubris undid him when he trampled on a fundamental tenet of American democracy, that the military must remain subservient to civilian authority. He flouted the dominant role of President Truman and was relieved of command, which ended the career of Douglas MacArthur. In his mirror he saw a figure of incorruptibility, courage, and wisdom caught in a web of schemers, mediocrities, detractors, and jealous rivals. He had a persecution complex, but then, complexes and genius often go hand in hand. Eric Larrabee, in *Commander in Chief*, paints a sharp-edged portrait of MacArthur. "He had the hunger that can never be satisfied: always to have been right, always perfect, always admired," Larrabee wrote. "As a human being he was a shell of tarnished magnificence, a false giant attended by real pygmies." Whatever MacArthur's defects, if symbolism and theater play a part in victory, who in the dark days of 1942, with America reeling in the Pacific, might Roosevelt have better picked to signal the country's perseverance than the American people's hero at the time, Douglas MacArthur?

IN THE ARMY HIERARCHY, George Patton had no direct link to President Roosevelt, though he delighted FDR with his dash. He owed his career to fellow officers, principally Marshall and Eisenhower. Eisenhower had read his old comrade wisely and elevated Patton to just the level of responsibility that the man's mercurial character could handle. General Jimmy Doolittle had it about right when he wrote, "I have often thought Ike used Georgie as one would use a pitbull. When there was a fight, he would tell George to 'sic 'em.' But when the fight was over, he would have to be put in isolation somewhere until the next scrap." The man's behavior was so bizarre that it raised questions about his sanity. Throughout his life Patton had been accident-prone, thrown from horses and banged up in automobiles. He once blacked out for two days after striking his head. The multiple cranial injuries likely produced long-term effects. So outlandish was his conduct that, after the victory in Europe, Major General Clarence L. Adcock, of the Fifth Army, had the Signal Corps tap Patton's phone and bug his quarters to plumb his behavior. The eavesdropping produced a record of a phone conversation between Patton and General Joseph McNarney in which Patton ranted against the Russians, "We are going to have to fight them sooner or later. . . . Why not do it now while our Army is intact and we can have their hind end kicked back into Russia in 3 months. We can do it easily with the German troops we have, if we just arm them and take them with us." During occupation duties in Bavaria, he told reporters, "The way I see it, this Nazi question is very much like a Democratic and Republican election fight." Patton was saying in effect that the Nazis who launched a world war and who murdered millions were just another party and that America had given its sons in what amounted to a political rivalry. Reported back in the United States, this comment ignited another firestorm. The man's life was a recurring cycle of self-doubt alternating with exhibitionism, driven by a constant need to prove himself exceptional. The nature of his death was the last that he would have wished for. The soldier who once told an aide, "The best end for an old campaigner is a bullet at the last minute of the last battle," was mortally injured in a minor, low-speed collision between his Army Cadillac and a truck near the German town of Neckarstadt. To his aides seeking to help him he groaned, "This is a helluva way to die."

IN ROOSEVELT'S PERFORMANCE as a recruiter selecting military chieftains capable of winning a global war, certain features stand out. First, his team was extraordinarily stable. The men he put in place to run each service in the beginning were all there at the end: Marshall for the Army, King for the Navy, and Arnold for the Air Force. Eric Larrabee has described the delicate balance that Roosevelt achieved: "Together the Joint Chiefs and their theater commanders gave a cohesion and decisiveness to the American High Command that allowed the President when it suited him to maintain, as far as the conduct of the war was concerned, that they were in charge. This was not the case: He was in charge." The stability that Roosevelt maintained stands in stark contrast to Churchill, or Hitler for that matter, who fired generals left and right. A high-ranking British navy officer observed, "There was not one admiral in an important command whom Churchill . . . did not attempt to have relieved." His chief military advisor, Alan Brooke, said of

Churchill, "He is quite the most difficult man to work with that I have ever struck, but I would not have missed the chance of working with him for anything on earth."

Contrasted with Churchill, FDR was a delegator and let his people run the daily war, while reserving to himself grand strategy. Nevertheless, he reveled in displaying his mastery of detail. Hap Arnold took to the president for approval the plan for striking the Ploesti oilfields by having B-24s fly at almost treetop level. The president consented. When Guadalcanal hung in the balance, FDR demanded that his service chiefs produce, over a weekend, a complete inventory of all munitions available that could be diverted to the island. His near photographic memory of the characteristics of weapons, along with his phenomenal knowledge of geography, rarely failed to amaze the military. When the president asked for Leahy's opinion, "I always gave him some kind of answer," the admiral remembered. "He would look at me quizzically and say, 'Bill that's not what you told me a year ago.' I frequently wondered if he was doing it on purpose." Two types of figures circled the president's military universe—planets such as Marshall, Leahy, and Eisenhower, steady in their orbits, untheatrical, dependable, and the shooting stars, fiery, unpredictable, sometimes flaming out, among them Patton, Stilwell, and Bill Donovan. The latter group, mold breakers, channel jumpers, and high-wire artists, mirrored FDR's character.

None of the service chiefs that Roosevelt chose thought parochially. All recognized that war is not war making alone, but requires a grasp of politics, economics, and psychology. If war, as it has been said, is too serious to leave to the generals, then generals must learn to see beyond the battlefield. Marshall displayed this talent in his success in gaining support from Congress, particularly in winning huge military appropriations even before the war began. Eisenhower, initially a politician naïf, learned his lessons bitterly during the Darlan wrangle in North Africa. And MacArthur never had to be taught to use politics to achieve his ends, as when he raised the specter of defeat in the 1944 presidential election campaign to FDR if he did not approve a campaign to liberate the Philippines.

Another common thread running through Roosevelt's choices was his single standard, merit. Almost to a man, none of the leading generals and admirals had voted for Roosevelt before the war or shared his political philosophy. There was not a Democrat in the lot. Yet, not in a single instance did political affiliation, social connections, or other irrelevancy influence FDR.

Not all those whom Roosevelt appointed to fight the war were in uniform. Henry Stimson, possessing the purest Republican credentials, made the wartime cabinet truly nonpartisan, as did his fellow Republican, Frank Knox. Harry Hopkins, without a single previous military credential, won Churchill's respect and his ear in shaping Allied policies, and served as something of a scout for military talent. If FDR could be overly optimistic about Russia, Averell Harriman fought mightily to have him see the true face of Stalin and his regime. Henry Morgenthau Jr., while overzealous in his plans to emasculate postwar Germany, was a gifted financier in funding the war. FDR turned fortuitously to Vannevar Bush to assemble the minds that conceived the potentiality of the atom bomb, which, however terribly, ended the war overnight.

Strategist in Chief

How able was Roosevelt as a strategist? The Constitution reads under Article II, Section II, "The President shall be commander in chief of the Army and Navy of the United States, and the militia of several states when called into the actual service of the United States." This power has been borne nominally, almost as an honorific, by most presidents without military backgrounds, particularly in time of peace. To presidents once soldiers themselves, the mantle was taken up naturally, among them, Washington, Jackson, Grant, and Eisenhower. Finally there are civilian presidents who seized the constitutional power granted them and used it to the fullest, Lincoln and FDR most notably, and to a lesser extent Woodrow Wilson, Harry Truman, and, more recently, Lyndon Johnson, Richard Nixon, George H. W. Bush, George W.

Bush, and Barack Obama. FDR's performance as a strategist must be judged by how well he achieved his political ends by military means since, as Clausewitz has written, "War is not a mere act of policy but a true political instrument, a continuation of political activity by other means."

The first strategic decision that FDR made, even before the United States went to war, was to rank Germany as the leading threat, hence the destroyer deal, Lend-Lease, and the undeclared war in the Atlantic. He saw Nazism as a cancer that, unless excised, could destroy democracy and Western civilization. He did not change his priority even after the attack on Pearl Harbor, when the American people were seething with rage against Japan and lukewarm about getting involved in a war against Germany. Hitler's December 11, 1941, declaration of war against the United States forced Roosevelt's next strategic decision. His military chiefs arrived early at a unanimous consensus. Massive American power must be assembled in England, alongside British forces, to mount an invasion of the continent across the English Channel, through occupied France, and into Germany. This operation, they believed, should be launched if possible in 1942 and certainly no later than 1943. Roosevelt overrode them all and instead accepted Churchill's case for going into France's North African colonies in 1942, producing the anomaly of American troops first fighting, not the Germans, but the French. Why Roosevelt chose to go against the very leaders he had chosen to run the war is explained largely by Churchill's powers of persuasion. Two motives underlay the prime minister's thinking: first, to avoid another head-on collision with Germany such as occurred in the First World War, leading to the charnel houses of the Somme, Passchendaele, and Ypres, which almost bled Britain's young manhood white. Secondly, Churchill thought not merely in terms of winning the war, but how to win it in a way that maximized Britain's postwar position. The country's greatness lay in her empire and the artery that sustained the empire ran from the British Isles along the Mediterranean, through the Suez Canal, to the Far Eastern jewels in the imperial crown. Axis control of the Mediterranean threatened that lifeline. Churchill's argument for North Africa shrewdly accommodated FDR's determination that American troops be engaged somewhere in 1942. The prime minister and his generals warned that the U.S. Army was not yet ready to take on the Wehrmacht in Hitler's Fortress Europa. North Africa offered an available, manageable training ground. Finally, at this early stage, Roosevelt bowed to Churchill's superior military credentials. FDR had never worn a uniform for a day in his life, while Churchill was a commissioned officer in the British army, a graduate of Sandhurst, Britain's military academy, who had actually seen combat in the Boer War and in the trenches in World War I; he had twice run the Royal Navy as first lord of the admiralty, and was now leading a nation that had been at war for over two years before the United States entered the conflict.

Marshall had warned Roosevelt that Torch would drain men and resources from the cross-Channel invasion and was proved right in that an army strong enough to invade the continent was not in place until mid-1944. However, the war in Europe was fought and won, leading to the assumption that the decisions that produced the victory must have been right. But even victories can be imperfectly fought, take too long, and cost more in lives and treasure than necessary. Roosevelt in his eagerness to fight in 1942 inadvertently was serving British imperial interests at the risk of lengthening the war. Hitler said that Torch cost the enemy at least six unnecessary months. Australia's prime minister, Robert Menzies, concluded, "Only Churchill's magnificent and courageous leadership compensated for his deplorable strategic sense." In his postwar histories, Churchill played down both his preference for the Mediterranean and his qualms about Overlord, saying, "I always considered that a decisive assault upon the German-occupied countries on the largest possible scale was the only way in which the War could be won." None of his actions at the time support this claim.

IF NORTH AFRICA WAS A MISTAKE, it was compounded by Sicily and Italy. Again, Roosevelt's key advisors, Marshall in the lead, judged these two campaigns unnecessary and a drag on Overlord. Over 150,000 men were siphoned off to invade Sicily within the first seventy-two hours, essentially the same number that took part in the Normandy landings. Once again, Roosevelt deferred to Churchill, who maintained that Italy would tie down German divisions, thus reducing enemy forces available to repel Overlord and take pressure off the Russian Front. In the latter case, quite the reverse occurred. In November 1943, a month after Allied troops went ashore at Salerno, the Germans actually *withdrew* divisions from Italy and sent them to Russia. "We have therefore failed," Churchill admitted to his chiefs, "to take the weight of the attack off the Soviets." Roosevelt would have been content to end the Italian campaign with the fall of Rome, and Marshall hoped so emphatically. The fighting, however, went on, and in his January 1945 State of the Union address, FDR felt compelled to rationalize the Italian war, saying, "The tremendous operations in Western Europe have overshadowed in the public mind the less spectacular but vitally important Italian front. . . . These valiant forces in Italy are continuing to keep a substantial portion of the German army under constant pressure—including some twenty first-line German divisions."

Churchill's case for Sicily and then Italy continued his Mediterranean First policy and his desire that the Western Allies win the war as far east as possible, using Italy as a wedge into Austria and Germany's weak allies, Bulgaria and Romania, thus keeping large stretches of Europe beyond the Red Army's grasp. The World War II historian Gerhard Weinberg concluded that assuming "a push into Northern Italy and into the Alps toward Austria would have gotten anywhere, is beyond belief." Congresswoman Clare Boothe Luce of Connecticut and wife of *Time* publisher Henry Luce, after visiting the Italian front, sent a stinging critique to Henry Stimson, declaring that low morale was "a result of widespread and deepening disbelief among the men in the purpose and importance of the whole Italian campaign."

Though Churchill exercised a disproportionate influence over Roosevelt, by war's end the power balance had shifted. In the early years of their association, FDR was clearly Churchill's junior partner in military matters. But as American industry began to outproduce all other powers, as Americans in uniform began to outnumber British forces, the center of gravity began to shift. Churchill's private secretary noted, "up until Overlord, he saw himself as the supreme authority to whom all military decisions were referred. Now he is by force of circumstances little more than a spectator." Churchill himself did not deny the change. "Up to July 1944 England had considerable say in things; after that I was conscious that it was America who made the decisions," he admitted. FDR was now in the saddle.

ANOTHER STRATEGIC QUESTION CONCERNS the efficacy and the morality of the indiscriminate Allied bombing of German cities. Here, Roosevelt's role was not direct but passive. Arnold, his Air Forces chief, working through his deputies, Spaatz and Eaker, in concert with the RAF, decided the air war. But Roosevelt had chosen Arnold and no evidence exists that he looked upon carpet bombing as anything but another necessary evil in achieving final victory. The verdict on the air offensive is mixed. Air superiority made D-Day possible, and the defense of German cities did divert manpower and airpower that the Germans could have thrown against Allied armies. The German arms minister, Albert Speer, told his captors after the war that 88-mm field guns that might have been used against enemy tanks and troops on the battlefield were instead diverted to defending cities. Freeman Dyson, a physicist who advised on bombing strategy, argued the opposite case, claiming that if the Allies had used the manpower and resources invested in bombing German cities elsewhere, the war in Europe "would probably have ended at least a year sooner." Astonishingly, under the day and night rain of destruction, German industrial production reached its peak in July 1944. Measuring the cost to the Allies in lives and matériel against the damage wrought upon the enemy, the military historian Major General J. F. C. Fuller concluded that the bombing campaign had been "a grotesque failure."

Whatever its merits or mistakes, the air campaign produced hell on earth for the people below. For every four German combat deaths a civilian died. In particularly hard-hit cities the death toll was higher at home than for the local men at the front. Harry Hopkins, while in Europe soon after the war, stared out of his airplane window at Berlin below and pronounced the city "another Carthage." As a weapon to destroy German morale the bombing has to be judged a flop. Morale could not be broken because the populace was numb from ceaseless pounding and little morale remained to be broken. The destruction falling down about their ears did not make the people resentful toward the regime that had brought them to this pass. Rather they saw themselves as a civilized, hardworking, law-abiding nation wantonly attacked by obtuse Western neighbors turned barbarian.

ROOSEVELT'S MAJOR STRATEGIC DECISION in the Pacific, to overrule his admirals and allow Douglas MacArthur to invade the Philippines, cost a steep price, but proved serendipitous. MacArthur's invasion combined with Nimitz's island hopping divided and weakened Japan's forces fatally. Eric Larrabee offers Roosevelt a backhanded compliment for deferring to MacArthur on the Philippine issue. The decision, he concluded, conferred "great credit on him not as a strategist but as a politician."

THE NEXT DECISION BY WHICH FDR's role as a strategist must be judged was his call at Casablanca in 1943 for unconditional surrender. The critics of unconditional surrender maintain that the words put steel into the German resistance, thus prolonging the war. They argue the preferability of negotiations. This position begs the question, negotiations with whom? One frequently mentioned German who supposedly could have brokered a peace was Admiral Wilhelm Canaris, chief of the Abwehr, the intelligence branch of the German High Command. But Canaris wound up with piano wire around his neck for his supposed complicity in the 20th of July plot to assassinate Hitler. Canaris's Abwehr was dissolved overnight and taken over by the arch-Nazi Heinrich Himmler. Germany's sterling war hero, Erwin Rommel, was pressured into committing suicide for an alleged connection to the plot. He was given the poison not by Nazi fanatics, but by two Regular Army generals. So crushed was the resistance after July 20 that no German hand was ever raised again against the Nazi regime. The party apparatus remained in control until the last building collapsed in Berlin. Dwight Eisenhower expressed doubts about unconditional surrender at the time Roosevelt announced it. But upon reflection, in his memoirs, he wrote that those who theorized negotiations could have shortened the war, "fail to appreciate the rigidity of the Nazi structure, the iron discipline imposed on the German people, or the failure of previous attempts to bring Hitler down. . . . So long as Hitler was alive, there could be no question about his control of the nation—and no alternative to unconditional surrender. His control over a cultured and civilized people was eerily hypnotic." Since Hitler and his accomplices could not be dislodged, the idea of conducting negotiations with the author of history's greatest calamity, or Himmler, the architect of extermination, or Joseph Goebbels, the mouthpiece of Nazism, or lesser but equally fanatic Nazi leaders was unthinkable. There simply was no respectable leadership left capable of taking control of Germany with whom the Allies could negotiate.

Giving the Soviet Union all-out support once Germany invaded Russia was also a strategic decision made by FDR. Roosevelt chose to come to Stalin's aid because at the time of the invasion, the Wehrmacht seemed unstoppable. And so he chose the ancient wisdom that the enemy of my enemy is my friend. Churchill, as anticommunist as a lord, reached the same conclusion when confronted with the choice of facing Germany alone or with Russia as an ally. FDR vigorously pushed for Lend-Lease to the Soviet Union totaling more than $11.3 billion, over five times the cost of the Manhattan Project. The aid ranged from a half million vehicles and aluminum to build Russian planes to foodstuffs. A *New Yorker* cartoon showed a Soviet official unloading a ship at a dock desperately searching his Russian-English dictionary for the word "Spam." Still the contribution went largely unacknowledged by the Russians. A display of too much gratitude would have forced the conclusion that a communist regime was incapable on its own of defeating Nazism and had to depend on the capitalists. Appreciated or not, Roosevelt saw in the outpouring of aid a fair exchange: Russia would continue to bear the brunt of the fighting while the Western Allies would preserve more lives.

Roosevelt was wrongheaded in his belief, almost to the end, that by obliging Stalin he could make the Soviet Union a benevolent member in the family of nations. Because his own postwar aims were so lofty, and his persuasive charm heretofore so irresistible, he failed to grasp that the Joseph Stalins of the world do not respond to goodwill, which they interpret as weakness, but to force, even bullying, which they fear and respect. Stalin and the rest of the Soviet leadership possessed not a single democratic impulse. The czarism of the czars had been replaced by the czarism of the commissars.

What might Roosevelt and Churchill have done differently at Yalta? Critics paint a picture of a feeble, dying president incapable of standing up to Stalin and giving away Eastern Europe. As recently as 2005, President George W. Bush, in a speech in Riga, Latvia, called Yalta "one of the greatest wrongs in history," and charged that "The agreement at Yalta followed in the unjust tradition of Munich and the Berlin-Molotov-Ribbentrop Pact." The argument has a superficial plausibility, powerful nations carving up smaller nations. But the analogy has an intrinsic defect. It ignored where the Red Army stood in 1945. A leading Cold War historian, Yale's John Lewis Gaddis, called the Bush comparison "a bit much" and countered that "Yalta didn't change a thing. If the Yalta Conference had never taken place, the division of Europe into two great spheres of influence would still have happened." Robert Dallek, respected Roosevelt foreign policy historian, adds "This idea that Roosevelt gave away Eastern Europe is nonsense." Later generations cannot re-create the mood of May 1945. Hitler had been defeated, the world was war-weary, and the only way that the Soviet Union might have been dislodged from the territory it held was if the Western Allies were willing to declare war against Russia after defeating Germany, which no leader advocated. Averell Harriman, deeply involved at the time, later concluded, "The postwar problems have resulted not from the understandings at Yalta but from the fact that Stalin failed to carry out those understandings in the postwar world." Churchill's famous denunciations of Soviet aggrandizement were not made at the time of Yalta, but after the war, most notably in his March 5, 1946, "Iron Curtain" speech in Fulton, Missouri. In the final tally, Roosevelt showered the Soviet Union with aid that America could easily afford to give and gave Stalin nothing that he did not already possess. The military historian Hanson Baldwin, however, has raised a provocative point: should the West have sided with Russia at all? Writing in *Great Mistakes of the War*, Baldwin ranked the decision to back the Soviet Union among the greatest. "There is no doubt whatever that it would have been in the interest of Britain, the United States, and the world," Baldwin concluded, "to have encouraged the world's two great dictatorships to fight each other to a frazzle." But that took hindsight. At the time Britain stood alone and Roosevelt saw Western civilization threatened, which ironically could be reversed by pitting the communist Soviet Union against the Nazis.

FDR's PERFORMANCE AS A STRATEGIST must be measured against a single standard: did his decisions advance or hinder successful prosecution of the war? As for his giving first priority to defeating Germany, the answer is a clear "Yes." The Reich presented a far greater threat than Japan. His decisions to support the invasions of North Africa, Sicily, and Italy rate an emphatic "No." They undoubtedly prolonged the war. His insistence on unconditional surrender rates a "Maybe." It may have stiffened enemy resistance, though that is not measurable; but it did give the Allies the moral high ground in a war against irredeemable enemies. As for backing MacArthur's case to retake the Philippines, if judged along with his parallel support of Nimitz's thrust through the Central Pacific, the answer is "Yes." Both hemmed in Japanese mobility. His tolerance of the bombing campaign against German cities is again a "Maybe." It distracted both the Allies and the Germans from possibly better use of their forces. The atom bomb, however pitiless, must be scored a "Yes." It brought World War II to an instant end. Churchill gave FDR high marks for his strategic decisions. He told his physician and confidant, Lord Moran, that the president was "the most skillful strategist of them all" and he ranked him "better than Marshall." The lofty grade may, however, reflect that Roosevelt usually sided with Churchill rather than Marshall on major issues. In sum, FDR's grade as a strategist is mixed. His best decisions advanced victory. His worst decisions delayed it.

Roosevelt, the Home Front Leader

Finally, we may judge how well Roosevelt performed as the president of a people at war. At the end of FDR's life, the columnist Walter Lippmann wrote, "The final test of a leader is that he leaves behind him in other men the conviction and the will to carry on." Clearly, Roosevelt left such a legacy. He exuded confidence and competence, thus his countrymen were willing to follow his lead. The very timbre of his voice, firm yet fatherly, the intimate fireside chats, the dazzling smile, the upturned hat brim, the jauntily angled cigarette, the air of insouciance, the quips and banter with the press, told them that if their president felt so upbeat, then how dark could the outcome be? All would turn out well. Like a schoolmaster, he urged his people over the radio to get out their maps and follow the war's progress with him. He drew more Americans into the war effort and enlarged democracy by creating the Women's Army Corps. He gingerly moved toward racially integrating 1.2 million blacks into the armed forces but at a snail's pace. He pressed to have films made to awaken civilians and those in uniform to what they were fighting for. He visited the defense plants and boosted War Bond drives. Roosevelt rewarded those who had risked all in creating the GI Bill, one of the most transformative social experiments in the nation's history. Over 10 million veterans participated, of whom 67,000 became physicians, 238,000 teachers, 14 Nobel laureates, 3 Supreme Court Justices, and 3 presidents. The GI Bill was described by one of its beneficiaries as "a magic carpet to the middle class." The bill assured men and women fighting the war that their sacrifices would not be forgotten the moment they took off the uniform.

✭

THE WELLSPRINGS OF ROOSEVELT'S ideas, such as Lend-Lease, baffled even those closest to him. His rambling, hopscotching conversations struck many as the meanderings of an undisciplined mind. What linear thinkers did not see were the hidden pathways of an intuitive imagination. What seemed to be non sequiturs were his way of thinking out loud to find out what he thought. His labor secretary, Frances Perkins, described him as "the most complicated human being I ever knew. . . . But this very complication of his nature made it possible for him to have insight and imagination into the most varied human experiences." FDR was the chess master looking down on the entire board. His seeming mental disarray obscured an overarching intelligence capable of envisioning simultaneously the multiple facets of military decision making, strategy, manpower, logistics, ships, planes, tanks, the enemy reaction, and synthesizing all these in deciding where he wanted to go. An old military axiom has it that "Amateurs talk about strategy, professionals talk about logistics." Roosevelt talked and thought knowledgeably about both.

He was bolder than the Congress or his generals and admirals; witness the destroyer deal done on his own hook, Lend-Lease with its rickety legality, his stretching the ocean boundaries to limits that would have astounded President James Monroe and his Doctrine, his willingness to fight an undeclared war in the Atlantic, his risking billions on an atomic weapon whose workability was uncertain at best. Had he been less bold, Britain could have collapsed and Hitler could have won the war.

By the time of his death, all his battles had been won. Allied victory was certain. He had promised the people an unconditional victory, not a halfhearted settlement, and that is what he delivered. His vision of a United Nations was about to be realized. An end to imperialism, which he preached and practiced, would become a hallmark of the postwar world. Roosevelt bore the burden of leading the nation in fighting two successful wars on opposite ends of the globe while enduring pain and immobility that would have broken a lesser spirit. There is no comparable case in history of anyone rising to the leadership of a great nation as severely crippled as was FDR. The president's life can only be regarded as heroic. The American people and all liberty-loving nations were blessed that when the world needed a giant, one emerged. Franklin Delano Roosevelt ranks with the immortals, with Washington and Lincoln, both as a president and as commander in chief.

Acknowledgments

ONCE AGAIN IN THIS MY THIRD BOOK ON PRESIDENT FRANKLIN Delano Roosevelt I am indebted to several people without whose involvement the work could never have been written. At Random House I was guided by two distinguished editors, Jon Meacham, who with his sure touch for narrative history and keen literary sensibilities led the way for me, and Robert Loomis, who initially saw merit in the project and who edited three of my previous books. Also at Random House, I am indebted to publisher and president Gina Centrello and the able Benjamin Steinberg. Esther Newberg, my agent, secured indispensable support for the project. The archives at the Roosevelt Library at Hyde Park proved the treasure trove for the book. The library's director at the beginning, Cynthia Koch, and Lynn Bassanese at the end, both put the resources of the library at my disposal. Among their colleagues I am most beholden to the library's supervising archivist, Robert Clark, who never failed to go above and beyond my requests for help. Among Bob's staff I wish to thank Mark Renovitch along with his assistant, Matthew Hanson, who did an extraordinary job of locating photos for me. Other FDR archivists who assisted at the library included Alycia Vivona, Karen Anson, and Virginia Lewick.

Through the intercession of Mary Redmond at the New York State Library, I benefited from the talents of one of the finest researchers in my experience, William Schilling, succeeded by the able Douglas O'Connor. At the library of the State University at Albany, my alma mater, through the backing of the director, Mary Casserly, I received superb research assistance contributions from Peter Bae and Gerald Burke. And, as usual, I was assisted by Margrit Krewson, formerly of the Library of Congress.

I have again benefited from the talent at my local library in Guilderland, New York. The director, Barbara Nichols Randall, and her assistant director, Margaret Garrett, along with reference librarians Mary Alingh, Maria Buhl, Margaret Lanoue, and Eileen Williams, and the rest of the reference staff were invaluable to me.

The involvement of historians in Congress Fred Beuttler, Matthew Wasniewski, and Anthony Wallis was crucial to my story. I was especially fortunate in having conversations with Curtis Roosevelt, whose memories of FDR, his grandfather, are still fresh and vivid. My colleague, Tanya Melich, aided me through her keen-eyed reading of the manuscript. Several people were helpful to me in ways they will recognize: Roger Hind, Dan Gerber, Henry Jurenka, John Foley, Wolfgang Neumann, Dr. Michael Mattioli, and Jim Burns.

Perhaps most fortunate was the support I enjoyed within my own family, my wife, Sylvia, for her work on the manuscript and her unfailing good judgment, and my daughter, Vanya Perez, my editorial assistant and photo editor, who proved indispensable.

Glossary

AEF: Allied Expeditionary Force

Anvil (also called Dragoon): Code name for invasion of southern France, August 1944

Arcadia: First Washington conference, December 1941

Avalanche: Code name for invasion of Italy, September 1943

B-17: Flying Fortress, backbone of the U.S. bombing fleet

B-24: Liberator, heavy long-range U.S. bomber

B-29: Superfortress

Barbarossa: German plan for invading Russia

Bodyguard: Allied deception plan for Normandy invasion

Bolero: Code name for buildup of U.S. forces in Britain

Cigs: Britain's chief of the Imperial General Staff

Cinc: Commander in chief

Cominch: Commander in chief, U.S. Fleet

ETOUSA: European Theater of Operations, U.S. Army

FCNL: French Committee of National Liberation

Fortitude: Code name for Normandy invasion deception plan

Frantic: Code name for U.S. shuttle bombing between West and Russia

FUSAG: First United States Army Group

Gold: Code name for beach British struck in Normandy

Gymnast: Code name for North Africa invasion

Husky: Code name for Sicily invasion

JCS: Joint Chiefs of Staff

Juno: Code name for beach Canadians struck in Normandy

Mulberry: Code name for Allied artificial harbor in Normandy

Neptune: Code name for land portion of Normandy invasion

Omaha: Code name for beach U.S. struck in Normandy

OSS: Office of Strategic Services

Overlord: Code name for invasion of northwest Europe

Pointblank: Allied bombing strategy for Germany

Quadrant: U.S.-British conference, Quebec, 1942

RAF: Royal Air Force

Sledgehammer: Code name for 1942 cross-Channel invasion

Sword: Code name for beach British struck in Normandy

Torch: Code name for invasion of North Africa

Trident: Code name for British-American 1943 Washington conference

Utah: Code name for beach U.S. struck in Normandy

V-1: First German pilotless flying bomb

V-2: German supersonic rocket

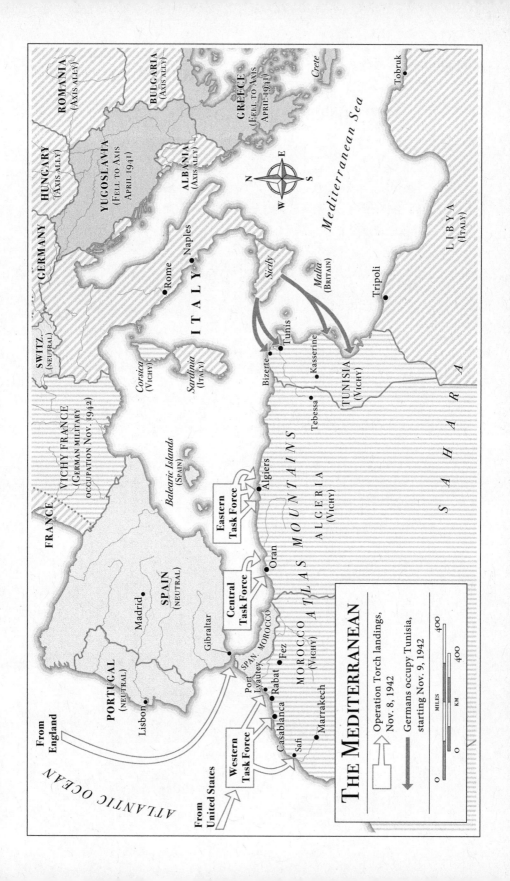

THE MEDITERRANEAN

→ Operation Torch landings, Nov. 8, 1942

→ Germans occupy Tunisia, starting Nov. 9, 1942

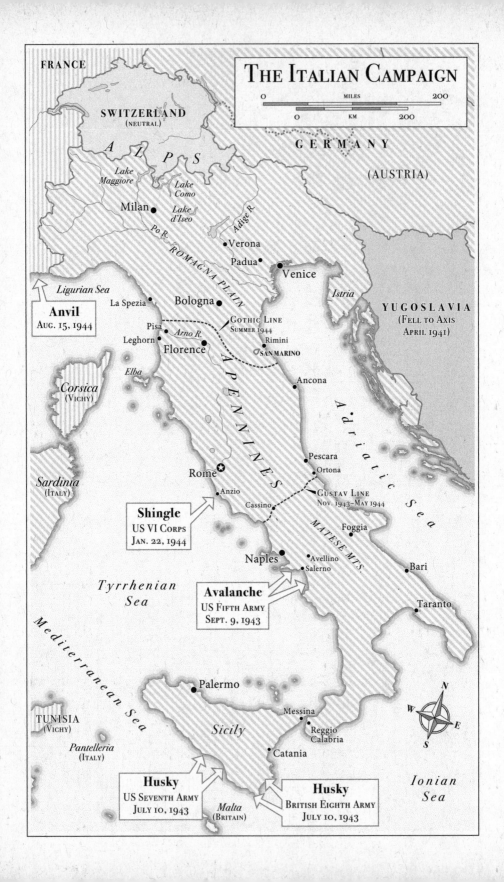

THE ITALIAN CAMPAIGN

MILES
0   200

KM
0   200

FRANCE

SWITZERLAND
(NEUTRAL)

GERMANY

(AUSTRIA)

A L P S

Lake
Maggiore

Lake
Como

Milan

Lake
d'Iseo

Adige R.

Verona

Padua

Po R.

ROMAGNA PLAIN

Venice

Istria

YUGOSLAVIA
(FELL TO AXIS
APRIL 1941)

Ligurian Sea

Anvil
AUG. 15, 1944

La Spezia

Bologna

GOTHIC LINE
SUMMER 1944

Pisa

Arno R.

Leghorn

Florence

Rimini

SAN MARINO

A P E N N I N E S

Elba

Ancona

Corsica
(VICHY)

Adriatic Sea

Sardinia
(ITALY)

Rome

Anzio

Pescara

Ortona

Shingle
US VI CORPS
JAN. 22, 1944

Cassino

GUSTAV LINE
NOV. 1943–MAY 1944

Foggia

MATESE MTS.

Naples

Avellino

Salerno

Bari

Avalanche
US FIFTH ARMY
SEPT. 9, 1943

Tyrrhenian
Sea

Taranto

Mediterranean Sea

TUNISIA
(VICHY)

Pantelleria
(ITALY)

Palermo

Messina

Reggio
Calabria

Sicily

Catania

N
W   E
S

Husky
US SEVENTH ARMY
JULY 10, 1943

Malta
(BRITAIN)

Husky
BRITISH EIGHTH ARMY
JULY 10, 1943

Ionian
Sea

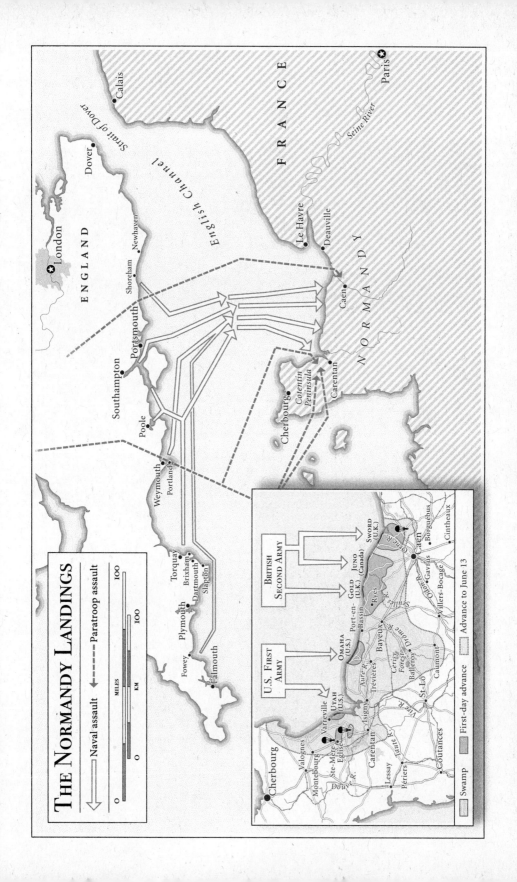

THE NORMANDY LANDINGS

Naval assault →
Paratroop assault ⇢

MILES
0   100
KM
0   100

London
ENGLAND
Dover
Strait of Dover
Calais
FRANCE
Paris
Seine River
Le Havre
Deauville
NORMANDY
Caen
English Channel
Shoreham
Newhaven
Portsmouth
Southampton
Poole
Weymouth
Portland
Slapton
Dartmouth
Brixham
Torquay
Plymouth
Fowey
Falmouth
Cherbourg
Cotentin Peninsula
Carentan

U.S. FIRST ARMY
BRITISH SECOND ARMY
Cherbourg
Valognes
Montebourg
Ste-Mère-Église
Varreville
UTAH (U.S.)
Carentan
Périers
Lessay
Coutances
St-Lô
Caumont
Villers-Bocage
Cintheaux
Bourguebus
Caen
SWORD (U.K.)
JUNO (Canada)
GOLD (U.K.)
Port-en-Bassin
OMAHA (U.S.)
Bayeux
Ryes
Trévières
Cerisy Forest
Balleroy
Gavrus
Orne R.
Odon R.
Seulles R.
Aure R.
Drôme R.
Vire R.
Taute R.
Douve R.
Dou(ve) R.

Swamp
First-day advance
Advance to June 13

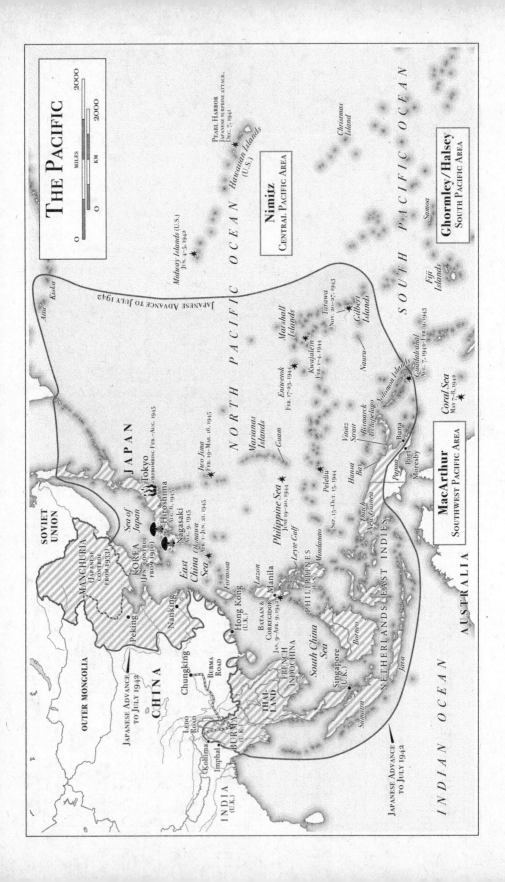

THE PACIFIC

MILES   0   2000
KM   0   2000

SOVIET UNION

OUTER MONGOLIA

MANCHURIA
(JAPANESE CONTROL FROM 1933)

CHINA

Peking
Nanking
Chungking

BURMA ROAD
LEDO ROAD

INDIA (U.K.)

KOHIMA
Imphal

BURMA (U.K.)

THAILAND

FRENCH INDOCHINA

Singapore (U.K.)
Sumatra

Hong Kong (U.K.)

South China Sea

Tara

Borneo

NETHERLANDS EAST INDIES

AUSTRALIA

INDIAN OCEAN

KOREA
(JPN. CONTROL FROM 1910)

JAPAN

Sea of Japan

Tokyo   FIREBOMBING: FEB.—AUG. 1945
Hiroshima   AUG. 6, 1945
Nagasaki   AUG. 9, 1945
Okinawa   APR. 1—JUN. 21, 1945

East China Sea

Formosa

Iwo Jima   FEB. 19—MAR. 16, 1945

Marianas Islands

Guam

Luzon
Manila
Batan & Corregidor   JAN. 9—APR. 9, 1942

PHILIPPINES (U.S.)

Leyte Gulf

Mindanao

Peleliu   SEP. 15—OCT. 15, 1944

Philippine Sea   JUNE 19—20, 1944

NORTH PACIFIC OCEAN

Attu
Kiska

JAPANESE ADVANCE TO JULY 1942

Midway Islands (U.S.)   JUN. 4—5, 1942

Marshall Islands

Eniwetok   FEB. 17—23, 1944
Kwajalein   FEB. 1—4, 1944

Tarawa   NOV. 20—27, 1943
Gilbert Islands

Nauru

Dutch New Guinea

Papua
Port Moresby

Hansa Bay

Vitiaz Strait
Bismarck Archipelago

Buna

Solomon Islands

Guadalcanal   AUG. 7, 1942—FEB. 9, 1943

Coral Sea   MAY 7—8, 1942

SOUTH PACIFIC OCEAN

PEARL HARBOR
JAPANESE SURPRISE ATTACK,
DEC. 7, 1941

Hawaiian Islands (U.S.)

Christmas Island

Samoa

Fiji Islands

Nimitz
CENTRAL PACIFIC AREA

Chormley/Halsey
SOUTH PACIFIC AREA

MacArthur
SOUTHWEST PACIFIC AREA

JAPANESE ADVANCE TO JULY 1942

Bibliography

Published Sources

Abramson, Rudy. *Spanning the Century: The Life of W. Averell Harriman.* New York: William Morrow, 1992.

Adolf Hitler: Speeches Before Generals, August 22, 1939. Reues Europa.

Allen, Frederick Lewis. "Marshall, Arnold, King: Three Snapshots." *Harper's Magazine,* Vol. 190, February 1945.

Allen, Robert S. "The Day Patton Quit." *Army,* June 1971.

Alsop, Joseph, and Robert Kinter. *American White Paper: The Story of American Diplomacy and the Second World War.* New York: Simon & Schuster, 1940.

————. *Men Around the President.* New York: Doubleday, Doran, 1939.

Ambrose, Stephen E. *Citizen Soldiers.* New York: Simon & Schuster, 1998.

————. *D-Day.* New York: Simon & Schuster, 1994.

————. *Eisenhower: Soldier, General of the Army, President-Elect.* New York: Simon & Schuster, 1983.

————. *The Supreme Commander: The War Years of General Dwight D. Eisenhower.* New York: Doubleday, 1969.

————. *The Victors: Eisenhower and His Boys.* New York: Simon & Schuster, 1998.

Andrew, Christopher. *For the President's Eyes Only.* New York: HarperCollins, 1995.

Armstrong, Anne. *Unconditional Surrender: The Impact of the Casablanca Policy on World War II.* New Brunswick, NJ: Rutgers University Press, 1961.

Arnold, Henry H. "Air War: Official Report of the Commanding General of the Army Air Forces to the Secretary of War." *The United States News,* January 4, 1944, Washington, DC.

————. *Global Mission.* New York: Harper & Brothers, 1949.

Atkinson, Rick. *An Army at Dawn: The War in North Africa, 1942–1943.* New York: Henry Holt, 2002.

————. *The Day of Battle: The War in Sicily and Italy, 1943–1944.* New York: Henry Holt, 2007.

Baldwin, Hanson. *Battles Lost and Won: Great Campaigns of World War II.* New York: Harper & Row, 1966.

————. *Great Mistakes of the War.* New York: Harper & Brothers, 1949.

Beevor, Anthony. *The Fall of Berlin, 1945.* New York: Viking, 2002.

Bernstein, Barton J. "Why We Didn't Use Gas in World War II." *American Heritage*, August–September 1985.

Berthon, Simon, and Joanna Potts. *Warlords.* London: Politicos, 2005.

Beschloss, Michael. *The Conquerors: Roosevelt, Truman and the Destruction of Hitler's Germany, 1941–1945.* New York: Simon & Schuster, 2002.

Biddle, Francis. *In Brief Authority.* New York: Doubleday, 1962.

Bishop, Jim. *FDR's Last Year.* New York: William Morrow, 1974.

Black, Conrad. *Franklin Delano Roosevelt: Champion of Freedom.* New York: PublicAffairs, 2003.

Blake, Robert, and William Roger Louis, eds. *Churchill: A Major New Assessment of His Life in War and Peace.* New York: W. W. Norton, 1993.

Bland, Larry I., and Sharon R. Ritenour, eds. *The Papers of George Catlett Marshall*, Vol. 1. Baltimore: Johns Hopkins University Press, 1981.

Bliss, Edward, Jr. *In Search of Light: The Broadcasts of Edward R. Murrow.* New York: Alfred A. Knopf, 1967.

Blum, John Morton. *From the Morgenthau Diaries*, Vol. 2: *Years of Urgency, 1938–1941.* Boston: Houghton Mifflin, 1965.

————. *From the Morgenthau Diaries*, Vol. 3: *Years of War, 1941–1945.* Boston: Houghton Mifflin, 1967.

Blum, John Morton, ed. *The Diary of Henry A. Wallace, 1942–1946.* Boston: Houghton Mifflin, 1973.

Blumenson, Martin. *The Battle of the Generals.* New York: William Morrow, 1994.

————. *Mark Clark.* New York: Congdon & Weed, 1984.

————. *Patton, The Man Behind the Legend, 1885–1945.* New York: William Morrow, 1985.

————. *The Patton Papers: 1940–1945.* Boston: Houghton Mifflin, 1974.

Bradley, Omar. *A Soldier's Story.* New York: Henry Holt, 1951.

Bradley, Omar N., with Clay Blair. *A General's Life.* New York: Simon & Schuster, 1981.

Brown, Anthony Cave. *Bodyguard of Lies.* New York: Harper & Row, 1975.

————. *The Last Hero: Wild Bill Donovan.* New York: Times Books, 1982.

Bryant, Arthur. *The Turn of the Tide: A History of the War Years Based on the Diaries of Field Marshall Lord Alanbrooke.* New York: Doubleday, 1957.

Buell, Thomas B. *Master of Sea Power: A Biography of Fleet Admiral Ernest J. King.* Boston: Little, Brown, 1980.

Bullard, Robert Lee. *Personalities and Reminiscences of the War.* Garden City, NY: Doubleday, Page, 1925.

Burns, James MacGregor. *Roosevelt: The Soldier of Freedom.* New York: Harcourt Brace Jovanovich, 1970.

Butcher, Harry. *My Three Years with Eisenhower.* New York: Simon & Schuster, 1946.

Butow, R. J. C. "The Story Behind the Tapes." *American Heritage,* Vol. 33, February–March, 1982.

Capra, Frank. *The Name Above the Title.* New York: Belvedere, 1982.

Charmley, John. *Churchill: The End of Glory.* New York: Harcourt Brace, 1993.

Chennault, Claire. *Way of a Fighter.* New York: Putnam, 1949.

Churchill, Winston S. *Memoirs of the Second World War.* Boston: Houghton Mifflin, 1959.

———. *The Second World War:* Vol. 1: *The Gathering Storm;* Vol. 2: *Their Finest Hour;* Vol. 3: *The Grand Alliance;* Vol. 4: *The Hinge of Fate;* Vol. 5: *Closing the Ring;* Vol. 6: *Triumph and Tragedy.* Boston: Houghton Mifflin, 1948–1953.

Clark, Mark. *Calculated Risk.* New York: Harper & Brothers, 1950.

Cline, Ray S. *Washington Command Post.* Washington, DC: Center of Military History, 1951.

Clodfelter, Micheal. *Warfare and Armed Conflicts: A Statistical Reference to Casualty and Other Figures, 1618–1991.* Jefferson, NC: McFarland, 1992.

Codman, Charles R. *Drive.* Boston: Little, Brown, 1957.

Coffey, Thomas M. *Hap: The Story of the U.S. Air Force and the Man Who Built It.* New York: Viking, 1982.

Cole, Wayne S. *Charles A. Lindbergh and the Battle Against American Intervention in World War II.* New York: Harcourt Brace Jovanovich, 1974.

Collis, Maurice. *Last and First in Burma.* New York: Macmillan, 1956.

Costello, John. *The Pacific War: 1941–1945.* New York: HarperPerennial, 2002.

Cowley, Robert, and Geoffrey Parker, eds. *The Reader's Companion to Military History.* New York: Houghton Mifflin, 1996.

Cross, Robert F. *Shepherds of the Sea.* Annapolis, MD: Naval Institute Press, 2010.

Dallek, Robert. *Franklin D. Roosevelt and American Foreign Policy, 1932–1945.* New York: Oxford University Press, 1979.

———. *Lone Star Rising: Lyndon Johnson and His Times.* New York: Oxford University Press, 1991.

Daniel, Clifton. *Lords, Ladies and Gentlemen.* New York: Arbor House, 1984.

Davis, Franklin M. *Across the Rhine.* Alexandria, VA: Time-Life Books, 1980.

Davis, Richard G. *Hap: Henry H. Arnold, Military Aviator.* Washington, DC: Air Force History and Museums Program, 1997.

de Gaulle, Charles. *The War Memoirs of Charles de Gaulle, 1944–1946.* New York: Simon & Schuster, 1960.

Deighton, Len. *Blood, Tears and Folly.* New York: HarperCollins, 1993.

DePastino, Todd. *Bill Mauldin: A Life Up Front.* New York: W. W. Norton, 2008.

D'Este, Carlo. *Eisenhower: A Soldier's Life.* New York: Henry Holt, 2002.

———. "MacArthur's Whipping Boy." *Military History Quarterly,* Winter 2004.

———. *Patton: A Genius for War.* New York: HarperCollins, 1995.

Divine, Robert A. *Roosevelt and World War II.* Baltimore: Johns Hopkins University Press, 1969.

Doolittle, General James H. *I Could Never Be So Lucky Again.* New York: Bantam, 1991.

Doyle, William. *Inside the Oval Office: The White House Tapes from FDR to Clinton.* New York: Kodansha, 1999.

Dyer, George D. *The Amphibians Came to Conquer: The Story of Richmond Kelly Turner,* Vols. 1 and 2. Washington, DC: Department of the Navy, 1969.

Dyson, Freeman. "Weapons and Hope II." *The New Yorker,* February 13, 1984.

Eade, Charles, ed. *Churchill, by His Contemporaries.* New York: Simon & Schuster, 1954.

Eaker, Ira C. "Hap Arnold: The Anatomy of Leadership." *Air Force Magazine,* September 1977.

Eisenhower, David. *Eisenhower: At War, 1943–1945.* New York: Random House, 1986.

Eisenhower, Dwight D. *At Ease: Stories I Tell My Friends.* Garden City, NY: Doubleday, 1967.

———. *Crusade in Europe.* Garden City, NY: Doubleday, 1955.

Eisenhower, John S. D. *Allies: Pearl Harbor to D-Day.* New York: Doubleday, 1982.

———. *The Bitter Woods: The Battle of the Bulge.* New York: Putnam, 1969.

———. *Strictly Personal.* Garden City, NY: Doubleday, 1974.

Eisenhower, Susan. *Mrs. Ike.* New York: Farrar, Straus & Giroux, 1996.

Emerson, William. "Franklin Roosevelt as Commander-in-Chief World War II." *Military History,* February 1959.

Erickson, John. *The Road to Berlin.* Boulder, CO: Westview, 1983.

Eubank, Keith. *Summit at Tehran.* New York: William Morrow, 1985.

Farago, Ladislas. *The Last Days of Patton.* New York: McGraw-Hill, 1981.

Feifer, George. *Tennozan: The Battle of Okinawa and the Atom Bomb.* New York: Ticknor & Fields, 1992.

Ferrell, Robert H. *The Dying President.* Columbia: University of Missouri Press, 1998.

Ferrell, Robert H., ed. *Off the Record: The Private Papers of Harry S. Truman.* New York: Harper & Row, 1980.

———. *The Eisenhower Diaries.* New York: W. W. Norton, 1981.

Finney, Nat S. "How FDR Planned to Use the A-Bomb." *Look,* March 14, 1950.

Fleming, Thomas. *The New Dealers' War.* New York: Basic Books, 2001.

———. "A Policy Written in Blood." *MHQ: The Military History Quarterly,* Winter 2009.

Flynn, George Q. *The Draft, 1940–1973.* Lawrence, University Press of Kansas, 1993.

Foreign Relations of the United States. Washington, DC: U.S. Government Printing Office, 1961.

Freidel, Frank. *Franklin D. Roosevelt: A Rendezvous with Destiny.* Boston: Little, Brown, 1970.

Fuchida, Mitsuo, and Masatake Okumiya. *Midway: The Battle That Doomed Japan.* Annapolis: Naval Institute Press, 1955.

Fuller, J. F. C. *The Second World War, 1939–45: A Strategical and Tactical History.* London: Eyre & Spottiswoode, 1948.

Gilbert, Martin. *Winston S. Churchill,* Vol. 6: *Finest Hour, 1939–1941.* Boston: Houghton Mifflin, 1983.

———. *Winston S. Churchill,* Vol. 7: *Road to Victory, 1941–1945.* Boston: Houghton Mifflin, 1986.

Gilbert, Martin, ed. *The Churchill War Papers,* Vol. 2. New York: W. W. Norton, 1993.

Goodwin, Doris Kearns. *No Ordinary Time.* New York: Simon & Schuster, 1994.

Gopnik, Adam. "Finest Hours." *The New Yorker,* August 30, 2010.

Grimsley, Mark. "What If the Allies Had Bombed Auschwitz?" *World War II Magazine,* January–February 2010.

Gunther, John. *D-Day.* New York: Harper & Brothers, 1943.

———. *Roosevelt in Retrospect.* New York: Harper & Brothers, 1950.

Halsey, William F., and J. Bryan III. *Admiral Halsey's Story.* New York: McGraw-Hill, 1947.

Harries, Meiron, and Susie Harries. *The Last Days of Innocence: America at War, 1917–1918.* New York: Random House, 1997.

Harriman, W. Averell. *Special Envoy to Churchill and Stalin: 1941–1946.* New York: Random House, 1975.

Hassett, William D. *Off the Record with FDR, 1942–1945.* New Brunswick, NJ: Rutgers University Press, 1958.

Hastings, Max. *Armageddon: The Battle for Germany, 1944–1945.* New York: Alfred A. Knopf, 2004.

Hayes, Grace P. *The History of the Joint Chiefs of Staff in World War II.* Annapolis, MD: Naval Institute Press, 1982.

Hinsley, F. H., with E. E. Thomas, C. F. G. Ransom, and R. C. Knight. *British Intelligence in the Second World War,* Vol. 1. New York: Cambridge University Press, 1979.

Hirshon, Stanley P. *General Patton: A Soldier's Life*. New York: HarperPerennial, 2003.

Hough, Frank O., with Verle Ludwig and Henry I. Shaw Jr. *History of U.S. Marine Corps Operations in World War II*, Vol. 1: *Pearl Harbor to Guadalcanal*. Washington, DC: Historical Branch, U.S. Marine Corps, 1958.

Howe, George F. *Northwest Africa: Seizing the Initiative in the West*. Washington, DC: Center of History, United States Army, 1993.

Hull, Cordell. *Memoirs of Cordell Hull*, Vols. 1 and 2. New York: Macmillan, 1948.

Hunt, Frazier. *The Untold Story of Douglas MacArthur*. New York: Devin-Adair, 1954.

Ickes, Harold L. *The Secret Diary of Harold L. Ickes*, Vol. 3: *The Lowering Clouds, 1939–1941*. New York: Simon & Schuster, 1954.

James, Clayton D. *The Years of MacArthur*, Vol. I: *1880–1941*; Vol. 2: *1941–1945*. Boston: Houghton Mifflin, 1970, 1975.

Kahn, David. *Codebreaking in World Wars I and II*. Urbana: University of Illinois Press, 1984.

———. *Hitler's Spies*. New York: Macmillan, 1978.

Keegan, John. *The Mask of Command*. New York: Penguin, 1988.

———. *The Second World War*. New York: Viking, 1990.

Kennedy, John. *The Business of War*. New York: William Morrow, 1958.

Kennedy, Paul, ed. *Grand Strategies in War and Peace*. New Haven: Yale University Press, 1991.

Kershaw, Ian. *Fateful Choices*. New York: Penguin, 2007.

Kimball, Warren F. *The Juggler: Franklin Roosevelt as Wartime Statesman*. Princeton: Princeton University Press, 1991.

Kimball, Warren F., ed. *Churchill and Roosevelt: The Complete Correspondence*. Princeton: Princeton University Press, 1984.

King, Ernest J., and Walter Muir Whitehall. *Fleet Admiral King: A Naval Record*. New York: W. W. Norton, 1952.

Knightley, Phillip. *The Second Oldest Profession*. New York: W. W. Norton, 1986.

Korda, Michael. *Ike: An American Hero*. New York: HarperCollins, 2007.

Kuter, Laurence S. "How Hap Arnold Built the AFF." *Air Force Magazine*, Washington, D.C., September 1973.

Lamb, Richard. *Montgomery in Europe: 1943–1945*. New York: Franklin Watts, 1984.

Larrabee, Eric. *Commander in Chief: Franklin Delano Roosevelt, His Lieutenants, and Their War*. Annapolis, MD: Naval Institute Press, 1987.

Lash, Joseph P. *Roosevelt and Churchill, 1939–1941*. New York: W. W. Norton, 1976.

Leahy, William D. *I Was There.* New York: McGraw-Hill, 1950.

Leckie, Robert. *Challenge for the Pacific.* Garden City, NY: Doubleday, 1965.

———. *Delivered from Evil: Saga of World War II.* New York: HarperCollins, 1989.

Lewis, Jon E., ed. *The Mammoth Book of Eyewitness World War II.* New York: Carroll & Graf, 2004.

Liebling, A. J. *Liebling Abroad.* New York: Worldview, 1981.

———. "Profiles: Chief of Staff." *The New Yorker,* October 26, 1940.

Loewenheim, Francis L., with Harold D. Langley and Manfred Jonas, eds. *Roosevelt and Churchill: Their Secret Wartime Correspondence.* New York: Saturday Review Press, 1975.

Lohbeck, Don. *Patrick J. Hurley.* Chicago: H. Regnery, 1956.

Lukacs, John. "Churchill Offers Toil and Tears to FDR." *American Heritage,* Vol. 58, No. 1, Spring–Summer 2008.

MacArthur, Douglas. *Reminiscences.* New York: McGraw-Hill, 1964.

Macmillan, Harold. *The Blast of War, 1939–1945.* New York: Carroll & Graf, 1983.

The Magic Background of Pearl Harbor, Vol. 1. Washington, DC: Department of Defense, 1978.

Manchester, William. *American Caesar: Douglas MacArthur, 1880–1964.* Boston: Little, Brown, 1978.

Marshall, Katherine Tupper. *Together: Annals of an Army Wife.* New York: Tupper & Love, 1946.

Matloff, Maurice. *Strategic Planning for Coalition Warfare, 1943–1944.* Washington, DC: Office of the Chief of Military History, Department of the Army, 1959.

McCarthy, Dudley. *Australia in the War of 1939–1945,* Vol. 5. Canberra: Australian War Memorial, 1959.

McJimsey, George. *Harry Hopkins.* Cambridge: Harvard University Press, 1987.

Meacham, Jon. *Franklin and Winston: An Intimate Portrait of an Epic Friendship.* New York: Random House, 2003.

Mead, Gary. *The Doughboys.* New York: Overlook, 2000.

Miller, Donald L. *Masters of the Air.* New York: Simon & Schuster, 2006.

———. *The Story of World War II.* New York: Simon & Schuster, 2001.

Millis, Walter (Foreword). *The War Reports of George C. Marshall, H. H. Arnold, Ernest J. King.* New York: Lippincott, 1947.

Millis, Walter, ed. *The Forrestal Diaries.* New York: Viking, 1951.

Montgomery, Sir Bernard L. *The Memoirs of Field Marshall the Viscount Montgomery.* New York: World, 1958.

Moran, Lord (Charles Wilson). *Churchill: Taken from the Diaries of Lord Moran.* New York: Random House, 1966.

Morgan, Kay Summersby. *Past Forgetting: My Love Affair with Dwight D. Eisenhower.* New York: Simon & Schuster, 1976.

Morison, Samuel E. *The History of United States Naval Operations in World War II,* Vols. 1–15. Boston: Atlantic Monthly Press, 1955–1962.

Murphy, Robert. *Diplomat Among Warriors.* Garden City, NY: Doubleday, 1964.

Nelson, Craig. *The First Heroes: The Extraordinary Story of the Doolittle Raid.* New York: Viking, 2002.

Nichols, David. *Ernie's War: The Best of Ernie Pyle's World War II Dispatches.* New York: Simon & Schuster, 1986.

Nixon, Edgar B., ed. *Franklin D. Roosevelt and Foreign Affairs,* Vols. 1–3. Cambridge: Harvard University Press, 1969.

Odom, Charles B. *General George S. Patton and Eisenhower.* New Orleans: Word Picture Productions, 1985.

Ossad, Steven. "Command Failures." *Army Magazine,* November 2008.

O'Sullivan, John. *From Voluntarism to Conscription.* New York: Garland, 1982.

Oxford, Edward. "The Draft." *American History,* 1994.

Paret, Peter. *Clausewitz and the State.* Princeton: Princeton University Press, 2007.

Parrish, Thomas. *Roosevelt and Marshall: Partners in Politics and War.* New York: William Morrow, 1989.

Patton, Robert H. *The Pattons: The Personal History of an American Family.* New York: Crown, 1994.

Pearson, Drew, and Robert S. Allen. "How the President Works." *Harper's,* June 1936.

Perkins, Frances. *The Roosevelt I Knew.* New York: Viking, 1946.

Perret, Geoffrey. *Old Soldiers Never Die: The Life of Douglas MacArthur.* New York: Random House, 1996.

Persico, Joseph E. *Edward R. Murrow: An American Original.* New York: McGraw-Hill, 1988.

———. *Eleventh Month, Eleventh Day, Eleventh Hour.* New York: Random House, 2004.

———. "The Flight of the Enola Gay." *Modern Maturity,* August–September 1985.

———. *Franklin and Lucy.* New York: Random House, 2008.

———. *Nuremberg: Infamy on Trial.* New York: Viking Penguin, 1994.

———. *Piercing the Reich.* New York: Viking, 1979.

———. *Roosevelt's Secret War: FDR and World War II Espionage.* New York: Random House, 2001.

Plaster, John L. *The History of Sniping and Sharpshooting.* Boulder, CO: Paladin, 2008.

Pogue, Forrest C. *George C. Marshall*, Vol. 1: *Education of a General, 1880–1939;* Vol. 2: *Ordeal and Hope, 1939–1942;* Vol. 3: *Organizer of Victory, 1943–1945.* New York: Viking, 1963, 1966, 1973.

———. *The Supreme Command.* Washington, DC: Center of Military History, United States Army, 1954.

Polmar, Norman, and Thomas B. Allen. *Spy Book: The Encyclopedia of Espionage.* New York: Random House, 1997.

Prange, Gordon W. *At Dawn We Slept: The Untold Story of Pearl Harbor.* New York: McGraw-Hill, 1981.

Rauch, Basil, ed. *Franklin D. Roosevelt: Selected Speeches, Messages, Press Conferences and Letters.* New York: Holt, Rinehart & Winston, 1957.

Rhodes, Richard. *The Making of the Atomic Bomb.* New York: Simon & Schuster, 1986.

Rigdon, William, and James Derieux. *White House Sailor.* Garden City, NY: Doubleday, 1962.

Roche, John. "Eisenhower Redux." *The New York Times Book Review,* June 28, 1981.

Romanus, Charles F., and Riley Sunderland. *Stilwell's Command Problems.* Washington, DC: Office of the Chief of Military History, 1956.

Roosevelt, Curtis. *Too Close to the Sun.* New York: Public Affairs, 2008.

Roosevelt, Eleanor. *The Autobiography of Eleanor Roosevelt.* New York: Harper & Brothers, 1961.

———. *This I Remember.* New York: Harper & Brothers, 1949.

Roosevelt, Elliott. *As He Saw It.* New York: Duell, Sloan & Pearce, 1946.

Roosevelt, Elliott, ed. *F.D.R.: His Personal Letters, 1928–1945,* Vol. 4. New York: Duell, Sloan & Pearce, 1950.

Roosevelt, Franklin D. *The Public Papers and Addresses of Franklin D. Roosevelt,* 1940 volume. New York: Macmillan Company, 1941.

———. *The Public Papers and Addresses of Franklin D. Roosevelt,* 1941, 1942, 1943, and 1944–1945 volumes. New York: Harper & Row, 1950.

Roosevelt, James. *Affectionately, FDR: A Son's Story of a Lonely Man.* New York: Harcourt Brace, 1959.

Roosevelt, James, and Bill Libby. *My Parents: A Differing View.* Chicago: Playboy, 1976.

Rose, Norman. *Churchill: The Unruly Giant.* New York: Free Press, 1994.

Rosenman, Samuel I. *Working with Roosevelt.* New York: Harper & Brothers, 1952.

Schlesinger, Arthur J. "FDR's Secret Romance." *Ladies' Home Journal,* November 1966.

Shaw, George Bernard. *Man and Superman.* New York: Macmillan, 1992.

Sherrod, Robert. *Tarawa: The Story of the Battle.* New York: Bantam, 1983.

Sherwood, Robert E. *Roosevelt and Hopkins: An Intimate History.* New York: Harper & Brothers, 1948.

Shirer, William L. *The Rise and Fall of the Third Reich.* New York: Simon & Schuster, 1960.

Shoumatoff, Elizabeth. *FDR: Unfinished Portrait.* Pittsburgh: University of Pittsburgh Press, 1990.

Simpson, B. Mitchell, III. *Admiral Harold R. Stark: Architect of Victory, 1939–1945.* Columbia: University of South Carolina Press, 1989.

Smith, Holland. *Coral and Brass.* Princeton Junction, NJ: Zenger, 1979.

Smith, Jean Edward. *FDR.* New York: Random House, 2007.

Smith, Merriman. *Thank You, Mr. President: A White House Notebook.* New York: Harper & Brothers, 1946.

Smith, Walter Bedell. *Eisenhower's Six Great Decisions.* New York: Longmans, Green, 1956.

Sorge, Martin K. *The Other Price of Hitler's War.* New York: Greenwood, 1986.

Spector, Ronald H. *Eagle Against the Sun: The American War with Japan.* New York: Free Press, 1985.

Spiller, Roger J. "Assessing Ultra." *Military Review,* Vol. 7, August 1979.

Stafford, David. *Churchill and Secret Service.* Toronto: Stoddart, 1997.

Stagg, J. M. *Forecast for Overlord.* London: Ian Allan, 1971.

Steele, Richard W. *The First Offensive 1942.* Bloomington: Indiana University Press, 1973.

Stettinius, Edward. *Roosevelt and the Russians.* Garden City, NY: Doubleday, 1949.

Stilwell, Joseph W., with Theodore H. White, ed. *The Stilwell Papers.* New York: William Sloane, 1948.

Stimson, Henry L., and McGeorge Bundy. *On Active Service in Peace and War.* New York: Harper & Brothers, 1947.

"The Strategic Bomber." *Air University Quarterly Review,* Vol. I, No. 1., Summer 1955.

Sudoplatov, Pavel, and Anatoli Sudoplatov. *Special Tasks.* New York: Back Bay Books/Little, Brown, 1994.

Summersby, Kay. *Eisenhower Was My Boss.* New York: Prentice Hall, 1948.

Sutherland, John P. "The Story General Marshall Told Me." *U.S. News & World Report,* November 2, 1959.

Thompson, Robert Smith. *A Time for War: Franklin Delano Roosevelt and the Path to Pearl Harbor.* New York: Prentice Hall, 1991.

Toland, John. *The Last 100 Days.* New York: Random House, 1965.

Totten, Christine M. "Remembering Sara Roosevelt." *Rendezvous,* Winter 2005.

Totten, Ruth Ellen (Patton). *The Button Box: A Daughter's Loving Memoir of Mrs. George S. Patton.* Columbia: University of Missouri Press, 2005.

Troy, Thomas F. *The Coordinator of Information and British Intelligence.* Washington, DC: Central Intelligence Agency, 1978.

Tuchman, Barbara W. *Stilwell and the American Experience.* New York: Macmillan, 1971.

Tully, Grace. *F.D.R.: My Boss.* New York: Charles Scribner's Sons, 1949.

U.S. Congress. House of Representatives Hearings Before the Committee on Military Affairs, July 10, 1940.

U.S. Congress. Joint Committee on the Investigation of the Pearl Harbor Attack, Washington, DC, December 5–12, 1945.

U.S. Congress. Joint Committee on the Investigation of the Pearl Harbor Attack, Washington, DC, April 9–11, May 23, 31, 1946.

Ward, Geoffrey C. *Closest Companion: The Unknown Story of the Intimate Friendship Between Franklin Roosevelt and Margaret Suckley.* Boston: Houghton Mifflin, 1995.

———. *A First-Class Temperament: The Emergence of Franklin Roosevelt.* New York: Harper & Row, 1989.

Watson, Mark S. *Chief of Staff: Prewar Plans and Preparations.* Washington, DC: Historical Division, Department of the Army, 1950.

Weinberg, Gerhard L. *A World at Arms.* Cambridge: Cambridge University Press, 1994.

Weintraub, Stanley. *15 Stars.* New York: Free Press, 2007.

White, Theodore H. *In Search of History.* New York: Harper & Row, 1978.

Whiting, Charles. *Patton.* New York: Ballantine, 1970.

Whitney, Courtney. *MacArthur: His Rendezvous with History.* New York: Alfred A. Knopf, 1956.

Wilson, Dale E. *Treat 'Em Rough: The Birth of American Armor, 1917–20.* Novato, CA: Presidio, 1990.

Wohlstetter, Roberta. *Pearl Harbor: Warning and Decision.* Stanford, CA: Stanford University Press, 1962.

Young, Peter, ed. *The World Almanac of World War II.* New York: World Almanac Publications, 1981.

Collections of Documents

Dwight D. Eisenhower Presidential Library, Dwight D. Eisenhower Papers, Abilene, Kansas.

George C. Marshall Papers, Marshall Foundation Research Library, Lexington, Virginia.

George S. Patton Papers, Manuscript Division, Library of Congress, Washington, DC.

George S. Patton Papers, United States Military Academy, West Point, New York.

Franklin D. Roosevelt Library, Hyde Park, New York.

Diaries, Henry Stimson, Yale University Library, New Haven, Connecticut.

U.S. Army Military History Institute, Carlisle Barracks, Pennsylvania.

Source Notes

SOURCE NOTES ARE KEYED TO THE BOOK'S PAGE NUMBER AND A QUO-
tation or phrase on that page. Sources are fully identified in the Bibli-
ography. Frequently used sources are abbreviated as follows:

COH: Oral History Project, Columbia University
DDE: Papers of Dwight D. Eisenhower, Johns Hopkins University
FDRL: Franklin D. Roosevelt Library
FRUS: *Foreign Relations of the United States,* U. S. State Department
GCM: Papers of George C. Marshall, Lexington, Virginia
MR: Map Room Files, FDRL
NYT: *New York Times*
POF: President's Official Files, FDRL
PPF: President's Personal Files, FDRL
PSF: President's Secretary's Files, FDRL
Suckley: Diaries of Margaret "Daisy" Suckley

Introduction

xii   "discarded overcoats": Ward, *A First-Class Temperament,* pp. 399–400.
xii   "we will no longer be able": Persico, *Roosevelt's Secret War,* p. 83.
xiii "When you see a rattlesnake": FDR, *Public Papers,* 1941, p. 390.
xiii "as commander in chief": Ibid., p. 514.
xiv "He has no system": Emerson, p. 190.
xiv "The helicopters": Lewis, p. 19.
xiv "the blackest day": Butcher, p. 29.
xv   "difficult if not impossible": MR, Box 26.
xv   He told his secretary of war: Stimson and Bundy, p. 435.
xv   "against the advice": Larrabee, p. 15.
xv   "If your decision be to bypass": Whitney, p. 125.

xvi "The elimination of German": FDR, *Public Papers*, 1943, p. 39.

xvi hasten the day: Harriman, p. 269.

xvi "If you were given two choices": Brown, *Bodyguard of Lies*, p. 248.

xvi "How can any German": Fleming, "A Policy Written in Blood," p. 28.

xvi "This requires action": PSF, Box 5.

xvi "No matter how long": FDR, *Public Papers*, 1941, pp. 514–15.

xvi "itch of historians": Gopnik, "Finest Hours," *The New Yorker*, August 30, 2010.

xvii "most disastrous human experience": Hastings, p. xi.

Chapter One: The Day We Almost Lost the Army

3 "the great naval base": Ibid., p. 43.

4 Wadsworth's measure: Fleming, *The New Dealers' War*, cover page.

4 Initially, public opinion: Kershaw, pp. 30–41.

4 Still, opponents were vigorous and organized: Ibid.

5 The House doorkeeper described: O'Sullivan, p. 76.

5 On September 14, after being: Ibid., p. 86.

6 "If someone attacks us": Sherwood, p. 191.

6 "If I don't say I hate war": James Roosevelt and Bill Libby, *My Parents*, p. xii.

6 On November 5, FDR defeated Willkie: Black, p. 598.

6 "Greeting: . . . you are hereby notified": Kershaw, pp. 30–41.

6 "go just as fast as the batboy": Flynn, p. 27.

7 Ten days after the lottery: O'Sullivan, p. 105.

7 "You put the case": Pogue, *George C. Marshall*, Vol. 2, p. 153.

7 "The President has sent in": Marshall, p. 93.

8 "To an extent": Senate Committee on Military Affairs, July 17–24, 1941.

8 "beginning this Autumn": Message of the President to the House of Representatives, July 21, 1941.

8 On July 28, Mrs. Rosa Farber: House Military Affairs Committee hearing, July 28, 1941.

8 "You talk about breaking faith": Congressional Record, August 8, 1941, pp. 6908–9.

8 "resembling a paunchy": *Current Biography*, 1943.

9 They now threatened to go home: O'Sullivan, p. 142.

9 "the Administration has not yet": *NYT*, August 1, 1941.

9 "lost control of his people": Stimson Diary, August 6, 1941.

9 "For probably the first time": *NYT*, August 13, 1941.

10 The House resolved itself: *Current Biography*, 1941.

10 "warning me": Congressional Record, August 12, 1941, p. 7012.

10 "Germany has not yet": Ibid., p. 7002.

10 "the method which has": Ibid., p. 6999.

10 "now dominates and has": Ibid., p. 7018.

10 The session was now approaching: *Newsweek*, August 28, 1941.

11 Rayburn's adroit parliamentary: O'Sullivan, p. 151.

11 "you'll have to knock me through": Ibid., pp. 157–58.

11 "The question is on the passage": Congressional Record, August 12, 1941, p. 7074.

12 "The vote stands": Ibid., p. 7075.

12 The Senate had already passed: *Life*, August 18, 1941, p. 15.

12 "give their time in order": *NYT*, August 13, 1941.

12 "Then it's happened": Gunther, *Roosevelt in Retrospect*, p. 303.

12 To Roosevelt, the moment had: Elliott Roosevelt, ed., *F.D.R.: His Personal Letters*, p. 196.

13 He thereupon was promoted: Weintraub, p. 101.

14 "If it was history": Pogue, *George C. Marshall*, Vol. 1, p. 22.

14 "People made fun of me": Ibid., p. 20.

14 "I was humiliated": Ibid., pp. 18–19.

15 "painful and humiliating": Ibid., p. 35.

15 "every boy in a democracy": Ibid., p. 36.

15 His aura of quiet authority: *Time*, January 3, 1944.

16 "first great emotional": Pogue, *George C. Marshall*, Vol. 1, pp. 52–53.

17 "large numbers of men": Larrabee, p. 98.

17 "I never spoke French again": Persico, *Eleventh Month, Eleventh Day, Eleventh Hour*, p. 198.

17 "There is something to be said here": Pogue, *George C. Marshall*, Vol. 2: *Ordeal and Hope*, pp. 152–53.

18 "spoke for a moment": Pogue: *George C. Marshall*, Vol. 1: *Education of a General*, p. 245.

18 Marshall's relations with: Ibid., p. 267.

18 "a technique and methods": Ambrose, *Citizen Soldiers*, p. 158.

19 "I would prefer to serve": Bland and Ritenour, eds., pp. 445–46.

19 "Request refused": Weintraub, pp. 87–88.

19 "George had a gray": Marshall, p. 18.

20 "the most instructive service": Larrabee, p. 108.

20 "General Pershing asks": Pogue, *George C. Marshall*, Vol. 1: *Education of a General*, p. 295.

20 "Don't you think so, George?": Black, p. 496.

20 "I am sorry, Mr. President, but": Pogue, *George C. Marshall*, Vol. 1: *Education of a General*, p. 323.

21 Yet FDR, who was: FDR, *Public Papers*, 1940, p. 615.

21 "Is that all right?": Pogue, *George C. Marshall*, Vol. 1: *Education of a General*, p. 330.

21 Again, Roosevelt dismissed: Larrabee, p. 106.

21 "For years I feared": Bland and Ritenour, eds., p. 714.

22 "I was in his office one day": Dwight D. Eisenhower, *Crusade in Europe*, p. 34.

22 Eisenhower further noted that: Ibid., p. 35.

23 On one wall: Frederick Lewis Allen, pp. 286–88.

23 "The situation had resulted": Forrest Pogue Interview, February 15, 1957, p. 477, GCM.

23 "I would forfeit my career": Ibid.

24 "The President just laughs": Ibid., pp. 477–78, GCM.

24 Marshall kept his job: Weintraub, p. 1.

24 "I get enthusiastic": FDR, *Public Papers*, 1940, p. 126.

24 "He brought a big notebook": GCM, Vol. 2, p. 623.

24 "I felt that he was going": Sutherland, pp. 50–56.

25 "If I can only keep": Sherwood, p. 281.

25 "I am not always able": Parrish, p. 137.

25 "because when he takes the": Ibid.

25 A nation with a population: Larrabee, p. 114.

25 Troops trained with broomsticks: *Washington Post*, October 22, 1939.

Chapter Two: An End of Neutrality

27 "We have no selfish ends": Harries and Harries, pp. 71–72.

28 "It is not possible": Dallek, *Franklin D. Roosevelt and American Foreign Policy*, p. 86.

28 So out of fashion was: Kershaw, p. 191.

28 Roosevelt signed it: Fleming, *The New Dealers' War*, p. 4.

28 "If we face the choice": Divine, p. 9.

29 "The government had to choose": Black, p. 476.

29 "Good man": Ibid.

29 The deed was done: Ibid., p. 466.

30 "It was relief money": FDRL, Freidel Interview Collection, Box 1.

30 "You certainly are using": POF, 198-D.

30 "You have repeatedly asserted": Ibid.

30 "Our enemies are little worms": *Adolf Hitler: Speeches Before Generals*, August 22, 1939.

31 "Can we stay out": Jean Edward Smith, *FDR*, p. 435.

31 "consequently this country is at war": Lewis, p. 32.

31 "The most incomprehensible": *NYT,* January 5, 1943.

31 "the United States should do everything": Meacham, p. 50.

32 "my sage old friend": Divine, p. 29.

32 The Norwegians lasted two weeks: Jean Edward Smith, *FDR,* p. 444.

32 A *Fortune* magazine poll: Lash, p. 147.

32 "an appeaser and will always": Blum, *From the Morgenthau Diaries,* Vol. 3, p. 102.

32 Morgenthau, a Jew, was: Persico, *Roosevelt's Secret War,* p. 69.

33 FDR was pleased to see: Ibid.

33 "It makes me dizzy": GCM, Vol. 2, p. 168.

33 "When you go to see": Lash, p. 184.

33 "It was quite evident": GCM, Vol. 2, p. 168.

34 "tremendously impressed with": Ibid.

34 "You have sat here": Jean Edward Smith, *FDR, p.* 444.

35 "I felt as if I were": Churchill, *Memoirs,* p. 227.

35 "You ask what is our policy?": Lewis, pp. 58–59.

35 "I trust you must realize": Lukacs, pp. 28–33.

35 "an extra push every": Blum, *From the Morgenthau Diaries,* Vol. 3, p. 155.

35 "We shall fight on the beaches": Gilbert, *War Papers,* p. 247.

36 "We had lost the whole equipment": Blum, *From the Morgenthau Diaries,* Vol. 3, p. 155.

36 "The hand that held the dagger": PSF, Box 2.

36 "With Roosevelt's speech": *Time,* June 17, 1940.

36 "Today, the enemy is almost": FDR, *Public Papers,* 1940, p. 265.

36 "only the Congress can make": Divine, p. 33.

36 However, as with Britain: FDR, *Public Papers,* 1940, p. 159.

37 "repeal the provisions": Stimson and Bundy, p. 319.

37 "Adolf Hitler today handed": Lewis, p. 76.

37 "I have prepared a landing": Churchill, *Memoirs,* p. 347.

37 "Hitler knows that he will have": Ibid., p. 326.

38 "in a towering rage": Lash, pp. 161–62.

38 "absolutely illegal": Ibid., p. 162.

38 "If I should guess wrong": Ickes, p. 200.

39 "fried mush with what": Ibid.

39 "The plan on the destroyers": Blum, *From the Morgenthau Diaries,* Vol. 3, p. 180.

39 "should he conclude the deal": Ibid.

39 "May such an action": POF, 4101.

40 "the most important action": Ibid.

40 "a high school track meet": Merriman Smith, *Thank You, Mr. President.*

40 "Some people will say": FDR, *Public Papers,* 1940, p. 375.

40 "I need not tell you how": Churchill, *Their Finest Hour,* p. 406.

41 "Hitler screamed with rage": Ickes, p. 314.

41 "In Washington the working day": Jean Edward Smith, *FDR, p.* 483.

41 "The moment approaches when": Persico, *Roosevelt's Secret War,* p. 83.

41 "a decisive act of constructive": Kershaw, p. 226.

42 "The most destructive attack": Churchill, *The Grand Alliance,* p. 41.

42 "Mr. President": PSF, Box 38.

42 "We turned over fifteen": "George C. Marshall: A Study in Character," paper delivered on January 28–29, 1999, GCM.

42 "wanted them to bomb Berlin": GCM interview, November 13, 1956, pp. 619–29.

42 "one evening he suddenly": Kershaw, p. 226.

42 "I have been thinking very hard": Blum, *From the Morgenthau Diaries,* Vol. 3, p. 209.

43 "He simply liked mystery": Persico, *Roosevelt's Secret War,* p. 97.

43 "I tried . . . to look beyond": Sherwood, p. 882.

43 The president's military team: Kershaw, p. 226.

43 "for us to pay for all": Rauch, ed., p. 270.

43 Several months before: Kershaw, p. 228.

43 "Well, let me give you": Rauch, ed., p. 271.

44 "New Deal triple A": *NYT,* January 15, 1941.

44 "the most untruthful": Ibid.

44 "A tiger": FDR, *Public Papers,* 1941, p. 643.

45 "I don't know how you feel": Persico, *Roosevelt's Secret War,* p. 249.

45 "After the war we must make": Harriman, p. 11.

45 He had been diagnosed: Ickes, p. 82.

45 "His lips are blanched": Moran, p. 13.

46 "The President didn't send me here": Larrabee, p. 637.

46 The two men withdrew alone: Harriman, p. 11.

46 "Lord Root of the Matter": Meacham, p. 92.

46 "I suppose you want to know": FDRL, Pamela Harriman Collection, Newton Interview.

46 "His was a soul": Churchill, *The Grand Alliance,* p. 21.

46 "Jesus Christ!": Meacham, p. 94.

46 "I think this applies": PSF, Box 37.

46 Soon after he told reporters: FDR, *Public Papers,* 1941, p. 113.

47 "it will come to war": Kershaw, p. 399.

47 "may be regarded as a declaration": Ibid.

47 "The Jew Frankfurter": *NYT,* March 13, 1941.

47 Hitler added that he regretted: Kershaw, p. 399.

47 "Government includes the art": FDR, *Public Papers,* 1941, p. xviii.

48 When the vessel slid down: *NYT,* April 10, 1941.
48 "could damage major fleet": Costello, p. 63.
48 A month later, France surrendered: Larrabee, p. 74.
49 "God," Roosevelt thundered: Butow, p. 12.
49 Roosevelt thereafter ordered: Morgan, p. 299.
49 "that the disappearance of": Stimson and Bundy, p. 386.
49 "the poorest administrator": Beschloss, p. 88.
50 Further, as no one else dared: Kershaw, p. 204.
50 "telling stories and doing": *PSF Secretary's File,* Box 6.
50 "I used to get a little bite": Stimson and Bundy, p. 562.
50 "He is trying to see how far": Ibid., p. 368.
50 "I think you know what a horse": FDR, *Public Papers,* 1941, p. 133.
50 "he is going to have a patrol": Blum, *From the Morgenthau Diaries,* Vol. 3, p. 91.
50 "The President is loath to": Fleming, *The New Dealers' War,* p. 86.
51 "I don't think anyone could beat": Perkins, p. 33.
51 Ironically, while FDR may have: Lukacs, pp. 28–33.
51 "I have talked to a number": Rauch, ed., p. 229.
51 "to bring Greenland within": *NYT,* April 11, 1941.
52 "We have some submarines down there": Sherwood, p. 295.
52 "Should he order submarines": Brown, *The Last Hero,* p. 162.
52 On May 27, British battleships: Rosenman, p. 283.
53 "what started as a European war": Persico, *Roosevelt's Secret War,* p. 86.
53 "He was an expert at dividing": Ibid., p. 355.
53 "They're ninety-five percent": Sherwood, p. 298.
53 In mid-June 1941: *NYT,* June 11, 1941.
54 On June 20, in response to the sinking: FDR, *Public Papers,* 1941, pp. 227–30.

Chapter Three: From Barbarossa to the Atlantic Charter

56 "The Soviet Union . . . is run by": FDR, *Public Papers,* 1940, p. 93.
57 "If we see that Germany is winning": Weintraub, p. 144.
57 "If I were a Russian": Elliott Roosevelt, *ed., F.D.R.: His Personal Letters,* p. 1195.
57 "The Nazi regime is": Churchill, *The Grand Alliance,* p. 331.
57 "We should go all out": Gilbert, *Winston S. Churchill: Finest Hour,* p. 1119.
58 "No one has been": Churchill, *Memoirs,* p. 469.
59 "The heat in Washington": Persico, *Roosevelt's Secret War,* p. 119.
59 "Then he smiled and": Elliott Roosevelt, *As He Saw It,* p. 224.
60 "Dropping the cares": *NYT,* August 5, 1941.
60 "I think I see my way": Meacham, p. 51.

60 "Former Naval Person": Churchill, *The Grand Alliance*, p. 381.

60 "I wonder if he will": Harriman, p. 75.

61 "Exactly as a princess": Persico, *Roosevelt's Secret War*, p. 252.

61 "will come alongside": Buell, p. 142.

62 "Here," he said: Elliott Roosevelt, *As He Saw It*, p. 19.

62 "Watch and see if": Ibid., p. 23.

62 "If they closed to within": Arnold, "Notes Relative to President Roosevelt's and Prime Minister Churchill's Conference Held Aboard Ship at Placentia Bay, Newfoundland August 9–12, 1941," MS, Arnold Papers, Manuscript Division, Library of Congress, pp. 248–53.

62 "She was magnificent": Buell, p. 143.

63 "short and stout with a": Ibid., p. 144.

63 "I am so devoured by": Charmley, p. 141.

63 "I don't like standing": Moran, p. 179.

64 "Even the slightest pitch": Meacham, pp. 106–8.

64 "acted like a stinker": HistoryNet.com.

64 "At last we've gotten": Persico, *Roosevelt's Secret War*, p. 122.

65 "My information": Elliott Roosevelt, *As He Saw It*, p. 27.

65 "He reared back": Ibid., p. 29.

65 "I would rather have an American": Kershaw, p. 188.

66 "A St. George who has": Meacham, p. 114.

66 "I think everybody, officers": FDR, *Public Papers*, 1941, p. 279.

66 "sharing the same book": Hayes, pp. 431–32.

66 "compliments of": Black, p. 653.

67 "seemed to be talking": Buell, p. 144.

67 "clad in a one piece": Elliott Roosevelt, *As He Saw It*, p. 40.

67 "Highjinks in high places": Ibid.

67 "He is a tremendously vital": Suckley, Binder 20, p. 61.

67 "with all his sparkle and": Gilbert, *Winston S. Churchill: Road to Victory*, p. 1292.

68 "America won't help England": Elliott Roosevelt, *As He Saw It*, p. 25.

68 "Let me, however, make this": *NYT*, November 11, 1942.

69 "was skating on pretty thin": Freidel, p. 387.

69 "I may never declare": Churchill, *The Grand Alliance*, p. 528.

69 "Betty, please don't ask": Buell, p. 139.

Chapter Four: An Undeclared War

70 "Once upon a time": *NYT*, September 6, 1941.

71 "What vitality I have": Christine Totten, "Remembering Sara Roosevelt."

71 "The United States destroyer": Persico, *Roosevelt's Secret War*, p. 126.

71 you don't wait for a rattlesnake: FDR, *Public Papers,* 1941, pp. 384–91.

71 "That means, very simply": Ibid., p. 139.

71 "Roosevelt Orders Navy": *NYT,* September 12, 1941.

71 "Hitler will have to choose": Thompson, p. 355.

72 "There is no longer": Ibid., p. 125.

72 "has every excuse in the world": Lash, p. 426.

72 "shoot on sight": PSF, Box 157.

72 "the *Kearny* incident": Buell, p. 149.

73 "I have in my possession": FDR, *Public Papers,* 1941, p. 439.

73 "would dry up the source": Thompson, pp. 357–59.

74 "defeat our potential enemies": Davis, *Hap,* p. 21.

74 "It is, in my opinion": Sherwood, p. 410.

74 "FDR's War Plans!": *Chicago Tribune,* December 5, 1941.

75 "I was the one": Forrest Pogue Interview, October 9, 1957, p. 600, GCM.

75 "an army was passé": Forrest Pogue Interview, January 15, 1952, p. 279, GCM.

75 "at their worst": Ibid., pp. 280–83.

76 "I don't know whether": Arnold, *Global Mission,* p. 97.

76 "it is highly unlikely": Coffey, p. 41.

76 "a new field artillery": Arnold, *Global Mission,* p. 177.

77 "achieved its Magna Carta": Ibid., p. 179.

77 "a staunch member of the": Ibid., p. 5.

78 "All of a sudden there it was": Ibid., pp. 1–3.

78 "an official letter arrived": Ibid., p. 15.

78 "Young man, I know of": Ibid., p. 15.

78 "I could fly": Coffey, p. 45.

78 "they gave me a sense": Larrabee, p. 207.

78 "gave up everything as lost": Coffey, p. 63.

79 "At the present time": Ibid.

79 "I cannot even look": Ibid.

79 "That's it": Ibid.

80 "The airplane is one of the": Arnold, *Global Mission,* p. 65.

80 "would stand bareheaded": Ibid., p. 102.

81 "I had just met a man": Ibid., p. 44.

82 "Colonel Arnold was the most": Eaker, p. 83.

82 "The difficult we do today": Ibid., p. 92.

83 "air power would win it": Coffey, p. 82.

83 "I was severely taken": Arnold, *Global Mission,* p. 213.

83 "give the wrong person": Kuter, pp. 89–90.

83 "Hap Arnold never sat": Ibid., p. 89.

84 "Does the Secretary": Arnold, *Global Mission,* p. 184.

84 "The President in unmistakable": Ibid., p. 186.

84 "I was received genially": Ibid., p. 194.

85 "There was no back slapping": Coffey, p. 209.

85 "Who are you?": Ibid., p. 347.

85 "Hundreds of people": Arnold, *Global Mission,* p. 227.

86 "must be turned out": *NYT,* May 6, 1941.

87 "One of my earliest": FDRL, McCrea Memoirs, Small Collections.

87 "All I had been told": Halsey, p. 18.

87 "Numerous officers commented": FDRL, Friedel Interview Collection, Box 1.

88 "How come we were shipping": Elliott Roosevelt, *As He Saw It,* pp. 11–12.

Chapter Five: Pearl Harbor

89 "the fervent hope that": FDR, *Public Papers,* 1941, p. 513.

89 "This means war": Black, p. 679.

90 "was clasping hands with": *NYT,* December 7, 1941.

91 "I got him there": Prange, pp. 247–48.

92 "I was disappointed but": Eleanor Roosevelt, *Autobiography,* p. 226.

92 "FDR enjoyed Harry's": Author interview with Curtis Roosevelt, November 12, 2008.

92 "the worst cook": James Roosevelt, *Affectionately,* p. xxiv.

92 "Mr. President": Gunther, *Roosevelt in Retrospect,* p. 319.

93 "His reaction to any great": Ward, *A First-Class Temperament,* p. xxiv.

93 "My God, there's another": Black, p. 687.

94 "The Japanese are presenting at": U.S. Congress, Joint Committee on the Investigation of the Pearl Harbor Attack, p. 1112.

94 "Show this to your naval officers": Ibid., p. 1109.

95 "Sit down, Grace": Tully, p. 356.

95 "Yesterday comma": Ibid.

95 "The President nodded as we": Perkins, p. 379.

96 "to divert the American mind": Doyle, p. 36.

96 "It looks as if": Ibid., pp. 35–39.

97 "How did it happen": Ibid., p. 39.

97 "Oh God, if I only": Persico, *Edward R. Murrow,* p. 193.

97 "would be regarded as utterly": *NYT,* December 9, 1941.

98 "If they were not surprised": Spector, pp. 193–95.

98 "The only geographical": Andrew, p. 117.

98 "The Prime Minister seemed": Harriman, p. 111.

98 "The news has just been given": Ibid.

98 "We shall declare war": Churchill, *The Grand Alliance,* p. 538.

99 "So we had won": Paul Kennedy, ed., *Grand Strategies in War and Peace*, p. 47.

99 "Oh, that is the way": John S. D. Eisenhower, *Allies*, pp. 18–19.

99 "No matter how long it may": FDR, *Public Papers*, 1941, pp. 514–15.

100 "Now, it is impossible": Keegan, *The Second World War*, p. 240.

100 "Roosevelt comes from a rich": Black, p. 698.

100 "there has been revealed": Persico, *Roosevelt's Secret War*, p. 150.

101 "the great distances which": Parrish, p. 208.

101 "Army preparations were primarily": Secret Report by the Secretary of the Navy to the President, December 14, 1941, National Archives.

101 "a defense against": Prange, p. 403.

102 "Essential fact is that": Elliott Roosevelt, ed., *F.D.R.: His Personal Letters*, pp. 1253–55.

102 "The Commanders in Hawaii": Jean Edward Smith, *FDR*, p. 535.

103 "all evidence conclusively points": FDR, *Public Papers*, 1941, pp. 563–67.

103 "The Committee found no evidence": Ibid.

103 "We are likely to be attacked": Persico, *Roosevelt's Secret War*, p. 152.

104 "the strongest fortress in the": Spector, p. 2.

104 "worst informed ambassador": Persico, *Roosevelt's Secret War*, p. 150.

105 "There was nobody in either": Ibid., p. 152.

105 "Saying that an enemy fleet": GCM, Vol. 3, p. 14.

105 "Reliable information that an attack": Stilwell, p. 5.

105 "from such an attack": Costello, p. 150.

106 "The necessity for mass evacuation": Andrew, pp. 127–28.

106 "about the craziest proposition": Persico, *Roosevelt's Secret War*, p. 168.

106 "I do not think he was": Biddle, p. 219.

107 "the commanding General, Hawaiian": PSF, Box 4.

107 "Tell Nimitz to get the hell": Larrabee, p. 354.

107 "You always thought that would be": Ibid.

108 "When they get in trouble": Ibid., p. 153.

108 "If I had thought of it": Buell, p. 573.

108 "He's a grand Navy man": Larrabee, p. 154.

108 "Don't worry": Buell, p. 178.

109 "may be combined and devolve": FDR, *Public Papers*, 1942, p. 157.

109 "He's always in a rage": *NYT*, June 20, 2010.

111 "Praise was given grudgingly": Buell, p. 91.

111 "He didn't need a megaphone": Ibid., p. 80.

111 "Take this to the head": Ibid., p. 232.

111 "King was the only Naval": Ibid., p. 106.

111 "His weaknesses": Ibid., p. 89.

111 "You ought to be very": Ibid.

112 "a has been": Larrabee, p. 158.

112 "I believe that Rear Admiral": Buell, pp. 123–27.

112 "your trouble is that": Ibid., 148–49.

112 "put a premium on": Ibid., p. 95.

113 "Well that was finished": FDR, *Public Papers,* 1941, p. 331.

113 "a tall man, bald": *Harper's,* February 1945, p. 228.

115 "He's never been in a bus": Moran, p. 265.

115 "Now Fields, we want to leave": Goodwin, p. 302.

116 "very important to morale": GCM, Vol. 3, p. 28.

116 "gave one the impression": Moran, p. 233.

116 "I was too awestruck": Lash, pp. 15–16.

116 "He would slurp his soup": Morgan, *Past Forgetting,* p. 156.

116 "The Prime Minister of Great Britain": Sherwood, p. 442.

117 "I can not help reflecting": Black, p. 705.

117 "What kind of people do they": Costello, p. 179.

117 "It was hot last night": Moran, pp. 17–18.

118 "in bed and propped up": Forrest Pogue Interview, October 5, 1956, p. 595, GCM.

118 "Marshall remains the key": Larrabee, p. 98.

118 "One evening the general": Churchill, *The Grand Alliance,* p. 624.

119 "There was a violent explosion": Moran, p. 33.

120 "Here, where the sword": Lash, pp. 17–18.

121 "This country is the most": John S. D. Eisenhower, *Allies,* p. 34.

121 "like two little boys": Author interview with Curtis Roosevelt, November 12, 2008.

122 "the number of people, your senior": Larrabee, p. 23.

122 "Briefly, I would like": Parrish, p. 233.

122 "Say John": FDRL, McCrea Papers.

122 "about the size of a couple": Ibid.

123 "the President took to that": Larrabee, p. 22.

Chapter Six: The President and General MacArthur

124 "I wouldn't be surprised": Weintraub, p. 17.

124 "the greatest concentration of": Baldwin, *Great Mistakes,* p. 65.

125 "You know General MacArthur": Perret, p. 247.

125 "My first recollection": Manchester, p. 54.

126 "Doug . . . be self-confident": Ibid. p. 60.

126 "It was a lesson": Ibid. p. 61.

127 "Never lie. Never tattle": Ibid. p, 65.

128 "Begging the lieutenant's pardon": Perret, p. 49.

128 "The 42nd Division stretches": Persico, *Roosevelt's Secret War*, p. 162.

128 "It's the orders you disobey": Manchester, p. 101.

128 "this sensitive, high-strung": Ibid. p. 94.

130 "I told that dumb": D'Este, *Eisenhower*, p. 224.

130 "at 4:30 this afternoon": *NYT,* July 29, 1932.

130 "was very much annoyed": Perret, p. 159.

131 he had made sure: Ibid.

131 "I was in the midst": MacArthur, p. 95.

131 "the American Communist Party": Ibid. p. 93.

131 "one of the two most dangerous": Perret, p. 172.

131 "Well, Felix": Weintraub, p. 84.

132 "were answered by a": MacArthur, p. 101.

132 "In my emotional exhaustion": Ibid.

132 "You must not talk to": Ibid.

132 "Don't be foolish": Ibid.

132 "I just vomited": Ibid.

132 "that cripple in the White House": Perret, p. 169.

132 "Douglas," he said, "if war": Manchester, p. 174.

133 "to be the Field Marshal": Ibid. p. 190.

133 "the whiteness of MacArthur's skin": Perret, p. 237.

133 "I studied dramatics": Ibid., p. 216.

134 "Probably no one had tougher": D'Este, "MacArthur's Whipping Boy," p. 141.

134 "if that door opened": Larrabee, p. 418.

134 "Effective this date": Perret, p. 227.

134 "had changed a local feeling": Forrest Pogue Interview, January 15, 1957, p. 297, GCM.

134 "It is the policy of": Perret, p. 233.

Chapter Seven: Philippines Lost, China on the Brink

135 "General," he told MacArthur: Weintraub, p. 101.

136 "Members of his staff": Pogue, *George C. Marshall*, Vol. 2: *Ordeal of Hope.*

136 "That man Eisenhower": Weintraub, p. 36.

136 "very sensitive to the fact": Ibid.

136 "I've got to relieve": Blumenson, *Mark Clark*, p. 54.

136 "I'll give you one name": Ibid.

136 "Is that you, Ike?": Ambrose, *The Supreme Commander*, p. 3.

137 "an eye that seemed": Ibid., p. 6.

137 "What should be our general": Manchester, p. 274.

137 "Steps to Be Taken": Ambrose, *The Supreme Commander*, p. 5.

137 "General, it will be a long time": Manchester, p. 275.

137 "Influence Russia to enter": Ambrose, *The Supreme Commander*, p. 5.

138 "The yielding of the": DDE, p. 36.

138 "it is now eight o'clock": Ibid., p. 33.

138 "MacArthur is as big": Perret, p. 268.

138 "Eisenhower," he told him: Ambrose, *The Supreme Commander*, p. 6.

139 "not give a damn about": David Eisenhower, *Eisenhower*, p. 41.

139 "The nearest that": Ambrose, *The Supreme Commander*, p. 22.

139 "I have felt terribly": DDE, pp. 183–84.

139 "We've got to go": Ambrose, *The Supreme Commander*, p. 15.

140 "I don't think that": Weintraub, p. 35.

141 "incapable of stopping": Costello, p. 172.

141 "My heart ached": Weintraub, p. 41.

141 "Help is on the way": Manchester, p. 260.

142 "Militarily it is evident": *FRUS*, 1942, Vol. 1, p. 894.

142 "You must determine whether": Manchester, p. 281.

143 "For thirty years": MacArthur, p. 138.

143 "I remonstrated with Quezon": Ibid.

143 "We can't do this": Black, p. 717.

143 "Whatever happens to the present": Stimson and Bundy, p. 403.

143 "I immediately discarded": Black, p. 717.

143 "will share the fate": Ibid.

144 "a moral and philanthropic": Persico, *Roosevelt's Secret War*, p. 13.

144 "Remember that I have a little": Larrabee, p. 568.

145 "burn out the industrial": Persico, *Roosevelt's Secret War*, p. 60.

145 "asking for 500 planes": Ibid.

145 "It would be a nice thing": Blum, *From the Morgenthau Diaries*, Vol. 2, p. 367.

145 "Is he still willing to fight?": Ibid.

145 "The four of you": Ibid.

145 "he liked to try new": Burns, pp. 83–84.

146 "try to get some": Blum, *From the Morgenthau Diaries*, Vol. 3, p. 368.

147 "The main Japanese fleet": Stilwell, p. 4.

147 "Reliable information": Ibid.

147 "is a rush of clerks": Stilwell, p. 15.

147 "wiry, ugly in the most": White, p. 134.

147 "a rank amateur": Baldwin, *Great Mistakes*, p. 77.

148 "He is utterly ignorant": Tuchman, pp. 153–56.

148 "Me? No thank you": Larrabee, p. 512.

148 "if I have command": Stilwell, p. 26.

149 "Tell him we are in this": Ibid., p. 36.

149 "Very pleasant and": Ibid.

149 "greatest disaster to British": John S. D. Eisenhower, *Allies,* p. 49.

149 "have voiced the opinion": *NYT,* February 12, 1942.

150 "are all under the command": DDE, p. 181.

150 "the American general only thinks": Collis, p. 122.

151 "Under existing conditions": PSF, FDRL online.

151 "a hell of a beating": Weinberg, p. 322.

151 "They will never take me": Manchester, p. 285.

151 "The most important question": DDE, pp. 97–98.

152 "The president directs that you": Perret, p. 273.

152 "walked around like a man": Ibid.

152 "Please be guided by me": MacArthur, p. 141.

152 "I'm dubious about": Ferrell, ed., *The Eisenhower Diaries,* p. 49.

153 "Jonathan, I want you": Manchester, p. 293.

153 "had just been bathed": *NYT,* March 25, 1942.

154 "would have been certain": MacArthur, p. 141.

154 "Memories of frontier days": *NYT,* March 25, 1941.

154 "The President of the United States": MacArthur, p. 145.

154 "We the parents of boys": POF, 4771.

155 Dugout Doug MacArthur: Manchester, p. 269.

155 "To offset any propaganda": PSF, Box 83.

155 "Wainwright states that doubtful": PSF, Box 62, McCrea Folder.

155 "With broken heart and head": Costello, p. 265.

155 "temporarily unbalanced and": Ibid., p. 266.

156 "The Bataan forces went": Perret, p. 289.

156 "Through the dust clouds": *NYT,* January 28, 1944.

156 "The President was insistent": Arnold, *Global Mission,* p. 298.

157 "it would take a few months": Nelson, p. 111.

157 "By the time we had": FDR, *Public Papers,* 1942, p. 214.

157 "I assured him it was": Arnold, *Global Mission,* p. 298.

157 "Colonel, there is a man": Ibid., p. 91.

157 "I'll bet you five bucks": Ibid.

158 "an air force commander": COH, p. 152.

158 "there is no substitute": Halsey, p. 23.

159 "Desire that there be": DDE, p. 258.

159 "Just after noon": *NYT,* April 18, 1942.

160 "How about the story": Nelson, p. 214.

160 "the idea that Tokyo": Larrabee, p. 366.

161 "It is with feeling": FDR, *Public Papers,* 1943, p. 178.

Chapter Eight: Europe a Debate, Pacific a Victory

162 "got what he wanted": Parrish, p. 227.
163 "I had to be very careful": Ibid., p. 282.
163 "In a sense": Forrest Pogue Interview, February 14, 1957, p. 431, GCM.
163 "I found that he had left": Ibid., p. 436.
163 "if you and I begin": Ibid.
163 "Well, you have been very": Ibid.
163 "And we did get along": Buell, p. 404.
163 "yes man": Buell, p. 404.
163 "Admiral King is an arbitrary": Ferrell, *The Eisenhower Diaries*, p. 49.
164 "the relative advantages": Parrish, p. 447.
164 "We must have a neutral": Forrest Pogue Interview, August 13, 1956, p. 623, GCM.
164 "I'm the Chief-of-Staff": Forrest Pogue Interview, February 14, 1957, p. 431, GCM.
164 "You are not Superman": Parrish, p. 250.
164 "Of course, General Arnold": Forrest Pogue Interview, January 22, 1957, p. 298, GCM.
165 "First thing you know": Hough, p. 86.
165 "How would you like to be": Ibid.
165 "I just gave up": Forrest Pogue Interview, February 20, 1957, pp. 519–20, GCM.
166 "Bill, if we have": Leahy, p. 4.
166 "the possibility that France": Ibid., p. 6.
166 "feeble, frightened": Sherwood, p. 487.
166 "had lost his incentive": *NYT*, July 22, 1942.
166 "Mr. President, can you tell": FDR, *Public Papers*, 1942, pp. 301–2.
166 "The President made clear": *NYT*, July 22, 1942.
167 "look awfully good": Buell, p. 187.
167 "Ernie, I can't tell you": FDRL, JLM Memoirs, Parts 1–5.
168 "King was furious": Forrest Pogue Interview, November 13, 1956, p. 624, GCM.
168 "There are a million": FDR, *Public Papers*, 1941, p. 415.
169 "the great decision of the war": Larrabee, p. 134.
169 "Some people want the": Rauch, ed., p. 311.
169 "we must win": DDE, p. 146.
169 "the difficulty of attacking": Dwight D. Eisenhower, *Crusade in Europe*, p. 43.
169 "It's going to be a hell": DDE, p. 75.
169 "successful attack in": PSF, Box 3.
169 "if the imminence": Ibid.

170 "I personally estimate": Ambrose, *The Supreme Commander*, p. 71.

170 "desperate operation to save": Ibid.

170 "would eliminate the": Dwight D. Eisenhower, *Crusade in Europe*, p. 70.

170 "This is it": Ibid., p. 47.

170 "the United States would no": Steele, pp. 110–11.

171 "what Harry and George": Meacham, pp. 177–78.

171 "Your people and mine": Ibid., p. 178.

171 "I know that the previous": Ibid. p. 434.

172 "gave us a long talk": Bryant, p. 285.

172 "I liked what I saw": Ibid.

172 "icy and condescending": John S. D. Eisenhower, *Allies*, p. 66.

172 "We all agreed": Churchill, *Memoirs*, pp. 569–71.

172 "our two nations": Sherwood, p. 535.

174 "the United States should adopt": Cline, p. 148.

175 "to do the necessary": FDRL, Small Collections, John McCrea, parts 10–18.

175 "Tell me," he asked: Ibid.

176 "Oshima often impressed": Polmar and Allen, p. 417.

176 "I told him that he should": Persico, *Roosevelt's Secret War*, p. 105.

176 "It looks at the moment": Burns, p. 226.

177 "Imperative this information": DDE, pp. 306–7.

178 "They'll come in from": Leckie, p. 67.

180 "Two carriers and battleships": Ibid., pp. 266–70.

180 Four of their carriers: Black, p. 741.

180 "essentially a victory": Persico, *Roosevelt's Secret War*, p. 189.

181 "prints lies and": Black, p. 771.

182 "The advance information": Persico, *Roosevelt's Secret War*, p. 189.

182 "Treat the operation": GCM, Vol. 3, p. 26.

182 "After General Doolittle's raid": GCM, Vol. 3, p. 216.

Chapter Nine: North Africa: FDR Versus the Generals

184 "control by Britain of the whole": Churchill, *The Grand Alliance*, p. 578.

184 "had the feeling that the President": Steele, p. 36.

185 "French invitation for a direct": GCM, Vol. 3, p. 41.

185 "bomb and shell trap": Churchill, *Memoirs*, p. 575.

185 "Where then could this": Ibid., p. 516.

185 "If the Bolero project": DDE, p. 281.

185 "American soldiers will land": *NYT*, May 30, 1942.

186 "Large sums of money": PSF, Box 37.

186 "I would rather lose": Blum, *From the Morgenthau Diaries*, Vol. 2, p. 82.

186 "If you postpone": John S. D. Eisenhower, *Allies*, p. 87.

187 "say to Mr. Stalin": *FRUS,* 1942, Vol. 2, pp. 575–77.

187 "The only surprise to me": Blum, ed., *The Diary of Henry A. Wallace,* p. 210.

188 "would not favor an operation": GCM, Vol. 3, p. 228.

188 "If you answer in the": MR, Box 165.

188 "not taken a single": *Time,* June 8, 1942.

188 "then we must attack": MR, Box 165, Folder 3.

189 "you know Grace": Tully, p. 305.

189 "is certainly a dead ringer": Ibid., p. 302.

189 "His powerful torso": Black, p. 747.

189 "for being so badly": Bryant, p. 328.

189 "Accustomed to their vast": Ibid., p. 339.

189 "The President had no great": Ibid., p. 355.

190 "Churchill's pink cheeks": Parrish, p. 286.

190 "What can we do": Meacham, p. 185.

190 "Give us as many": Churchill, *The Hinge of Fate,* p. 383.

190 "Mr. President," he said: Churchill, *Memoirs,* p. 583.

190 "There are a couple": Larrabee, pp. 412–13.

191 "was an overthrow": PSF, Safe Box 3.

191 "The occupation of Northwest": Ibid.

191 "The operation, Gymnast": GCM, Vol. 3, p. 229.

192 "definite plans for a second": *NYT,* June 26, 1942, p. 2.

192 "big, bland Kansan": Butcher, p. 31.

193 "we were poor": Ambrose, *Eisenhower,* p. 19.

193 "a cross word pass": Korda, p. 69.

194 "the best amateur": Dwight D. Eisenhower, *At Ease,* p. 101.

194 "my feeling of regret": Ibid., p. 83.

195 "We were all harassed": Ibid., p. 4.

195 "raw-boned, gawky": Ibid.

195 "Mr. Dumgard," he shouted: Ibid., p. 18.

196 "make the world safe": Persico, *Eleventh Month, Eleventh Day, Eleventh Hour,* p. 137.

197 "Today when I think of it": Dwight D. Eisenhower, *At Ease,* pp. 181–82.

198 "I could hear the monkeys": Susan Eisenhower, *Mrs. Ike,* p. 83.

198 "it is our opinion": GCM, Vol. 3, p. 251.

198 "that is exactly": Larrabee, p. 136.

199 "now our principal": Atkinson, *An Army at Dawn,* p. 16.

199 "I'm right back to": Butcher, p. 29.

199 "always to be very strong": Cowley and Parker, eds., p. 92.

199 "Many times in his study": Buell, p. 172.

199 "King wobbled around": Ibid., p. 206.

200 "the Pacific problem is no": PSF, Safe Box 4.

200 "because of the repercussions": King, p. 385.

200 "Not just the fate of Australia": Perret, p. 297.

201 "a truly beautiful sight": Dyer, *the Amphibian Came to Conquer*, Vol. 1, p. 328.

201 "Blue green mountains": Larrabee, p. 266.

201 "They must have decoded": Buell, p. 223.

202 "I couldn't kill a": Hassett, p. 175.

Chapter Ten: Sea War, Air War

203 "like carrying a large": Churchill, *Memoirs*, p. 619.

203 "Stalin took issue": MR, Box 12, Folder 1.

203 "that we had broken": Churchill, *Memoirs*, p. 619.

203 "about being too much": Ibid.

203 "Why stick your mouth": Clark, pp. 9–10.

203 "hit Rommel in the back": Churchill, *The Hinge of Fate*, p. 482.

204 Prince of the Kremlin: Bryant, p. 384.

204 "Wild scenes that crowded": *NYT*, August 21, 1942.

205 "I can tell you": DDE, p. 617.

205 "Butcher's job": Ambrose, *The Supreme Commander*, p. 50.

205 "as picturesque as": Summersby, *Eisenhower Was My Boss*, p. 26.

205 "Ike was fine": Blumenson, *The Patton Papers*, p. 123.

206 "if there are any pretty": Ibid., p. 82.

206 "I've got it": Morgan, p. 77.

206 "indicating that your relations": GCM, Vol. 3, p. 327.

206 "Few who watched him": Roche, p. 12.

207 "like a football team": Ambrose, *The Supreme Commander*, p. 55.

207 "no longer just a question": DDE, p. 617.

207 "He only called me": Ambrose, *The Supreme Commander*, p. 81.

208 "It seems to me that": Persico, *Roosevelt's Secret War*, p. 202.

209 "another month or two": GCM, Vol. 3, p. 227.

209 "This furnishes excellent": Roosevelt to King, July 7, 1942; King to Roosevelt, July 9, 1942, King Papers, Library of Congress.

210 "just a nice old lady": Ferrell, ed., *The Eisenhower Diaries*, p. 50.

210 "I am doing my best": Larrabee, p. 178.

212 "the inhumane barbarism": FDR, *Public Papers*, 1941, p. 454.

213 "Give me 20,000": *NYT*, April 7, 1984.

213 "not tough and hard": Ferrell, ed., *The Eisenhower Diaries*, p. 95.

213 "I'm tired of hearing": Forrest Pogue Interview, February 14, 1957, p. 437, GCM.

214 "With all those guns": Arnold, *Global Mission*, p. 156.

214 "We'd like him to go in as": Coffey, p. 268.

215 "by order of the Führer": Jean Edward Smith, *FDR,* p. 437.

215 "a little too suave": Cole, p. 68.

215 "full of striking": Arnold, *Global Mission,* p. 188.

215 "I shall count it a great": Arnold to Lindbergh, October 8, 1938, Arnold Papers, Manuscript Division, Library of Congress.

215 "Lindbergh gave me the most": Arnold, *Global Mission,* pp. 188–89.

216 "a defense hysteria": Persico, *Roosevelt's Secret War,* p. 38.

216 "If I should die": Cole, pp. 128–29.

216 "could not have been better": Ibid.

216 "The President put the colonel": *NYT,* April 29, 1941.

Chapter Eleven: Torch: The Political Education of Dwight Eisenhower

219 "arrogance, bumptiousness": Atkinson, *The Day of Battle,* pp. 125–26.

219 "Break ranks": Ambrose, *The Supreme Commander,* p. 347.

220 "Who's smoking?": Ibid., p. 44.

220 "proud to have 'em": Butcher, p. 96.

221 "he held up his hands": Forrest Pogue Interview, October 5, 1956, p. 573, GCM.

221 "When I found out": DDE, p. 491.

222 "My friends, who suffer": FDR, *Public Papers,* 1942, pp. 451–52.

223 "We needed shallow": Theadvocate.com/features/higginsstory.

223 "The President took a pencil": Leahy, p. 128.

223 "The boss's hand": Tully, p. 264.

224 "Stop the game": Marshall, p. 130.

225 "Come back here!": D'Este, *Patton,* p. 436.

225 "One soldier who was pushing": Blumenson, *The Patton Papers,* p. 108.

225 "You and I fought": Murphy, p. 151.

226 "I am the best of the best": D'Este, *Patton,* p. 83.

226 "I am a characterless": Ibid., p. 79.

226 "You have done your": Ibid., p. 93.

227 "in order to be clean": Ibid., p. 95.

227 "pranced up and down": Ibid.

227 "I reported more men": Ibid., p. 93.

227 "To the end of his": Ibid., p. 106.

228 "I will never apply": Ibid., p. 149.

228 "We don't want to waste": Ibid.

228 "Mexican Bandit Killer": Ibid., p. 176.

229 "Why you God damned": Ibid., p. 220.

229 "They were all": Ibid., p. 235.

229 "I felt a great": Ibid., p. 257.

230 "just at the crack": Ibid., p. 259.

230 "I have been cited": Harriman, p. 263.

230 "I would rather be a": Ibid., p. 275.

230 "It is time for another": D'Este, *Patton*, p. 259.

230 "he drank urine": Ibid., p. 323.

230 Yet that damned Boche: George S. Patton Papers, Box 60, Manuscript Division, Library of Congress.

231 We can but hope: Persico, *Roosevelt's Secret War*, pp. 372–73.

231 "Like most great men": Blumenson, *The Patton Papers*, p. 838.

232 "Your father needs me": D'Este, *Patton*, p. 359.

232 "A man who does not": Blumenson, *The Patton Papers*, p. 222.

232 "no matter how we get": D'Este, *Patton*, p. 390.

232 "It would be great to be": Ibid.

232 "He not only swore": Ibid., p. 347.

232 "Patton is by far": Ibid., p. 378.

233 "Admiral Hewitt and I": Blumenson, *The Patton Papers*, p. 94.

233 "would be fatal": Ibid., pp. 93–94.

233 "we can stall": Ibid., p. 94.

233 "whether he had his old": D'Este, *Patton*, p. 425.

233 "Sir, all I want": Ibid.

233 "Patton is a joy": Larrabee, p. 486.

233 "Himmler Program Kills": *NYT*, November 25, 1942.

234 "enemies of the German": PSF, Box 2.

234 "What kinds of people do you object": Persico, *Roosevelt's Secret War*, p. 217.

234 "The practice of executing": FDR, *Public Papers*, 1942, p. 330.

235 "I now think he travelled": Bullard, p. 219.

235 "One of the things that": COH, Rosenman, p. 163.

235 "some very wonderful": Blum, *From the Morgenthau Diaries*, Vol. 3, p. 207.

235 "I would actually put a barbed": Ibid., p. 208.

236 "I now declare it to be": Ibid.

236 "new order": *NYT*, August 13, 1941.

236 "Reichsfuehrer Hitler has received": *NYT*, May 13, 1941.

237 "short, bald-headed": Black, p. 786.

237 "Is this then what": Ambrose, *The Supreme Commander*, p. 127.

238 "Are we at some future": Persico, *Edward R. Murrow*, p. 201.

238 "war carries with it": DDE, p. 795.

238 "I walk a soapy": Ibid.

238 "The actual state of": Larrabee, p. 426.

238 "ten minutes": Ambrose, *The Supreme Commander,* pp. 128–29.

238 "I have accepted General": Sherwood, p. 653.

238 "a Serbian proverb": Blum, ed., *The Diary of Henry A. Wallace,* p. 134.

238 "I am therefore not disposed": Sherwood, p. 654.

239 "I am but a lemon": Butcher, p. 206.

239 "the effect of a statement": MR, Box 12, Folder 1.

239 "carried the honor": John S. D. Eisenhower, *Allies,* p. 7.

240 "I first met him in the hall": Moran, p. 87.

240 "how to deal with": GCM, Vol. 3, p. 270.

240 "You have been fighting": de Gaulle, p. 58.

Chapter Twelve: The Home Front

241 "appoint fifty Negroes": *NYT,* January 1, 1940.

242 "It is the policy of the War": GCM, Vol. 3, p. 287.

242 "Our government seemed": Bullard, p. 292.

242 "America makes the Negro clean": Shaw, p. 191.

242 "Mr. President . . . the Negro people": Butow, p. 23.

243 "Now suppose you have": Ibid, p. 24.

243 "stab in the back": Ibid., p. 24.

243 "to prevent discrimination": FDR, *Public Papers,* 1941, p. 216.

244 "we ran into things": Forrest Pogue Interview, February 20, 1957, pp. 499–500, GCM.

244 "recommends withdrawal of": DDE, pp. 208–9.

245 "There were many in the": FDR, *Public Papers,* 1942, p. 241.

246 "Will we ever get over": *Newsweek,* June 21, 1943.

246 "It was common for": Arnold, *Global Mission,* p. 358.

246 "the WASPs have completed": Ibid.

247 "a very necessary consideration": Hassett, p. 127.

248 "I'm going to ask the American": Rosenman, p. 330.

248 "From Berlin, Rome and": Rauch, ed., p. 307.

248 "I honestly feel that it would": FDR, *Public Papers,* 1942, p. 62.

249 "What I am a little": Ibid., p. 449.

249 "Mr. President, does the ban": Ibid. p. 424.

250 "Dear George, you won again": Weintraub, p. 134.

250 "a piano company": Arnold, *Global Mission,* p. 291.

250 "Grass will grow": FDR, *Public Papers,* 1940, p. 487.

250 "presented after lunch": Forrest Pogue Interview, February 14, 1957, p. 463, GCM.

250 "Capra," Marshall answered: Capra, p. 302.

251 "amusing, they were": Forrest Pogue Interview, February 14, 1957, p. 463, GCM.

251 "to enable the young men": FDR, *Public Papers,* 1942, p. 470.

252 "the biggest sonovabitch": Capra, p. 426.

252 "About that duty": Rhodes, p. 425.

253 "it may be possible": PSF, Box 5.

253 "use it exclusively in": FDRL, Alexander Sachs Papers.

253 "This requires action": Ibid.

253 "prepare a nice note of thanks": PSF, Box 5.

254 "If atomic bombs could": Persico, *Roosevelt's Secret War,* p. 176.

254 "I think the whole thing": PSF, Box 2.

254 "a young Einstein": Rhodes, p. 443.

254 "He's a genius": Ibid., pp. 448–49.

255 "Can a leopard change": *NYT,* December 24, 1943.

256 "getting rid of the": Ibid.

256 "an opportunity for members": Rauch, ed., pp. 330–31.

257 "Almost everything important": Goodwin, p. 513.

Chapter Thirteen: Unconditional Surrender

258 "To the United States of America": Sherwood, p. 665.

258 "the reason the President wanted": John S. D. Eisenhower, *Allies,* pp. 174–75.

258 "We are off to find": Sherwood, p. 671.

259 "It was his first long trip": Eleanor Roosevelt, *This I Remember,* p. 279.

259 "acted like a 16-year-old": Parrish, p. 319.

259 "worried about the President's": Sherwood, p. 671.

260 "Crowds of semi-dressed": Berthon and Potts, p. 177.

260 "Now all we need": Larrabee, p. 184.

260 "I christened the two": Kimball, *The Juggler,* p. 79.

260 "most anxious not to": MR, Box 65, Folder 7.

261 "Since the PM is short": Kimball, *The Juggler,* p. 225.

261 "noble procession of wines": Ibid.

261 "more and more pompous": Black, p. 796.

261 "The English mean to maintain": Elliott Roosevelt, *As He Saw It,* p. 71.

261 "Oh yes, those West": Andrew, p. 99.

262 "biting everyone": D'Este, *Patton,* p. 451.

262 "There, now try to use it": Ibid., p. 466.

262 "He could become intensely": Eade, ed., p. 159.

263 "I was astounded by": Summersby, p. 19.

263 "his famous siren suit": Morgan, p. 84.

263 "would have been just": Weintraub, p. 146.

264 "I have a general feeling": MR, Box 154, Folder 7.

264 "I never meant the": Bryant, p. 428.

264 "would be a difficult if not": MR, Box 26, Folder 1.

264 "we came, we listened": Keegan, *The Second World War,* p. 318.

264 "I spent many hours": Sherwood, p. 70.

265 "Well, what do you think": Marshall, p. 60.

265 "You could hear 'em": Elliott Roosevelt, *As He Saw It,* p. 106.

265 "the President abominated": D'Este, "MacArthur's Whipping Boy," p. 240.

266 "at least five times": D'Este, *Patton,* p. 451.

266 "really appeared as a great statesman": D'Este, *Patton,* p. 451.

267 "I was born without": *PM* (newspaper), January 27, 1943.

267 "I think we have all had": FDR, *Public Papers,* 1943, p. 39.

267 "I agree with everything": Rauch, p. 319.

267 "I heard the words": Brown, *Bodyguard of Lies,* p. 247.

267 "with the assumption": *FRUS*, Washington Conference II, May 1943, p. 506.

268 "Mr. Stalin probably felt out": MR, Box 29.

268 "of the firm intention": Churchill, *Memoirs,* p. 670.

268 "Perfect! I can just see": Armstrong, p. 11.

268 "Notes for my use": MR, Box 165, Folder 7.

269 "We certainly do not want": Churchill, *Closing the Ring,* pp. 573–74.

269 "with the despairing": Fleming, "A Policy Written in Blood," p. 28.

269 "If you were given": Brown, *Bodyguard of Lies,* p. 248.

269 "I do not remember": Rosenman, p. 371.

269 "If our Western enemies": Fleming, "A Policy Written in Blood," p. 28.

270 "ate and drank enormously": Larrabee, p. 184.

270 "you cannot come all": Churchill, *Memoirs,* p. 674.

270 "paralyzed legs dangling": Atkinson, *An Army at Dawn,* p. 295.

270 "If anything happens": Goodwin, p. 408.

271 "hold their positions": Lewis, p. 252.

Chapter Fourteen: From Pacific Islands to Desert Sands

272 "It now appears that": Morison, Vol. 4, p. 385.

272 "to make certain that": Sherwood, pp. 624–25.

272 "The President was really": Larrabee, p. 293.

272 "at great risk to himself": *NYT,* January 14, 1943.

273 "you get hardened to these": Pogue, *George C. Marshall,* Vol. 3: *Organizer of Victory,* p. 316.

273 "It occurs to me that": FDRL, McCrea Memoirs, parts 1–5.

273 "We've got the bastards licked": Larrabee, p. 301.

274 "It would now seem": Ibid.

274 "would take too long": Arnold, *Global Mission,* p. 372.

274 "the end of the beginning": ChurchillSocietyLondon.org.uk.

275 "I should bring to your notice": Buell, p. 187.

275 "So what, old top?": Buell, p. 187.

276 "The Japanese will pay": Perret, p. 369.

276 "unable to match": McCarthy, p. 334.

276 "the Australians were not": Weintraub, p. 133.

276 "a brilliant mind obsessed": John S. D. Eisenhower, *Allies,* p. 133.

277 "Malaria, dengue fever": Larrabee, p. 326.

278 "Good luck and good hunting": Costello, p. 401.

279 "a juggler, and I never": Kimball, p. 7.

279 "If the Army remained in": Lewis, p. 193.

280 "like a spark": Ibid.

280 "The Germans are natural": Forrest Pogue Interview, February 15, 1957, p. 472, GCM.

280 "I bless the day you urged": DDE, p. 690.

280 "a son of a bitch": D'Este, *Patton,* p. 460.

281 "I'm sure you must have": Ibid.

281 "deep sense of duty": Ibid., pp. 500–501.

281 "And just where": Ambrose, *The Supreme Commander,* p. 12.

282 "I kissed him on the": D'Este, *Patton,* p. 479.

282 "The President greeted me": Butcher, p. 278.

282 "On the other hand": Ibid.

283 "When Patton talked to officers": Spartacus.schoolnet.co.uk.

283 "a godsend": D'Este, *Patton,* p. 501.

283 "a teacher outlining": Liebling, *Liebling Abroad,* pp. 313–14.

285 "We failed to see": Pogue, *George C. Marshall,* Vol. 2: *Ordeal and Hope,* p. 330.

285 "convinced that a mistake": Ambrose, *The Supreme Commander,* p. 67.

285 "out all previous": Weinberg, p. 436.

286 "the main purpose for which": Churchill, *Memoirs,* p. 691.

286 "the most powerful group": Leahy, p. 158.

286 "bronze bust of Mrs. R": Bryant, p. 505.

286 "cause a chill of": GCM, Vol. 3, p. 669.

287 "Churchill made no mention": Leahy, pp. 158–59.

287 "had always shrunk": GCM, Vol. 3, p. 669.

287 "landing ground forces": Ibid.

287 "the Americans are taking": Bryant, p. 507.

287 "I find it hard even now": MacArthur, p. 508.

287 "This is Joe at this end": Meacham, p. 218.

288 "The President sat back": Ibid.

288 "For [this] we have": John S. D. Eisenhower, *Allies,* p. 298.

288 "The President is not willing": Moran, p. 104.

288 "an invasion of Europe": Leahy, p. 159.

289 "We ought to divert": Atkinson, *The Day of Battle,* p. 15.

289 "appealed personally to the": Churchill, *Memoirs,* p. 691.

289 "on a difficult and rather": GCM, Vol. 3, p. 69.

290 "The Generalissimo does not": Coffey, p. 302.

290 "Aid to China!": Arnold, *Global Mission,* p. 427.

290 "If a Chinese soldier": Ibid., p. 434.

290 "about $6,000": Ibid.

290 "A gang of thugs": Stilwell, pp. 190–91.

290 Pappy's done his bit: Ibid., p. 185.

291 "it would slow up": PSF, Box 3.

291 "Stilwell has exactly": MR, Box 165, Folder 2.

291 "The boys have got to": White, p. 139.

291 "had the morality of": Ibid., pp. 139–40.

292 "accomplish the downfall": Chennault, p. 5.

292 "the beautiful small hand": Eleanor Roosevelt, *This I Remember,* p. 284.

292 "Nobody was interested in": John S. D. Eisenhower, *Allies,* p. 296.

292 "I wanted Stilwell to resign": Forrest Pogue Interview, November 21, 1956, p. 373, GCM.

293 "twelve layers of bodies": Erickson, p. 88.

293 "the campaign of calumny": MR, Box 8.

293 "Mr. Stalin, Moscow": Ibid.

294 "In light of all": Kimball, ed., *Churchill and Roosevelt,* pp. 389–94.

294 "a grim, well written": Ibid., p. 389.

294 "are attempting to continue": Sudoplatov, p. 477.

295 "indirectly but convincingly": *New York Times,* April 14, 1990.

Chapter Fifteen: Italy Invaded, Germany Blasted

296 "Is Sicily to be a means": Ambrose, *The Supreme Commander,* p. 104.

296 "In reality, we will get": Clark, p. 166.

296 "Sicily cannot replace": DDE, p. 1043.

296 "I have just had word": FDR, *Public Papers,* 1943, p. 291.

297 "You frequently give": DDE, p. 1353.

297 "great and generous": Montgomery, p. 148.

297 "I know well that I am": Ibid., p. 160.

299 "I want you to get": D'Este, *Patton,* p. 526.

299 "considered the blood of": GCM, Interview, July 25, 1949.

299 "did not believe in destruction": *NYT,* July 24, 1943.

299 "so that Sicily may become": John S. D. Eisenhower, *Allies,* p. 328.

299 "to revoke, repeat, revoke": MR, Box 16.

300 "What will the Russians": MR, Box 33.

300 "I think the personal": *NYT,* July 29, 1943.

300 "At this moment you are": John S. D. Eisenhower, *Allies,* p. 329.

301 "The war continues": Ibid., p. 330.

301 "Good treatment of the": MR, Box 34.

301 "We commend the Italian": MR, Box 12.

301 "Our terms to Italy": John S. D. Eisenhower, *Allies,* p. 335.

302 "turning the tide": D'Este, *Patton,* p. 508.

302 "a combination of Buck": Ibid., p. 454.

302 "The Marquis": Atkinson, *The Day of Battle,* p. 143.

302 "Monty never starts until": Perkins, p. 382.

302 "this is one hell": GCM, from Arnold to Marshall, May 10, 1943, Marshall to Arnold, May 14, 1943, Folder 41, p. 56.

303 "If he continues as commanding": Coffey, p. 309.

304 "the antiaircraft defenses": EyewitnesstoHistory.com.

304 "Hitler built walls": Miller, *Masters of the Air,* p. 202.

305 "One tail flipper": Arnold, *Global Mission,* p. 446.

305 "a battle between large": *NYT,* January 18, 1945.

306 "will soon have to": GCM, Vol. 4, p. 190.

306 "As the effects of the bombing": PSF, Box 83.

307 "There is no substantial": MR, Box 164.

307 "adored the President": Suckley, Binder 27, pp. 230–31.

307 "The shadows of Passchendaele": Stimson and Bundy, pp. 431–38.

308 "A difference of opinion": Buell, p. 394.

308 "very undiplomatic language": Ibid.

309 "There is no question": *FRUS,* Washington Conference III, p. 2.

309 "made a firm commitment": FDRL, HH, Box 132.

309 "to bring the Tube Alloys": *FRUS,* Quebec Conference, August 19, 1943.

309 "magnificent in reconciliation": Persico, *Roosevelt's Secret War,* p. 225.

310 "PM called me in": Bryant, pp. 540–41.

310 "took a year off my life": Atkinson, *An Army at Dawn,* pp. 14–15.

310 "down on that wonderful": Bryant, p. 579.

310 "He asked me how I felt": Ibid., p. 578.

310 "not for one moment": Ibid., p. 579.

310 "then said that Eisenhower": Weinberg, p. 1079.

311 "I shall require sworn verification": MR, Box 16.

311 "he gets bright ideas": Jean Edward Smith, *FDR,* p. 578.

311 "small American force": Young, ed., pp. 220–24.

311 "Among an area commander's": Halsey, p. 166.

312 "She is especially anxious": Elliott Roosevelt, ed., *F.D.R.: His Personal Letters*, p. 1439.

312 "That set me back": Halsey, p. 166.

312 "I need every fighter": Ibid., p. 167.

312 "When I say she inspected": Ibid.

312 "I was ashamed of my": Ibid., pp. 166–67.

312 "None of us had never": Goodwin, p. 464.

313 "Badoglio has gummed up": Ambrose, *The Supreme Commander*, p. 166.

314 "it seemed that he was becoming": Ferrell, ed., *The Eisenhower Diaries*, p. 94.

314 "it was a shock": Blumenson, *Mark Clark*, p. 111.

314 "These things always": Moran, p. 127.

314 "Hitler, through his": FDR, *Public Papers*, 1943, p. 382.

314 "crawl up the leg": Baldwin, *Battles Lost and Won*, p. 218.

315 "he was not insisting": Stimson and Bundy, p. 433.

315 "It is true, I suppose": Baldwin, *Battles Lost and Won*, p. 218.

315 "We want to see what": Clark, pp. 242–43.

316 "co-belligerent": MR, Box 34.

Chapter Sixteen: From Tarawa to Tehran

317 "had a right to be": Miller, *The Story of World War II*, p. 210.

317 "I have seen the dead": Divine, p. 9.

318 "the reason we print": *Life*, September 20, 1943.

319 "an unqualified no": Holland Smith, *Coral and Brass*, pp. 111–12.

320 "pretty raw, pretty rugged": Sherrod, p. 113.

321 "John, I am sailor": FDRL, McCrea Papers.

321 "The trouble is": Buell, pp. 420–21.

322 "Lion! Lion!": Sherwood, p. 768.

322 "a tremendous explosion": FDRL, McCrea Papers.

323 "Can you imagine our own": Sherwood, p. 768.

323 "I revel in an old": Beschloss, p. 22.

323 "It was a very dramatic": Buell, p. 424.

323 "He spoke of his pleasure": Butcher, p. 445.

324 "That's an awfully nice place": Summersby, p. 93.

324 "Won't you come back": Ibid., p. 94.

324 "No one could have": Dwight D. Eisenhower, *Crusade in Europe*, p. 195.

324 "Ike, you and I know": Sherwood, p. 770.

325 "But it is dangerous": Dwight D. Eisenhower, *Crusade in Europe*, p. 197.

325 "I answered nothing": Ibid.

325 "My Friend the Sphinx": Black, p. 856.

325 "Resting her hand firmly": Elliott Roosevelt, *As He Saw It*, p. 152.

325 "The accepted belief": Churchill, *Memoirs*, p. 753.

326 "FDR doesn't like me to": Stilwell, p. 245.

326 "My God, you have": Forrest Pogue Interview, October 29, 1956, p. 605, GCM.

326 "It has been decided": GCM, Vol. 4, p. 137.

326 "flopped over to Stilwell": Ibid.

326 "a waste of time": Black, p. 857.

327 "we talked over the air": Arnold, *Global Mission*, p. 463.

327 "was not only useless": White, p. 56.

328 "God forbid": Forrest Pogue Interview, November 13, 1956, p. 622, GCM.

328 "He had calculated": Churchill, *Closing the Ring*, p. 238.

328 "For a couple of hours": Ibid.

328 "It is a pity": Lohbeck, p. 201.

329 "the top of his head": Blumenson, *The Patton Papers*, p. 315.

329 "I guess I can't": D'Este, *Patton*, p. 533.

329 "It's my nerves": Atkinson, *The Day of Battle*, p. 148.

329 "serious doubt in my mind": DDE, p. 1340.

330 "who would shoot Patton": D'Este, *Patton*, p. 536.

330 "It is rather a commentary": Patton Papers, August 21, 1943, Manuscript Division, Library of Congress.

330 "Pistol Packing Patton": *Time*, December 6, 1943.

330 "if you want to write": FDR, *Public Papers*, 1943, p. 552.

330 "Don't let anything that SOB": D'Este, *Patton*, p. 550.

331 "Part of this was perhaps": Blumenson, *The Patton Papers*, p. 6.

331 "maintain constant direction": MR, Box 12, Folder 2.

331 "I know you will not": *FRUS*, 1942, Vol. 3, pp. 542–43.

333 "Stalin came to call": Suckley, Binder 17, p. 91.

333 "who's promoting that": Sherwood, p. 780.

334 "We Russians believe": Eubank, p. 259.

334 "He felt that to leave": Harriman, p. 269.

335 "suddenly, in the flick": Ferrell, *The Dying President*, p. 17.

335 "It was like talking": Sherwood, pp. 343–44.

335 "knowledge of our planes": Arnold, *Global Mission*, p. 467.

335 "the most inscrutable": Jean Edward Smith, *FDR*, p. 588.

335 "in regard to me": Forrest Pogue Interview, November 15, 1956, p. 342, GCM.

335 "rough SOB": Pogue, *George C. Marshall*, Vol. 3: *Organizer of Victory*, p. 313.

336 "The conference is over": Bryant, p. 484.

336 "Withdrawal behind a river": David Eisenhower, *Eisenhower,* p. 29.

336 "just so much talk": Leahy, p. 304.

336 "That old Bolshevik": Ibid., p. 208.

337 "a mustard-colored uniform": Moran, pp. 146–47.

337 "Stalin the great": Beschloss, p. 26.

337 "At least fifty thousand": Ibid., p. 27.

337 "say, forty-nine thousand": Ibid.

337 "Russia is like": Arnold, *Global Mission,* p. 230.

338 "was correct, stiff": Perkins, pp. 83–85.

338 "he pledged that": *FRUS,* Vol. 5, p. 577.

339 "Together we controlled": Churchill, *Closing the Ring,* p. 65.

339 "That is an indication": Leahy, p. 211.

339 "I suggested that the value": Churchill, *Closing the Ring,* p. 396.

340 "who made the President's": Persico, *Roosevelt's Secret War,* p. 276.

340 "surreptitiously": Marshall, p. 142.

340 "Chief of Staff Will Head": *NYT,* October 1, 1943.

340 "I believe that Marshall's": FDRL, Stimson to Hopkins, November 10, 1943.

340 "I believe General Marshall is": MR, Box 17.

340 "Any soldier would prefer": Stimson and Bundy, p. 440.

341 "We have the winning": Weintraub, p. 195.

341 "To transfer [Marshall]": PSF, Box 83.

341 "You are absolutely right": Ibid.

341 "My grandfather went out": Stilwell, p. 251.

341 "First time in history": Ibid., pp. 266–67.

341 "After a great deal": Forrest Pogue Interview, November 15, 1956, pp. 344–45, GCM.

341 "in as convincing": Ibid.

342 "Well, I didn't feel": Ibid.

342 "I would not command": Sherwood, p. 761.

343 "Never had he wanted": Ibid.

343 "The appointment of General": Parrish, p. 416.

343 "Dear Eisenhower, I thought": Dwight D. Eisenhower, *Crusade in Europe,* p. 208.

343 "one of my most": Ibid.

343 "Well, Ike, you are going": David Eisenhower, *Eisenhower,* p. 46.

344 "You will have an Army": Atkinson, *The Day of Battle,* p. 297.

344 "perhaps really preferred": Stimson and Bundy, p. 442.

344 "I had seen a good deal": Harriman, p. 272.

345 "Eisenhower is the best": James Roosevelt and Bill Libby, *My Parents,* p. 167.

Chapter Seventeen: D-Day

346 "in hush-hush tones": Summersby, p. 105.

346 "Discussed Kay": Atkinson, *An Army at Dawn*, p. 330.

346 "I'm very out of practice": Weintraub, p. 223.

346 "Goddamit, can't you tell": Morgan, p. 151.

347 "You will be under": Weintraub, p. 221.

347 "no-nonsense life": D'Este, *Patton*, p. 56.

347 "I still have some fear": DDE, p. 1646.

348 "so the troops could": DDE, p. 1721.

348 "kept me by his bedside": Dwight D. Eisenhower, *Crusade in Europe*, p. 218.

348 "almost an egomaniac": Ibid.

348 *"Adiós"*: David Eisenhower, *Eisenhower*, p. 64.

349 "leading a rather": *Washington Post*, March 1, 1998.

349 "Leave Kay and Ike": *Washington Post*, March 1, 1998.

350 "we should content": Dwight D. Eisenhower, *Crusade in Europe*, p. 212.

350 "launching the attack": Blumenson, *Mark Clark*, p. 160.

350 "lance the abscess": Cowley and Parker, eds., p. 25.

351 "I thought we were throwing": Churchill, *Memoirs*, p. 800.

351 "any higher commander": Clark, p. 318.

351 "If the New Zealand": Ibid., p. 317.

351 "That's beautiful": *NYT*, February 16, 1944.

351 "other than to take": Clark, p. 312.

352 "I may be able quietly": GCM, Vol. 5, p. 535.

352 "A blessed numbness": Marshall, p. 196.

352 "I am terribly distressed": Sherwood, p. 805.

352 Your son, my lord: Ibid.

353 "We can, if necessary": MR, Box 29.

353 "He would have been": Rose, p. 366.

353 "the faces that": Churchill, *The Hinge of Fate*, p. 619.

353 "When I think of": *Time*, June 6, 1944.

353 "Dammit, everybody knows": Meacham, p. 228.

354 "overwhelming all others": Summersby, p. 126.

354 "You asked the other": GCM, Vol. 4, p. 255.

355 "crawled half a mile": Ambrose, *The Supreme Commander*, pp. 214–15.

355 "By George": Perkins, p. 383.

355 "My dear Mr. Prime Minister": PSF, 37.

356 "Regarding gas": FDR, *Public Papers*, 1943, pp. 242–43.

357 "I rather expected": Buell, p. 449.

357 "My guess is that": Blum, *From the Morgenthau Diaries*, Vol. 3: *Years of War*, p. 167.

357 "I would put in": Ibid.

357 "I am anti de Gaulle": PSF, Safe Box 4.

358 "We call him Joan": Persico, *Roosevelt's Secret War*, p. 304.

358 "I wonder how he": PSF, Box 4.

358 "I am personally": Loewenheim, Langley, and Jonas, eds., p. 493.

358 "the bombing of these": DDE, p. 1809.

358 "Do not let the Germans": *NYT*, May 28, 1944.

359 "a cover plan": Brown, *Bodyguard of Lies*, p. 389.

359 "Truth is so precious": Ibid.

359 "I will have to battle": DDE, p. 399.

360 "A man must be": Blumenson, *The Patton Papers*, pp. 222–23.

360 "When he shook hands": Summersby, p. 21.

360 "I now have the pleasure": Blumenson, *The Patton Papers*, p. 440.

360 "The sooner our soldiers": GCM, Vol. 4, p. 378.

360 "Since it is": D'Este, *Patton*, p. 585.

360 "succeeded in slapping": GCM, Vol. 4, p. 378.

361 "General Patton has progressed": GCM, Vol. 4, p. 378.

361 "On all the evidence": DDE, p. 1840.

361 "George, you have gotten": Patton Papers, May 1, 1944, Manuscript Division, Library of Congress.

361 "put his head on": D'Este, *Patton*, pp. 588–89.

361 "I am once more": Ibid, p. 590.

362 "I have learned that": GCM, Vol. 4, p. 246.

362 "I am inclined to believe": Kahn, *Codebreaking in World Wars I and II*, p. 148.

362 "No matter when or": National Archives Record Group 457, Decrypts, Japanese Messages, 76–77.

362 "I wonder what ideas": Ibid.

362 "most indications point": Ibid.

363 "I cannot agree": MR, Box 33.

363 "I would never survive": Ibid.

363 "was one of the": Clark, p. 370.

363 "We are committed to": MR, Box 29.

364 "by a small German force": Ibid.

364 "would seem far": Ibid.

364 "For if the trumpet": Kimball, *Roosevelt and Churchill*, p. 228.

364 "but fear of": Pogue, *The Supreme Command*, p. 340.

365 "Please note that I am": Beschloss, p. 35.

365 "Lee wanted to talk": Elliott Roosevelt, *F.D.R.: His Personal Letters*, Vol. 4, p. 1486.

367 "In the greatest mass": *NYT*, May 22, 1944.

368 "dour but canny Scot": Stagg, pp. 96–97.

368 "could agree on the": Armchairgeneral.com.

368 "six foot two": Larrabee, p. 453.

368 "full of menace": Ibid.

368 "Probably no one who does": Ibid.

369 "I think they're frightful": Summersby, p. 28.

369 "just how long": Ambrose, *The Supreme Commander*, p. 416.

371 "The Boss was keeping": Tully, p. 265.

371 "that the 5th Army": Blumenson, *Mark Clark*, p. 202.

371 "I wonder how [Russell] Linaka": Eleanor Roosevelt, *This I Remember*, p. 252.

372 "Ike has the forecasters": Ambrose, *The Supreme Commander*, p. 264.

372 "The eyes of the world": DDE, pp. 1908, 1913.

373 "I reluctantly contemplated": Ambrose, *The Supreme Commander*, p. 271.

373 "Almighty God: our sons": *NYT*, June 7, 1944.

373 "the history of warfare": Churchill, *Memoirs*, p. 813.

374 "not a single unit": Kahn, *Hitler's Spies*, p. 515.

374 "I wish you would": PSF, Box 82.

375 "Daylight bombing": Harriman, p. 296.

375 "about the octane": Ibid., p. 297.

375 "agreed to provide": MR, Box 35.

376 "He could not afford": Ibid.

376 "General Staff": *Time*, January 13, 1947.

376 "bubbled over with joy": Harriman, p. 313.

376 "Dammit, we all can": Ibid.

376 "For a while": Arnold, *Global Mission*, p. 470.

377 "London would be leveled": National Archives Record Group 457, Decrypts, Japanese Messages, 76–77.

377 "Devastating robot land": MR, Box 13.

378 "stratospheric attacks": Ibid.

378 "during the last six": Churchill, *Closing the Ring*, p. 197.

378 "new toy": *NYT*, June 17, 1944.

378 "I am opposed to": DDE, p. 1975.

379 "that crippled son of a bitch": Persico, *Roosevelt's Secret War*, p. 338.

379 "he feared that in": Suckley, Binder 8, p. 237.

379 "every precaution should": MR, Box 20, p. 164.

379 "The thing to do": *NYT*, January 8, 1944.

380 "Bill Donovan is also": Ibid., pp. 63–64.

380 "Wild Bill is a": Brown, *The Last Hero*, p. 56.

381 "Strategy, without information": Donovan to FDR memorandum, June 10, 1941, FDRL.

382 "He would grasp": Persico, *Piercing the Reich*, p. 6.

382 "the sort of guy who": Stafford, p. 204.

382 "There is a possibility": *The Magic Background,* p. A-224.

383 "Those opposed to the Nazis": PSF, Box 149.

383 "A revolution is not to be": Ibid.

383 "Colonel Stauffenberg": National Archives Record Group 457, Decrypts, Japanese Messages, 76-77.

384 "I don't think I know": Beschloss, p. 7.

384 "From a strictly": FDR, *Public Papers,* 1944–45, pp. 147–48.

384 "I see no great purpose": GCM, Vol. 4, p. 296.

384 "I called it the": Churchill, *Memoirs,* p. 739.

384 "who diverted whom?": Baldwin, *Great Mistakes,* p. 228.

385 "Hitler valued Italy": Keegan, *The Second World War,* p. 349.

385 "All roads led to": Baldwin, *Great Mistakes,* p. 228.

385 "stepped from the": Hassett, p. 259.

385 "I did not fail to": de Gaulle, p. 268.

Chapter Eighteen: MacArthur Versus King: FDR's Decision

387 "Arrange your plans": Whitney, p. 405.

387 "felt reasonably certain": MacArthur, p. 196.

388 "The humiliation of": Hunt, pp. 331–32.

388 "to present fully": GCM, Vol. 4, p. 422.

389 "the poor dog was": Jean Edward Smith, *FDR,* p. 620.

389 "We assumed": Rosenman, p. 456.

390 "a terrific automobile": Manchester, p. 423.

390 "When I last saw": Perret, pp. 403–4.

391 "patently of Japanese": Leahy, p. 252.

391 "of everything but": Larrabee, p. 343.

391 "He is just the shell": Manchester, p. 424.

391 "Well, Douglas": Ibid., p. 426.

392 "All of my American": MacArthur, p. 97.

392 "If I could secure": Ibid., p. 197.

392 "We must now allow": GCM, Vol. 4, p. 422.

393 "apparently felt that": MacArthur, p. 183.

393 "We have cut off": FDR, *Public Papers,* 1944–45, p. 175.

393 "If your decision be to bypass": Whitney, p. 125.

393 "We will not bypass": Ibid.

393 "Give me an aspirin": Manchester, p. 427.

394 "But Douglas": MacArthur, p. 198.

394 "He wanted to display": Rosenman, pp. 458–59.

394 "What chance do you": Perret, p. 406.

395 "MacArthur seems to have": Hassett, p. 88.

395 "I'll beat the son of": Manchester, p. 424.

395 "If the war with": Perret, p. 407.

395 "planning his life": Suckley, Binder 18.

396 "Quick, get a shot of it": Manchester, p. 427.

396 "At your conference": Rosenman, pp. 371–72.

396 "Tell FBI Hoover": MR, 19.

396 "I like your climate": MR, 24, Folder 1.

396 "You have been doing": MacArthur, p. 199.

397 "It is my considered": PSF, Box 83.

397 "the President has accepted": Costello, p. 493.

Chapter Nineteen: Europe: Broad Axe Versus the Spear

398 "didn't tell me about": Forrest Pogue Interview, October 5, 1956, p. 597, GCM.

399 "I have prepared": MR, Box 33.

399 "I am mindful": Churchill, *Triumph and Tragedy*, p. 66.

399 "I am impressed": MR, Box 33.

399 "the first major": Ibid.

400 "Good God": Ibid.

400 "lay down the mantle": DDE, p. 2066.

400 "with all that might": Churchill, *Triumph and Tragedy*, pp. 504–5.

401 "This would mean": Dwight D. Eisenhower, *Crusade in Europe*, p. 228.

401 "aggressive action on": Montgomery, p. 235.

401 "one really powerful": Lamb, pp. 207–8.

401 "dead, wounded": Miller, *The Story of World War II*, p. 318.

402 "pissed in the river": D'Este, *Patton*, p. 463.

402 "troubled by doubt": Ibid., p. 643.

402 "There isn't a correspondent": Nichols, pp. 328, 358.

402 "It was literally possible": Dwight D. Eisenhower, *Crusade in Europe*, pp. 279–80.

402 "He's colorful": D'Este, *Patton*, p. 636.

402 "Compared to war": Ibid., p. 634.

402 "every ounce of fuel": Dwight D. Eisenhower, *Crusade in Europe*, p. 296.

403 "It is the duty": Miller, *The Story of World War II*, p. 326.

403 "Paris must not fall": DDE, p. 2090.

403 "in better physical form": Henry Stimson Diary, August 23, 1944, Yale University.

403 "The Republic has never ceased": de Gaulle, p. 346.

404 "stretched to the limit": Ferrell, ed., *The Eisenhower Diaries*, p. 127.

404 "Well, they're balls": Butcher, p. 659.

404 "my arguments were": Montgomery, p. 242.

405 "embarrassing, not only": Weintraub, p. 252.

405 "never felt like": Ibid.

405 "General Ike pinned": Summersby, p. 195.

406 "the hour for action": Harriman, p. 336.

406 "refused to help": Ibid., p. 337.

406 "calumny against": MR, Box 15.

407 "it had proved impossible": MR, Box 35.

407 "wanted it understood": D'Este, *Patton*, p. 337.

407 "an adventuristic affair": Harriman, p. 339.

407 "We hope that you": Ibid., p. 343.

407 "For the first time": PSF, Box 48.

408 "I do not believe": MR, Box 35.

409 "We had to regain": Buell, p. 470.

409 "The offer has been": Ibid., p. 471.

409 "he had always been": *FRUS,* Quebec II, p. 314.

409 "Our objective": Ibid.

410 "if the President": Dwight D. Eisenhower, *Crusade in Europe,* p. 284.

410 "Winston never talks": Moran, p. 185.

410 "You could have put": Ibid., p. 192.

410 "It was 1862": Ibid.

410 "Never at any time": DDE, p. 2164.

410 "After all": Montgomery, p. 256.

411 "ninety percent successful": Ibid., p. 243.

411 "we could push on": D'Este, *Patton*, p. 650.

411 "We got no gas": Ibid., p. 649.

412 "if it took every": Ibid., p. 666.

412 "condoms became": Hastings, p. 69.

412 "our troops will simply": D'Este, *Patton,* p. 653.

412 "absolutely unacceptable": Ibid.

412 "tell the men": Ibid.

412 "It is highly improbable": Hastings, p. 178.

413 "These photographs are": DDE, p. 2176.

413 "We've got to be": Perret, p. 342.

413 "The prisoners of 17": FDR, *Public Papers,* 1944, p. 233.

414 "a nation of seventy": Stimson and Bundy, p. 578.

414 "he was thinking of": Blum, *From the Morgenthau Diaries,* Vol. 3, p. 363.

414 "for the purpose of": Stimson and Bundy, p. 574.

414 "the industries referred": Ibid., p. 581.

414 "We have got": Beschloss, p. 143.

415 "ten fresh German": Blum, *From the Morgenthau Diaries*, Vol. 3, p. 382.
415 "He had no intention": Stimson and Bundy, p. 581.

Chapter Twenty: Stilwell Leaves China, MacArthur Returns to the Philippines

416 "overrunning eastern China": GCM, Vol. 4, p. 538.
417 "It is inconceivable": Romanus and Sunderland, pp. 309–10.
417 "clouds of war planes": Stimson and Bundy, p. 533.
417 "He hates the Reds": Stilwell, p. 322.
417 "They are allied": White, p. 134.
418 "It appears to be": MR, Box 165.
418 "areas where": Ibid.
418 "We were fighting": Stilwell, p. 320.
418 "headed by an": Ibid.
418 "The Chinese ground forces": GCM, Vol. 4, p. 434.
419 "directly under you": GCM, Vol. 4, p. 439.
419 "I have urged": GCM, Vol. 4, p. 510.
420 "I handed this bundle": Ibid.
420 "Throw out General": Stilwell, p. 336.
420 "has been done at": GCM, Vol. 4, p. 538.
420 "bleeding us white": Stimson and Bundy, p. 538.
420 "so much American": White, p. 167.
421 "you will lose Chiang": Costello, p. 523.
421 "If Old Softy": Stilwell, p. 339.
421 "You will be ordered": GCM, Vol. 4, p. 547.
421 "Stilwell told his aide": White, p. 178.
421 "never really made": Stimson and Bundy, p. 535.
421 "just a case of": *NYT,* November 1, 1944.
422 "The situation is just": PSF, Box 83.
422 MacArthur would command: *NYT,* September 19, 1944.
422 "Ships to the front": MacArthur, p. 214.
423 "the smoke from": Ibid., p. 216.
423 "People of the Philippines": Ibid., pp. 216–17.
424 "Please excuse": PSF, Box 83.
424 "I know well what this means": MR, Box 12.
424 "We have landed": FDR, *Public Papers,* 1944–45, p. 377.
425 "The Japanese Navy": Halsey, p. 226.
426 "The New Deal": *Time,* January 3, 1944.
426 "I regret very much": GCM, Vol. 4, p. 160.
426 "General Marshall would": Marshall, p. 150.

427 "If the Republicans ran": DDE, p. 1463.

427 "When Mr. Winchell": Ibid.

427 "He was exasperated": DDE, p. 1535.

427 "That night we had": Harriman, pp. 374–75.

428 "all the resources": MacArthur to Churchill, April 12, 1943; Churchill to
        Ismay, May 7, 1943, Public Records Office, London.

428 "FDR will find some": Wilkinson Journal mss., Churchill College,
        Cambridge.

428 "My chief talked": Manchester, p. 411.

428 "If the war is over": PSF, Box 157.

429 "fearful and small-minded": Perret, p. 213.

429 "Boy, did the general": Ferrell, ed., *The Eisenhower Diaries*, p. 22.

429 "tell on him": Ibid.

429 "I am most grateful": Perret, p. 384.

429 "unless this New Deal": Manchester, p. 418.

430 "destroy this monstrosity": Ibid.

430 "General MacArthur has one": Perret, p. 383.

430 "were generally construed": *NYT*, April 14, 1944.

431 "were never intended": Manchester, p. 419.

431 "I request that": Ibid.

431 "I think you are": MacArthur, p. 96.

431 "These Republican leaders": Hassett, p. 273.

432 "Information has come": PSF, Box Navy 62.

432 "For Mr. Dewey's eyes only": GCM, Vol. 4, p. 530.

432 "I should much have": Ibid.

433 "based on deciphered": Wohlstetter, p. 177.

433 "Why in hell": GCM, Vol. 4, p. 530.

434 "a few of Roosevelt's": Murphy, p. 247.

434 "It would be a": Rauch, ed., p. 373.

434 "I have as little": FDR, *Public Papers,* 1944–45, p. 197.

434 "speaking of the glorious": Rosenman, p. 487.

435 "full of fight": Meacham, p. 309.

435 "had voted against": Sherwood, p. 913.

435 "let him know": DDE, p. 2321.

Chapter Twenty-one: From the Home Front to Yalta

436 "recognize the fact": Buell, p. 384.

436 "I didn't want any": Forrest Pogue Interview, February 14, 1957, p. 456,
        GCM.

437 "Allied Forces yesterday": Baldwin, *Battles Lost and Won,* p. 315.

437 "The Germans took": John S. D. Eisenhower, *The Bitter Woods,* p. 29.

437 "getting ready": Forrest Pogue Interview, February 4, 1957, p. 392, GCM.

437 "Americans Capture": *NYT,* December 17, 1944.

437 "completing the defeat": GCM, Vol. 4, p. 552.

437 "I still have nine": Pogue, *The Supreme Command,* p. 370.

437 "fighting a defensive": DDE, p. 2350.

437 "The men are done": Sorge, p. 15.

438 "public statements by": FDR, *Public Papers,* 1944–45, p. 433.

438 "I have made a": Keegan, *The Second World War,* p. 440.

438 "ghost front": John S. D. Eisenhower, *The Bitter Woods,* p. 27.

439 "If we can deliver": Ibid., p. 7.

439 "It is plain": Ibid., p. 171.

439 "I believe the Germans": D'Este, *Patton,* p. 673.

440 "Soldiers of the west front": *NYT,* December 18, 1944.

441 "He doesn't seem to be": Blum, ed., *The Diary of Henry A. Wallace,* p. 416.

441 "There will be only": John S. D. Eisenhower, *The Bitter Woods,* p. 35.

441 "opportunity, and not": D'Este, *Patton,* p. 679.

442 "Brad, this time": Ambrose, *The Supreme Commander,* p. 472.

442 "Well, it will only": Dwight D. Eisenhower, *At Ease,* p. 174.

442 "it is the Russian": MR, Box 34.

442 "decide whether they": Beschloss, p. 171.

443 "I'm mighty glad": Hastings, p. 227.

443 "That's it": Ibid.

444 "Here is a question": Ambrose, *Citizen Soldiers,* pp. 345–46.

444 "to promote tolerance": *NYT,* March 6, 1944.

444 "the average Negro": Ibid.

444 "will not ordinarily": MR, Box 171.

445 "the worst in Europe": Miller, *The Story of World War II,* p. 248.

445 "would have settled": Ibid.

445 "characteristics that are": Ibid., p. 247.

445 "I did not send": Ibid., pp. 247–48.

445 "America wasn't perfect": Ibid., p. 248.

445 "I don't care what": Ibid., p. 331.

446 "the Negro type has": Ibid., p. 474.

447 "haven't been treated": FDR, *Public Papers,* 1944–45, pp. 66–67.

447 "We had a [Japanese]": Forrest Pogue Interview, February 15, 1957, p. 470, GCM.

448 "The more I think": Elliott Roosevelt, ed., *F.D.R.: His Personal Letters,* p. 1577.

448 "the worst single": Burns, p. 216.

449 "scraping the bottom": Paul V. McNutt, Radio Address, Washington, DC, February 13, 1943.

449 "We are holding here": GCM, Vol. 4, p. 127.

449 "because he had": GCM, Vol. 4, p. 164.

450 "several of them": Buell, p. 243.

450 "about the best thing": GCM, Vol. 3, p. 550.

450 "I consider the commemoration": FDR, *Public Papers,* 1943, p. 528.

451 "We're not a war industry": James C. Petrillo entry, Britannica Online Encyclopedia.

451 "I hope that no": DDE, p. 538.

451 "greeted me at": Summersby, p. 156.

451 "Some of the Army": Ibid., p. 161.

453 "The war must be": Ambrose, *Citizen Soldiers,* p. 54.

453 "The whole world": Armstrong, p. 128.

453 "Goebbels has twisted": Persico, *Roosevelt's Secret War,* p. 323.

454 "Nobody will make peace": Ambrose, *Citizen Soldiers,* p. 54.

454 "realizes what is": Persico, *Nuremberg,* pp. 330–31.

454 "no evidence that": MR, Box 73.

454 "At the present time": *FRUS,* Quebec II, p. 489.

455 "several million": MR, Box 12.

456 "will be summarily shot": Larrabee, p. 504.

456 "We've got everything": John S. D. Eisenhower, *The Bitter Woods,* p. 434.

456 "I have been thinking": MR, Box 21.

457 "any change of climate": MR, Box 35.

457 "He says that": MR, Box 21.

458 "If you go they will": Persico, *Franklin and Lucy,* p. 322.

458 "I had too many": Toland, p. 52.

458 "He is very thin": Meacham, p. xiii.

458 "instead of improvement": Sherwood, p. 849.

458 "we ought to occupy": Churchill, *Memoirs,* p. 913.

459 "most terrifying experience": MR, Box 21.

459 "The curves were short": Rigdon and Derieux, p. 145.

459 "Look how many are girls": Toland, p. 56.

459 "even more to want": Beschloss, p. 178.

460 "a block to the bath": Ibid.

460 "his powerful head": Stettinius, p. 99.

461 "I mention this only": Toland, p. 62.

462 "Whoever occupies": Meacham, p. 319.

462 "It must never be": Parrish, p. 486.

463 "I have found out": Ferrell, *The Dying President,* p. 108.

463 "Russia's entry at": Parrish, p. 494.

464 "We've just saved": Meacham, p. 317.

464 "the bravest government": Black, pp. 1062–63.

465 "That's my Himmler": Ibid., p. 1062.

465 "absolutely charming": Harriman, p. 391.

465 "mosquitoes under": Leahy, p. 311.

465 "In this palace": Moran, p. 237.

465 "rose and gripped": Ibid., p. 246.

467 "justify and surpass": MR, Box 22.

467 "The conference has produced": Ibid.

467 "The President is to be": Ibid.

467 "I just thought that": Perkins, p. 142.

467 "You have 400 years": Kimball, *The Juggler*, p. 66.

468 "It would be a grand": Toland, p. 324.

468 "have set themselves up": Knightley, p. 230.

468 "France has had": Elliott Roosevelt, ed., *F.D.R.: His Personal Letters*, p. 1489.

468 "He made a statement": FDR, *Public Papers*, 1944–45, p. 564.

469 "I hope you will pardon": Ibid., pp. 570–86.

469 "I remember of the moment": COH, Frances Perkins.

469 "The Roosevelts are not": FDR, *Public Papers*, 1944–45, pp. 574–76.

471 "Everyone seemed to agree": Moran, p. 239.

471 "Honestly, FDR spoke": Meacham, p. 319.

471 "worn, wasted": Abramson, p. 371.

471 "President looked better": Black, p. 1074.

471 "was lethargic": Meacham, p. 319.

Chapter Twenty-two: Leveling Japan, Invading Okinawa

473 "I understand the big parade": Manchester, p. 482.

474 "are likely to have": Weinberg, p. 865.

474 "no reason why we": *American Heritage*, August–September 1985, p. 44.

474 "We Should Have Used": Ibid.

474 "I state categorically": Ibid., pp. 41–45.

476 "At one time": Miller, *The Story of World War II*, p. 556.

476 "I swung my camera": Ibid., p. 547.

477 "On Iwo Island": Ibid., p. 555.

477 "I am going to see": Larrabee, p. 304.

478 "I do not know": PPF, p. 7177.

478 "Following a successful": Finney, pp. 23–24.

482 "pastoral and handsomely": Miller, *The Story of World War II*, p. 563.

482 "My chances of becoming": Ibid., p. 561.

482 "Goddam—this is": *NYT,* April 2, 1945.

483 "It is an honor": Feifer, p. 206.

483 "at the price of": Halsey, p. 232.

484 "the most important": *NYT,* April 6, 1945.

Chapter Twenty-three: To Take Berlin?

486 "the loveliest city": Miller, *The Story of World War II,* p. 480.

486 "a center of a railway": GCM, Vol. 5, p. 55.

487 "Today we can only speak": *NYT,* March 5, 1945.

487 "when the occasion warrants": Miller, *Masters of the Air,* p. 454.

488 "every person in Germany": Miller, *The Story of World War II,* p. 481.

488 "Dispersion is one of": Dwight D. Eisenhower, *Crusade in Europe,* p. 370.

490 "Patton's forces seemed": D'Este, *Patton,* p. 711.

490 "for God's sake": Ibid., p. 712.

490 "Thus William": Ambrose, *Citizen Soldiers,* p. 434.

490 "So far in my": Blumenson, *Patton,* p. 635.

490 "George, you are not": D'Este, *Patton,* p. 711.

491 "He knew damn well": Hirshon, p. 623.

491 "I didn't know": D'Este, *Patton,* p. 716.

491 "John Waters": Ibid., p. 715.

492 "Because I'll recognize": Hirshon, p. 621.

492 "sent off a little": DDE, p. 2617.

492 "Tell your nation": Beschloss, p. 66.

492 "wouldn't have done": Ibid., p. 40.

493 "Germans!": DDE, p. 2224.

493 "To see the whole": Grimsley, pp. 84–85.

493 "he did not want": Rosenman, pp. 518–19.

494 "This time": Ibid.

494 "Men and boys": Bliss, p. 96.

495 "When the Red Army": PSF, Safe Box 5.

496 "ruthless attitude": MR, Box 13.

496 "It would be completely": MR, Box 28.

497 "a matter in which": Persico, *Roosevelt's Secret War,* p. 426.

497 "the Germans have already": MR, Box 28.

497 "I feel that your": Ibid.

497 "has agreed to open": MR, Box 28.

497 "The Germans on the": Ibid.

497 "I cannot avoid": Ibid.

498 "continue to fight": Ibid.

498 "Averell is right": Harriman, p. 444.

498 "Stalin has been deceiving": Bishop, p. 509.

498 "there would definitely": Hastings, p. 412.

499 "Clearly Berlin": Montgomery, pp. 248–49.

499 "I say quite frankly": Meacham, p. 332.

499 "Who do you think": Ambrose, *The Supreme Commander*, p. 630.

499 "a pretty stiff price": Ibid., p. 535.

500 "Through bombings": MR, Box 33.

500 "to divide the enemy's": DDE, p. 2551.

500 "hold 15–25 divisions": Persico, *Roosevelt's Secret War*, p. 423.

500 "the best briefed invasion": Ibid., p. 354.

500 "If the German": Dwight D. Eisenhower, *Crusade in Europe*, p. 397.

501 "Berlin has lost": Harriman, p. 435.

501 "Who is going to take": Hastings, p. 462.

501 "he has no business": Toland, p. 311.

501 "the complete confidence": MR, Box 23.

502 "had become": Toland, p. 312.

502 "I deem it highly": DDE, p. 2579.

502 "completely broken up": MR, Box 23.

502 "Whilst Berlin remains": DDE, p. 2563.

502 "upset E. quite a bit": DDE, p. 2563.

502 "I would cheerfully": MR, Box 33.

502 "in an almost": MR, Box 23.

502 "I consider that Berlin": DDE, pp. 2594–95.

503 "the so-called National": Toland, pp. 311–12.

503 "I think that it is": Blumenson, *Patton*, p. 694.

503 "exploit any opportunity": Hastings, p. 412.

503 "about sixty miles from": Churchill, *Memoirs*, p. 756.

503 "I regard the matter": MR, Box 23.

503 "but the Germans": Ambrose, *The Supreme Commander*, p. 456.

503 "I alone had to be": Ibid.

504 "his most controversial": Ambrose, *Citizen Soldiers*, p. 457.

504 "I cannot see exactly": DDE, p. 2615.

505 "safeguard us against more": Black, p. 1100.

505 "In thirty years of": Ambrose, *The Victors*, p. 341.

Chapter Twenty-four: Death of the Commander in Chief

506 "It's no good": Bishop, p. 520.

506 "with an overpowering": FDRL, Hassett Diary, Box 22.

506 "As I reined in": Merriman Smith, *Thank You, Mr. President*, p. 186.

507 "We can hear the laughter": Suckley, Binder 19.

507 "He says that he can": Ibid.

507 "The work, my friends": FDR, *Public Papers,* 1944–45, p. 615.

507 "come hell or high water": Hassett, p. 332.

507 "We are going to": Perkins, p. 396.

508 "the greatest reception": Rosenman, p. 546.

508 "Although we were alone": Perkins, p. 396.

509 "a minor misunderstanding": MR, Box 23.

509 "It is my desire": Ibid.

509 "I would minimize": Rosenman, p. 538.

509 "those photos look": Persico, *Franklin and Lucy,* p. 330.

510 "was quite a jolly": Shoumatoff, p. 103.

510 "He is slipping away": Hassett, p. 327.

510 "His condition was not": Ibid., p. 328.

510 "I understood his position": Ibid.

510 "Lucy is so sweet": Suckley, Binder 19.

510 "removing all industry": Blum, *From the Morgenthau Diaries,* Vol. 3, p. 433.

510 "I was terribly shocked": Ibid.

511 "His hands shook": Ibid.

511 "at three o'clock": Ibid., p. 417.

511 "I get the gruel": Suckley, Binder 19.

512 "The trouble is that": Ibid.

512 "Here's where I make a law": *NYT,* April 13, 1945.

512 "I was struck by": Shoumatoff, p. 116.

512 "Have you dropped": Suckley, Binder 19.

513 "His eyes were closed": Hassett, p. 335.

513 "sat up late": Dwight D. Eisenhower, *Crusade in Europe,* p. 409.

513 "I had failed": Blumenson, *Patton,* p. 285.

513 "We were doubtful": Dwight D. Eisenhower, *Crusade in Europe,* p. 409.

513 "It seems very": Blumenson, *Patton,* p. 285.

513 "from our distance": Weintraub, p. 332.

514 "The news was": Arnold, *Global Mission,* p. 549.

514 "He had greatly": Stimson and Bundy, p. 154.

514 "Darlings": MR, Box 14.

515 "Bring out the champagne": Shirer, p. 1110.

515 "My Führer": Ibid.

515 "Fate has removed": Beevor, p. 204.

515 "Do not make personal": GCM, Vol. 5, p. 102.

515 "The following are the": Burns, p. 602.

516 "complete silence spread": Marshall, p. 244.

516 "bewilderment, as though": Rosenman, p. 348.

516 "What an enviable": Black, p. 1121.

517 "It is difficult not": Hastings, p. 512.

517 "a more complicated": Meacham, p. 350.

517 "Churchill's decision was": Blake, p. 14.

518 "My first impulse": Churchill, *Memoirs*, p. 945.

518 "However, so many": Meacham, p. 350.

518 "In the afterlight": Churchill, *Memoirs*, p. 945.

519 "There were a good": Elliott Roosevelt, ed., *F.D.R.: His Personal Letters*, p. 771.

519 "At that time I was": Ibid., p. 271.

519 "I will not fall": Beschloss, p. 226.

520 "The smell of death": Miller, *The Story of World War II*, p. 521.

520 "be held responsible": *American Heritage*, April–May 1985, p. 72.

520 "The mission of this": Walter Bedell Smith, *Eisenhower's Six Great Decisions*, p. 229.

521 "the Wehrmacht": Hastings, p. 6.

522 "by sentiments in": *World War II Magazine*, October–November 2008, p. 13.

523 "The boss wants": Gunther, *Roosevelt in Retrospect*, p. 304.

524 "The explosion was visible": Lewis, ed., p. 552.

524 "I've gotten what I": Weinberg, p. 837.

524 "The full application": Ferrell, *Off the Record*, p. 56.

525 "Some wanted it dropped": Sutherland, pp. 50–56.

526 "Let us pray": Perret, p. 479.

526 "against the Japanese": Gilbert, *Winston S. Churchill*, Vol. 7, p. 970.

526 "At no time": Stimson and Bundy, p. 613.

526 "James, there will be": James Roosevelt, *Affectionately, FDR*, pp. 169–70.

Chapter Twenty-five: Anatomy of Victory

529 "That is the noblest": Moran, p. 38.

529 "the commanding general": GCM, Vol. 5, p. 116.

529 "I know that General Marshall": Harriman, p. 272.

531 "an efficient little shit": Hastings, p. 26.

531 "an intelligent terrier": Atkinson, *The Day of Battle*, p. 125.

531 "I would not class": Ambrose, *The Supreme Commander*, p. 325.

532 "His real strength": Ibid.

532 "the best rounded": Ferrell, ed., *The Eisenhower Diaries*, p. 94.

532 "Corresponding Secretary": Dwight D. Eisenhower, *Crusade in Europe*, p. 133.

533 "Four individuals that could": DDE, p. 1995.

533 "odd job handler": Summersby, p. 223.

533 "Let me tell you": Churchill, *Triumph and Tragedy,* p. 229.

533 "The success of this": Beschloss, p. 283.

534 "We never could have": Ambrose, *D-Day,* p. 45.

537 "I would send my": Forrest Pogue Interview, October 29, 1956, p. 609, GCM.

537 "every mistake that": Manchester, p. 438.

537 "supreme among": Manchester, p. 322.

537 "outshone Marshall": Ibid.

538 "He had the hunger": Larrabee, p. 335.

538 "I have often thought": D'Este, *Patton,* p. 758.

538 "We are going to": Ibid., pp. 756–58.

539 "The way I see it": Ibid., p. 766.

539 "The best end": Ibid., p. 729.

539 "This is a helluva": Ibid., p. 785.

539 "Together the Joint Chiefs": Larrabee, p. 623.

539 "There was not one": Bryant, p. 592.

540 "I always gave him": Leahy, p. 298.

542 "War is not a mere": Halsey, p. 393.

543 "Only Churchill's magnificent": John Kennedy, *The Business of War,* p. 115.

543 "I always considered": Churchill, *The Grand Alliance,* p. 581.

544 "We have therefore": Rose, p. 370.

544 "The tremendous operations": GCM, Vol. 5, p. 17.

544 "a push into Northern": Weinberg, p. 677.

544 "a result of widespread": GCM, Vol. 5, p. 17.

545 "up until Overlord": Hastings, p. 5.

545 "Up to July 1944": Ibid.

545 "would probably have ended": Dyson, pp. 89–93.

545 "a grotesque failure": Larrabee, p. 599.

546 "another Carthage": Sherwood, p. 887.

546 "great credit on him": Larrabee, p. 641.

547 "fail to appreciate": Dwight D. Eisenhower, *At Ease,* p. 312.

548 "one of the greatest": Presidentialrhetoric.com/speeches.

548 "Yalta didn't change": *NYT,* May 16, 2005.

548 "This idea that": Ibid.

548 "The postwar problems": Harriman, p. 396.

549 "There is no doubt": Baldwin, *Great Mistakes of the War,* p. 10.

550 "The final test": *New York Herald Tribune,* April 14, 1945.

550 "a magic carpet": *PBS NewsHour,* July 4, 2000.

551 "the most complicated human being": Perkins, p. 134.

Index

in North African campaign,
220–21, 237, 239
Clarke, Carter, 432–33
Clausewitz, Carl Philipp Gottfried
von, 199, 488, 542
Clinton, Bill, 103
Coast Guard, U.S., 246
Cochran, Jacqueline, 86, 246
Colby, William, 382
Cold War, 470, 504
Columbia Broadcasting System,
159–60
Commager, Henry Steele, 307
Compiègne, Forest of, 37
Compton, Arthur, 254
Conant, James B., 254, 308–9
concentration camps, 492–95, 520
see also Jews, Nazi extermination
of
Congress, U.S.:
Churchill's addresses to, 116–17,
288
December 7 resolution in, 450
draft battle in, 3–5, 7–12
FDR's Pearl Harbor address to,
xiii, 95, 99
FDR's Yalta address to, 468–70
isolationism in, 4, 5, 38, 39, 44, 54,
65, 68, 83, 84, 116
Jewish refugee bill in, 234
Lend-Lease program in, 44, 46,
65
Marshall's status in, 3, 7, 25,
249–50, 344, 540
military bonus controversy in,
129, 130
Neutrality Acts in, 28, 29, 31–32,
37, 39–40, 76
New Deal in, 164, 242, 300
Pearl Harbor probe in, 102–3
southern Democrats in, 241–42,
447

see also House of Representatives,
U.S.; Senate, U.S.
Connally, Tom, 95, 97
Consolidated B-24 Liberator, 303
Cooper, Isabel Rosario, 129, 132
Coral Sea, Battle of, 174–75, 433, 535
Corregidor, Philippines, 138, 140,
141, 151, 152, 155
Crim, Howell, 122
Crusade in Europe (Eisenhower),
410, 532
Cullen, John C., 207–8
Curtin, John, 155
Curtiss Jenny, 79
Curzon, Lord, 462
Czechoslovakia, 245, 253
in Munich agreement, 29, 58, 215

Daladier, Edouard, 29
Daniels, Josephus, xi, 80, 87, 321
Darlan, Alain, 237, 239
Darlan, François, 236–37, 238, 239,
531, 540
Dasch, George, 207, 208, 209
Dauntless, 112–13
Davis, Benjamin O., Sr., 243, 446
Davis, Bob, 194
Davis, Elmer, 174, 175, 317, 318
Davis, Norman, 267
Dawes, Charles G., 19
D-Day, *see* Normandy invasion
Deane, John R., 376, 495, 500
"Declaration of the United Nations,"
120
de Gaulle, Charles, 239–40, 266, 348,
357–58, 369, 385–86, 403–4
Delano, Laura "Polly," 507, 509, 511,
513
Delano, Warren, II, 144
Democratic Party, U.S.:
in 1942 elections, 221, 224
draft opposition in, 9

PHOTO: © JOSEPH SCHUYLER

JOSEPH E. PERSICO is the author of *Roosevelt's Secret War; Franklin and Lucy; Eleventh Month, Eleventh Day, Eleventh Hour; Piercing the Reich;* and *Nuremberg: Infamy on Trial,* which was made into a television docudrama. He also collaborated with Colin Powell on his autobiography, *My American Journey.* He lives in Guilderland, New York.